ACCA
STUDY TEXT

Professional Paper 14

Financial Strategy

New in this June 2000 edition

- Updating for all examinable topic developments up to 1 June 2000

- Revisions to reflect exam trends

FOR DECEMBER 2000 AND JUNE 2001 EXAMS

BPP Publishing
June 2000

First edition 1993
Eighth edition June 2000

ISBN 0 7517 0197 1 (Previous edition 0 7517 0169 6)

British Library Cataloguing-in-Publication Data
A catalogue record for this book is available from the British Library

Published by

BPP Publishing Limited
Aldine House, Aldine Place
London W12 8AW

www.bpp.com

Printed in Great Britain by Ashford Colour Press, Gosport, Hants

We are grateful to the Association of Chartered Certified Accountants for permission to reproduce in this text the syllabus and teaching guide of which the Association holds the copyright.

We are also grateful to the Association of Chartered Certified Accountants, the Institute of Chartered Accountants in England and Wales and the Chartered Institute of Management Accountants for permission to reproduce past examination questions in our Exam Question Bank. The Exam Answer Bank has been prepared by BPP Publishing Limited.

Contents

		Page

BPP
PUBLISHING

Contents

HOW TO USE THIS STUDY TEXT

Aims of this Study Text

To provide you with the knowledge and understanding, skills and applied techniques required for passing the exam

The Study Text has been written around the ACCA's Official Syllabus and the ACCA's Official Teaching Guide (reproduced below, and cross-referenced to where in the text each topic is covered).

- It is **comprehensive**. We do not omit sections of the syllabus as the examiner is liable to examine any angle of any part of the syllabus - and you do not want to be left high and dry.

- It is **up-to-date as at 1 June 2000**, which means that it fulfils the requirement for the December 2000 exams that students should be up-to-date as at 1 June 2000.

- And it is **on-target**. We do not include any material which is not examinable. You can therefore rely on the BPP Study Text as the stand-alone source of all your information for the exam, without worrying that any of the material is irrelevant.

To allow you to study in the way that best suits your learning style and the time you have available, by following your personal Study Plan (see below)

You may be studying at home on your own until the date of the exam, or you may be attending a full-time course. You may like to (and have time to) read every word, or you may prefer to (or only have time to) skim-read and devote the remainder of your time to question practice. Wherever you fall in the spectrum, you will find the BPP Study Text meets your needs in designing and following your personal Study Plan.

To tie in with the other components of the BPP Effective Study Package to ensure you have the best possible chance of passing the exam

BPP PUBLISHING

How to use this Study Text

Recommended period of use	Elements of the BPP Effective Study Package
3-12 months before exam	**Study Text** Acquisition of knowledge, understanding, skills and applied techniques.

1-6 months before exam	**Practice & Revision Kit** Tutorial questions and helpful checklists of the key points lead you into each area. There are then numerous Examination questions to try, graded by topic area, along with realistic suggested solutions prepared by BPP's own authors in the light of the Examiner's Reports. June 2000 examinees will find the 2001 edition of the Kit invaluable for bringing them up-to-date as at 1 December 2000, the cut-off date for the June 2001 examinable material.

last minute - 3 months before exam	**Passcards** Short, memorable notes focused on what is most likely to come up in the exam you will be sitting.

1-6 months before exam	**Success Tapes** Audio cassettes covering the vital elements of your syllabus in less than 90 minutes per subject. Each tape also contains exam hints to help you fine tune your strategy.

3-12 months before exam	**Breakthrough Videos** These supplement your Study Text, by giving you clear tuition on key exam subjects. They allow you the luxury of being able to pause or repeat sections until you have fully grasped the topic.

3-12 months before exam	**Master CD** Interactive CD-ROM containing questions on all aspects of the syllabus, cross referenced to help topics.

Settling down to study

By this stage in your career you are probably a very experienced learner and taker of exams. But have you ever thought about *how* you learn? Let's have a quick look at the key elements required for effective learning. You can then identify your learning style and go on to design your own approach to how you are going to study this text - your personal Study Plan.

Key element of learning	Using the BPP Study Text
Motivation	You can rely on the comprehensiveness and technical quality of BPP. You've chosen the right Study Text - so you're in pole position to pass your exam!
Clear objectives and standards	Do you want to be a prizewinner or simply achieve a moderate pass? Decide.
Feedback	Follow through the examples in this text and do the Questions and the Quick quizzes. Evaluate your efforts critically - how are you doing?
Study Plan	You need to be honest about your progress to yourself - don't be over-confident, but don't be negative either. Make your Study Plan (see below) and try to stick to it. Focus on the short-term objectives - completing two chapters a night, say - but beware of losing sight of your study objectives
Practice	Use the Quick quizzes and Chapter roundups to refresh your memory regularly after you have completed your initial study of each chapter

These introductory pages let you see exactly what you are up against. However you study, you should:

- **Read through the syllabus and teaching guide** - this will help you to identify areas you have already covered, perhaps at a lower level of detail, and areas that are totally new to you

- **Study the examination paper section**, where we show you the format of the exam (how many and what kind of questions etc) and analyse all the papers set since the 1995 change in exam format.

Key study steps

The following steps are, in our experience, the ideal way to study for professional exams. You can of course adapt it for your particular learning style (see below). Tackle the chapters in the order you find them in the Study Text. Taking into account your individual learning style, follow these key study steps for each chapter.

Key study steps	Activity
Step 1 *Chapter topic list*	Study the list. Each numbered topic denotes a numbered section in the chapter
Step 2 *Introduction*	Read it through. It is designed to show you *why* the topics in the chapter need to be studied - how they lead on from previous topics, and how they lead into subsequent ones
Step 3 *Knowledge brought forward boxes*	In these we highlight information and techniques that it is assumed you have 'brought forward' with you from your earlier studies. If there are matters which have changed recently due to legislation etc then these topics are explained in full. Do not panic if you do not feel instantly comfortable with the content - it should come back to you as we develop the subject for this paper. If you are really unsure, we advise you to go back to your previous notes
Step 4 *Explanations*	Proceed methodically through the chapter, reading each section thoroughly and making sure you understand. Where a topic has been examined, we state the month and year of examination against the appropriate heading. You should pay particular attention to these topics
Step 5 *Key terms* and *Exam focus points*	• **Key terms** can often earn you *easy marks* if you state them clearly and correctly in an appropriate exam answer (and they are indexed at the back of the text so you can check easily that you are on top of all of them when you come to revise) • **Exam focus points** give you a good idea of how the examiner tends to examine certain topics - and also pinpoint *easy marks*
Step 6 *Note taking*	Take brief notes if you wish, avoiding the temptation to copy out too much
Step 7 *Examples*	Follow each through to its solution very carefully
Step 8 *Case examples*	Study each one, and try if you can to add flesh to them from your own experience - they are designed to show how the topics you are studying come alive (and often come unstuck) in the real world
Step 9 *Questions*	Make a very good attempt at each one
Step 10 *Answers*	Check yours against ours, and make sure you understand any discrepancies
Step 11 *Chapter roundup*	Check through it very carefully, to make sure you have grasped the major points it is highlighting

BPP PUBLISHING

Key study steps	Activity
Step 12 *Quick quiz*	When you are happy that you have covered the chapter, use the **Quick quiz** to check your recall of the topics covered. The answers are in the paragraphs in the chapter that we refer you to
Step 13 *Examination question(s)*	Either at this point, or later when you are thinking about revising, make a full attempt at the **Examination question(s)** suggested at the very end of the chapter. You can find these at the end of the Study Text, along with the **Answers** so you can see how you did. We highlight for you which ones are introductory, and which are of the full standard you would expect to find in an exam

Developing your personal Study Plan

Preparing a Study Plan (and sticking closely to it) is one of the key elements in learning success.

First you need to be aware of your style of learning. There are four typical learning styles. Consider yourself in the light of the following descriptions. and work out which you fit most closely. You can then plan to follow the key study steps in the sequence suggested.

Learning styles	Characteristics	Sequence of key study steps in the BPP Study Text
Theorist	Seeks to understand principles before applying them in practice	1, 2, 3, 4, 7, 8, 5, 9/10, 11, 12, 13 (6 continuous)
Reflector	Seeks to observe phenomena, thinks about them and then chooses to act	
Activist	Prefers to deal with practical, active problems; does not have much patience with theory	1, 2, 9/10 (read through), 7, 8, 5, 11, 3, 4, 9/10 (full attempt), 12, 13 (6 continuous)
Pragmatist	Prefers to study only if a direct link to practical problems can be seen; not interested in theory for its own sake	9/10 (read through), 2, 5, 7, 8, 11, 1, 3, 4, 9/10 (full attempt), 12, 13 (6 continuous)

Next you should complete the following checklist.

Am I motivated?   (a) [ ]

Do I have an objective and a standard that I want to achieve?   (b) [ ]

Am I a theorist, a reflector, an activist or a pragmatist?   (c) [ ]

How much time do I have available per week, given: (d) [ ]

- the standard I have set myself
- the time I need to set aside later for work on the Practice and Revision Kit and Passcards
- the other exam(s) I am sitting, and (of course)
- practical matters such as work, travel, exercise, sleep and social life?

BPP
PUBLISHING

Now:

- take the time you have available per week for this Study Text (d), and multiply it by the number of weeks available to give (e).

(e) [ ]

- divide (e) by the number of chapters to give (f)

(f) [ ]

- set about studying each chapter in the time represented by (f), following the key study steps in the order suggested by your particular learning style

This is your personal **Study Plan**.

Short of time?

Whatever your objectives, standards or style, you may find you simply do not have the time available to follow all the key study steps for each chapter, however you adapt them for your particular learning style. If this is the case, follow the Skim Study technique below (the icons in the Study Text will help you to do this).

Skim Study technique

Study the chapters in the order you find them in the Study Text. For each chapter, follow the key study steps 1-3, and then skim-read through step 4. Jump to step 11, and then go back to step 5. Follow through steps 7 and 8, and prepare outline Answers to Questions (steps 9/10). Try the Quick quiz (step 12), following up any items you can't answer, then do a plan for the Examination question (step 13), comparing it against our answers. You should probably still follow step 6 (note-taking), although you may decide simply to rely on the BPP Passcards for this.

Moving on...

However you study, when you are ready to embark on the practice and revision phase of the BPP Effective Study Package, you should still refer back to this Study Text:

- as a source of **reference** (you should find the list of key terms and the index particularly helpful for this)

- as a **refresher** (the Chapter roundups and Quick quizzes help you here)

And remember to keep careful hold of this Study Text - you will find it invaluable in your work

ACCA OFFICIAL SYLLABUS

BPP PUBLISHING

6 International financial management decisions

(i) payments between companies
(ii) cash management
(iii) transfer pricing
(iv) judging the performance of companies within a group
(v) the financial control of a group of companies.

(i) strategic objectives
(ii) the principle of home country versus host country returns
(iii) the form of foreign investment, branch versus subsidiary, European Economic Interest Groups (EEIGs)
(iv) the effect of taxation on the foreign investment decision (basic principles only)
(v) discounted cash flows
(vi) adjusted present value
(vii) political risk analysis
(viii) an analysis of the different methods of financing the investment.

ACCA OFFICIAL TEACHING GUIDE

This is the Official Teaching Guide, for the December 2000 and June 2001 exams.

Syllabus reference

Session 1 Financial strategy: its nature and scope

1a

- describe what is meant by financial strategy
- identify the importance of financial strategy to the organisation
- discuss the relationship between financial strategy and overall corporate strategy

Corporate governance
- identify the aims and objectives of organisations
- describe the goals of different interest groups
- understand the significance of changing share ownership patterns for the company
- define the meaning of corporate governance from a UK perspective and briefly contrast between UK practices and those of other countries especially the USA, Continental Europe and the Far East
- understand the debate regarding corporate governance, including the Cadbury Report
- identify the role of auditors, audit committees, non-executive directors etc in corporate governance

Session 2 Conflicts of interest and their resolution

1b, 1c, 1d

- identify directors' powers and behaviour, including the significance of creative accounting, off-balance sheet finance and the influence of the threat of takeover
- understand the principles of agency theory and their contribution to the debate on governance
- understand the potential for conflict between owners, directors, managers and other interest groups
- discuss the meaning of goal congruence, and understand how it might be achieved through the use of alternative reward systems including share option schemes and profit related pay
- discuss the role of non-executive directors, administrators etc with respect to the organisation

Session 3 Translating market disciplines

2c, 3a

- explain and quantify what is meant by adequate financial return, contrasting profit based measures with net present value of expected cash flows
- understand the benefits of using net present value, and how the use of net present value can serve as a unifying long-term objective for the enterprise as a whole
- revise NPV analysis, including the identification of relevant cash flows and the impact of price level changes
- describe the efficient markets hypothesis including weak, semi-strong and strong form efficiency
- understand the meaning of market efficiency and its significance to financial decision-making based upon NPV
- explain the meaning of the term structure of interest rates, including the forms of the yield curve and the expectations, liquidity preference and market segmentation theories
- understand the significance of yield curves to financial managers

Session 4   The valuation of securities

- understand models for the valuation of shares and bonds, dividend growth models, earnings growth models and use such models to estimate value from given information
- be aware of the theoretical and practical limitations of such models
- discuss the relevance of accounting information to share valuation
- be aware of practical influences on share price, including reasons why share prices differ from their theoretical values
- understand and apply models for the valuation of debt and other securities

Session 5   Portfolio theory

- understand the benefits of portfolio diversification
- estimate the risk and return of portfolios
- understand the meaning of mean-variance efficiency for two asset portfolios and portfolios of many assets, efficient portfolios and the efficient frontier
- understand the concept of utility and its importance to portfolio selection
- explain portfolio selection when both risky and risk free assets are available
- discuss the nature and significance of the Capital Market Line
- discuss the relevance of portfolio theory to practical financial management
- discuss the limitations of portfolio theory

Session 6   Capital asset pricing model

- understand the meaning and significance of systematic and unsystematic risk
- discuss the Security Market Line
- understand what is meant by alpha and beta factors, their interpretation and how they are calculated
- discuss the problems of using historic data as the basis for future decision-making, and the evidence of the stability of beta over time
- describe the assumptions of CAPM
- understand the uses of the model in financial management
- discuss the limitations of the model, including some of the instances when it does not perform as expected (eg low beta investments, low PE investments, day of week effects etc)

Session 7   The cost of capital

- estimate the cost of equity, using the CAPM and dividend valuation models
- estimate the cost of debt, for both redeemable and irredeemable debt
- understand the weighted average cost of capital of a company, and how it is estimated
- discuss the theories of Modigliani and Miller including their assumptions, and the value and limitations of their theories and their implications for the capital structure decision
- estimate the cost of capital for individual investments and divisions, including the use of the 'pure play' method with ungearing and regearing beta
- discuss the relevance of the cost of capital for unlisted companies and public sector organisations
- explain the practical problems of estimating an appropriate discount rate, and understand the margin of error that is involved in cost of capital estimates

Session 8   The interaction of investment and financing decisions

- understand the adjusted present value technique of investment appraisal including how to estimate the base case NPV and the financing side effects of an investment
- discuss the practical problems of using the APV technique
- discuss alternatives to the capital asset pricing model, including the Arbitrage Pricing Theory (n.b. detailed knowledge is not required)

Session 9   Corporate dividend policy

- describe the practical influences on dividend policy, including the possible effects of both corporate and personal taxation
- discuss the role of dividends as signals of future prospects
- discuss the alternative arguments with respect to the effect of dividend policy on share prices

Case scenario
- practise a detailed investment appraisal question or mini-case

Session 10 Business planning

- review the nature of financial control - the three levels of control: strategic, tactical and operational
- discuss the information requirements for financial control, forecasts, decision support and monitoring

Short-term financial planning
- understand the information needs of short-term financial planning
- explain how budgeting, monitoring and controlling cash flows, including pricing, raising finance, repaying debt etc may be used to meet short and medium term financial objectives
- understand how business plans are developed and analysed to meet specified objectives
- analyse past, current and expected future performance of the organisation through ratios and other techniques to provide relevant information for business planning
- compare actual and expected performance, highlighting areas for further investigation
- nature of free cash flow and its impact on financial planning and strategy

Session 11 Long-term planning

- understand the relationship between short-term and long-term financial planning, and the potential conflict between short-term and long-term objectives
- describe top-down versus bottom-up planning systems
- understand the use of budgets to influence the success of financial planning
- describe the relationship of investment decisions to long-term planning
- describe alternative strategies for long-term growth, organic growth versus external growth, and the key dimensions of strategy that need to be addressed if a business is considering organic growth

Session 12 Mergers and acquisitions

2e

- understand the arguments for and against mergers and acquisitions
- contrast merger and acquisition activity in the UK and USA with activity in continental Europe and Japan, and discuss the implications of the differences that exist for corporate governance
- describe the alternative strategies and tactics of mergers and acquisitions
- discuss how possible acquisition targets may be identified using financial or other information
- estimate the value of potential target companies
- distinguish between the various methods of financing mergers and acquisitions - cash, debt equity and hybrids, and assess the attractiveness of different financing alternatives to vendors
- evaluate the various defences against takeovers, and be aware of any restrictions on their use as specified by the City Code
- identify key issues that influence the success of acquisitions, and recommend appropriate actions for a given situation
- understand the importance of post-audit and monitoring of post-acquisition success

Session 13 Financial restructuring alternatives and decisions

2e

- describe the nature of, and reasons for, divestments
- describe 'unbundling' and 'de-merging' of quoted companies

Management buy-outs
- discuss the advantages of buy-outs, and understand the issues that a management team should address when in the preparation of a buy-out proposal
- identify situations in which a management buy-out is likely to offer the best value for a disposer
- evaluate alternative sources of finance for buy-outs
- assess the viability of buy-outs from the viewpoint of both the buy-out team and the financial backers
- identify the advantages and disadvantages of management buy-ins

Capital reconstruction schemes
- identify and justify when a capital reconstruction may be required or appropriate
- be aware of the importance of taking into account the interests of the various suppliers of capital in a reconstruction situation
- formulate a feasible reconstruction from given information

Session 14 Economic influences on international financial management decisions

5a, 5b, 5c,
5d, 5e, 5f

Multinational companies and trends in global competition
- understand the nature, size and significance of multinational companies in the world economy
- discuss the influence of exchange rates, international capital markets and changes in global competition patterns on the strategies of multinational companies, with particular reference to the EU, USA and Japan

BPP PUBLISHING

International trade and protectionism
- understand the theory and practice of free trade, and the problems of protectionism, through tariff and non-tariff barriers
- describe the major trade agreements and customs unions (the European Union, North American Free Trade Area, EFTA etc)
- understand the nature and significance of the balance of payments and the possible effects of national balance of payments problems on the financial decisions of companies
- explain the objectives and function of GATT and the World Trade Organisation (WTO), and describe the major rounds of GATT and their achievements

Self study
- most of these items, especially where description of the institutional framework is concerned, could be undertaken by self study

Session 15 The international financial system

5h, 5i, 6b

- understand the role of the major international financial institutions, including the IMF, the Bank of International Settlements and the International Bank for Reconstruction and Development (The World Bank)

International banking
- understand the workings of international money markets
- outline the major factors affecting the development of international banking
- understand the role of international banks in international finance, including international bank lending through syndication and multi-option facilities and other means

International capital markets
- describe the nature and development of the Euromarkets, including the Eurocurrency, Eurobond and Euroequity markets
- explain the types of financing instruments that are available to corporate treasurers on the Euromarkets, for both borrowing and financial investment
- understand the role of domestic capital markets, especially stock exchanges, in financing the activities of multinational companies

Self study
- understand the nature of the global debt problem and its effects on relations between developed and developing countries
- be aware of the role of international financial markets and institutions in the global debt problem, and the effect of the problem on multinational companies and international banks
- be aware of the methods that have been suggested for dealing with the problem

Session 16 Foreign trade

6a

- advise clients on the alternative methods of exporting and importing
- understand the risks of foreign trade, currency, credit/commercial and political
- explain the advantages and disadvantages of using documentary letters of credit, bills of exchange, acceptances etc in foreign trade
- describe the insurance that is available to protect against the risks of foreign trade
- describe and evaluate the sources of finance for foreign trade, including forfaiting and international factoring
- describe the main features of countertrade, and various alternatives that exist for foreign trade deals other than for monetary payments

Session 17 Exchange rate systems

- describe the major developments in exchange rate systems since Bretton Woods, including the European Monetary System, the ERM, EMU and the development of the Euro
- explain the workings of the foreign exchange markets, types of quotation, spot and forward rates

The determinants of exchange rates

- discuss the relationship between foreign exchange rates and interest rates in different countries
- explain the meaning and significance of the purchasing power parity theory
- discuss whether exchange rates may be successfully forecast using modelling or other techniques

Session 18 Currency risk

- discuss the types of currency risk - transaction, translation and economic exposure, and their importance to companies
- evaluate alternative strategies that companies might adopt with respect to currency exposure
- discuss and evaluate traditional methods of currency risk management, including currency of invoice, leading and lagging, netting, matching, and internal asset and liability management
- evaluate hedging strategies using forward foreign exchange contracts

Session 19 Risk management

- outline the recent volatility of interest rates and exchange rates
- describe the main instruments that are available to help manage the volatility of such rates

Futures markets and contracts

- explain the nature of futures contracts
- discuss the use of margin requirements and the functions of futures clearing houses
- explain how price movements are recognised within futures markets
- describe the major interest rate futures (short-term and long-term) and currency futures contracts
- evaluate hedging strategies with both interest rate and currency futures using given information
- contrast the use of currency futures with forward contracts

Session 20 Options

- describe the main features of options including puts and calls, the exercise price, American and European options, in and out of the money
- differentiate between traded options and over-the-counter options
- discuss the determinants of options prices, including the Black-Scholes model and its limitations
- explain the advantages and disadvantages of options compared to futures
- describe the various types of interest rate options, including short-term options, caps, collars and floors, and the nature of currency options
- be aware of the nature of benefits of low cost or zero cost options
- evaluate alternative hedging scenarios using interest rate and currency options

Session 21 Swaps

4b

- describe nature of interest rate and currency swaps
- understand the value of swaps to the corporate treasurer
- understand the role of banks in swap activity
- describe the various types of risk that are associated with swaps
- describe hybrid forms of instruments such as swaptions, and the value of financial engineering
- evaluate hedging scenarios using swaps and swaptions

6c

Session 22 Transfer pricing

- explain the importance of transfer pricing to multinational companies
- understand the legal regulations affecting transfer pricing, particularly with respect to the attitude of tax authorities
- discuss the use of tax havens to try to maximise the benefits of transfer pricing
- explain the potential adverse motivational effects of transfer pricing on individual subsidiaries or divisions

Performance measurement
- describe the guidelines appropriate to the regular financial reports required from overseas operations
- evaluate the performance of all or part of the international group of companies using ratio and other forms of analysis

Session 23 The international treasury function

4a, 6c

- discuss the merits of defining the treasury as a cost centre or profit centre
- discuss the arguments for the centralisation versus decentralisation of international treasury activities
- describe the main forms of international cash transfer mechanisms
- describe the short-term investment opportunities that exist in international money markets and in international marketable securities

Session 24 International operations

6d

- describe the forms of entity that are available for international operations, including the relative merits of branch, subsidiary, joint venture licensing and economic interest groups

Foreign direct investment
- discuss the complexities of foreign direct investment, including the possible forms and implications of political risk and its importance to the investment decision process
- discuss the impact of blocked funds and restrictions on the remittance of funds to the parent company, and the use of royalties, management charges etc to avoid restrictions on remittances

Session 25 International capital budgeting

- estimate the international cost of capital for an organisation, using the CAPM
- evaluate how APV might be used in international investment appraisal
- illustrate the effect of taxation on international investment, including the possibility of double taxation
- discuss the advantages and disadvantages of international portfolio diversification

Session 26 The international capital structure decision

- discuss the factors that influence the type of finance used in international operations
- describe the strategic implications of international financing, with respect both to the type of finance used, and the currency in which the financing is denominated
- undertake a detailed appraisal of an international capital investment proposal using given information - this could be either by organic growth or acquisition

Session 27/28 Question practice

- As an alternative to a block of question practice at the end of the course, individual sessions could be used during the course. The emphasis during these sessions should be on detailed case scenario questions of the format that are likely to appear in the examination

BPP PUBLISHING

THE EXAMINATION PAPER

Format of the paper

The format of the examination paper is as follows.

		Number of marks
Section A:	2 compulsory questions	
	(both questions at least 30 marks)	70
Section B:	3 (out of 5) questions of 10 marks each	30
		100

Time allowed: 3 hours

Section A will consist of mini case studies/scenario type questions.

Present value table, annuity table and formula sheet will be provided in the exam.

Analysis of past papers

The analysis below shows the topics which have been examined under the current syllabus since the change in exam format in 1995.

December 1999

Section A

1   Evaluation of an international joint venture (40 marks)
2   Interest rate hedging using futures and options; exchange traded *versus* OTC interest rate options (30 marks)

Section B

3   Valuation of shares of a company comprising four investment projects
4   Convertible debentures: impact of conversion on company's cost of capital
5   Expected value calculation for debt and equity of a merged company
6   Share ownership patterns
7   Financial post-audits of a merger or takeover

June 1999

Section A

1   Report on performance and strategy of a group and subsidiaries (40 marks)
2   Methods of estimating cost of capital (30 marks)

Section B

3   Appraisal of an investment for a pension fund
4   Foreign exchange risk; currency futures; basis risk
5   A company's dividend policy
6   Factors explaining the growth of multinationals
7   Exchange rate systems

December 1998

Section A

1   Assessments of post-acquisition EPS, share price and APV (40 marks)
2   Top-down and bottom-up financial planning; sources of finance; financial gearing; gap analysis (30 marks)

Section B

3   Interest rate risk strategy using interest rate options
4   Foreign project in high inflation country: calculations; foreign exchange risks
5   Use of country data to indicate political risk and in investment decisions
6   Executive share option schemes and role congruence
7   Foreign direct investment; implications for home country

June 1998

Section A

1   Synergy in mergers and takeovers; company valuation for an acquisition; use of cash, shares or bonds for the acquisition (30 marks)
2   Transaction and translation exposure; hedging of foreign exchange risk (40 marks)

Section B

3   Efficiency of portfolios
4   The yield curve; liquidity preference hypothesis; zero coupon bond calculations
5   Blocked funds, including calculation
6   Steps of a strategic financial plan
7   International transfer of cash

December 1997

Section A

1   Report on reconstruction of a company in financial difficulties (30 marks)
2   NPV evaluation; CAPM and arbitrage pricing theory (40 marks)

Section B

3   Balance of payments policy
4   Conflicts between objectives of directors and shareholders
5   International portfolio diversification
6   Interest rate swap
7   Exchange rate forecasts

June 1997

Section A

1   Report on financing mix for a management buyout; evaluation of gearing; information required by venture capitalist (30 marks)
2   Organic growth v acquisition; evaluation of decision to set up an overseas subsidiary; implications of European single currency (40 marks)

Section B

3   Alpha values and beta values
4   Futures hedge; basis risk
5   Benefits and problems of Treasury centralisation
6   Corporate governance; international differences
7   Modigliani and Miller's model, adjusted for corporate taxation, to estimate cost of capital

BPP PUBLISHING

The examination paper

5   Discussion of how a company can comply with the Cadbury Code
6   Comparison of portfolio theory and CAPM; estimation of portfolio risk and return
7   Discussion of non-tariff trade barriers

FURTHER GUIDANCE

Bear in mind the following points as you study Paper 14.

Knowledge brought forward from Paper 8 is very important. We have indicated some of the key areas which you should check you are familiar with in **boxes** within the text. If you are unclear on any topics, you should go back to your earlier notes. Part of the Paper 8 knowledge which you will often need to use in Paper 14 is that relating to different **financial instruments** and to different **sources of finance**.

Questions will require you to **think flexibly**. You may be dealing with problems relating to **different parts of the economy** and to **different parts of the world**. The techniques you can use are often not spelt out. You will need to select appropriate techniques yourself. Often, more than one technique is valid, and there may be no single right answer. (This last point should be remembered when you review our answers to the question bank: if your answer may be different from ours, it does not necessarily mean that it is wrong.)

You will be tested in different questions on your ability to **understand strategic implications** of problems you are faced with.

Be prepared for topical questions on **recent events**, eg developments on EMU; corporate governance.

Be prepared for questions which integrate **theory** with **practice**: so, be ready to point out the practical limitations of theory, but also to show *how* it can be applied.

The ACCA provides the following guidance on Paper 14 *Financial Strategy*.

Aim of Paper 14

To equip students with the underpinning knowledge and competence to make reasoned decisions in the area of financial management and to be able to adapt to changes in factors affecting those decisions.

On completion of this paper students should be able to:

(a) Understand the concepts behind available theoretical models and assess the relevance of developments in financial management theory to an enterprise

(b) Select the techniques most appropriate to optimise the employment of resources including the most effective method of financing

(c) Understand the workings of the financial system and evaluate alternative sources of finance and assess investment possibilities

(d) Understand the treasury management function, in particular the working capital aspects and international considerations

(e) Demonstrate the skills expected at the Professional Stage

Prerequisite knowledge

Students will require a thorough understanding of the financial management section of Paper 8 *Managerial Finance*. Paper 14 develops the introduction to financial management provided in Paper 8 by:

(a) Considering further aspects relating to long-term investments, including the capital asset pricing model and portfolio theory

(b) Examining the strategic implications of short-term and long-term financial planning

(c) Introducing the international considerations of the treasury management function

(d) Extending the appraisal of capital investments within an international environment

(e) Considering the economic influences on international financial management decisions

(f) Providing a more critical appraisal of corporate governance

(g) Evaluating financial restructuring schemes

Extent of integration

Questions will demand an application of quantitative techniques covered in Paper 3 *Management Information* to appraise capital investment decisions.

Paper 14 develops an awareness of the international environment and considers the economic influences on international decisions - students will have made reference to this area in their study of economics in Paper 4 *The Organisational Framework*.

Students need to be aware of the links between the personal finance coverage in Paper 11 *Tax Planning* and the portfolio theory dimension of Paper 14. Paper 14 will draw upon the strategic management and business planning issues covered in Paper 12 *Management and Strategy* in the context of financial planning. Paper 14 examines mergers and acquisitions in the context of long-term financial planning - an area covered in Paper 13 *Financial Reporting Environment*.

Key areas of the syllabus

The examiner has identified the following areas as being core topics:

(a) *Investment decisions* (portfolio theory; CAPM; cost of capital; interactions between investment and financing decisions).

(b) *Risk management* (foreign exchange risk; interest rate risk; identification of exposure; options; futures; swaps; hybrids).

(c) *Corporate restructuring* (mergers and acquisitions; management buy-outs, management buy-ins and capital reconstructions; Divestment; demergers, all of these should include associated valuation, financing and corporate governance effects).

(d) *Financial planning* (short and long term planning; strategic, tactical and operational planning; top down versus bottom up; organic and external growth, analysis of current and expected future performance).

(e) *International finance* (international investment; international treasury management; financing and capital structure; control of international operations).

Other points

The examiner emphasised that any part of the current syllabus may be examined. Therefore minor areas that have not been examined recently should not be ignored.

Candidates will be expected to have an awareness of APV, but will not be required to detail the implications of foreign exchange.

Free cash flows are unlikely to be examined in depth in future examination papers; however, should this change then appropriate warning will be provided in the *ACCA Students' Newsletter*.

Part A

Financial strategy, investment and capital structure

Chapter 1

FINANCIAL STRATEGY AND OBJECTIVES

Chapter topic list	Syllabus reference
1 Corporate strategy and financial strategy	1(a), 1(b), 1(d)
2 Objectives of business enterprises	1(a), 2(b)
3 Financial objectives	1(a)
4 Non-financial objectives	1(a)
5 Objectives of publicly owned and non-commercial bodies	1(a)

Introduction

In this chapter, we introduce the subject of this Study Text - **financial strategy** - in the context of the objectives of organisations. Many of the concepts introduced are relevant to the debate on **corporate governance** which is discussed in Chapter 2.

1 CORPORATE STRATEGY AND FINANCIAL STRATEGY

1.1 **Strategy** may be defined as a course of action, including the specification of resources required, to achieve a specific objective. Strategy can be **short-term** or **long-term**, depending on the time horizon of the objective it is intended to achieve. This definition also indicates that since strategy depends on objectives or targets, the obvious starting point for a study of corporate strategy and financial strategy is the **identification and formulation of objectives**.

1.2 Johnson and Scholes (*Exploring corporate strategy*) have summarised the characteristics of strategic decisions for an organisation as follows.

(a) Strategic decisions will be concerned with the **scope** of the organisation's activities.

(b) Strategy involves the matching of an organisation's activities to the **environment** in which it operates.

(c) Strategy also involves the matching of an organisation's activities to its **resource capability**.

(d) Strategic decisions therefore involve major decisions about the **allocation** or **re-allocation of resources**.

(e) Strategic decisions will **affect operational decisions,** because they will set off a chain of 'lesser' decisions and operational activities, involving the use of resources.

  BPP PUBLISHING

(f) Strategic decisions will be affected not just by (1) environmental considerations and (2) resources availability, but also by (3) the **values and expectations of the people in power** within the organisation.

(g) Strategic decisions are likely to affect the **long-term direction** that the organisation takes.

(h) Strategic decisions have implications for change throughout the organisation, and so are likely to be **complex in nature**.

1.3 **Financial strategy** is the area of strategy which falls within the scope of financial management, including for example decisions relating to the sources from which funds are obtained and the amount which should be paid out by a company in dividends.

1.4 Three levels of strategy can be identified.

(a) **Corporate strategy** is concerned with broader issues, such as that of 'what business are we in?' Financial aspects of this level of strategic decision-making include the choice of method in entering a market or business. Whether entry should be accomplished through an acquisition or through organic growth, for example, is a question with financial implications.

(b) **Business strategy** or **competitive strategy** covers the question of how strategic business units compete in individual markets, and therefore of the resources which should be allocated to them. For example, what is the threat from potential entrants to the market? What is the bargaining power of buyers and of suppliers? What competition is there among existing companies? What pressure is there from substitute products? Porter (1985) identified these competitive forces as determining profitability of an industry.

(c) **Operational strategy** is to do with how different functions within the business - including the finance function - contribute to corporate and business strategies. For example, a strategy to implement a new policy on dividends formulated as a part of corporate strategy may be developed by the finance function.

What determines strategies?

1.5 The evolution of strategies can be seen as the result of the following.

(a) General and environmental influences
(b) The power and influence of stakeholder groups and internal coalitions
(c) Economic objectives
(d) Social responsibilities of the organisation

Environmental influences

1.6 General environmental influences consist of the following.

(a) **External influences**

(i) The values of society

(ii) The influence of organised groups, such as government departments, consumer groups and environmentalist groups

(b) The influence of the **nature of the business** itself

   (i) The market situation and market conditions it is in (eg depressed market, growth market)

   (ii) The products it makes

   (iii) The technology it uses (influencing its methods of operating, the skills of its employees and so on)

(c) The influence of the **organisation's culture**

   (i) Its tradition (history)
   (ii) Its organisation structure
   (iii) Its management/leadership style

Stakeholder groups   6/96

1.7 There is a variety of different groups or individuals whose interests are directly affected by the activities of a firm. These groups or individuals are referred to as **stakeholders** in the firms. Sharplin (*Strategic management*) has listed the various stakeholder groups in a firm as follows.

- Common (equity) shareholders
- Preferred shareholders
- Trade creditors
- Holders of unsecured debt securities
- Holders of secured debt securities
- Intermediate (business) customers
- Final (consumer) customers
- Suppliers
- Employees
- Past employees
- Retirees
- Competitors
- Neighbours
- The immediate community
- The national society
- The world society
- Corporate management
- Organisational strategists
- The chief executive
- The board of directors
- Government
- Special interest groups

Objectives of stakeholder groups

1.8 The various groups of stakeholders in a firm will have different goals which will depend in part on the particular situation of the enterprise. Some of the more important aspects of these different goals are as follows.

(a) **Ordinary (equity) shareholders** are the providers of the risk capital of a company and usually their goal will be to maximise the wealth which they have as a result of the ownership of the shares in the company.

(b) **Trade creditors** have supplied goods or services to the firm. Trade creditors will generally be profit-maximising firms themselves and have the objective of being paid the full amount due by the date agreed. On the other hand, they usually wish to ensure that they continue their trading relationship with the firm and may sometimes be prepared to accept later payment to avoid jeopardising that relationship.

(c) **Long-term creditors,** which will often be banks, have the objective of receiving payments of interest and capital on the loan by the due date for the repayments. Where the loan is secured on assets of the company, the creditor will be able to appoint a receiver to dispose of the company's assets if the company defaults on the repayments. To avoid the possibility that this may result in a loss to the lender if the assets are not sufficient to cover the loan, the lender will wish to minimise the risk of default and will not wish to lend more than is prudent.

(d) **Employees** will usually want to maximise their rewards paid to them in salaries and benefits, according to the particular skills and the rewards available in alternative employment. Most employees will also want continuity of employment.

(e) **Government** has objectives which can be formulated in political terms. Government agencies impinge on the firm's activities in different ways including through taxation of the firm's profits, the provision of grants, health and safety legislation, training initiatives and so on. Government policies will often be related to macroeconomic objectives such as sustained economic growth and high levels of employment.

(f) **Management** has, like other employees (and managers who are not directors will normally be employees), the objective of maximising their own rewards. It is the duty of the directors and the managers to whom they delegate responsibilities to manage the company for the benefit of shareholders. The objective of reward maximisation might conflict with the exercise of this duty, in ways which we shall examine a little later.

1.9 The situation of a company in financial distress presents the possibility that a **receiver** or an **administrator** may be appointed.

(a) Where a receiver is appointed by a secured creditor following default by the company, the receiver's primary duty is to the creditor, usually a bank, who pays his fees. The receiver may sell the business, or parts of it, as a going concern or may sell the assets of the business separately. Once sufficient money has been raised to repay the loan, the receiver has no incentive to maximise proceeds from the sale of remaining assets or to keep the business operating.

(b) Administration is a procedure introduced under the Insolvency Act 1986 in order to help rescue companies in difficulties and to protect jobs. The administrator attempts to reorganise the finances and operating structure of the company while the company continues to trade. Appointed by the court at the request of the directors, the administrator has an equal duty to all creditors. As with the 'Chapter 11' bankruptcy provisions in the USA, the administration procedure is intended to provide a 'breathing space' during which the company is protected from legal action by its creditors and has a chance to get back on its feet again.

Stakeholder groups and strategy

1.10 The actions of stakeholder groups in pursuit of their various goals can exert influence on strategy. The greater the power of the stakeholder, the greater his influence will be. Johnson and Scholes separate power groups into 'internal coalitions' and 'external stakeholder groups'. Internal coalitions will include the marketing department, the finance department, the manufacturing department, the chairman and board of directors and so on.

1.11 Each internal coalition or external stakeholder group will have different expectations about what it wants, and the expectations of the various groups will conflict. Each group, however, will influence strategic decision-making.

Case example

As just one example, the Ferranti 'scandal' in the late 1980s brought to the public attention the disagreement a few years earlier between the chairman of Ferranti and some of the company's major institutional shareholders, who opposed (unsuccessfully) the company's strategy to take over ISC, the secretive US defence equipment manufacturer. When details of a fraud within ISC eventually emerged, the institutional shareholders were accused in the press of having failed to use their influence more powerfully to prevent the takeover in the first place.

1.12 Many managers acknowledge that the interests of some stakeholder groups - eg themselves and employees - should be recognised and provided for, even if this means that the interests of shareholders might be adversely affected. Not all stakeholder group interests can be given specific attention in the decisions of management, but those stakeholders for whom management recognises and accepts a responsibility are referred to as **constituents** of the firm.

1.13 The **stakeholder view** of company objectives is that many groups of people have a stake in what the company does. Shareholders own the business, but there are also suppliers, managers, workers and customers. Each of these groups has its own objectives so that a compromise or balance is required. Management must balance the profit objectives with the pressures from the non-shareholder groups in deciding the strategic targets of the business.

> 'There can be no debate about whether corporations should acknowledge and respond to the interest of every stakeholder to the extent that the interests are embodied in law or enforced by market forces .... The debate is ongoing, however, about whether the plural stakeholders should be served as legitimate claimants in their own right rather than simply as a way of serving the primary corporate constituency, the common shareholder' (Sharplin).

1.14 The **consensus theory** of company objectives was developed by Cyert and March. They argued that managers 'run' a business but do not own it and that 'organisations do not have objectives, only people have objectives'. Managers do not necessarily set objectives for the company but rather they look for objectives which suit their own inclinations. However, objectives emerge as a consensus of the differing views of shareholders, managers, employees, suppliers, customers and society at large, but (in contrast to the stakeholder view) they are not all selected nor controlled by management.

Financial reporting and accounting concepts

1.15 As you will be aware, limited companies and their directors are bound by the provisions of the Companies Act 1985 (CA 1985). This legislation governs the preparation and publication of the annual financial statements of companies.

1.16 The form and content of a company's accounts are regulated primarily by CA 1985, but must also comply with the accounting standards published by the Accounting Standards Board (Financial Reporting Standards) and by the Accounting Standards Committee, which the ASB has now replaced (Statements of Standard Accounting Practice).

2 OBJECTIVES OF BUSINESS ENTERPRISES   12/96, 12/97

Mission, corporate objectives and unit objectives

2.1 Objectives of organisations will be heavily influenced by the 'coalition' or stakeholder group that has the most power. This is usually an organisation's senior management. However, this group will be influenced by the expectations of other coalitions and stakeholders. Objectives come in hierarchies, with the objectives lower down in the hierarchy contributing to the objectives higher up.

2.2 Granger identifies three types of objectives: **mission**; **corporate objectives**; **unit objectives**.

Mission

2.3   A mission is a general objective, visionary, often unwritten, and very open-ended, without any time limit for achievement. Thus, the mission of a democratic government should be to improve the well-being of its people in ways which are compatible with their wishes and have a general consensus of support. A commercial company in the leisure industry might have a mission of improving the quality of people's lives, by providing them with all the leisure activities they want.

Corporate objectives

2.4   Corporate objectives are those which are concerned with the firm as a whole. Objectives should be explicit, quantifiable and capable of being achieved. The corporate objectives outline the expectations of the firm and the strategic planning process is concerned with the means of achieving the objectives.

2.5   Objectives should relate to the **key factors for business success**, which are typically as follows.

   (a)   Profitability (return on investment)
   (b)   Market share
   (c)   Growth
   (d)   Cash flow
   (e)   Customer satisfaction
   (f)   The quality of the firm's products
   (g)   Industrial relations
   (h)   Added value

Unit objectives

2.6   Unit objectives are objectives that are specific to individual units of an organisation, and are often 'operational' objectives. Examples are as follows.

   (a)   From the **commercial sector**:

      (i)   Increasing the number of customers by x% (an objective of a sales department)

      (ii)   Reducing the number of rejects by 50% (an objective of a production department)

      (iii)   Producing monthly reports more quickly, within 5 working days of the end of each month (an objective of the management accounting department)

   (b)   From the **public sector**:

      (i)   To provide cheap subsidised bus travel (an objective of a local authority transport department)

      (ii)   To introduce more nursery education (an objective of a borough education department)

      (iii)   Responding more quickly to calls (an objective of a local police station, fire department or hospital ambulance service)

Primary and secondary objectives

2.7   Some objectives are more important than others, and it could be argued that in the hierarchy of objectives, there is a **primary corporate objective** (restricted by certain constraints on corporate activity) and other **secondary objectives** which are strategic objectives which should combine to ensure the achievement of the overall corporate objective.

2.8 Many writers accept that profitability must be the primary objective for a profit-making commercial organisation, but there are different ways of measuring profitability, in one form or another. It is not clear, however, whether there should be a single primary objective or several objectives, nor how different aims and objectives inter-relate.

Argenti cited the creation of customers, servicing society, providing employment and maximising profits as various objectives, and concluded that an objective must be expressed as follows.

(a) It must identify the beneficiaries.
(b) It must state what the nature of the benefit is to be.
(c) It must state the size of the benefit.

For a public sector organisation, the primary objective is unlikely to be quite so simple.

2.9 Whereas the primary objective of a profit-oriented organisation is to make money, it must fulfil certain secondary objectives to do so. For example, the secondary objective of a motor company whose primary objective might be to make money for its shareholders must be to build the best cars for its market or market niche. Other secondary objectives include areas such as promoting environmentally friendly production processes, if that is what consumers indicate they require, or what the law stipulates. In the public sector, the primary objective is an output of services (for example, patient care), not the pursuit of profit.

Trade-off between objectives

2.10 When there are several key objectives, some might be achieved only at the expense of others. For example, a company's objective of achieving good profits and profit growth might have adverse consequences for the cash flow of the business, or the quality of the firm's product. Attempts to achieve a good cash flow or good product quality, or to improve market share, might call for some sacrifice of profits.

2.11 There will be a trade-off between objectives when strategies are formulated, and a choice will have to be made. For example, there might be a choice between the following two options.

Option A   15% sales growth, 10% profit growth, a £2 million negative cash flow and reduced product quality and customer satisfaction.

Option B   8% sales growth, 5% profit growth, a £500,000 surplus cash flow, and maintenance of high product quality/customer satisfaction.

If the firm chose option B in preference to option A, it would be trading off sales growth and profit growth for better cash flow, product quality and customer satisfaction.

Long-term and short-term objectives

2.12 Objectives may be **long-term** and **short-term**. A company that is suffering from a recession in its core industries and making losses in the short term might continue to have a primary objective in the long term of achieving a steady growth in earnings or profits, but in the short term, its primary objective might switch to survival.

BPP PUBLISHING

2.13 Secondary objectives will range from short-term to long-term. Planners will formulate secondary objectives within the guidelines set by the primary objective, after selecting strategies for achieving the primary objective.

2.14 For example, a company's primary objective might be to increase its earnings per share from 30p to 50p in the next five years. Strategies for achieving the objective might be selected to include the following.

   (a) Increasing profitability in the next 12 months by cutting expenditure
   (b) Increasing export sales over the next three years
   (c) Developing a successful new product for the domestic market within five years

   Secondary objectives might then be re-assessed to include the following.

   (a) The objective of improving manpower productivity by 10% within 12 months

   (b) Improving customer service in export markets with the objective of doubling the number of overseas sales outlets in selected countries within the next three years

   (c) Investing more in product-market research and development, with the objective of bringing at least three new products to the market within five years

2.15 Objectives, targets and plans are inter-related aspects of the strategic planning process. Targets cannot be set without an awareness of what is realistic. For example, setting an objective of doubling profits within the next three years might seem fine on paper, but if it is not a realistic aim, it will not be worth the paper it is written on. Quantified targets for achieving the primary objective, and targets for secondary objectives, must therefore emerge from a realistic 'situation audit' of the organisation's position and resources, and from the planning process.

Trade-offs between short-term and long-term objectives

2.16 Just as there may have to be a trade-off between different objectives, so too might there be a need to make trade-offs between short-term and long-term (S/L) objectives.

2.17 In practice, managers' performance is usually judged by short-term achievements.

   (a) Middle and senior management are expected to achieve budget targets, and are criticised if they do not.

   (b) The board of directors of a public company are expected by City analysts to achieve a certain growth in profits and earnings per share each year. If they do not, the share price will be marked down, and the board will be criticised for poor corporate results.

2.18 Since performance is often judged by short-term achievements, it is hardly surprising that the natural tendency for managers is to sacrifice longer term aims in order to achieve short-term targets. In some situations, this might be the 'right' thing to do; in others, it might be a short-sighted and ultimately a bad decision.

2.19 Decisions which involve the sacrifice of longer term objectives include: **postponing or abandoning capital expenditure projects**, which would eventually contribute to (longer term) growth and profits, in order to protect short-term cash flow and profits; and **cutting research and development expenditure** to save operating costs, and so reducing the prospects for future product development.

Question 1

See if you can think of other examples of how an organisation might be sacrificing longer term objectives for shorter term ones.

Answer

Here are a couple of examples you could have chosen.

(a) Reducing quality control, to save operating costs
(b) Reducing the level of customer service, to save operating costs

Profitability and profit measurement

2.20 The shorter term financial objectives of companies include targets for profitability. The measurement of profit under historical cost accounting follows the principles of the generally accepted fundamental accounting concepts (going concern, accruals, consistency and prudence) set out in the accounting standard SSAP 2.

Although profits do matter, they are not the best measure of a company's achievements.

(a) Accounting profits are not the same as 'economic' profits. Accounting profits can be manipulated to some extent by choices of accounting policies.

Question 2

Can you give three examples of how accounting profits might be so manipulated?

Answer

Here are some examples you might have chosen.

(i)   Provisions, such as provisions for depreciation or anticipated losses
(ii)   The capitalisation of various expenses, such as development costs
(iii) Adding overhead costs to stock valuations

(b) A company might make an accounting profit without having used its resources in the most profitable way possible. There is a difference between the accounting concept of 'historical cost' and the economic concept of 'opportunity cost', which is the value that could have been obtained by using resources in their most profitable alternative way.

(c) Profits on their own take no account of the volume of investment that it has taken to earn the profit. Profits must be related to the volume of investment to have any real meaning. Hence measures of financial achievement include:

(i)   Accounting return on capital employed
(ii)   Earnings per share
(iii) Yields on investment, eg dividend yield as a percentage of stock market value

(d) Profits are reported every year (with half-year interim results for quoted companies). They are measures of **short-term** performance, whereas a company's performance should ideally be judged over a longer term.

3   FINANCIAL OBJECTIVES   12/97

3.1 **Financial management** is the management of the finances of a business; that is, financial planning and financial control in order to achieve the financial objectives of the business.

The prime financial objective of a company

3.2 The theory of company finance is based on the assumption that the objective of management is to **maximise the market value of the company's shares**. Specifically, the main objective of a company should be to maximise the wealth of its ordinary shareholders.

3.3 A company is financed by ordinary shareholders, preference shareholders, loan stock holders and other long-term and short-term creditors. All surplus funds, however, belong to the legal owners of the company, its ordinary shareholders. Any retained profits are undistributed wealth of these equity shareholders.

How are the wealth of shareholders and the value of a company measured?

3.4 If the financial objective of a company is to maximise the value of the company, and in particular the value of its ordinary shares, we need to be able to put values on a company and its shares. How do we do it? Three possible methods of valuation might occur to us.

    (a) A balance sheet valuation, with assets valued on a going concern basis. Certainly, investors will look at a company's balance sheet. If retained profits rise every year, the company will be a profitable one. Balance sheet values are not a measure of 'market value', although retained profits might give some indication of what the company could pay as dividends to shareholders.

    (b) The valuation of a company's assets on a **break-up basis**. This method of valuing a business is only of interest when the business is threatened with liquidation, or when its management is thinking about selling off individual assets (rather than a complete business) to raise cash.

    (c) **Market values**. The market value is the price at which buyers and sellers will trade stocks and shares in a company. This is the method of valuation which is most relevant to the financial objectives of a company.

        (i) When shares are traded on a recognised stock market, such as the London Stock Exchange, the market value of a company can be measured by the price at which shares are currently being traded.

        (ii) When shares are in a private company, and are not traded on any stock market, there is no easy way to measure their market value. Even so, the financial objective of these companies should be to maximise the wealth of their ordinary shareholders.

3.5 The **wealth** of the shareholders in a company comes from dividends received and the market value of the shares. A shareholder's **return** on investment is obtained in the form of dividends received and capital gains from increases in the market value of his or her shares.

3.6 Dividends are generally paid by UK public companies just twice a year at most (interim and final dividends), whereas a current market value is (for quoted shares) always known from share prices. There is also a theory, supported by much empirical evidence (and common sense) that market prices are influenced strongly by expectations of what future dividends will be. So we might conclude that the wealth of shareholders in quoted companies can be measured by the market value of the shares.

How is the value of a business increased?

3.7 If a company's shares are traded on a stock market, the wealth of shareholders is increased when the share price goes up. Ignoring day-to-day fluctuations in price caused by patterns of supply and demand, and ignoring fluctuations caused by 'environmental' factors such as changes in interest rates, the price of a company's shares will go up when the company makes attractive profits, which it pays out as dividends or re-invests in the business to achieve future profit growth and dividend growth. However, to increase the share price the company should achieve its profits without taking business risks and financial risks which worry shareholders.

3.8   If there is an increase in earnings and dividends, management can hope for an increase in the share price too, so that shareholders benefit from both higher revenue (dividends) and also capital gains (higher share prices). Management should set targets for factors which they can influence directly, such as profits and dividend growth. And so a financial objective might be expressed as the aim of increasing profits, earnings per share and dividend per share by, say, 10% a year for each of the next five years.

3.9   Following FRS 3, earnings are the profits attributable to equity (that is, to ordinary shareholders) after tax and after any extraordinary gains or losses (although 'extraordinary items' were effectively outlawed by FRS 3). Earnings per share (EPS) are the earnings attributable to each equity share.

3.10   Dividends are the direct reward to shareholders that a company pays out, and so dividends are evidence of a company's ability to provide a return for its shareholders. Companies might therefore set targets for growth in dividend per share.

Financial targets

3.11   In addition to targets for earnings, EPS, and dividend per share, a company might set other financial targets, such as:

(a)   A restriction on the company's level of gearing, or debt. For example, a company's management might decide that:

(i)   The ratio of long-term debt capital to equity capital should never exceed, say, 1:1

(ii)   The cost of interest payments should never be higher than, say, 25% of total profits before interest and tax

(b)   A target for profit retentions. For example, management might set a target that dividend cover (the ratio of distributable profits to dividends actually distributed) should not be less than, say, 2.5 times.

(c)   A target for operating profitability. For example, management might set a target for the profit/sales ratio (say, a minimum of 10%) or for a return on capital employed (say, a minimum ROCE of 20%). (The calculation of ROCE is explained later in the Study Text.)

3.12   These financial targets are not primary financial objectives, but they can act as subsidiary targets or constraints which should help a company to achieve its main financial objective without incurring excessive risks.

Case examples

Some recently privatised companies act within regulatory financial constraints imposed by 'consumer watchdog' bodies set up by government. For example, BT (British Telecom) is overseen by the telecommunications regulator OFTEL, which restricts price rises to protect consumers.

BPP PUBLISHING

Short-term and long-term objectives

3.13 Targets such as those mentioned in Paragraph 3.11 are usually measured over a year rather than over the long term, and it is the maximisation of shareholder wealth in the long term that ought to be the corporate objective. As already stated, short-term measures of return can encourage a company to pursue short-term objectives at the expense of long-term ones, for example by deferring new capital investments, or spending only small amounts on research and development and on training.

Multiple financial targets

3.14 A major problem with setting a number of different financial targets, either primary targets or supporting secondary targets, is that they might not all be consistent with each other, and so might not all be achievable at the same time. When this happens, some compromises will have to be accepted.

4 NON-FINANCIAL OBJECTIVES

4.1 An enterprise may have important non-financial objectives, which could limit the achievement of financial objectives.

Question 3

Before looking at what follows, write out your own list of the various non-financial objectives which an enterprise might have.

Examples of non-financial objectives are as follows.

(a) **Welfare of employees.** A company might try to provide good wages and salaries, comfortable and safe working conditions, good training and career development, and good pensions. If redundancies are necessary, many companies will provide generous redundancy payments, or spend money trying to find alternative employment for redundant staff.

(b) **Welfare of management.** Managers will often take decisions to improve their own circumstances, even though their decisions will incur expenditure and so reduce profits. High salaries, company cars and other perks are all examples of managers promoting their own interests.

(c) **Welfare of society as a whole.** The management of some companies are aware of the role that their company has to play in providing for the well-being of society. As an example, oil companies are aware of their role as providers of energy for society, faced with the problems of protecting the environment and preserving the Earth's dwindling energy resources.

(d) **Provision of a service.** The major objectives of some companies will include the provision of a service to the public. Examples are the recently privatised companies such as BT, British Gas and the regional electricity distribution companies. For some of these companies (including BT), the regulatory regime imposed by government specifies certain service standards.

(e) **Fulfilment of responsibilities towards customers and suppliers.** Responsibilities towards customers include providing a product or service of a quality that customers expect, and dealing honestly and fairly with customers. Responsibilities towards **suppliers** are expressed mainly in terms of trading relationships. A company's size could give it considerable power as a buyer. The company should not use its power unscrupulously. Suppliers might rely on getting prompt payment, in accordance with the agreed terms of trade.

The relationship between financial and non-financial objectives

4.2 Non-financial objectives do not negate financial objectives, but they do mean that the simple theory of company finance, that the objective of a firm is to maximise the wealth of ordinary shareholders, is too simplistic. Financial objectives may have to be compromised in order to satisfy non-financial objectives.

5 OBJECTIVES OF PUBLICLY OWNED AND NON-COMMERCIAL BODIES

Nationalised industries

5.1 The framework of financial management in state-owned (or nationalised) industries consists of: **strategic objectives**; **rules about investment plans and their appraisal**; **corporate plans, targets and aims**; **external financing limits**.

Following the privatisation programme of the 1980s and early 1990s, the UK's nationalised industries are much fewer in number than they were. The largest nationalised industry remaining is the Post Office. Another is the London Underground transport system. Some other countries, however, have much more extensive state ownership of industries.

Strategic objectives for the nationalised industries

5.2 Nationalised industries are financed by government loans, and some borrowing from the capital markets. They do not have equity capital, and there is no stock exchange to give a day-by-day valuation of the business.

5.3 The financial objective cannot be to maximise the wealth of its owners, the government or the general public, because this is not a concept which can be applied in practice. Nevertheless, there will be a financial objective, to contribute in a certain way to the national economy. This objective may be varied according to the political views of the government. There may be an objective to earn enough profits for the industry to provide for a certain proportion of its **investment needs** from its own resources. A very **profitable** state-owned industry may be expected to transfer surplus funds to the government.

5.4 Even so, the principal objective of a nationalised industry will in most cases not be a financial one at all. The financial objectives will therefore be subordinated to a number of political and social considerations.

(a) A nationalised industry may be expected to provide a certain standard of service to all customers, regardless of the fact that some individuals will receive a service at a charge well below its cost. For example, the postal service must deliver letters to remote locations for the price of an ordinary first or second class stamp.

(b) The need to provide a service may be of such overriding social and political importance that the government is prepared to subsidise the industry. There is a strong body of opinion, for example, which argues that public transport is a social necessity and a certain level of service must be provided, with losses made up by government subsidies.

Corporate plans, targets and aims for nationalised industries

5.5   Each nationalised industry has financial targets and a series of performance aims. These targets and performance aims are set for a period of three to five years ahead, and may be included within a broader corporate plan. Financial targets vary from industry to industry, depending on how profitable or unprofitable it is expected to be. For profitable industries, the financial target has so far been set in terms of achieving a target rate of return. The return is measured as a current cost operating profit on the net replacement cost of assets employed.

5.6   Performance aims are intended to back up the financial targets, and may be expressed in terms of target cost reductions or efficiency improvements. Achieving cost reduction through efficiency improvements has been a prime target of nationalised industries in the UK in recent years. The Post Office, for example, has in the past had a target to reduce real unit costs in its mail business and in its counters business.

External financing limits (EFLs) for nationalised industries

5.7   External financing limits (EFLs) control the flow of finance to and from nationalised industries. They set a limit on the amount of finance the industry can obtain from the government, and in the case of very profitable industries, they set requirements for the net repayment of finance to the government.

Not-for-profit organisations

5.8   Some organisations are set up with a prime objective which is not related to making profits. Charities and government organisations are examples. These organisations exist to pursue non-financial aims, such as providing a service to the community. However, there will be financial constraints which limit what any such organisation can do.

   (a)   A not-for-profit organisation needs finance to pay for its operations, and the major financial constraint is the amount of funds that it can obtain.

   (b)   Having obtained funds, a not-for-profit organisation should seek to use the funds:

      (i)   **Economically**: not spending £2 when the same thing can be bought for £1
      (ii)   **Efficiently**: getting the best use out of what money is spent on
      (iii) **Effectively**: spending funds so as to achieve the organisation's objectives

Government departments

5.9   Financial management in government departments is different from financial management in an industrial or commercial company for various reasons.

   (a)   Government departments do not operate to make a profit, and the objectives of a department or of a programme of spending cannot be expressed in terms of maximising the return on capital employed.

   (b)   Government services are provided without the commercial pressure of competition. There are no competitive reasons for controlling costs, being efficient or, when services are charged for (such as medical prescriptions), keeping prices down.

   (c)   Government departments have full-time professional civil servants as their managers, but decisions are also taken by politicians.

(d) The government gets its money for spending from taxes, other sources of income and borrowing (such as issuing gilts) and the nature of its fund-raising differs substantially from fund-raising by companies.

5.10 Since managing government is different from managing a company, a different framework is needed for planning and control. This is achieved by:

(a) Setting objectives for each department
(b) Careful planning of public expenditure proposals
(c) Emphasis on getting value for money

Executive agencies

5.11 A development in recent years has been the creation of agencies to carry out specific functions (such as vehicle licensing). These **executive agencies** are answerable to the government for providing a certain level of service, but are independently managed on business principles.

Chapter roundup

- In this chapter, we have discussed **financial strategy** and its relationship with overall corporate strategy.

- One of the most important influences on strategy is the **goals of different interest groups**, or **stakeholder groups.**

- In financial management, the key objective is the **maximisation of shareholders' wealth**.

- **Non-financial objectives** also need to be considered.

Quick quiz

1 List six types of stakeholder groups. (see para 1.7)

2 Explain what is meant by the consensus theory of corporate objectives. (1.14)

3 What is meant by the 'mission' of an organisation? (2.3)

4 According to the theory of company finance, what is the central financial objective of a company? (3.2)

5 What might be the objectives of a publicly owned industry? (5.3, 5.4)

Question to try	Level	Marks	Time
1	Exam standard	10	18 mins

BPP PUBLISHING

Chapter 2

ISSUES IN CORPORATE GOVERNANCE

Chapter topic list	Syllabus reference
1 Patterns of share ownership	1(b)
2 Potential sources of conflict	1(b), (c), (d)
3 Issues in corporate governance	1(b), (d)

Introduction

Following on from Chapter 1, we discuss here:

(a) The system of **corporate governance**, by which companies are directed and controlled, and
(b) The possible **conflicts of interest** which may arise in corporate governance

In recent years, the debate on corporate governance has been intensifying, leading to a re-examination of shareholders' relationships with management. Corporate governance should be studied as an underpinning to the study of strategic financial decisions in Paper 14.

Knowledge brought forward from Paper 8

The following points were covered in Paper 8, *Managerial Finance*. Go back to your Paper 8 notes if you feel you need to.

Stock market listing

In the UK, a company can bring its shares to the market for the first time (in a flotation) by the following methods.

- An offer for sale at either a set price, or (more rarely) by tender
- A placing, usually with institutional investors
- A prospectus issue
- A stock exchange introduction

The Alternative Investment Market

Key points on the AIM are as follows.

- The AIM is a 'second tier' market of the London Stock Exchange, the first tier being the 'main market' or official list

- Launched in 1995 as a market for smaller, growing, companies

- Not a direct replacement for the earlier Unlisted Securities Market (USM), as it has more lax entry requirements and regulations

- No eligibility criteria concerning size, profitability or length of track record

- Any type of security can be offered, provided no restrictions on transferability

- No Stock Exchange requirements for the percentage of shares in public hands or the number of shareholders

- Few obligations to issue shareholder circulars; public announcements will generally sufficient

- Admission documents are the responsibility of the directors: not reviewed by the Stock Exchange

- AIM companies must have an approved Nominated Adviser and a Nominated Broker

  - The Adviser will advise the directors on obligations under AIM rules
  - The Broker will support trading if there is no market maker

- AIM shares are treated as unquoted for tax purposes, meaning that a number of reliefs are available to investors

AIM companies might be new business 'start-ups' or well established family businesses, from high technology firms to traditional manufacturers. The AIM offers the advantages of wider access to capital, enhanced credibility among financial institutions and a higher public profile, at a much lower cost than a full listing.

1   PATTERNS OF SHARE OWNERSHIP   12/97

1.1   Who are the shareholders of the company? The governance of a company will depend in part on the answer to this question. The most important distinction to be made here is between private companies, which cannot offer their shares to the public, and public companies, which include all companies quoted on the Stock Exchange.

Private companies

1.2   A **private company** is likely to be 'owner-managed', in which case it will be run by a small group of shareholder/directors. Outside shareholders are relatively uncommon, although the UK Government's Enterprise Investment Scheme, set up in 1994, offers tax incentives to encourage individuals to hold shares in private companies.

1.3   **Minority shareholders** in private companies are usually in a weak position if they are not on the board, since the small group controlling more than 50% of the voting shares will be able to control the make-up of the board of directors.

Quoted companies

1.4   Under London Stock Exchange rules, at least 25% of the shares of **quoted companies** must be held by members of the public. Although a small group might still control the majority of voting shares, the minority shareholder of a quoted company has the advantage that there is a secondary market for the shares. If the shareholder does not like the way the company is run, it is possible simply to sell the shares - an alternative which is often not available to the private company minority shareholder.

1.5   The existence of a secondary market in existing shares of Stock Exchange quoted companies acts as an incentive to directors to manage the company effectively and in accordance with the general wishes of shareholders and potential shareholders. If demand for the company's shares falls, the share price will fall and it may become more difficult for the company to raise the finance it needs.

Types of institutional investor

1.6   **Institutional investors** channel funds invested by individuals making investments on their behalf which may be in government ('gilt-edged') stocks, shares of unquoted companies and other financial instruments or other assets (such as gold or works of art), as well as the predominant form of investment: shares in companies quoted on the Stock Exchange.

19 **BPP**
PUBLISHING

1.7 The institutional investors are now the biggest investors on the stock market but they might also invest venture capital, or lend directly to companies.

Question 1

Before looking at the following paragraph, see if you can list the major types of institutional investor in the UK.

1.8 The major institutional investors in the UK are: **pension funds**; **insurance companies**; **investment trusts**; **unit trusts**; **venture capital organisations**. Of these, pension funds and insurance companies have the largest amounts of funds to invest.

Pension funds as institutional investors

1.9 **Pension funds** comprise funds set aside to provide for retirement pensions. They are financed from pension contributions paid into a fund by a company and its employees, and private individuals.

1.10 Pension funds are continually receiving large amounts of money from pension contributions. They are also continually paying out money for pensions, as lump sums and regular pension payments to beneficiaries.

1.11 Money coming in can be diverted to meet payment obligations, but there will usually be an excess of contributions coming in over pensions going out, and this excess must be invested.

1.12 A fund manager is the person who makes the investment decisions, buying and selling securities. Fund managers must attempt to ensure that their investments will provide enough income to meet future pension commitments. Generally speaking, most holdings are considered to be long-term. Few fund managers would expect to make a substantial profit from short term speculation as such dealing is highly risky. Often a portion of the fund is invested in high yield securities, such as gilts which will, hopefully, give enough income to meet current commitments, and the balance is invested in growth assets such as equities or property.

Insurance companies

1.13 **Insurance companies** sell insurance policies (life assurance policies, car insurance, house insurance, pension policies and so on). They need cash to pay out for claims or other entitlements under the terms of their policies, but they will have substantial cash income to invest.

1.14 The investment strategy of insurance companies is similar to the investment strategy of pension fund managers. They invest in a **portfolio** of company stocks and shares, government securities (gilts), direct loans and mortgages and other investments. They **limit investment risks,** investing most of their funds in secure companies. They deal in **large blocks** of stocks and shares, because the potential return from small investments is often not worth the trouble.

Investment trusts

1.15 **Investment trusts** are companies whose business is to invest in the securities of a wide range of other companies. Their portfolios may change continually, as circumstances require.

(a) Having a capital structure like any other company, they pay dividends to shareholders from profits which arise from their investment income. An investment trust company with a Stock Exchange listing must have a clause in its Memorandum or Articles prohibiting the distribution as dividend of any surpluses arising from the sale of investments it holds.

(b) Most of the funds of investment trusts are invested directly through the Stock Exchange, and little money goes into unquoted shares. Normally they are only interested in larger unquoted companies but some investment trusts might be prepared to take a block of shares in a smaller unquoted company.

Unit trusts

1.16 **Unit trusts** cater for small investors who wish to spread their investment risk over a wide range of securities, but have insufficient funds to create such a portfolio by themselves. A 'unit' is a portfolio of shares or other investments managed by a unit trust company in which individual investors are invited to take a stake (sub-unit). Since 1991, the Securities and Investments Board has sanctioned the creation of authorised unit trusts dealing in futures and options.

1.17 The unit trust is based on a trust deed. Unit holders receive their income as a proportionate share of the investment income from the securities in the unit after deducting expenses of the management company. When a unit holder wants to realise his investment, he can sell his unit. Unit prices vary in market value according to the value of the shares or other securities which make up the unit's portfolio.

The growth of institutional investment

1.18 Over the last four decades or so, there has been a radical change in the pattern of shareholdings in the UK. Research has shown that, while in 1957 over 60% of equities were held by private individuals, by the 1990s it was institutions which held nearly two-thirds of all shares in UK companies. The market worth of pension funds stood at around £200 billion by the beginning of the 1990s, over 50% of which was invested in UK equities. The decline in the proportion of shares held by individuals continued through the 1980s, a trend which also occurred in the USA, Japan and Germany. In the 1990s, there was some increase in the number of individual shareholdings following UK privatisations. However, in value terms, institutional investment (including investment on behalf of individuals, such as unit trusts, investment trusts and pensions), remains dominant. The UK trends show that institutional investors or fund managers wield great power with the potential to exert influence over the various companies in which they invest.

1.19 In some respects the existence of the institutional investor seems desirable. It is desirable that more people should be in pensionable employment or have personal pension plans and that the funds from which their pensions will be payable should be held separately from the companies by whom they are employed. Similarly, it is desirable that investors should have the opportunity to invest through the medium of insurance companies, unit trusts and investment trusts. These forms of collective investment are often best for the small investor whose knowledge of the market is limited and who has insufficient funds to build up his own balanced portfolio of investments.

1.20 However, the dominance of the equity markets by institutional investors has possibly undesirable consequences as well.

(a) For capital markets to be truly competitive there should be no investors who are on their own of such size that they can influence prices. In the UK, transactions by the largest institutions are now on such a massive scale that considerable price movements can result. For example if an insurance company decided to sell, at one time, a 5% holding in a large public company the effect on the price would, at least in the short term, be substantial. The problem will be compounded if other institutions follow and sell their holdings.

(b) Many institutions tend to avoid shares which are seen as speculative as they feel that they have a duty to their 'customers' to invest only in 'blue chip' shares (ie those of leading commercially sound companies). As a result, the shares of such companies tend to be relatively expensive.

(c) Because of their collective power the institutions have to some extent become **elite investors**. They are sometimes, for example, invited to meet the top management of companies. At such meetings it is almost inevitable that they will obtain information not generally available to other investors. The Stock Exchange is concerned about trends of this type, believing that all shareholders should be treated as equal. One consequence of their concern has been the Takeover Code. This is aimed, among other things, at preventing a bidder from seeking institutional support by offering better terms than those available to other shareholders.

(d) Fund managers are sometimes accused of **'short-termism'** in that they will tend to seek short-term speculative gains or simply sell their shares and invest elsewhere rather than use their collective power constructively if they feel that there are management shortcomings.

1.21 The advantages of having a **wide range of shareholders** include the following.

(a) There is likely to be greater activity in the market in the firm's shares, ie greater 'market liquidity'.

(b) There is less likelihood of one shareholder having a controlling interest.

(c) Since shareholdings are smaller on average, there is likely to be less effect on the share price if one shareholder sells his holding.

(d) There is a greater likelihood of the threat of a takeover bid being frustrated.

Disadvantages of a large number of shareholders include the following.

(a) Administrative costs will be high. These include the costs of sending out copies of the annual report and accounts, counting proxy votes, registering new shareholders and paying dividends.

(b) Shareholders will have varying tax rates and objectives in holding the firm's shares, which makes a dividend/retention policy more difficult for the management to decide upon.

Should managers know who the shareholders are?

1.22 A company's senior management should remain aware of who its major shareholders are, and it will often help to retain shareholders' support if the chairman or the managing director meets occasionally with the major shareholders, to exchange views. The advantages of knowing who the company's shareholders are can be listed as follows.

(a) The company's management might learn about shareholders' preferences for either high dividends or high retained earnings for profit growth and capital gain.

(b) For public companies, changes in shareholdings might help to explain recent share price movements.

(c) The company's management should be able to learn about shareholders' attitudes to both risk and gearing. If a company is planning a new investment, its management might have to consider the relative merits of seeking equity finance or debt finance, and shareholders' attitudes would be worth knowing about before the decision is taken.

(d) Management might need to know its shareholders in the event of an unwelcome takeover bid from another company, in order to identify key shareholders whose views on the bid might be crucial to the final outcome.

2 POTENTIAL SOURCES OF CONFLICT 12/96, 12/97

The role of shareholders and the role of managers

2.1 Although ordinary **shareholders** (equity shareholders) are the owners of the company to whom the board of directors are accountable, the actual powers of shareholders tend to be restricted, except in companies where the shareholders are also the directors. Shareholders are often ignorant about their company's current situation and future prospects. They have no right to inspect the books of account, and their forecasts of future prospects are gleaned from the annual report and accounts, stockbrokers, investment journals and daily newspapers.

2.2 The day-to-day running of a company is the responsibility of the directors and other management staff to whom they delegate, and although the company's results are submitted for shareholders' approval at the annual general meeting (AGM), there is often apathy and acquiescence in directors' recommendations. AGMs are often very poorly attended. For these reasons, there is the potential for **conflicts of interest** between management and shareholders.

Agency theory and the 'agency problem'

2.3 The relationship between management and shareholders is sometimes referred to as an agency relationship, in which managers act as agents for the shareholders, using delegated powers to run the affairs of the company in the shareholders' best interests.

2.4 **Agency theory** proposes that, although individual members of the business team act in their own self-interest, the well-being of each individual depends on the well-being of other team members and on the performance of the team in competition with other teams. The firm is seen as constituted by contracts among the different factors of production. Agency theory was advanced by two American economists, Jensen and Meckling, in 1976 as a theory to explain relationships within corporations. It has been used to explain management control practices as well as relationships between management and investors: here we are concerned with the latter.

2.5 Jensen and Meckling proposed that corporations be viewed as a set of contracts between management, shareholders and creditors, with management as agents and providers of finance as principals. Financial reports and external audit are two mechanisms by which the agents demonstrate compliance with their obligations to the principals.

2.6 The agency relationship arising from the separation of ownership from management is sometimes characterised as the **'agency problem'**. For example, if managers hold none or very little of the equity shares of the company they work for, what is to stop them from:

working inefficiently, not bothering to look for profitable new investment opportunities, or giving themselves high salaries and perks?

2.7 One power that shareholders possess is the right to remove the directors from office. But shareholders have to take the initiative to do this, and in many companies, the shareholders lack the energy and organisation to take such a step. Even so, directors will want the company's report and accounts, and the proposed final dividend, to meet with shareholders' approval at the AGM.

2.8 For management below director level, it is the responsibility of the directors to ensure that they perform well. Getting the best out of subordinates is one of the functions of management, and directors should be expected to do it as well as they can.

2.9 Another reason why managers might do their best to improve the financial performance of their company is that managers' pay is often related to the size or profitability of the company. Managers in very big companies, or in very profitable companies, will normally expect to earn higher salaries than managers in smaller or less successful companies.

2.10 As explained by G Cosserat (ACCA *Students' Newsletter*, December 1994), agency theory is based on a number of behavioural and structural assumptions. The most important **behavioural assumptions** are individual welfare maximisation, individual rationality, and the assumption that individuals are risk-averse. Structural assumptions include the assumption that investments are not infinitely divisible, and that individuals vary in their access to funds and their entrepreneurial ability. Some criticisms of the theory have attacked these various assumptions. For example, are individuals satisficers rather than maximisers? And are individuals truly 'rational' or perhaps rather gullible?

2.11 The assumptions of the theory suggest that investors and entrepreneurs have incentives for sharing risks and rewards of entrepreneurial activity, for example where the entrepreneur, who may enjoy limited liability, borrows from investors at fixed rates of interest.

2.12 The key feature of an efficient agency contract, for example within a company, is that it allows full delegation of decision-making authority over the use of invested funds to management without excessive risk of abuse of that authority. In the real world, an 'agency cost' arises, being the difference between the return expected if managers truly maximised shareholder wealth and the actual return, given that managers will actually be seeking to maximise their own wealth.

2.13 **'Bonding'** and **'monitoring'** procedures help to act as safeguards to minimise the risk of investors incurring agency costs. An example of 'bonding' is a condition attached to a loan (eg security over assets, conditions not to raise further loans). A bank lending money to a business will also expect information to be supplied to enable it to monitor compliance with the loan agreement.

2.14 Agency theory suggests that audited accounts of limited companies are an important source of 'post-decision' information minimising investors' agency costs, in contrast to alternative approaches which see financial reports as primarily a source of 'pre-decision' information for equity investors. The theory is advanced as an explanation for the continued use of absorption costing and historic costs in management accounts in spite of their apparent lack of relevance in decision making.

Goal congruence

2.15 Agency theory sees employees of businesses, including managers, as individuals, each with his or her own objectives. Within a department of a business, there are departmental objectives. If achieving these various objectives leads also to the achievement of the objectives of the organisation as a whole, there is said to be **goal congruence**.

> **KEY TERM**
>
> **Goal congruence:** accordance between the objectives of agents acting within an organisation and the objectives of the organisation as a whole.

2.16 Goal congruence may be better achieved and the 'agency problem' better dealt with by giving managers some profit-related pay, or by providing incentives which are related to profits or share price. Examples of such remuneration incentives are:

(a) Pay or bonuses related to the size of profits (**profit-related pay**).

(b) Rewarding managers with shares. This might be done when a private company 'goes public' and managers are invited to subscribe for shares in the company at an attractive offer price. In a **management buy-out** or buy-in (the latter involving purchase of the business by new managers; the former by existing managers), managers become owner-managers.

(c) **Executive share options plans (ESOPs)**. In a share option scheme, selected employees are given a number of share options, each of which gives the holder the right after a certain date to subscribe for shares in the company at a fixed price. The value of an option will increase if the company is successful and its share price goes up. For example, an employee might be given 10,000 options to subscribe for shares in the company at a price of £2.00 per share. If the share price goes up to, say, £5 per share by the time that the exercise date for the options arrives, the employee will be able to profit by £30,000 (by buying £50,000 worth of shares for £20,000).

2.17 Such measures might merely encourage management to adopt '**creative accounting**' methods which will distort the reported performance of the company in the service of the managers' own ends. However, creative accounting methods such **as off-balance sheet finance** present a temptation to management at all times given that they allow a more favourable picture of the state of the company to be presented than otherwise, to shareholders, potential investors, potential lenders and others.

2.18 An alternative approach is to attempt to monitor managers' behaviour, for example by establishing 'management audit' procedures, to introduce additional reporting requirements, or to seek assurances from managers that shareholders' interests will be foremost in their priorities.

Shareholders, managers and the company's long-term creditors

2.19 The relationship between long-term creditors of a company, the management and the shareholders of a company encompasses the following factors.

(a) Management may decide to raise finance for a company by taking out long-term or medium-term loans. They might well be taking risky investment decisions using outsiders' money to finance them.

BPP PUBLISHING

(b) Investors who provide debt finance will rely on the company's management to generate enough net cash inflows to make interest payments on time, and eventually to repay loans. Long-term creditors will often take **security** for their loan, perhaps in the form of a fixed charge over an asset (such as a mortgage on a building). Debentures are also often subject to certain restrictive covenants, which restrict the company's rights to borrow more money until the debentures have been repaid. If a company is unable to pay what it owes its creditors, the creditors may decide to exercise their security or to apply for the company to be wound up.

(c) The money that is provided by long-term creditors will be invested to earn profits, and the profits (in excess of what is needed to pay interest on the borrowing) will provide extra dividends or retained profits for the shareholders of the company. In other words, shareholders will expect to increase their wealth using creditors' money.

3 ISSUES IN CORPORATE GOVERNANCE   6/94, 6/95

The Cadbury Report

3.1 Financial aspects of corporate governance in the UK have been addressed recently in the report of the Cadbury Committee, which was formed in 1991. The terms of reference of the committee were to consider, along with any other relevant matters, the following issues.

(a) The responsibilities of executive and non-executive directors for reviewing and reporting on performance to shareholders and other financially interested parties, and the frequency, clarity and form in which information should be provided

(b) The case for audit committees of the board, including their composition and role

(c) The principal responsibilities of auditors and the extent and value of the audit

(d) The links between shareholders, boards, and auditors

Corporate governance

> ### KEY TERM
>
> The Cadbury Report defines **corporate governance** as 'the system by which companies are directed and controlled'.

3.2 The roles of those concerned with the financial statements are described in the Cadbury Report.

(a) The **directors** are responsible for the corporate governance of the company.

(b) The **shareholders** are linked to the directors via the financial reporting system.

(c) The **auditors** provide the shareholders with an external objective check on the directors' financial statements.

(d) Other concerned **users**, particularly employees (to whom the directors owe some responsibility) are indirectly addressed by the financial statements.

3.3 The Cadbury Committee was set up because of the lack of confidence which was perceived in financial reporting and in the ability of auditors to provide the assurances required by the users of financial statements. The main difficulties were considered to be in the relationship between auditors and boards of directors. In particular, the commercial pressures on both directors and auditors caused pressure to be brought to bear on auditors by the board and the auditors often capitulated. Problems were also perceived in the ability of the board of directors to control their organisations. These problems have been debated for some time, but recent company collapses, often sudden and unexpected, intensified the worries of regulating bodies, the Stock Exchange and the government. The lack of board accountability in many of these company collapses intensified the perceived need for action.

3.4   The committee aims to set out the responsibilities of each group involved in the reporting process and to make recommendations on good practice.

Code of Best Practice

3.5   The **Code of Best Practice** included in the Cadbury Report is aimed at the directors of all UK public companies, but the directors of all companies are encouraged to use the Code for guidance. Pressure should be brought by all the relevant parties on the directors to ensure compliance with the Code. In particular, institutional investors will have a lot of power to influence the directors. Key points in the Code are summarised in the following paragraphs.

3.6   Directors should state in the annual report and accounts whether they comply with the Code and give reasons for any non-compliance. This statement of compliance should only be published after a review by the auditors.

The board of directors

3.7   The **board of directors** must meet on a regular basis, retain full control over the company and monitor the executive management. A clearly accepted division of responsibilities is necessary at the head of the company, so no one person has complete power, answerable to no-one. (Compare this to the Robert Maxwell situation.)

3.8   The report encourages the separation of the posts of Chairman and Chief Executive. Where they are not separate, a strong independent group should be present on the board, with their own leader.

3.9   There should be a formal schedule of matters which must be referred to the board stating which decisions require a single director's signature and which require several signatures. Procedures should be in place to make sure the schedule is followed. The schedule should include **acquisitions and disposals of assets of the company** or its subsidiaries that are material to the company and **investments, capital projects, bank borrowing** facilities, **loans** and their repayment, foreign currency transactions, all above a certain size (to be determined by the board).

Non-executive directors

3.10 The following points are made about **non-executive directors**, who are those directors not running the day to day operations of the company.

(a)   They should bring independent judgement to bear on important issues, including key appointments and standards of conduct.

(b)   There should be no business, financial or other connection between the non-executive directors and the company, apart from fees and shareholdings.

(c)   Fees should reflect the time they spend on the business of the company, so extra duties could earn extra pay.

(d) They should not take part in share option schemes and their service should not be pensionable, to maintain their independent status.

(e) Appointments should be for a specified term and reappointment should not be automatic. The board as a whole should decide on their nomination and selection.

(f) Procedures should exist whereby non-executive directors may take independent advice, at the company's expense if necessary.

Executive directors

3.11 In relation to the **executive directors**, who run companies on a day to day basis, the main points in the Code relate to service contracts (contracts of employment) and pay. The length of such contracts should be three years at most, unless the shareholders approve a longer contract.

3.12 Directors' emoluments and those of the highest paid directors should be fully disclosed and analysed between salary and performance-related pay. The basis of measuring performance should also be shown. A remuneration committee of non-executive directors should decide on the level of executive pay.

The audit committee

3.13 A major recommendation in the Code is that all listed companies must establish effective **audit committees** if they have not already done so. The Code takes its example from countries such as Canada and the USA where audit committees for listed companies are compulsory.

3.14 The audit committees should have formal terms of reference dealing with their membership, authority and duties. They should meet at least three times every year and membership of the committee, which should be comprised of **non-executive directors**, should be shown in the annual report.

3.15 The committee must have the authority, resources and means of access to investigate anything within its terms of reference. The duties of the audit committee should include the following.

(a) Recommendations to the board on the appointment of the auditor, resignation or dismissal and the audit fee

(b) Review of the half yearly and annual statements before they are submitted to the board

(c) Discussion with the auditors

(d) Review of the internal audit programme and any significant findings

(e) Review of the external auditors' management letter and the company's statement on the internal control system

Smaller companies

3.16 Many **smaller companies** have complained that the Cadbury Code is too burdensome for them, raising fears that if its requirements are not diluted then many smaller companies will simply fail to comply with them. In response to this, a special version of the code aimed at listed companies with market capitalisation below £250 million was published in 1994 by the City Group for Smaller Companies ('Cisco'), with the endorsement of the Cadbury Committee. Differences between the Cisco code and the Cadbury code include reduction of the number of non-executives on a company board from three to two and not requiring smaller companies to split the roles of Chief Executive and Chairman.

The Greenbury Code

3.17 In 1995, the **Greenbury Committee** published a Code which established principles for the determination of directors' pay and detailing disclosures to be given in the annual reports and accounts. Most of the Greenbury Code principles have been adopted by The Stock Exchange in its Listing Rules.

3.18 The Greenbury Code goes beyond The Cadbury Code of Best Practice. Under the Greenbury Code, it is recommended that the remuneration committee determines, and not merely recommends, executive directors' remuneration and that this committee should be comprised solely of non-executive directors. (However, the Chairman or Chief Executive may be consulted.) Directors' service contracts, it is recommended, should be limited to one year.

3.19 The implementation of two of the most controversial recommendations of the Greenbury Committee have been deferred.

(a) The first of these is the prohibition on issuing share options at a discount. The Stock Exchange is to issue a Consultative Document to explore the possibility of exempting discounted options granted as a part of approved schemes.

(b) The second is the disclosure of pension entitlements earned by each director in the year. Guidance from the actuarial profession is awaited on this issue.

3.20 Two further recommendations have been included in the Listing Rules (Annex B), but the Stock Exchange has not yet made them mandatory by including them in the Listing Rules themselves, pending further consultation. These are recommendations that:

(a) Long-term incentive schemes should be approved by shareholders

(b) Awards under share option and other incentive schemes should normally be phased rather than awarded in one block

The Hampel Report

3.21 The **Hampel Committee on Corporate Governance** produced a final report in January 1998. The committee followed up matters raised in the Cadbury and Greenbury reports, aiming to restrict the regulatory burden on companies and substituting principles for detail whenever possible. The introduction to the report also states that whilst the Cadbury and Greenbury reports concentrated on the prevention of abuses, Hampel was equally concerned with the positive contribution good corporate governance can make.

3.22 Hampel proposed combining the various best practices, principles and codes of **Cadbury, Greenbury and Hampel** into one single **supercode**. The London Stock Exchange has issued a combined corporate governance code, which was derived from the recommendations of the Cadbury, Greenbury and Hampel reports. In June 1998 the Stock Exchange Listing Rules were amended to make compliance with the new code obligatory for listed companies for **accounting periods ending after 31 December 1998**.

3.23 The introduction to the Hampel Report points out that the **primary duty of directors is to shareholders**, to enhance the value of shareholders' investment over time. Relationships

BPP PUBLISHING

with other stakeholders are important, but making the directors responsible to other stakeholders would mean there was no clear yardstick for judging directors' performance.

3.24 The Hampel Committee is also against treating the corporate governance codes as sets of prescriptive rules, and judging companies by whether they have complied. The report states that there can be guidelines which will normally be appropriate but the differing circumstances of companies mean that sometimes there are valid reasons for exceptions.

3.25 The major recommendations of the report were as follows.

Directors

3.26 **Executive** and **non-executive directors** should continue to have the same duties under the law. New directors should be properly trained. The majority of non-executive directors should be independent, and boards should disclose in the annual report which of the non-executive directors are considered to be independent. Non-executive directors should comprise at least one third of the membership of the board. The roles of chairman and chief executive should generally be separate. Whether or not the roles of chairman and chief executive are combined, a senior non-executive director should be identified. All directors should submit themselves for **re-election** at least once every three years. Boards should assess the **performance** of individual directors and collective board performance.

Directors' remuneration

3.27 Boards should establish a **remuneration committee**, made up of independent non-executive directors, to develop policy on remuneration and devise remuneration packages for individual executive directors. Remuneration committees should use their judgement in devising schemes appropriate for the specific circumstances of the company. Total rewards from such schemes should not be excessive. Boards should try and reduce directors' contract periods to one year or less, but this cannot be achieved immediately. The accounts should include a general statement on remuneration policy, but this should not be the subject of an AGM vote.

Shareholders and the AGM

3.28 Companies should consider providing a business presentation at the **AGM**, with a question and answer session. Shareholders should be able to vote separately on each substantially separate issue; and that the practice of 'bundling' unrelated proposals in a single resolution should cease. The number of proxy votes for or against a resolution should be announced after votes on a show of hands. Companies should propose a resolution at the AGM relating to the report and accounts. Notice of the AGM and related papers should be sent to shareholders at least 20 working days before the meeting.

Accountability and audit

3.29 Each company should establish an **audit committee** of at least three non-executive directors, at least two of them independent. The audit committee should keep under review the overall financial relationship between the company and its auditors, to ensure a balance between the maintenance of objectivity and value for money. Directors should report on **internal control**, but should not be required to report on effectiveness of controls. Auditors should report privately on internal controls to directors. Directors should maintain and review controls relating to all relevant control objectives, and not merely financial controls. Companies which do not already have a separate internal audit function should consider the need for one.

Reporting

3.30 The accounts should contain a **statement** of how the company applies the corporate governance principles, and should **explain their policies**, including any circumstances justifying departure from best practice.

Criticisms of the Hampel report

3.31 Some commentators have criticised the Hampel report for stating that the debate on accountability has obscured the first responsibility of a board, to enhance the prosperity of a company over time. Critics have argued that accountability and prosperity should be seen as compatible. In addition, Hampel has been criticised for dropping the requirement for the board to report publicly on the effectiveness of internal controls and for the auditors to report publicly on the statement made by the board.

3.32 Indications are that the UK government is contemplating certain statutory changes to reinforce the work of the corporate governance committees, but will otherwise leave the approach of **voluntary compliance** alone for now. However Margaret Beckett, Trade and Industry Secretary, has stated that there should be an emphasis on **growth**, **investment**, **accountability** and **transparency**.

> **Exam focus point**
> Be prepared to take a broad view of corporate governance in the exam, not just considering the Cadbury Report. Below we take an international perspective.

Corporate governance: comparisons with other countries 6/97

3.33 The establishment of a voluntary code of practice on corporate governance in the Cadbury Report characterises a different approach to that adopted in many other countries.

(a) In the USA, the system of corporate governance is rather more oriented to **stock exchange regulation**, through the Securities and Exchange Commission (SEC), which imposes stringent quarterly reporting requirements on listed US companies and requires all such companies to maintain independent audit committees.

There is more emphasis on control through legislation than in the UK. The board of directors and the auditors have similar roles to the UK, but there is more legislation on directors' conduct in the USA than the UK. Unlike the UK, it is relatively common to have major creditors and chief executive officers of other companies represented on boards of directors in the USA.

(b) In continental Europe, **reporting requirements** tend to be more statutorily based in tax law. In **Germany**, the common two-tier board system, with a separate management board and supervisory board, may be claimed to encourage management to take shareholders' interests more closely into account than the typical one-tier UK system.

(c) **Japanese** companies are characterised by what is sometimes called a flexible approach to corporate governance, with a low level of regulation. All stakeholders are supposed to collaborate in the company's best interests, unlike the UK and US traditions of directors working primarily in the interests of shareholders.

We examine some aspects of the corporate environment in Germany and Japan in more detail below.

Germany: institutional differences

3.34   A significant difference between companies in the UK and many German companies is the **distribution of power** between **workers and managers,** and **shareholders and managers**.

3.35   In the UK, ownership is something which can be easily traded on the Stock Exchange in the form of shares. Buyers of shares seek the best combination of risk and return. While managers have most power for practical purposes, in theory they are acting in the shareholders' interests. From the company's point of view, the stock market is the principal source of investment capital, especially for large companies. Banks generally provide credit, not capital.

3.36   In Germany the role of stock markets in company finance and management is not so important, although it is quite possible that other changes will give them an enhanced role in future, especially with financial deregulation. German banks specialising in lending to industry and commercial enterprises have a relatively long-term interest in a company, and might even have an equity investment in it, as the sign of a long-term business relationship. It is argued that this makes them more sympathetic to a company's problems.

3.37   Institutional arrangements in German companies, typified by the **two-tiered board**, allow employees to have a formal say in the running of the company. A **supervisory board** has workers' representatives, and perhaps shareholders' representatives, in equal numbers. The board has no executive function, although it does review the company's direction and strategy. An **executive board**, composed entirely of managers, will be responsible for the running of the business.

Japan: cross shareholdings

3.38   In Japan, the stock market does have an important role to play, particularly in savings. However, the separation between investment and management is in practice drawn differently to the UK. The stock market is less 'open'. The corporate sector has close links with the banks, who are often represented on boards of directors.

3.39   There are three different types of board of director.

(a)   **Policy boards** - concerned with long-term strategic issues
(b)   **Functional boards** - made up of the main senior executives with a functional role
(c)   **Monocratic boards** - with few responsibilities and having a more symbolic role

3.40   Japanese companies generally set up long-term business relationships with suppliers and customers, even to the extent of buying each other's shares as a symbol of the relationship. When share prices fall, friendly companies do not sell shares in each other. If the web of interrelated companies is large enough, it may possibly include a bank which provides credit to participants in the group.

3.41   These arrangements have enabled some companies to be protected from the rigours of profit-performance, so that long-term objectives such as market share have been traditionally favoured instead. There is evidence, however, that this system is gradually coming to an end.

The effect of institutional differences

3.42   Assessing the **impact of institutional arrangements on financial performance** is difficult, especially as there are a multitude of factors which are responsible for commercial success or failure. It has become fashionable to talk of the failure of the 'Anglo-Saxon' model of corporate governance (ie that prevalent in the USA, the UK, Canada and Australia for example), and to compare it unfavourably with the success of German and Japanese industries since World War II. However, this probably understates the differences between the Anglo-Saxon economies (eg the USA is one of the most important markets in the world, while Australia's economy has been based on natural resources) and the significance of other economic and cultural factors. Moreover, even the most precisely defined institutional arrangements will still have little impact if other factors, such as government economic decisions, past trading patterns, culture and so on militate against commercial success.

Differences in management culture

3.43 Another factor which has an impact on multinational enterprises, or organisations competing in global markets, is the management culture. This comprises the views about managing held by managers, their shared educational experiences, and the 'way business is done'. Obviously, this reflects wider cultural differences between countries, and conversely national cultures can sometimes be subordinated to the corporate culture of the organisation (eg the efforts to ensure that staff of Disneyland in Paris are as enthusiastic as their American counterparts).

Question 2

Examine the recently published annual report of any listed public company. Many can be obtained from the *FT Annual Reports Service* - see the *Financial Times* for further details.

Bearing in mind our discussion of corporate objectives and corporate governance in Chapters 1 and 2, look for:

(a)   A statement regarding the Cadbury Report Code of Best Practice

(b)   Any references to the corporate objectives and financial strategy of the company (examine the Chairman's Statement especially)

Chapter roundup

- A company should be aware of its shareholding **clientele**: in the UK, **institutional investors** now account for the majority of quoted company shares.

- The system of **corporate governance** - which is the directors' responsibility - should seek to ensure **congruence** between the objectives of the organisation and those of its teams or departments and individual team members. The **agency problem** arises when agents do not act in the best interests of their principals.

- The UK **perspective on corporate governance** can be contrasted with that of other parts of the world.

- The **Cadbury Report** has clarified many of the contentious issues of corporate governance and sets standards of best practice in relation to financial reporting and accountability, while the **Greenbury Code** has made recommendations on directors' pay. The **Hampel Report** has reviewed the Cadbury and Greenbury recommendations.

BPP PUBLISHING

Quick quiz

1   What advantages are there for management in knowing who the company's shareholders are? (see para 1.22)

2   What is the relevance of agency theory to corporate governance? (2.4 - 2.5)

3   What is meant by 'goal congruence'? (2.15)

4   According to the Cadbury Report, what should be the role of the audit committee? (3.13 - 3.15)

5   Outline the main provisions of the Greenbury Code. (3.17 - 3.20)

6   What is the 'supercode'? (3.22)

7   Describe the main differences affecting corporate governance between companies in the UK and (i) Germany and (ii) Japan. (3.33 - 3.42)

Question to try	Level	Marks	Time
2	Exam standard	10	18 mins

Chapter 3

EVALUATING FINANCIAL RETURNS

Chapter topic list	Syllabus reference
1 Financial returns and profit	2(c), 3(a)
2 Discounting cash flows	2(c), 3(a)
3 Net present value (NPV) analysis	2(c), 3(a)
4 NPV analysis and inflation	2(c), 3(a)
5 The NPV method and separation of ownership and control	2(c), 3(a)
6 Interest rates	2(c), 3(a)

Introduction

Having considered general aspects of financial strategy and corporate governance in Part A, we now begin to examine more specific issues in financial strategy. In this chapter, we seek to explain and quantify what is meant by an adequate **financial return**. We also discuss the significance of interest rates and what is called the term structure of interest rates.

Knowledge brought forward from Papers 3 and 8

Paper 14 questions involving capital investment appraisal may demand application of quantitative techniques covered in Paper 3 *Management information* and the investment appraisal techniques covered in Paper 8 *Managerial finance*. We revise NPV analysis in this chapter.

1   FINANCIAL RETURNS AND PROFIT

1.1   Firms are in business to make a **financial return**. Firms seek to make a financial return overall, and they will also need to consider the financial return to be made from an individual project or venture when deciding whether to select it. Shareholders similarly wish to make a financial return from their investment and will select shares and other alternative investments accordingly.

1.2   What do we mean by financial return? How do we measure it? Economists assume that firms make decisions on what to supply and at what price so as to maximise profits. A central aim of accounting is to provide a way of measuring financial return in the form of 'profit' for a firm in a given accounting period. Yet accountants and economists use different concepts of profit.

1.3   **Accounting profits** consist of sales revenue minus the explicit costs of the business. Explicit costs are those which are clearly stated and recorded, such as:

(a)   Material costs - prices paid to suppliers

BPP PUBLISHING

    (b)   Labour costs - wages paid

    (c)   Depreciation costs on fixed assets

    (d)   Other expenses, such as rates and rents on buildings

1.4   **Economic profits** consist of sales revenue minus both the explicit and the implicit costs of the business. Implicit costs are benefits forgone by not using the factors of production (labour, capital and so on) in their next most profitable way.

1.5   For example, suppose that a business hires labour which is paid a wage of £200,000. The labour is used to provide a service A, which means that it could not be used to do an alternative task, which was to provide a service B, which would have earned a contribution to profit of £100,000. The economic cost of the labour would be the sum of its explicit and implicit costs, which is its total **opportunity cost.**

	£
Explicit cost - wages paid	200,000
Implicit cost - contribution forgone	100,000
Economic cost (opportunity cost) of labour	300,000

1.6   Using the economists' concept of profit, it can be shown that firms in a perfectly competitive market reach a long-term equilibrium in which profits are zero. In the light of what we have said above about different ways of defining profit, it is important to realise that these 'zero' profits are profits *after* the deduction of a 'risk premium' due to entrepreneurs or investors to compensate them for providing risk capital. No such deduction is made in arriving at accounting profit.

1.7   **Profitability** of a firm in accounting terms can be measured in different ways. For example, as you will be aware, gross profit margins and net profit margins are both widely used performance measures. The fact that opportunity costs are ignored for the purposes of measuring accounting profits means that the acceptability of a particular level of profitability for a project must be judged by comparison of that level of profitability with that available from other projects.

The accounting rate of return (ARR) method

1.8   A capital investment project may be assessed by calculating the return on investment (ROI) or **accounting rate of return** (ARR) and comparing it with a pre-determined target level. You should recall these methods, and the payback method, from your earlier studies.

$$\text{ARR} = \frac{\text{Estimated average profits}}{\text{Estimated average investment}} \times 100\%$$

1.9   The accounting rate of return method of appraising a capital project is to estimate the accounting rate of return that the project will yield. If it exceeds a target rate of return, the project should be undertaken.

The comparison of mutually exclusive projects

1.10   The ARR method of capital investment appraisal can be used to compare two or more projects which are mutually exclusive, that is, only one of them can be undertaken. The project with the highest ARR should be selected (provided that its expected ARR is higher than the company's target ARR).

Drawbacks of the ARR method

1.11 The ARR method of capital investment appraisal has the serious drawback that it does not take account of the **timing of the profits** from an investment. Whenever capital is invested in a project, money is tied up until the project begins to earn profits which pay back the investment. Money tied up in one project cannot be invested anywhere else until the profits are realised. Management should be aware of the benefits of early repayments from an investment, which will provide money for other investments.

The payback method

1.12 The payback method is another profit based measure which evaluates projects by considering how long a project would take to pay back the initial investment made in it. This is the **payback period**.

Using the payback method

1.13 Payback is often used as a first screening method. A company might have a target payback period, and it would reject a capital project unless its payback period is less than a certain number of years, perhaps five years. However, payback should not be used on its own to evaluate capital investments because projects with short payback periods might make much smaller profits overall than other projects which have longer payback periods but which make high profits at the end of their lives.

2   DISCOUNTING CASH FLOWS   6/94, 12/95, 12/97

2.1 The financial manager needs an approach to measuring returns which will allow choices to be made between different investment or financing proposals, within the overall remit that the wealth of shareholders is to be maximised. Choosing only proposals which enhance the wealth of shareholders means choosing those for which the total of the benefits less the costs attributable to the decision exceeds zero. How are these benefits and costs to be measured? To answer this question, we need a clear understanding of the importance of **cash flows** and the **time value of money.**

2.2 The value of money depends on when the cash flow occurs, for a number of reasons.

(a) **Inflation.** If inflation is expected, the purchasing power of money, and therefore its 'value' or utility, falls over time.

(b) **Risk.** There is likely to be greater risk associated with future cash flows than with present ones, because of the possible consequences of intervening events.

(c) **Individuals' consumption preferences.** In general, people appear to prefer consumption now to consumption in the future. After all, in the future we may not be around to do the consuming.

(d) **Opportunity costs.** £100 now is better than £100 in a year's time because we would have the opportunity of investing £100 at, say, a 6% interest rate to produce £106 at the end of the year instead.

2.3 The ARR method of project evaluation considered earlier ignores the timing of cash flows and the opportunity cost of capital tied up. Payback considers the time it takes to recover the original investment cost, but ignores total profits over a project's life. Discounted cash flow, or DCF for short, is an investment appraisal technique which takes into account both

BPP PUBLISHING

the time value of money and also total returns over the life of the investment proposal or project.

(a) DCF looks at the **cash flows** of a project, not the accounting profits. As a decision accounting technique, DCF is concerned with **relevant costs**.

(b) The **timing of cash flows** is taken into account by discounting them. The effect of discounting is to give a bigger value per £1 for cash flows that occur earlier: £1 earned after one year will be worth more than £1 earned after two years, which in turn will be worth more than £1 earned after five years, and so on.

Discounting

2.4 **Discounting** is compounding in reverse.

Suppose that a company has £10,000 to invest. If it could be invested at 10% compound, the value of the investment with interest would build up as follows.

(a) After one year £10,000 × 1.10 = £11,000
(b) After two years £10,000 × 1.10^2 = £12,100
(c) After three years £10,000 × 1.10^3 = £13,310, and so on.

2.5 This is **compounding**. The formula for the future value of an investment plus accumulated interest after n time periods is:

$$FV = PV (1 + r)^n$$

where   FV is the future value of the investment with interest
PV is the present value of the investment
r is the compound rate of return per time period, expressed as a proportion (so 10% = 0.10, 5% = 0.05 and so on)
n is the number of time periods.

2.6 Discounting starts with the future value, and converts a future value to a present value. For example, if a company expects to earn a compound rate of return of 10% on its investments, how much would it need to invest now to have an investment of:

(a) £11,000 after 1 year?
(b) £12,100 after 2 years?
(c) £13,310 after 3 years?

2.7 The answer is £10,000 in each case, and we can calculate it by discounting, as follows.

(a) £11,000 × $\dfrac{1}{1.10}$ = £10,000

(b) £12,100 × $\dfrac{1}{1.10^2}$ = £10,000

(c) £13,310 × $\dfrac{1}{1.10^3}$ = £10,000

2.8 The discounting formula to calculate the present value of a future sum of money at the end of n time periods is:

$$PV = FV \dfrac{1}{(1 + r)^n}$$

where the symbols have the same meanings as above.

2.9 Discounting can be applied to both money **receivable** and money **payable**. By discounting all payments and receipts from a capital investment to present values, we can compare them on a common basis at values which take account of the timing of cash flows.

Question 1

Spender Ltd expects the cash inflow from an investment to be £40,000 after two years and another £30,000 after three years. Its target rate of return is 12%.

(a) What is the present value of these future returns?
(b) What does this present value signify?

Answer

Year	Cash flow £	Discount factor at 12%	Present value £
2	40,000	$\frac{1}{1.12^2} = 0.797$	31,880
3	30,000	$\frac{1}{1.12^3} = 0.712$	21,360
		Total PV	53,240

The present value of the future returns, discounted at 12%, is £53,240. This means that if Spender Ltd can invest now to earn a return of 12% on its investments, it would have to invest £53,240 now to earn £40,000 after two years plus £30,000 after three years.

Non-annual cash flows

2.10 For non-**annual cash flows,** the period interest rate r is related to the annual interest rate R by the following formula. Where n is the number of periods per annum:

$$r = \sqrt[n]{1+R} - 1$$

2.11 For example, if the annual interest rate is 18%, the monthly interest rate $r = \sqrt[12]{1.18} - 1 = 0.0139$, ie 1.39%

Changes in interest rate

2.12 **Changes in interest rate** can be dealt with as in the following example. Say, in years 1, 2 and 3, the interest rate is 10%, 12% and 14% respectively.

$$\text{Then: Year 3 discount factor} = \frac{1}{(1+r_1)(1+r_2)(1+r_3)} = \frac{1}{1.10 \times 1.12 \times 1.14} = 0.7120$$

Relevant cash flows

2.13 The cash flows to consider when making decisions are only those that are directly relevant to the decision under consideration.

2.14 Remember that a relevant cost is a future cash flow arising as a consequence of a decision. It follows that any **costs incurred in the past,** and any **committed costs** which will be incurred regardless of whether or not an investment is undertaken are **not relevant cash flows** because they have occurred, or will occur whatever investment decision is taken.

BPP
PUBLISHING

3 NET PRESENT VALUE (NPV) ANALYSIS $\quad$ 6/94, 12/95, 12/97

> **KEY TERM**
>
> The **net present value (NPV)** of a project is the value obtained by discounting all cash outflows and inflows at a chosen target rate of return or 'cost of capital', and taking the net total (inflows minus outflows).

3.1 **If the NPV is positive**, then the cash inflows from the investment will yield a return in excess of the cost of capital, and so the project should be undertaken. **If the NPV is negative**, then the cash inflows from the investment will yield a return below the cost of capital, and so the project should not be undertaken. **If the NPV is exactly zero**, then the cash inflows from the investment will yield a return which is exactly the same as the cost of capital, so the company should be indifferent between undertaking and not undertaking the project.

3.2 EXAMPLE: NET PRESENT VALUE METHOD (1)

Slogger Ltd has a cost of capital of 15%. The company is considering a capital investment, where the estimated cash flows are as follows.

Year	Cash flow
	£
0	(100,000)
1	60,000
2	80,000
3	40,000
4	30,000

What is the NPV of the project, and should it be undertaken?

3.3 SOLUTION

Year	Cash flow	Discount factor		Present value
	£	15%		£
0	(100,000)		1.000	(100,000)
1	60,000	$\dfrac{1}{(1.15)}$	= 0.870	52,200
2	80,000	$\dfrac{1}{(1.15)^2}$	= 0.756	60,480
3	40,000	$\dfrac{1}{(1.15)^3}$	= 0.658	26,320
4	30,000	$\dfrac{1}{(1.15)^4}$	= 0.572	17,160
			NPV =	56,160

The discount factor for any cash flow now, that is, at year 0, is always 1.0, regardless of what the cost of capital is.

The PV of cash inflows exceeds the PV of cash outflows by £56,160, which means that the project has a yield in excess of 15%. It should therefore be undertaken.

Discount tables for the present value of £1

3.4 The discount factor that we use in discounting is $\dfrac{1}{(1+r)^n} = (1+r)^{-n}$

Instead of having to calculate this factor every time we can use tables. **Discount tables** for the present value of £1, for different values of r and n, are shown in the **Appendix** to this Study Text.

The timing of cash flows

3.5 To use discounting, we must attach precise times to cash flows. The following guidelines may be applied.

(a) A cash outlay to be incurred at the beginning of an investment project occurs in year 0. The present value of £1 now, in year 0 is:

$$\frac{1}{(1+r)^0} = £1$$

regardless of the value of r (the cost of capital).

(b) A cash outlay, saving or inflow which occurs during the course of a year is assumed to occur all at once at the end of the year. Therefore receipts of £10,000 spread over the first year are taking to occur 'at year 1', the time one year from now.

(c) A cash outlay, saving or inflow which occurs at the beginning of a year is taken to occur at the end of the previous year. Therefore a cash outlay of £5,000 at the beginning of the second year is taken to occur at the end of the first year, that is, 'at year 1'.

Annuity tables

3.6 In Question 2, the calculations could have been simplified for years 1 to 3 as follows.

	30,000	×	0.893	
+	30,000	×	0.797	
+	30,000	×	0.712	
=	¯30,000	×	2.402	

3.7 Where there is a constant cash flow for several years (in this case £30,000 a year for years 1 to 3) we can calculate the present value by adding together the discount factors for the individual years. These total factors are 'cumulative present value' factors or 'annuity' factors. They are shown in the table of cumulative present value factors at the start of this Text. (2.402, for example, is in the column for 12% and the year 3 row).

The formula which yields the cumulative present value factors is:

$$\frac{1}{r}\left(1 - \frac{1}{(1+r)^n}\right)$$

where   r is the discount rate as a proportion
             n is the number of years.

A table of cumulative present value factors can be found in the Appendix to this Study Text.

Question 2

(a) What is the present value of £1,000 earned each year from years 1 to 10, when the required return on investment is 11%?

(b) What is the present value of £100 earned each year from years 3 to 6 when the cost of capital is 5%?

Answer

(a) The PV of £1,000 earned each year from year 1 to year 10 at 11% is £1,000 × 5.889 = £5,889.

(b) The PV of £100 earned each year from year 3 to year 6 at 5% is as follows.

PV of £1 a year for years 1 to 6	= 5.076
Less PV of £1 a year for years 1 to 2	= 1.859
PV of £1 a year for years 3 to 6	= 3.217

£100 × 3.217 = £321.7, say £322

Annual cash flows in perpetuity

3.8 How do we calculate the cumulative present value of £1 a year for ever? When the cost of capital is r, the cumulative PV of £1 a year in perpetuity (starting one year from now) is £1/r.

3.9 EXAMPLE: NET PRESENT VALUE METHOD

A company with a cost of capital of 14% is considering an investment in a project costing £500,000 that would yield cash inflows of £100,000 a year in perpetuity. Should the project be undertaken?

3.10 SOLUTION

Year	Cash flow £	Discount factor 14%	Present value £
0	(500,000)	1.0	(500,000)
1 - ∞	100,000	1/0.14 = 7.14	714,000
		Net present value	214,000

The NPV is positive and so the project should be undertaken.

4 NPV ANALYSIS AND INFLATION 6/99

4.1 We need now to consider the effect of inflation on the net present value (NPV) analysis of investment proposals. As the inflation rate increases so will the minimum return required by an investor. You might be happy with a return of 5% in an inflation-free world, but if inflation was running at 15% you would expect a considerably greater yield.

4.2 EXAMPLE: INFLATION (1)

A company is considering investing in a project with the following cash flows.

Time	Actual cash flows £
0	(15,000)
1	9,000
2	8,000
3	7,000

The company requires a minimum return of 20% under the present and anticipated conditions. Inflation is currently running at 10% a year, and this rate of inflation is expected to continue indefinitely. Should the company go ahead with the project?

4.3 SOLUTION

Let us first look at the company's required rate of return. Suppose that it invested £1,000 for one year on 1 January, then on 31 December it would require a minimum return of £200. With the initial investment of £1,000, the total value of the investment by 31 December must therefore increase to £1,200. During the course of the year the purchasing value of the pound would fall due to inflation. We can restate the amount received on 31 December in terms of the purchasing power of the pound at 1 January as follows.

Amount received on 31 December in terms of the value of the pound at 1 January $= \dfrac{£1,200}{(1.10)^1} = £1,091$

4.4 In terms of the value of the pound at 1 January, the company would make a profit of £91 which represents a rate of return of 9.1% in 'today's money' terms. This is known as the **real rate of return**. The required rate of 20% is a **nominal rate** of return (sometimes called a 'money' rate of return). The nominal rate measures the return in terms of the pound which is, of course, falling in value. The real rate measures the return in constant price level terms.

The two rates of return and the inflation rate are linked by the equation:

$(1 + \text{nominal rate}) = (1 + \text{real rate}) \times (1 + \text{inflation rate})$

where all the rates are expressed as proportions.

In our example: $(1 + 0.20) = (1 + 0.091) \times (1 + 0.10) = 1.20$

Which rate is used in discounting?

4.5 We must decide which rate to use for discounting, the real rate or the nominal rate. If the cash flows are expressed in terms of the actual number of pounds that will be received or paid on the various future dates, we must use the nominal rate for discounting. If the cash flows are expressed in terms of the value of the pound at time 0 (that is, in constant price level terms), we must use the **real rate**.

4.6 The cash flows given in Paragraph 4.2 are expressed in terms of the actual number of pounds that will be received or paid at the relevant dates. We should, therefore, discount them using the nominal rate of return.

Time	Cash flow £	Discount factor 20%	PV £
0	(15,000)	1.000	(15,000)
1	9,000	0.833	7,497
2	8,000	0.694	5,552
3	7,000	0.579	4,053
		NPV =	+ 2,102

The project has a positive net present value of £2,102.

4.7 The future cash flows can be re-expressed in terms of the value of the pound at time 0 as follows, given inflation at 10% a year.

Time	Actual cash flow £	Cash flow at time 0 price level £
0	(15,000)	(15,000)
1	9,000	$9,000 \times \dfrac{1}{1.10} = 8,182$
2	8,000	$8,000 \times \dfrac{1}{(1.10)^2} = 6,612$
3	7,000	$7,000 \times \dfrac{1}{(1.10)^3} = 5,259$

4.8 The cash flows expressed in terms of the value of the pound at time 0 can now be discounted using the real rate of 9.1%.

Time	Cash flow £	Discount factor 9.1%	PV £
0	(15,000)	1.00	(15,000)
1	8,182	$\dfrac{1}{1.091}$	7,500
2	6,612	$\dfrac{1}{(1.091)^2}$	5,555
3	5,259	$\dfrac{1}{(1.091)^3}$	4,050
		NPV	+2,105

4.9 The NPV is the same as before (and the present value of the cash flow in each year is the same as before) apart from rounding errors with a net total of £3.

Costs and benefits which inflate at different rates

4.10 Not all costs and benefits will rise in line with the general level of inflation. In such cases, we can **apply the money rate to inflated values** to determine a project's NPV.

4.11 EXAMPLE: INFLATION (2)

Rice Ltd is considering a project which would cost £5,000 now. The annual benefits, for four years, would be a fixed income of £2,500 a year, plus other savings of £500 a year in year 1, rising by 5% each year because of inflation. Running costs will be £1,000 in the first year, but would increase at 10% each year because of inflating labour costs. The general rate of inflation is expected to be 7½% and the company's required money rate of return is 16%.

Is the project worthwhile? (Ignore taxation.)

4.12 SOLUTION

The cash flows at inflated values are as follows.

Year	Fixed income £	Other savings £	Running costs £	Net cash flow £
1	2,500	500	1,000	2,000
2	2,500	525	1,100	1,925
3	2,500	551	1,210	1,841
4	2,500	579	1,331	1,748

The NPV of the project is as follows.

Year	Cash flow £	Discount factor 16%	PV £
0	(5,000)	1.000	(5,000)
1	2,000	0.862	1,724
2	1,925	0.743	1,430
3	1,841	0.641	1,180
4	1,748	0.552	965
		NPV	+ 299

The NPV is positive and the project would seem to be worthwhile.

Variations in the expected rate of inflation

4.13 If the rate of inflation is expected to change, the calculation of the money cost of capital is slightly more complicated.

4.14 EXAMPLE: INFLATION (3)

Mr Gable has just received a dividend of £1,000 on his shareholding in Gonwithy Windmills plc. The market value of the shares is £8,000 ex div. What is the (money) cost of the equity capital, if dividends are expected to rise because of inflation by 10% in years 1, 2 and 3, before levelling off at this year 3 amount?

4.15 SOLUTION

The money cost of capital is the internal rate of return of the following cash flows.

Year	Cash flow £	Discount factor 15%	PV at 15% £	Discount factor 20%	PV at 20% £
0	(8,000)	1.000	(8,000)	1.000	(8,000)
1	1,100	0.870	957	0.833	916
2	1,210	0.756	915	0.694	840
3 - ∞*	1,331 pa	5.041	6,710	3.472	4,621
			582		(1,623)

* Discount factors $= \dfrac{1}{r} -$ 2-year annuity factor:

(a) Discount factor at 15%: 6.667 − 1.626 = 5.041
(b) Discount factor at 20%: 5.000 − 1.528 = 3.472

Interpolation gives an IRR of about 16.3%.

Expectations of inflation and the effects of inflation

4.16 When managers evaluate a particular project, or when shareholders evaluate their investments, they can only guess at what the rate of inflation is going to be. Their expectations will probably be wrong, at least to some extent, because it is extremely difficult to forecast the rate of inflation accurately. The only way in which uncertainty about inflation can be allowed for in project evaluation is by **risk and uncertainty analysis**.

4.17 You should note that **inflation** has the following effects.

(a) Since fixed assets and stocks will increase in money value, the same quantities of assets must be financed by increasing amounts of capital. If the future rate of inflation **can be predicted,** management can work out how much extra finance the company will need, and take steps to obtain it (for example by increasing retentions of earnings, or borrowing). If the future rate of inflation **cannot be predicted** with accuracy, management should guess at what it will be and plan to obtain extra finance accordingly. However, plans should also be made to obtain 'contingency funds' if the rate of inflation exceeds expectations. For example, a higher bank overdraft facility might be negotiated, or a provisional arrangement made with a bank for a loan.

(b) Inflation means higher costs and higher selling prices. The effect of higher prices on demand is not necessarily easy to predict. A company that raises its prices by 10% because the general rate of inflation is running at 10% might suffer a serious fall in demand.

Exam focus point

The standard rate of UK corporation tax for Financial Year 2000 is 30%. Check any exam question carefully for the tax rate: you will normally be told which rate should be assumed.

Knowledge brought forward from Paper 8

DCF and taxation

The effects of taxation on cash flows should be included in DCF analysis, with after-tax cash flows discounted at an after-tax cost of capital

- Taxation on profits is typically assumed payable one year in arrears. As a general convention (but not a hard and fast rule) taxation is assessed as percentage of cash profits.

- Capital allowances on capital equipment purchases could be in the form of a writing down allowance, but check capital allowance details in any question you attempt.

Rules in investment appraisal

Include	**Exclude**
• Effect of tax allowances	• Depreciation
• After-tax incremental cash flows	• Dividend/interest (∴ dividend/borrowing decisions analysed separately)
• Working capital requirements	• Sunk costs
• Opportunity costs	• Allocated costs and overheads

Internal rate of return method

With the **NPV method**, present values are calculated by discounting at a target rate of return or cost of capital. The **internal rate of return (IRR) method** is to calculate instead the exact DCF rate of return which the project is expected to achieve, ie the rate at which the NPV is zero.

- The first step is to calculate two NPVs, preferably one positive and one negative and both close to zero

- Interpolation is then used to find an estimated IRR

Capital rationing

When capital for investments is in restricted supply, a choice must be made between projects that all have a positive NPV.

Soft or **internal capital rationing** is where capital is rationed by constraints within the business (which might include management reluctance to raise further capital and thus dilute EPS or allow in new outside shareholders).

Hard or **external capital rationing** is where external forces limit the amount of capital available to a business (which might include government policies on credit).

If capital rationing is in the current time period only

- And projects/investments are **not divisible**, the feasible combination of projects that give the highest total NPV should be selected

- And projects/investments are **divisible**, the projects for selection should be ranked according to a **profitability index (PI)**, ie descending order of NPV of future net cash flows per £1 of current outlay, since this will give the highest achievable NPV

---

5 THE NPV METHOD AND SEPARATION OF OWNERSHIP AND CONTROL

5.1 The concept of **net present value** accords with the separation of ownership and control found in the large or medium-sized company. The reasoning for this is as follows. Managers are assumed to act in the best interests of the shareholders, the owners of the company. This is achieved by management trying to increase shareholders' wealth by maximising the net present value of cash flows. The rate of interest reflects the market discount of future wealth in relation to current wealth.

The NPV rule as a long-term objective for the enterprise

5.2 The NPV method prescribes acceptance of all investment proposals which offer positive net present values when discounted at the market rate of interest. Thus, using this method, managers will ensure that all projects will be accepted up to the point at which the marginal rate of return on the investment equals the rate of interest prevailing on alternative investments in the capital market. This will lead to an increase in the market value of the firm and therefore of the shareholder's share in it. We can thus see that the NPV rule can serve as a unifying long-term objective for the enterprise as a whole.

5.3 In relatively liquid capital markets, shareholders are able to invest and disinvest at appropriate times in order to meet their own consumption requirements. They can also combine different investments with different degrees of risk as they require. Because of these possibilities, the manager of an individual enterprise does not need to be concerned with the consumption requirements or risk preferences of individual shareholders.

6 INTEREST RATES   6/95, 6/98

6.1 Interest rates are an important element in the economic environment faced by financial managers.

(a) Interest rates measure the **cost of borrowing**. If a company wants to raise money, it must pay interest on its borrowing, and the rate of interest payable will be one which is 'current' at the time the borrowing takes place. When interest rates go up, companies will pay more interest on some of their borrowing (including on bank overdrafts).

(b) Interest rates in a country influence the **exchange rate** of the country's currency.

(c) Interest rates act as a guide to the sort of **return** that a company's shareholders might want, and changes in market interest rates will affect share prices.

The main interest rates in the financial markets

6.2 The interest rates in the UK financial markets which are most commonly quoted are as follows.

(a) The clearing banks' **base rates.** Banks will lend money to small companies and individual customers at certain margins above their base rate. The base rate is set independently by each clearing bank, although in practice, an increase in the base rate of one bank will be followed by similar changes by other banks.

(b) The inter-bank lending rate on the London inter-bank money market (**LIBOR**). For large loans to big companies, banks will set interest rates at a margin above LIBOR rather than at a margin above base rate.

(c) The **Treasury bill rate**. This is the rate at which the Bank of England sells Treasury bills to the discount market. It is an average rate, since discount houses tender for bills and tender prices vary.

(d) The **yield on long-dated gilt-edged securities** (20 years to maturity). Gilt-edged securities are securities issued by the government.

KEY TERM

LIBOR or the London Inter-Bank Offered Rate is the rate of interest applying to wholesale money market lending between London banks.

6.3 There are many other different interest rates you might see quoted, for example:

(a) The yield on bank deposit accounts or building society accounts

(b) The bank overdraft rate for personal customers

(c) Various money market rates, such as the yield on deposits with discount houses, the rate of discount on bank bills or 'fine' trade bills, the yield on sterling certificates of deposit, and the yield on local authority deposits

(d) The rate of discount offered by the Bank of England for its purchase of different types of eligible bills from the discount market

Why are there so many different interest rates?

6.4 There are several reasons why interest rates differ in different markets and market segments.

(a) **Risk**. Higher risk borrowers must pay higher rates on their borrowing, to compensate lenders for the greater risk involved (see Paragraph 6.13 below on **default risk**).

(b) The **need to make a profit on re-lending**. Financial intermediaries make their profits from re-lending at a higher rate of interest than the cost of their borrowing.

(c) The **duration of the lending**. Normally, long-term loans will earn a higher yield than short-term loans. The reasons for this term structure of interest rates are discussed later.

(d) The **size of the loan**. Deposits above a certain amount with a bank or building society might attract higher rates of interest than smaller deposits.

(e) **International interest rates**. The level of interest rates varies from country to country. The reasons for these variations are:

(i) Differing rates of inflation from country to country
(ii) Government policies on interest rates and foreign currency exchange rates

(f) **Different types of financial asset**. Different types of financial asset attract different rates of interest. This is largely because of the competition for deposits between different types of financial institution.

The term structure of interest rates: the yield curve

6.5 Suppose that an investor decides to buy some government securities (gilts). Since the securities represent borrowing by the government, it might seem reasonable to expect that the nominal rate of interest paid would be the same, no matter what the type of security.

6.6 Obviously, this is not the case. One reason why is that the government borrows by issuing new securities from time to time, and the rate of interest offered on a new issue of securities will depend on conditions in the market at the time. This will explain why the nominal interest rate on new gilt-edged securities might be 12% on one occasion, 10% on another and 8% on another.

6.7 There is another important reason why interest rates on the same type of financial asset might vary. This is that interest rates depend on the term to maturity of the asset. For example, Treasury Stock might be short-dated, medium-dated, or long-dated. The **term structure** of interest rates refers to the way in which the yield on a security varies according to the term of the borrowing, that is the length of time until the debt will be repaid as shown by the **yield curve**. Normally, the longer the term of an asset to maturity, the higher the rate of interest paid on the asset.

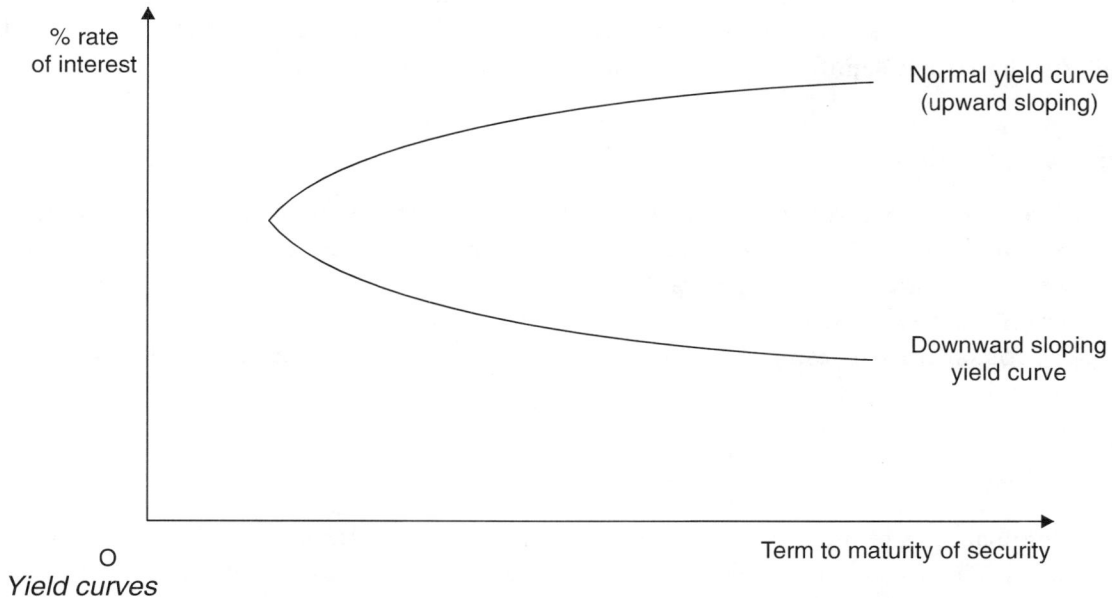

Yield curves

6.8 The reasons why, in theory, the yield curve will normally be upward sloping, so that long-term financial assets offer a higher yield than short-term assets, are as follows.

(a) The investor must be compensated for tying up his money in the asset for a longer period of time. In other words, if the government were to make two issues of 9% Treasury Stock on the same date, one with a term of five years and one with a term of 20 years (and if there were no expectations of changes in interest rates in the future) then the **liquidity preference** of investors would make them prefer the five year stock.

The only way to overcome the liquidity preference of investors is to compensate them for the loss of liquidity; in other words, to offer a higher rate of interest on longer dated stock.

(b) There is a greater risk in lending long-term than in lending short-term. To compensate investors for this risk, they might require a higher yield on longer dated investments.

6.9 So why might a yield curve slope downwards, with short-term rates higher than longer-term rates?

(a) **Expectations** about the way that interest rates will move in the future affect the term structure of interest rates. When interest rates are expected to fall, short-term rates might be higher than long-term rates, and the yield curve would be downward sloping. Thus, the shape of the yield curve gives an indication to the financial manager about how interest rates are expected to move in the future.

(b) **Government policy** on interest rates might be significant too. In the UK, government influence over interest rates is directed mainly towards short-term interest rates. A policy of keeping interest rates relatively high might therefore have the effect of forcing short-term interest rates higher than long-term rates.

(c) The **market segmentation theory** of interest rates suggests that the slope of the yield curve will reflect conditions in different segments of the market. This theory holds that the major investors are confined to a particular segment of the market and will not switch segment even if the forecast of likely future interests rates changes. For instance, banks, building societies and general insurance companies invest mainly at the 'short end' of the market (with short periods to maturity) while life assurance and pension funds invest mainly at the 'long end'. Although there may be some truth in this theory, the fact that the shape of the yield curve is used in practice to predict interest rate movements suggests that expectations of future interest rates must also have some significant influence on the slope of the yield curve.

The reverse yield gap

6.10 Because debt involves lower risk than equity investment, we might expect yields on debt to be lower than yields on shares. In fact, the opposite has applied in recent years, so that the yields on shares are lower than on low-risk debt: this situation is known as a **reverse yield gap.** A reverse yield gap can occur because shareholders may be willing to accept lower returns on their investment in the short term, in anticipation that they will make capital gains in the future.

Nominal rates and real rates of interest

6.11 Nominal rates of interest or 'money' rates of interest are interest rates expressed in money terms. The real rate of interest is the nominal rate of interest adjusted downwards the rate of inflation. The real rate is therefore a measure of the increase in the real wealth, expressed in terms of buying power, of the investor or lender.

(a) The real rate of interest is calculated as:

$$\frac{1 \; + \; \text{nominal rate of interest}}{1 \; + \; \text{rate of inflation}} - 1$$

If the nominal rate of interest is 12% and the rate of inflation is 8%, the real rate of interest would be:

$$\frac{1.12}{1.08} - 1 = 0.037 = 3.7\%$$

(b) The real rate of interest is more commonly estimated (for arithmetical simplicity) as the difference between the nominal rate of interest and the rate of inflation. In our example, this would be 12% – 8% = 4%.

6.12 The real rate of interest will usually be positive, although when the rate of inflation is very high, the real rate of interest might become negative (the rate of inflation exceeding the nominal interest rate). Nominal rates of interest will tend to rise when the rate of inflation increases, because lenders will want to earn a real return and will therefore want nominal rates to exceed the inflation rate.

Default risk

6.13 As mentioned earlier, the relative **risks of default** by different borrowers is reflected in differences in the interest rates which different borrowers will have to pay. It can be appreciated that the risks of default by the Government is rather less than the risk of default by companies, and this accounts for why the government typically has to pay lower interest rates than companies on its borrowings.

6.14 EXAMPLE: DEFAULT RISK

Drainforth plc issues 9% loan stock redeemable at par after one year, at a time when the interest rate for one-year government stocks is 8%. There is a 10% probability that Drainforth plc will default on payment, with the loan stock holders then receiving nothing. Calculate the value of the loan stock and the yield that it offers. (Ignore taxation and general risks in the markets.)

6.15 SOLUTION

If there was no default risk, the loan stock will have a value of: $\dfrac{£109}{1.08} = £100.93$

However, given the default risk, the expected value of the loan stock after one year will be:
$(0.9 \times £109) + (0.1 \times 0) = £98.10$

If we discount at the risk-free rate, we have a present value of:

$$\frac{£98.10}{1.08} = £90.83$$

This is the value at which the loan stock will now sell.

The yield is:

$$\frac{109}{90.83} - 1 = 20\%$$

6.16 It can be seen that the expected yield has risen to compensate for the default risk.

Interest rates, inflation and capital gains or losses

6.17 A positive real rate of interest adds to an investor's real wealth from the income he earns from his investments. However, when interest rates go up or down, perhaps due to a rise or fall in the rate of inflation, there will also be a potential capital loss or gain for the investor. In other words, the market value of interest-bearing securities will alter. Market values will fall when interest rates go up.

6.18 For example, when the Government issues long-term gilts at a coupon interest rate of, say, 10% and the market rate of interest is also 10%, the market value of the securities will be £100 per £100 face value of the stock (or '£100 per cent').

(a) Now if nominal interest rates in the market subsequently rise to, say, 14% the re-sale value of the gilts will fall to:

$£100 \times \dfrac{10\%}{14\%} = £71.43$ per £100 face value of the stock

An investor in the gilts will make a capital loss of £28.57 per cent (plus selling costs) if he decides to sell the securities.

(b) If nominal interest rates subsequently fall to, say, 8%, the re-sale value of the gilts will rise to:

$£100 \times \dfrac{10\%}{8\%} = £125$ per cent

An investor could then sell his asset for a capital gain of £25 per cent (less selling costs).

Interest rates and share prices

6.19 When interest rates change, the return expected by investors from shares will also change.

For example, if interest rates fell from 14% to 12% on government securities, and from 15% to 13% on company debentures, the return expected from shares (dividends and capital growth) would also fall.

6.20 By the fundamental theory of share values, it is predicted that if a shareholder expects a 15% return on his investment in equities, and the annual dividend on one of his shares is 21p, then the market value of the share should be 21p/15% = £1.40 (ignoring any prospect of capital growth).

However, if interest rates fell, the shareholder would probably be satisfied with a lower return from his shares, say 14%, and the price of a share offering an annual dividend of 21p should then rise to 21p/14% = £1.50.

Equally, if interest rates went up, the shareholder would probably want a higher return from his shares, and share prices would fall. If, in our example, the investor wanted a 16% return, the predicted share price would fall to 21p/16% = £1.31.

Changes in interest rates and financing decisions

6.21 Interest rates are important for financial decisions by companies.

(a) When interest rates are low, it might be financially prudent:

(i) To borrow more, preferably at a fixed rate of interest, and so increase the company's gearing

(ii) To borrow for long periods rather than for short periods

(iii) To pay back loans which incur a high interest rate, if it is within the company's power to do so, and to take out new loans at a lower interest rate

(b) When interest rates go up:

(i) A company might decide to reduce the amount of its debt finance, and to substitute equity finance, such as retained earnings

(ii) A company which has a surplus of cash and liquid funds might switch some of its short-term investments out of equities and into interest-bearing securities

(iii) A company might opt to raise new finance by borrowing short-term funds and debt at a variable interest rate (for example on overdraft) rather than long-term funds at fixed rates of interest, in the hope that interest rates will soon come down again

Interest rates and new capital investments

6.22 When interest rates go up, and so the cost of finance to a company goes up, the **minimum return that a company will require** on its own new capital investments will go up too. Some new capital projects might be in the pipeline, with purchase contracts already signed with suppliers, and so there will often be a time lag before higher interest rates result in fewer new investments. A company's management should give close consideration, when interest rates are high, to keeping investments in assets, particularly unwanted or inefficient fixed assets, stocks and debtors, down **to a minimum**, in order to reduce the company's need to borrow.

Chapter roundup

- In this chapter, we have worked through some of the mathematics of **investment appraisal**. While it is of course important to practise calculations, do not neglect the pros and cons of different methods of investment appraisal. It is important to understand the central concept of the **time value of money**.

- The **fundamental analysis theory of share values**, which we discuss in the next chapter, is based on the discounted cash flow principles which we have revised in this chapter.

- The **payback period** is the time taken for cash inflows from a project to equal the cash outflows. This ignores the time value of money.

- **Interest rates** are, for corporate and individual borrowers, the cost of borrowing. The **term structure** of interest rates is shown by yield curve.

Quick quiz

1 Give a formula for the accounting rate of return. (see para 1.8)

2 What is a project's payback period? (1.12)

3 Why is £1 now worth more than £1 at a later time? (2.2)

4 A cost of £20,000 is expected to occur near the beginning of the third year. To what year should the £20,000 be allocated in DCF analysis? (3.5)

5 How is the NPV method consistent with the separation of ownership and control in a company? (5.1 - 5.4)

6 Why might a yield curve for interest rates slope downwards? (6.9)

7 What is meant by the market segmentation theory of interest rates? (6.9)

8 How do interest rates affect share prices? (6.19, 6.20)

Question to try	Level	Marks	Time
3	Introductory	n/a	25 mins

Chapter 4

VALUATION OF SECURITIES AND MARKET EFFICIENCY

Chapter topic list	Syllabus reference
1 Share prices and investment returns	2(d), (e)
2 The fundamental analysis theory of share values	2(e)
3 Charting or technical analysis	2(e)
4 Random walk theory	2(e)
5 The efficient market hypothesis	2(e)
6 Stock market ratios	2(c), (e)
7 Convertibles and warrants	2(e)

Introduction

In this chapter, we look at methods of **valuing individual shares**, and then at the question of how **share price movements** may be explained.

In aiming to maximise the share value, and hence shareholders' wealth, the financial manager must face the need to convince the stock market of the worth of the company. It is therefore important to appreciate the meaning and importance of the various **stock market ratios**.

We also look at the special features of **convertibles** and **warrants**.

Knowledge brought forward from Paper 8

Recall from Paper 8 that the role of a stock market for companies is:

- As a **primary market**, bringing companies and investors together through the issue of new securities, whereby
  - o   Investors put new long-term funds into a company, and
  - o   A company can raise capital for investing in its business
- As a **secondary market** for existing stocks and shares, whereby
  - o   Investors can sell their stocks or shares if and when they wish to do so, and
  - o   Other investors can acquire existing stocks or shares in a company

A readily available market gives existing stocks and shares greater **liquidity**, which makes them much more attractive as investments.

Further functions of a stock market are as follows.

- To enable the owners of a company to realise some of their investment by bringing a hitherto private company to the market
- To allow companies to take over other companies by issuing new shares as the purchase consideration. Stock market companies can thus use their market status to finance expansion through acquisitions

As well as forming the most important markets for shares in the UK, the London Stock Exchange is the capital market for UK government stocks (gilts).

1 SHARE PRICES AND INVESTMENT RETURNS

1.1 Investors will buy shares to obtain an income from dividends and/or to make a capital gain from an increase in share prices. The market price of a security will depend on the return that investors expect to get from it.

1.2 The return from an **ordinary share** consists of dividends plus any capital gain. The **capital gain** (or **loss**) is the difference between the price at which the investor bought the share, and the share's current market value. Capital gains are not taxable until the shareholder sells his or her shares, and realises the capital gain.

1.3 Returns on **fixed interest** securities consist of:

(a) Interest payments, and

(b) Either:

(i) Changes in the market value of the security, if the investor sells it before maturity, or

(ii) The redemption value of the security when it eventually matures, less the price paid

1.4 With redeemable loan stock, return is measured by:

(a) Interest up to the date of redemption, *plus*
(b) The redemption value of the stock

The return is the **discounted yield** that equates the cost of investment in the stock with the present value (PV) of future interest payments and cash receivable on redemption.

1.5 Generally speaking, investors who buy ordinary shares are taking a bigger financial risk than investors in fixed interest securities. This is because holders of debt receive interest out of pre-tax profits and have a prior claim over shareholders in the event that the company goes into liquidation. Ordinary shareholders, in contrast, can only receive dividends if the company has enough distributable profits, and might suffer capital losses if the share price goes down.

1.6 If the purpose of investing is to earn dividend income, an investor will try to buy shares which are expected to provide a satisfactory dividend in relation to their market value. The movement in share prices, which occurs from day to day on the stock market, means that an investor can improve his return by **buying at the right time**. For example, if the share price is £1.50 on day 1, rising to £1.55 on day 2, falling to £1.48 on day 3 and rising to £1.50 on day 4, the investor will obtain the best return if he buys shares on day 3. However, if he predicts that the share price will fall even lower than £1.48 in one or two weeks time, he will prefer to wait until then before buying.

1.7 Similarly, the prediction of share price movements may help an investor to maximise his capital gain from buying and selling shares. Shares should be bought when prices are at their lowest and sold when they are at their highest. Since stockbrokers and investment advisers give advice to clients about when to buy and sell shares, they need a method of foretelling which way share prices will move, up or down, and when. It is therefore useful to consider the extent to which share prices and share price movements can be predicted.

Theories of share price behaviour

1.8 There are differing views about share price movements, which may be broadly classified as: **fundamental analysis theory; technical analysis (chartist theory); random walk theory.** These different theories about how share prices are reached in the market, especially fundamental analysis, have important consequences for financial management.

2 THE FUNDAMENTAL ANALYSIS THEORY OF SHARE VALUES

2.1 The **fundamental theory of share values** is based on the theory that the 'realistic' market price of a share can be derived from a valuation of estimated future dividends. The value of a share will be the discounted present value of all future expected dividends on the share, discounted at the shareholders' cost of capital.

Exam focus point
You need to learn the two formulae given below for use in the exam.

2.2 (a) When the company is expected to pay constant dividends every year into the future, 'in perpetuity':

$$P_0 = \frac{D}{K_e}$$

where P_0 is the market price of the share ex div, that is, excluding any current dividend that might be payable

D is the expected annual dividend per share in the future

K_e is the shareholders' cost of capital (the required rate of return).

(b) When the company is expected to pay a dividend which increases at a constant rate, g, every year into the future, the following **dividend growth model** may be used:

$$P_0 = \frac{D_0(1+g)}{(K_e - g)} = \frac{D_1}{(r - g)}$$

where D_0 is the dividend in the current year (year 0) and so $D_0(1+g)$ is the expected future dividend in year 1(D_1). Again, P_0 is the market value of the share ex div.

2.3 EXAMPLE: CONSTANT DIVIDEND

Hocus plc expects to pay a constant dividend of £450,000 at the end of every year for ever (in perpetuity). Assuming that a dividend has just been paid, calculate what the market value of Hocus plc's shares ought to be if its shareholders' cost of capital is 15%.

2.4 SOLUTION

$$P_0 = \frac{£450,000}{(1.15)} + \frac{£450,000}{(1.15)^2} + \frac{£450,000}{(1.15)^3} + \text{.... and so on, in perpetuity.}$$

The present value of £1 a year for ever at a rate of interest r% (r expressed as a proportion) is 1/r.

Therefore, the present value of £450,000 a year at a rate of interest of 15% is:

$$£450,000 \times \frac{1}{0.15} = £3,000,000.$$

The value of Hocus plc's shares will be £3,000,000.

2.5 EXAMPLE: DIVIDEND GROWTH

Pocus plc paid a dividend this year of £3,000,000. The company expects the dividend to rise by 2% a year in perpetuity. This expectation is shared by the investors in the stock market. The current return expected by investors from shares in the same industry as Pocus plc is 11%.

(a) What would you expect the total market value of the shares of Pocus plc to be?

(b) If it is now rumoured in the stock market that interest rates are about to rise and so shareholders will want to earn an extra 1% on their shares. What change would you expect in the value of the shares of Pocus plc?

(c) What conclusion do you draw from this example?

2.6 SOLUTION

$$P_0 = \frac{D_0(1+g)}{K_e - g}$$

(a) Predicted share value (return of 11%) $= \dfrac{£3,000,000(1.02)}{(0.11-0.02)} = £34,000,000$

(b) Predicted share value (return of 12%) $= \dfrac{£3,000,000(1.02)}{(0.12-0.02)} = £30,600,000$

The value of the company's shares would fall by £3,400,000.

(c) When interest rates are expected to go up, there may well be a fall in share prices. Similarly, expectations of a fall in interest rates may well result in an increase in share prices. This is because the required return on shares is likely to move approximately in step with changes in rates of interest on other investments.

Question 1

The management of Crocus plc are trying to decide on the dividend policy of the company.

There are two options that are being considered.

(a) The company could pay a constant annual dividend of 8p per share.

(b) The company could pay a dividend of 6p per share next year, and use the retained earnings to achieve an annual growth of 3% in dividends for each year after that.

The shareholders' cost of capital is thought to be 18%. Which dividend policy would maximise the wealth of shareholders, by maximising the share price?

Answer

(a) *With a constant annual dividend*

Share price $= \dfrac{8p}{0.18} = 44.4p$

(b)   *With dividend growth*

Share price $= \dfrac{6p(1.03)}{(0.18-0.03)} = \dfrac{6.18}{0.15} = 41.2p$

The constant annual dividend would be preferable.

Question 2

Lupin plc has paid a constant annual dividend of 8.4p a share for some years, and is expected to go on doing so in the future. The current dividend of 8.4p is about to be paid.

The return expected by shareholders is currently 14%.

(a)   What would you expect the share price cum div for Lupin plc shares to be?

(b)   What should the share price cum div move to if the return required by shareholders falls to 12%?

(c)   Can you see a simplifying assumption about the payment of the annual dividend that is being made in the computations you make?

Note. The market value (MV) cum div is the market value including the value of the dividend that is soon to be paid out. The MV cum div equals the MV ex div (P_0) plus the dividend.

Answer

(a) $P_0 = \dfrac{8.4}{0.14} = 60p$

MV cum div   = P_0 + current dividend

                 = 60p + 8.4p

                 = 68.4p

(b) $P_0 = \dfrac{8.4}{0.12} = 70p$

MV cum div   = 70p + 8.4p

                 = 78.4p

Since the shareholders' required rate of return will go down, the share price will go up.

(c)   The simplifying assumption is that the annual dividend will be paid in full all in one go. In practice, companies (especially public companies) will probably pay the dividend in two parts:

(i)   an interim dividend part way through the year;
(ii)   a final dividend after the end of the year.

In general, however, this simplifying assumption is accepted as giving a sufficiently accurate estimate of share values.

The value of debentures

2.7   The same valuation principle can be applied to the valuation of **debentures and other loan stock**. However, the future income from fixed interest debentures is predictable, which should make the process of valuation more straightforward.

(a)   For irredeemable debentures or loan stock, where the company will go on paying interest every year in perpetuity, without ever having to redeem the loan:

$$P_0 = \frac{i}{K_d}$$

where P_0 the market price of the stock ex interest, that is, excluding any interest payment that might soon be due

                i is the annual interest payment on the stock

                K_d is the return required by the loan stock investors

(b) For redeemable debentures or loan stock, the market value is the discounted present value of future interest receivable, up to the year of redemption, **plus** the discounted present value of the redemption payment.

2.8 EXAMPLE: DEBENTURES

A company has issued some 9% debentures, which are now redeemable at par in three years time. Investors now require an interest yield of 10%. What will be the current market value of £100 of debentures?

2.9 SOLUTION

Year		Cash flow £	Discount factor 10%	Present value £
1	Interest	9	0.909	8.18
2	Interest	9	0.826	7.43
3	Interest	9	0.751	6.76
3	Redemption value	100	0.751	75.10
				97.47

£100 of debentures will have a market value of £97.47.

The importance of the fundamental theory of share values

2.10 If the fundamental analysis theory of share values is correct, the price of any share will be predictable, provided that all investors have the **same information** about a company's expected future profits and dividends and a **known cost of capital**. So is it correct? Are share prices predictable? And if not, why not?

2.11 In general terms, fundamental analysis seems to be valid. This means that if an investment analyst can foresee before anyone else that:

(a) A company's future profits and dividends are going to be different from what is currently expected, or

(b) Shareholders' cost of capital will rise or fall (for example in response to interest rate changes)

then the analyst will be able to predict a future share price movement, and so recommend clients to buy or sell the share before the price change occurs.

2.12 In practice, share price movements are affected by day to day fluctuations, reflecting supply and demand in a particular period, investor confidence, market interest rate movements, and so on. Investment analysts want to be able to predict these fluctuations in prices, but fundamental analysis might be inadequate as a technique. Some analysts, known as **chartists**, therefore rely on technical analysis of share price movements.

3 CHARTING OR TECHNICAL ANALYSIS

3.1 **Chartists** or 'technical analysts' attempt to predict share price movements by assuming that past price patterns will be repeated. There is no real theoretical justification for this approach, but it can at times be spectacularly successful. Studies have suggested that the degree of success is greater than could be expected merely from chance. Nevertheless not

BPP PUBLISHING

even the most extreme chartist would claim that every major price movement can be predicted accurately and sufficiently early to make correct investment decisions.

3.2 Chartists do not attempt to predict every price change. They are primarily interested in trend reversals, for example when the price of a share has been rising for several months but suddenly starts to fall. There are several features of charts that are considered important. These include: **resistance levels**; **double tops** and **double bottoms**; 'head and shoulders' patterns.

3.3 Consider Figure 1. The dotted line represents the lower **resistance level** on a rising trend. It will be noticed that many of the troughs lie on this line, but only at the end is it breached. The chartist would claim that this breach is a good indication that the trend has been reversed.

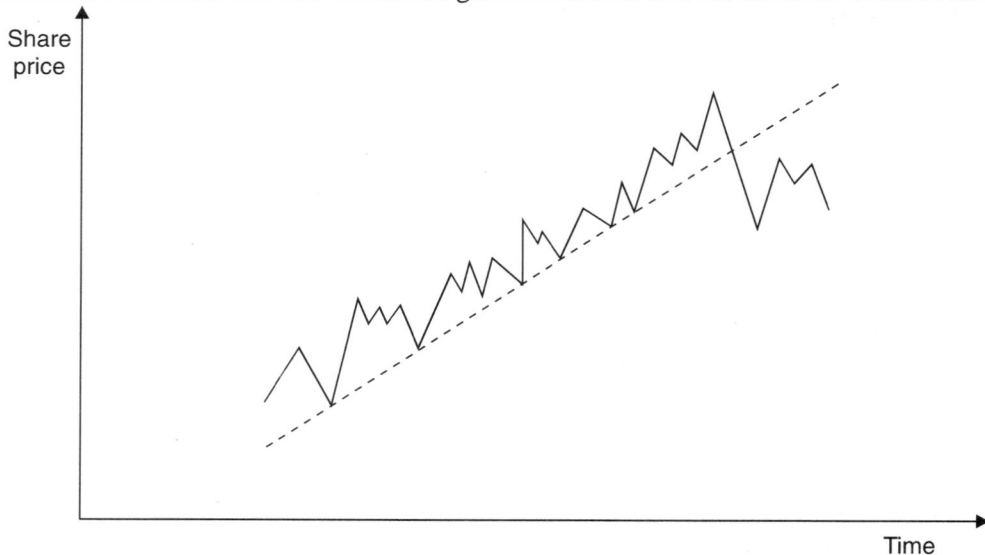

Figure 1 Resistance level

3.4 Let us now look at a resistance level on a **double top**. Suppose that the price of a share has been rising steadily for some time. Recently the price fell as some investors sold to realise profits and it then rose to its maximum level for a second time before starting to fall again. This is known as a double top and based on experience the chartist would predict that the trend has reversed. A typical double top might appear as in Figure 2.

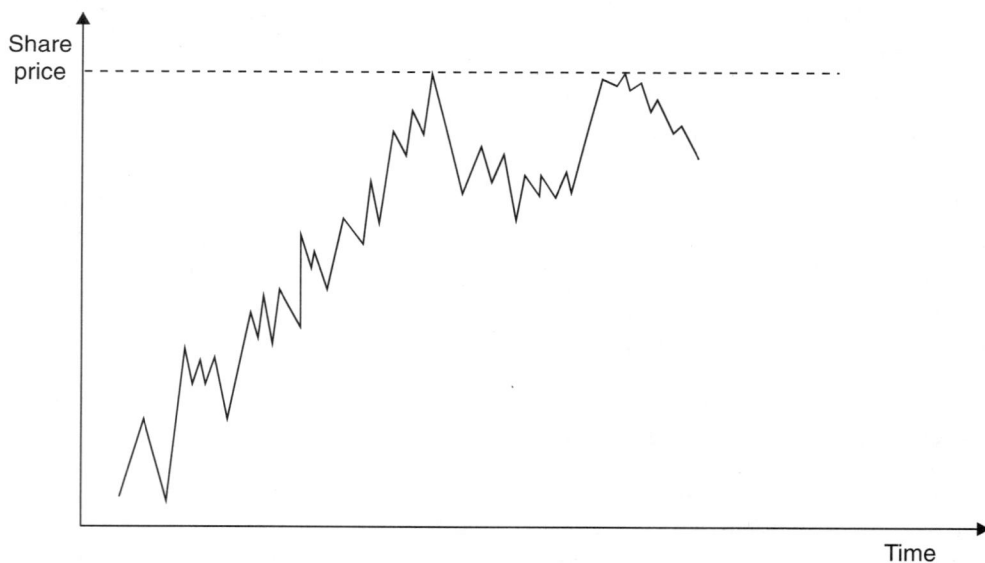

Figure 2 Double top

Double bottoms can be interpreted in a similar but opposite way.

3.5 Another indication of a trend reversal is the '**head and shoulders**'. In Figure 3, the price has been rising for some time before, at the left shoulder, profit taking has caused the price to drop. The price has then risen steeply again to the head before more profit taking causes the price to drop to more or less the same level as before (the neck). Although the price rises again the gains are not as great as at the head. The level of the right shoulder together with the frequent dips down towards the neck would suggest to the chartist that the upward trend previously observed is over and that a fall is imminent. The breach of the neckline is the indication to sell. An **inverse head and shoulders** can be interpreted in a similar manner.

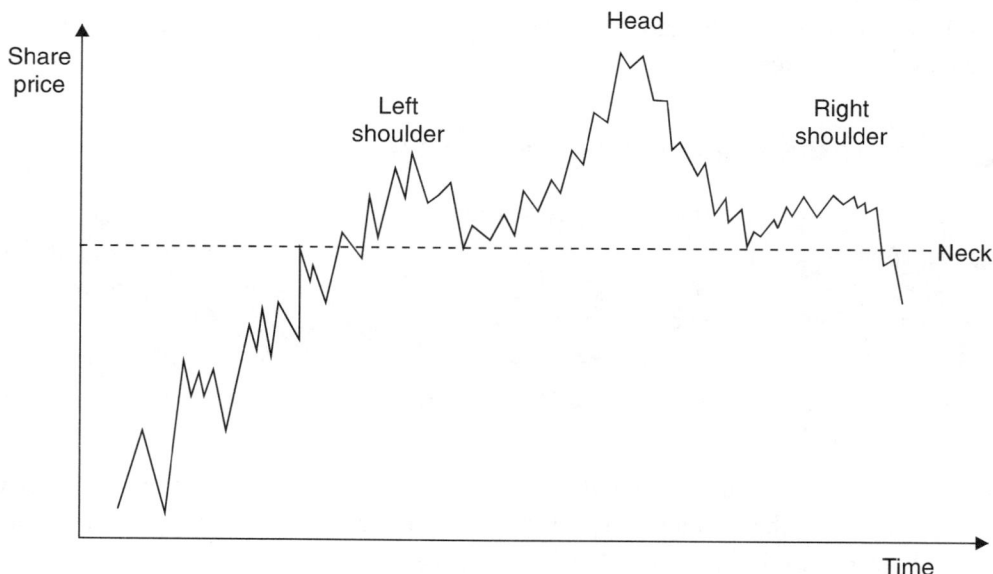

Figure 3 Head and shoulders

3.6 Moving averages help the chartist to examine overall trends. For example, he may calculate and plot moving averages of share prices for 20 days, 60 days and 240 days. The 20 day figures will give a reasonable representation of the actual movement in share prices after eliminating day to day fluctuations. The other two moving averages give a good idea of longer term trends.

4 RANDOM WALK THEORY

4.1 **Random walk theory** is consistent with the fundamental theory of share values. It accepts that a share should have an intrinsic price dependent on the fortunes of the company and the expectations of investors. One of its underlying assumptions is that all relevant information about a company is available to all potential investors who will act upon the information in a rational manner.

4.2 The key feature of random walk theory, however, is that although share prices will have an intrinsic or fundamental value, this value will be altered as new information becomes available, and that the behaviour of investors is such that the actual share price will fluctuate from day to day around the intrinsic value.

4.3 Random walk theory emerged in the late 1950s as an attempt to disprove chartist theory. H V Roberts challenged the idea that share price movements were systematic, and showed how sequences of random numbers can exhibit the same pattern as actual recorded changes of share prices on the Stock Exchange. Roberts was able to duplicate the 'head and shoulders' pattern of share price movements with random numbers, and he concluded that such 'patterns' are illusory and of no value for predicting share prices.

Random walks and an efficient stock market

4.4 Research was carried out in the late 1960s to explain why share prices in the stock market display a random walk phenomenon. This research led to the development of the efficient market hypothesis. It can be shown that random movements in share prices will occur if the stock market operates 'efficiently' and makes information about companies, earnings, dividends and so on, freely (or cheaply) available to all customers in the market. In displaying efficiency, the stock market also lends support to the fundamental analysis theory of share prices.

5   THE EFFICIENT MARKET HYPOTHESIS

Exam focus point
Rather than forming the basis of a full question, the efficient market hypothesis is more likely to be examined in questions on the cost of capital.

5.1 It has been argued that the UK and US stock markets are efficient capital markets, that is, markets in which:

(a) The prices of securities bought and sold reflect all the relevant information which is available to the buyers and sellers (In other words, share prices change quickly to reflect all new information about future prospects.)

(b) No individual dominates the market and so there is competition

(c) Transaction costs of buying and selling are not so high as to discourage trading significantly

5.2 If the stock market is efficient, share prices should vary in a rational way.

(a) If a company makes an investment with a positive net present value (NPV), shareholders will get to know about it and the market price of its shares will rise in anticipation of future dividend increases.

(b) If a company makes a bad investment shareholders will find out and so the price of its shares will fall.

(c) If interest rates rise, shareholders will want a higher return from their investments, so market prices will fall.

The definition of efficiency

5.3 Different types of efficiency can be distinguished in the context of the operation of financial markets.

(a) If financial markets allow funds to be directed towards firms which make the most productive use of them, then there is **allocative efficiency** in these markets. Allocative efficiency will be at its maximum or 'optimum' level if there is no alternative allocation of funds, channelled from savings, which would result in higher economic prosperity.

(b) Transaction costs are incurred by participants in financial markets, for example commissions on share transactions, margins between interest rates for lending and for borrowing, and loan arrangement fees. Financial markets have **operational efficiency** if transaction costs are kept as low as possible. Transaction costs are kept low where there is open competition between brokers and other market participants.

(c) The **information processing efficiency** of a stock market means the ability of a stock market to price stocks and shares fairly and quickly. An efficient market in this sense is one in which the market prices of all the securities traded on it reflect all the available information. There is no possibility of 'speculative bubbles' in which share prices are pushed up or down, by speculative pressure, to unrealistically high or low levels.

Varying degrees of information processing efficiency

5.4 There are three degrees or 'forms' of this 'information processing' efficiency: **weak form**; **semi-strong form**; **strong form**.

5.5 Tests can be carried out on the workings of a stock market to establish whether the market operates with a particular form of efficiency. **Weak form tests** are made to assess whether a stock market shows at least weak form efficiency. **Semi-strong form tests** are made to assess whether a market shows at least semi-strong form efficiency. **Strong form tests** are made to assess whether a market shows strong form efficiency.

Weak form tests and weak form efficiency

5.6 The **weak form hypothesis** of market efficiency explains changes in share prices as the result of new information which becomes available to investors. In other words, share prices only change when new information about a company and its profits have become available. Share prices do *not* change *in anticipation* of new information being announced.

5.7 Since new information arrives unexpectedly, changes in share prices should occur in a random fashion: a weak form test seeks to prove the validity of the random walk theory of share prices. In addition, since the theory states that current share prices reflect all information available from past changes in the price, if it is correct then chartist or technical analysis cannot be based on sound principles.

5.8 Research to prove that the stock market displays weak form efficiency has been based on the principle that if **share price changes are random**, and if there **is no connection between past price movements and new share price changes**, then it should be possible to prove statistically there is no correlation between successive changes in the price of a share, that is, that trends in prices cannot be detected. Proofs of the absence of trends have been claimed in the work of various writers.

Semi-strong form tests and semi-strong form efficiency

5.9 **Semi-strong form** tests attempt to show that the stock market displays semi-strong efficiency, by which we mean that current share prices reflect **both** all relevant information about past price movements and their implications, **and** all knowledge which is available publicly.

5.10 Tests to prove semi-strong efficiency have concentrated on the ability of the market to anticipate share price changes before new information is formally announced. For example, if two companies plan a merger, share prices of the two companies will inevitably change once the merger plans are formally announced. The market would show semi-strong

BPP PUBLISHING

efficiency, however, if it were able to *anticipate* such an announcement, so that share prices of the companies concerned would change in advance of the merger plans being confirmed.

5.11 Research in both the UK and the USA has suggested that **market prices anticipate mergers** several months before they are formally announced, and the conclusion drawn is that the stock markets in these countries *do* exhibit semi-strong efficiency. It has also been argued that the market displays sufficient efficiency for investors to see through '**creative accounting**' or '**window dressing**' of accounts by companies which use accounting conventions to overstate profits.

5.12 Suppose that a company is planning a rights issue of shares in order to invest in a new project. A semi-strong form efficient market hypothesis (unlike the weak form hypothesis) would predict that if there is public knowledge before the issue is formally announced, of the issue itself and of the expected returns from the project, then the market price (cum rights) will change to reflect the anticipated profits before the issue is announced.

Strong form tests and strong form efficiency

5.13 A **strong form test** of market efficiency attempts to prove that the stock market displays a strong form of efficiency, by which we mean that share prices reflect all information available:

   (a) From past price changes

   (b) From public knowledge or anticipation, and

   (c) From insider knowledge available to specialists or experts (such as investment managers)

   It would then follow that in order to maximise the wealth of shareholders, management should concentrate simply on maximising the net present value of its investments and it need not worry, for example, about the effect on share prices of financial results in the published accounts because investors will make allowances for low profits or dividends in the current year if higher profits or dividends are expected in the future.

5.14 In theory, an expert such as an investment manager should be able to use his privileged access to additional information about companies to earn a higher rate of return than an ordinary investor. Unit trusts should in theory therefore perform better than the average investor. Research has suggested, however, that this expert skill does not exist (or at least, that any higher returns earned by experts are offset by management charges).

How efficient are stock markets?

5.15 Evidence so far collected suggests that stock markets show efficiency that is at least weak form, but tending more towards a semi-strong form. In other words, current share prices reflect all or most publicly available information about companies and their securities. However, it is very difficult to assess the market's efficiency in relation to shares which are not usually actively traded.

5.16 Fundamental analysis and technical analysis, which are carried out by analysts and investment managers, play an important role in creating an efficient stock market. This is because an efficient market depends on the widespread availability of cheap information about companies, their shares and market conditions, and this is what the firms of market makers and other financial institutions **do** provide for their clients and for the general investing public.

The implications of the efficient market hypothesis

5.17   If the strong form of the efficient market hypothesis is correct, a company's real financial position will be reflected in its share price. Its real financial position includes both its current position and its expected future profitability. Making profits from insider dealing would not be possible, since all information is available to the market. If the management of a company attempts to maximise the net present value of their investments and to make public any relevant information about those investments then current share prices will in turn be maximised.

5.18   The semi-strong form EMH has the most supporters. If the semi-strong EMH is true, it will not be possible for investors to make a speculative gain on the basis of publicly available information. Indeed studies have shown that not even fund managers can consistently 'beat the market'. Of course this does not preclude a 'fair' profit being made over time for the risk taken by investing. If the semi-strong form EMH is correct, then the directors should 'manage' both the underlying projects and information made publicly available concerning the company and its projects. Such information may 'signal' important facts that might be used to predict future equity cashflows.

5.19   The implication for an investor is that if the market shows strong form or semi-strong form efficiency, he can rarely spot shares at a bargain price that will soon rise sharply in value. This is because the market will already have anticipated future developments, and will have reflected these in the share price. All the investor can do, instead of looking for share bargains, is to concentrate on building up a good spread of shares (a portfolio) in order to achieve a satisfactory balance between risk and return.

5.20   As already pointed out, the weak form EMH challenges the claim of chartists - those who claim to identify trends and pattern in share values.

5.21   EXAMPLE: EFFICIENT MARKET HYPOTHESIS

Company X has 3,000,000 shares in issue and company Y 8,000,000.

(a)   On day 1 the market value per share is £3 for X and £6 for Y.

(b)   On day 2 the management of Y decide, at a private meeting, to make a takeover bid for X at a price of £5 per share. The takeover will produce large operating savings with a present value of £8,000,000.

(c)   On day 5 Y publicly announces an unconditional offer to purchase all shares of X at a price of £5 per share with settlement on day 20. Details of the large savings are not announced and are not public knowledge.

(d)   On day 10 Y announces details of the savings which will be derived from the takeover.

Ignoring tax and the time value of money between day 1 and 20, and assuming the details given are the only factors having an impact on the share price of X and Y, determine the day 2, day 5 and day 10 share price of X and Y if the market is:

(a)   Semi-strong form efficient
(b)   Strong form efficient

in each of the following separate circumstances.

(i)   The purchase consideration is cash as specified above.

(ii)   The purchase consideration, decided on day 2 and publicly announced on day 5, is five newly issued shares of Y for six shares of X.

BPP PUBLISHING

5.22 SOLUTION

(a) *Semi-strong form efficient market (i) cash offer*

With a semi-strong form of market efficiency, shareholders know all the relevant historical data and publicly available current information.

(i) Day 1   Value of X shares: £3 each, £9,000,000 in total.

Value of Y shares: £6 each, £48,000,000 in total.

(ii) Day 2   The decision at the *private* meeting does not reach the market, and so share prices are unchanged.

(iii) Day 5   The takeover bid is announced, but no information is available yet about the savings.

(1) The value of X shares will rise to their takeover bid price of £5 each, £15,000,000 in total.

(2) The value of Y shares will be as follows.

	£
Previous value (8,000,000 × £6)	48,000,000
Add value of X shares to be acquired,	
at previous market worth (3,000,000 × £3)	9,000,000
	57,000,000
Less purchase consideration for X shares	15,000,000
New value of Y shares	42,000,000
Price per share	£5.25

The share price of Y shares will fall on the announcement of the takeover.

(iv) Day 10   The market learns of the potential savings of £8,000,000 (present value) and the price of Y shares will rise accordingly to:

$$\frac{£42,000,000 + £8,000,000}{8,000,000 \text{ shares}} = £6.25 \text{ per share}$$

The share price of X shares will remain the same as before, £5 per share.

Semi-strong form efficient market (ii) share exchange offer

(i) The share price will not change until the takeover is announced on day 5, when the value of the combined company will be perceived by the market to be (48 + 9) £57,000,000.

The number of shares in the enlarged company Y would be as follows.

Current	8,000,000
Shares issued to former X shareholders (3,000,000 × 5/6)	2,500,000
	10,500,000

The value per share in Y would change to reflect what the market expects the value of the enlarged company to be.

$$\frac{£57,000,000}{10,500,000} = £5.43 \text{ per share}$$

The value per share in X would reflect this same price, adjusted for the share exchange terms.

$$\frac{5}{6} \text{ of } £5.43 = £4.52$$

(ii) Day 10 The value of the enlarged company would now be seen by the market to have risen by £8,000,000 to £65,000,000 and the value of Y shares would rise to:

$$\frac{£65,000,000}{10,500,000} = £6.19 \text{ per share}$$

The value per X share would be:

$$\frac{5}{6} \text{ of } £6.19 = £5.16$$

(b) *Strong form efficient market (i) cash offer*

In a strong form efficient market, the market would become aware of *all* the relevant information when the private meeting takes place. The value per share would change as early as *day 2* to:

(i)   X: £5
(ii) Y: £6.25

The share prices would then remain unchanged until day 20.

Strong form efficient market (ii) share exchange offer

In the same way, for the same reason, the value per share would change *on day 2* to:

(i)   X: £5.16
(ii) Y: £6.19

and remain unchanged thereafter until day 20.

5.23 The different characteristics of a semi-strong form and a strong form efficient market thus affect the timing of share price movements, in cases where the relevant information becomes available to the market eventually. The difference between the two forms of market efficiency concerns when the share prices change, not by how much prices eventually change. You should notice, however, that in neither case would the share prices remain unchanged until day 20. In a **weak form** efficient market, the price of Y's shares would not reflect the expected savings until after the savings had been achieved and reported, so that the takeover bid would result in a fall in the value of Y's shares for a considerable time to come.

Explaining share price movements

5.24 Events such as the 'crash' of October 1987, in which share prices fell suddenly by 20% to 40% on the world's stock markets, raised serious questions about the validity of random walk theory, the fundamental theory of share values and the efficient market hypothesis. If these theories are correct, how can shares that were valued at one level on one day suddenly be worth 40% less the next day, without any change in expectations of corporate profits and dividends? On the other hand, a widely feared crash late in 1989 failed to happen, suggesting that stock markets may not be altogether out of touch with the underlying values of companies.

5.25 Various types of anomaly appear to support the view that 'irrationality' often drives the stock market, including the following.

(a) Seasonal month-of-the-year effects, day-of-the-week effects and also hour-of-the-day effects seem to occur, so that share prices might tend to rise or fall at a particular time of the year, week or day.

(b) There may be a short-run overreaction to recent events.

(c) Individual shares or shares in small companies may be neglected.

5.26 According to 'speculative bubble theory', stock market behaviour is non-linear and based on inflating and bursting **speculative bubbles**, rather than economic forecasts. Security prices rise above their intrinsic prices reflecting expected cash returns because some investors believe that others will pay more for them in the future. This behaviour feeds upon itself and prices rise for a period, producing a bull market. However, at some point, investors will eventually react to all the information which they have previously ignored, losing confidence that prices can rise still further, and a market crash then occurs.

5.27 Zeeman (1974) divided all investors into two (non-mutually exclusive) classes: 'fundamentalists', who are guided in their investment strategies by economic analyses to construct forecasts based on rational expectations; and 'speculators', whose decisions reflect adaptive behaviour in response to technical analysis of recent stock market patterns. Instability in financial markets occurs if there is a substantial proportion of speculators, amplifying changes in market indices. If the index begins to rise/fall, there will be a rapid move into a bull/bear phase respectively.

The coherent market hypothesis

5.28 An approach developed by Vaga in a 1991 publication and drawing upon catastrophe theory, is that known as the **coherent market hypothesis** (CMH). The CMH holds that financial markets may be in one of the following four states depending on the combination of economic fundamentals and group sentiment or crowd behaviour:

(a) Random walks (an efficient market with neutral fundamentals)
(b) Unstable transition (an inefficient market with neutral fundamentals)
(c) Coherence (crowd behaviour with bullish fundamentals)
(d) Chaos (crowd behaviour with mildly bearish fundamentals)

5.29 According to Vaga, the 1987 crash was pure crowd behaviour characteristic of a chaotic market and had little to do with information on economic fundamentals.

6 STOCK MARKET RATIOS 6/99

6.1 **Investors** are interested in:

(a) The value (market price) of the securities that they hold
(b) The return that the security has obtained in the past
(c) Expected future returns
(d) Whether their investment is reasonably secure

6.2 Information that is relevant to market prices and returns is available from published stock market information, and in particular from certain **stock market ratios**.

Dividend yield

6.3 The dividend yield is given by $\dfrac{\text{Gross dividend per share}}{\text{Market price per share}} \times 100\%$

The gross dividend is the dividend paid plus any tax credit. The **gross dividend yield** is used in preference to a net dividend yield, so that investors can make a direct comparison with (gross) interest yields from loan stock and gilts.

6.4 EXAMPLE: DIVIDEND YIELD

A company pays a dividend of 15p (net) per share. The market price is 240p. What is the dividend yield if the tax credit is 10%?

$$\text{Gross dividend per share} = 15p \times \frac{100}{(100-10)} = 16.67p$$

$$\text{Dividend yield} = \frac{16.67p}{240p} \times 100\% = 6.95\%$$

Interest yield

6.5 **Interest yield** $= \dfrac{\text{Gross interest}}{\text{Market value of loan stock}} \times 100\%$

6.6 EXAMPLE: INTEREST YIELD

An investor buys £1,000 (nominal value) of a bond with a coupon of 8% for the current market value of £750.

$$\text{Interest yield} = \frac{1,000 \times 8\%}{750} \times 100\% = 10.67\%$$

> **Exam focus point**
>
> Note that the interest yield, which is the investor's rate of return, is different from the coupon rate of 8%. (Many students confuse these.)

> **KEY TERM**
>
> **Coupon**: the rate of gross interest on loan stock expressed as a percentage of the nominal value of the stock.

Dividend yield and interest yield

6.7 In practice, we usually find with quoted companies that: the dividend yield on shares is less than the interest yield on debentures and loan stock (and also less than the yield paid on gilt-edged securities); and the share price often rises each year, giving shareholders capital gains. In the long run, shareholders will want the return on their shares, in terms of dividends received plus capital gains, to exceed the return that investors get from fixed interest securities.

Earnings per share (EPS) 12/98

6.8 **Earnings per share** is widely used as a measure of a company's performance and is of particular importance in comparing results over a period of several years. A company must be able to sustain its earnings in order to pay dividends and re-invest in the business so as to achieve future growth. Investors also look for **growth in EPS** from one year to the next.

6.9 EPS is defined (in FRS 3) as the profit in pence attributable to each equity (ordinary) share, based on:

(a) The profit (or in the case of a group the consolidated profit) of the period after tax, minority interests and extraordinary items, and after deducting preference dividends

(b) Divided by the number of equity shares in issue and ranking for dividend

(Extraordinary items are unusual, non-repeating items that affect profit but, as already mentioned, they have been effectively outlawed by FRS 3.)

Question 3

Walter Wall Carpets plc made profits before tax in 20X8 of £9,320,000. Tax amounted to £2,800,000.

The company's share capital is as follows.

	£
Ordinary shares (10,000,000 shares of £1)	10,000,000
8% preference shares	2,000,000
	12,000,000

Calculate the EPS for 20X8.

Answer

	£
Profits before tax	9,320,000
Less tax	2,800,000
Profits after tax	6,520,000
Less preference dividend (8% of £2,000,000)	160,000
Earnings	6,360,000
Number of ordinary shares	10,000,000
EPS	63.6p

6.10 EPS on its own does not tell us anything. It must be seen in the context of several other matters.

(a) EPS is used for comparing the results of a company over time. Is its EPS growing? What is the rate of growth? Is the rate of growth increasing or decreasing?

(b) Is there likely to be a significant dilution of EPS in the future, perhaps due to the exercise of share options or warrants, or the conversion of convertible loan stock into equity?

(c) EPS should not be used blindly to compare the earnings of one company with another. For example, if A plc has an EPS of 12p for its 10,000,000 10p shares and B plc has an EPS of 24p for its 50,000,000 25p shares, we must take account of the numbers of shares. When earnings are used to compare one company's shares with another, this is done using the P/E ratio or perhaps the earnings yield.

(d) If EPS is to be a reliable basis for comparing results, it must be calculated consistently. The EPS of one company must be directly comparable with the EPS of others, and the EPS of a company in one year must be directly comparable with its published EPS figures for previous years. Changes in the share capital of a company during the course of a year cause problems of comparability.

6.11 Note that, firstly, EPS is a figure based on **past data**; and secondly it is **easily manipulated** by changes in accounting policies and by mergers or acquisitions. The use of the measure in calculating management bonuses makes it particularly liable to manipulation. The attention given to EPS as a performance measure by City analysts is arguably disproportionate to its true worth. Investors should be more concerned with future earnings, but of course estimates of these are more difficult to reach than the readily available EPS figure.

6.12 A **fully diluted EPS** (FDEPS) can be measured where the company has issued securities that might be converted into ordinary shares at some future date, such as convertible loan stock, share warrants or share options. The FDEPS measures a hypothetical EPS, based on earnings in the period under review, if the company's ordinary shares were increased to their maximum number by the exercise of all existing share options and warrants, and the conversion of existing convertible loan stock etc. The FDEPS gives investors an appreciation of by how much EPS might be affected if and when the options, warrants or conversion rights are exercised.

6.13 Total earnings are increased by:

(a) The savings in interest (net of tax) from the conversion of loan stock into shares

(b) In the case of share options or warrants, the addition to profits (net of tax) from investing the cash obtained from their exercise (estimated on the assumption that the cash is invested in 2½% Consolidated Stock at their market price on the first day of the period)

$$\text{FDEPS} = \frac{\text{Adjusted earnings}}{\text{Maximum number of ordinary shares}}$$

6.14 EXAMPLE: FULLY DILUTED EARNING PER SHARE

Suppose that Walter Wall Carpets plc (see Question 3 above) has in issue £4,000,000 8% convertible unsecured loan stock, convertible in three years' time, with a conversion ratio of 5 shares per £100 of loan stock. The company pays tax at 30%. What is the fully diluted EPS?

6.15 SOLUTION

Undiluted EPS is 63.6 pence, as shown in Question 3. If all holders of the convertible stock convert their holding to ordinary shares, an additional 200,000 ($= 4,000,000/100 \times 5$) shares will be issued in three years' time.

The interest saving on conversion (with tax at 30%) is:

£4,000,000 × 8% × 0.7 = £224,000.

Therefore:

$$\text{FDEPS} = \frac{£6,360,000 + £224,000}{10,000,000 + 200,000}$$

$$= \frac{£6,584,800}{10,200,000} = 64.6 \text{ pence}$$

The price earnings (P/E) ratio   6/98

6.16 The **P/E ratio** is the most important yardstick for assessing the relative worth of a share. It is:

$$\frac{\text{Market price in pence}}{\text{EPS in pence on the net basis}}$$

which is the same as:

Total market value of equity
       Total earnings

6.17 The value of the P/E ratio reflects the market's appraisal of the shares' future prospects. In other words, if one company has a higher P/E ratio than another it is because investors either expect its earnings to increase faster than the other's or consider that it is a less risky company or in a more 'secure' industry.

6.18 The P/E ratio is, simply, a measure of the relationship between the market value of a company's shares and the earnings from those shares. It is an important ratio because it relates two key considerations for investors, the market price of a share and its earnings capacity. It is however significant only as a measure of this relationship between earnings and value.

6.19 EXAMPLE: PRICE EARNINGS RATIO (1)

A company has recently declared a dividend of 12p per share. The share price is £3.72 cum div and earnings for the most recent year were 30p per share. Calculate the P/E ratio.

6.20 SOLUTION

$$\text{P/E ratio} = \frac{\text{MV ex div}}{\text{EPS}} = \frac{£3.60}{30p} = 12$$

Changes in EPS: the P/E ratio and the share price

6.21 The dividend valuation model or fundamental theory of share values is the theory that share prices are related to expected future dividends on the shares. Another approach to assessing what share prices ought to be, which is often used in practice, is a P/E ratio approach. It is a commonsense approach to share price assessment (although not as well founded in theory as the dividend valuation model), which is that:

(a) The relationship between the EPS and the share price is measured by the P/E ratio

(b) There is no reason to suppose, in normal circumstances, that the P/E ratio will vary much over time

(c) So if the EPS goes up or down, the share price should be expected to move up or down too, and the new share price will be the new EPS multiplied by the constant P/E ratio

6.22 For example, if a company had an EPS last year of 30p and a share price of £3.60, its P/E ratio would have been 12. If the current year's EPS is 33p, we might expect that the P/E ratio would remain the same, 12, and so the share price ought to go up to 12 × 33p = £3.96.

6.23 EXAMPLE: EFFECTS OF A RIGHTS ISSUE

Annette Cord Sports Goods plc has 6,000,000 ordinary shares in issue, and the company has been making regular annual profits after tax of £3,000,000 for some years. The share price is £5. A proposal has been made to issue 2,000,000 new shares in a rights issue, at an issue price of £4.50 per share. The funds would be used to redeem £9,000,000 of 12% debenture stock. The rate of corporation tax is 30%.

What would be the predicted effect of the rights issue on the share price, and would you recommend that the issue should take place?

6.24 SOLUTION

If the stock market shows semi-strong form efficiency, the share price will change on announcement of the rights issue, in anticipation of the change in EPS. The current EPS is 50p per share, and so the current P/E ratio is 10.

	£	£
Current annual earnings		3,000,000
Increase in earnings after rights issue		
Interest saved (12% × £9,000,000)	1,080,000	
Less tax on extra profits (30%)	324,000	
		756,000
Anticipated annual earnings		3,756,000
Number of shares (6,000,000 + 2,000,000)		8,000,000
EPS		£0.4695
Current P/E ratio		10
The anticipated P/E ratio is assumed to be the same		
Anticipated share price		£4.695

The proposed share issue is a one for three rights issue, and we can estimate the theoretical ex rights price.

	£
Current value of three shares (× £5)	15.00
Rights issue price of one share	4.50
Theoretical value of four shares	19.50
Theoretical ex rights price $\quad \frac{£19.50}{4} = £4.875$	

6.25 The anticipated share price after redeeming the debentures would be £4.695 per share, which is less than the theoretical ex rights price. If the rights issue goes ahead and the P/E ratio remains at 10, shareholders should expect a fall in share price below the theoretical ex rights price, which indicates that there would be a capital loss on their investment. The rights issue is for this reason not recommended.

Changes in the P/E ratio over time

6.26 Changes in the P/E ratios of companies over time will depend on several factors.

(a) If interest rates go up, investors will be attracted away from shares and into debt capital. Share prices will fall, and so P/E ratios will fall.

Similarly, if interest rates go down, shares will become relatively more attractive to invest in, so share prices and P/E ratios will go up.

(b) If prospects for company profits improve, share prices will go up, and P/E ratios will rise. Share prices depend on expectations of future earnings, not historical earnings, and so a change in prospects, perhaps caused by a substantial rise in international trade, or an economic recession, will affect prices and P/E ratios.

(c) Investors' confidence might be changed by a variety of circumstances, such as:

(i) The prospect of a change in government
(ii) The prospects for greater exchange rate stability between currencies

The dividend cover

6.27 The **dividend cover** is the number of times the actual dividend could be paid out of current profits.

The dividend cover is equal to:

$$\frac{\text{Maximum possible equity dividend that could be paid out of current profits}}{\text{Actual dividend for ordinary shareholders}}$$

6.28 The dividend cover indicates the proportion of distributable profits for the year that is being retained by the company, and the level of risk that the company will not be able to maintain the same dividend payments in future years, should earnings fall. **A high dividend cover** means that a high proportion of profits are being retained, which might indicate that the company is investing to achieve earnings growth in the future.

6.29 EXAMPLE: DIVIDEND COVER

The EPS of York plc is 20p. The dividend was 20% on the 25p ordinary shares. Calculate the dividend cover.

6.30 SOLUTION

$$\text{Dividend cover} = \frac{20p}{20\% \text{ of } 25p} = 4$$

A dividend cover of 4 means that the company is retaining 75% of its earnings for reinvestment.

7 CONVERTIBLES AND WARRANTS

Convertible loan stock   12/96

7.1 Convertible securities are fixed return securities that may be converted, on pre-determined dates and at the option of the holder, into ordinary shares of the company at a predetermined rate. Once converted they cannot be converted back into the original fixed return security. For example, the conversion terms of convertible stock might be that on 1 April 2000, £2 of stock can be converted into one ordinary share, whereas on 1 April 2001, the conversion price will be £2.20 of stock for one ordinary share.

The conversion value and the conversion premium

7.2 The current market value of ordinary shares into which a unit of stock may be converted is known as the **conversion value**. The conversion value will be below the value of the stock at the date of issue, but will be expected to increase as the date for conversion approaches on the assumption that a company's shares ought to increase in market value over time. The difference between the issue value of the stock and the conversion value as at the date of issue is the implicit **conversion premium**.

7.3 EXAMPLE: CONVERTIBLE LOAN STOCK

The 10% convertible loan stock of Starchwhite plc is quoted at £142 per £100 nominal. The earliest date for conversion is in four years time, at the rate of 30 ordinary shares per £100 nominal loan stock. The share price is currently £4.15. Annual interest on the stock has just been paid.

(a) What is the average annual growth rate in the share price that is required for the stockholders to achieve an overall rate of return of 12% a year compound over the next four years, including the proceeds of conversion?

(b) What is the implicit conversion premium on the stock?

7.4 SOLUTION

(a)

Year	Investment £	Interest £	Discount 12%	Present value £
0	(142)		1.000	(142.00)
1		10	0.893	8.93
2		10	0.797	7.97
3		10	0.712	7.12
4		10	0.636	6.36
				(111.62)

The value of 30 shares on conversion at the end of year 4 must have a present value of at least £111.62, to provide investors with a 12% return.

The money value at the end of year 4 needs to be £111.62 ÷ 0.636 = £175.50.

The current market value of 30 shares is (× £4.15) £124.50.

The growth factor in the share price over four years needs to be:

$$\frac{175.50}{124.50} = 1.4096$$

If the annual rate of growth in the share price, expressed as a proportion, is g, then:

$(1 + g)^4 = 1.4096$

$1 + g = 1.0896$

$g = 0.0896$, say 0.09

Conclusion. The rate of growth in the share price needs to be 9% a year (compound).

(b) The conversion premium can be expressed as an amount per share or as a percentage of the current conversion value.

(i) As an amount per share $\frac{£142 - £(30 \times 4.15)}{30}$ = £0.583 per share

(ii) As a % of conversion value $\frac{£0.583}{£4.15} \times 100\%$ = 14%

The issue price and the market price of convertible loan stock

7.5 A company will aim to issue loan stock with the greatest possible conversion premium as this will mean that, for the amount of capital raised, it will, on conversion, have to issue the lowest number of new ordinary shares. The premium that will be accepted by potential investors will depend on the company's growth potential and so on prospects for a sizeable increase in the share price.

7.6 Convertible loan stock issued at par normally has a lower coupon rate of interest than straight debentures. This lower yield is the price the investor has to pay for the conversion rights. It is, of course, also one of the reasons why the issue of convertible stock is attractive to a company.

7.7   When convertible loan stock is traded on a stock market, its **minimum market price** will be the price of straight debentures with the same coupon rate of interest. If the market value falls to this minimum, it follows that the market attaches no value to the conversion rights.

7.8   The actual market price of convertible stock will depend not only on the price of straight debt but also on the current conversion value, the length of time before conversion may take place, and the market's expectation as to future equity returns and the risk associated with these returns. If the conversion value rises above the straight debt value then the price of convertible stock will normally reflect this increase.

7.9   Most companies issuing convertible stocks expect them to be converted. They view the stock as **delayed equity**. They are often used either because the company's ordinary share price is considered to be particularly depressed at the time of issue or because the issue of equity shares would result in an immediate and significant drop in earnings per share. There is no certainty, however, that the security holders will exercise their option to convert; therefore the stock may run its full term and need to be redeemed.

Warrants (or subscription rights)

> **KEY TERMS**
>
> A **warrant** is a right given by a company to an investor, allowing him to buy new shares at a future date or dates at a fixed, pre-determined price (the **exercise price**).

7.10   Warrants are usually issued as **part of a package** with unsecured loan stock: an investor who buys stock will also acquire a certain number of warrants. The purpose of warrants is to make the loan stock more attractive. Once issued, warrants are **detachable from the stock** and can be sold and bought separately before or during the 'exercise period' (the period during which the right to use the warrants to subscribe for shares is allowed). The market value of warrants will depend on expectations of actual share prices in the future.

7.11   During the exercise period, the price of a warrant should not fall below the higher of:

(a)   Nil, and

(b)   The 'theoretical value', which equals:

(Current share price – Exercise price) × Number of shares obtainable from each warrant

7.12   If, for example, a warrant entitles the holder to purchase two ordinary shares at a price of £3 each, when the current market price of the shares is £3.40, the minimum market value ('theoretical value') of a warrant would be (£3.40 – £3) × 2 = 80p.

7.13   If the price fell below the theoretical value during the exercise period, then arbitrage would be possible. For example, suppose the share price is £2.80 and the warrant exercise price is £2.20. The warrants are priced at 50p with each entitled to one share. Ignoring transactions costs, investors could make an instant gain of 10p per share by buying the warrant, exercising it and then selling the share.

7.14   For a company with good growth prospects, the warrant will usually be quoted at a premium above the minimum prior to the exercise period. This premium is known as the warrant conversion premium. It is sometimes expressed as a percentage of the current share price.

7.15 EXAMPLE: WARRANT CONVERSION PREMIUM

An investor holds some warrants which can be used to subscribe for ordinary shares on a one for one basis at an exercise price of £2.50 at a specified future date. The current share price is £2.25 and the warrants are quoted at 50p. What is the warrant conversion premium?

7.16 SOLUTION

The easiest way of finding the premium is to deduct the current share price from the cost of acquiring a share using the warrant, treating the warrant as if it were currently exercisable.

	£
Cost of warrant	0.50
Exercise price	2.50
	3.00
Current share price	2.25
Premium	0.75

7.17 **Attractions of warrants to the investor**

(a) **Low initial outlay**. The investor only has to spend 50p per share as opposed to £2.25. This means that he could buy 4½ times as many warrants as shares or, alternatively, he could invest the remaining £1.75 in other, less risky investments.

(b) **Lower downside potential**. The maximum loss per share is 50p instead of £2.25. Of course the risk of the loss of 50p is much greater than the risk of losing £2.25. The share price of £2.25 is below the exercise price. If it remained at this level until the beginning of the exercise period, the warrants would become worthless as it would not be worthwhile exercising them.

(c) **High potential returns** - see below.

The gearing effect of warrants

7.18 In a similar way to share options, warrants offer the investor the possibility of making a high profit as a percentage of initial cost. This is because the price of the warrants will tend to move more or less in line with the price of the shares. Thus, if the share price rises by 50p the increase in the value of the warrant will be similar. Using the previous prices, a 50p increase in share price is about 22% but a 50p increase in the warrant price is 100%. This illustrates the gearing effect of warrants.

7.19 Let us now recalculate the premium, assuming a 50p rise in the share price and a 50p rise in the warrant price.

	£
Cost of warrant (50p + 50p)	1.00
Exercise price	2.50
	3.50
Current share price (£2.25 + 50p)	2.75
Premium	0.75

7.20 The premium has stayed the same. Note also that the share price is now above the exercise price. The warrants now have an 'intrinsic' value of 25p (ie 275p – 250p).

7.21 In the short run, the warrant price and share price normally move fairly closely in line with each other. **In the longer term** the price of the warrant and hence the premium will depend on:

(a) The length of time before the warrants may be exercised

BPP PUBLISHING

(b) The current price of the shares compared with the exercise price, and

(c) The future prospects of the company

7.22 As the exercise period approaches, any premium will reduce. Towards the end of the exercise period the premium will disappear because, if there were a premium, it would be cheaper to buy the shares directly rather than via the warrant.

Chapter roundup

- In this chapter, we have seen how **share values** may be arrived at. We can now start to see how a financial manager should act, in order to maximise shareholders' wealth.

- **Fundamental analysis** assesses share values on the basis of a study of the company and its business.

- **Chartism** (or **technical analysis**) looks for patterns in share price movements in an attempt to forecast future movements.

- The **efficient market hypothesis** is concerned with how efficient the market is at **processing information**.

- In practice, factors affecting the market value of company shares of which the financial manager should be aware also include the following.

  ◦ Announcement of results
  ◦ Other information about the company's prospects, products and management
  ◦ Information about industry prospects
  ◦ Takeover speculation
  ◦ The state of the economy
  ◦ Exchange rate changes
  ◦ Interest rate changes
  ◦ New legislation

Quick quiz

1   What is the fundamental theory of share values? (see para 2.1) State the formulae for the valuation of shares, assuming (a) no dividend growth (b) a constant rate of dividend growth in perpetuity. (2.2)

2   What is chartism? (3.1)

3   What is random walk theory? (4.1 - 4.3) How is this theory related to the efficient market hypothesis? (4.4)

4   What does efficiency mean, in the context of the efficient market hypothesis? (5.3)

5   What is weak form efficiency? (5.6)

6   What is semi-strong form efficiency? (5.9, 5.10)

7   What is strong form efficiency? (5.13)

8   How does the difference between weak form and semi-strong form efficiency matter, in terms of by how much or when share prices change? (5.23)

9   How is dividend yield calculated? (6.3)

10   How might EPS be used to judge the returns that a company is making for its equity investors? (6.10)

11   What is the P/E ratio? (6.16)

12   What is the dividend cover? (6.27) What does it indicate? (6.28, 6.29)

13   What is the earnings yield? (6.31)

14   Distinguish between convertible loan stocks and warrants. (7.1, 7.10)

Question to try	Level	Marks	Time
4	Exam standard	10	18 mins

BPP PUBLISHING

Chapter 5

THE COST OF CAPITAL

Chapter topic list	Syllabus reference
1 Investment decisions, financing decisions and the cost of capital	3(d)
2 The costs of different sources of finance	3(d)
3 Special problems	3(d)
4 The weighted average cost of capital	3(d)
5 The cost of capital, the NPV of new projects and the value of shares	3(d)

Introduction

While in the previous chapter we looked at investments mainly from the investor's point of view, in this chapter we assess costs from the perspective of the company (or other business enterprise). Every source of finance has a **cost**. In deciding how to finance a company, the costs of all sources must be considered.

Financial managers need a **cost of capital** to use in making decisions. A weighted average might seem a reasonable cost to use, but you should appreciate the arguments against, as well as those for, using it.

Knowledge brought forward from Paper 8

Your knowledge of sources of finance gained in Paper 8 is liable to be tested again in the context of strategic decision making in Paper 14. Some points to jog your memory are set out below, but if you think you need to, go back to your Paper 8 study material.

The following factors should be considered when raising long-term finance.

- Minimum/maximum loan limits
- Expense of raising funds
- Dilution of ownership
- Interference in decision making
- Security required
- Marketability - how easy will it be to persuade investors to invest?
- Market liquidity - are funds available?
- Signalling - how will the market react?

Companies, whether public or private, obtain long-term funds from a variety of sources.

- New issues of equity (ordinary) shares, preference shares, loan stock or bonds
- Retained profits
- Bank borrowing (medium-term)

Retained profits are the main source of long-term finance.

Loan stock and bonds

'**Bonds**' is a term used to describe various forms of long-term debt. Bonds or loans come in a variety of forms, for example as follows.

- **Floating rate** debentures are loans on which the coupon rate of interest can be varied at regular intervals, in line with changes in current market rates of interest

- **Zero coupon bonds** are bonds issued at a large discount to their eventual redemption value, but on which no interest is paid. Investors obtain all their return from the capital gain on redemption

- **Convertible loan stock** (see the previous chapter).

- Loans might be **secured** or **unsecured.**

- Mortgage loans are loans secured on property

- Bank loans might have a fixed charge over certain fixed assets (eg property) and a floating charge over current assets (eg stocks and debtors)

- Companies might be able to issue **subordinated debt** or **junior debt** which is debt over which 'senior debt' takes priority in a liquidation. Being more risky for investors, junior debt carries a higher rate of interest

Other sources of long-term funds include the following.

- Private loans (fairly common with small private companies)
- Loans/equity capital from venture capital organisations
- Government grants
- Leasing - a form of finance for fixed assets

There are two steps in arriving at a **lease or buy decision.**

- Establish whether it is worth having the equipment by discounting the project's cash flows at a suitable cost of capital

- If the equipment is worth having, compare the cash flows of purchasing and leasing. The cash flows can be discounted at an after-tax cost of borrowing, and the financing method with the lowest PV of cost selected

Venture capital is money put into a risky new enterprise, which may all be lost if the enterprise fails.

- The investment is usually in return for an equity stake

- The investing company also often puts a director on the board, and might get involved in management as well

- Venture capital will usually be viewed as short-term from the investor's point of view, the aim being to provide an exit route for the venture capitalist, such as taking the company to the AIM.

---

1 INVESTMENT DECISIONS, FINANCING DECISIONS AND THE COST OF CAPITAL 6/99, 12/99

1.1 The cost of capital has two aspects to it. It is the **cost of funds** that a company raises and uses, and the return that investors expect to be paid for putting funds into the company. It is therefore the **minimum return** that a company should make on its own investments, to earn the cash flows out of which investors can be paid their return. The cost of capital can therefore be measured by studying the returns required by investors, and then used to derive a discount rate for DCF analysis and investment appraisal.

The cost of capital as an opportunity cost of finance

1.2 The cost of capital, however it is measured, is an opportunity cost of finance, because it is the minimum return that investors require. If they do not get this return, they will transfer some or all of their investment somewhere else. Here are two examples.

    (a) If a bank offers to lend money to a company, the interest rate it charges is the yield that the bank wants to receive from investing in the company, because it can get just as good a return from lending the money to someone else. In other words, the interest rate is the opportunity cost of lending for the bank.

(b) When shareholders invest in a company, the returns that they can expect must be sufficient to persuade them not to sell some or all of their shares and invest the money somewhere else. The yield on the shares is therefore the opportunity cost to the shareholders of not investing somewhere else.

The cost of capital and risk

1.3 The cost of capital has three elements.

(a) The **risk-free rate of return** is the return which would be required from an investment if it were completely free from risk. Typically, a risk-free yield would be the yield on government securities.

(b) The **premium for business risk** is an increase in the required rate of return due to the existence of uncertainty about the future and about a firm's business prospects. The actual returns from an investment may not be as high as they are expected to be. Business risk will be higher for some firms than for others, and some types of project undertaken by a firm may be more risky than other types of project that it undertakes.

(c) The **premium for financial risk** relates to the danger of high debt levels (high gearing). For ordinary shareholders, financial risk is evident in the variability of earnings after deducting payments to holders of debt capital. The higher the gearing of a company's capital structure, the greater will be the financial risk to ordinary shareholders, and this should be reflected in a higher risk premium and therefore a higher cost of capital.

1.4 Because different companies are in different types of business (varying business risk) and have different capital structures (varying financial risk) the cost of capital applied to one company may differ radically from the cost of capital of another.

2 THE COSTS OF DIFFERENT SOURCES OF FINANCE   6/96, 12/97, 12/99

2.1 Where a company uses a mix of equity and debt capital its overall cost of capital might be taken to be the weighted average of the cost of each type of capital, but before discussing this we must look at the cost of each source of capital: equity, preference shares, debt capital and so on.

The cost of ordinary share capital

2.2 New funds from equity shareholders are obtained either from new issues of shares or from cash deriving from retained earnings. Both of these sources of funds have a cost. Shareholders will not be prepared to provide funds for a **new issue of shares** unless the return on their investment is sufficiently attractive. **Retained earnings** also have a cost. This is an opportunity cost, the dividend forgone by shareholders.

The dividend valuation model

2.3 If we begin by ignoring share issue costs, the cost of equity, both for new issues and retained earnings, could be estimated by means of a **dividend valuation model**, on the assumption that the market value of shares is directly related to expected future dividends on the shares.

If the future dividend per share (D_1) is expected to be *constant* in amount then the ex dividend share price (P_o) will be calculated by the formula:

$$P_o = \frac{D_1}{(1+K_e)} + \frac{D_1}{(1+K_e)^2} + \frac{D_1}{(1+K_e)^3} + \ldots = \frac{D_1}{K_e}, \text{ so } K_e = \frac{D_1}{P_o}$$

where K_e is the shareholders' cost of capital

D_1 is the annual dividend per share, starting at year 1 and then continuing annually in perpetuity

2.4   Assumptions in the dividend valuation model

(a)   The dividends from projects for which the funds are required will be of the same risk type or quality as dividends from existing operations.

(b)   There would be no increase in the cost of capital, for any other reason besides (a) above, from a new issue of shares.

(c)   All shareholders have perfect information about the company's future, there is no delay in obtaining this information and all shareholders interpret it in the same way.

(d)   Taxation can be ignored.

(e)   All shareholders have the same marginal cost of capital.

(f)   There would be no issue expenses for new shares.

Share issue costs and the cost of equity

2.5   The issue of shares, whether to the general public or as a rights issue, costs money and these costs should be considered in investment appraisal. Two approaches have been suggested.

(a)   One approach is to deduct issue costs as a year 0 cash outflow of the project or projects for which the share capital is being raised. The issue costs would not affect the cost of equity capital.

(b)   An alternative approach you might come across is to calculate the cost of new equity with the formula:

$$K_e = \frac{D_1}{P_o - X}$$

where X represents the issue costs. Thus, if the issue price of a share is £2.50, issue costs are 20p per share, and new shareholders expect constant annual dividends of 46p, the cost of new equity would be:

$$\frac{46}{(250 - 20)} = 0.2 = 20\%$$

Approach (a) is recommended.

The dividend growth model

2.6   Shareholders will normally expect dividends to increase year by year and not to remain constant in perpetuity. The fundamental theory of share values states that the market price of a share is the present value of the discounted future cash flows of revenues from the share, so the market value given an expected constant annual growth in dividends would be:

$$P_o = \frac{D_0(1+g)}{(1+K_e)} + \frac{D_0(1+g)^2}{(1+K_e)^2} + \ldots$$

BPP PUBLISHING

where P_0 is the current market price (ex div)

           D_0 is the current net dividend

           K_e is the shareholders' cost of capital

           g   is the expected annual growth in dividend payments

               and both r and g are expressed as proportions.

2.7   This formula assumes a constant growth rate in dividends, but it could easily be adapted for uneven growth. Capital growth through increases in the share price will arise from changed expectations about future dividend growth, or changes in the required return, r.

2.8   It is often convenient to assume a constant expected dividend growth rate in perpetuity. The formula in Paragraph 2.6 then simplifies to:

$$P_o = \frac{D_0(1+g)}{(r-g)}$$

2.9   Re-arranging this, we get a formula for the ordinary shareholders' cost of capital.

$$K_e = \frac{D_0(1+g)}{P_o} + g$$

2.10   This is equivalent to the following equation, which is included on the **Paper 14 Formulae sheet** (see the Appendix to this Study Text).

EXAM FORMULA

$$K_e = \frac{D_1}{P_o} + g$$

where D_1 is the dividend in year 1, so that $D_1 = D_0(1 + g)$.

2.11   The dividend growth model is sometimes called **Gordon's growth model**.

Question 1

A share has a current market value of 96p, and the last dividend was 12p. If the expected annual growth rate of dividends is 4%, calculate the cost of equity capital.

Answer

Cost of capital   = $\dfrac{12(1+0.04)}{96}$ + 0.04 = 0.13 + 0.04 = 0.17 = 17%

Exam focus point

If an examination question requires you to calculate a cost of equity using the growth model, it is likely that you will be expected to predict the future growth rate from an analysis of the growth in dividends over the past few years.

2.12 EXAMPLE: COST OF CAPITAL (2)

The dividends and earnings of Hall Shores plc over the last five years have been as follows.

Year	Dividends £	Earnings £
20X1	150,000	400,000
20X2	192,000	510,000
20X3	206,000	550,000
20X4	245,000	650,000
20X5	262,350	700,000

The company is financed entirely by equity and there are 1,000,000 shares in issue, each with a market value of £3.35 ex div.

What is the cost of equity?

What implications does dividend growth appear to have for earnings retentions?

2.13 SOLUTION

The dividend growth model will be used.

(a) Dividends have risen from £150,000 in 20X1 to £262,350 in 20X5. The increase represents four years growth. (Check that you are aware that there are four years growth, and not five years growth, in the table.) The average growth rate, g, may be calculated as follows.

$$\text{Dividend in 20X1} \times (1+g)^4 = \text{Dividend in 20X5}$$

$$(1+g)^4 = \frac{\text{Dividend in 20X5}}{\text{Dividend in 20X1}}$$

$$= \frac{£262,350}{£150,000} = 1.749$$

$$1+g = \sqrt[4]{1.749} = 1.15$$

$$g = 0.15 = 15\%$$

(b) The growth rate over the last four years is assumed to be expected by shareholders into the indefinite future, so the cost of equity, r, is:

$$\frac{d_0(1+g)}{P_0} + g = \frac{0.26235(1.15)}{3.35} + 0.15 = 0.24 = 24\%$$

(c) Retained profits will earn a certain rate of return and so growth will come from the yield on the retained funds. It might be assumed that g = bR where b is the yield on new investments and R is the proportion of profits retained for reinvestment. In our example, if we applied this assumption the future annual growth rate would be 15% if bR continued to be 15%. If the rate of return on new investments averages 24% (which is the cost of equity) and if the proportion of earnings retained is 62.5% (which it has been, approximately, in the period 20X1 – 20X5) then g = bR = 24% × 62.5% = 15%.

The cost of debt capital and the cost of preference shares

Knowledge brought forward from Paper 8

Preference shares - now uncommon - usually carry the following rights.

- A constant dividend expressed as % of nominal value
- Priority of dividends over ordinary shareholders
- Sometimes cumulative
- Priority over ordinary shareholders in a winding up (if stated in the Articles)

BPP PUBLISHING

> Why issue preference shares?
>
> - Unlike interest payments on loans or debentures, the dividend payments can be missed in a poor year and preference shareholders cannot then appoint a receiver
>
> - Compared with ordinary shares, there is no dilution of control since preference shares do not carry voting rights
>
> - Unless they are redeemable, issuing preference shares will reduce gearing
>
> - The company's borrowing powers will not be restricted, since there is no security against assets
>
> - Preference shares are attractive to corporate investors as dividends received are not subject to corporation tax, unlike interest received. *But*, for the issuing company, dividend payments are not tax-deductible, unlike interest payments.

2.14 Estimating the cost of fixed interest or fixed dividend capital is much easier than estimating the cost of ordinary share capital because the interest received by the holder of the security is fixed by contract and will not fluctuate. The cost of debt capital already issued is the rate of interest (the internal rate of return) which equates the current market price with the discounted future cash receipts from the security. Ignoring taxation for the moment, in the case of **irredeemable debt** (or **preference shares**) the future cash flows are the interest (or dividend) payments in perpetuity so that:

$$P_0 = \frac{I}{(1+K_d)} + \frac{I}{(1+K_d)^2} + \frac{I}{(1+K_d)^3} \dots$$

where P_0 is the current market price of debt capital after payment of the current interest (dividend)

       I is the interest (dividend) received

       K_d is the cost of debt (preference share) capital

$$\frac{1}{(1+K_d)} + \frac{1}{(1+K_d)^2} + \frac{1}{(1+K_d)^3} \dots$$

simplifies to $\dfrac{1}{K_d}$ so:

$$P_0 = \frac{I}{K_d} \qquad \text{and} \qquad K_d = \frac{I}{P_0}$$

2.15 If the debt is **redeemable** then in the year of redemption the interest payment will be received by the holder as well as the amount payable on redemption, so:

$$P_0 = \frac{I}{(1+K_d)} + \frac{I}{(1+K_d)^2} + \dots + \frac{I+P_n}{(1+K_d)^n}$$

where P_n = the amount payable on redemption in year n.

2.16 The above equation cannot be simplified so 'K_d' will have to be calculated by trial and error, as an IRR. The best trial and error figure to start with in calculating the cost of redeemable debt is to take the cost of debt capital as if it were irredeemable and then add the annualised capital profit that will be made from the present time to the time of redemption.

2.17 EXAMPLE: COST OF CAPITAL (3)

Owen Allot plc has in issue 10% debentures of a nominal value of £100. The market price is £90 ex interest. Ignoring taxation, calculate the cost of this capital if the debenture is:

(a) Irredeemable

(b) Redeemable at par after 10 years

2.18 SOLUTION

(a) The cost of irredeemable debt capital is $\dfrac{i}{P_0} = \dfrac{£10}{£90} \times 100\% = 11.1\%$

(b) The cost of debt capital is 11.1% if irredeemable. The capital profit that will be made from now to the date of redemption is £10 (£100 – £90). This profit will be made over a period of ten years which gives an annualised profit of £1 which is about 1% of current market value. The best trial and error figure to try first is, therefore, 12%.

Year		Cash flow	Discount factor 12%	PV £	Discount factor 11%	PV £
0	Market value	(90)	1.000	(90.00)	1.000	(90.00)
1-10	Interest	10	5.650	56.50	5.889	58.89
10	Capital repayment	100	0.322	32.20	0.352	35.20
				(1.30)		4.09

The approximate cost of debt capital is, therefore, $\left(11 + \dfrac{4.09}{(4.09 - -1.30)} \times 1\right) = 11.76\%$

2.19 The cost of debt capital estimated above represents the cost of continuing to use the finance rather than redeem the securities at their current market price. It would also represent the cost of raising additional fixed interest capital if we assume that the cost of the additional capital would be equal to the cost of that already issued. If a company has not already issued any fixed interest capital, it may estimate the cost of doing so by making a similar calculation for another company which is judged to be similar as regards risk.

Debt capital and taxation

2.20 The interest on debt capital is an allowable deduction for purposes of taxation and so the cost of debt capital and the cost of share capital are not properly comparable costs. This tax relief on interest ought to be recognised in DCF computations. One way of doing this is to include tax savings due to interest payments in the cash flows of every project. A simpler method, and one that is normally used, is to allow for the tax relief in computing the cost of debt capital, to arrive at an 'after-tax' cost of debt. The **after-tax cost of irredeemable debt capital** is:

$$K_d = \frac{I}{P_0}(1-t)$$

where K_d is the cost of debt capital

         I is the annual interest payment

         P_0 is the current market price of the debt capital ex interest (that is, after payment of the current interest)

         t is the rate of corporation tax.

2.21 Therefore if a company pays £10,000 a year interest on irredeemable debenture stock with a nominal value of £100,000 and a market price of £80,000, and the rate of corporation tax is 30%, the cost of the debentures would be:

$\dfrac{10,000}{80,000}(1 - 0.30) = 0.0875 = 8.75\%.$

2.22 The higher the rate of corporation tax is, the greater the tax benefits in having debt finance will be compared with equity finance. In the example above, if the rate of tax had been 40%, the cost of debt would have been, after tax:

$$\frac{10,000}{80,000}(1-0.40) = 0.075 = 7.5\%$$

2.23 The relative attraction of debt over equity has been enhanced by the abolition in 1997 of the tax credit on dividends which **pension funds** - a major category of investor - could previously reclaim.

2.24 In the case of **redeemable debentures**, the capital repayment is not allowable for tax. To calculate the cost of the debt capital to include in the weighted average cost of capital, it is necessary to calculate an internal rate of return which takes account of tax relief on the interest.

2.25 EXAMPLE: COST OF CAPITAL (4)

(a) A company has outstanding £660,000 of 8% debenture stock on which the interest is payable annually on 31 December. The stock is due for redemption at par on 1 January 19X6. The market price of the stock at 28 December 19X2 was 103 cum interest. Ignoring any question of personal taxation, what do you estimate to be the current market rate of interest?

(b) If a new expectation emerged that the market rate of interest would rise to 12% during 19X3 and 19X4 what effect might this have in theory on the market price at 28 December 19X2?

(c) If the effective rate of corporation tax was 30% what would be the percentage cost to the company of debenture stock in (a) above? Tax is paid each 31 December on profits earned in the year ended on the previous 31 December.

2.26 SOLUTION

(a) The current market rate of interest is found by calculating the pre-tax internal rate of return of the cash flows shown in the table below. We must subtract the current interest (of 8% per £100 of stock) from the current market price, and use this 'ex interest' market value. A discount rate of 10% is chosen for a trial-and-error start to the calculation.

Item and date		*Year*	*Cash flow*	*Discount factor*	*Present value*
			£	10%	£
Market value (ex int)	28.12.X2	0	(95)	1.000	(95.00)
Interest	31.12.X3	1	8	0.909	7.28
Interest	31.12.X4	2	8	0.826	6.61
Interest	31.12.X5	3	8	0.751	6.01
Redemption	1.1.X6	3	100	0.751	75.10
				NPV	0

By coincidence, the market rate of interest is 10% since the NPV of the cash flows above is zero.

(b) If the market rate of interest is expected to rise in 19X3 and 19X4 it is probable that the market price in December 19X2 will fall to reflect the new rates obtainable. The probable market price would be the discounted value of all future cash flows up to 19X6, at a discount rate of 12%.

Item and date		Year	Cash flow £	Discount factor 12%	Present value £
Interest	31.12.X2	0	8	1.000	8.00
Interest	31.12.X3	1	8	0.893	7.14
Interest	31.12.X4	2	8	0.797	6.38
Interest	31.12.X5	3	8	0.712	5.70
Redemption	1.1.X6	3	100	0.712	71.20
				NPV	98.42

The estimated market price would be £98.42 per cent *cum* interest.

(c) Again we must deduct the current interest payable and use ex interest figures.

At a market value of 103

Item and date		Year	Cash flow ex int £	PV 5% £	PV 8% £
Market value		0	(95.00)	(95.00)	(95.00)
Interest	31.12.X3	1	8.00	7.62	7.41
Tax saved	31.12.X4	2	(2.40)	(2.18)	(2.06)
Interest	31.12.X4	2	8.00	7.26	6.86
Tax saved	31.12.X5	3	(2.40)	(2.07)	(1.91)
Interest	31.12.X5	3	8.00	6.91	6.35
Tax saved	31.12.X6	4	(2.40)	(1.98)	(1.76)
Redemption	1. 1.X6	3	100.00	86.40	79.40
NPV				6.96	(0.71)

The estimated cost of capital is:

$$5\% + (\frac{6.96}{(6.96 - -0.71)} \times 3\%) = 7.7\%$$

The cost of floating rate debt

2.27 If a firm has **floating rate debt,** then the cost of an equivalent fixed interest debt should be substituted. 'Equivalent' usually means fixed interest debt with a similar term to maturity in a firm of similar standing, although if the cost of capital is to be used for project appraisal purposes, there is an argument for using debt of the same duration as the project under consideration.

The cost of convertible securities

2.28 The cost of fixed interest securities which are convertible into ordinary shares is found as follows, allowing for taxation and assuming that conversion will take place.

$$P_0 = \frac{I(1-t)}{(1+r)} + \frac{I(1-t)}{(1+r)^2} + \ldots + \frac{I(1-t)}{(1+r)^n} + \frac{P_n \times R}{(1+r)^n}$$

where
- P_0 is the current market price of the convertible security, convertible in year n, after paying the current year's interest
- I is the annual interest payment
- t is the rate of corporation tax
- r is the cost of capital of the convertible security holders
- P_n is the market value of an ordinary share in year n
- R is the conversion ratio, that is the number of shares into which the security is convertible.

BPP PUBLISHING

The cost of capital, r, would be calculated by finding the IRR which equates P_0 with the present value of the future cash flows. If the cost of capital found by treating the convertibles as non-convertible debentures is higher, that higher cost should be used on the basis that the debenture holders will choose not to convert, so as to secure the higher rate of return for themselves.

2.29 EXAMPLE: COST OF CAPITAL (5)

Some 8% convertible debentures have a current market value of £106 per cent. An interest payment was made recently. The debentures will be convertible into equity shares in three years time, at a rate of four shares per £10 of debentures. The shares are expected to have a market value of £3.50 each at that time, and all the debenture holders are expected to convert their debentures.

What is the cost of capital to the company for the convertible debentures? Corporation tax is at 30%. Assume that tax savings occur in the same year that the interest payments arise.

2.30 SOLUTION

Year	Item	Cash flow	*Try 12 %* Discount factor	PV £	*Try 15%* Discount factor	PV £
0	Current MV	(106.00)	1.000	(106.00)	1.000	(106.00)
1-3	Interest less tax (I(1–t))	5.60	2.402	13.45	2.283	12.78
3	Value of shares on conversion (40 × £3.5)	140.00	0.712	99.68	0.658	92.12
				7.13		(1.10)

$$\text{Cost of capital} = 12\% + \left[\frac{7.13}{(7.13 - -1.10)} \times (15 - 12) \right]\%$$

$$= 12\% + 2.6\% = 14.6\%$$

The cost of short-term funds

2.31 The cost of short-term funds such as bank loans and overdrafts is the current interest being charged on such funds.

Depreciation

2.32 Depreciation, being a non-cash item of expense, is ignored in our cost of capital computations, but depreciation is a means of retaining funds within a business for new investments or replacements. For our purposes, it is sufficient to say that the cost of funds retained by depreciation *is ignored*, because it is argued that they should be taken as having a cost equal to the company's weighted average cost of capital, and so are irrelevant to the calculation of the cost of capital.

3 SPECIAL PROBLEMS

Private companies and the cost of equity

3.1 The cost of capital cannot be calculated from market values for **private companies** in the way that has been described so far, because the shares in a private company do not have a quoted market price. Since private companies do not have a cost of equity that can be readily estimated, it follows that a big problem for private companies which want to use DCF for evaluating investment projects is how to select a cost of capital for a discount rate.

3.2 Suitable approaches might be: to estimate the cost of capital for similar public companies, but then add a further premium for additional business and financial risk; or to build up a cost of capital by adding estimated premiums for business risk and financial risk to the risk-free rate of return.

Government organisations and the cost of capital

3.3 The same problem faces government organisations. Government organisations do not have a market value, and most of them do not pay interest on much or all of the finance they receive. Government activities do not involve business risk, and there is no financial risk either for the investor, which is mainly the government itself. In practice, the problem is overcome in the case of nationalised industries by using a target 'real' rate of return set by the Treasury rather than a cost of capital.

The cost of equity capital: gross dividend or net dividend yield?

3.4 We have seen that the cost of equity is calculated on the basis of **net dividends** (perhaps with dividend growth). The net dividend is chosen because the cost of capital is used as the discount rate for the evaluation of capital projects by a company, and the company must have sufficient profits from its investments to pay shareholders the net dividends they require out of after-tax profits.

3.5 Tax on profits is allowed for in the cash flows of each project. The discount rate is therefore applied to the cash flows of the project after tax. If a company were to make a payment of dividends out of profits, the amount available would be the net dividend, related to the after-tax profits earned.

3.6 Since the company's cost of equity is connected with the net dividends payable by the company, the company need not be concerned with the net dividends received by the shareholders after personal taxation has been deducted from the shareholders' gross dividend income. The cash return to a shareholder from his investment in the shares may well differ from the cash which the company pays out. That is, the cost of equity to the company will differ from the required net return of the shareholder.

3.7 Different shareholders have different tax positions, and may therefore have different preferences as to the amount of dividends they receive and the amount of retained earnings kept within the business for capital growth.

4 THE WEIGHTED AVERAGE COST OF CAPITAL 12/99

Computing a discount rate

4.1 We have now looked at the costs of individual sources of capital for a company. But how does this help us to work out the **cost of capital** as a whole, or the **discount rate** to apply in DCF investment appraisals? In many cases it will be difficult to associate a particular project with a particular form of finance. A company's funds may be viewed as a pool of resources. Money is withdrawn from this pool of funds to invest in new projects and added

BPP
PUBLISHING

to the pool as new finance is raised or profits are retained. Under these circumstances it might seem appropriate to use an average cost of capital as the discount rate.

4.2 The correct cost of capital to use in investment appraisal is the **marginal cost** of the funds raised (or earnings retained) to finance the investment. The weighted average cost of capital (WACC) might be considered the most reliable guide to the marginal cost of capital, but only on the assumption that the company continues to invest in the future, in projects of a standard level of business risk, by raising funds in the same proportions as its existing capital structure.

General formula for the WACC

4.3 A general formula for the weighted average cost of capital is:

$$\text{WACC} = K_{eg}\left(\frac{E}{E+D}\right) + K_d\left(\frac{D}{E+D}\right)$$

where
K_{eg} is the cost of equity
K_d is the cost of debt
E is the market value of equity in the firm
D is the market value of debt in the firm

4.4 The above formula ignores taxation. Bringing in corporation tax, we should calculate the cost of debt net of tax, where the tax rate is t, as follows.

EXAM FORMULA

$$\text{WACC} = K_{eg}\left(\frac{E}{E+D}\right) + K_d(1-t)\left(\frac{D}{E+D}\right)$$

Exam focus point

This second formula - included on the Paper 14 **Formulae Sheet** - works only for irredeemable debt. If you are given a pre-tax cost of debt, and no details about the nature of the debt, then you can assume that it is irredeemable.

If you need to calculate WACC where debt is redeemable, you should calculate the after-tax cost of debt using the techniques set out earlier in this chapter and substitute this into the formula in place of $K_d(1-t)$.

4.5 EXAMPLE: WEIGHTED AVERAGE COST OF CAPITAL

Prudence plc is financed partly by equity and partly by debentures. The equity proportion is always kept at two thirds of the total. The cost of equity is 18% and that of debt 12%. A new project is under consideration which will cost £100,000 and will yield a return before interest of £17,500 a year in perpetuity. Should the project be accepted? Ignore taxation.

4.6 SOLUTION

Since the company will maintain its gearing ratio unchanged, it is reasonable to assume that its marginal cost of funds equals its WACC. The weighted average cost of capital is as follows.

	Proportion	Cost	Cost × proportion
Equity	$\frac{2}{3}$	18%	12%
Debt	$\frac{1}{3}$	12%	4%
		WACC	16%

The present value of the future returns in perpetuity can be found using the WACC as the discount rate, as follows.

$$\text{Present value of future cash flows} = \frac{\text{Annual cash flow}}{\text{Discount rate}} = \frac{£17,500}{0.16} = £109,375$$

The NPV of the investment is £109,375 – £100,000 = £9,375.

Another way of looking at the investment shows how using the WACC as the discount rate ensures that equity shareholders' wealth is increased by undertaking projects with a positive NPV when discounted at the WACC.

The amount of finance deemed to be provided by the debenture holders will be $^1/_3$ × £100,000 = £33,333. The interest on this will be 12% × £33,333 = £4,000, leaving £13,500 available for the equity shareholders. The return they are receiving based on their 'investment' of £66,667 will be as follows.

$$\text{Return to equity} = \frac{£13,500}{£66,667} = 0.2025 \text{ or } 20.25\%$$

As this return exceeds the cost of equity capital, the project is acceptable.

Weighting

4.7 In the last example, we simplified the problem of **weighting the different costs of capital** by giving the proportions of capital. Two methods of weighting could be used.

(a) Weights could be based on market values (by this method, the cost of retained earnings is implied in the market value of equity).

(b) Weights could be based on book values.

Although the latter are often easier to obtain they are of doubtful economic significance. It is, therefore, more meaningful to use market values when data are available. For unquoted companies estimates of market values are likely to be extremely subjective and consequently book values may be used. When using market values it is not possible to split the equity value between share capital and reserves and only one cost of equity can be used. This removes the need to estimate a separate cost of retained earnings.

Question 2

The management of Custer Ackers plc are trying to decide on a cost of capital to apply to the evaluation of investment projects. The company has an issued share capital of 500,000 ordinary £1 shares, with a current market value cum div of £1.17 per share. It has also issued £200,000 of 10% debentures, which are redeemable at par in two years time and have a current market value of £105.30 per cent, and £100,000 of 6% preference shares, currently priced at 40p per share. The preference dividend has just been paid, and the ordinary dividend and debenture interest are due to be paid in the near future.

The ordinary share dividend will be £60,000 this year, and the directors have publicised their view that earnings and dividends will increase by 5% a year into the indefinite future. The fixed assets and working capital of the company are financed by the following.

	£
Ordinary shares of £1	500,000
6% £1 Preference shares	100,000
Debentures	200,000
Reserves	380,000
	1,180,000

Required

Advise the management. Ignore inflation, and assume corporation tax of 30%. Assume also that tax savings occur in the same year as the interest payments to which they relate.

Note. The cost of capital of a security is the IRR which equates the current market value of the security with its expected future cash flows. The balance sheet (accounting) values of the securities and reserves should be ignored.

Answer

(a) *Equity.* Given a 5% annual increase in dividend in perpetuity, the cost of equity capital may be estimated as:

$$\frac{60,000(1+0.05)}{585,000-60,000 \ *}+0.05 = 0.17 = 17\%$$

* MV ex div

(b) *Preference shares.* The cost of capital is $\frac{6p}{40p} \times 100\% = 15\%$

(c) *Debentures.* The cost of capital is the IRR of the following cash flows.

Year	Cost £	Interest £	Tax relief £	Net cash flows £
0	(95.30)			(95.30)
1		10	(3.00)	7.00
2	100.00	10	(3.00)	107.00

	Try 10%		*Try 8%*	
Net cash flow £	Discount factor	PV £	Discount factor	PV £
(95.30)	1.000	(95.30)	1.000	(95.30)
7.00	0.909	6.36	0.926	6.48
107.00	0.826	88.38	0.857	91.70
		(0.56)		2.88

The IRR is approx $8\% + \dfrac{2.88}{(2.88 - -0.56)} \times (10 - 8)\%$

$= 9.67\%$

(d) *Weighted average cost of capital*

Item	Market value £	Cost of capital	Product £
Ordinary shares*	525,000	17%	89,250
Preference shares	40,000	15%	6,000
Debentures*	190,600	9.57%	18,240
	755,600		113,490

* ex div and ex interest

$$\text{WACC} = \frac{113,490}{755,600} = 0.150 = 15.0\%$$

(e) The management of Custer Ackers plc may choose to add a premium for risk on top of this 15% and apply a discount rate of, say, 18% to 20% in evaluating projects.

Arguments for using the WACC

4.8   The weighted average cost of capital can be used in investment appraisal if we make the following assumptions.

(a)   The project is small relative to the overall size of the company.

(b)   The weighted average cost of capital reflects the company's long-term future **capital structure**, and capital costs. If this were not so, the current weighted average cost would become irrelevant because eventually it would not relate to any actual cost of capital.

(c)   The project has the same degree of **business risk** as the company has now.

(d)   New investments must be financed by new **sources of funds**: retained earnings, new share issues, new loans and so on.

(e)   The cost of capital to be applied to project evaluation reflects the **marginal cost of new capital** (see below).

KEY TERMS

Business risk (or **systematic risk**) is risk arising from the existing operations of an enterprise (eg relating to macroeconomic factors) which cannot be reduced by diversification of investments.

Arguments against using the WACC

4.9   The arguments against using the WACC as the cost of capital for investment appraisal (as follows) are based on criticisms of the assumptions that are used to justify use of the WACC.

(a)   New investments undertaken by a company might have different **business risk** characteristics from the company's existing operations. As a consequence, the return required by investors might go up (or down) if the investments are undertaken, because their business risk is perceived to be higher (or lower).

(b)   The finance that is raised to fund a new investment might substantially change the capital structure and the perceived **financial risk** of investing in the company. Depending on whether the project is financed by equity or by debt capital, the perceived financial risk of the entire company might change. This must be taken into account when appraising investments.

(c)   Many companies raise **floating rate** debt capital as well as fixed interest debt capital. With floating rate debt capital, the interest rate is variable, and is altered every three or six months or so in line with changes in current market interest rates. The cost of debt capital will therefore fluctuate as market conditions vary. Floating rate debt is difficult to incorporate into a WACC computation, and the best that can be done is to substitute an 'equivalent' fixed interest debt capital cost in place of the floating rate debt cost.

Marginal cost of capital approach

4.10   The **marginal cost of capital approach** involves calculating a marginal cut-off rate for acceptable investment projects by:

(a)   Establishing rates of return for each component of capital structure, except retained earnings, based on its value if it were to be raised under current market conditions

(b) Relating dividends or interest to these values to obtain a marginal cost for each component

(c) Applying the marginal cost to each component depending on its proportionate weight within the capital structure and adding the resultant costs to give a weighted average

4.11 It can be argued that the current weighted average cost of capital should be used to evaluate projects where a company's capital structure changes only very slowly over time; then the marginal cost of new capital should be roughly equal to the weighted average cost of current capital. If this view is correct, then by undertaking investments which offer a return in excess of the WACC, a company will increase the market value of its ordinary shares in the long run. This is because the excess returns would provide surplus profits and dividends for the shareholders.

4.12 Where gearing levels fluctuate significantly, or the finance for a new project carries a significantly different level of risks to that of the existing company, there is good reason to seek an alternative marginal cost of capital.

4.13 Note that the marginal cost of capital approach outlined above only takes into account the incremental financing costs of the new project. The financing of a major project may change the risk profile of the existing capital structure, in which case the **adjusted present value (APV) method**, discussed in the next chapter, is likely to be more appropriate.

5 THE COST OF CAPITAL, THE NPV OF NEW PROJECTS AND THE VALUE OF SHARES

5.1 Using the **dividend valuation model**, it can be argued that the total value of a company's shares will increase by the NPV of any project that is undertaken, provided that there is no change in the company's WACC. We begin considering this argument for companies financed entirely by equity, so that the WACC and the cost of equity are the same.

5.2 Suppose that a company relying on equity as its only source of finance wishes to invest in a new project. If the money is raised by issuing new share capital to the existing shareholders and the inflows generated by the new project are used to increase dividends, then the project will have to show a positive net present value (NPV) at the shareholders' marginal cost of capital, because otherwise the shareholders would not agree to provide the new capital.

5.3 The gain to the shareholders after acceptance of the new project will be the difference between the market value of the company before acceptance of the new project and the market value of the company after acceptance of the new project less the amount of funds raised from the shareholders to finance the project.

The market value of the shares will increase by:

$$\frac{A_1}{(1+K_e)} + \frac{A_2}{(1+K_e)^2} + \frac{A_3}{(1+K_e)^3} + \ldots - (\text{Cost of project})$$

where $A_1, A_2 \ldots$ are the additional dividends at years 1, 2 and so on

K_e is the shareholders' marginal cost of capital

This is the NPV of the project.

Investments financed by retained profits

5.4 If for some reason there is a limit to the number of new shares that a company can issue to its shareholders and a company could undertake many projects with positive net present values, then reducing its dividend payment would increase the supply of capital available. Even though in the short term dividends will be reduced, this will be more than compensated for in the long term by the fact that extra cash inflows generated by the investments will increase dividends in the future. Indeed, it can be argued that no dividends should be paid until all projects with positive net present values have been financed.

5.5 EXAMPLE: INCREASE IN THE MARKET VALUE OF SHARES

Hubble plc, which has just paid its current dividend, expects to pay dividends of £6,000 at year 1, £6,000 at year 2 and £8,000 a year from then onwards. A new project has just been discovered which will require an outlay of £3,000 at year 1 and will yield cash inflows of £2,000 each year for two years. If the project is accepted, dividends will be adjusted accordingly.

The shareholders' marginal cost of capital is estimated at 15%.

If the shareholders were told at year 0 that the project was going to be accepted and they were given full information about the project, what should be the theoretical increase in the market value of the company's shares?

5.6 SOLUTION

(a) The market value of company at year 0 before acceptance of the new project is:

$$\frac{£6,000}{1.15} + \frac{£6,000}{1.15^2} + \frac{£8,000}{1.15^3} + \frac{£8,000}{1.15^4} + \dots \text{ (£8,000 pa in perpetuity)}$$

The value at year 2 of £8,000 receivable each year from year 3 onwards is:

$$\frac{£8,000}{0.15} = £53,333 \text{ which means that the computation above can be simplified to:}$$

$$\frac{£6,000}{1.15} + \frac{£6,000}{1.15^2} + \frac{£53,333}{1.15^2} = £50,080$$

(b) The market value of the company at year 0 after acceptance of the new project is:

$$\frac{£3,000}{1.15} + \frac{£8,000}{1.15^2} + \frac{£10,000}{1.15^3} + \frac{£8,000}{1.15^4} + \dots \text{ (£8,000 pa in perpetuity)}$$

The year 1 dividend will be £3,000 lower than before and the years 2 and 3 dividends will be £2,000 higher than before.

$$\frac{£3,000}{1.15} + \frac{£8,000}{1.15^2} + \frac{£10,000}{1.15^3} + \frac{£53,333}{1.15^3} = £50,300$$

(c) The market value of the company at year 0 would increase by £220 (£50,300 − £50,080) after acceptance of the project. The £220 can be proved as follows.

(i) NPV of the project at year 1 $= \dfrac{£2,000}{1.15^2} + \dfrac{£2,000}{1.15} - £3,000$

$= £(1,512 + 1,739 - 3,000) = £251$

(ii)   NPV at year 0 of £251 receivable at the end of year 1

$$= \frac{£251}{1.15} = £218$$

This NPV of £218 is the same as the increase in the market value of £220, allowing for a rounding error of £2.

5.7   In the example above, the shareholders would in theory benefit from a sudden rise in the price equal to the net present value of the new project as soon as the project was accepted. This would only happen if there is a strong form efficient market, or if dividend forecasts are published and are believed. Furthermore, shareholders do not necessarily make rational decisions, so market values may not in practice respond to changes in future dividend expectations.

Conclusions for ungeared companies

5.8   If an all equity company undertakes a project, and it is financed in such a way that its cost of capital remains unchanged, the total market value of ordinary shares will increase by the amount of the NPV of the project. If the market has strong form efficiency the shares will increase in value as soon as details of the intended project become available in advance of extra profits actually being earned and extra dividends actually being received from the project. The situation is the same if a company is geared (ie has **debt capital** in its capital structure).

5.9   EXAMPLE: GEARED COMPANY

Trubshaw plc is financed 50% by equity and 50% by debt capital. The cost of equity is 20% and the cost of debt is 14%. Ignoring tax, this means that Trubshaw's WACC is 17%.

The company currently pays out all its profits as dividends, and expected dividends are £800,000 a year into the indefinite future.

A project is under consideration which would cost £1,200,000, to be financed half by a new issue of equity and half by a new loan. It would increase annual profits before interest by £340,000. The costs of equity and debt capital would be unchanged.

(a)   What is the NPV of the project?
(b)   By how much would the value of equity increase if the project is undertaken?

5.10   SOLUTION

The NPV of the project is as follows.

Year	Cash flow £	Discount factor 17%	Present value £
0	(1,200,000)	1.0	(1,200,000)
1 - ∞	340,000	1/0.17	2,000,000
		NPV	800,000

The market value of the company as a whole will increase by £2,000,000, which is the project's NPV plus the cost of the investment. Of this, £1,000,000 will be debt capital and £1,000,000 will be equity.

To maintain the 50:50 debt:equity ratio, the cost of the investment will be financed by £1,000,000 debt capital and £200,000 equity. It would not be financed by £600,000 of each. This is because the NPV of £800,000 will add to the value of equity *only*, not to the value of the debt capital.

If new equity of £200,000 is issued, the NPV of £800,000 will increase the market value of equity by £1,000,000 in total, which matches the new loan capital of £1,000,000.

The increased value of equity can be proved as follows.

	£
Annual profit from project, before interest	340,000
Less interest cost (£1,000,000 × 14%)	140,000
Increase in annual profits and dividends	200,000
Cost of equity	÷20%
Increase in the market value of equity	£1,000,000

This example therefore illustrates that given an unchanged WACC, the value of equity will be increased by the NPV of any project which is undertaken (plus the extra funds invested in equity, in this case £200,000) with the NPV calculated using a discount rate equal to the WACC.

Chapter roundup

- The **cost of capital** is the rate of return that the enterprise must pay to satisfy the providers of funds, and it reflects the riskiness of the funding transaction.

- The **dividend valuation model** can be used to estimate a cost of equity, on the assumption that the market value of share is directly related to the expected future dividends on the shares.

- Expected **growth in dividends** can be allowed for, using Gordon's growth model.

- The **cost of debt** is the return an enterprise must pay to its lenders.

    ○ For **irredeemable debt**, this is the (post-tax) interest as a percentage of the ex div market value of the loan stock (or preference shares).

    ○ For **redeemable debt**, the cost is given by the internal rate of return of the cash flows involved.

- The **weighted average cost of capital** can be used to evaluate a company's investment projects if:

    ○ The project is small relative to the company

    ○ The existing capital structure will be maintained (same financial risk)

    ○ The project has the same business risk as the company

    ○ New investments are financed by new sources of funds, and a marginal cost of capital approach is used

BPP PUBLISHING

Quick quiz

1   A cost of capital can be said to consist of three elements. What are they? (see para 1.4)

2   What are the dividend valuation model formulae for the cost of equity:

    (a)   with no dividend growth? (2.3)
    (b)   with dividend growth? (2.6 - 2.10)

3   How is the after-tax cost of debt capital calculated? (2.20 - 2.24)

4   How is the cost of convertible securities calculated? (2.28)

5   Why should a weighted average cost of capital be used as the discount rate, instead of the cost of the funds that are specifically used to finance each new investment? (4.1)

6   What are the arguments against using the WACC as the discount rate? (4.9)

Question to try	Level	Marks	Time
5	Introductory	n/a	35 mins

Chapter 6

THE EFFECT OF CAPITAL STRUCTURE

Chapter topic list	Syllabus reference
1 Gearing, financial risk and the cost of capital	3(d)
2 Traditional and net operating income views of WACC	3(d)
3 Modigliani-Miller (MM) theory without taxation	3(d)
4 Modigliani-Miller theory adjusted for taxation	3(d)
5 The adjusted present value method of project evaluation	3(e)

Introduction

As well as looking in this chapter at the theories of **Modigliani and Miller** we explain a rather different topic: the **adjusted present value (APV) method** in project appraisal. The APV method provides a way of taking into account the **financing effects** of a project.

1   GEARING, FINANCIAL RISK AND THE COST OF CAPITAL

1.1   A high level of debt creates financial risk. The **financial risk** of a company's capital structure can be measured by a gearing ratio. The method of calculating a gearing ratio which is appropriate for investment evaluation is one based on market values. **Capital gearing** can be measured as:

$$\frac{\text{Market value of debt (including preference shares)}}{\text{Market value of equity + market value of debt}} \quad \text{or} \quad \frac{D}{D+E}$$

1.2   Because of the financial risk associated with gearing, higher gearing will increase the rate of return required by ordinary shareholders, and may also affect the yield required by long-term creditors. It follows that a company's gearing level could have a bearing on its weighted average cost of capital.

Knowledge brought forward from Paper 8

Practical limits to financial gearing

Financial gearing can reach very high levels, with companies preferring to raise additional capital for expansion by means of loans rather than issuing new equity, but there are limits.

- Restrictions on further borrowing might be contained in the debenture trust deed for a company's current debenture stock in issue

- Occasionally, there might be borrowing restrictions in the Articles of Association

- Lenders might want *security* for extra loans which the would-be borrower cannot provide

- Lenders might simply be unwilling to lend more to a company with high gearing/low interest cover

BPP PUBLISHING

- Extra borrowing beyond a safe level will cost more in interest. Companies might not be *willing* to borrow at these rates

Policies to lower a company's financial gearing ratio might include the following.

- Revaluation of fixed assets (to boost book values)
- Place a value on brands, if any
- Tighten control over working capital
- Issue more shares

Gearing, project appraisal and the source of funds to finance a new project

1.3   It can be suggested that a project which has a positive NPV when its cash flows are discounted at the WACC might be financially harmful to shareholders if it is financed in the wrong way. This suggestion can be taken one step further. If a project is viable (has a positive NPV) when it is discounted at the current WACC, then it would be worthwhile provided that the new funds which are raised to finance it leave the company's WACC unchanged.

Gearing and shareholders' investment decisions

1.4   The value of equity is related, not only to the size of dividends and the cost of equity, but also to the weighted average cost of capital. This connection will now be investigated in some detail. We will assume that a shareholder would be prepared to accept a change in the gearing of a company, and therefore a change in the required rate of return for equity, provided that the effect of this change in gearing would be to increase the value of his shares, or at the very least to leave them unchanged.

2   TRADITIONAL AND NET OPERATING INCOME VIEWS OF WACC

2.1   There are two main theories about the effect of changes in gearing on the weighted average cost of capital (WACC) and share values. These are the **'traditional' view,** and the **net operating income approach** (Modigliani and Miller).

2.2   The assumptions on which these theories are based are as follows.

(a)   The company pays out all its earnings as dividends.

(b)   The gearing of the company can be changed immediately by issuing debt to repurchase shares, or by issuing shares to repurchase debt. There are no transaction costs for issues.

(c)   The earnings of the company are expected to remain constant in perpetuity and all investors share the same expectations about these future earnings.

(d)   Business risk is also constant, regardless of how the company invests its funds.

(e)   Taxation, for the time being, is ignored.

The traditional view of WACC

2.3   The **traditional view** is as follows.

(a)   As the level of gearing increases the cost of debt remains unchanged up to a certain level of gearing. Beyond this level, the cost of debt will increase.

(b) The cost of equity rises as the level of gearing increases.

(c) The weighted average cost of capital does not remain constant, but rather falls initially as the proportion of debt capital increases, and then begins to increase as the rising cost of equity (and possibly of debt) becomes more significant.

(d) The optimum level of gearing is where the company's weighted average cost of capital is minimised.

2.4 The traditional view about the cost of capital is illustrated in Figure 1. It shows that the weighted average cost of capital will be minimised at a particular level of gearing P.

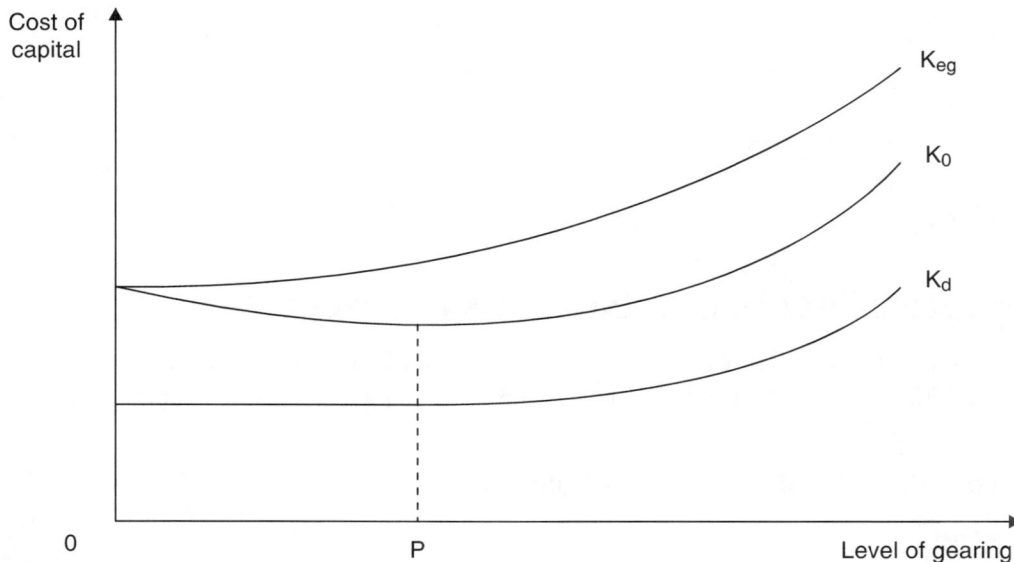

Figure 1

K_{eg} is the cost of equity in the geared company
K_d is the cost of debt
K_o is the weighted average cost of capital

2.5 The traditional view is that the weighted average cost of capital, when plotted against the level of gearing, is saucer shaped. The optimum capital structure is where the weighted average cost of capital is lowest, at point P.

The net operating income view of WACC

2.6 The **net operating income** approach takes a different view of the effect of gearing on WACC. It assumes that the weighted average cost of capital is unchanged, regardless of the level of gearing, because of the following two factors.

(a) The cost of debt remains unchanged as the level of gearing increases.

(b) The cost of equity rises in such a way as to keep the weighted average cost of capital constant.

This would be represented on a graph as shown in Figure 2.

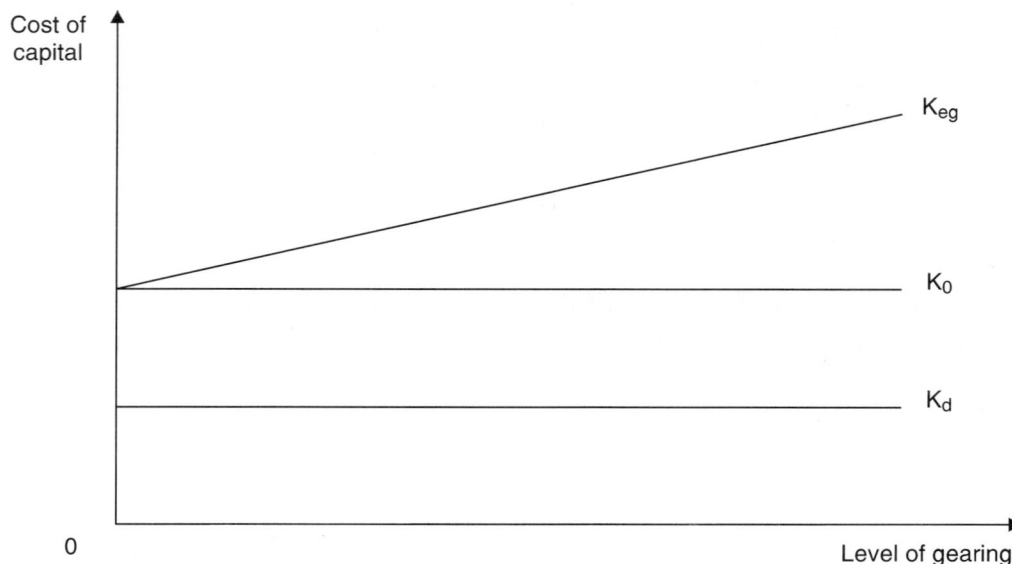

Figure 2

2.7 EXAMPLE: NET OPERATING INCOME APPROACH

A company has £5,000 of debt at 10% interest, and earns £5,000 a year before interest is paid. There are 2,250 issued shares, and the weighted average cost of capital of the company is 20%.

The market value of the company should be as follows.

Earnings	£5,000
Weighted average cost of capital	0.2
	£
Market value of the company (£5,000 ÷ 0.2)	25,000
Less market value of debt	5,000
Market value of equity	20,000

The cost of equity is therefore $\dfrac{5,000 - 500}{20,000} = \dfrac{4,500}{20,000} = 22.5\%$

and the market value per share is $\dfrac{4,500}{2,250} \times \dfrac{1}{0.225} = £8.89$

2.8 Suppose that the level of gearing is increased by issuing £5,000 more of debt at 10% interest to repurchase 562 shares (at a market value of £8.89 per share) leaving 1,688 shares in issue.

The weighted average cost of capital will, according to the net operating income approach, remain unchanged at 20%. The market value of the company should still therefore be £25,000.

Earnings	£5,000
Weighted average cost of capital	0.2
	£
Market value of the company	25,000
Less market value of debt	10,000
Market value of equity	15,000

Annual dividends will now be £5,000 − £1,000 interest = £4,000.

The cost of equity has risen to $\dfrac{4,000}{15,000} = 26.667\%$ and the market value per share is still

$$\dfrac{4,000}{1,688} \times \dfrac{1}{0.2667} = £8.89$$

2.9 The conclusion of the net operating income approach is that the level of gearing is a matter of indifference to an investor, because it does not affect the market value of the company, nor of an individual share. This is because as the level of gearing rises, so does the cost of equity in such a way as to keep both the weighted average cost of capital and the market value of the shares constant. Although, in our example, the dividend per share rises from £2 to £2.37 the increase in the cost of equity is such that the market value per share remains at £8.89.

Question 1

AB plc has a WACC of 16%. It is financed partly by equity (cost 18%) and partly by debt capital (cost 10%). The company is considering a new project which would cost £5,000,000 and would yield annual profits of £850,000 before interest charges. It would be financed by a loan at 10%. As a consequence of the higher gearing, the cost of equity would rise to 20%. The company pays out all profits as dividends, which are currently £2,250,000 a year.

(a) What would be the effect on the value of equity of undertaking the project?

(b) To what extent can you analyse the increase or decrease in equity value into two causes, the NPV of the project at the current WACC and the effect of the method of financing?

Ignore taxation. The traditional view of WACC and gearing is assumed in this exercise.

Answer

(a)

	£
Current profits and dividends	2,250,000
Increase in profits and dividends	
(£850,000 less extra interest 10% x £5,000,000)	350,000
New dividends, if project is undertaken	2,600,000

New cost of equity	20%
	£
New MV of equity	13,000,000
Current MV of equity (£2,250,000 ÷ 0.18)	12,500,000
Increase in shareholder wealth from project	500,000

(b) (i) NPV of project if financed at current WACC

$$= \dfrac{£850,000}{0.16} - £5,000,000 = + £312,500$$

(ii) The effect of financing on share values must be to increase the MV of equity by the remaining £187,500, which indicates that the effect of financing the project in the manner proposed will be to increase the company's gearing, but to reduce its WACC.

---

3 MODIGLIANI-MILLER (MM) THEORY WITHOUT TAXATION

Exam focus point

Modigliani and Miller's theories are unlikely to be the subject of a whole question, except possibly a 10-mark question. A question on the topic could contain a numerical part, but the main emphasis is likely to be on practical aspects.

3.1 **Modigliani and Miller** developed a defence of the net operating income approach to the effect of gearing on the cost of capital. Their view was that investors would use **arbitrage** to keep the weighted average cost of capital constant when changes in a company's gearing occur.

KEY TERM

Arbitrage: the exploitation for profit of differences in prices of an asset in different markets.

3.2 EXAMPLE: ARBITRAGE

Consider two companies, Ordinary plc and Levered plc, in the same risk class, which are identical in all respects except that Ordinary plc is financed entirely by equity whereas the capital structure of Levered plc includes £40,000 of debt at 8% interest. We will assume that the annual earnings of both companies (before interest) are the same, £20,000, and we will begin by considering the traditional view of the cost of capital, and suppose that the cost of equity in the unlevered company is 13½%, and in the levered company, it is higher at 14%.

3.3 The market valuation of each company, according to the traditional view, would be as follows.

	Ordinary plc	Levered plc
	£	£
Annual earnings	20,000	20,000
Less interest	-	3,200
Available for equity (earnings = dividends)	20,000	16,800
Cost of equity	0.135	0.14
	£	£
Market value of equity	148,148	120,000
Market value of debt	-	40,000
Market value of company	148,148	160,000
Weighted average cost of capital (PBIT ÷ market value)	13.5%	12.5%
Gearing ratio	0%	25%

3.4 The two companies, identical in every respect except their gearing, are therefore assumed by the traditional view to have different market values. MM argue that this situation could not last for long because investors in Levered plc would soon see that they could get the same return for a smaller investment by investing in Ordinary plc. Exercising arbitrage, they would sell their shares in Levered plc and buy shares in Ordinary plc.

This sale would drive up the price of Ordinary plc shares (thereby lowering the cost of its equity capital) and force down the price of Levered plc shares (thereby raising the cost of its equity capital) until the total market value of each company is the same. Arbitrage would then cease.

3.5 **Arbitrage** would occur as follows. Suppose Mr Onepercent owns 1% of the equity in Levered plc. These would have a market value of (1% × £120,000) = £1,200. He would notice that Ordinary plc makes the same annual earnings as Levered plc (£20,000) but with a smaller investment (£148,148 compared to £160,000). He would therefore take the following steps.

(a)   He would sell his shares in Levered plc for £1,200.

(b)   He would borrow £400 at 8% interest. This amount is equivalent to 1% of the debt of Levered plc (£40,000 at 8%). In this way, Mr Onepercent would have substituted personal gearing for the corporate gearing of Levered plc. His assets would be as follows.

£	
1,200	from the sale of his shares
400	borrowed at 8%
1,600	which is 1 % of the value of Levered plc

His personal gearing ratio (400/1,600 = 25%) is the same as the gearing ratio of Levered plc, and so MM would argue that his financial risk is in no way changed by this process of arbitrage.

(c)   He would then buy 1% of the equity of Ordinary plc for £148,148 × 1% = £1,481.48. To do this, he would use the borrowed £400 plus £1081.48 of his own money.

(d)   His annual earnings from Ordinary plc would be as follows.

	£
1% of £20,000	200
₣Less the interest he must repay on his personal loan (8% of £400)	32
Net earnings	168

This is exactly the same as he would earn from keeping 1% of the equity of Levered plc (1% of £16,800) but he can earn this from a smaller net investment of £1,081.48 rather than £1,200.

(e)   Alternatively, if he spends the entire £1,600 in purchasing shares of Ordinary plc, his annual earnings would be a dividend of:

$$\frac{1,600}{148,148} \times £20,000 = £216 \text{ less loan repayments of £32, leaving him with £184, which is}$$

£16 more than he currently earns from his Levered plc investment.

3.6   Rational investors will continue to substitute personal gearing for corporate gearing, and buy shares in Ordinary plc, until the price of these shares has risen, the price of Levered plc shares has fallen, and the market values of the two companies are the same. At this point:

(a)   The cost of equity in the company with the higher gearing (Levered plc) will be higher than the cost of equity in the other company

(b)   Because both the market values and the annual earnings of the companies are the same, the weighted average costs of capital must be the same, despite the difference in gearing

The Modigliani-Miller propositions, ignoring taxes

3.7   We can now set out the propositions of Modigliani and Miller, ignoring tax relief on the interest charged on debt capital.

3.8   The following symbols will be used.

V_u =   the market value of an ungeared (all equity) company

D =   the market value of the debt capital in a geared company which is similar in every respect to the ungeared company (same profits before interest and same business

BPP PUBLISHING

risk) except for its capital structure. The debt capital is assumed, for simplicity, to be irredeemable

E = the market value of the equity in the geared company

K_{eu} = the cost of equity in an ungeared company

K_{eg} = the cost of equity in the geared company

K_d = the cost of debt capital

The total market value of the geared company (V_g) is then equal to (E + D).

Proposition 1 (ignoring taxation): the total market value of a company and the WACC

3.9 MM suggested that the total market value of any company is independent of its capital structure, and is given by discounting its expected return at the appropriate rate. The value of a geared company is therefore as follows.

$$V_g = V_u$$

$$V_g = \frac{\text{Profit before interest}}{\text{WACC}}$$

$$V_u = V_g = \frac{\text{Earnings in an ungeared company}}{K_{eu}}$$

Proposition 2 (ignoring taxation): the cost of equity in a geared company

3.10 MM went on to argue that the expected return on a share in a geared company equals the expected cost of equity in a similar but ungeared company, plus a premium related to financial risk.

3.11 The premium for financial risk can be calculated as the debt/equity ratio multiplied by the difference between the cost of equity for an ungeared company and the risk-free cost of debt capital.

$$K_{eg} = K_{eu} + [(K_{eu} - K_d) \times \frac{D}{E}]$$

Note the following points.

(a) The part of the formula to the right of the plus sign is the value of the premium for financial risk.

(b) The formula requires the debt ratio (debt : equity) to be used rather than the more common debt : (debt + equity).

(c) Market values are used - not book values.

3.12 EXAMPLE: MM, IGNORING TAXATION (1)

The cost of equity in Dunquin plc, an all equity company, is 15%. The WACC is therefore also 15%. Another company, Bantry plc, is identical in every respect to the first, except that it is geared, with a debt:equity ratio of 1:4. The cost of debt capital is 5% and this is a risk-free cost of debt. What is Bantry plc's WACC?

SOLUTION

3.13 $K_{eg} = 15\% + \left[(15-5)\% \times \dfrac{1}{4} \right] = 17.5\%$

	Weighting	*Cost*	*Product*
Equity	80%	17.5%	14%
Debt	20%	5.0%	1%
		WACC =	15%

The WACC in the geared company is the same as in the ungeared company.

3.14 EXAMPLE: MM, IGNORING TAXATION (2)

Loesch plc is an all equity company and its cost of equity is 12%. Berelco plc is similar in all respects to Loesch plc, except that it is a geared company, financed by £1,000,000 of 3% debentures (current market price £50 per cent) and 1,000,000 ordinary shares (current market price £1.50 ex div). What is Berelco's cost of equity and weighted average cost of capital?

3.15 SOLUTION

$K_d = 3\% \times \dfrac{100}{50} = 6\%$

$K_{eg} = 12\% + \left[(12\% - 6\%) \times \dfrac{500}{1,500} \right] = 14\%$

	Market value £'000		*Cost*		£'000
Equity	1,500	×	0.14	=	210
Debt	500	×	0.06	=	30
	2,000				240

$WACC = \dfrac{240}{2,000} = 0.12 = 12\%$

This is the same as Loesch plc's WACC. As gearing is introduced, the cost of equity rises, but in such a way that the WACC does not change.

Weaknesses in MM theory

3.16 MM theory has been criticised on four main grounds.

(a) The risks for the investor may differ between personal gearing and corporate gearing. In the example in Paragraph 3.5 Mr Onepercent stands, financially, to lose no more than £1,200, which is in his stake in a company (Levered plc) with limited liability. If he practises arbitrage, he would stand to lose his personal investment in Ordinary plc (£1,481.48 – £400 = £1,081.48) plus his debt repayment (£400), a total of £1,481.48. The financial risk is consequently greater.

(b) The cost of borrowing for an individual is likely to be higher than the cost of borrowing for a company. MM assume that the cost is the same for personal and corporate borrowers.

(c) Transaction costs will restrict the arbitrage process.

(d) MM theory initially ignored tax implications (discussed below).

3.17 Further weaknesses in the MM theory are as follows.

(a) In practice, it may be impossible to identify firms with identical business risk and operating characteristics.

(b) Some earnings may be retained and so the simplifying assumption of paying out all earnings as dividends would not apply.

(c) Investors are assumed to act rationally which may not be the case in practice.

3.18 MM also acknowledge that when the level of gearing gets high, the cost of debt will rise. They argue, however, that this does not affect the weighted average cost of capital because the cost of equity falls at the same time as risk seeking investors are attracted to buying shares in the company.

3.19 When a company's gearing reaches very high levels, it may be perceived as being in danger of insolvency, and its market value will be very low (instead of being very high, as MM would predict). MM ignored the possibility of bankruptcy, and so their theory may not be valid at very high levels of gearing.

4 MODIGLIANI-MILLER THEORY ADJUSTED FOR TAXATION 6/97

4.1 Allowing for **corporate taxation** reduces the cost of debt capital by multiplying it by a factor $(1 - t)$ where t is the rate of corporation tax (assuming the debt to be irredeemable). So far, our analysis of MM theory has ignored the tax relief on debt interest, which makes debt capital cheaper to a company, and therefore reduces the weighted average cost of capital where a company has debt in its capital structure.

4.2 MM modified their theory to admit that tax relief on interest payments does lower the weighted average cost of capital. They claimed that the weighted average cost of capital will continue to fall, up to very high levels of gearing.

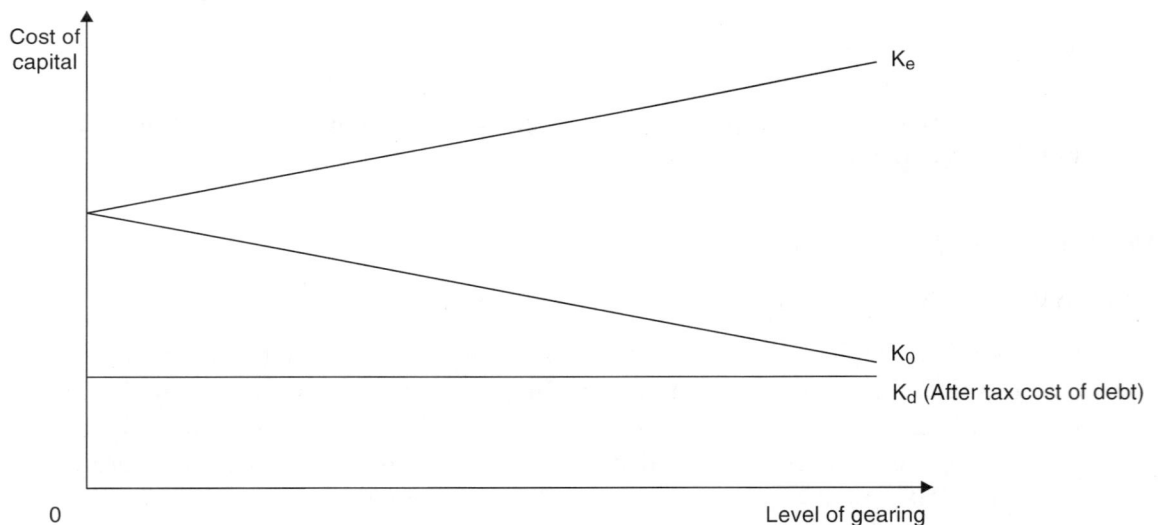

Figure 3

The adjustment to the MM cost of equity formula to allow for taxes

4.3 The formula for the cost of equity in a geared company becomes:

$$K_{eg} = K_{eu} + (1-t)\left((K_{eu} - K_d) \times \frac{D}{E} \right)$$

where t is the corporation tax rate and K_d is the pre-tax (gross) cost of debt capital.

The financial risk premium is adjusted by a factor of $(1 - t)$.

4.4 From this formula we can derive the following formula.

EXAM FORMULA

$$WACC_g = K_{eu}\left[1 - \frac{Dt}{E+D}\right]$$

where $WACC_g$ is the weighted average cost of capital of a geared company
              K_{eu} is the cost of equity and the WACC of a similar ungeared company

(You are not required to know the derivation, and so this is not given here.)

4.5 Thus assuming a corporation tax rate of 30%, Bantry plc's cost of equity in the example in Paragraphs 3.12 and 3.13 would be:

$$15\% + (1-0.30)[(15\% - 5\%) \times \tfrac{1}{4}] = 16.75\%$$

and its WACC would be:

$$15\%\left[1 - \frac{1 \times 0.30}{(1+4)}\right] = 15\% \times 0.94 = 14.1\%$$

4.6 This is below the ungeared company's WACC, which is 15%. So higher gearing reduces the WACC.

Question 2

Apply the formula given in Paragraphs 4.3 and 4.4 to find the cost of equity and WACC for Berelco plc (using the information given in Paragraph 3.14). The corporation tax rate is 30%.

Answer

Berelco plc's cost of equity would be:

$$12\% + (1 - 0.30) \times \left[(12 - 6)\% \times \frac{500}{1,500}\right]$$

$$= 13.4\%$$

and its WACC would be:

$$12\%\left[1 - \frac{500 \times 0.30}{1,500 + 500}\right] = 12\% \times 0.925 = 11.1\%$$

This is below Loesch plc's WACC of 12%.

4.7 The WACC in a geared company will be lower than the WACC in an ungeared company $(WACC_u = K_{eu})$ by a measurable amount. WACC will fall as gearing increases.

$$WACC_g = WACC_u \times \frac{V_u}{V_g}$$

where $V_g = E + D$

Is there an optimum level of gearing?

4.8 We have now seen that MM modified their theory to say that when taxation is taken into account, the WACC will continue to fall as the level of gearing increases. The arbitrage process still operates, although the actions of investors will be influenced by their marginal rates of personal taxation.

4.9 MM argued that since WACC falls as gearing rises, and the value of a company should rise as its WACC falls, the value of a geared company will always be greater than its ungeared counterpart, but only by the amount of the debt-associated tax saving of the geared company, assuming a permanent change in gearing.

$$V_g = V_u + Dt$$

where V_g is the value of the similar geared company.

4.10 However, the positive tax effects of debt finance will be exhausted where there is insufficient tax liability to use the tax relief which is available. This is known as **tax shield exhaustion**.

4.11 EXAMPLE: MM, WITH TAXES

Notnil plc and Newbegin plc are companies in the same industry. They have the same business risk and operating characteristics, but Notnil is a geared company whereas Newbegin is all equity financed. Notnil plc earns three times as much profit before interest as Newbegin plc. Both companies pursue a policy of paying out all their earnings each year as dividends.

The market value of each company is currently as follows.

		Notnil plc £m		*Newbegin plc* £m
Equity	(10m shares)	36	(20m shares)	15
Debt	(£12m of 12% loan stock)	14		—
		50		15

The annual profit before interest of Notnil is £3,000,000 and that of Newbegin is £1,000,000. The rate of corporation tax is 30%. It is thought that the current market value per ordinary share in Newbegin plc is at the equilibrium level, and that the market value of Notnil's debt capital is also at its equilibrium level. There is some doubt, however, about whether the value of Notnil's shares is at its equilibrium level.

Apply the MM formula to establish the equilibrium price of Notnil's shares.

4.12 SOLUTION

$$V_g = V_u + Dt$$

V_u = the market value of an ungeared company. Since Notnil's earnings (before interest) are three times the size of Newbegin's, V_u is three times the value of Newbegin's equity:

$3 \times £15,000,000 = £45,000,000$

$Dt = £14,000,000 \times 30\% = £4,200,000$

$V_g = £45,000,000 + £4,200,000 = £49,200,000$

Since the market value of debt in Notnil plc is £14,000,000, it follows that the market value of Notnil's equity should be £49,200,000 – £14,000,000 = £35,200,000.

$$\text{Value per share} = \frac{£35,200,000}{10,000,000} = £3.534 \text{ per share}$$

Since the current share price is £3.60 per share, MM would argue that the shares in Notnil are currently over-valued by the market, but only by £800,000 in total or 8p per share.

4.13 Now let us relate the MM company valuation formula to the process of arbitrage.

4.14 EXAMPLE: MM AND ARBITRAGE

Lenox plc and Groves plc are two companies operating in the same industry. They have the same business risk, and are identical in most other respects. The annual earnings before interest and tax are £40,000 for each company. The only differences between the companies are in their financial structures and their market values. Details of these are given below.

Lenox plc

	£
Ordinary shares of £1	30,000
Share premium account	10,000
Profit and loss account	110,000
Shareholders' funds	150,000
12% loan stock (newly issued)	100,000
	250,000

Lenox's ordinary shares have a market value of 600 pence, and the 12% loan stock is trading at £100.

Groves plc

	£
Ordinary shares of £1	50,000
Share premium account	16,000
Profit and loss account	100,000
Shareholders' funds	166,000

Groves' shares have a market value of 400 pence. Corporation tax is at 30%. Suppose that you are the owner of 1% of the equity of Lenox plc. If you agreed with the propositions of Modigliani and Miller, would you retain your shares in Lenox or could you improve your financial position? Ignore personal taxes.

4.15 SOLUTION

A difficulty with this problem is the need to allow for tax relief on corporate debt, when working out how an investor should gear himself up so as to achieve personal gearing which is the same as the geared company. Check the solution carefully on this point.

According to MM theory, where there are corporate taxes, the value of a geared company will always be greater than the value of its ungeared counterpart, but only by the amount of the debt-associated tax saving of the geared company. This is expressed by the formula:

$$V_g = V_u + Dt$$

If actual market values do not conform to this formula, it would follow that one company is incorrectly valued by the market relative to the other.

113 BPP
PUBLISHING

Let us assume that the shares of Groves, the ungeared company, are correctly valued by the market at 400 pence. We would then predict that the total market value of Lenox, the geared company, should be $(V_u + Dt)$.

	£
Market value of Groves shares (50,000 × £4)	200,000
Market value of Lenox debt multiplied by tax rate (100,000 × 30%)	30,000
Correct market value of Lenox plc	230,000

Actual market value of Lenox

	£
Market value of Lenox shares (30,000 × £6)	180,000
Market value of Lenox debt capital	100,000
	280,000

We can conclude that Lenox plc is over-valued by the market and so an investor in Lenox shares can improve his or her financial position by:

(a) Selling all their shares in Lenox
(b) Gearing, by personal borrowing, so as to achieve the same personal gearing as Lenox
(c) Buying shares in Groves

This action will increase the investor's income without any change in the investor's business or financial risk. This process of arbitrage should continue until the equilibrium of $V_g = V_u + Dt$ is restored.

1% of the equity of Lenox has a current market value of 1% × £180,000 = £1,800.

	£
Sell 1% holding of shares in Lenox to receive	1,800
Borrow, through personal borrowing★, an amount equal to 1% of the market value of Lenox's debt capital, adjusted to allow for the tax relief that Lenox gets on the debt interest (1% × £100,000 × 0.70)	700
	2,500

(★ The rate of interest on personal borrowing is assumed to be the same as the market rate of interest on corporate debt, which is 12%.)

The investor should now invest £2,500 in the equity of Groves plc, and can buy £2,500 ÷ £200,000 = 1.25% of Groves' shares. The investor's income will now be higher than before, but because personal gearing has been substituted for corporate gearing, there is no change in the investor's financial risk. The increase in income can be illustrated as follows.

	Holding 1% shares in Lenox plc £	*Holding 1.25% of shares in Groves plc with personal gearing* £
Earnings before interest and tax	40,000	40,000
Less interest charge for the company	12,000	0
	28,000	40,000
Less tax (30%)	8,400	12,000
Earnings, assumed equal to dividends	19,600	28,000
Investor's share (1% of Lenox/1.25% of Groves)	196.00	350.00
Less interest on personal debt (12% × £700)	-	84.00
Investor's net income	196.00	266.00

The investor can increase his or her annual income by £(266.00 − 196.00) = £70.00 through this arbitrage process.

Empirical testing and conclusion

4.16 It might be imagined that empirical testing should have been carried out by now either to prove or to disprove MM theory. Given, however, that MM accept that the weighted average cost of capital declines after allowing for tax, and that traditional theorists argue in favour of a flattish bottom to the weighted average cost of capital curve, it is very difficult to prove that one theory is preferable to the other.

Question 3

The cost of equity in an ungeared company is 18%. The cost of risk free debt capital is 8%.

(a) What is the cost of equity in a similar geared company, according to MM, which is 75% equity financed and 25% debt financed, assuming corporation tax at a rate of 30%?

(b) What is the WACC of the geared company, allowing for taxation?

Answer

(a) $K_{eg} = 18\% + (1 - 0.30)[(18 - 8)\% \times \frac{25}{75}] = 20.3\%$

(b) $WACC_g = 18\% \left[1 - \frac{0.30 \times 25}{25 + 75} \right]$

$= 18\% \times 0.925 = 16.7\%$

5 THE ADJUSTED PRESENT VALUE METHOD OF PROJECT EVALUATION
6/94, 12/96, 12/98

5.1 We have seen that a company's gearing level has implications for both the value of its equity shares and its WACC. The viability of an investment project will depend partly on how the investment is financed, and how the method of finance affects gearing. The **net present value method of investment appraisal** is to discount the cash flows of a project at a cost of capital. This cost of capital might be the WACC, but it could also be another cost of capital, perhaps one which allows for the risk characteristics of the individual project.

5.2 An alternative method of carrying out project appraisal is to use the **adjusted present value** or **APV** method.

The APV method involves two stages.
Step 1. Evaluate the project first of all as if it were all equity financed, and so as if the company were an all equity company to find the 'base case NPV'.
Step 2. Make adjustments to allow for the effects of the method of financing that has been used.

Exam focus point
The examiner plans to give APV a little more emphasis than in the past. While acknowledging that it is not widely used in practice, he considers it important for people to be aware of it.

5.3 EXAMPLE: NPV METHOD AND APV METHOD

A company is considering a project that would cost £100,000 to be financed 50% by equity (cost 21.6%) and 50% by debt (pre-tax cost 12%). The financing method would maintain the company's WACC unchanged. The cash flows from the project would be £36,000 a year in perpetuity, before interest charges. Corporation tax is at 30%.

Appraise the project using firstly the NPV method and secondly the APV method.

5.4 SOLUTION

We can use the **NPV method** because the company's WACC will be unchanged.

	Cost	Weighting	Product
	%		%
Equity	21.6	0.5	10.8
Debt (70% of 12%)	8.4	0.5	4.2
		WACC	15.0

Annual cash flows in perpetuity from the project are as follows.

	£
Before tax	36,000
Less tax (30%)	10,800
After tax	25,200

$$\text{NPV of project} = -£100,000 + (£25,200 \div 0.15)$$

$$= -£100,000 + £168,000 = +£68,000$$

Since £100,000 of new investment is being created, the value of the company will increase by £100,000 + £68,000 = £168,000, of which 50% must be debt capital.

The company must raise 50% × £168,000 = £84,000 of 12% debt capital, and (the balance) £16,000 of equity. The NPV of the project will raise the value of this equity from £16,000 to £84,000 thus leaving the gearing ratio at 50:50.

5.5 The **APV method** is as follows.

(a) First, we need to know the cost of equity in an ungeared company. The MM formula we can use to establish this is:

$$K_{eg} = K_{eu} + (1-t)\left((K_{eu} - K_d)\frac{D}{E}\right)$$

$$21.6\% = K_{eu} + (0.70)\left((K_{eu} - 12\%)\frac{50}{50}\right)$$

$$21.6\% = K_{eu} + 0.70K_{eu} - 8.4\%$$

$$1.70K_{eu} = 30\%$$

$$K_{eu} = 17.647\%$$

(b) Next, we calculate the NPV of the project as if it were all equity financed. The cost of equity would be 17.647%.

$$\text{NPV} = \frac{£25,200}{0.17647} - £100,000 = +£42,800$$

(c) Next, we can use the MM formula for the relationship between the value of geared and ungeared companies, to establish the effect of gearing on the value of the project. £84,000 will be financed by debt.

$$V_g = V_u + Dt$$

$$= +£42,800 + (£84,000 \times 0.30) = £68,000$$

5.6 The value Dt represents the present value of the **tax shield** on debt interest, that is the present value of the savings arising from tax relief on debt interest.

Annual interest charge = 12% of £84,000		=	£10,080
Tax saving (30% × £10,080)		=	£3,024.00
Cost of debt (pre-tax)		=	12%
PV of tax savings in perpetuity		=	$\dfrac{£3,024}{0.12}$
		=	£25,200

Dt = £84,000 × 0.30 = £25,200 is a quicker way of deriving the same value.

5.7 The APV and NPV approaches produce the same conclusion. However, the APV method can also be adapted to allow for financing which changes the gearing structure and the WACC. In this respect, it is superior to the NPV method. Suppose, for example, that in the previous example, the entire project were to be financed by debt. The APV of the project would be calculated as follows.

(a) The NPV of project if all equity financed is:

$$\frac{£25,200}{0.17647} - £100,000 = + £42,800 \text{ (as before)}$$

(b) The adjustment to allow for the method of financing is the present value of the tax relief on debt interest in perpetuity.

Dt = £100,000 × 0.30 = £30,000

(c) APV = £42,800 + £30,000 = + £72,800

The project would increase the value of equity by £72,800.

Question 4

A project costing £100,000 is to be financed by £60,000 of irredeemable 12% debentures and £40,000 of new equity. The project will yield an annual cash flow of £21,000 in perpetuity. If it were all equity financed, an appropriate cost of capital would be 15%. The corporation tax rate is 30%. What is the project's APV?

Answer

	£
NPV if all equity financed: £21,000/0.15 − £100,000	40,000
PV of the tax shield: £60,000 × 12% × 30%/0.12	18,000
APV	58,000

The advantages and disadvantages of the APV method

5.8 The main **advantage of the APV method** is that it can be used to evaluate all the effects of the method of financing a project. The NPV technique can allow for the financing side-effects implicitly, by adjusting the discount rate used. In contrast, the APV technique allows for the financing side-effects explicitly.

5.9 The main **difficulties with the APV method** are those of establishing a suitable cost of equity for the initial DCF computation as if the project were all-equity financed, and of identifying all the costs associated with the method of financing.

BPP
PUBLISHING

Chapter roundup

- **Financial gearing** or **leverage** is the increased variability of earnings resulting from having debt in the capital structure.

- Both traditional and MM theories agree that:

  ○ The optimal level of financial gearing will be that at which the WACC is minimised
  ○ The cost of equity increases as financial gearing increases

- The **traditional theory** finds that there is a minimum WACC at a level somewhere between 0% and 100% gearing. **Modigliani and Miller** argue that, ignoring corporate tax, the rise in the cost of equity as gearing rises would offset exactly the benefits of an increasing proportion of low-cost debt capital, resulting in a constant WACC.

- **With taxation**, the tax relief available on debt will, according to MM, cause the WACC to fall, right up to a 100% level of gearing. This suggests that companies should gear to as high a level as possible.

- The **APV method of project evaluation** is a technique which can be used when the method of financing a project precludes use of the WACC method.

Quick quiz

1 Outline the traditional view of WACC. (see para 2.3)

2 Outline the net operating income view of WACC. (2.6)

3 What weaknesses are there in MM's theory? (3.16, 3.17)

4 Taking taxation into account in MM's theory, is there an optimum level of gearing? (4.8 - 4.10)

5 Outline the adjusted present value method of project evaluation. (5.3)

Question to try	Level	Marks	Time
6	Introductory	n/a	35 mins

Chapter 7

PORTFOLIO THEORY

Chapter topic list	Syllabus reference
1 Portfolios and portfolio theory	3(b)
2 Investors' preferences	3(b)
3 Portfolio theory and financial management	3(b)

Introduction

The **diversification of portfolios** is an important concept in financial management. Both individuals and firms diversify their investments. Individuals have portfolios of shares and firms have portfolios of business operations. In this chapter, we explain the benefits of portfolio diversification. We explain **portfolio theory**, its relevance and its limitations.

1 PORTFOLIOS AND PORTFOLIO THEORY   6/95, 6/98

1.1 A **portfolio** is the collection of different investments that make up an investor's total holding. A portfolio might be the investments in stocks and shares of an **investor**, or the investments in capital projects of a **company**.

1.2 **Portfolio theory**, which originates from the work of Markowitz, is concerned with establishing guidelines for building up a portfolio of stocks and shares, or a portfolio of projects. The same theory applies to both stock market investors and to companies with capital projects to invest in.

Factors in the choice of investments

1.3 There are five major factors to be considered when an investor chooses investments, whether the investor is an institutional investor, a company making an investment or a private individual investor.

(a) **Security.** Investments should at least maintain their capital value.

(b) **Liquidity.** Where the investments are made with short-term funds, they should be convertible back into cash at short notice.

(c) **Return.** The funds are invested to make money. The highest return compatible with safety should be sought.

(d) **Spreading risks.** The investor who puts all his funds into one type of security risks everything on the fortunes of that security. If it performs badly, his entire investment will make a loss. A better (and more secure) policy is to spread investments over several types of security, so that losses on some may be offset by gains on others.

BPP
PUBLISHING

(e) **Growth prospects**. The most profitable investments are likely to be in businesses with good growth prospects.

Portfolios: expected return and risk

1.4 When an investor has a portfolio of securities, he will expect the portfolio to provide a certain return on his investment. The **expected return** of a portfolio will be a weighted average of the expected returns of the investments in the portfolio, weighted by the proportion of total funds invested in each.

The expected return $\bar{r}_p$ of a two-asset portfolio can thus be stated as the following formula:

$$\bar{r}_p = x\bar{r}_a + (1-x)\bar{r}_b$$

where   x is the proportion of investment A in the portfolio

$\bar{r}_a$, $\bar{r}_b$ are the expected returns of investments A and B

For example, if 70% of the portfolio relates to a security which is expected to yield 10% and 30% to a security expected to yield 12%, the portfolio's expected return is (70% × 10%) + (30% × 12%) = 10.6%.

1.5 The **risk** in an investment, or in a portfolio of investments, is the risk that the actual return will not be the same as the expected return. The actual return may be higher, but it may be lower. A prudent investor will want to avoid too much risk, and will hope that the actual returns from his portfolio are much the same as what he expected them to be. The risk of a security, and the risk of a portfolio, can be measured as the **standard deviation of expected returns**, given estimated probabilities of actual returns.

1.6 EXAMPLE: PORTFOLIOS (1)

Suppose that the return from an investment has the following probability distribution.

Return x %	Probability p	Expected value px
8	0.2	1.6
10	0.2	2.0
12	0.5	6.0
14	0.1	1.4
		11.0

The expected return is 11%, and the standard deviation of the expected return is as follows. The symbol $\bar{x}$ refers to the expected value of the return, 11%.

Return

x %	$x - \bar{x}$ %	p	$p(x - \bar{x})^2$
8	−3	0.2	1.8
10	−1	0.2	0.2
12	1	0.5	0.5
14	3	0.1	0.9
		Variance	3.4

Standard deviation   = $\sqrt{3.4}$ = 1.84%

Thus, the expected return is 11% with a standard deviation of 1.84%.

1.7 The risk of an investment might be high or low, depending on the nature of the investment. **Low risk** investments usually give **low returns**. **High risk** investments might give **high returns,** but with more risk of disappointing results. So how does holding a **portfolio** of investments affect expected returns and investment risk?

Diversification as a means of reducing risk

1.8 Portfolio theory states that individual investments cannot be viewed simply in terms of their risk and return. The relationship between the return from one investment and the return from other investments is just as important. The relationship between investments can be one of three types.

(a) **Positive correlation**. When there is positive correlation between investments, if one investment does well (or badly) it is likely that the other will perform likewise. Thus if you buy shares in one company making umbrellas and in another which sells raincoats you would expect both companies to do badly in dry weather.

(b) **Negative correlation**. If one investment does well the other will do badly, and vice versa. Thus if you hold shares in one company making umbrellas and in another which sells ice cream, the weather will affect the companies differently.

(c) **No correlation**. The performance of one investment will be independent of how the other performs. If you hold shares in a mining company and in a leisure company, it is likely that there would be no relationship between the profits and returns from each.

1.9 This relationship between the returns from different investments is measured by the correlation coefficient. A figure close to +1 indicates high positive correlation, and a figure close to −1 indicates high negative correlation. A figure of 0 indicates no correlation. If investments show high negative correlation, then by combining them in a portfolio overall risk would be reduced. Risk will also be reduced by combining in a portfolio investments which have no significant correlation.

1.10 EXAMPLE: PORTFOLIOS (2)

Security A and Security B have the following expected returns.

Probability	Security A Return	Security B Return
0.1	15%	10%
0.8	25%	30%
0.1	35%	50%

1.11 The expected return from each security is as follows.

	Security A			Security B	
Probability	Return	EV		Return	EV
	%	%		%	%
0.1	15	1.5		10	1
0.8	25	20.0		30	24
0.1	35	3.5		50	5
	Expected return =	25.0		Expected return =	30

1.12 The variance of the expected return for each security is $\sum p(x - \bar{x})^2$

BPP PUBLISHING

Probability	Return	Security A		Return		Security B	
p	x	x - $\bar{x}$	p(x - $\bar{x}$)²	y	y – $\bar{y}$	p(y – $\bar{y}$)²
0.1	15	(10)	10	10	(20)	40
0.8	25	0	0	30	0	0
0.1	35	10	10	50	20	40
	$\bar{x}$ = 25	Variance =	20	$\bar{y}$ = 30	Variance =	80

1.13 The standard deviation is the square root of the variance.

Security A: $\sqrt{20} = 4.472\%$

Security B: $\sqrt{80} = 8.944\%$

Security B therefore offers a higher return than security A, but at a greater risk.

1.14 Let us now assume that an investor acquires a portfolio consisting of 50% A and 50% B. The **expected return** from the portfolio will be $0.5 \times 25\% + 0.5 \times 30\% = 27.5\%$. This is less than the expected return from security B alone, but more than that from security A. The combined portfolio should be less risky than security B alone (although in this example of just a two-security portfolio, it will be more risky than security A alone except when returns are negatively correlated).

1.15 We can work out the standard deviation of the expected return:

(a) If there is perfect positive correlation between the returns from each security, so that if A gives a return of 15%, then B will give a return of 10% and so on

(b) If there is perfect negative correlation between the returns from each security, so that if A gives a return of 15%, B will yield 50%, if A gives a return of 35%, B will yield 10%, and if A gives a return of 25%, B will yield 30%

(c) If there is no correlation between returns, and so the probability distribution of returns is as follows

A	B		p
%	%		
15	10	(0.1×0.1)	0.01
15	30	(0.1×0.8)	0.08
15	50	(0.1×0.1)	0.01
25	10	(0.8×0.1)	0.08
25	30	(0.8×0.8)	0.64
25	50	(0.8×0.1)	0.08
35	10	(0.1×0.1)	0.01
35	30	(0.1×0.8)	0.08
35	50	(0.1×0.1)	0.01
			1.00

Perfect positive correlation

1.16 The standard deviation of the portfolio may be calculated as follows, given an expected return of 27.5%.

Probability	Return from 50% A	Return from 50% B	Combined portfolio return		
p			x	x − x̄	p(x − x̄)²
	%	%	%		
0.1	7.5	5	12.5	(15)	22.5
0.8	12.5	15	27.5	0	0
0.1	17.5	25	42.5	15	22.5
				Variance =	45.0

The standard deviation is $\sqrt{45} = 6.71\%$

Perfect negative correlation

1.17   The standard deviation of the portfolio, given an expected return of 27.5%, is as follows.

Probability p	Return from 50% A	Return from 50% B	Combined portfolio return x	x − x̄	p(x − x̄)²
	%	%	%		
0.1	7.5	25	32.5	5	2.5
0.8	12.5	15	27.5	0	0
0.1	17.5	5	22.5	(5)	2.5
				Variance =	5.0

The standard deviation is $\sqrt{5} = 2.24\%$

No correlation

1.18   The standard deviation of the portfolio, given an expected return of 27.5%, is as follows.

Probability p	Return from 50% A	Return from 50% B	Combined portfolio return x	x − x̄	p(x − x̄)²
	%	%	%		
0.01	7.5	5	12.5	(15)	2.25
0.08	7.5	15	22.5	(5)	2.00
0.01	7.5	25	32.5	5	0.25
0.08	12.5	5	17.5	(10)	8.00
0.64	12.5	15	27.5	0	0.00
0.08	12.5	25	37.5	10	8.00
0.01	17.5	5	22.5	(5)	0.25
0.08	17.5	15	32.5	5	2.00
0.01	17.5	25	42.5	15	2.25
				Variance =	25.00

The standard deviation is $\sqrt{25} = 5\%$

Conclusion

1.19   You should notice that for the same expected return of 27.5%, the standard deviation (the risk):

(a)   Is highest when there is perfect positive correlation between the returns of the individual securities in the portfolio

(b)   Is lower when there is no correlation

(c)   Is lowest when there is perfect negative correlation – the risk is then less than for either individual security taken on its own.

Another way of calculating the standard deviation of a portfolio

1.20   The standard deviation of the returns from a portfolio of two investments can be calculated using the following formula.

EXAM FORMULA

$$\sigma_p = \sqrt{\sigma_a^2 x^2 + \sigma_b^2 (1-x)^2 + 2x(1-x)\,p_{ab}\,\sigma_a\,\sigma_b}$$

where:

σ_p is the standard deviation of a portfolio of two investments, A and B

σ_a is the standard deviation of the returns from investment A

σ_b is the standard deviation of the returns from investment B

σ_a^2, σ_b^2 are the variances of returns from investment A and B (the squares of the standard deviations)

x   is the weighting or proportion of investment A in the portfolio

p_{ab} is the correlation coefficient of returns from investment A and B

$$= \frac{\text{Covariance of investments A and B}}{\sigma_a \times \sigma_b}$$

1.21   EXAMPLE: PORTFOLIOS (3)

We will use the previous example of the portfolio of 50% security A and 50% security B.

(a)   When there is perfect positive correlation between the returns from A and B, $p_{ab} = 1$.

$$\begin{aligned}\sigma_p^2 &= (20 \times 0.5^2) + (80 \times 0.5^2) + (2 \times 0.5 \times 0.5 \times 1 \times \sqrt{20} \times \sqrt{80}) \\ &= 5 + 20 + (0.5 \times 4.472 \times 8.944) \\ &= 45\end{aligned}$$

The standard deviation of the portfolio is $\sqrt{45} = 6.71\%$

(b)   When there is perfect negative correlation between returns from A and B, $p_{ab} = -1$.

$$\begin{aligned}\sigma_p^2 &= (20 \times 0.5^2) + (80 \times 0.5^2) + (2 \times 0.5 \times 0.5 \times -1 \times \sqrt{20} \times \sqrt{80}) \\ &= 5 + 20 - (0.5 \times 4.472 \times 8.944) \\ &= 5\end{aligned}$$

The standard deviation of the portfolio is $\sqrt{5} = 2.24\%$

(c)   When there is no correlation between returns from A and B, $P_{ab} = 0$.

$$\begin{aligned}\sigma_p^2 &= (20 \times 0.5^2) + (80 \times 0.5^2) + (2 \times 0.5 \times 0.5 \times 0 \times \sqrt{20} \times \sqrt{80}) \\ &= 5 + 20 + 0 \\ &= 25\end{aligned}$$

The standard deviation of the portfolio is $\sqrt{25} = 5\%$

1.22   These are exactly the same figures for standard deviations that were calculated earlier.

2   INVESTORS' PREFERENCES   6/98

2.1   Investors must choose a portfolio which gives them a satisfactory **balance** between the **expected returns** from the portfolio and the **risk** that actual returns from the portfolio will be higher or lower than expected. Some portfolios will be more risky than others.

2.2   Traditional investment theory suggests that rational investors wish to maximise return and minimise risk. Thus if two portfolios have the same element of risk, the investor will choose the one yielding the higher return. Similarly, if two portfolios offer the same return the investor will select the portfolio with the lesser risk. This is illustrated by Figure 1.

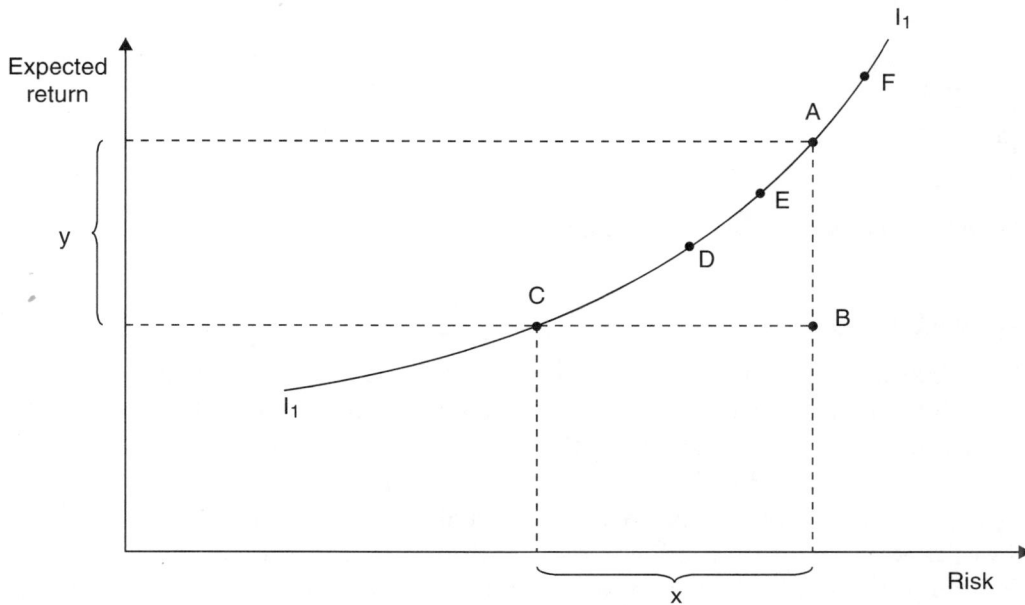

Figure 1 An investor's indifference curve

2.3   Portfolio A will be preferred to portfolio B because it offers a higher expected return for the same level of risk. Similarly, portfolio C will be preferred to portfolio B because it offers the same expected return for lower risk. (A and C are said to **dominate** portfolio B). But whether an investor chooses portfolio A or portfolio C will depend on the individual's attitude to risk, whether he wishes to accept a greater risk for a greater expected return.

2.4   The curve I_1 is an investor's indifference curve. The investor will have no preference between any portfolios which give a mix of risk and expected return which lies on the curve, since he derives equal **utility** from each of them. Thus, to the investor the portfolios A, C, D, E and F are all just as good as each other, and all of them are better than portfolio B. Remembering that the risk of a portfolio can be measured as the standard deviation of expected returns, this may be expressed by saying that portfolio B is dispreferred on grounds of **mean-variance inefficiency**.

2.5   An investor would prefer combinations of return and risk on **indifference curve** A to those on curve B (Figure 2) because curve A offers higher returns for the same degree of risk (and less risk for the same expected returns). For example, for the same amount of risk x, the expected return on curve A is y_1, whereas on curve B it is only y_2.

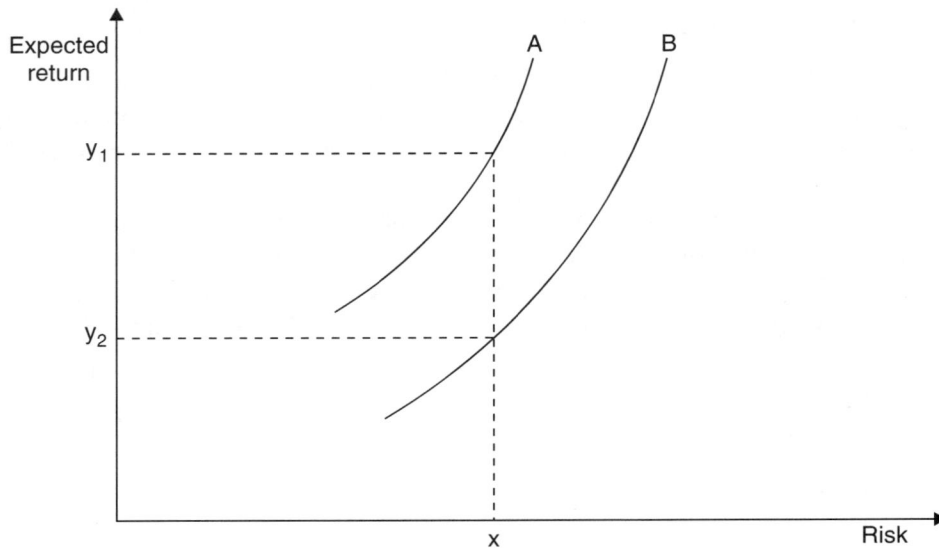

Figure 2 Indifference curves compared

Efficient portfolios

2.6   If we drew a graph (Figure 3) to show the expected return and the risk of the many possible portfolios of investments, we could (according to portfolio theory) plot an egg-shaped cluster of dots on a scattergraph. In this graph, there are some portfolios which would not be as good as others. However, there are other portfolios which are neither better nor worse than each other, because they have either a higher expected return but a higher risk, or a lower expected return but a lower risk. These portfolios lie along the so-called **efficient frontier of portfolios** which is shown as a dotted line in Figure 3. Portfolios on this efficient frontier are called 'efficient' portfolios.

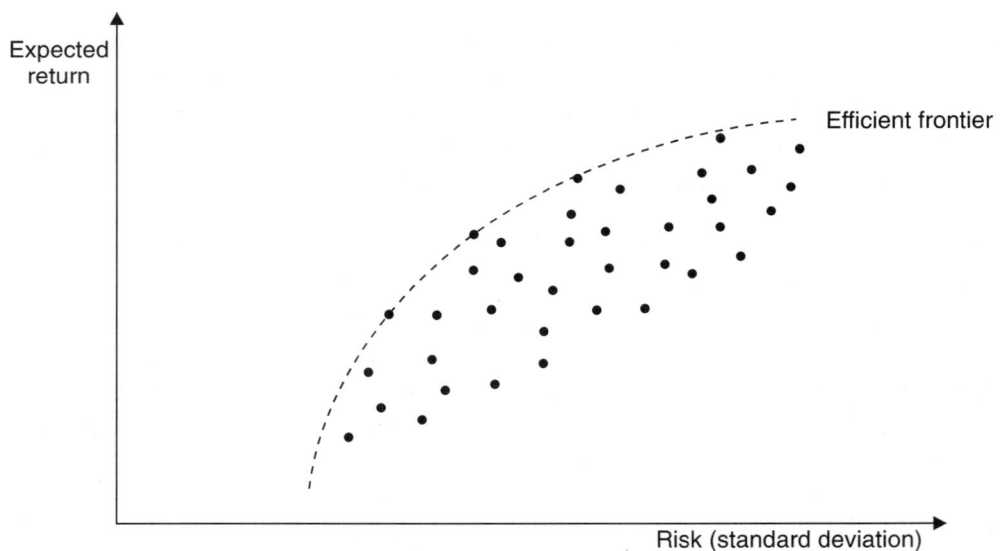

Figure 3 The efficient frontier of available investment portfolios

2.7   We can now place an investor's indifference curves on the same graph as the possible portfolios of investments (the **egg-shaped scatter graph**), as in Figure 4. An investor would prefer a portfolio of investments on indifference curve A to a portfolio on curve B, which in turn is preferable to a portfolio on curve C which in turn is preferable to curve D. No portfolio exists, however, which is on curve A or curve B.

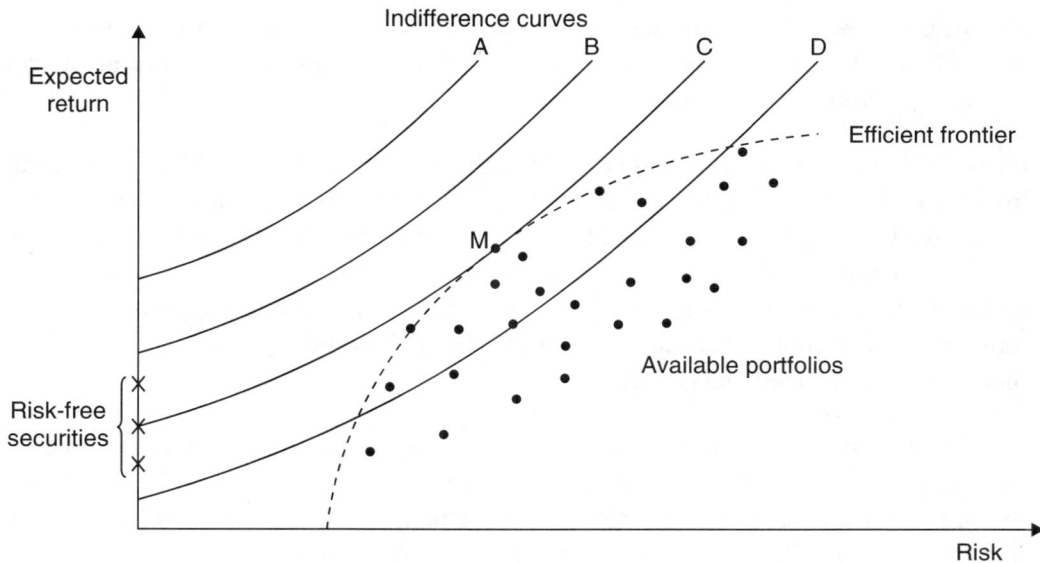

Figure 4 The optimum portfolio (ignoring risk-free securities)

2.8 The optimum portfolio (or portfolios) to select is one where an indifference curve touches the efficient frontier of portfolios at a tangent. In Figure 4, this is the portfolio marked M, where indifference curve C touches the efficient frontier at a tangent. Any portfolio on an indifference curve to the right of curve C, such as one on curve D, would be worse than M.

Risk-free investments

2.9 The efficient frontier is a curved line, not a straight line. This is because the additional return for accepting a greater level of risk will not be constant. The curve eventually levels off because a point will be reached where no more return can be offered to an investor for accepting more risk.

2.10 All the portfolios under consideration carry some degree of risk. But some investments are risk-free. It is extremely unlikely that the British Government would default on any payment of interest and capital on its stocks. Thus government stocks can be taken to be risk-free investments. If we introduce a **risk-free investment** into the analysis we can see that the old efficient frontier is superseded (Figure 5).

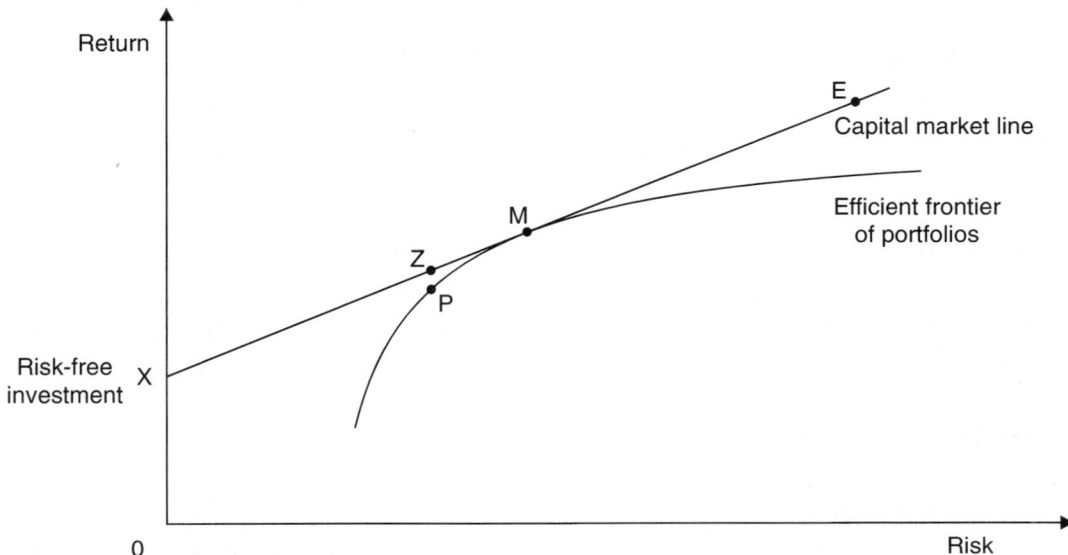

Figure 5 The capital market line

2.11 The straight line XZME is drawn at a tangent to the efficient frontier and cuts the y axis at the point of the risk-free investment's return. The line (known as the **capital market line** (CML)) becomes the new efficient frontier.

2.12 Portfolio M is the same as in Figure 4. It is the efficient portfolio which will appeal to the investor most, ignoring risk-free investments. Portfolio Z is a mixture of the investments in portfolio M and risk-free investments. Investors will prefer portfolio Z (a mixture of risky portfolio M and the risk-free investment) to portfolio P because a higher return is obtained for the same level of risk. The only portfolio consisting entirely of **risky investments** a rational investor should want to hold is portfolio M. All other risky portfolios are inefficient (because they are below the CML).

2.13 As with the curvilinear frontier, one portfolio on the capital market line is as attractive as another to a rational investor. One investor may wish to hold portfolio Z, which lies 2/3 of the way along the CML between risk-free investment X and portfolio M (that is, a holding comprising 2/3 portfolio M and 1/3 risk-free securities). Another investor may wish to hold portfolio E, which entails putting all his funds in portfolio M and borrowing money at the risk-free rate to acquire more of portfolio M.

2.14 We have said that investors will only want to hold one portfolio of risky investments: portfolio M. This may be held in conjunction with a holding of the risk-free investment (as with portfolio Z). Alternatively, an investor may borrow funds to augment his holding of M (as with portfolio E). Therefore, since all investors wish to hold portfolio M, and all shares quoted on the Stock Exchange must be held by investors, it follows that **all shares quoted on the Stock Exchange must be in portfolio M**.

2.15 Thus portfolio M is the **market portfolio** and each investor's portfolio will contain a proportion of it. (Although in the real world, investors do not hold every quoted security in their portfolio, in practice a well-diversified portfolio will 'mirror' the whole market in terms of weightings given to particular sectors, high income and high capital growth securities, and so on.) In practice, investors *might* be able to build up a small **portfolio that 'beats the market'** or might have a portfolio which performs worse than the market average. The following question illustrates this.

Question

The following data relate to four different portfolios of securities.

Portfolio	Expected rate of return %	Standard deviation of return on the portfolio %
K	11	6.7
L	14	7.5
M	10	3.3
N	15	10.8

The expected rate of return on the market portfolio is 8.5% with a standard deviation of 3%. The risk-free rate is 5%. Identify which of these portfolios could be regarded as 'efficient'.

Answer

To answer this question, we can start by drawing the CML (see below).

(a) When risk = 0, return = 5.
(b) When risk = 3, return = 8.5.

These points can be plotted on a graph and joined up, and the line can be extended to produce the CML. The individual portfolios K, L, M and N can be plotted on the same graph.

(a)   Any portfolio which is above the CML is efficient.

(b)   Any portfolio which is below the CML is inefficient.

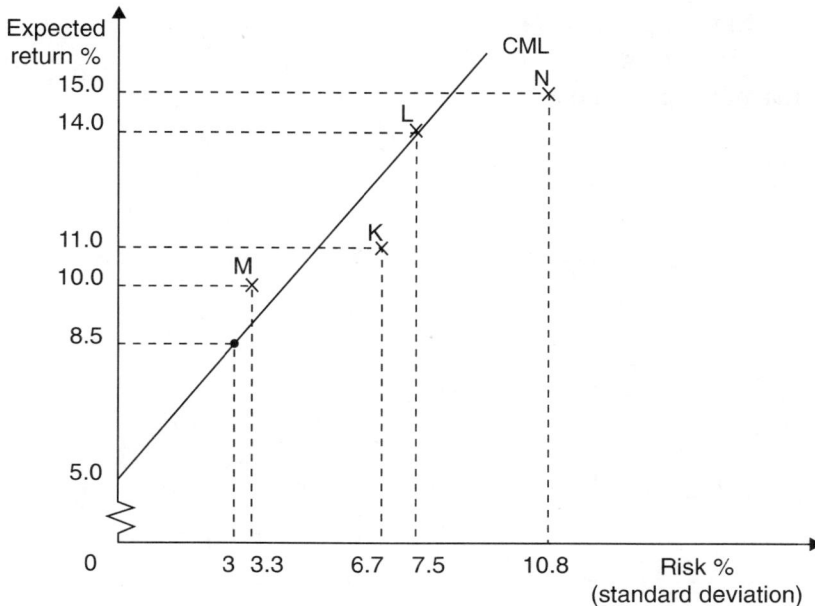

(a)   Portfolio M is very efficient.

(b)   Portfolio L is also efficient.

(c)   Portfolios K and N are inefficient.

If you prefer numbers to graphs, we can tackle the problem in a slightly different way, by calculating the equation of the CML.

Let the standard deviation of a portfolio be x.

Let the return from a portfolio be y.

The CML equation is $y = r_f + bx$.

where r_f is the risk-free rate of return. Here, this is 5.

To calculate b, we can use the high-low method.

When   x = 3, y = 8.5

When   x = 0, y = 5

Therefore $b = \dfrac{(8.5 - 5)}{(3 - 0)} = \dfrac{3.5}{3} = 1.16667$

The CML is y = 5 + 1.16667x

Portfolio	Standard deviation x	CML return		Actual return %	Efficient or inefficient portfolio
			%		
K	6.7	5 + (1.16667 × 6.7)	12.8	11	Inefficient
L	7.5	5 + (1.16667 × 7.5)	13.8	14	Efficient
M	3.3	5 + (1.16667 × 3.3)	8.9	10	Very efficient
N	10.8	5 + (1.16667 × 10.8)	17.6	15	Inefficient

If the actual return exceeds the CML return for the given amount of risk, the portfolio is efficient.

Here, L is efficient and M is even more efficient, but K and N are inefficient.

The return on the market portfolio M

2.16   The expected returns from portfolio M will be higher than the return from risk-free investments because the investors expect a greater return for accepting a degree of investment risk. The size of the **risk premium** will increase as the risk of the market portfolio increases. We can show this with an analysis of the capital market line (CML) as in Figure 6 in which:

r_m = return from portfolio M
r_f = risk-free return
σ_m = risk of the portfolio M

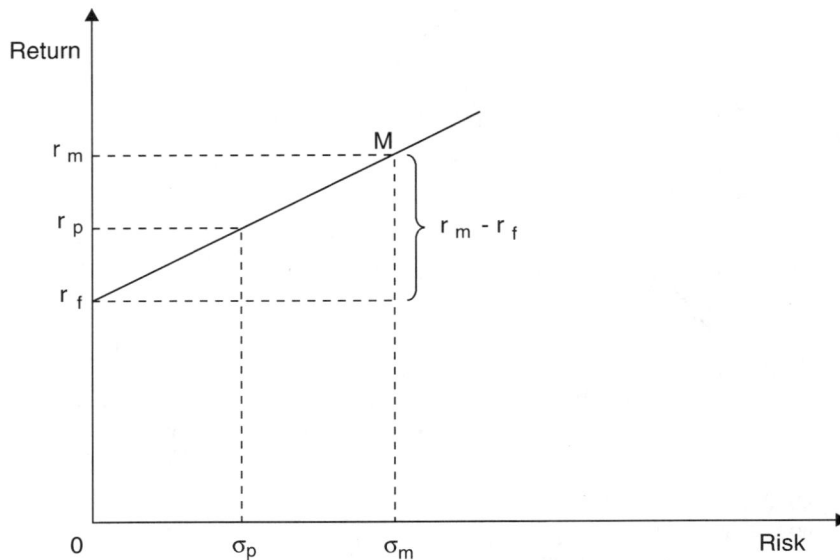

Figure 6 The risk premium in required returns from a portfolio

2.17 The formula for the CML was expressed as y = a + bx in the previous question, where a is the risk-free rate of return and b represents the increase in the return as the risk increases.

2.18 Let

r_f = the risk-free rate of return
r_m = the return on market portfolio M
r_p = the return on portfolio P, which is a mixture of investments in portfolio M and risk-free investments
σ_m = the risk (standard deviation) of returns in portfolio M
σ_p = the risk (standard deviation) of returns in portfolio P

The gradient of the CML can be expressed as $\dfrac{r_m - r_f}{\sigma_m}$

This represents the extent to which the required returns from a portfolio should exceed the risk-free rate of return, to compensate investors for risk.

The beta factor

2.19 The equation of the CML can be expressed as $\qquad r_p = r_f + \left(\dfrac{r_m - r_f}{\sigma_m} \right) \sigma_p$

where $\left(\dfrac{r_m - r_f}{\sigma_m} \right) \sigma_p$ is the risk premium that the investor should require as compensation for accepting portfolio risk σ_p. You can see that the risk premium is the gradient of the CML multiplied by the portfolio risk.

2.20 A high level of diversification leads to the investor holding the market portfolio, with investments reflecting the risk and return characteristics of all shares in the market. It has been shown that in practice only 10 to 12 or so diverse shares are needed to reach this position, at which:

$$\sigma_p = \sigma_m$$

2.21 The risk premium can be arranged into:

$$\frac{\sigma_p}{\sigma_m}(r_m - r_f)$$

The expression $\frac{\sigma_p}{\sigma_m}$ is referred to as a **beta factor,** so that an investor's required return from a portfolio can be stated as $r_p = r_f + (r_m - r_f)\beta$

2.22 The beta factor (β) can therefore be used to measure the extent to which a portfolio's return (or indeed an individual investment's return) should exceed the risk-free rate of return. The beta factor is multiplied by the difference between the average return on market securities (r_m) and the risk-free return (r_f) to derive the portfolio's or investment's risk premium. This risk premium will include both a business risk and a financial risk element in it. This equation forms the basis of the **capital asset pricing model (CAPM)**, which we shall look at in the next chapter.

KEY TERMS

Beta factor: in portfolio theory, a measure of the volatility of the price of a security, and thus of its **systematic risk** (see next chapter), used to calculate appropriate discount rates in the **capital asset pricing model.**

3 PORTFOLIO THEORY AND FINANCIAL MANAGEMENT 6/94

3.1 Our discussion of portfolio theory has concentrated mainly on portfolios of stocks and shares. Investors can reduce their investment risk by diversifying, but what about individual companies choosing a range of businesses or projects to invest in?

3.2 Just as an investor can reduce the risk of variable returns by diversifying into a portfolio of different securities, a company can reduce its own risk and so stabilise its profitability if it invests in a portfolio of different projects or operations, assuming that any positive correlation between returns is weak.

(a) If a company which manufactures garden tables diversifies into manufacturing umbrellas for garden tables, it is unlikely that the diversification will reduce risk, because the returns from trading in garden tables and garden table umbrellas will be positively correlated, both depending on the strength of demand for garden furniture.

(b) On the other hand, if a company which manufactures and sells computer equipment were to diversify into trading in video recorders, children's clothing, industrial paints, domestic plumbing and electrical services, it is probable that its risk of variable profits would be reduced.

Should companies try to diversify?

Case example

The answer to this question is not clear-cut, and you can probably think of examples of large companies today which concentrate mainly on a single industry or product range (for example BT, formerly British Telecom) and 'conglomerates' which are widely diversified (for example Hanson Trust).

3.3 Diversification may have the following **advantages** for shareholders.

(a) **Internal cash flows** will become less volatile. This makes it less risky to service the company's current level of debt and may consequently allow the company to make use of more debt without additional risk. This could reduce the cost of capital generally, increasing the wealth of shareholders.

(b) Diversification into foreign markets may enable shareholders to reduce the level of their **systematic risk** where exchange controls or other barriers to direct investment exist. The diversifying company can enable this to occur by investing in markets which have a combination of risk and return which shareholders would not otherwise be able to obtain.

(c) A diversified company may have a lower probability of **corporate failure** because of the reduced total risk for the company. This will reduce the likely impact of insolvency costs.

3.4 However, there are a number of reasons why a company should **not try to diversify too far**.

(a) A company may employ people with **particular skills**, and it will get the best out of its employees by allowing them to stick to doing what they are good at. A manager with expert knowledge of the electronics business, for example, might not be any good at managing a retailing business. *Some* managers can adapt successfully to running a diversified business.

(b) When companies try to grow, they will often find the best opportunities to make extra profits in industries or markets with which they are **familiar**. If a market opens up for say, a new electronic consumer product, the companies which are likely to exploit the market most profitably are those which already have experience in producing electronic consumer products.

(c) Conglomerates are **vulnerable to takeover bids** where the buyer plans to 'unbundle' the companies in the group and sell them off individually at a profit, particularly because their returns will often be mediocre rather than high, and so the stock market will value the shares on a fairly low P/E ratio. Separate companies within the group would be valued according to their individual performance and prospects, often at P/E ratios that are much higher than for the conglomerate as a whole.

(d) Except where restrictions apply to direct investment, investors can probably reduce investment risk **more efficiently** than companies. They have a wider range of investment opportunities. Investments with uncorrelated or negatively correlated returns will be easier to identify. Estimates of beta factors will be more reliable for quoted companies' shares than for companies' capital expenditure projects.

3.5 These arguments suggest that a company should not necessarily diversify widely into completely different products and markets. On the other hand, it would be against the interests of shareholders if a company were to be so unprofitable that it went into liquidation. Companies should try to obtain some protection against short-term profit changes, and diversification can help to provide this.

Limitations of portfolio analysis for the financial manager

3.6 Portfolio analysis is useful for diversifying through the firm's investment decisions. Applied to the selection of investment proposals, portfolio theory has a number of limitations.

(a) **Probabilities** of different outcomes must be estimated: fairly easy for (eg) machine replacement; more difficult for (eg) new product development.

(b) **Shareholders' preferences between risk and return** may be difficult to know.

(c) Portfolio theory is based on the idea of managers assessing the relevant probabilities and deciding the combination of activities for the business. Managers have their job security to consider, while the shareholder can easily buy and sell securities. Managers may therefore be more risk-averse than shareholders, and this may distort managers' investment decisions (the **'agency problem'** - see Chapter 2).

(d) Projects may be of such a **size** that they are not easy to divide in accordance with recommended diversification principles.

(e) The theory assumes that there are **constant returns to scale**, in other words that the percentage returns provided by a project are the same however much is invested in it. In practice, there may be economies of scale to be gained from making a larger investment in a single project.

(f) Other aspects of **risk** not covered by the theory may need to be considered, eg bankruptcy costs.

Chapter roundup

- **Portfolio theory** takes account of the fact that many investors have a range of investments which are unlikely all to changes values in step. The investor should be concerned with his or her overall position, not with the performance of individual investments. **Diversification** is equally an important consideration for the financial manager in making investment decisions.

- **Portfolio theory** has limitations in its use by the financial manager, although it provides the basis of the more sophisticated **CAPM** approach to making investment decisions under risk, which we turn to in the next chapter.

Quick quiz

1   What are the factors in choosing a portfolio of investments? (see para 1.3)

2   How is the expected return from a portfolio measured? (1.4)

3   Returns from investments might be positively correlated, negatively correlated, or uncorrelated. How does correlation of returns from individual investments affect the risk of a portfolio? (1.19)

4   What is the formula for calculating the standard deviation of returns from a two-investment portfolio? (1.20)

5   Give an example of a risk-free investment. (2.10)

6   What is the equation of the capital market line? (2.19) Use this to derive an expression for the beta factor. (2.21)

7   How is the beta factor used? (2.22)

8   What limitations are there in using portfolio analysis in financial management decisions? (3.6)

Question to try	Level	Marks	Time
7	Exam standard	10	18 mins

BPP PUBLISHING

Chapter 8

THE CAPITAL ASSET PRICING MODEL

Chapter topic list	Syllabus reference
1 Risk and the CAPM	3(c)
2 Calculating a beta factor	3(c)
3 CAPM and portfolios	3(c)
4 Gearing and the β values of companies' equity	3(c), (d)
5 Practical implications of the CAPM	3(c), (d)
6 The arbitrage pricing model	3(c)

Introduction

The **Capital Asset Pricing Model (CAPM)** brings together aspects of topics covered in earlier chapters: portfolio theory, share valuations, the cost of capital and gearing. Towards the end of the chapter, we discuss a possible replacement for the CAPM - the **arbitrage pricing model (APM)**. *Detailed* knowledge of the APM is not required for the Paper 14 examination.

1   RISK AND THE CAPM   6/94, 6/95, 12/95, 12/96, 12/97, 6/99

1.1   The uses of the capital asset pricing model (CAPM) include:

(a) Trying to establish the 'correct' equilibrium market value of a company's shares

(b) Trying to establish the cost of a company's equity (and the company's average cost of capital), taking account of the risk characteristics of a company's investments, both business and financial risk

The CAPM thus provides an approach to establishing a cost of equity capital which is an alternative to the dividend valuation model.

Systematic risk and unsystematic risk

1.2   Whenever an investor invests in some shares, or a company invests in a new project, there will be some risk involved. The actual return on the investment might be better or worse than that hoped for. To some extent, risk is unavoidable (unless the investor settles for risk-free securities such as gilts). Investors must take the rough with the smooth and for reasons outside their control, returns might be higher or lower than expected. Provided that the investor diversifies his investments in a suitably wide portfolio, the investments which perform well and those which perform badly should tend to cancel each other out, and much risk can be diversified away. In the same way, a company which invests in a number of projects will find that some do well and some do badly, but taking the whole portfolio of investments, average returns should turn out much as expected.

1.3 Risks that can be diversified away are referred to as **unsystematic risk**. Some investments are by their very nature more risky than others. This has nothing to do with chance variations up or down in actual returns compared with what an investor should expect. This inherent risk - the **systematic risk** or **market risk** - cannot be diversified away (see Figure 1).

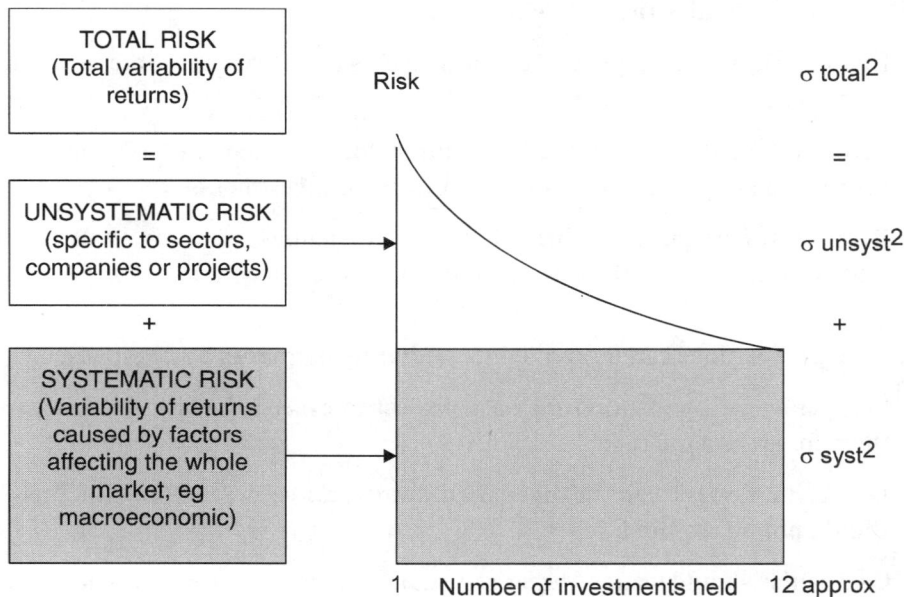

Figure 1

1.4 Systematic risk must be accepted by any investor, unless he invests entirely in risk-free investments. In return for accepting systematic risk, an investor will expect to earn a return which is higher than the return on a risk-free investment. The amount of systematic risk in an investment varies between different types of investment.

(a) The systematic risk in the operating cash flows of a tourism company which will be highly sensitive to consumers' spending power might be greater than the systematic risk for a company which operates a chain of supermarkets.

(b) Some individual projects will be more risky than others and so the systematic risk involved in an investment to develop a new product would be greater than the systematic risk of investing in a replacement asset.

Systematic risk and unsystematic risk: implications for investments

1.5 If an investor wants to avoid risk altogether, he must invest entirely in **risk-free securities**. If an investor holds shares in just a few companies, there will be some unsystematic risk as well as systematic risk in his portfolio, because he will not have spread his risk enough to diversify away the unsystematic risk. To eliminate unsystematic risk, he must build up a well-diversified portfolio of investments.

1.6 If an investor holds a **balanced portfolio** of all the stocks and shares on the stock market, he will incur systematic risk which is exactly equal to the average systematic risk in the stock market as a whole.

1.7 Shares in individual companies will have systematic risk characteristics which are different to this market average. Some shares will be less risky and some will be more risky than the stock market average. Similarly, some investments will be more risky and some will be less risky than a company's 'average' investments.

Systematic risk and the CAPM

1.8 The capital asset pricing model is mainly concerned with how systematic risk is measured (using **beta factors**) and with how systematic risk affects required returns and share prices.

1.9 **CAPM theory includes the following propositions.**

(a) Investors in shares require a return in excess of the risk-free rate, to compensate them for systematic risk.

(b) Investors should not require a premium for unsystematic risk, because this can be diversified away by holding a wide portfolio of investments.

(c) Because systematic risk varies between companies, investors will require a higher return from shares in those companies where the systematic risk is greater.

1.10 The same propositions can be applied to **capital investments by companies**.

(a) Companies will want a return on a project to exceed the risk-free rate, to compensate them for systematic risk.

(b) Unsystematic risk can be diversified away, and so a premium for unsystematic risk should not be required.

(c) Companies should want a bigger return on projects where systematic risk is greater.

Market risk and returns

1.11 The CAPM was first formulated for investments in stocks and shares on the market, rather than for companies' investments in capital projects. It is based on a comparison of the systematic risk of individual investments (shares in a particular company) and the risk of all shares in the market as a whole. Market risk (systematic risk) is the average risk of the market as a whole. Taking all the shares on a stock market together, the total expected returns from the market will vary because of systematic risk. The market as a whole might do well or it might do badly.

Risk and returns from an individual security

1.12 In the same way, an individual security may offer prospects of a return of x%, but with some risk (business risk and financial risk) attached. The return (the x%) that investors will require from the individual security will be higher or lower than the market return, depending on whether the security's systematic risk is greater or less than the market average. A major assumption in CAPM is that there is a **linear relationship** between the return obtained from an individual security and the average return from all securities in the market.

1.13 EXAMPLE: CAPM (1)

The following information is available about the performance of an individual company's shares and the stock market as a whole.

	Individual company	Stock market as a whole
Price at start of period	105.0	480.0
Price at end of period	110.0	490.0
Dividend during period	7.6	39.2

1.14 The return on the company's shares (r$_j$) and the return on the 'market portfolio' of shares (r$_m$) may be calculated as:

$$\frac{\text{Capital gain (or loss)} + \text{dividend}}{\text{Price at start of period}}$$

$$r_j = \frac{(110-105)+7.6}{105} = 0.12 \qquad r_m = \frac{(490-480)+39.2}{480} = 0.1025$$

1.15 A statistical analysis of 'historic' returns from a security and from the 'average' market may suggest that a linear relationship can be assumed to exist between them. A series of comparative figures could be prepared (month by month) of the return from a company's shares and the average return of the market as a whole. The results could be drawn on a scattergraph and a 'line of best fit' drawn (using linear regression techniques) as shown in Figure 2.

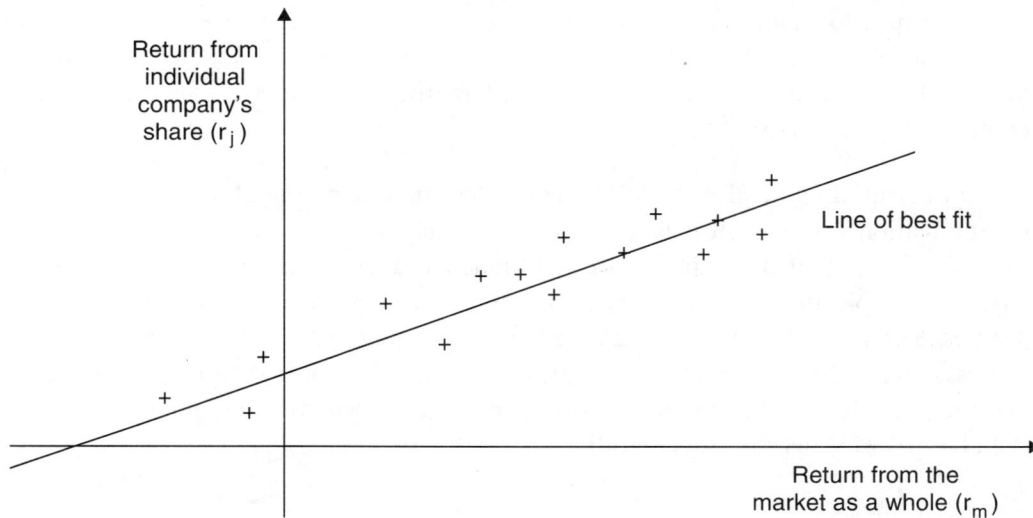

Figure 2

1.16 This analysis would show three things. (Note that returns can be negative. A share price fall represents a capital loss, which is a negative return.)

(a) The return from the security (r$_j$) and the return from the market as a whole will tend to rise or fall together.

(b) The return from the security may be higher or lower than the market return. This is because the systematic risk of the individual security differs from that of the market as a whole. The graph above corresponds to a security which is riskier than the market (higher returns).

(c) The scattergraph may not give a good line of best fit, unless a large number of data items are plotted, because actual returns are affected by unsystematic risk as well as by systematic risk.

1.17 The conclusion from this analysis is that individual securities will be either more or less risky than the market average in a fairly predictable way. The measure of this relationship between market returns and an individual security's returns, reflecting differences in systematic risk characteristics, can be developed into a beta factor for the individual security.

The beta factor and the market risk premium

1.18 A share's **beta factor** is the measure of its volatility in terms of market risk. The beta factor of the **market as a whole** is **1.0**. Market risk makes market returns volatile and the beta factor is simply a basis or yardstick against which the risk of other investments can be measured.

1.19 For example, suppose that returns on shares in XYZ plc tend to vary twice as much as returns from the market as a whole, so that if market returns went up 3%, say, returns on XYZ plc shares would be expected to go up by 6% and if market returns fell by 3%, returns on XYZ plc shares would be expected to fall by 6%. The beta factor of XYZ plc shares would be 2.0.

1.20 Thus if the average market return rises by, say, 2%, the return from a share with a beta factor of 0.8 should rise by 1.6% in response to the *same conditions* which have caused the market return to change. The *actual* return from the share might rise by, say, 2.5%, or even fall by, say, 1%, but the difference between the actual change and a change of 1.6% due to general market factors would be attributed to unsystematic risk factors unique to the company or its industry.

1.21 It is an essential principle of CAPM theory that unsystematic risk can be cancelled out by diversification. In a well-balanced portfolio, an investor's gains and losses from the unsystematic risk of individual shares will tend to cancel each other out. In other words, if shares in X plc do worse than market returns and the beta factor of X's shares would predict, shares in Y plc will do better than predicted, and the net effect will be self-cancelling elimination of the specific (unsystematic) risk from the portfolio, leaving the average portfolio return dependent only on **changes in the average market return** and **the beta factors of shares in the portfolio**.

Excess returns over returns on risk-free investments

1.22 The CAPM also makes use of the principle that returns on shares in the market as a whole are expected to be higher than the returns on risk-free investments. The difference between market returns and risk-free returns is called an **excess return**. For example, if the return on British Government stocks is 9% and market returns are 13%, the excess return on the market's shares as a whole is 4%.

1.22 The difference between the risk-free return and the expected return on an individual security can be measured as the excess return for the market as a whole multiplied by the security's beta factor. Thus, if shares in DEF plc have a beta of 1.5 when the risk-free return is 9% and the expected market return is 13%, then the expected return on DEF plc shares would exceed the risk- free return by $(13 - 9) \times 1.5\% = 6\%$ and the total expected return on DEF shares would be $(9 + 6)\% = 15\%$. If the market returns fall by 3% to 10%, say, the expected return on DEF plc shares would fall by $1.5 \times 3\% = 4.5\%$ to 10.5%, being 9% $+(10 - 9) \times 1.5\% = 10.5\%$.

The CAPM formula   6/96

1.24 The capital asset pricing model is a statement of the principles explained above. It can be stated as follows.

$$E(r_j) - r_f = (E(r_m) - r_f)\beta$$

where $E(r_j)$ is the expected return from an individual security

           r_f is the risk-free rate of return

           (r_m) is the expected return from the market as a whole

           β_j is the beta factor of the individual security

1.25   The CAPM equation or security market line (SML) can be rearranged into the following.

EXAM FORMULA

$E(r_j) = r_f + (E(r_m) - r_f)\,\beta_j$

Alpha values

1.26   A share's **alpha value** is a measure of its abnormal return, which is the amount by which the share's returns are currently above or below the required return, given the level of systematic risk.

1.27   EXAMPLE: CAPM (2)

ABC plc's shares have a beta value of 1.2 and an alpha value of +2%. The market return is 10% and the risk-free rate of return is 6%.

Expected return $6\% + (10 - 6) \times 1.2\% = 10.8\%$

Current return   =   expected return ± alpha value

                  = $10.8\% + 2\% = 12.8\%$

1.28   Alpha values:

(a)   Reflect only temporary, abnormal returns, if CAPM is a realistic model

(b)   Can be positive or negative

(c)   Over time, will tend towards zero for any individual share, and for a well-diversified portfolio taken as a whole will be 0

(d)   If positive, might attract investors into buying the share to benefit from the abnormal return, so that the share price will temporarily go up

(e)   May exist due to the inaccuracies and limitations of the CAPM (which we examine later)

The CAPM and share prices

1.29   The CAPM can be used not only to estimate expected returns from securities with differing risk characteristics, but also to **predict the values of shares**.

1.30   EXAMPLE: CAPM (3)

Company X and company Y both pay an annual cash return to shareholders of 34.048 pence per share and this is expected to continue in perpetuity. The risk-free rate of return is 8% and the current average market rate of return is 12%. Company X's β coefficient is 1.8 and company Y's is 0.8. What is the expected return from companies X and Y respectively, and what would be the predicted market value of each company's shares?

BPP PUBLISHING

1.31 SOLUTION

(a) The expected return for X is $8\% + (12\% - 8\%) \times 1.8 = 15.2\%$

(b) The expected return for Y is $8\% + (12\% - 8\%) \times 0.8 = 11.2\%$

The dividend valuation model can now be used to derive expected share prices.

(c) The predicted value of a share in X is $\dfrac{34.048p}{0.152} = 224$ pence

(d) The predicted value of a share in Y is $\dfrac{34.048p}{0.112} = 304$ pence

The actual share prices of X and Y might be higher or lower than 224p and 304p. If so, CAPM analysis would conclude that the share is currently either overpriced or underpriced.

Question 1

The risk-free rate of return is 7%. The average market return is 11%.

(a) What will be the return expected from a share whose β factor is 0.9?

(b) What would be the share's expected value if it is expected to earn an annual dividend of 5.3p, with no capital growth?

Answer

(a) $7\% + (11\% - 7\%) \times 0.9 = 10.6\%$

(b) $\dfrac{5.3p}{10.6\%} = 50$ pence

2 CALCULATING A BETA FACTOR   6/97, 12/99

2.1 The beta factor for a particular security can be calculated by plotting its return against the market return and drawing the line of best fit. The equation of this line can be derived by regression analysis. The β factor is the gradient of the line. It can be calculated by using the following formula.

$$\beta = \frac{n\sum xy - \sum x \sum y}{n\sum x^2 - (\sum x)^2}$$

where   β = the beta coefficient
            x = the return from the market
            y = the return from the security
            n = the number of pairs of data for x and y.

2.2 Another formula for calculating the beta value of a company's shares is:

$$\beta = \frac{\text{cov}(x, y)}{\text{var}(x)}$$

where cov (x, y) is the covariance of returns on the individual company's shares (y) with returns for the market as a whole (x) and var(x) is the variance of returns for the market as a whole.

Exam focus point

In the 6/97 exam, you needed to use the above formula to find beta values and compare the required returns with forecast returns to find the alpha values (see previous section).

2.3 EXAMPLE: CAPM (4)

The risk-free rate of return is 6% and the market rate of return is 11%. The standard deviation of returns for the market as a whole is 40%. The covariance of returns for the market with returns for the shares of Peapod plc is 19.2%. Since the variance is the square of a standard deviation, the beta value for Peapod plc is:

$$\frac{0.192}{0.4^2} = \frac{0.192}{0.16} = 1.20$$

The cost of equity capital for Peapod plc would therefore be $6\% + (11 - 6) \times 1.2\% = 12\%$.

2.4 Yet another formula for calculating a share's beta factor is:

$$\beta = \frac{\sigma_s \rho_{sm}}{\sigma_m}$$

where
- σ_s is the standard deviation of returns on the shares of a company
- σ_m is the standard deviation of returns on equity for the market as a whole
- ρ_{sm} is the correlation coefficient between total returns on equity for the stock market as a whole and total returns on the shares of the individual company.

2.5 EXAMPLE: CAPM (5)

We are given the following information.

The average stock market return on equity	= 15%
The risk-free rate of return (pre-tax)	= 8%
Company X: dividend yield	= 4%
Company X: share price rise (capital gain)	= 12%
Standard deviation of total stock market return on equity	= 9%
Standard deviation of total return on equity of Company X	= 10.8%
Correlation coefficient between Company X return on equity and average stock market return on equity	= 0.75

What is the beta factor for Company X shares, and what does this information imply for the actual returns and actual market value of Company X shares?

2.6 SOLUTION

(a) $\beta = \dfrac{\sigma_s \rho_{sm}}{\sigma_m}$

$= \dfrac{10.8\% \times 0.75}{9\%} = 0.9$

(b) The cost of Company X equity should therefore be:

$E(r_j) = 8\% + (15 - 8) \times 0.9\% = 14.3\%$

2.7 The actual returns on Company X equity are $4\% + 12\% = 16\%$. This implies that:

(a) The actual returns include extra returns due to unsystematic risk factors, or

(b) If there are no unsystematic risk factors, the price of Company X shares is currently lower than it should be

BPP PUBLISHING

Question 2

The standard deviation of market returns is 50%, and the expected market return ($E(r_m)$) is 12%. The risk-free rate of return is 9%. The covariance of returns for the market with returns on shares in Deancourt plc has been 20%. Calculate a beta value and a cost of capital for Deancourt plc equity.

Answer

(a) The variance of market returns is $0.50^2 = 0.25$

$$\beta = \frac{0.20}{0.25} = 0.8$$

(b) Cost of Deancourt plc equity $= 9\% + (12 - 9) \times 0.8\%$

$= 11.4\%$

3 CAPM AND PORTFOLIOS

3.1 Just as an individual security has a beta factor, so too does a portfolio of securities.

(a) A portfolio consisting of all the securities on the stock market (in the same proportions as the market as a whole), excluding risk-free securities, will have an expected return equal to the expected return for the market as a whole, and so will have a beta factor of 1.

(b) A portfolio consisting entirely of risk-free securities will have a beta factor of 0.

(c) The beta factor of an investor's portfolio is the weighted average of the beta factors of the securities in the portfolio.

3.2 EXAMPLE: CAPM (6)

A portfolio consisting of five securities could have its beta factor computed as follows.

Security	Percentage of portfolio	Beta factor of security	Weighted beta factor
A plc	20%	0.90	0.180
B plc	10%	1.25	0.125
C plc	15%	1.10	0.165
D plc	20%	1.15	0.230
E plc	35%	0.70	0.245
	100%	Portfolio beta =	0.945

3.3 If the risk-free rate of return is 12% and the average market return is 20%, the expected return from the portfolio would be $12\% + (20 - 12) \times 0.945\% = 19.56\%$

3.4 The calculation could have been made as follows.

Security	Beta factor	Expected return $E(r_i)$	Weighting %	Weighted return %
A plc	0.90	19.2	20	3.84
B plc	1.25	22.0	10	2.20
C plc	1.10	20.8	15	3.12
D plc	1.15	21.2	20	4.24
E plc	0.70	17.6	35	6.16
			100	19.56

4 GEARING AND THE β VALUES OF COMPANIES' EQUITY
6/94, 6/96, 12/96

4.1 The **gearing** of a company will affect the risk of its equity. If a company is geared and its financial risk is therefore higher than the risk of an all-equity company, then the β value of the geared company's equity will be higher than the β value of a similar ungeared company's equity.

4.2 The CAPM is consistent with the propositions of **Modigliani and Miller**. MM argue that as gearing rises, the cost of equity rises to compensate shareholders for the extra financial risk of investing in a geared company. This financial risk is an aspect of systematic risk, and ought to be reflected in a company's beta factor.

Beta values and the effect of gearing: geared betas and ungeared betas

4.3 The connection between MM theory and the CAPM means that it is possible to establish a mathematical relationship between the β value of an ungeared company and the β value of a similar, but geared, company. The β value of a geared company will be higher than the β value of a company identical in every respect except that it is all-equity financed. This is because of the extra financial risk. The mathematical relationship between the 'ungeared' and 'geared' betas is as follows.

> **EXAM FORMULA**
>
> $$\beta_a = \beta_e \frac{E}{E + D(1-t)} + \beta_d \frac{D(1-t)}{E + D(1-t)}$$

where β_a is the beta factor of an ungeared company: the ungeared beta

β_e is the beta factor of equity in a similar, but geared company: the geared beta

β_d is the beta factor of debt in the geared company

D   is the market value of the debt capital in the geared company

E   is the market value of the equity capital in the geared company

t   is the rate of corporation tax

The formula above can be used to calculate the ungeared beta as a weighted average of a company's equity and debt beta factor.

4.4 Debt is often assumed to be risk-free and its beta (β_d) is then taken as zero, in which case the formula above reduces to the following form.

$$\beta_a = \beta_e \frac{E}{E + D(1-t)}$$

> **Exam focus point**
> Debt should be assumed to be risk-free unless the question indicates otherwise.

4.5 Re-arranging the formula in the previous paragraph, we have:

$$\beta_e = \beta_a \times \frac{E + D(1-t)}{E} = \beta_a \left(1 + \frac{D(1-t)}{E}\right) = \beta_a + \beta_a \left(\frac{D(1-t)}{E}\right)$$

BPP PUBLISHING

Note that the geared beta is equal to the ungeared beta plus a premium for financial risk which equals:

$$\beta_a \left(\frac{D\,(1-t)}{E} \right)$$

4.6 EXAMPLE: CAPM (7)

Two companies are identical in every respect except for their capital structure. Their market values are in equilibrium, as follows.

	Geared plc £'000	Ungeared plc £'000
Annual profit before interest and tax	1,000	1,000
Less interest (4,000 × 8%)	320	0
	680	1,000
Less tax at 30%	204	300
Profit after tax = dividends	476	700

	Geared plc £'000	Ungeared plc £'000
Market value of equity	3,900	6,600
Market value of debt	4,180	0
Total market value of company	8,080	6,600

The total value of Geared plc is higher than the total value of Ungeared plc, which is consistent with MM's proposition that $V_g = V_u + Dt$. All profits after tax are paid out as dividends, and so there is no dividend growth.

The beta value of Ungeared plc has been calculated as 1.0. The debt capital of Geared plc can be regarded as risk-free.

Calculate:

(a) The cost of equity in Geared plc
(b) The market return r_m
(c) The beta value of Geared plc

4.7 SOLUTION

(a) Since its market value is in equilibrium, the cost of equity in Geared plc can be calculated as:

$$\frac{d}{MV} = \frac{476}{3,900} = 12.20\%$$

(b) The beta value of Ungeared plc is 1.0, which means that the expected returns from Ungeared plc are exactly the same as the market returns, and the r_m = 700/6,600 =10.6%.

(c) $\beta_e = \beta_a \times \dfrac{E + D(1-t)}{E}$

$$= 1.0 \times \frac{3,900 + (4,180 \times 0.70)}{3,900} = 1.75$$

The beta of Geared plc, as we should expect, is higher than the beta of Ungeared plc.

Using the geared and ungeared beta formula to estimate a beta factor for a company

4.8 Another way of estimating a beta factor for a company's equity is to use data about the returns of other quoted companies which have similar operating characteristics: that is, to **use the beta values of other companies' equity to estimate a beta value** for the company under consideration. The beta values estimated for the firm under consideration must be adjusted to allow for differences in gearing from the firms whose equity beta values are known. The formula for geared and ungeared beta values can be applied.

4.9 EXAMPLE: CAPM (8)

The management of Crispy plc wish to estimate their company's equity beta value. The company, which is an all-equity company, has only recently gone public and insufficient data is available at the moment about its own equity's performance to calculate the company's equity beta. Instead, it is thought possible to estimate Crispy's equity beta from the beta values of quoted companies operating in the same industry and with the same operating characteristics as Crispy.

Details of three similar companies are as follows. The tax rate is 30%.

(a) Snapp plc has an observed equity beta of 1.15. Its capital structure at market values is 70% equity and 30% debt. Snapp plc is very similar to Crispy plc except for its gearing.

(b) Crackle plc is an all-equity company. Its observed equity beta is 1.25. It has been estimated that 40% of the current market value of Crackle is caused by investment in projects which offer high growth, but which are more risky than normal operations and which therefore have a higher beta value. These investments have an estimated beta of 1.8, and are reflected in the company's overall beta value. Crackle's normal operations are identical to those of Crispy.

(c) Popper plc has an observed equity beta of 1.35. Its capital structure at market values is 60% equity and 40% debt. Popper has two divisions, X and Y. The operating characteristics of X are identical to those of Crispy but those of Y are thought to be 50% more risky than those of X. It is estimated that X accounts for 75% of the total value of Popper, and Y for 25%.

Required

(a) Assuming that all debt is virtually risk-free, calculate three estimates of the equity beta of Crispy, from the data available about Snapp, Crackle and Popper respectively.

(b) Now assume that Crispy plc is not an all-equity company, but instead is a geared company with a debt:equity ratio of 2:3 (based on market values). Estimate the equity beta of Crispy from the data available about Snapp.

4.10 SOLUTION

(a) *Snapp plc - based estimate*

$$\beta_e = \beta_a \times \frac{E + D(1 - t)}{E}$$

$$1.15 = \beta_a \times \frac{70 + 30(1 - 0.30)}{70}$$

$$1.15 = 1.3\beta_a$$

$$\beta_a = 0.88$$

(b) *Crackle plc - based estimate*

If the beta value of normal operations of Crackle is β_n, and we know that the high-risk operations have a beta value of 1.8 and account for 40% of Crackle's value, we can estimate a value for β_n.

Overall beta = 0.4(high risk beta) + 0.6(normal operations beta)

1.25 = 0.4(1.8) + 0.6 β_n

β_n = 0.88

Since Crackle is an all-equity company, this provides the estimate of Crispy's equity beta.

(c) *Popper plc - based estimate*

It is easiest to arrive at an estimate of Crispy's equity beta by calculating the equity beta which Popper would have had if it had been an all-equity company instead of a geared company.

$$\beta_e = \beta_a \times \frac{E + D(1-t)}{E}$$

$$1.35 = \beta_a \times \frac{0.6 + 0.4(1-0.30)}{0.6}$$

$$\beta_a = \frac{1.35}{1.47} = 0.92$$

This equity beta estimate for Popper plc is a weighted average of the beta values of divisions X and Y, so that:

$$0.92 = 0.75\beta_x + 0.25\beta_y$$

where β_x and β_y are the beta values for divisions X and Y respectively. We also know that Y is 50% more risky than X, so that $\beta_y = 1.5\beta_x$.

$$0.92 = 0.75\beta_x + 0.25(1.5\beta_x)$$

$$(0.75 + 0.375)\beta_x = 0.92$$

$$\beta_x = 0.82$$

Since Crispy plc is similar in characteristics to division X, the estimate of Crispy's equity beta is 0.82.

4.11 If Crispy plc is a geared company with a market-value based gearing ratio of 2:3, we can use the geared and ungeared beta formula again. The ungeared beta value, based on data about Snapp, was 0.88. The geared beta of Crispy would be estimated as:

$$\beta_e = 0.88 \times \frac{3 + 2(1-0.30)}{3} = 1.29$$

Weaknesses in the formula

4.12 (a) It is difficult to identify other firms with identical operating characteristics.

(b) Estimates of beta values from share price information are not wholly accurate. They are based on statistical analysis of historical data, and as the previous example shows, estimates using one firm's data will differ from estimates using another firm's data. The beta values for Crispy estimated from Snapp, Crackle and Popper are all different.

(c) There may be differences in beta values between firms caused by different cost structures (eg the ratio of fixed costs to variable costs), by size differences between firms and by debt capital not being risk-free.

(d) If the firm for which an equity beta is being estimated has opportunities for growth that are recognised by investors, and which will affect its equity beta, estimates of the equity beta based on other firms' data will be inaccurate, because the opportunities for growth will not be allowed for.

4.13 Perhaps the most significant simplifying assumption is that to link MM theory to the CAPM, it must be assumed that the cost of debt is a risk-free rate of return. This is obviously unrealistic. Companies may default on interest payments or capital repayments on their loans. It has been estimated that corporate debt has a beta value of 0.2 or 0.3.

4.14 The consequence of making the assumption that debt is risk-free is that the formulae tend to **overstate** the financial risk in a geared company and to **understate** the business risk in geared and ungeared companies by a compensating amount. In other words β_a will be slightly higher and β_e will be slightly lower than the formulae suggest.

5 PRACTICAL IMPLICATIONS OF THE CAPM 12/95, 12/99

5.1 Practical **implications of CAPM theory for an investor** are as follows.

(a) He should decide what beta factor he would like to have for his portfolio. He might prefer a portfolio beta factor of greater than 1, in order to expect above-average returns when market returns exceed the risk-free rate, but he would then expect to lose heavily if market returns fall. On the other hand, he might prefer a portfolio beta factor of 1 or even less.

(b) He should seek to invest in shares with low beta factors in a bear market, when average market returns are falling. He should then also sell shares with high beta factors.

(c) He should seek to invest in shares with high beta factors in a bull market, when average market returns are rising.

An investor can measure the beta factor of his portfolio by obtaining information about the beta factors of individual securities. These are obtainable from investment analysts, or from the London Business School's Risk Management Service.

Limitations of the CAPM for the selection of a portfolio of securities

5.2 Under the CAPM, the return required from a security is related to its systematic risk rather than its total risk. If we relax some of the assumptions upon which the model is based, then the total risk may be important. In particular, the following points should be considered.

(a) The model assumes that the costs of insolvency are zero, or in other words, that all assets can be sold at going concern prices and that there are no selling, legal or other costs. In practice, the costs of insolvency cannot be ignored. Furthermore, the risk of insolvency is related to a firm's total risk rather than just its systematic risk.

(b) The model assumes that the investment market is efficient. If it is not, this will limit the extent to which investors are able to eliminate unsystematic risk from their portfolios.

(c) The model also assumes that portfolios are well diversified and so need only be concerned with systematic risk. However, this is not necessarily the case, and undiversified or partly-diversified shareholders should also be concerned with unsystematic risk and will seek a total return appropriate to the total risk that they face.

5.3 The major sources of difficulty in applying the CAPM in practice are:

(a) The need to determine the excess return $(E(r_m) - r_f)$ (Expected, rather than historical, returns should be used, although historical returns are used in practice.)

(b) The need to determine the risk-free rate (A risk-free investment might be a government security. However, interest rates vary with the term of the lending.)

(c) Errors in the statistical analysis used to calculate β values

5.4 Beta factors based on historical data may be a poor basis for future decision-making. Evidence from a US study suggests that stocks with high or low betas tend to be fairly stable over time, but this may not always be so. Financial managers should preferably use betas for industrial sectors rather than individual company betas, as measurement errors will tend to cancel each other out. Beta values may change over time, for example if luxury items produced by a company become regarded as necessities, or if the cost structure (eg the proportion of fixed costs) of a business change. The CAPM is also unable to forecast accurately returns for **companies with low price/earnings ratios** and to take account of seasonal 'month-of-the-year' or 'day-of-the-week' effects which appear to influence returns on shares. Beta factors measured over different timescales may differ.

The CAPM and project appraisal

5.5 The CAPM can be used instead of the dividend valuation model to establish an equity cost of capital to use in project appraisal.

The cost of equity is $K_{eg} = r_f + (E(r_m) - r_f) \times \beta_e$ where β_e is the beta value for the company's equity capital.

5.6 EXAMPLE: CAPM (9)

A company is financed by a mixture of equity and debt capital, whose market values are in the ratio 3:1. The debt capital, which is considered risk-free, yields 10% before tax. The average stock market return on equity capital is 16%. The beta value of the company's equity capital is estimated as 0.95. The tax rate is 31%.

What would be an appropriate cost of capital to be used for investment appraisal of new projects with the same systematic risk characteristics as the company's current investment portfolio?

5.7 SOLUTION

An appropriate cost of capital to use, assuming no change in the company's financial gearing, is its WACC. However, the CAPM can be used to estimate the cost of the company's equity.

$K_{eg} = 10\% + (16 - 10) \times 0.95\% = 15.7\%$

The after tax cost of debt is $0.70 \times 10\% = 7.0\%$.

The WACC is therefore:

$(¾ \times 15.7\%) + (¼ \times 7.0\%) = 13.5\%$.

The cost of capital to use in project appraisal is 13.5%.

How is the WACC different using the CAPM?

5.8 You might be wondering how the weighted average cost of capital (WACC) is different when we use the CAPM compared to the method of calculating the WACC which was described in the earlier chapter on the cost of capital. The only difference, in fact, is the method used to calculate the cost of the firm's equity: the dividend valuation model or the CAPM. Using the different techniques for measuring the cost of equity will produce two different values, for these reasons.

(a) The dividend valuation model uses expectations of actual dividends and current share values. Dividends may include extra or lower returns caused by unsystematic risk variations, as well as systematic risk. Share prices might not be in equilibrium.

(b) The CAPM considers systematic risk only, and assumes equilibrium in the stock market.

5.9 If dividends reflect systematic risk only, and if stock market prices are in equilibrium, the dividend valuation model and the CAPM should produce roughly the same estimates for the cost of a firm's equity and for its WACC.

Using the CAPM to establish a discount rate for the appraisal of major projects

5.10 If a company plans to invest in a project which involves diversification into a new business, the investment will involve a different level of systematic risk from that applying to the company's existing business. A discount rate should be calculated which is specific to the project, and which takes account of both the project's systematic risk and the company's gearing level.

5.11 A discount rate can be found using the CAPM, although the discount rate that is calculated is not exactly correct. A method that can be used is as follows.

(a) ***Step 1***. Get an estimate of the systematic risk characteristics of the project's operating cash flows by obtaining published beta values for companies in the industry into which the company is planning to diversify.

(b) ***Step 2***. Adjust these beta values to allow for the company's capital gearing level. This adjustment is done in two stages.

    (i) ***Step 2A***. Convert the beta values of other companies in the industry to ungeared betas, using the formula:

$$\beta_a = \frac{\beta_e}{\left(1 + \dfrac{D\,(1-t)}{E}\right)}$$

    (ii) ***Step 2B***. Having obtained an ungeared beta value β_a, convert it back to a geared beta β_e, which reflects the company's own gearing ratio, using the formula:

$$\beta_e = \beta_a \left(1 + \frac{D\,(1-t)}{E}\right)$$

(c) ***Step 3***. Having estimated a project-specific geared beta, use the CAPM to estimate:

    (i) A project-specific cost of equity, and

    (ii) A project-specific cost of capital, based on a weighting of this cost of equity and the cost of the company's debt capital

5.12 EXAMPLE: CAPM (10)

A company's debt:equity ratio, by market values, is 2:5. The corporate debt, which is assumed to be risk-free, yields 11% before tax. The beta value of the company's equity is currently 1.1. The average returns on stock market equity are 16%.

The company is now proposing to invest in a project which would involve diversification into a new industry, and the following information is available about this industry.

(a) Average beta coefficient of equity capital = 1.59
(b) Average debt:equity ratio in the industry = 1:2 (by market value).

The rate of corporation tax is 30%. What would be a suitable cost of capital to apply to the project?

5.13 SOLUTION

Convert the geared beta value for the industry to an ungeared beta for the industry.

$$\beta_a = \frac{1.59}{1 + \frac{1(1 - 0.30)}{2}} = 1.18$$

Convert this ungeared industry beta back into a geared beta, which reflects the company's own gearing level of 2:5.

$$\beta_e = 1.18 \left(1 + \frac{2(1 - 0.30)}{5}\right) = 1.51$$

5.14 This is a project-specific beta for the firm's equity capital, and so using the CAPM, we can estimate the project-specific cost of equity as:

$$K_{eg} = 11\% + 1.51(16\% - 11\%) = 18.55\%$$

5.15 The project will presumably be financed in a gearing ratio of 2:5 debt to equity, and so the project-specific cost of capital ought to be:

$$[\frac{5}{7} \times 18.55\%] + [\frac{2}{7} \times 70\% \times 11\%] = 15.45\%$$

Question 3

Two companies are identical in every respect except for their capital structure. XY plc has a debt: equity ratio of 1:3, and its equity has a β value of 1.20. PQ plc has a debt:equity ratio of 2:3. Corporation tax is at 30%. Estimate a β value for PQ plc's equity.

Answer

Estimate an ungeared beta from XY plc data.

$$\beta_a = \frac{1.20}{1 + \frac{1(0.70)}{3}} = 0.973$$

Estimate a geared beta for PQ plc using this ungeared beta.

$$\beta_e = 0.973 \left[1 + \frac{2(0.70)}{3}\right] = 1.427.$$

The usefulness and the limitations of the CAPM for capital investment decisions   12/97

5.16   The CAPM produces a required return based on the expected return of the market, expected project returns, the risk-free interest rate and the variability of project returns relative to the market returns. Its main advantage when used for investment appraisal is that it produces a discount rate which is based on the systematic risk of the individual investment. It can be used to compare projects of all different risk classes and is therefore superior to an NPV approach which uses only one discount rate for all projects, regardless of their risk.

5.17   The model was developed with respect to securities; by applying it to an investment within the firm, the company is assuming that the shareholder wishes investments to be evaluated as if they were securities in the capital market and thus assumes that all shareholders will hold diversified portfolios and will not look to the company to achieve diversification for them.

5.18   The greatest **practical problems** with the use of the CAPM in capital investment decisions are as follows.

  (a)   It is hard to estimate returns on projects under **different economic environments**, market returns under different economic environments and the probabilities of the various environments.

  (b)   The CAPM is really just a **single period model**. Few investment projects last for one year only and to extend the use of the return estimated from the model to more than one time period would require both project performance relative to the market and the economic environment to be reasonably stable.

   In theory, it should be possible to apply the CAPM for each time period, thus arriving at successive discount rates, one for each year of the project's life. In practice, this would exacerbate the estimation problems mentioned above and also make the discounting process much more cumbersome.

  (c)   It may be hard to determine the risk-free rate of return. Government securities are usually taken to be risk-free, but the return on these securities varies according to their term to maturity.

6   THE ARBITRAGE PRICING MODEL   12/95, 12/97

> **Exam focus point**
>
> What is important here is to be aware that there are other models apart from the CAPM, and to know the benefits and limitations of the arbitrage pricing model relative to the CAPM.
>
> A common error in the 12/97 exam was to confuse the model with adjusted present value (APV) or with arbitrage as applied to Modigliani and Miller's theory of capital structure.

6.1   The CAPM is seen as a useful analytical tool by financial managers as well as by financial analysts. However, critics suggest that the relationship between risk and return is more complex than is assumed in the CAPM. One model which could replace the CAPM in the future is the **arbitrage pricing model** (APM).

6.2   Unlike the CAPM, which analyses the returns on a share as a function of a single factor - the return on the market portfolio, the APM assumes that the return on each security is based on a number of independent factors. The actual return r on any security is shown as:

$$r = E(r_j) + \beta_1 F_1 + \beta_2 F_2 \dots + e$$

where $E(r_j)$ is the expected return on the security
β_1 is the sensitivity to changes in factor 1
F_1 is the difference between actual and expected values of factor 1
β_2 is the sensitivity to changes in factor 2
F_2 is the difference between actual and expected values of factor 2
e is a random term

6.3   **Factor analysis** is used to ascertain the factors to which security returns are sensitive. Four key factors identified by researchers have been: unanticipated inflation; changes in the expected level of industrial production; changes in the risk premium on bonds (debentures); and unanticipated changes in the term structure of interest rates.

6.4   If a certain combination of securities is expected to produce higher returns than is indicated by its risk sensitivities, then traders will engage in arbitrage trading to improve the expected returns. It has been demonstrated that when no further arbitrage opportunities exist, the expected return $E(r_j)$ can be shown as:

$$E(r_j) = r_f + \beta_1(r_1 - r_f) + \beta_2(r_2 - r_f) \dots$$

where r_f is the risk-free rate of return
r_1 is the expected return on a portfolio with unit sensitivity to factor 1 and no sensitivity to any other factor
r_2 is the expected return on a portfolio with unit sensitivity to factor 2 and no sensitivity to any other factor

6.5   This implies that the expected rate of return on a security is a function of the risk-free rate of return plus risk premiums $((r_1 - r_f), (r_2 - r_f)$ etc) depending on the sensitivity of the security to various factors such as the four factors identified in Paragraph 6.3 above.

6.6   With the APM, the CAPM's problem of identifying the market portfolio is avoided, but this replaced with the problem of identifying the macroeconomic factors and their risk sensitivities. As is the case with the CAPM, what empirical evidence is available is inconclusive and neither proves nor disproves the theory of the APM. Both the CAPM and the APM do however provide a means of analysing how risk and return may be determined in conditions of competition and uncertainty.

6.7   In an article published in the ACCA *Students' Newsletter* (January 1995), R A Hill points out that the APM has the advantage over the CAPM that it explains the pricing of securities in relation to each other, rather than relative to a market portfolio.

6.8   While the CAPM focuses upon the linear relationship between beta factors and returns, the APM breaks systematic risk into smaller components which need not be specified in advance. Any factor affecting investor returns, for example an unexpected change in the rate of inflation, can be incorporated into the APM. Research corroborates the 4-factor APM. Although the APM differs in detail from the CAPM, the model is still something of a simplification, relying as it does on portfolio theory (originally developed by Markowitz) and its accompanying assumptions, including the questionable efficient markets hypothesis (EMH).

Chapter roundup

- The **CAPM** has many applications, as we have seen in this chapter. However, you should not think of it as the only approach to the cost of equity, or to project appraisal. You should learn the formulae, not only to be able to use them but also to be able to criticise the CAPM.

- The **risk** involved in holding securities (shares) divides into risk specific to the company and risk due to variations in market activity.

- **Unsystematic** or **business risk** can be diversified away, while **systematic** or **market risk** cannot. Investors may mix a diversified market portfolio with risk-free assets to achieve a preferred mix of risk and return on the Capital Market Line (see Chapter 7). The required return on shares includes a risk premium in respect of systematic risk only.

- If we assume a perfect capital market, then the following equations link CAPM and Modigliani and Miller, and are all consistent with one another.

$$V_g = V_u + Dt$$

$$WACC = Ke_u \left[1 - \frac{Dt}{E + D} \right] \qquad *$$

$$E(r_j) = r_f + [E(r_m) - r_f]\beta_j \qquad *$$

$$\beta_a = \beta_e \frac{E}{E + D(1 - t)} + \beta_d \frac{D(1 - t)}{E + D(1 - t)} \qquad *$$

*These formulae are included on the Paper 14 **Formulae Sheet**.

- You should be aware of the **arbitrage pricing model**, which could replace the capital asset pricing model in the future as a tool for analysing the determination of risk and return.

Quick quiz

1 Distinguish between systematic risk and unsystematic risk. (see para 1.3)

2 What is meant by a share's beta factor? (1.18)

3 State the formula for the CAPM (the security market line). (1.25)

4 What is meant by a share's alpha value? (1.26)

5 Which portfolios will have a beta factor of (a) one and (b) zero? (3.1)

6 Explain briefly how the gearing of a company affects its beta value. (4.1)

7 What is the difference between using the CAPM and using the dividend valuation model for calculating a cost of equity and a WACC? (5.8 - 5.9)

8 Outline the main practical problems in using the CAPM in capital investment decisions. (5.18)

9 Outline the main features of the arbitrage pricing model (APM). (6.2 - 6.5)

Question to try	Level	Marks	Time
8	Exam standard	35	63 mins

BPP PUBLISHING

Chapter 9

CORPORATE DIVIDEND POLICY

Chapter topic list	Syllabus reference
1 Dividends and retentions	3(f)
2 Dividend growth and market value	3(f)
3 Theories of dividend policy	3(f)
4 Practical aspects of dividend policy	3(f)

Introduction

In this chapter, we deal with the question of how much should be paid out by a company to its shareholders in the form of **dividends**. What is the effect of dividend policy on share prices? What are the practical influences on dividend policy, including the effects of taxation?

We shall be discussing the views on dividend policy of **Modigliani and Miller**, whose theories were discussed in Chapter 6. Part of the chapter is based on the **fundamental theory of share values**, which was described in Chapter 4.

1 DIVIDENDS AND RETENTIONS 12/95

1.1 Funds generated from **retained earnings** are the single most important source of finance for UK companies. For any company, the amount of earnings retained within the business has a direct impact on the amount of dividends. Profit re-invested as retained earnings is profit that could have been paid as a dividend.

1.2 The major reasons for using retained earnings to finance new investments, rather than to pay higher dividends and then raise new equity funds for the new investments, are as follows.

   (a) The dividend policy of a company is in practice determined by the directors. From their standpoint, funds from retained earnings are an attractive source of finance because investment projects can be undertaken without involving either the shareholders or any outsiders.

   (b) The use of retained earnings as opposed to new shares or debentures avoids issue costs.

   (c) The use of funds from retained earnings avoids the possibility of a change in control resulting from an issue of new shares.

1.3 Another factor that may be of importance is the **financial and taxation position of the company's shareholders**. If, for example, because of taxation considerations, they would rather make a capital profit (which will only be taxed when the shares are sold) than receive current income, then finance through retained earnings would be preferred to other methods.

1.4 A company must restrict its self-financing through retained profits because shareholders should be paid a reasonable dividend, in line with realistic expectations, even if the directors would rather keep the funds for re-investing. At the same time, a company that is looking for extra funds will not be expected by investors (such as banks) to pay generous dividends, nor over-generous salaries to owner-directors.

1.5 Dividends are usually paid by UK public companies twice a year. An **interim dividend** is paid after the publication of the interim results of the company for the first half year. A **final dividend** is paid after the annual accounts for the year have been published, and after the proposed dividend has been agreed by shareholders at the Annual General Meeting.

1.6 It is usual for shareholders to have the power to vote to **reduce** the size of the final (proposed) dividend at the AGM, but not the power to **increase** the dividend. The directors of the company are therefore in a strong position, with regard to shareholders, when it comes to determining dividend policy. For practical purposes, shareholders will usually be obliged to accept the dividend policy that has been decided on by the directors, or otherwise to sell their shares.

2   DIVIDEND GROWTH AND MARKET VALUE

Dividend policy and share prices

2.1 The purpose of a dividend policy should be to maximise shareholders' wealth, which depends on both current dividends and capital gains. Capital gains can be achieved by retaining some earnings for reinvestment and dividend growth in the future.

2.2 According to what can be termed the **'residual theory'**, maximisation of shareholder wealth will be achieved by applying the following rules.

(a) If a company can identify projects with positive NPVs, it should invest in them.
(b) Only when these investment opportunities are exhausted should dividends be paid.

Growth in dividends

2.3 The rate of growth in dividends is sometimes expressed, theoretically, as:

$g = rb$

where   g is the annual growth rate in dividends
         r is the rate of return on new investments
         b is the proportion of profits that are retained

2.4   EXAMPLE: DIVIDEND GROWTH

(a) If a company has a payout ratio of 40%, and retains the rest for investing in projects which yield 15%, the annual rate of growth in dividends could be estimated as $15\% \times 60\% = 9\%$.

(b) If a company pays out 80% of its profits as dividends, and retains the rest for reinvestment at 15%, the current dividend would be twice as big as in (a), but annual dividend growth would be only $15\% \times 20\% = 3\%$.

An approach to dividend policy, based on fundamental analysis of share values

2.5   A theoretical approach to dividend and retentions policy can be based on the fundamental theory of share values. We will make the following assumptions.

   (a)   The market value of a company's shares depends on the **size of dividends paid**, the **rate of growth in dividends** and the **shareholders' required rate of return**.

   (b)   The rate of growth in dividends depends on how much money is reinvested in the company, and so on the rate of earnings retention.

   (c)   Shareholders will want their company to pursue a retentions policy that maximises the value of their shares.

2.6   The basic dividend-based formula for the market value of shares P_0 is:

$$P_0 = \frac{D_1}{r}$$

where D_1 is a constant annual dividend, and r is the shareholders' required rate of return. Given that this formula assumes a **constant dividend**, with no dividend growth at all, an assumption on which this formula is based is that all earnings are paid out as dividends.

2.7   Using the **dividend growth model**, we have:

$$P_0 = \frac{D_0(1+g)}{(r-g)}$$

where D_0 is the current year's dividend (year 0) and g is the growth rate in earnings and dividends, so $D_0(1 + g)$ is the expected dividend in one year's time. P_0 is the market value excluding any dividend currently payable.

2.8   EXAMPLE: DIVIDEND GROWTH MODEL

Tantrum plc has achieved earnings of £800,000 this year. The company intends to pursue a policy of financing all its investment opportunities out of retained earnings. There are considerable investment opportunities, which are expected to be available indefinitely. However, if Tantrum plc does not exploit any of the available opportunities, its annual earnings will remain at £800,000 in perpetuity. The following figures are available.

Proportion of earnings retained	Growth rate in earnings	Required return on all investments by shareholders
%	%	%
0	0	14
25	5	15
40	7	16

The rate of return required by shareholders would rise if earnings are retained, because of the risk associated with the new investments.

What is the optimum retentions policy for Tantrum plc? The full dividend payment for this year will be paid in the near future in any case.

2.9 SOLUTION

Since $P_0 = \dfrac{D_0(1+g)}{(r-g)}$

the market value cum dividend is given by:

$$\text{MV cum div} = \frac{D_0(1+g)}{(r-g)} + D_0$$

We are trying to maximise the value of shareholder wealth, which is currently represented by the *cum div* market value, since a dividend will soon be paid.

(a) If retentions are 0%, the market value cum dividend is given by:

$$\text{MV cum div} = \frac{800,000}{0.14} + 800,000$$

$$= £6,514,286$$

(b) If retentions are 25%, the current dividend will be £600,000 and:

$$\text{MV cum div} = \frac{600,000(1.05)}{(0.15-0.05)} + 600,000$$

$$= £6,900,000$$

(c) If retentions are 40%, the current dividend will be £480,000 and:

$$\text{MV cum div} = \frac{480,000(1.07)}{(0.16-0.07)} + 480,000$$

$$= £6,186,667$$

The best policy (out of the three for which figures are provided) would be to retain 25% of earnings.

Dividend policy and shareholders' personal taxation

2.10 The market value of a share has been defined as the sum of all future dividends, discounted at the shareholder's marginal cost of capital. When constant dividends are expected, we have:

$$P_0 = \frac{D_0}{r}$$

2.11 The cost of capital is generally taken to be a **tax-free** rate, ignoring the actual rates of personal taxation paid on dividends by different shareholders. To each individual shareholder, however, the dividends are subject to income tax at a rate which depends on his own tax position, and it is possible to re-define his valuation of a share as:

$$P_0 = \frac{D_g(1-t)}{r_t}$$

where D_g is the gross dividend (assumed to be constant each year)
         t is the rate of personal tax on the dividend
         r_t is the shareholder's after tax marginal cost of capital

2.12 Presumably, a company should choose between dividend payout and earnings retention so as to maximise the wealth of its shareholders; however, if not all shareholders have the same tax rates and after tax cost of capital, there might not be an optimum policy which satisfies all shareholders. By what is referred to as the **clientele effect**, companies may attract particular types of shareholders seeking particular dividend policies.

> **KEY TERM**
>
> The term **clientele effect** describes the tendency of companies to attract particular types of shareholders because of their management organisation and policies, particularly dividend policies.

2.13 A further problem occurs when income from dividends might be taxed either more or less heavily than capital gains. Note that in the UK, individuals have an annual capital gains exemption which is not available for setting against income, and companies are taxed on capital gains but not on dividend income.

2.14 Since the purpose of a dividend policy should be to maximise the wealth of shareholders, it is important to consider whether it would be better to pay a dividend now, subject to tax on income, or to retain earnings so as to increase the shareholders' capital gains (which will be subject to capital gains tax when the shareholders eventually sell their shares).

2.15 A major set of shareholders for UK listed companies is the **pension funds** sector. Up to 1997, these investors were able to claim back tax credits on dividends received, but this was changed in 1997 by the new Labour Government. This change could have a significant effect on the way that this particular **clientele** views dividends. Dividend yield becomes less important, and the pension funds no longer have the same reason to prefer dividends over capital gains.

3 THEORIES OF DIVIDEND POLICY

Residual theory

3.1 A '**residual**' theory of **dividend policy** can be summarised as follows.

(a) If a company can identify projects with positive NPVs, it should invest in them.
(b) Only when these investment opportunities are exhausted should dividends be paid.

Traditional view

3.2 The '**traditional**' view of dividend policy, implicit in our earlier discussion, is to focus on the effects on share price. The price of a share depends upon the mix of dividends, given shareholders' required rate of return, and growth. Accordingly, the rate at which dividends are paid does matter to shareholders.

$$r = \frac{d_1}{p_0} + g \qquad\qquad \therefore P_0 = \frac{d_1}{(r-g)} = \frac{d_0(1+g)}{(r-g)}$$

Irrelevancy theory

3.3 In contrast to the traditional view, **Modigliani and Miller** (MM) proposed that in a tax-free world, shareholders are indifferent between dividends and capital gains, and the value of a company is determined solely by the 'earning power' of its assets and investments.

3.4 MM argued that if a company with investment opportunities decides to pay a dividend, so that retained earnings are insufficient to finance all its investments, the shortfall in funds will be made up by obtaining additional funds from outside sources. The consequent loss of value in the existing shares, as a result of obtaining outside finance instead of using retained earnings, is exactly equal to the amount of the dividend paid. A company should therefore be indifferent between paying a dividend (and obtaining new outside funds) and retaining earnings.

3.5 In answer to criticisms that certain shareholders will show a preference either for high dividends or for capital gains, MM argued that if a company pursues a consistent dividend policy, 'each corporation would tend to attract to itself a clientele consisting of those preferring its particular payout ratio, but one clientele would be entirely as good as another in terms of the valuation it would imply for the firm'.

The case in favour of the relevance of dividend policy (and against MM's views)

3.6 There are strong arguments against MM's view that dividend policy is irrelevant as a means of affecting shareholder's wealth.

(a) Differing rates of taxation on dividends and capital gains can create a preference for a high dividend or one for high earnings retention.

(b) Dividend retention should be preferred by companies in a period of capital rationing.

(c) Due to imperfect markets and the possible difficulties of selling shares easily at a fair price, shareholders might need high dividends in order to have funds to invest in opportunities outside the company.

(d) Markets are not perfect. Because of transaction costs on the sale of shares, investors who want some cash from their investments should prefer to receive dividends rather than to sell some of their shares to get the cash they want.

(e) Information available to shareholders is imperfect, and they are not aware of the future investment plans and expected profits of their company. Even if management were to provide them with profit forecasts, these forecasts would not necessarily be accurate or believable.

   (i) As a consequence of imperfect information, companies are normally expected at least to maintain the same level of dividends from one year to the next. They are expected to pay a constant dividend or an increased dividend, but not a lower dividend than the year before. Failure to maintain the dividend level would undermine investors' confidence in the future.

   (ii) In practice, undertaking a new investment project with a positive NPV will not immediately increase the market value of shares by the amount of the NPV because markets do not show strong-form efficiency. It is only gradually, as the profits from the investment begin to show up in the profits and dividends in historical financial statements, that the market value of the shares will rise.

(f) Perhaps the strongest argument against the MM view is that shareholders will tend to prefer a current dividend to future capital gains (or deferred dividends) because the future is more uncertain.

4 PRACTICAL ASPECTS OF DIVIDEND POLICY   12/96, 6/99

4.1 So far, we have concentrated on theoretical approaches to establishing an optimal dividend and retentions policy. A practical approach to dividends and retentions should take various factors into consideration.

BPP PUBLISHING

(a) The **need to remain profitable**. Dividends are paid out of profits, and an unprofitable company cannot for ever go on paying dividends out of retained profits made in the past.

(b) The **law on distributable profits**.

(c) Any **dividend restraints** which might be imposed by loan agreements.

(d) The **effect of inflation**, and the need to retain some profit within the business just to maintain its operating capability unchanged.

(e) The company's **gearing level**. If the company wants extra finance, the sources of funds used should strike a balance between equity and debt finance. Retained earnings are the most readily available source of growth in equity finance.

(f) The company's **liquidity position**. Dividends are a cash payment, and a company must have enough cash to pay the dividends it declares.

(g) The ease with which the company could raise **extra finance** from sources other than retained earnings. Small companies which find it hard to raise finance might have to rely more heavily on retained earnings than large companies.

4.2 If a company wants extra finance to invest, retained earnings can be obtained without incurring transaction costs. Costs of raising new share capital can be high, and even bank borrowings can be quite expensive.

Dividends as a signal to investors

> **KEY TERM**
>
> **Signalling**: the use of dividend policy to indicate the future prospects of an enterprise.

4.3 Although the market would like to value shares on the basis of underlying cash flows on the company's projects, such information is not readily available to investors. however, the directors do have this information. The dividend declared can be interpreted as a **signal** from directors to shareholders about the strength of underlying project cash flows. Directors can signal to the market in other ways also: the issue of debt, which commits the company to paying interest, can be interpreted as a signal of strong project cash flows, as compared with the issue of equity. Such 'signals' are likely to be taken as more reliable than anything which the directors say, since they involve actual commitments or movements of cash.

4.4 Investors usually expect a consistent dividend policy from the company, with stable dividends each year or, even better, steady dividend growth. A large rise or fall in dividends in any year can have a marked effect on the company's share price. Stable dividends or steady dividend growth are usually needed for share price stability. A cut in dividends may be treated by investors as signalling that the future prospects of the company are weak. Thus, the dividend which is paid acts, possibly without justification, as a signal of the future prospects of the company.

4.5 The signalling effect of a company's dividend policy may also be used by management of a company which faces a possible takeover. The dividend level might be increased as a defence against the takeover: investors may take the increased dividend as a signal of improved future prospects, thus driving the share price higher and making the company more expensive for a potential bidder to take over.

> ## Exam focus point
> You should make a point of showing in exam answers, where it is relevant, that you appreciate the signalling effect of dividends.

Scrip dividends, scrip issues and stock splits

4.6 A **scrip dividend** is a dividend payment which takes the form of new shares instead of cash. Effectively, it converts profit reserves into issued share capital. When the directors of a company would prefer to retain funds within the business but consider that they must pay at least a certain amount of dividend, they might offer equity shareholders the choice of a cash dividend or a scrip dividend of more shares in the company. Recently (particularly since 1993) **enhanced scrip dividends** have been offered by a number of companies. With enhanced scrip dividends, the value of the shares offered is much greater than the cash alternative, giving investors an incentive to choose the shares.

4.7 A **scrip** or **bonus issue** (also known as a **capitalisation issue**) involves the issue of new shares to existing shareholders in proportion to their existing holdings. Such an issue has the effect of reducing the retained earnings (profit and loss) account and increasing the called up share capital account. Obviously there is no net raising of cash, nor any increase in the value of shareholders' equity. Whether there is any point to the process (other than reducing the price per share and hence possibly increasing share trading liquidity) is open to debate. If there is, then it is either because shareholders are not as clever as we think they are, or because there are associated 'signals' that commonly accompany the scrip issue, eg perhaps that the dividend per share is to be maintained on the increased number of shares and hence the directors believe future company cashflows will be favourable.

4.8 This possible advantage of a scrip issue is also the reason for a **stock split**. A stock split occurs where, for example, each ordinary share of £1 each is split into two shares of 50p each, thus creating cheaper shares with greater marketability. There is possibly an added psychological advantage, in that investors may expect a company which splits its shares in this way to be planning for substantial earnings growth and dividend growth in the future. As a consequence, the market price of shares may benefit. For example, if one existing share of £1 has a market value of £6, and is then split into two shares of 50p each, the market value of the new shares might settle at, say, £3.10 instead of the expected £3, in anticipation of strong future growth in earnings and dividends.

4.9 The difference between a stock split and a scrip issue is that a scrip issue converts equity reserves into share capital, whereas a stock split leaves reserves unaffected. Both are popular with investors as they are seen as likely to lead to increased dividends. Scrip dividends can, however, lead to tax complications for individual investors.

Question

Ochre plc is a company that is still managed by the two individuals who set it up 12 years ago. In the current year, the company acquired plc status and was launched on the second tier Alternative Investment Market (AIM). Previously, all of the shares had been owned by its two founders and certain employees. Now, 40% of the shares are in the hands of the investing public. The company's profit growth and dividend policy are set out below. Will a continuation of the same dividend policy as in the past be suitable now that the company is quoted on the AIM?

Year	Profits £'000	Dividend £'000	Shares in issue
4 years ago	176	88	800,000
3 years ago	200	104	800,000
2 years ago	240	120	1,000,000
1 year ago	290	150	1,000,000
Current year	444	222 (proposed)	1,500,000

Answer

Year	Dividend per share	Dividend as % of profit
4 years ago	11.0	50%
3 years ago	13.0	52%
2 years ago	12.0	50%
1 year ago	15.0	52%
Current year	14.8	50%

The company appears to have pursued a dividend policy of paying out half of after-tax profits in dividend. This policy is only suitable when a company achieves a stable EPS or steady EPS growth. Investors do not like a fall in dividend from one year to the next, and the fall in dividend per share in the current year is likely to be unpopular, and to result in a fall in the share price.

The company would probably serve its shareholders better by paying a dividend of at least 15p per share, possibly more, in the current year, even though the dividend as a percentage of profit would then be higher.

Chapter roundup

- **Retained earnings** remain the most important single course of finance for UK companies, and financial managers should take account of the proportion of earnings which are retained as opposed to being paid as dividends.

- Companies generally **smooth out** dividend payments by adjusting only gradually to changes in earnings: large fluctuations might undermine **investors'** confidence.

- The dividends a company pays may be treated as a **signal** to investors. A company needs to take account of different **clienteles** of shareholders in deciding what dividends to pay.

- **Modigliani and Miller's theories** suggest that dividend policy is irrelevant to shareholder wealth in perfect capital markets. Given the imperfections in real-world markets and in taxation policies, the position is not so clear.

Quick quiz

1 What reasons are there for using retained earnings to finance new investments? (see para 1.2)

2 Explain the clientele effect. (2.12 - 2.15)

3 Outline Modigliani and Miller's views on the irrelevance of dividend policy. (3.4 - 3.6)

4 What is meant by 'signalling' in the context of dividends? (4.3 - 4.5)

Question to try	Level	Marks	Time
9	Introductory	n/a	25 mins

Part B

Business planning

Chapter 10

BUSINESS PLANNING AND FINANCIAL PLANNING

Chapter topic list	Syllabus reference
1 Planning and control	2(a), (b), (c), (d)
2 Strategic planning, management control and operational control	2(a), (b), (c), (d)
3 Capital structure and cash flow	2(a), (b), (c), (d)
4 Pricing	2(d)

Introduction

Before covering **ratio analysis** as a part of business financial planning (in Chapter 12), we look in Chapters 10 and 11 at more general aspects of **business planning**, **financial planning** and **control**. Your knowledge from Paper 12 *Management and Strategy* will be relevant here.

1   PLANNING AND CONTROL   12/95

1.1   Koontz (1958) wrote:

> 'Planning and control are so closely interconnected as to be singularly inseparable'.

> 'The fact that there seem ... to be so many fewer principles of control than principles of planning indicates the extent to which control depends upon planning and how it is largely a technique for assuring that plans are realised.'

1.2   As an alternative analysis of planning and control systems, Robert N Anthony (*Planning and control systems: A framework for analysis*) suggested that there are three levels or tiers within a decision-making hierarchy.

(a)   **Strategic planning**: 'the process of deciding on objectives of the organisation, on changes in these objectives, on the resources used to attain these objectives, and on the policies that are to govern the acquisition, use and disposition of these resources'

(b)   **Management control**: 'the process by which managers assure that resources are obtained and used effectively and efficiently in the accomplishment of the organisation's objectives'. Management control can alternatively be called **tactical control**

(c)   **Operational control**: 'the process of assuring that specific tasks are carried out effectively and efficiently'

1.3   In spite of the possibly misleading use of the words 'planning' and 'control' in these three titles, each level of decision-making includes elements of both planning and control (although perhaps in varying proportions).

BPP PUBLISHING

2 STRATEGIC PLANNING, MANAGEMENT CONTROL AND OPERATIONAL CONTROL

Strategic planning

2.1 We discussed objectives of organisations in the first chapter of this text. **Strategic plans** are those which set or change the objectives, or strategic targets of an organisation. They include such matters as the selection of products and markets, the required levels of company profitability, the purchase and disposal of subsidiary companies or major fixed assets, and whether employees should share in company profits. Johnson and Scholes suggest that strategy within an organisation might be classified into three levels, as we saw in Chapter 1.

Question 1

Think about, and jot down notes on, aspects of the three levels of strategy identified by Johnson and Scholes in your own organisation.

Reminder: these are corporate strategy; business or competitive strategy; operational strategy.

Management control

2.2 **Management control** is at the level below strategic planning in Anthony's decision-making hierarchy. Whilst strategic planning is concerned with setting objectives and strategic targets, management control is concerned with decisions about the efficient and effective use of an organisation's resources to achieve these objectives or targets.

(a) Resources are: personnel, materials, machines and money.

(b) Efficiency in the use of resources means that optimum output is achieved from the input resources used.

(c) Effectiveness in the use of resources means that the resources are used to reach the intended objectives or targets.

2.3 Management control planning is **tactical planning** and would include activities such as the following.

(a) Preparing budgets of production, stock levels
(b) Establishing departmental measures of performance (eg return on capital employed)
(c) Developing a product for launching in the market
(d) Planning advertising and marketing campaigns
(e) Establishing a line-of-authority structure for the organisation

2.4 **Long-term financial plans** are implemented by converting them into short-term plans or **budgets**. Most operating budgets cover a period of one year. Some budgets, notably capital expenditure budgets, might cover a period of several years.

2.5 No corporate plan has the detail or 'accuracy' that a budget has. Consequently, the tolerance limits giving 'early warning' or deviations from the plan should be wider. For example, if tolerance limits in budgetary control are variance $\pm$ 5% from standard, then corporate planning tolerance limits might be set at $\pm$ 10% or more from targets.

2.6 Data about actual results can be used to **revise forecasts** about what is likely to happen in the future. Managers need information about whether actual results so far show that short-term targets have been met. They also need to know whether longer-term targets are likely to be met.

2.7 Control at a strategic level calls for the continuous revision of forecasts. A simple numerical example might help to explain this. Suppose that in 20X1, a company forecasts its future return on capital employed, year by year for the next five years, as follows.

Year	20X2	20X3	20X4	20X5	20X6
Return	12%	13.5%	15%	16%	17%

In 20X2, the forecast might be revised in view of actual results in 20X2, as follows.

Year	20X2 *(actual result)*	20X3 *(forecast)*	20X4	20X5	20X6	20X7
Return	11.5%	12.5%	14%	15.5%	16.5%	17%

The revised forecast in 20X2 would show that the forecast return each year will be less than originally planned in 20X1, and that a return of 17% would not now be achieved until 20X7. This revised forecast could be used as either to take control action to try to improve the forecast return each year, back to the levels that were originally planned in 20X1, or to revise the strategic planning targets.

2.8 **Control at a strategic level**, and the **review of strategic plans**, should therefore be an iterative process, with **revised forecasts** for the future being an important part of the control information.

Management control and strategic planning compared

2.9 The dividing line between **strategic planning** and **management control** is not a clear one. Matters such as the optimum siting of a transport depot, for example, include issues ranging from the strategic to the tactical. Nevertheless, there is a basic distinction between the two levels of decision.

(a) The decision to launch a new brand of calorie-controlled frozen foods is a strategic plan (business strategy), but the choice of ingredients for the frozen meals involves a management control decision.

(b) A decision that the market share for a product should be 25% is a strategic plan (competitive strategy), but the selection of a sales price of £2 per unit, supported by other marketing decisions about sales promotion, direct sales effort etc to achieve the required market share, would be a series of management control decisions.

2.10 Management control tends to be carried out in a series of **regular planning and comparison procedures** (annually, monthly or weekly). For example, a budget is usually prepared annually, and control reports issued every month or four weeks. Strategic planning, in contrast, might be irregular and occur when opportunities arise or are identified.

Information requirements

2.11 The **information** required for management control embraces the entire organisation, just as a master budget includes all aspects of the organisation's activities. A system must exist for planning, measuring, comparing and controlling the efforts of every department or profit centre. The information is often quantitative (eg labour hours, quantities of materials consumed, volumes of sales and production) and is commonly expressed in money terms.

2.12 Management control information may by analysed in several different ways, for example an analysis may be made of production costs or departmental costs, but the total costs will be the same, whatever analysis is used. It will also be apparent that much management control information is obtained by measuring the activities and output of the organisation, as **feedback**.

2.13 In contrast, strategic planning information is obtained to some extent from **internally measured data**, but to a far greater extent from **environmental data** - external data about competitors, customers, suppliers, new technology, the state of markets and the economy, government legislation, political unrest and so on. It also tends to be more approximate and imprecise than management control information.

Conflict between management control and strategic planning activities

2.14 It is quite common for strategic plans to be in conflict with the shorter term objectives of management control. Examples are as follows.

(a) It might be in the long-term interests of a company to buy more expensive or technologically advanced machinery to make a product, in the expectation that when market demand for the product eventually declines, customers will buy from producers whose output is of a slightly better quality - ie made on better machinery. In the short run, however, new and expensive machinery will incur higher depreciation charges and therefore higher unit costs for the same volume of production. Since higher costs will reduce profit, considerations of 'management control' would suggest the existing old machinery should be worn out before replacement.

(b) Similarly, it may be in the long-term interests of a company to invest in research and development, in spite of the costs and loss of profits in the short term.

Operational control

2.15 The third and lowest tier in Anthony's hierarchy of decision-making consists of **operational control** decisions. As we have seen, it is the task of ensuring that **specific tasks** are carried out effectively and efficiently. Just as 'management control' plans are set within the guidelines of strategic plans, so too are 'operational control' plans set within the guidelines of both strategic planning and management control.

2.16 Here is an example.

(a) Senior management may decide that the company should increase sales by 5% per annum for at least five years - a **strategic plan**.

(b) The sales director and senior sales managers will make plans to increase sales by 5% in the next year, with some provisional planning for future years. This involves planning direct sales resources, advertising, sales promotion and so on. Sales quotas are assigned to each sales territory - a **tactical plan** (management control).

(c) The manager of a sales territory specifies the weekly sales targets for each sales representative. This is **operational planning** - individuals are given tasks which they are expected to achieve.

Operational control and management control compared

2.17   Whereas tactical information for management control is often expressed in money terms, operational information, although quantitative, is more often expressed in terms of units, hours, quantities of material and so on. **Management control** decisions are generally taken by managers senior in the organisation to those who take operational control decisions.

2.18   Management control reports are often prepared monthly (although sometimes annually, or weekly). **Operational control** is exercised during and after the completion of individual tasks - ie more frequently. In the case of automated production, control is exercised minute by minute.

3   CAPITAL STRUCTURE, CASH FLOW AND PRICING

3.1   In this section of the chapter, we look at how capital structure, cash flow and pricing can influence business planning.

Capital structure

3.2   The assets of a business must be financed somehow, and when a business is growing, the additional assets must be financed by additional capital. There are different ways in which the funding of current and fixed assets can be achieved by employing long and short-term sources of funding. As you will already know, **capital structure** refers to the way in which an organisation is financed, by a combination of long-term capital (ordinary shares and reserves, preference shares, debentures, bank loans, convertible loan stock and so on) and short-term liabilities such as a bank overdraft and trade creditors.

3.3   The diagram below illustrates three alternative types of policy A, B and C. The dotted lines A, B and C are the cut-off levels between short-term and long-term financing for each of the policies A, B and C respectively: assets above the relevant dotted line are financed by short-term funding while assets below the dotted line are financed by long-term funding.

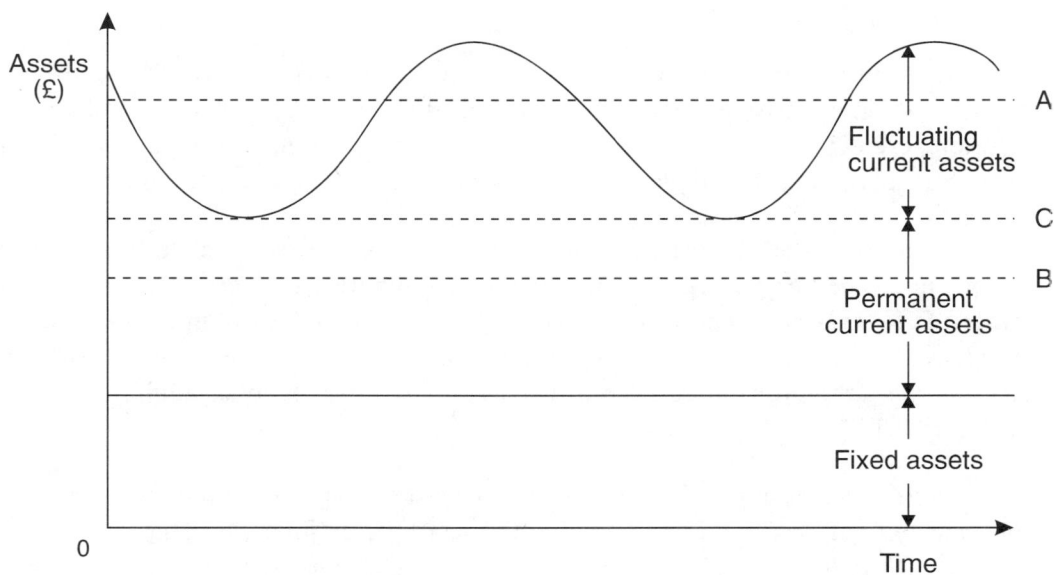

Financing policies

3.4   Fluctuating current assets together with permanent current assets form part of the working capital of the business, which may be financed by either long-term funding (including

BPP
PUBLISHING

equity capital) or by current liabilities (short-term funding). This can be seen in terms of policies A, B and C.

(a) Policy A can be characterised as a **conservative funding policy**. All fixed assets and permanent current assets, as well as part of the fluctuating current assets, are financed by long-term funding. There is only a need to call upon short-term financing at times when fluctuations in current assets push total assets above the level of dotted line A. At times when fluctuating current assets are low and total assets fall below line A, there will be surplus cash which the company will be able to invest in marketable securities.

(b) Policy B is a more **aggressive funding policy** in its approach to financing working capital. Not only are fluctuating current assets all financed out of short-term sources, but so are some of the permanent current assets. This policy represents an increased risk of liquidity and cash flow problems, although potential returns will be increased if short-term financing can be obtained more cheaply than long-term finance.

(c) A **balance** between risk and return might be best achieved by policy C, in which long-term funds finance permanent assets while short-term funds finance non-permanent assets.

Business confidence and expectations

3.5 **Business confidence** and **expectations of future profits** are crucial factors in the determination of how much debt capital investors are prepared to lend. The level of gearing which the market will allow will therefore depend on the nature of the company wishing to borrow more funds, and the industry in which it is engaged.

(a) A company which is involved in a cyclical business, where profits are subject to periodic ups and downs, should have a relatively low gearing.

(b) A company in a business where profits are stable should be able to raise a larger amount of debt.

Cash flow planning

3.6 A business must maintain an adequate inflow of cash in order to survive. If a business owes money and cannot pay its debts when they fall due, it can be put into liquidation by its creditors, even if it is making profits. Since a company must have adequate cash inflows to survive, management should plan and control cash flows as well as profitability.

3.7 **Cash budgeting** is an important element in short-term cash flow planning. Cash budget periods might be for one year, or less (for example monthly budgets). The purpose of cash budgets is to make sure that the organisation will have enough cash inflows to meet its cash outflows. If a budget reveals that a short-term cash shortage can be expected, steps will be taken to meet the problem and avoid the cash crisis (perhaps by arranging a bigger bank overdraft facility).

3.8 Cash budgets and cash flow forecasts on their own do not give full protection against a cash shortage and enforced liquidation of the business by creditors. There may be unexpected changes in cash flow patterns. Examples of unforeseen changes include the following.

(a) A change in the general **economic environment** (An economic recession will cause a slump in trade.)

(b) A **new product**, launched by a competitor, which takes business away from a company's traditional and established product lines

(c) New cost-saving product technology, which forces the company to invest in the new technology to remain competitive

(d) Moves by competitors which have to be countered (for example a price reduction or a sales promotion)

(e) Changes in consumer preferences, resulting in a fall in demand

(f) Government action against certain trade practices or against trade with a country that the company has dealings with

(g) Strikes or other industrial action

(h) Natural disasters, such as floods or fire damage, which curtail an organisation's activities

3.9 When unforeseen events have an adverse effect on cash inflows, a company will only survive if it can maintain adequate cash inflows despite the setbacks.

Strategic fund management

3.10 **Strategic fund management** is an extension of cash flow planning, which takes into consideration the ability of a business to overcome unforeseen problems with cash flows, recognising that the assets of a business can be divided into three categories.

(a) Assets which are needed to carry out the 'core' activities of the business. A group of companies will often have one or several main activities, and in addition will carry on several peripheral activities. The group's strategy should be primarily to develop its main activities, and so there has to be enough cash to maintain those activities and to finance their growth.

(b) Assets which are not essential for carrying out the main activities of the business, and which could be sold off at fairly short notice. These assets will consist mainly of short-term marketable investments.

(c) Assets which are not essential for carrying out the main activities of the business, and which could be sold off to raise cash, although it would probably take time to arrange the sale, and the amount of cash obtainable from the sale might be uncertain. These assets would include: long-term investments (for example, substantial shareholdings in other companies); subsidiary companies engaged in 'peripheral' activities, which might be sold off to another company or in a management buyout; and land and buildings.

3.11 If an unexpected event takes place which threatens a company's cash position, the company could meet the threat by:

(a) Working capital management to improve cash flows by reducing stocks and debtors, taking more credit, or negotiating a higher bank overdraft facility

(b) Changes to dividend policy

(c) Arranging to sell off non-essential assets.

The assets in category (b) above would be saleable at short notice, and arrangements could also be made to dispose of the assets in category (c), should the need arise and provided that there is enough time to arrange the sale.

Strategic cash flow planning

3.12 It is essential for the survival of any business to have an adequate inflow of cash. Cash flow planning at a strategic level is similar to normal cash budgeting, with the following exceptions.

BPP
PUBLISHING

(a) The **planning horizon** is longer.

(b) The **uncertainties** about future cash inflows and cash outflows are much greater.

(c) The business should be able to respond, if necessary, to an **unexpected need** for cash. Where could extra cash be raised, and in what amounts?

(d) A company should have planned cash flows which are consistent with:

    (i)   Its **dividend payment policy,** and
    (ii)   Its policy for **financial structuring, debt and gearing**

Question 2

Suppose that WXY plc had the following balance sheet as at 31 December 20X8.

	£
Fixed assets	3,500,000
Current assets less current liabilities	500,000
	4,000,000
Share capital	500,000
Reserves	1,600,000
Long-term 10% debt	1,900,000
	4,000,000

The company's strategic planners have formulated the following policies.

(a) By the end of the next year (31 December 20X9), gearing should not exceed 100% - ie long term debt should not exceed the total of share capital and reserves.

(b) The company shall pay out 50% of its profits as dividend to shareholders.

The following estimates have been made.

(a) Each £10,000 of assets generates profits of £2,000 pa, before interest.
(b) The current market cost of debt capital is 10% pa.

The company would like to invest a further £500,000 but does not intend to make a share issue to raise the finance. Advise its management. Could it borrow the money and still achieve its strategic targets by the end of 20X9? (Ignore taxation and fixed asset depreciation.)

Answer

The company's strategic aims *can* all be achieved, without a new share issue, even though it is already near the gearing limit it has set itself, of 100%.

A further £500,000 investment in capital would yield extra annual profits of £100,000 pa before interest.

Without a share issue, the £500,000 would have to be raised as a loan at 10%, raising the total company debt to £2,400,000 and total assets at the beginning of the year to £4,500,000.

		£
(1)	Profits before interest in 20X9 (£4,500,000 × 20%)	900,000
(2)	Interest (10% of £2,400,000)	240,000
(3)	Profits before dividend	660,000
(4)	Dividend (NB: taxation ignored)	330,000
(5)	Retained profits	330,000

Balance sheet at 31 December 20X9

Total assets (depreciation ignored)	£
At 31.12.X8	4,000,000
New investment	500,000
Retained profits	330,000
	4,830,000

Financed by	£
Share capital	500,000
Reserves	1,930,000
Debt capital	2,400,000
	4,830,000

The company's gearing would just about remain below the maximum target limit of 100%.

New investments/product developments

3.13 Investments in new projects, such as new product developments, use up cash in the short term, and it will not be for some years perhaps that good profits and cash inflows are earned from them.

3.14 One aspect of strategic cash flow planning is to try to achieve a balance between the following.

(a) Making and selling products which are still in their early stages of development, and are still 'soaking up' cash

(b) Making and selling products which are **'cash cows'** - ie established products which are earning good profits and good cash inflows

Cash-rich companies

3.15 A company should try to plan for adequate cash inflows, and be able to call on 'emergency' sources of cash in the event of an unforeseen need, but it might be unwise to hold too much cash.

3.16 When a company is **cash-rich**, it can invest the money, usually in short-term investments or deposits, such as the money market, to earn interest. However, for companies which are not in financial services or banking, the main function of money is to be spent. A cash-rich company could do one of the following.

(a) Plan to use the cash, for example for a project investment or a takeover bid for another company

(b) Pay out the cash to shareholders as dividends, and let the shareholders decide how best to use the cash for themselves

(c) Re-purchase its own shares

4 PRICING

4.1 There are three categories of pricing decision: **short-term pricing**; **competitive bidding**; **strategic pricing**.

Short-term pricing

4.2 There is an inter-relationship between sales price and the volume of demand, expressed as a demand curve. The extent to which sales demand varies with price changes is expressed as the **elasticity of demand**. Marketing management should have the responsibility for estimating the price-demand inter-relationship for their organisation's products.

4.3 An aspect of pricing is the offer of **discounts** for bulk purchases, or to major customers. The scope for offering discounts is dependent on the ratio of variable cost to gross selling price.

For example, if variable costs are 90% of gross sales value, a discount of 10% would wipe out all contribution, whereas if variable costs are, say, 40% of gross sales value, there is much more scope for discounts. Sales staff might be keen to offer attractive discounts to win sales, but data about variable costs and contribution margins must be available to make sure that the discounts offered are prudent.

Competitive bidding

4.4 **Competitive bidding** calls for the preparation of cost data for the purpose of submitting a bid to a potential customer, in the hope of securing his order. Many sales contracts, for example local government authority contracts, are not awarded without having to resort to competitive tender.

4.5 A balance has to be drawn between putting in a bid which is too low to make an adequate profit, but keeping the bid low enough to stand a good chance of winning the contract. Consideration must be given to the following.

 (a) The contribution to profit that would be obtained from the contract

 (b) The consequences for the company if it failed to win the order

 (c) The probability of winning the order, which might be assessed on the basis of past experience

4.6 Three other factors in the competitive pricing equation might be as follows.

 (a) A general price level may well exist, so that there is little likelihood of winning a contract on the basic price alone.

 (b) There may be scope for a quantity discount.

 (c) There may be some non-price product differentiation in favour of the supplier eg quality of service, reliable delivery times, finance facilities offered.

Strategic pricing

4.7 The Boston Consulting Group research (in the USA) has identified substantial empirical evidence to support the theory that costs are related to the **learning** or **experience curve**. The implications of the learning curve for pricing are as follows.

 (a) New products often hold their price in their early stages of life, while costs are going down, creating increasing profit margins.

 (b) A policy of reducing prices as costs fall can help a company to win a dominant share of the market and pursue a strategy of overall cost leadership.

4.8 **Strategic pricing decisions** might well depend crucially on whether the organisation achieves its estimated cost reductions from the learning curve, and close co-operation between the management accountant, marketing management and strategic planners will be necessary, to agree in advance what the size of the unit cost reductions ought to be and then to try to ensure that they are achieved in practice.

Chapter roundup

- The **hierarchical level** of planning and control decisions is important to recognise, because decision-makers can only make plans or take control action within the sphere of the authority that has been delegated to them.

- The **time span** of decisions, and the importance of the potential consequences of individual decisions, are also important to bear in mind.

- Three types of **pricing decision** are short-term pricing, competitive bidding and strategic pricing.

Quick quiz

1   Identify three levels within a decision-making hierarchy. (see para 1.2)

2   Distinguish between strategic planning and management control. (2.9)

3   Distinguish between operational control and management control. (2.15)

4   What unforeseen circumstances could lead to a business running out of cash? (3.8)

5   Identify three categories of pricing decision. (4.1)

Question to try	Level	Marks	Time
10	Introductory	30	54 mins

Chapter 11

LONG-TERM FINANCIAL PLANNING

Chapter topic list	Syllabus reference
1 Financial management decisions	2(b), 3(a)
2 Financial planning	2(b), 3(a)
3 Gap analysis	2(e)
4 Strategies for long-term growth	2(e)

Introduction

This chapter follows on from topics raised in Chapter 10 to look at **financial planning** and **strategies for long-term growth**, including mergers, acquisitions and organic growth (developed further in Chapter 13). We outline the approach to strategy known as **shareholder value analysis** in part of Section 2 of this Chapter.

1   FINANCIAL MANAGEMENT DECISIONS

1.1   Maximising the wealth of shareholders generally implies maximising profits consistent with long-term stability. It is often found that short-term gains must be sacrificed in the interests of the company's long-term prospects. In the context of this overall objective, there are three main types of decisions facing financial managers.

Question 1

Identify the three main types of decision facing financial managers.

Answer

(a)   Investment decisions
(b)   Financing decisions
(c)   Dividend decisions

In practice, these three areas are interconnected and should not be viewed in isolation.

Investment decisions

1.2   Investment decisions involve committing funds to:

(a)   **Internal investment projects** (and withdrawing from such projects should they turn out to be unprofitable)

(b)   **External investment decisions,** involving the takeover of another company or a merger

(c) **Disinvestment decisions**, involving selling a part of the business, such as an unwanted subsidiary company

Financing decisions

1.3 The assets of a company must be financed by a combination of share capital and reserves, long-term liabilities and short-term liabilities. When a company is growing, it will need additional finance from one or more of these sources.

1.4 The financial manager must know:

(a) Where additional funds can be obtained and at what cost
(b) The effect on a company's profitability and value of using any particular source of funds
(c) The effect on financial risk of using any particular source of funds

1.5 A company ought to be profitable, but it must be 'liquid' too, so that it always has access to enough cash to pay creditors and employees. **Financing decisions** therefore include cash management.

The opportunity cost of finance

1.6 Financial management is concerned with obtaining funds for investment, and investing those funds profitably so as to maximise the value of the firm. It is not enough to invest at a profit; it is necessary to invest so that the profits are sufficient to pay lenders a satisfactory amount of interest. If a company cannot pay interest at the market rate demanded by lenders, the lenders will prefer to invest elsewhere on the capital market, where they can get this rate. There is a market **'opportunity cost' of funds** which a company must expect to pay for new finance.

1.7 Similarly, if a company cannot make big enough profits, shareholders will be dissatisfied. The company will not be able to raise funds from new issues of shares, because investors will not be attracted. Existing shareholders who wish to sell their shares will find that buyers, who can invest in whatever securities they choose, will offer a comparatively low price, and the market price of the shares will be depressed. Since investors have a wide range of shares available to them, there is a market opportunity cost of equity.

Dividend decisions

1.8 Ordinary shareholders expect to earn dividends, and the value of a company's shares will be related to the amount of dividends that a company has been paying, and also to prospects of future dividends.

1.9 **Dividend decisions**, which were discussed in Chapter 9, are also directly related to financing decisions, since retained profits are the most important source of new funds for companies. What a company pays as dividends out of profits cannot be retained in the business to finance future growth, and profits retained represent a withholding of dividends.

2 FINANCIAL PLANNING   12/94, 6/98

2.1 Financial objectives will not be achieved, except by luck, unless management know what they are trying to achieve, and plan how to achieve the objectives. **Quantified targets** for the achievement of financial objectives should therefore be set out in a financial plan. The

financial plan should cover a number of years, perhaps three to five years, or ten years, or even longer. The financial plan should be a part of the overall **strategic plan** of the organisation.

2.2   With good financial planning, a business can assess in advance:

(a)   Just **how much finance** it needs for **long-term investment** and **short-term cash flow needs**

(b)   Whether it is likely to have surplus cash, and if so for how long and what can best be done with the surplus cash when it arises

(c)   How any required finance should be **raised**

(d)   Whether the company is likely to be **profitable** and to achieve its main and subsidiary financial objectives, for example to carry out its policy of a 10% annual growth in dividends

The business plan and forecasting

2.3   Financial plans will be based on forecasts.

Question 2

See if you can identify the different types of forecast on which financial plans may be based before looking at the remainder of this paragraph.

(a)   **Environmental forecasts** are needed to assess future economic and political events which will influence an organisation's prospects. Economic factors might include the rate of growth in the economy, the rate of inflation, foreign exchange rates and the level of interest rates.

(b)   **Market or industry forecasts** can be formulated within the framework of environmental forecasts. These forecasts will cover the likely rate of growth or decline in an industry or market, technological changes which might alter product design or production methods, the possible break-up of a market into separate segments and so on. An organisation ought to be aware of the likely conditions in the markets and industries where it operates, and plan accordingly.

(c)   **Forecasts for the organisation** itself can then be prepared within the framework of market and industry forecasts. Forecasts can be made for sales; costs and profits; new product development; the work force; and finance needs.

2.4   **Further steps in the financial planning process**

(a)   Establishing the **financial requirements** of the business plan and arranging to secure the necessary funding from the most appropriate sources

(b)   **Monitoring and review** of the business plan against actual events

2.5   EXAMPLE: BUSINESS PLAN

Lion Grange Ltd has recently introduced a formal scheme of long range planning. At a meeting called to discuss the first draft plans, the following estimates emerged.

(a)   Sales in the current year reached £10,000,000, and forecasts for the next five years are £10,600,000, £11,400,000, £12,400,000, £13,600,000 and £15,000,000.

(b) The ratio of net profit after tax to sales is 10%, and this is expected to continue throughout the planning period.

(c) Net asset turnover, currently 0.8 times, will remain more or less constant.

It was also suggested that:

(a) If profits rise, dividends should rise by at least the same percentage

(b) An earnings retention rate of 50% should be maintained

(c) The ratio of long-term borrowing to long-term funds (debt plus equity) is limited (by the market) to 30%, which happens also to be the current gearing level of the company

Prepare a financial analysis of the draft long range plan and suggest policies for dividends, retained earnings and gearing (the level of debt).

2.6 SOLUTION

The draft financial plan, for profits, dividends, assets required and funding, can be drawn up in a table, as follows.

	Current year £m	Year 1 £m	Year 2 £m	Year 3 £m	Year 4 £m	Year 5 £m
Sales	10.00	10.60	11.40	12.40	13.60	15.00
Net profit after tax	1.00	1.06	1.14	1.24	1.36	1.50
Dividends (50% of profit after tax)	0.50	0.53	0.57	0.62	0.68	0.75
Net assets (125% of sales)	12.50	13.25	14.25	15.50	17.00	18.75
Equity (increased by retained earnings)	8.75*	9.28	9.85	10.47	11.15	11.90
Maximum debt (30% of assets)	3.75	3.97	4.27	4.65	5.10	5.62
Funds available	12.50	13.25	14.12	15.12	16.25	17.52
Shortfalls in funds, given maximum gearing of 30% and no new issue of shares = funds available minus net assets required	0	0	(0.13)	(0.38)	(0.75)	(1.23)

* The current year equity figure is a balancing figure, equal to the difference between net assets and long-term debt, which is currently at the maximum level of 30% of net assets.

These figures show that the financial objectives of the company are not compatible with each other, and adjustments will have to be made.

(a) Given the assumptions about sales, profits, dividends and net assets required, there will be an increasing shortfall of funds from year 2 onwards, unless new shares are issued or the gearing level rises above 30%.

(b) In years 2 and 3, the shortfall can be eliminated by retaining a greater percentage of profits, but this may have a serious adverse effect on the share price. In year 4 and year 5, the shortfall in funds cannot be removed even if dividend payments are reduced to nothing.

(c) The net asset turnover appears to be low. The situation would be eased if investments were able to generate a higher volume of sales, so that fewer fixed assets and less working capital would be required to support the projected level of sales.

(d) If asset turnover cannot be improved, it may be possible to increase the profit to sales ratio by reducing costs or increasing selling prices.

(e) If a new issue of shares is proposed to make up the shortfall in funds, the amount of funds required must be considered very carefully. Total dividends would have to be increased in order to pay dividends on the new shares. The company seems unable to offer prospects of suitable dividend payments, and so raising new equity might be difficult.

(f) It is conceivable that extra funds could be raised by issuing new debt capital, so that the level of gearing would be over 30%. It is uncertain whether investors would be prepared to lend money so as to increase gearing. If more funds were borrowed, profits after interest and tax would fall so that the share price might also be reduced.

The problem of uncertainty

2.7 The main problem with planning and forecasting, especially in the longer term, is **uncertainty**. Forecasts about economic events and changes in a market or an industry will be very difficult to make, and planners must accept that even the best forecasts will not be wholly accurate.

(a) A sales forecast might be for an annual growth of 10% in sales for the next five years. But how reliable are the assumptions made?

(b) Similarly, a company might forecast that on the assumption that the exchange rate of sterling against the US dollar falls by 5% next year, export sales will rise by 8%. How can exchange rate movements be forecast accurately, and so how reliable is this forecast?

2.8 **Managers** should make forecasts based on **realistic assumptions** so as to be able to compare actual and expected performance.

2.9 Planners should also try to assess the consequences of forecasts being inaccurate. Three methods of assessing uncertainty are as follows.

(a) **Ask 'what if' questions.** A forecast is prepared, based on certain assumptions. The forecaster or planner can then carry out sensitivity analysis by finding the answers to questions such as the following.

    (i)   What if sales growth is only 5% a year, not 10%?

    (ii)   What if costs rise by 5% more than anticipated?

    (iii)   What if the introduction of a new project is held up by 12 months?

    (iv)   What if interest rates are 10% rather than 8%?

    (v)   What if the rate of corporation tax is put up to 40%, or what if the VAT rate is increased to 20%?

(b) **Prepare a probability distribution of possible outcomes.** An alternative technique for assessing uncertainty is to prepare a probability distribution for the range of different possible outcomes, for example as follows.

Annual sales growth	
%	*Probability*
0	0.05
1	0.15
2	0.25
3	0.25
4	0.30

A probability distribution could be prepared for any key variable in the business plan, such as wage levels, raw material costs, productivity levels, interest rates, foreign exchange rates, sales and so on. From the probability distributions, forecasts can be prepared of:

(i)   The expected value of (for example) sales or profits
(ii)   The probability distribution of (for example) sales or profits

(c) **Prepare pessimistic, optimistic and most likely forecasts**. A forecast can be prepared for each of three possible outcomes.

(i)   **The worst** that might happen
(ii)   **The best** that might happen
(iii)   **The most likely** outcome that might happen

2.10   Companies might also wish:

(a) To make **contingency plans**, for what should be done in the event that something occurs in the future that has not been allowed for in the main plan. For example, a company that exports many of its goods to an overseas country might have been warned of the possibility of import controls or exchange controls being imposed by the government of that country. The company might therefore draw up a contingency plan for what it should do if this occurs.

(b) To protect themselves whenever possible against adverse change, by means of **risk management**. Companies can, at a cost, protect themselves against adverse movements in interest rates or foreign exchange rates. We shall look in some detail at risk management in later chapters.

Long-term strategic planning

2.11   **Long-term strategic planning** may be defined as the formulation, evaluation and selection of strategies for the purpose of preparing a long-term plan of action to attain objectives.

The planning period

2.12   A 'stumbling block' to successful strategic planning centres around the critical decision as to how far ahead the company should be preparing its plans. There is little point in planning beyond the furthest point one can reasonably foresee with any certainty. Therefore, a business which is operating in an unstable environment (eg with material shortages) or an uncertain situation (eg marketing a new product) should plan for only a few months, whilst those operating in stable conditions may plan for a decade or more ahead.

2.13   Planners must decide what the planning period ought to be. The planning period ought to be the period of time which is most suitable for planning requirements and which enables the decision making and control processes to be most effectively exercised. The most suitable length for the planning period varies with circumstances. For example, forestry requires a period of many years whereas clothing manufacture may require only a few months.

The planning horizon

2.14   The **planning horizon** can be defined as the furthest time ahead for which plans can be quantified. It need not be the planning period. Thus, if there is a planning period of, say, 15 years or 20 years, the planning horizon for quantified plans might be shorter, say ten years.

Planning beyond the planning horizon involves plans which cannot be properly quantified yet, but which are nevertheless useful for management decision makers, to form a picture of how the organisation should be developing in the longer term.

'Top-down' and 'bottom-up' planning   12/98

2.15   The development of corporate planning can be seen as a response to the existence of **bottom-up planning systems**. In a 'bottom-up' organisation, information is accumulated at lower levels of the enterprise and consolidated as it is passed up through the organisation, with a summary covering the overall position being prepared for top levels of management. This brings the risk that management react only on the basis of the limited options which seem to be available on the basis of the information which is presented to them. A **top-down planning system**, in contrast, is based on the idea that directives emanating from the top management flow down through the organisational structure.

2.16   An example of a **bottom-up** organisation is a conglomerate in which there are many disparate subsidiaries, all having autonomy and not being linked by a synergistic relationship. Disadvantages of bottom-up planning in an organisation include the following.

   (a)   Overall control may become difficult.
   (b)   There may be a number of separate objectives which become difficult to reconcile.
   (c)   There may be a lack of sense of direction in the organisation as a whole.

2.17   **Top-down planning** recognises the position that top management has the ultimate managerial responsibility for the overall direction of the enterprise, and for providing a framework within which decision making by managers at lower levels in the organisation can operate. Nevertheless the 'top-down' principle should probably not be taken too far: planning should, where practicable, involve a wide range of people in the organisation and not just top managers or specialist planners.

The trade-off between short-term and long-term for control action

2.18   It is often the case that in order to rectify short-term results, control action will be at the expense of long-term targets. Similarly, controls over longer-term achievements might call for short-term sacrifices. This conflict between controls for achieving short-term and long-term targets, and the need to keep a balance between the short-term and long-term, is sometimes referred to as the 'S/L trade-off'.

2.19   Very often managers are under pressure to produce good short-term results (eg immediate profitability) in order to get their next promotion. The successfully promoted manager then goes on to another job where again he succeeds only if he produces good short-term results. And so it goes on up the management scale, with managers being rewarded for short-term results, even if they damage long-term prospects in the process.

External information sources for long-term planning

2.20   Planning and decision making rely on accurate and complete information. Financial managers often rely on **externally provided information systems** as the source of much current information about other companies (which might be targets for takeover bids), certain markets (such as commodity and foreign exchange markets), share prices, or business and economic matters.

2.21 Some companies specialise in providing an external 'electronic reference library' or on-line information retrieval system to make this information available to subscribers. This is an externally supplied database. Subscribers can gain access to the supplier's information from a terminal in their office and pay a fee for access to the data.

2.22 A number of firms provide on-line information systems on commercial and tax matters, such as Datastream, Data-Star, Extel and Butterworths.

2.23 The value of an on-line information retrieval system (OLIRS) or external database to companies arises from the need for:

(a) Comprehensive data, which the company's own information systems might not be able to provide. For example information on company accounts is available through Extel's database system.

(b) Rapid access to data.

(c) Up-to-date data. Some information changes so quickly (for example commodity market prices, share prices, money market interest rates and foreign exchange rates) that companies are unable to keep fully up-to-date information systems themselves, and so rely on a specialised OLIRS to do this for them.

Financial planning models

2.24 **Computer modelling** may be used to assist management in the financial planning process.

2.25 A model can be constructed (or a modelling package purchased) incorporating certain variables. These variables might include the following.

(a) Fixed assets
(b) Current assets
(c) Liabilities
(d) Revenues from the sale of different products
(e) Payments for various items of operating cost
(f) Taxation
(g) Sources of funds (equity, loans, preference shares)
(h) Dividends and interest rates

2.26 The inter-relationships between the variables will be specified in the model. For example, an increase in sales will affect the cost of sales, debtors, creditors, cash, fixed assets, profits, taxation and dividends in a way specified by the model, according to assumptions about the contribution/sales ratio, price inflation for various cost items, asset turnover ratios, taxation rates and dividend cover.

2.27 The model may be used to plan ahead, and the future profitability of the company can be estimated. If the company needs extra funds, the amount required can be assessed, and steps can be taken at an early stage to ensure that they will be available. If the model forecasts unsatisfactory profits and dividends, management will be aware that they need to devise long-term strategies now to improve results in future years.

Financial planning illustrated by decision trees

2.28 The process of financial planning can be viewed as the process of managing a set of options or decisions.

BPP PUBLISHING

Decision trees can be used to illustrate the choices and possible outcomes in financial planning. The two stages in preparing a decision tree are:

Step 1. Drawing the tree itself, to show all the choices and outcomes.

Step 2. Putting in the numbers. The probabilities, outcome values and expected values (EVs). (Expected value is calculated as probability × outcome.) For example, if you have a 1% chance of winning £100, the expected value of the winning is £1.

2.29 EXAMPLE: DECISION TREE

Beethoven Ltd has a new wonder product, the vylin, of which it expects great things. At the moment the company has two courses of action open to it, to test market the product or abandon it. If the company test markets it, the cost will be £100,000 and the market response could be positive or negative with probabilities of 0.60 and 0.40.

(a) If the response is positive the company could either abandon the product or market it full scale. If it markets the vylin full scale, the outcome might be low, medium or high demand, and the respective net payoffs would be (200), 200 or 1,000 in units of £1,000 (the result could range from a net loss of £200,000 to a gain of £1,000,000). These outcomes have probabilities of 0.20, 0.50 and 0.30 respectively.

(b) If the result of the test marketing is negative and the company goes ahead and markets the product, estimated losses would be £600,000. If, at any point, the company abandons the product, there would be a net gain of £50,000 from the sale of scrap. All the financial values have been discounted to the present.

Required

(a) Draw a decision tree.
(b) Include figures for cost, loss or profit on the appropriate branches of the tree.
(c) Evaluate each option.

2.30 SOLUTION

The starting point for the tree is to establish what decision has to be made now. What are the options? In this case, they are:

(a) To test market
(b) To abandon

The outcome of the 'abandon' option is known with certainty. There are two possible outcomes of the option to test market, positive response and negative response. Depending on the outcome of the test marketing, another decision will then be made, to abandon the product or to go ahead.

The **expected value (EV)** of each decision option can be evaluated, using the decision tree below to help with keeping the logic properly sorted out. The basic rules are as follows.

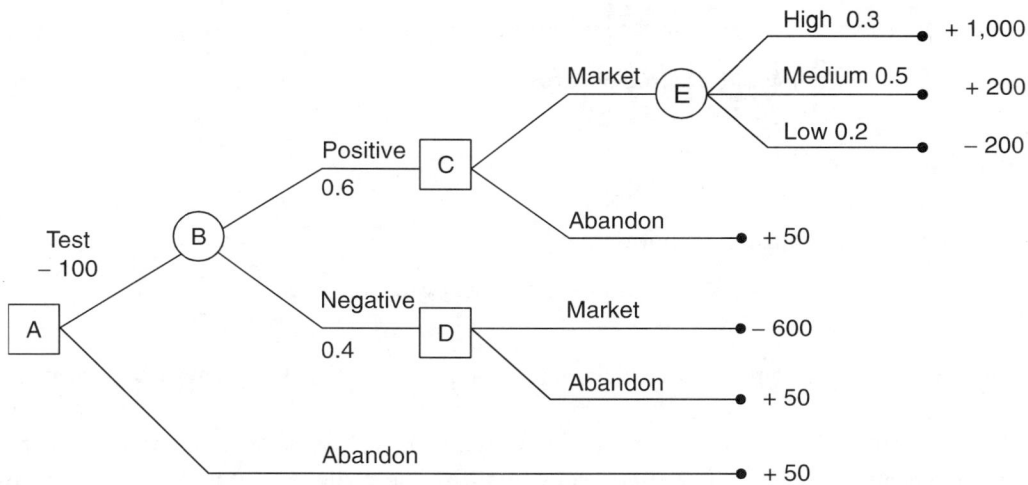

Figure 1 Evaluating the decision with a decision tree

We start on the right hand side of the tree and work back towards the left hand side and the current decision under consideration. Working from *right to left*, we calculate the EV of revenue, cost, contribution or profit at each outcome point on the tree. In the above example, the right-hand-most outcome point is point E, and the EV is as follows.

	Profit (£'000)	Probability	
	x	*p*	*px*
High	1,000	0.3	300
Medium	200	0.5	100
Low	(200)	0.2	(40)
		EV	360

This is the EV of the decision to market the product if the test shows positive response. It may help you to write the EV on the decision tree itself, at the appropriate outcome point (point E). We now make the second stage decisions.

(a)   At decision point C, the choice is:

(i)   Market, EV + 360 (the EV at point E), or
(ii)   Abandon, value + 50

The choice would be to market the product, and so the EV at decision point C is +360.

(b)   At decision point D, the choice is:

(i)   Market, value – 600, or
(ii)   Abandon, value +50

The choice would be to abandon, and so the EV at decision point D is +50.

If the original decision is to test market, the company will market the product if the test shows positive customer response, and will abandon the product if the test results are negative.

The evaluation of the decision tree is completed as follows.

(a) Calculate the EV at outcome point B.

$$
\begin{aligned}
& 0.6 \times 360 \ \ (\text{EV at C}) \\
+ \ \ & 0.4 \times 50 \ \ (\text{EV at D}) \\
= \ \ & 216 + 20 = 236.
\end{aligned}
$$

(b) Compare the options at point A, which are:

(i) Test: EV = EV at B minus test marketing cost = 236 − 100 = 136
(ii) Abandon: Value 50

The choice would be to test market the product, because it has a higher EV of profit.

2.31 Decision trees can be of use in strategic planning to assess which choices are mutually exclusive, and to try and give them some quantitative value. As such they are useful in:

(a) Clarifying strategic decisions when they are complex
(b) Using risk (in probability terms) as an input to quantifying the decision options
(c) Ranking the relative costs and benefits of the options

Shareholder value analysis

2.32 **Shareholder value analysis (SVA)** was developed during the 1980s from the work of Rappaport and focuses on value creation using the net present value (NPV) approach. Thus, SVA assumes that the value of a business is the net present value of its future cash flows, discounted at the appropriate cost of capital.

2.33 Many leading companies (including, for example, Pepsi, Quaker and Disney) have used SVA as a way of linking management strategy and decisions to the creation of value for shareholders.

2.34 SVA takes the following approach.

(a) **Key decisions** with implications for cash flow and risk are specified. These may be strategic, operational, related to investment, or financial.

(b) **Value drivers** are identified as the factors having the greatest impact on shareholder value, and management attention is focused on the decisions which influence the value drivers.

2.35 Value drivers include:

(a) Sales growth and margin
(b) Working capital and fixed capital investment
(c) The cost of capital

2.36 SVA may help managers to concentrate on activities which create value rather than on short-term profitability. A problem with the approach is that of specifying a terminal value at the end of the planning horizon, which will extend for perhaps five or ten years.

3   GAP ANALYSIS   6/98, 12/98

3.1 **Gap analysis is** 'the comparison of an entity's ultimate objective with the sum of projections and already planned projects', with the purpose of establishing:

(a) What are the organisation's targets for achievement over the planning period?

(b) What would the organisation be expected to achieve if it 'did nothing' - in other words, did not develop any new strategies, but simply carried on in the current way with the same products and selling to the same markets.

There will be a difference between the targets in (a) and expected achievements in (b). This difference is the 'gap'. New strategies will then have to be developed which will close this gap, so that the organisation can expect to achieve its targets over the planning period.

A forecast or projection based on existing performance: F_0 forecasts

3.2 An F_0 **forecast** (in Argenti's terminology) is a forecast of the company's future results assuming that it does nothing new. For example, if the company sells ten products in eight markets, produces them with a certain quantity and type of machinery in one factory, has a gearing structure of 30% etc, a forecast will be prepared, covering the corporate planning period, on the assumption that none of these items is changed. (Ansoff calls these forecasts 'reference projections'.)

3.3 Argenti identified four stages in the preparation of an F_0 forecast.

(a) The analysis of revenues, costs and volumes (for example fixed, variable, unit costs and revenue).

(b) Projections into the future based on past trends (for example using product life cycles to estimate sales volumes and examining forecasts for reasonableness).

(c) Identifying other factors affecting profits and return (for example external factors that might affect projections such as changes in government economic policy, technology, possible competitors' actions.)

(d) Finalising the forecast.

3.4 The purpose of the F_0 forecast and gap analysis is to determine the size of the task facing the company if it wishes to achieve its target profits.

Errors in the forecast

3.5 A forecast cannot be expected to guarantee accuracy and there must inevitably be some latitude for error. If possible, the error should be quantified in either of the following two ways.

(a) By predicting the profit and estimating likely variations. For example, 'in 1995 the forecast profit is £5 million with possible variations of plus or minus £2 million'.

(b) By providing a probability distribution for profits. For example, 'in 1995 there is a 20% chance that profits will exceed £7 million, a 50% chance that they will exceed £5 million and an 80% chance that they will exceed £2½ million. Minimum profits in 1995 will be £2 million.'

The profit gap

3.6 The **profit gap** is the difference between the target profits (according to the overall corporate objectives of the company) and the profits on the F_0 forecast (Figure 2).

'It is at this stage of the game that the company must turn its attention to deciding what options are open to it in trying to bridge the gap. This gap represents the extra task facing the company over and above the mere continuation of the existing business - it indicates how much extra profit has to be yielded from the decisions and the commitments that will be made over the next few years' (Bishop and Griffiths).'

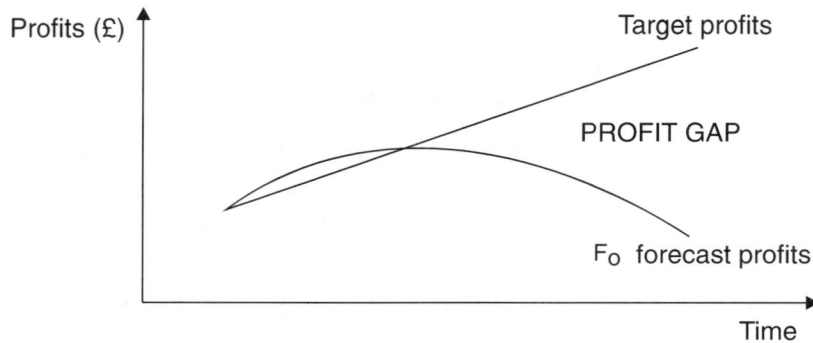

Figure 2 Profit gap

3.7 In deciding the size of the gap that must be closed, allowance must be made for errors in the forecast.

4 STRATEGIES FOR LONG-TERM GROWTH

Expansion, integration and diversification

4.1 Expansion is the growth of existing products and/or development of existing markets. It is sometimes referred to as market penetration. However, many companies actively seek new products and/or new markets.

4.2 A firm should have a clear idea about what it expects to gain from dealing in products or markets with which it is unfamiliar.

(a) New products and new markets should be selected which offer prospects for growth not found in the existing product-market mix.

(b) New operations might be more profitable than keeping the surplus funds as liquid resources, deposited with a bank, say, but with comparatively low rates of return. On the other hand, there is an argument that the funds should be returned to shareholders, who can make their own investment decisions.

(c) New products and/or markets might achieve greater profitability than mere expansion even though current objectives are being realised. This may occur because:

(i) Outstanding new products have been developed by the firm's research and development department

(ii) The profit opportunities from these new activities are high

(d) New activities might enable a firm to provide a more comprehensive service to customers.

4.3 Four product-market strategy options for growth are noted below.

(i) Horizontal integration } Confusingly, these are sometimes called
(ii) Vertical integration } **related diversification**

(iii) Concentric diversification } Confusingly, these are sometimes called
(iv) Conglomerate diversification } **unrelated diversification**

Integration (or 'related diversification')

4.4 **Horizontal integration** is characterised by a firm adding new products to its existing market, or new markets to its existing products (eg where a milk producer adds yoghurt to its product line or offers to deliver fruit juice with the early morning milk round). The stability of a firm is not greatly improved by horizontal integration because the firm still relies on the same markets or the same products as before.

4.5 **Vertical integration,** or vertical diversification, occurs when a company becomes either one of the following.

(a) Its own supplier of raw materials or components (ie **backward** vertical integration). For example, backward integration would occur where a milk producer acquires its own dairy farms rather than buying raw milk from independent farmers.

(b) Its own distributor or sales agent (ie **forward** vertical integration). For example, the Laura Ashley company not only make its goods but sells them in its own shops.

4.6 The purpose of vertical integration may be as follows.

(a) To provide a secure supply of components or raw materials with more control over quality, quantity and price

(b) To strengthen relationships and contacts of the manufacturer with the 'final consumer' of the product

(c) To win a share of the higher profits which might be obtainable in the raw materials market or end-user market

4.7 The disadvantages of vertical integration are as follows.

(a) The **acquired company** loses out on the industry-wide scale economies that might arise out of a merger with a similar firm. This might lead to higher costs or lower innovation.

(b) A company places 'more eggs in the same end-market basket' (Ansoff). Such a policy is fairly inflexible, more sensitive to instabilities and increases the firm's dependence on a particular aspect of demand.

Diversification (or 'unrelated diversification')

4.8 **Concentric diversification** occurs when a company seeks to add new products that have technological and/or marketing synergies with the existing product line. These products will normally appeal to new classes of customer. For example, Ansoff refers to a motor manufacturer who decides to make farm machinery because there is a technological similarity between the two, although the class of customer will be different.

4.9 **Conglomerate diversification** consists of making entirely new products for new classes of customers. These new products have no relationship to the company's current technology, products or markets.

Case examples

An example of conglomerate diversification is provided by BTR plc. BTR (now Invensys) bought up ailing companies in mature industries and sought to run them more efficiently than the previous management. The company had over 500 profit centres. More recently, it has sold off parts of the group in order to focus on core activities. Tomkins is another example.

4.10 **Advantages** to an organisation in pursuing a strategy of conglomerate diversification are as follows.

(a) Risk is spread. By entering new products into new markets, the organisation can obtain protection against failure of one or more of the firm's existing range.

(b) The firm's overall profitability and flexibility might improve through acquisition in industries which have better economic characteristics than those of the acquiring firms. (But shareholders can invest in those industries directly.)

(c) Management might wish to escape from the present business into another.

(d) Greater business 'substance' or 'status' might mean better access to capital markets.

(e) A company pursuing a policy of conglomerate diversification can quickly take advantage of **profit opportunities** which develop by acquiring a subsidiary company in the new product-market area.

(f) Conglomerate diversification and concentric diversification offer the chance of growth without creating a monopoly which would attract state regulation. This is an example of system goals overtaking mission.

(g) The firm can use surplus cash on the questionable assumption that managers are always better judges than shareholders.

(h) The firm can exploit under-utilised resources.

(i) **Synergistic possibilities** include:

    (i) A company which needs cash in the short term obtaining a cash-rich company or a company with large cash surpluses in the short term

    (ii) Using a company's image and reputation in one market to develop into another where corporate image and reputation could be vital ingredients for success

4.11 The **limitations** of conglomerate diversification may be as follows.

(a) The dilution of shareholders' earnings if diversification is into growth industries with high P/E ratios.

(b) Profitable businesses will be milked to support ailing ones.

(c) Resource allocation will be a political rather than an economic process, as different divisions compete with each other.

(d) The organisation might suffer more in conditions of recession, if more than one activity suffers from the recession. British Aerospace suffered when its property development subsidiary hit a slump in the commercial property market.

(e) The management of the acquiring firm may interfere in the running of the acquisition, to the detriment of its operations.

(f) A conglomerate will only be successful if it has a high quality of management and financial ability at central headquarters, where the diverse operations are brought together. Otherwise it lacks a common purpose.

(g) Failure in one of the businesses will drag down the rest, as it will eat up resources.

(h) Lack of management experience in the business area can spell trouble. Japanese steel companies have diversified into areas completely unrelated to steel, such as personal computers, with limited success.

Withdrawal or abandonment

4.12 Strategies of expansion and diversification imply some logic in carrying on operations. It might be a better decision, although a much harder one, to cease operations or to pull out of a market completely. There are likely to be **exit barriers** to so doing.

(a) Economic barriers include redundancy costs.

(b) Managers might fail to grasp the principles of opportunity costing ('we've spent all this money, so we must go on').

(c) Political barriers include government action.

(d) Marketing considerations may delay withdrawal. A product might be a 'loss-leader' for others, or might contribute to the company's reputation for its breadth of coverage.

(e) Psychology: managers hate to admit failure, and there might be a desire to avoid a 'bloodletting'. Furthermore, people might wrongly assume that carrying on is a low risk strategy.

(f) It will be better for entities to be 'going concerns' in order to achieve the best price.

4.13 That said, firms do withdraw from products or markets, and for good reasons.

(a) The company's business may be in buying businesses, selling their assets or improving their performance, and selling them at a profit.

(b) Resource limitations mean that less profitable businesses have to be abandoned. A business will be sold to a competitor, or occasionally to management (as a buy-out).

(c) A company may be forced to quit, because of bankruptcy.

(d) The company might change its generic strategy for competitive advantage. (For example, in the microprocessor industry, many American firms left high-volume DRAM chips to Japanese firms so as to concentrate on high value added niche products.)

(e) Decline in purchasing power of the market segment, or indeed a fall in the market size.

Mergers and acquisitions

4.14 Companies may expand or diversify by developing their own internal resources, but they are also likely to consider growth through acquisitions or mergers. A merger is the joining of two separate companies to form a single company. On the other hand, an acquisition is the purchase of a controlling interest in another company. In both situations the result is a sudden spurt in company growth, which can clearly cause 'corporate indigestion' typified by problems of communication, blurring of policy decisions and decline in the staff's identity with company and products.

4.15 It is important for a company to understand its reasons for acquisition and that these reasons should be valid in terms of its strategic plan. The classic reasons for acquisition as a part of the broader corporate strategy are as follows.

(a) **Marketing advantages:**

(i) To buy in a new product range

(ii) To buy a market presence (especially true if acquiring a company with overseas offices and contracts that can be utilised by the parent company)

      (iii)   To unify sales departments or to rationalise distribution and advertising (eg the merger between Schweppes and Cadbury, where both companies had many common customers)

      (iv)   To eliminate competition or to protect an existing market

(b) **Production advantages**:

      (i)   To gain a higher utilisation of production facilities and reap economies of scale by larger machine runs, less time spent on change-overs

      (ii)   To 'buy in' technology and skills

      (iii)   To obtain greater production capacity

      (iv)   To safeguard future supplies of raw materials

      (v)   To improve the purchasing position through better bulk purchase opportunities

(c) **Finance and management**:

      (i)   To buy a high quality management team, which exists in the acquired company
      (ii)   To obtain cash resources where the acquired company is very liquid
      (iii)   To gain undervalued assets or surplus assets that can be sold off ('asset stripping')
      (iv)   To obtain tax advantages (eg purchase of a tax loss company)

(d) **Risk-spreading**. The diversification of tobacco companies into other businesses has already been referred to. Diversification reduced the risk of reliance on a single market, which is always threatened by further anti-smoking legislation.

(e) To **retain independence**. A company threatened by a takeover might take over another company, just to make itself bigger and so a more expensive 'target' for the predator company. Alternatively, a company under threat from a takeover could try to establish a 'Pacman defence' in which it turns round and eats (ie takes over) the predator.

4.16 The aim of a merger or acquisition, however, should be to make profits in the long term as well as the short term. Acquisitions provide a means of entering a market, or building up a market share, more quickly and/or at a lower cost than would be incurred if the company tries to develop its own resources.

4.17 Acquisitions and mergers may not be successful in creating the anticipated profits and there is a need for corporate planners to consider the level of risk involved.

(a) The corporate planner must suggest product-market areas where acquisitions or mergers should be sought, and indicate the level of risk which would be acceptable in any particular 'deal'.

(b) It would then be the task of executive managers to find the acquisition and merger opportunities which conform to the strategic plan for products and markets and also for the level of risk which would be tolerable in view of the company's objectives.

4.18 A serious problem is the difficulty which planners will have in attempting to quantify monetary (and non-monetary) advantages to be expected from acquisitions, especially where planned growth will be into areas outside the company's previous experience (ie conglomerate diversification).

4.19 It will also be necessary to attempt an evaluation of the following.

(a) The prospects of technological change in the industry
(b) The size and strength of competitors
(c) The reaction of competitors to an acquisition

(d) The likelihood of government intervention and legislation

(e) The state of the industry and its long-term prospects

(f) The amount of synergy obtainable from the merger or acquisition

4.20 Whatever the reason for the merger or acquisition, it is unlikely to be successful unless it offers the company opportunities that cannot be found within the company itself and unless the new subsidiary fits closely into the strategic plan outlined for future growth.

Takeovers or mergers financed by a share exchange arrangement

4.21 A business might be able to achieve accelerated growth and the cost advantages of synergy by acquiring another firm without any additional major cash investment. Many acquisitions are paid for by issuing new shares in the acquiring company, which are then used to buy the shares of the company to be taken over in a **share exchange** arrangement. An enlarged company might then have the financial 'muscle' and borrowing power to invest further so as to gain access to markets closed to either company previously because they could not individually afford the investment.

Case example

It can be noted that, in the computer technology industry, where new business opportunities are continually arising, Sinclair proved itself to be a highly innovative company, but was restricted from greater expansion by lack of financial resources and inadequate profits, until it was eventually taken over by Amstrad.

4.22 Share exchange details are more easily agreed when the buying company is a quoted company - ie with shares that can readily be sold and bought on a stock market, and which have a **measurable market value**. For example, if the owners of a company were approached with a takeover bid by X plc, offering a share exchange of, say, two X plc shares for every five shares in the company, the company's owners would be paid in shares that they can eventually sell for cash. In contrast, if they were approached with a similar offer by a private company, all they would get for selling up would be a part of the equity of a private company, with the only cash returns being dividends, assuming of course, that the private company did choose to pay any dividends.

Acquisitions and earnings per share

4.23 Companies seek growth through acquisitions, and their success in achieving growth can be measured by the growth in earnings per share. Growth in EPS will only occur after an acquisition if either: the company that is acquired is bought on a lower P/E ratio; or the company that is acquired is bought on a higher P/E ratio, but there is profit growth to offset this.

4.24 A **corporate raid** occurs when share prices are low, and acquisitive companies are able to buy a substantial quantity of a target company's shares at a market price which would be below the offer price in a takeover bid. For example, suppose that shares in Wallow plc are currently trading at £1.50, on a P/E ratio of 8. Two similar companies in the industry have recently been taken over on a P/E ratio of 16. A corporate raid might then occur, in which the 007 Corporation purchases 20% of the shares of Wallow for £1.50 each. With 20% of the shares in its hands, the 007 Corporation could then go on to make a takeover bid for the remaining shares (at a price of around £3) or could wait before deciding what to do next.

4.25 Another feature of much takeover activity in the USA especially, but also in the UK, is the **debt-financed takeover**. This is a takeover bid where most or all of the purchase finance is provided by a syndicate of banks for the acquisitor. The acquisitor company, if the takeover bid is successful, will then become highly geared, with debts possibly well in excess of the company's equity. The **interest costs** of the borrowing will damage the acquisitor's profits and cash flows. To ease the debt burden, the acquisitor will usually **sell off parts of the target company** once the takeover has taken place.

4.26 A **leveraged management buy-out (LBO)** is a form of debt-financed takeover where the target company is bought up by a team of managers in the company, rather than by an external acquisitor. Management buyouts are discussed later in this Study Text.

Organic growth or acquisition? 6/97

> **Exam focus point**
> Eight marks - a significant allocation - were available in the 6/97 paper for an answer to this general question. Look out for such relatively easy mark-earning opportunities in your exam paper.

4.27 A company which is planning to grow must decide on whether to pursue a policy of 'organic' internal growth or a policy of taking over other established businesses, or a mix of the two.

4.28 **Organic growth** requires funding in cash, whereas acquisitions can be made by means of share exchange transactions. A company pursuing a policy of organic growth would need to take account of the following.

(a) The company must make the finance available, possibly out of retained profits. However, the company should then know how much it can afford, and with careful management, should not over-extend itself by trying to achieve too much growth too quickly.

(b) The company can use its existing staff and systems to create the growth projects, and this will open up career opportunities for the staff. In contrast, when expansion is achieved by taking over other businesses, the company usually acquires and assimilates the staff of those businesses.

(c) Overall expansion can be planned more efficiently. For example, if a company wishes to open a new factory or depot, it can site the new development in a place that helps operational efficiency (eg close to other factories, to reduce transport costs). With acquisitions, the company must take on existing sites no matter where they happen to be.

(d) Economies of scale can be achieved from more efficient use of central head office functions such as finance, purchasing, personnel and management services. With acquisitions, a company buys the head office functions of other companies and there will either be fewer economies of scale, or more redundancies.

4.29 **Acquisitions** are probably only desirable if organic growth alone cannot achieve the targets for growth that a company has set for itself.

Acquisitions can be made to enter new product areas, or to expand in existing markets, much more quickly. Organic growth takes time. With acquisitions, entire existing operations are assimilated into the company at one fell swoop. Acquisitions can be made without cash, if share exchange transactions are acceptable to both the buyers and sellers of any company which is to be taken over.

When an acquisition is made to diversify into new product areas, the company will be buying technical expertise, goodwill and customer contracts and so on, which it might take years to develop if it tried to enter the market by growing organically.

4.30　However, acquisitions do have their **strategic problems**.

(a) They might be too expensive. Some might be resisted by the directors of the target company. Others might be referred to the government under the terms of anti-monopoly legislation.

(b) Customers of the target company might resent a sudden takeover and consider going to other suppliers for their goods.

(c) In general, the problems of assimilating new products, customers, suppliers, markets, employees and different systems of operating might create 'indigestion' and management overload in the acquiring company.

(d) An example of growth which had to be pursued through diversification and acquisition is the case of Fujitsu. By acquiring the UK firm ICL, not only did it find an entry to the European market, but it also acquired ICL's experience in **open systems technologies**.

Chapter roundup

- **Financial planning** needs to be based on forecasts. The financial requirements of the business plan need to be established and the necessary funding arranged.

- Once in place, the business plan must be monitored and reviewed against actual events.

- **Shareholder value analysis** focuses on value creation using the net present value approach. Value drivers are the factors having greatest impact on shareholder value.

- **Acquisition** as a strategy for long-term growth may be desirable if **organic growth** alone does not allow the company's long-range targets to be met.

Quick quiz

1　What is meant by the 'opportunity cost of finance'? (see para 1.6)

2　On what different types of forecast might financial plans be based? (2.3)

3　What are the advantages of 'top-down' planning? (2.15 - 2.17)

4　What is meant by 'value drivers' in the context of shareholder value analysis? (2.34, 2.35)

5　Distinguish between 'concentric diversification' and 'conglomerate diversification'. (4.8, 4.9)

6　Outline some of the strategic problems of an acquisitions strategy. (4.30)

Question to try	Level	Marks	Time
11	Introductory	n/a	20 mins

Chapter 12

ANALYSIS OF PERFORMANCE

Chapter topic list	Syllabus reference
1 Ratio analysis	2(c)
2 Comparisons of accounting figures	2(c)
3 Predicting business failure	2(c)
4 Other information from companies' accounts	2(c)
5 Performance measurement in the public sector	2(c)

Introduction

The purpose of this chapter is to look at how **accounting information** can be interpreted so as to assess a company's financial position or the performance of business enterprises and other organisations. This topic is covered mainly as revision, since you will have covered **ratio analysis** and **other techniques** for the interpretation of financial statements in your earlier studies.

1   RATIO ANALYSIS   12/94, 12/95, 12/96, 6/99

1.1   The financial situation of a company will obviously affect its share price and its ability to raise finance. Is the company profitable? Is it growing? Does it have satisfactory liquidity? Is its gearing level acceptable? What is its dividend policy? The answers to some of these questions can be obtained from accounting reports produced by the company.

1.2   Within a group of companies, subsidiary companies or divisions will be expected to report on their performance to the holding company as a part of the process of short-term financial planning. A **group's performance** can be measured in terms of growth in EPS or growth in dividend per share. A **subsidiary's performance** cannot be measured in the same way, because its financial environment is artificial (funds are obtained from the holding company, not from the market) and dividends are decided on by the holding company.

1.3   Financial reporting systems are therefore likely to be based on an analysis of financial ratios. Such ratios need to be compared over a number of periods if the analysis is to be of value.

The broad categories of ratios

1.4   Ratios can be grouped into the following four categories:

- **Profitability and return**
- **Debt and gearing**
- **Liquidity**: control of cash and other working capital items

- Shareholders' investment ratios (or **stock market ratios**), which were covered earlier in this Study Text

1.5 Within each heading there are a number of standard measures or ratios that are normally calculated and generally accepted as meaningful indicators. It must be stressed however that each individual business must be considered separately, and a ratio that is meaningful for a manufacturing company may be completely meaningless for a financial institution. Try not to be too mechanical when working out ratios, and constantly think about what you are trying to achieve.

1.6 The key to obtaining meaningful information from ratio analysis is comparison: comparing ratios over time within the same business to establish whether the business is improving or declining, and comparing ratios between similar businesses to see whether the company you are analysing is better or worse than average within its own business sector.

Profitability

1.7 A company ought of course to be profitable, and obvious checks on profitability are:

(a) Whether the company has made a profit or a loss on its ordinary activities
(b) By how much this year's profit or loss is bigger or smaller than last year's profit or loss

It is probably better to consider separately the profits or losses on exceptional items if there are any.

1.8 **Profit on ordinary activities before taxation** is generally thought to be a better figure to use than profit after taxation, because there might be unusual variations in the tax charge from year to year which would not affect the underlying profitability of the company's operations.

1.9 Another profit figure that can be calculated is PBIT: profit before interest and tax. This is the amount of profit which the company earned before having to pay interest to the providers of loan capital. By loan capital, we usually mean **longer term** loan capital, such as debentures and medium-term bank loans, which will be shown in the balance sheet as 'Creditors: amounts falling due after more than one year'. This figure is of particular importance to bankers and lenders.

1.10 Profit before interest and tax is therefore:

(a) The profit on ordinary activities before taxation, *plus*
(b) Interest charges on long-term loan capital

1.11 To calculate PBIT, in theory, all we have to do is to look at the interest payments in the relevant note to the accounts. Do not take the net interest figure in the profit and loss account itself, because this represents interest payments less interest received, and PBIT is profit including interest received but before interest payments.

1.12 The note to the accounts on interest charges, unfortunately, does not give us the exact figure we want, and we have to take the most suitable figure available. Company law requires companies to show the amount of interest in respect of:

(a) Bank loans and bank overdrafts, and other loans which are repayable within five years
(b) Loans repayable by instalments (for example finance leases) beyond five years
(c) All other loans (for example long-term debentures)

BPP PUBLISHING

1.13 The interest cost we want is (c) plus (b) and probably a part of (a) (for interest on loans repayable within one to five years which are 'Creditors: amounts falling due after more than one year.'). Unless a company gives clear details of its interest costs, it is probably simplest to approximate the interest for PBIT as the total of (a), (b) and (c).

Profitability and return: the return on capital employed (ROCE)

1.14 It is impossible to assess profits or profit growth properly without relating them to the amount of funds (the capital) employed in making the profits. The most important profitability ratio is therefore **return on capital employed (ROCE),** which states the profit as a percentage of the amount of capital employed.

1.15 Profit is usually taken as PBIT, and capital employed is shareholders' capital plus long-term liabilities and debt capital. This is the same as total assets less current liabilities. The underlying principle is that we must compare like with like, and so if capital means share capital and reserves plus long-term liabilities and debt capital, profit must mean the profit earned by all this capital together. This is PBIT, since interest is the return for loan capital.

Thus **ROCE** $= \dfrac{\text{Profit on ordinary activities before interest and taxation (PBIT)}}{\text{Capital employed}}$

Capital employed $=$ Shareholders' funds plus 'creditors: amounts falling due after more than one year' plus any long-term provisions for liabilities and charges

Evaluating the ROCE

1.16 What does a company's ROCE tell us? What should we be looking for?

1.17 There are three comparisons that can be made.

(a) The change in ROCE from one year to the next.

(b) The ROCE being earned by other companies, if this information is available.

(c) A comparison of the ROCE with current market borrowing rates.

 (i) What would be the cost of extra borrowing to the company if it needed more loans, and is it earning an ROCE that suggests it could make high enough profits to make such borrowing worthwhile?

 (ii) Does the company have an ROCE which suggests that it is making profitable use of its current borrowing?

1.18 However, it is possible that a company's ROCE is artificially high. This is because a company's fixed assets, especially property, might be undervalued in its balance sheet, and if they are, the company would be undervaluing its capital employed. This in turn would make its ROCE higher. For example, a profit of £10,000 on capital employed of £100,000 gives an ROCE of 10%, but if capital employed is valued lower, say at £80,000, the ROCE would be 12½% for the same profit figure. What this means is that if a company's ROCE is, say 20%, you cannot assume that this is a good performance without first deciding whether the result has been due to good profits or whether it has been due to an undervaluation of capital employed.

Analysing profitability and return in more detail: the secondary ratios

1.19 We may analyse the ROCE, to find out why it is high or low, or better or worse than last year. There are two factors that contribute towards a return on capital employed, both related to turnover.

(a) **Profit margin**. A company might make a high or a low profit margin on its sales. For example, a company that makes a profit of 25p per £1 of sales is making a bigger return on its turnover than another company making a profit of only 10p per £1 of sales.

(b) **Asset turnover**. Asset turnover is a measure of how well the assets of a business are being used to generate sales. For example, if two companies each have capital employed of £100,000, and company A makes sales of £400,000 a year whereas company B makes sales of only £200,000 a year, company A is making a higher turnover from the same amount of assets and this will help company A to make a higher return on capital employed than company B. Asset turnover is expressed as 'x times' so that assets generate x times their value in annual turnover. Here, company A's asset turnover is 4 times and company B's is 2 times.

1.20 Profit margin and asset turnover together explain the ROCE, and if the ROCE is the primary profitability ratio, these other two are the secondary ratios. The relationship between the three ratios is as follows.

Profit margin × Asset turnover = ROCE

$$\frac{PBIT}{Sales} \times \frac{Sales}{Capital\ employed} = \frac{PBIT}{Capital\ employed}$$

A warning about comments on profit margin and asset turnover

1.21 It might be tempting to think that a high profit margin is good, and a low asset turnover means sluggish trading. In broad terms, this is so. But there is a trade-off between profit margin and asset turnover, and you cannot look at one without allowing for the other. A **high profit margin** means a high profit per pound of sales, but if this also means that sales prices are high, there is a strong possibility that sales turnover will be depressed, so that asset turnover will be lower. A **high asset turnover** means that the company is generating a lot of sales, but to do this, it might have to keep its prices down and so accept a low profit margin.

1.22 Consider the following figures.

	Company A		*Company B*	
Sales	£1,000,000	Sales	£4,000,000
Capital employed	£1,000,000	Capital employed	£1,000,000
PBIT	£200,000	PBIT	£200,000

These figures would give the following ratios.

		Company A					*Company B*		
ROCE	=	200,000 / 1,000,000	=	20%	ROCE	=	200,000 / 1,000,000	=	20%
		Company A					*Company B*		
Profit margin	=	200,000 / 1,000,000	=	20%	Profit margin	=	200,000 / 4,000,000	=	5%
Asset turnover	=	1,000,000 / 1,000,000	=	1	Asset turnover	=	4,000,000 / 1,000,000	=	4

1.23 The companies have the same ROCE, but it is arrived at in very different ways. Company A operates with a low asset turnover and a comparatively high profit margin whereas company B carries out much more business, but on a lower profit margin. Company A could be operating at the luxury end of the market, whilst company B is perhaps operating at the popular end of the market. Company B may be under-capitalised. It would be wrong to over-generalise, but there will be a tendency for **service industries** to operate with a higher profit margin than **manufacturing industries**.

The gross profit margin, the net profit margin and profit analysis

1.24 Depending on the format of the profit and loss account, you may be able to calculate the gross profit margin as well as the net profit margin. Looking at the two together can be quite informative.

Question 1

A company has the following summarised profit and loss accounts for two consecutive years.

	Year 1 £	Year 2 £
Turnover	70,000	100,000
Less cost of sales	42,000	55,000
Gross profit	28,000	45,000
Less expenses	21,000	35,000
Net profit	7,000	10,000

Required

Analyse the net profit margin and gross profit margin, indicating the implications of any changes between the two years.

Answer

Although the net profit margin is the same for both years at 10%, the gross profit margin is not.

In year 1 it is: $\dfrac{28,000}{70,000}$ = 40%

and in year 2 it is: $\dfrac{45,000}{100,000}$ = 45%

Is this good or bad for the business? An increased profit margin must be good because this indicates a wider gap between selling price and cost of sales. However, given that the net profit ratio has stayed the same in the second year, expenses must be rising. In year 1 expenses were 30% of turnover, whereas in year 2 they were 35% of turnover. This indicates that administration or selling and distribution expenses or interest costs require tight control.

A percentage analysis of profit between year 1 and year 2 is as follows.

	Year 1 %	Year 2 %
Cost of sales as a % of sales	60	55
Gross profit as a % of sales	40	45
	100	100
Expenses as a % of sales	30	35
Net profit as a % of sales	10	10
Gross profit as a % of sales	40	45

Debt and gearing ratios   12/98

1.25 Debt ratios are concerned with how much the company owes in relation to its size and whether it is getting into heavier debt or improving its situation.

(a) When a company is heavily in debt, and seems to be getting even more heavily into debt, the thought that should occur to you is that this cannot continue. If the company carries on wanting to borrow more, banks and other would-be lenders are very soon likely to refuse further borrowing and the company might well find itself in trouble.

(b) When a company is earning only a modest profit before interest and tax, and has a heavy debt burden, there will be very little profit left over for shareholders after the interest charges have been paid. And so if interest rates were to go up or the company were to borrow even more, it might soon be incurring interest charges in excess of PBIT. This might eventually lead to the liquidation of the company.

1.26 These are the two main reasons why companies should keep their debt burden under control. Four ratios that are particularly worth looking at are the **debt ratio**, the **gearing ratio**, **interest cover** and the **cash flow ratio**.

The debt ratio

1.27 The **debt ratio** is the ratio of a company's total debts to its total assets. **Assets** consist of fixed assets at their balance sheet value, plus current assets. **Debts** consist of all creditors, whether amounts falling due within one year or after more than one year. You can ignore **long-term provisions** and liabilities, such as deferred taxation.

1.28 There is no absolute rule on the maximum safe debt ratio, but as a very general guide, you might regard 50% as a safe limit to debt. In practice, many companies operate successfully with a higher debt ratio than this, but 50% is nonetheless a helpful benchmark. In addition, if the debt ratio is over 50% and getting worse, the company's debt position will be worth looking at more carefully.

Gearing

1.29 **Capital gearing,** defined at the beginning of Chapter 6, is concerned with a company's **long-term capital structure.** As with the debt ratio, there is no absolute limit to what the gearing ratio ought to be. Many companies are highly geared, but if a highly geared company is increasing its gearing, it is likely to have difficulty in the future when it wants to borrow even more, unless it can also boost its shareholders' capital, either with retained profits or with a new share issue.

Operating gearing

1.30 **Operating gearing** is concerned with the relationship in a company between its variable/fixed cost operating structure and its profitability. It can be calculated as the ratio of contribution (sales minus variable costs of sales) to profit before interest and tax (PBIT). The possibility of rises or falls in sales revenue and volume means that operating gearing has possible implications for a company's business risk.

Interest cover

1.31 The **interest cover** ratio shows whether a company is earning enough profits before interest and tax to pay its interest costs comfortably, or whether its interest costs are high in relation to the size of its profits, so that a fall in PBIT would then have a significant effect on profits available for ordinary shareholders.

1.32 Interest cover equals:

$$\frac{\text{PBIT}}{\text{Interest charges}}$$

1.33 An interest cover of 2 times or less would be low, and it should really exceed 3 times before the company's interest costs can be considered to be within acceptable limits.

The cash flow ratio

1.34 The **cash flow ratio** is the ratio of a company's net annual cash inflow to its total debts:

$$\frac{\text{Net annual cash inflow}}{\text{Total debts}}$$

(a) Net annual cash inflow is the amount of cash which the company has coming into the business each year from its operations. This will be shown in a company's cash flow statement for the year.

(b) Total debts are short-term and long-term creditors, together with provisions for liabilities and charges.

1.35 Obviously, a company needs to earn enough cash from operations to be able to meet its foreseeable debts and future commitments, and the cash flow ratio, and changes in the cash flow ratio from one year to the next, provides a useful indicator of a company's cash position.

Liquidity ratios: cash and working capital

1.36 **Profitability** is of course an important aspect of a company's performance, and debt or gearing is another. Neither, however, addresses directly the key issue of liquidity. A company needs liquid assets so that it can meet its debts when they fall due.

1.37 **Liquidity** is the amount of cash a company can obtain quickly to settle its debts (and possibly to meet other unforeseen demands for cash payments too). Liquid funds consist of:

(a) Cash

(b) Short-term investments for which there is a ready market, such as investments in shares of other companies (Short-term investments are distinct from investments in shares in subsidiaries or associated companies.)

(c) Fixed term deposits with a bank or building society, for example six month deposits with a bank

(d) Trade debtors (These are not cash, but ought to be expected to pay what they owe within a reasonably short time.)

(e) Bills of exchange receivable (Like ordinary trade debtors, these represent amounts of cash due to be received soon.)

1.38 Some assets are more liquid than others. Stocks of goods are fairly liquid in some businesses. Stocks of finished production goods might be sold quickly, and a supermarket will hold consumer goods for resale that could well be sold for cash very soon. Other stocks are not so liquid. Raw materials and components in a manufacturing company have to be used to make a finished product before they can be sold to realise cash, and so they are less liquid than finished goods. Just how liquid they are depends on the speed of stock turnover and the length of the production cycle.

1.39 Fixed assets are not liquid assets. A company can sell off fixed assets, but unless they are no longer needed, or are worn out and about to be replaced, they are necessary to continue the company's operations. Selling fixed assets is certainly not a solution to a company's cash needs, and so although there may be an occasional fixed asset item which is about to be sold off, probably because it is going to be replaced, it is safe to disregard fixed assets when measuring a company's liquidity.

1.40 In summary, liquid assets are current asset items that will or could soon be converted into cash, and cash itself. Two common **definitions of liquid assets** are:

(a) All current assets

(b) All current assets with the exception of stocks

1.41 The main source of liquid assets for a trading company is sales. A company can obtain cash from sources other than sales, such as the issue of shares for cash, a new loan or the sale of fixed assets. But a company cannot rely on these at all times, and in general, obtaining liquid funds depends on making sales and profits. A company must be able to pay its debts when they fall due, and in the balance sheet, foreseeable creditors to be paid are represented by current liabilities, that is, amounts falling due within one year. There are also other payments that a company might want to make, such as the purchase of a new fixed asset for cash.

Why does profit not provide an indication of liquidity?

1.42 If a company makes profits, it should earn money, and if it earns money, it might seem that it should receive more cash than it pays out. In fact, profits are not always a good guide to liquidity. Two examples will show why this is so.

(a) Suppose that company X makes all its sales for cash, and pays all its running costs in cash without taking any credit. Its profit for the year just ended was as follows.

		£	£
Sales			400,000
Less costs:	running costs	200,000	
	depreciation	50,000	
			250,000
Profit			150,000
Less dividends (all paid)			80,000
Retained profits			70,000

During the year, the company purchased a fixed asset for £180,000 and paid for it in full.

Depreciation is not a cash outlay, and so the company's 'cash profits' less dividends were sales less running costs less dividends = £120,000. However, the fixed asset purchase required £180,000, and so the company's cash position worsened in the year by £60,000, in spite of the profit.

(b) Suppose that company Y buys three items for cash, each costing £5,000, and resells them for £7,000 each. The buyers of the units take credit, and by the end of the company's accounting year, they were all still debtors.

(i) The profit on the transactions is £2,000 per unit and £6,000 in total.

(ii) The company has paid £15,000 to buy the goods, but so far it has received no cash back from selling them, and so its cash position is so far £15,000 worse off from the transactions.

(iii) The effect so far of the transactions is:

Reduction in cash	£15,000
Increase in debtors	£21,000
Increase in profit	£6,000

The increase in assets is £6,000 in total, to match the £6,000 increase in profit, but the increase in assets is the net change in cash (reduced balance) and debtors (increased balance).

1.43   Both these examples show ways in which a company can be profitable but at the same time get into cash flow problems. If an analysis of a company's published accounts is to give us some idea of the company's liquidity, profitability ratios are not going to be appropriate for doing this. Instead, we look at liquidity ratios and working capital turnover ratios.

The current ratio and the quick ratio

1.44   The standard test of liquidity is the **current ratio**:

$$\frac{\text{Current assets}}{\text{Current liabilities}}$$

A company should have enough current assets that give a promise of 'cash to come' to meet its commitments to pay its current liabilities. A ratio comfortably in excess of 1 should be expected. Otherwise, the company might be unable to pay its debts on time.

1.45   Companies are not able to convert all their current assets into cash very quickly. In particular, some manufacturing companies might hold large quantities of raw material stocks, which must be used in production to create finished goods. Finished goods might be warehoused for a long time, or sold on lengthy credit. In such businesses, where stock turnover is slow, most stocks are not very liquid assets, because the cash cycle is so long. For these reasons, we calculate an additional liquidity ratio, known as the quick ratio or acid test ratio.

1.46   The **quick ratio**, or **acid test ratio**, is:

$$\frac{\text{Current assets less stocks}}{\text{Current liabilities}}$$

This ratio should ideally be at least 1 for companies with a slow stock turnover. For companies with a fast stock turnover, a quick ratio can be less than 1 without suggesting that the company is in cash flow difficulties.

1.47   Do not forget the other side of the coin. The current ratio and the quick ratio can be bigger than they should be. A company that has large volumes of stocks and debtors might be over-investing in working capital, and so tying up more funds in the business than it needs to. This would suggest poor management of debtors or stocks by the company.

The debtors' payment period

1.48   A rough measure of the average length of time it takes for a company's debtors to pay what they owe is the 'debtor days' ratio, or average **debtors' payment period**.

$$\frac{\text{Trade debtors}}{\text{Sales}} \times 365 \, \text{days}$$

1.49   The figure for sales should be the turnover figure in the profit and loss account. The trade debtors are not the *total* figure for debtors in the balance sheet, which includes prepayments and non-trade debtors. The trade debtors figure will be itemised in an analysis of the total debtors, in a note to the accounts.

1.50 The estimate of debtor days is only approximate.

(a) The balance sheet value of debtors might be abnormally high or low compared with the normal level the company usually has.

(b) Turnover in the profit and loss account excludes VAT, but the debtors' figure in the balance sheet includes VAT. We are not strictly comparing like with like.

1.51 Sales are often made on terms of payment within 30 days, or at the end of the month following the month in which the invoice is sent out. Debtor days *significantly* in excess of this might indicate poor management of the funds of a business. However, some companies must allow generous credit terms to win customers. Exporting companies in particular may have to carry large amounts of debtors, and so their average collection period might be well in excess of 30 days.

1.52 The **trend of the collection period** (debtor days) over time is probably the best guide. If debtor days are increasing, this indicates a poorly managed credit control function.

The stock turnover period

1.53 Another ratio which can be calculated is the **stock turnover period**, or **stock days**. This is another estimated figure, obtainable from published accounts, which indicates the average number of days that items of stock are held for. As with the average debt collection period, however, it is only an approximate figure, but one which should be reliable enough for finding changes over time.

1.54 The number of **stock days** is:

$$\frac{\text{Stock}}{\text{Cost of sales}} \times 365$$

1.55 The reciprocal of the fraction:

$$\frac{\text{Cost of sales}}{\text{Stock}}$$

is called the **stock turnover**, and is another measure of how vigorously a business is trading. A lengthening stock turnover period indicates a slowdown in trading, or a build-up in stock levels, perhaps suggesting that the investment in stocks is becoming excessive.

1.56 If we add together the stock days and the debtor days, this should give us an indication of **how soon stock is convertible into cash.** Both debtor days and stock days therefore give us a further indication of the company's liquidity.

Question 2

Calculate liquidity and working capital ratios from the accounts of the RMC Group, a manufacturer of products for the construction industry, and comment on the ratios.

	Year 2 £m	Year 1 £m
Turnover	2,065.0	1,788.7
Cost of sales	1,478.6	1,304.0
Gross profit	586.4	484.7

BPP PUBLISHING

Part B: Business planning

	Year 2 £m	Year 1 £m
Current assets		
Stocks	119.0	109.0
Debtors (note 1)	400.9	347.4
Short-term investments	4.2	18.8
Cash at bank and in hand	48.2	48.0
	572.3	523.2
Creditors: amounts falling due within one year		
Loans and overdrafts	49.1	35.3
Corporation taxes	62.0	46.7
Dividend	19.2	14.3
Creditors (note 2)	370.7	324.0
	501.0	420.3

	Year 2 £m	Year 1 £m
Net current assets	71.3	102.9

Notes

	Year 2 £m	Year 1 £m
Trade debtors	329.8	285.4
Trade creditors	236.2	210.8

Answer

	Year 2		Year 1	
Current ratio	$\frac{572.3}{501.0}$	= 1.14	$\frac{523.2}{420.3}$	= 1.24
Quick ratio	$\frac{453.3}{501.0}$	= 0.90	$\frac{414.2}{420.3}$	= 0.99
Debtors' payment period	$\frac{329.8}{2,065.0} \times 365$	= 58 days	$\frac{285.4}{1,788.7} \times 365$	= 58 days
Stock turnover period	$\frac{119.0}{1,478.6} \times 365$	= 29 days	$\frac{109.0}{1,304.0} \times 365$	= 31 days
Creditors' turnover period	$\frac{236.2}{1,478.6} \times 365$	= 58 days	$\frac{210.8}{1,304.0} \times 365$	= 59 days

RMC is a manufacturing group serving the construction industry, and so would be expected to have a comparatively lengthy debtors' turnover period, because of the relatively poor cash flow in the construction industry. It is clear that RMC compensates for this by ensuring that they do not pay for raw materials and other costs before they have sold their stocks of finished goods (hence the similarity of debtors' and creditors' turnover periods).

RMC's current ratio is a little lower than average but its quick ratio is better than average and very little less than the current ratio. This suggests that stock levels are strictly controlled, which is reinforced by the low stock turnover period. It would seem that working capital is tightly managed, to avoid the poor liquidity which could be caused by a high debtors' turnover period and comparatively high creditors.

Creditors' turnover is ideally calculated by the formula:

$$\frac{\text{Average stock}}{\text{Purchases}} \times 365$$

However, it is rare to find purchases disclosed in published accounts and so cost of sales serves as an approximation. The creditors' turnover ratio often helps to assess a company's liquidity; an increase in creditor days is often a sign of lack of long-term finance or poor management of current assets, resulting in the use of extended credit from suppliers, increased bank overdraft and so on.

Shareholders' investment ratios

1.57 A further set of ratios to consider are the ratios which help equity shareholders and other investors to assess the value and quality of an investment in the ordinary shares of a company. The following stockmarket ratios were described in Chapter 4.

- Dividend yield
- Earnings per share
- P/E ratio
- Dividend cover
- Earnings yield

The value of an investment in ordinary shares in a listed company is its market value, and so investment ratios must have regard not only to information in the company's published accounts, but also to the current share price, and ratios (a), (c) and (e) all involve using the share price.

2 COMPARISONS OF ACCOUNTING FIGURES

2.1 Useful information is obtained from ratio analysis largely by means of comparisons. Comparisons that might be made are:

(a) Between the company's results in the most recent year and its results in previous years

(b) Between the company's results and the results of other companies in the same industry

(c) Between the company's results and the results of other companies in other industries

Results of the same company over successive accounting periods

2.2 Although a company might present useful information in its five year or ten year summary, it is quite likely that the only detailed comparison you will be able to make is between the current year's and the previous year's results. The comparison should give you some idea of whether the company's situation has improved, worsened or stayed much the same between one year and the next.

2.3 Useful comparisons over time include:

(a) The percentage growth in profit (before and after tax) and the percentage growth in turnover

(b) Increases or decreases in the debt ratio and the gearing ratio

(c) Changes in the current ratio, the stock turnover period and the debtors' payment period

(d) Increases in the EPS, the dividend per share, and the market price

2.4 The principal advantage of making comparisons over time is that they give some indication of progress: are things getting better or worse? However, there are some weaknesses in such comparisons.

(a) The **effect of inflation** should not be forgotten.

(b) The progress a company has made needs to be set in the context of:

(i) What other companies have done

(ii) Whether there have been any special 'environmental' or economic influences on the company's performance

Allowing for inflation

2.5 Ratio analysis is not usually affected by price inflation, except as follows.

(a) Return on capital employed (ROCE) can be misleading if fixed assets, especially property, are valued at historical cost net of depreciation rather than at current value. As time goes by and if property prices go up, the fixed assets would be seriously undervalued if they were still recorded at their historical cost, and so the return on capital employed would be misleadingly high.

(b) Some growth trends can be misleading, in particular:

(i) The growth in sales turnover
(ii) The growth in profits or earnings

2.6 For example, suppose that a company achieved the following results.

	20X8	*20X7*	*% growth*
	£m	£m	
Turnover	46	43	7.0
Profit	12	11	9.1

However, if price inflation from 20X7 to 20X8 was 10%, the performance of the company would show a drop in turnover and profit in real terms, of about 3% in turnover and of about 0.9% in profit.

Putting a company's results into context

2.7 The financial and accounting ratios of one company should be looked at in the context of what other companies have been achieving, and also any special influences on the industry or the economy as a whole. Here are two examples.

(a) If a company achieves a 10% increase in profits, this performance taken in isolation might seem commendable, but if it is then compared with the results of rival companies, which might have been achieving profit growth of 30% the performance might in comparison seem very disappointing.

(b) An improvement in ROCE and profits might be attributable to a temporary economic boom, and an increase in profits after tax might be attributable to a cut in the rate of corporation tax. When improved results are attributable to factors outside the control of the company's management, such as changes in the economic climate and tax rates other companies might be expected to benefit in the same way.

Comparisons between different companies in the same industry

2.8 Making comparisons between the results of different companies in the same industry is a way of assessing which companies are outperforming others.

(a) Even if two companies are in the same broad industry (for example retailing) they might not be direct competitors. Even so, they might still be expected to show broadly similar performance, in terms of growth, because a boom or a depression in retail markets should affect all retailers in much the same way. The results of two such companies can be compared, and the company with the better growth and accounting ratios might be considered more successful than the other.

(b) If two companies are direct competitors, a comparison between them would be particularly interesting. Which has achieved the better ROCE, sales growth, or profit growth? Does one have a better debt or gearing position, a better liquidity position or better working capital ratios? How do their P/E ratios, dividend cover and dividend yields compare? And so on.

2.9 Comparisons between companies in the same industry can help investors to rank them in order of desirability as investments, and to judge relative share prices or future prospects. It is important, however, to make comparisons with caution: a large company and a small company in the same industry might be expected to show different results, not just in terms of size, but in terms of:

(a) Percentage rates of growth in sales and profits

(b) Percentages of profits re-invested (Dividend cover will be higher in a company that needs to retain profits to finance investment and growth.)

(c) Fixed assets (Large companies are more likely to have freehold property in their balance sheet than small companies.)

Comparisons between companies in different industries

2.10 Useful information can also be obtained by comparing the financial and accounting ratios of companies in different industries. An investor ought to be aware of how companies in one industrial sector are performing in comparisons with companies in other sectors. For example, it is important to know the following.

(a) Whether sales growth and profit growth is higher in some industries than in others. For example how does growth in the financial services industry compare with growth in heavy engineering, electronics or leisure?

(b) How the return on capital employed and return on shareholder capital compare between different industries.

(c) How the P/E ratios and dividend yields vary between industries. For example, if a publishing company has a P/E ratio of, say, 20, which is average for its industry, whereas an electronics company has a P/E ratio of, say, 14, do the better growth performance and prospects of the publishing company justify its higher P/E ratio?

3 PREDICTING BUSINESS FAILURE

3.1 The analysis of financial ratios is largely concerned with the efficiency and effectiveness of the use of resources by a company's management, and also with the financial stability of the company. Investors will wish to know whether additional funds could be lent to the company with reasonable safety, and whether the company would fail without additional funds.

3.2 One method of predicting business failure is the use of **liquidity ratios** (the **current ratio** and the **quick ratio**). A company with a current ratio well below 2:1 or a quick ratio well below 1:1 might be considered illiquid and in danger of failure. Research seems to indicate, however, that the current ratio and the quick ratio and trends in the variations of these ratios for a company, are poor indicators of eventual business failure.

Z scores

3.3 E I Altman researched into the simultaneous analysis of several financial ratios as a combined predictor of business failure. Altman analysed 22 accounting and non-accounting variables for a selection of failed and non-failed firms in the USA and from these, five key indicators emerged. These five indicators were then used to derive a **Z score**. Firms with a Z score above a certain level would be predicted to be financially sound, and firms with a Z score below a certain level would be categorised as probable failures. Altman also identified a range of Z scores in between the non-failure and failure categories in which eventual failure or non-failure was uncertain.

3.4 Altman's Z score model (derived in 1968) emerged as:

$$Z = 1.2X_1 + 1.4X_2 + 3.3X_3 + 0.6X_4 + 1.0X_5$$

where

X_1 = working capital/total assets
X_2 = retained earnings/total assets
X_3 = earnings before interest and tax/total assets
X_4 = market value of equity/book value of total debt (a form of gearing ratio)
X_5 = sales/total assets

3.5 In Altman's model, a Z score of 2.7 or more indicated non-failure, and a Z score of 1.8 or less indicated failure.

3.6 Altman's sample size was small, and related to US firms. Subsequent research based on the similar principle of identifying a Z score predictor of business failure has produced different prediction models, using a variety of financial ratios and different Z score values as predictors of failure. It would be argued, for example, that different ratios and Z score values would be appropriate for conditions in the UK.

The value of Z scores

3.7 A current view of the link between financial ratios and business failure would be as follows.

(a) The financial ratios of firms which fail can be seen in retrospect to have deteriorated significantly prior to failure, and to be worse than the ratios of non-failed firms. In retrospect, financial ratios can be used to suggest why a firm has failed.

(b) No fully accepted model for **prediction** of future business failures has yet been established, although some form of Z score analysis would appear to be the most promising avenue for progress. In the UK, several Z score-type failure prediction models exist.

(c) Because of the use of X_4: market value of equity/book value of debt, Z score models cannot be used for unquoted companies which lack a market value of equity.

3.8 Z score models are used widely in the banking sector, in risk assessment, loan grading and corporate finance activities. They are also used by accountancy firms, fund management houses, stockbrokers and credit insurers, including Trade Indemnity.

Other corporate failure models

3.9 **Beaver** conducted a study which showed that the worst predictor of failure is the current ratio (current assets/current liabilities) and the best predictor of failure is cash flow borrowings. Other writers have put forward alternative models designed to predict whether a business will fail.

3.10 **Taffler's** approach is based on the following measures.

(a) Earnings before tax/current liabilities

(b) Current assets/total liabilities

(c) Current liabilities/total assets

(d) Sales/total assets

3.11 From historical data on a wide range of actual cases, **Argenti** developed a model which is intended to predict the likelihood of company failure. The model is based on calculating scores for a company based on (a) defects of the company; (b) management mistakes and (c) the symptoms of failure. For each of the scores (a), (b) and (c) there is a 'danger mark'.

3.12 Among the most important factors in the model are:

(a) **Defects**

(i) Autocratic Chief Executive (Robert Maxwell is an example here)

(ii) Passive board

(iii) Lack of budgetary control

(b) **Mistakes**

(i) Over-trading (expanding faster than cash funding)

(ii) Gearing - high bank overdrafts/loans

(iii) Failure of large project jeopardises the company (eg Laker Airways)

(c) **Symptoms**

(i) Deteriorating ratios

(ii) Creative accounting - signs of window-dressing

(iii) Declining morale and declining quality

Weaknesses of corporate failure models

3.13 Weaknesses of corporate failure models include the following.

(a) In common with all correlation models, they relate to the past, without taking into account the current state of the macroeconomic environment (the level of inflation and interest rates, and so on).

(b) The models share the limitations of the accounting model (including the accounting concepts and conventions) on which they are based.

(c) The publication of accounting data by companies is subject to a delay. Failure might occur before the data becomes available.

(d) If the measures incorporated in the models become used as objectives, as some suggest, then the model is likely to become less useful as a predictive tool as the measures will be subject to manipulation.

(e) The definition of corporate failure is not clear, given that various forms of rescue or restructuring are possible, short of liquidation, for a company which is in trouble.

Other indicators of financial difficulties

3.14 You should not think that ratio analysis of published accounts and correlation models such as Z score analysis are the only ways of spotting that a company might be running into financial difficulties. There are other possible indicators too.

(a) **Other information in the published accounts**
Some information in the published accounts might not lend itself readily to ratio analysis, but still be an indicator of financial difficulties, for example:

(i)   Very large increases in intangible fixed assets

(ii)   A worsening net liquid funds position, as shown by the cash flow statement

(iii) Very large contingent liabilities

(iv)   Important post balance sheet events

(b) **Information in the chairman's report and the directors' report**

The report of the chairman or chief executive that accompanies the published accounts might be very revealing. Although this report is not audited, and will no doubt try to paint a rosy picture of the company's affairs, any difficulties the company has had and not yet overcome will probably be discussed in it. There might also be warnings of problems to come in the future.

The directors' report is usually restricted to the minimum information required by law, but it might be interesting to check whether there have been any changes in the composition of the board since last year. Have many of last year's directors gone? Are there many new directors, and if so, what are their qualifications?

(c) **Published information in the press**

Newspapers and financial journals are a source of information about companies, and the difficulties or successes they are having. There may be reports of strikes, redundancies and closures. Reports of **sales of shares by directors** may also be found.

There are often articles in newspapers which focus on particular companies. If a company is in financial difficulty, adverse comments might well appear in one of these articles.

(d) **Published information about environmental or external matters**

There will also be published information about matters that will have a direct influence on a company's future, although the connection may not be obvious. Examples of external matters that may affect a company adversely are as follows.

(i)   New legislation, for example on product safety standards or pollution controls, which affect a company's main products

(ii)   International events, for example political disagreements with a foreign country, leading to a restriction on trade between the countries (The foreign country concerned might be a major importer of a company's products.)

(iii) New and better products being launched on to the market by a competitor

(iv)   A big rise in interest rates, which might affect a highly geared company seriously

(v)   A big change in foreign exchange rates, which might affect a major importer or exporter seriously

4   OTHER INFORMATION FROM COMPANIES' ACCOUNTS

Fixed assets

4.1   Two features of a company's fixed assets which can be looked at are:

(a)   How the company has accounted for the **revaluation of fixed assets**

(b)   The amount of **intangible fixed assets** in the balance sheet

The revaluation of fixed assets

4.2   Fixed assets may be stated in the balance sheet at cost less accumulated depreciation. They may also be revalued from time to time to a current market value. When this happens:

(a) The increase in the balance sheet value of the fixed asset is matched by an increase in the **revaluation reserve**

(b) Depreciation in subsequent years is based on the revalued amount of the asset, its estimated residual value and its estimated remaining useful life

4.3 It has been usual for companies to revalue their land and buildings periodically, but not their other fixed assets such as plant and machinery. There has been nothing to stop companies revaluing all their fixed assets regularly, but land and buildings have been an obvious example of fixed assets that can increase substantially in value. To avoid a serious understatement of their balance sheet value, companies have therefore revalued their land and buildings from time to time, typically every two or three years.

Intangible fixed assets

4.4 Intangible fixed assets are assets which do not have any physical substance, but are of use to a business over a number of years in helping to provide goods or services. Intangible assets include **trademarks, patents, copyrights, development expenditure** and **goodwill.**

4.5 Companies are allowed to include intangible fixed assets in their balance sheet, but if they do, they must depreciate them over their estimated useful lives. Instead of having intangible fixed assets, many companies write off the cost of intangible items in the year of acquisition.

4.6 An important area of recent debate is the extent to which companies should be allowed to include the values of **brand names** in their balance sheets. Valuations of such assets are likely to be highly subjective.

Share capital and reserves

4.7 The capital and reserves section of a company's accounts contains information which appears to be mainly the concern of the various classes of shareholder. However, because the shareholders' interest in the business acts as a buffer for the creditors in the event of any financial problems, this section is also of some importance to creditors.

4.8 The nature of any increase in reserves will be of some interest. For example, if a company has increased its total share capital and reserves in the year:

(a) Did it do so by issuing new shares resulting in a higher allotted share capital and share premium account?

(b) Did it do so by revaluing some fixed assets, resulting in a higher revaluation reserve?

(c) Did it make a substantial profit and retain a good proportion of this profit in the business resulting in a higher profit and loss account balance?

4.9 A **scrip issue** might also be of some interest. It will result in a fall in the market price per share. If it has been funded from a company's profit and loss account reserves, a scrip issue would indicate that the company recognised and formalised its long-term capital needs by now making some previously distributable reserves non-distributable.

4.10 If a company has issued shares in the form of a dividend, are there obvious reasons why this should be so? For example, does the company need to retain capital within the business because of poor trading in the previous year, making the directors reluctant to pay out more cash dividend than necessary?

Debentures, loans and other liabilities

4.11 Two points of interest about debentures, loans and other liabilities are **whether or not loans are secured**, and the **redemption dates of loans**.

Secured loans

4.12 For debentures and loan stock which are **secured**, the details of the security are usually included in the terms of a trust deed. Details of any **fixed or floating charges** against any assets must be disclosed in a note to the accounts.

Redemptions of debentures and loan stock

4.13 In analysing a set of accounts, particular attention should be paid to some significant features concerning **debenture or loan stock redemption**. These are:

   (a) The closeness of the redemption date which would indicate how much finance the company has to find in the immediate future to repay its loans. It is not unusual, however, to repay one loan by taking out another, and so a company does not necessarily have to find the money to repay a loan from its own resources.

   (b) The percentage interest rate on the loans being redeemed, compared with the current market rate of interest. This would give some idea, if a company decides to replace loans by taking out new loans, of the likely increase (or reduction) in interest costs that it might face, and how easily it might accommodate any interest cost increase.

4.14 There are classes of debentures which do not have a redemption date attached. This does not mean that they will never be redeemed because a company can always buy back its own debentures in the market. The holder of an irredeemable debenture does not, however, have a date by which redemption must take place, so he cannot demand repayment. Consequently, not being very attractive to investors, this is a rare form of finance.

A geographical analysis of trading

4.15 When you study a company's published accounts, a useful item of information to look for might be the analysis of the company's turnover in each part of the world. It could show in which markets the company is making good progress, and where it is losing ground to competitors.

Post balance sheet events

4.16 **Post balance sheet events** are those events both favourable and unfavourable which occur between the balance sheet date and the date on which the financial statements are approved by the board of directors, such as:

   (a) Mergers and acquisitions
   (b) The issue of new shares and debentures
   (c) The purchase and sales of major fixed assets and investments
   (d) Losses of fixed assets or stocks as a result of a catastrophe such as fire or flood
   (e) The opening of new trading activities
   (f) The closure of a significant part of the trading activities
   (g) A decline in the value of property and investments held as fixed assets
   (h) Changes in exchange rates where the company has significant overseas interests
   (i) Government action, such as nationalisation

    (j)   Strikes and other labour disputes

    (k)   The augmentation of pension benefits to employees

Contingencies

4.17   Contingencies are conditions which exist at the balance sheet date where the outcome will be confirmed only on the occurrence or non-occurrence of one or more uncertain future events.

4.18   Contingencies can result in **contingent gains** or **contingent losses**. The fact that the condition exists at the balance sheet date distinguishes a contingency from a post balance sheet event, which arises between the balance sheet date and the date of the formal approval of the financial statements by the board of directors.

The usual types of reported contingencies

4.19   Some of the principal types of contingencies disclosed by companies are as follows.

    (a)   Guarantees given by the company:

        (i)   For other group companies

        (ii)   For associated companies

        (iii)   For staff pension schemes

        (iv)   For the completion of contracts

    (b)   Discounted bills of exchange

    (c)   Uncalled liabilities on shares or loan stock

    (d)   Lawsuits or claims pending

    (e)   Tax on profits where the basis on which the tax should be computed is unclear

5   PERFORMANCE MEASUREMENT IN THE PUBLIC SECTOR

5.1   In public sector organisations, an increasing volume of information on performance and 'value for money' is produced for internal and external use.

5.2   Targets are likely to fall under the following broad headings.

- **Financial performance targets**
- **Volume of output targets**
- **Quality of service targets**
- **Efficiency targets**

Performance measurement in central government

5.3   Over recent years, much of the work of central government has been reorganised into semi-autonomous **executive agencies**. The following are examples of targets related to **financial performance** in executive agencies.

    (a)   Full cost recovery (Civil Service College, Central Office of Information and others), plus unit cost targets

    (b)   Commercial revenue to offset costs (Met Office)

    (c)   Non-Exchequer income as a percentage of total income (National Engineering Laboratory)

BPP PUBLISHING

Volume of output targets

5.4 Targets related to **output** can be difficult to set. While the output of the Vehicle Inspectorate can be measured on the number of tests performed, and the output of the Hydrographic Office consists of charts for navigators, in many other cases the output of executive agencies is less tangible. For example, the Historic Royal Palaces Agency not only deals with visitors, whose numbers can be counted, but is also responsible for maintaining the fabric of royal palaces - an output which is more difficult to measure. In such cases, performance will be best measured by appraising the progress of the project as a whole.

Quality of service targets

5.5 Example of **quality** targets set for executive agencies include the following.

(a) **Timeliness**

(i) Time to handle applications (Passport Office, Vehicle Certification Agency and many others)

(ii) Car driving tests to be reduced to 6 weeks nationally and 10 weeks in London (Driving Standards Agency)

(iii) All cheques to be banked within 35 hours (Accounts Services Agency)

(b) **Quality of product**

(i) Number of print orders delivered without fault (Stationery Office)

(ii) Error rate in the value of benefit payments (Employment Service)

(iii) 95% business complaints handled within 5 days (Radio Communications Agency)

(iv) 85% overall customer satisfaction rating (Recruitment and Assessment Services Agency)

(v) Meetings of creditors held within 12 weeks in 90% of cases (Insolvency Service)

Efficiency targets

5.6 Efficiency improvements may come through reducing the cost of inputs without reducing the quality of outputs. Alternatively, areas of activity affecting total costs may be reduced. Targets related to **efficiency** include the following.

(a) Percentage reduction in price paid for purchases of stationery and paper (Stationery Office)

(b) Reduction in the ratio of cost of support services to total cost (Laboratory of the Government Chemist)

(c) 8.7% efficiency increase in the use of accommodation (Recruitment and Assessment Services Agency)

Performance measurement in local government

5.7 The performance measures chosen by local authorities usually consist of comparative statistics and unit costs. These measures do two things.

(a) They give details, statistics and unit costs of an authority's own activities.

(b) They show statistical and cost comparisons with other authorities or clusters of authorities.

5.8 Reporting on comparative statistics was recommended by the Department of the Environment in its code of practice *Local authority annual reports* (1982). The following list illustrates the types of comparative statistics suggested in the code of practice.

Performance measures in local government	
For the authority's total expenditure and for each function	Net cost per 1,000 population Manpower per 1,000 population
Primary education, secondary education	Pupil/teacher ratio Cost per pupil
School meals	Revenue/cost ratio Pupils receiving free meals as a proportion of school roll
Children in care	As a proportion of total under-18 population Cost per child in care
Care of elderly	Residents of council homes as a proportion of total over-75 population Cost per resident week
Home helps	Contract hours per 1,000 population over 65
Police	Population per police officer Serious offences per 1,000 population
Fire	Proportion of area at high risk
Public transport	Passenger journeys per week per 1,000 population
Highways	Maintenance cost per kilometre
Housing	Rents as a proportion of total cost Management cost per dwelling per week Rent arrears as a percentage of year's rent income Construction cost per dwelling completed
Trading services	Revenue/gross cost ratio

Chapter roundup

- Analysis of company performance may serve a number of purposes:

  ○ To examine the company's financial position and growth potential
  ○ To focus on weaknesses in the company's financial structure
  ○ To evaluate the risk to an investor of holding shares or loan stocks in the company
  ○ To compare performance with that of other companies

- Comments on a company based on such ratios are far more likely to be right than comments based on a casual read through a set of accounts. However, you should always make use of whatever **other information** can be gleaned from a company's accounts.

- You should be aware of the use of **corporate failure models** such as those of Altman and Taffler, but numerical questions will not be set on them. Although they are used in practice, such models have a number of weaknesses.

Quick quiz

1   Define return on capital employed. (see para 1.15)

2   What is the debt ratio? (1.27)

3   How can a profitable company run out of cash? (1.42, 1.43)

4   What is the quick ratio? (1.46)

5   What is the stock turnover? (1.55)

6   Does inflation affect ratio analysis? (2.5)

7   What is a Z score? (3.3)

8   Outline the weaknesses of corporate failure models. (3.13)

9   Why should creditors be interested in a company's share capital and reserves? (4.7)

10   Under what broad headings do individual targets for public sector organisations fall? (5.2)

Question to try	Level	Marks	Time
12	Introductory	n/a	45 mins

Chapter 13

AMALGAMATIONS AND RESTRUCTURING

Chapter topic list	Syllabus reference
1 Amalgamations and takeovers	2(e)
2 Trends in takeover activity	2(e)
3 The conduct and financing of a takeover	2(e)
4 The position of shareholders	2(e)
5 Other matters in takeovers	2(e)
6 Post-acquisition integration	2(e)
7 Demergers	2(e)
8 Management buyouts	2(e)
9 Share repurchase	2(e)

Introduction

The forms of business reorganisations undertaken in the modern industrialised economy are various, as companies seek the optimal form of enterprise. In this and the following chapter, we are concerned with the issues of business combinations and restructuring from the point of view of financial management and financial strategy.

Mergers and acquisitions in the context of long-term financial planning are also covered, from a slightly different perspective, in Paper 13 *Financial Reporting Environment*.

1   AMALGAMATIONS AND TAKEOVERS   6/94, 6/96, 6/98, 12/98

1.1   A **takeover** is the purchase of a controlling interest in one company by another company. Takeovers are also referred to as **acquisitions**, and are a form of 'external' investment. An amalgamation is a **merger** between two separate companies to form a single company.

1.2   The distinction between amalgamations and takeovers is not always clear, for example when a large company 'merges' with another smaller company. The methods used for mergers are often the same as the methods used to make takeovers. In practice, the number of genuine mergers is small relative to the number of takeovers.

The reasons for an amalgamation or a takeover

1.3   When two or more companies join together, there should be a **'synergistic' effect**. Synergy can be described as the $2 + 2 = 5$ effect, whereby a group after a takeover achieves combined results that reflect a better rate of return than was being achieved by the same resources used in two separate operations before the takeover. If company A, which makes annual profits of £200,000 merges with company B, which also makes annual profits of £200,000, the combined annual profits of the merged companies should be more than £400,000.

1.4 The main reasons why one company may wish to acquire the shares or the business of another may be categorised as follows.

(a) **Operating economies**. Duplicate (and competing) facilities can be eliminated.

(b) **Management acquisition**. If a company lacks a management team of sufficient quality to ensure continued growth, it may be best to seek an amalgamation with another company with aggressive and competent management.

(c) **Diversification**. The long-term interest of shareholders might be best served by spreading risk through diversification.

(d) **Asset backing**. A company in a risky industry with a high level of earnings relative to the net assets may try to reduce its overall risk by acquiring a company with substantial assets.

(e) **The quality of earnings**. A company may reduce its risk by acquiring another with less risky earnings.

(f) **Finance and liquidity**. A company may be able to improve its liquidity and its ability to raise new finance through the acquisition of another more financially stable company.

(g) **Growth**. A company may achieve growth through acquisition more cheaply than through internal expansion.

(h) **Tax factors.** In exceptional cases, a cash-financed takeover may be a tax-efficient method of transferring cash out of the corporate sector. However, UK tax law precludes using amalgamations as a way of utilising tax losses by setting them against profits of another company.

(i) **Defensive merger**. Companies may merge in order to prevent competitors from obtaining an advantage in some way.

1.5 The aim of a merger or acquisition should be to make profits in the long term as well as in the short term.

(a) Acquisitions may provide a **means of entering a market** at a lower cost than would be incurred if the company tried to develop its own resources, or a **means of acquiring the business of a competitor**. Acquisitions or mergers which might reduce or eliminate competition in a market may be prohibited by the Monopolies and Mergers Commission.

(b) Mergers, especially in Britain, have tended to be more common in industries with a history of little growth and low returns. Highly profitable companies tend to seek acquisitions rather than mergers.

Factors in a takeover decision

1.6 Several factors will influence a decision to try to take over a target business. These include the following.

Price factors

(a) What would the cost of acquisition be?

(b) Would the acquisition be worth the price?

(c) Alternatively, factors (a) and (b) above could be expressed in terms of the highest price that it would be worth paying to acquire the business.

The value of a business could be assessed in terms of its earnings, its assets, its prospects for sales and earnings growth, or how it would contribute to the short-term and long-term strategy of the 'predator' company.

Different methods for the valuation of companies are covered in Chapter 14 of this Study Text.

Other factors

(a) Would the takeover be regarded as desirable by the predator company's shareholders and (in the case of quoted companies) the stock market in general?

(b) Are the owners of the target company amenable to a takeover bid? Or would they be likely to adopt defensive tactics to resist a bid?

(c) What form would the purchase consideration take? An acquisition is accomplished by buying the shares of a target company. The purchase consideration might be cash, but the purchasing company might issue new shares (or loan stock) and exchange them for shares in the company taken over. If purchase is by means of a share exchange, the former shareholders in the company taken over will acquire an interest in the new, enlarged company.

(d) How would the takeover be reflected in the published accounts of the predator company?

(e) Would there be any other potential problems arising from the proposed takeover, such as future dividend policy or service contracts for key personnel?

Question

Flycatcher Ltd wishes to make a takeover bid for the shares of an unquoted company, Mayfly Ltd. The earnings of Mayfly Ltd over the past five years have been as follows.

20X0	£50,000	20X3	£71,000
20X1	£72,000	20X4	£75,000
20X2	£68,000		

The average P/E ratio of quoted companies in the industry in which Mayfly Ltd operates is 10. Quoted companies which are similar in many respects to Mayfly Ltd are:

(a) Bumblebee plc, which has a P/E ratio of 15, but is a company with very good growth prospects;
(b) Wasp plc, which has had a poor profit record for several years, and has a P/E ratio of 7.

What would be a suitable range of valuations for the shares of Mayfly Ltd?

Answer

(a) *Earnings.* Average earnings over the last five years have been £67,200, and over the last four years £71,500. There might appear to be some growth prospects, but estimates of future earnings are uncertain.

A low estimate of earnings in 19X5 would be, perhaps, £71,500. A high estimate of earnings might be £75,000 or more. This solution will use the most recent earnings figure of £75,000 as the high estimate.

(b) *P/E ratio.* A P/E ratio of 15 (Bumblebee's) would be much too high for Mayfly Ltd, because the growth of Mayfly Ltd earnings is not as certain, and Mayfly Ltd is an unquoted company. On the other hand, Mayfly Ltd's expectations of earnings are probably better than those of Wasp plc. A suitable P/E ratio might be based on the industry's average, 10; but since Mayfly is an unquoted company and therefore more risky, a lower P/E ratio might be more appropriate: perhaps 60% to 70% of 10 = 6 or 7, or conceivably even as low as 50% of 10 = 5.

The valuation of Mayfly Ltd's shares might therefore range between:

high P/E ratio and high earnings: 7 × £75,000 = £525,000; and

low P/E ratio and low earnings: 5 × £71,500 = £357,500.

A strategic approach to takeovers

1.7 A strategic approach to takeovers would imply that acquisitions are only made after a full analysis of the underlying strengths of the acquiror company, and identification of candidates' **strategic fit** with its existing activities. Possible strategic reasons for a takeover are matched with suggested ways of achieving the aim in the following list from a publication of 3i (Investors in Industry), which specialises in offering advice on takeovers.

Strategic opportunities	
Where you are	**How to get to where you want to be**
Growing steadily but in a mature market with limited growth prospects	Acquire a company in a younger market with a higher growth rate
Marketing an incomplete product range, or having the potential to sell other products or services to your existing customers	Acquire a company with a complementary product range
Operating at maximum productive capacity	Acquire a company making similar products operating substantially below capacity
Under-utilising management resources	Acquire a company into which your talents can extend
Needing more control of suppliers or customers	Acquire a company which is, or gives access to, a significant customer or supplier
Lacking key clients in a targeted sector	Acquire a company with the right customer profile
Preparing for flotation but needing to improve your balance sheet	Acquire a suitable company which will enhance earnings per share
Needing to increase market share	Acquire an important competitor
Needing to widen your capability	Acquire a company with the key talents and/or technology

Are takeovers good for business?

1.8 Stuart Manson, Andrew Stark and Hardy Thomas addressed this question in an article published in *Certified Accountant* (October 1994), making the following points.

(a) Because of the volume of takeover, acquisition and merger activity, there is concern about the effect that takeover activity has on industrial structure, monopoly power and economic performance. Most previous research focuses on whether gains or losses arise from acquisitions: that is, the effect of acquisitions on economic performance.

(b) In contrast to previous accounting profit-based studies, the analysis presented in the article concludes that the average takeover does produce improvements in operating performance. This conclusion conflicts with the commonly held view that changes in corporate control result from managers pursuing their own self-interest at the expense of shareholders. If that were so, the authors argue, then the only gains would be gains to management. The authors found some support for the proposition that the takeover market provides a disciplinary mechanism over management, helping to ensure that managers act in the interests of shareholders. Recent studies in the USA have produced some similar conclusions.

(c) A key problem in analysing the effect of a takeover is that of how to choose a yardstick for revaluating post-takeover performance when investigating improvements in operating performance or any other type of performance.

2 TRENDS IN TAKEOVER ACTIVITY

UK takeover activity

2.1 There was a boom in takeover activity in the UK at the end of the 1980s and another at the end of the first half of the 1990s. As the increased level of expenditure on acquisitions took place at the same time as a surge in capital expenditure by industrial and commercial companies (ICCs), it appears that the increase in takeover activity must partly have reflected a desire of companies to expand.

2.2 The annual expenditure on UK takeovers peaked at £27 billion in 1989, following by a fall to £8.2 billion in 1990 which reflected diminished business confidence with the onset of higher interest rates and the subsequent economic recession. A new surge in takeover activity in the mid 1990s included the £9 billion takeover of Wellcome by Glaxo, Europe's largest ever takeover at the time.

2.3 The 1990s surge in activity has been much more focused on particular sectors than the earlier boom. For example, the sectors of investment banking and the privatised regional electricity companies have both experienced substantial levels of bid activity. In a significant shift in ownership, foreign banks took over various companies including (in 1995) Kleinwort Benson, Barings, Smith New Court and the investment banking businesses of SG Warburg. Deals completed in the electricity sector included the bid for South Western Electricity by Southern Company of the USA, and Hanson's £2.4 billion bid for Eastern Group.

Some major UK takeovers	
Acquiror	**Acquiree**
Guinness	Distillers
Burton Group	Debenhams
Hanson Trust	Imperial Group
Nestlé	Rowntree Mackintosh
HSBC	Midland Bank
Glaxo	Wellcome

International aspects of UK takeovers

2.4 Acquisition is one of the chief ways of carrying out **foreign direct investment (FDI)**. Over the past fifteen years or so, approximately half of the UK's FDI was in the form of acquisition of share and loan capital overseas, of which a substantial proportion was related to takeovers.

2.5 After the stock market crash of October 1987, there was a switch to 'leveraged' takeovers, with the cost of acquisitions being paid for by loan finance. With the 1990s recession, highly developed takeovers are having a severe impact on firms which borrowed heavily.

BPP PUBLISHING

The US, where leveraged financing was made fashionable, had a large number of indebted firms which fell on hard times.

> **KEY TERM**
>
> A **leveraged takeover** is a takeover which is achieved using a high proportion of debt.

2.6 A number of reasons for the expansion of UK companies in the USA, which occurred particularly during the late 1980s, can be identified.

   (a) The same factors which led to the expansion in takeovers at home can be cited, especially the strong financial position of companies in this period.

   (b) US capital markets are open and large bids, often hostile, can be made relatively easily.

   (c) The US product markets are large and diverse.

   (d) There is no language barrier.

   (e) The depreciation of the dollar during the mid to late 1980s made acquisition targets more attractive.

2.7 Takeover transactions conducted by UK companies in the EU have on average been much smaller than for takeovers in the USA in past recent years. However, the Single European Act and financial deregulation are factors contributing to a growth in importance of UK takeovers in the rest of the EU.

International comparisons of takeover activity

2.8 Official statistics for acquisitions are not available on a fully comparable basis internationally. However, it is clear that takeover activity was buoyant in the major OECD economies generally in the latter half of the 1980s, especially in the USA, Germany, France and Canada. However, distinctive features of the UK takeover boom have been the frequency of hostile bids (relative to other EU countries) and the greater emphasis on equity finance than in the USA. Hostile bids involve payment of a substantial premium over the pre-bid share price of the target firm and are therefore only feasible if the profitability of the joint assets can be improved to compensate for this premium.

Takeovers in the UK compared with other European countries

2.9 It has been suggested that UK companies are more vulnerable to takeover than their counterparts in other European countries. There are a number of reasons why this should be so.

2.10 Firstly, the **equity markets** in Britain are more highly developed than in other European countries and a greater proportion of companies are either quoted or are subsidiaries of quoted firms with publicly traded shares. In the rest of Europe by contrast there is a much greater proportion of firms which are still in private hands; this is especially true in Germany. Thus access to ownership in Britain is easier.

2.11 In addition the **capital structure** of British firms is generally different to their European counterparts. In European firms there is frequently a large class of shares that do not have voting rights, unlike the ordinary shares that make up the major part of the equity for most

UK companies. Thus in Europe there is a greater division between ownership and control, and access to the controlling shares is harder to obtain.

2.12   It has also been argued that it has been easier to build a stake in a UK firm due to the **3% rule** whereby a shareholder does not have to declare an interest until he holds 3% of the shares or 10% of any particular class of share. This is enhanced by the rule that a full bid need not be triggered until he owns 30%. It is difficult for a firm to mount a defence until a bid is declared, by which time the bidder already has a strong hand.

2.13   **Government attitudes** to the issues of ownership and control are also different to those in many other European countries. The prevalent non-interventionist policies mean that the government holds much fewer stakes and controlling interests in companies than say in France, and the 'national interest' lobby in the UK is also weaker.

2.14   **Reporting requirements** in the UK have been generally more rigorous than in Continental Europe. Annual reports contain more information and are more transparent than those of comparable European firms, and thus it is easier for a predator to obtain a meaningful preliminary valuation of a potential target. Although reporting rules in Europe have become stricter, enforcement is relatively weak, and annual accounts do not provide as full a picture of the company's position as in the UK.

Friendly and hostile takeovers: the UK, USA, Japan, Europe

2.15   In contrast to the UK and the USA, takeovers in Continental Europe and Japan are nearly always friendly. It has been argued that this difference results from different approaches to corporate governance in the Anglo-US markets compared with others.

2.16   In Continental Europe and Japan, the prevailing philosophy is that the objective of the organisation should be the maximisation of corporate wealth. In contrast to the Anglo-American emphasis on maximisation of shareholder wealth, this objective gives much more emphasis to the interests of other interest groups such as management, trade unions and suppliers. There are more often dual classes of voting shares, and strategic alliances (eg exchanges of shares between firms) and networks of close personal relationships play an important role. These factors mean that there are many more defences against unfriendly takeovers.

Competition policy differences in the USA and the UK

2.17   In the USA, the term 'trust' is used for a monopoly. The USA has a long history of legislation aimed at outlawing monopolies, starting with the Sherman Anti-Trust Act of 1890. From 1968, US guidelines on mergers and takeovers involved analysing the power held by the four largest companies in a market.

2.18   Since 1982, guidelines on which mergers should receive detailed scrutiny have been based on the **Herfindahl-Hirschman Index**, which sums the squares of the percentage market shares of all the companies in the market. Thus a pure monopoly will have a value of 10,000 (100^2) while a perfectly competitive market will have a value close to zero. A duopoly in which the two companies each have a 50% share will have a value of 5,000 (= $50^2 + 50^2$). The guidelines are based on the zone of index values within which a market lies, and the change in index value which an amalgamation would cause. For example, in highly concentrated markets (1,800 to 10,000), amalgamations increasing the index by more than 100 points are likely to be prohibited, while the central zone (1,000 to 1,800) is a 'grey' area, necessitating greater scrutiny of the proposed amalgamation.

2.19   The US guidelines leave an area of uncertainty about the US Justice Department's reaction relating to 'non-horizontal' amalgamations between companies in different industries or market sectors. This uncertainty is serious for the greater majority of US takeovers which are of a 'conglomerate' type (ie involving companies in different industries).

2.20   The approach to legislation on takeovers and mergers has been more tentative in the UK than in the US. (UK policy on takeovers and mergers is discussed later in this chapter.) In overview, the current regulatory regime in the UK is designed neither to inhibit nor to encourage takeovers, but to encourage competition and to ensure fair treatment of shareholders.

3   THE CONDUCT AND FINANCING OF A TAKEOVER   6/94, 6/96

Takeover tactics

3.1   It is common for a company to build up a holding of the shares of a takeover target company by buying the shares in the marketplace. Such buying may be undertaken over a very short space of time, in an effort to avoid an upward move in share prices which may occur if the buying company's tactics become known in the market. Such a tactic gives rise to the phrase 'dawn raid'. Once a holding of 3% is reached, the shareholding company is obliged to notify the company. When a holding of 30% or more is reached, the company becomes obliged under the **City Code** (discussed later in this chapter) to make an offer to the other remaining shareholders.

3.2   The offer price decided at this point should be set below the maximum worth of the takeover target but above the current market price of the shares. An offer addressed to the board of the target company, which may be communicated either through a merchant bank or directly, will establish the board's reaction as hostile or not.

3.3   Although secrecy should be sought for this stage in negotiations, it may in fact be in the target company's interests to 'leak' information to the market in the hope of either raising the market perception of an acceptable price or inducing the acquiror company to abandon its bid. Secrecy is relaxed when a formal offer document is sent to all shareholders.

Will the bidding company's shareholders approve of a takeover?

3.4   When a company is planning a takeover bid for another company, its board of directors should give thought to **how its own shareholders might react** to the bid.

3.5   A company does not have to ask its shareholders for their approval of every takeover, but:

(a)   When a large takeover is planned by a listed company involving the issue of a substantial number of new shares by the predator company (to pay for the takeover), Stock Exchange rules may require the company to obtain the formal approval of its shareholders to the takeover bid at a general meeting (probably an extraordinary general meeting, called specifically to approve the takeover bid)

(b)   If shareholders, and the stock market in general, think the takeover is not a good one, then the market value of the company's shares is likely to fall (The company's directors have a responsibility to protect their shareholders' interests, and are accountable to them at the annual general meeting of the company.)

3.6   A takeover bid might seem unattractive to shareholders of the bidding company for the following reasons.

(a) It might reduce the EPS of their company.

(b) The target company is in a risky industry, or is in danger of going into liquidation.

(c) It might reduce the net asset backing per share of the company, because the target company will probably be bought at a price which is well in excess of its net asset value.

Will a takeover bid be resisted by the target company?

3.7 Quite often, a takeover bid will be resisted. **Resistance** may come from the target company's board of directors, who adopt defensive tactics, and eventually from the target company's shareholders, who can refuse to sell their shares to the bidding company.

3.8 Resistance can be overcome by offering a higher price. In cases where an **unquoted** company is the target company, if resistance to a takeover cannot be overcome, the takeover will not take place, and negotiations would simply break down.

3.9 In cases where the target company is a **quoted** company, the situation is different. The target company will have many shareholders, some of whom will want to accept the offer for their shares, and some of whom will not. In addition, the target company's board of directors might resist a takeover, even though their shareholders might want to accept the offer.

3.10 Because there are likely to be major differences of opinion about whether to accept a takeover bid or not, the Stock Exchange has issued formal rules for the conduct of takeover bids, in the **City Code on Takeovers and Mergers**.

Contesting an offer: defensive tactics

3.11 The directors of a target company must act in the interests of their shareholders, employees and creditors. They may decide to **contest an offer** on several grounds.

(a) The offer may be unacceptable because the terms are poor. Rejection of the offer may lead to an improved bid.

(b) The merger or takeover may have no obvious advantage.

(c) Employees may be strongly opposed to the bid.

(d) The founder members of the business may oppose the bid, and may appeal to the loyalty of other shareholders.

3.12 When a company receives a takeover bid which the board of directors considers **unwelcome**, the directors must act quickly to fight off the bid. It should be borne in mind that the tactics that can be used in fighting off a takeover bid are restricted by the City Code (discussed later).

The steps that might be taken to thwart a bid or make it seem less attractive include:

(a) Issuing a forecast of attractive future profits and dividends to persuade shareholders that to sell their shares would be unwise, that the offer price is too low, and that it would be better for them to retain their shares to benefit from future profits, dividends and capital growth (Such profit and dividend forecasts can be included in 'defence documents' circulated to shareholders, and in press releases.)

(b) Lobbying the Office of Fair Trading and/or the Department of Trade and Industry to have the offer referred to the Monopolies and Mergers Commission

(c) Launching an advertising campaign against the takeover bid. (One technique is to attack the accounts of the predator company.)

(d) Finding a 'white knight', a company which will make a welcome takeover bid

(e) Making a counter-bid for the predator company (This can only be done if the companies are of reasonably similar size.)

(f) Arranging a management buyout

(g) Introducing a **'poison-pill'** anti-takeover device (see the case example below)

Case example

An example of a poison pill anti-takeover device was that used by Time Warner, the US media group in which Canada's Seagram drinks company had built up an 11 per cent stake, early in 1994. Seagram had announced plans to buy up to 15 per cent of Time Warner shares for investment purposes.

The Time Warner device was formally known as a 'shareholder rights plan' and is triggered if one investor buys more than 15 per cent of the company's stock. If that occurs, all other shareholders are given the right to buy stock at a large discount, thus diluting the 15 per cent shareholding. Time Warner pointed out that the device would not preclude a *bona fide* all-cash offer for the company which treated all shareholders equally; the 'poison pill' was designed to protect against 'abusive takeover tactics'. Seagram, on the other hand, questioned whether poison pills were in the best interests of shareholders, since they could interfere with choice and adversely affect share values.

Costs of contested takeover bids

3.13 Takeover bids, when contested, can be very expensive, involving:

(a) Costs of professional services, such as a merchant bank and a public relations agency
(b) Advertising costs
(c) Underwriting costs
(d) Interest costs

Gaining the consent of the target company shareholders

3.14 A takeover bid will only succeed if the predator company can persuade enough shareholders in the target company to sell their shares. Shareholders will only do this if they are **dissatisfied with the performance of their company** and its shares, or they are **attracted by a high offer** and the chance to make a good capital gain.

The Competition Commission

3.15 A company may have to consider whether its proposed takeover would be drawn to the attention of the **Competition Commission** (formerly called the **Monopolies and Mergers Commission**). The **Office of Fair Trading** (the OFT) is entitled to scrutinise all mergers and takeovers above a certain size. If the OFT thinks that a merger or takeover might be against the public interest, it can refer it to the Competition Commission. Proposed mergers can be notified to the OFT in advance. If no referral is made to the Competition Commission within (normally) 20 days, the merger can proceed without fear of a referral.

3.16 The function of the Competition Commission is to advise the government. The Commission can make recommendations to the Department of Trade and Industry (or to any other body, including the companies involved in the bid).

3.17 The result of an investigation by the Competition Commission might be:

(a) A withdrawal of the proposal for the merger or takeover, in anticipation of its rejection by the Commission

(b) Acceptance or rejection of the proposal by the Commission

(c) Acceptance of the proposal by the Commission subject to the new company agreeing to certain conditions laid down by the Commission, for example on prices, employment or arrangements for the sale of the group's products

European Union regulations on mergers

3.18 In the past, EU competition policy was criticised for its limited scope. However, under a regulation introduced during 1990, the European Commission gained, for the first time, the power to intervene and to either block or authorise mergers above a certain threshold size. If the Commission finds that the merger raises some serious doubts as to its compatibility with the European common market, it will initiate proceedings to block the merger.

The purchase consideration   6/98

3.19 The terms of a takeover will involve a purchase of the shares of the target company for cash or for '**paper**' (**shares**, or possibly **loan stock**). In a **share exchange**, a target company's shares is purchased with shares of the predator company.

Cash purchases

3.20 If the purchase consideration is in **cash**, the shareholders of the target company will simply be bought out. For example, suppose that the following information applies to two companies.

	Big Ltd	*Small Ltd*
Net assets (book value)	£1,500,000	£200,000
Number of shares	100,000	10,000
Earnings	£2,000,000	£40,000

Big Ltd negotiates a takeover of Small Ltd for £400,000 in cash.

3.21 As a result, Big Ltd will end up with:

(a) Net assets (book value) of:

£1,500,000 + £200,000 − £400,000 cash = £1,300,000

(b) 100,000 shares (no change)

(c) Expected earnings of £2,040,000, minus the loss of interest (net of tax) which would have been obtained from the investment of the £400,000 in cash which was given up to acquire Small Ltd

Purchases with paper

3.22 One company can acquire another company by issuing shares to pay for the acquisition. The new shares might be issued:

(a) In exchange for shares in the target company. Thus, if A plc acquires B Ltd, A plc might issue shares which it gives to B Ltd's shareholders in exchange for their shares. The B Ltd shareholders therefore become new shareholders of A plc. This is a takeover for a 'paper' consideration. Paper offers will often be accompanied by a cash alternative.

(b) To raise cash on the stock market, which will then be used to buy the target company's shares. To the target company shareholders, this is a cash bid.

3.23 Sometimes, a company might acquire another in a share exchange, but the shares are then sold immediately on a stock market to raise cash for the seller. For example, A plc might acquire B Ltd by issuing shares which it gives to B's shareholders; however A plc's stockbrokers arrange to 'place' these shares with other buyers, and so sell the newly issued shares for cash on behalf of the ex-shareholders of B Ltd. This sort of arrangement, which is a mixture of (a) and (b), is called a **vendor placing**.

3.24 Whatever the detailed arrangements of a takeover with paper, the end result will be an increase in the issued share capital of the company making the takeover.

The choice between a cash offer and a paper offer

3.25 The choice between **cash** and **paper offers** (or a combination of both) will depend on how the different methods are viewed by the company and its existing shareholders, and on the attitudes of the shareholders of the target company.

The factors that the directors of the bidding company must consider include the following.

(a) **The company and its existing shareholders**

  (i) **Dilution of earnings per share**. A fall in the EPS attributable to the existing shareholders is undesirable but it might occur when the purchase consideration is in equity shares.

  (ii) The **cost to the company**. The use of loan stock (or of cash borrowed elsewhere) will be cheaper to the acquiring company than equity as the interest will be allowable for tax purposes. A direct consequence of this is that dilution of earnings may be avoided. If convertible loan stock is used, the coupon rate could probably be slightly lower than with ordinary loan stock.

  (iii) **Gearing**. A highly geared company may find that the issue of additional loan stock either as consideration or to raise cash for the consideration may be unacceptable to some or all of the parties involved.

  (iv) **Control**. In takeovers involving a relatively large new issue of ordinary shares the effective control of the company can change considerably. This could be unpopular with the existing shareholders.

  (v) An **increase in authorised share capital**. If the consideration is in the form of shares, it may be necessary to increase the company's authorised capital. This would involve calling a general meeting to pass the necessary resolution.

  (vi) **Increases in borrowing limits**. A similar problem arises if a proposed issue of loan stock will require a change in the company's borrowing limit as specified in the Articles.

(b) **The shareholders in the target company**

  (i) **Taxation**. If the consideration is in cash many investors may find that they face an immediate liability to tax on a realised capital gain, whereas the liability would be postponed if the consideration consisted of shares.

  (ii) **Income**. Where the consideration is other than cash, it is normally necessary to ensure that existing income is at least maintained. A drop may, however, be accepted if it is compensated for by a suitable capital gain or by reasonable expectations of future growth.

(iii) **Future investments**. Shareholders in the target company might want to retain a stake in the business after the takeover, and so would prefer the offer of shares in the bidding company, rather than a cash offer.

(iv) **Share price**. If shareholders in the target company are to receive shares, they will want to consider whether the shares are likely to retain their value.

Mezzanine finance and takeover bids

3.26 When the purchase consideration in a takeover bid is cash, the cash must be obtained somehow by the bidding company, in order to pay for the shares that it buys. Occasionally, the company will have sufficient cash in hand to pay for the target company's shares. More frequently, the cash will have to be raised, possibly from existing shareholders, by means of a **rights issue**, or more probably by **borrowing** from banks or other financial institutions. When cash for a takeover is raised by borrowing, the loans would normally be medium-term and secured.

3.27 However, there have been many takeover bids, with a cash purchase option for the target company's shareholders, where the bidding company has arranged loans that:

(a) Are short-to-medium term

(b) Are unsecured (that is, 'junior' debt, low in the priority list for repayment in the event of liquidation of the borrower)

(c) Because they are unsecured, attract a much higher rate of interest than secured debt (typically 4% or 5% above LIBOR)

(d) Often, give the lender the option to exchange the loan for shares after the takeover

This type of borrowing has been called **mezzanine finance** (because it lies between equity and debt financing).

4   THE POSITION OF SHAREHOLDERS   6/96

The market values of the companies' shares during a takeover bid

4.1 **Market share prices** can be very important during a takeover bid. Suppose that Velvet plc decides to make a takeover bid for the shares of Noggin plc. Noggin plc shares are currently quoted on the market at £2 each. Velvet shares are quoted at £4.50 and Velvet offers one of its shares for every two shares in Noggin, thus making an offer at current market values worth £2.25 per share in Noggin. This is only the value of the bid so long as Velvet's shares remain valued at £4.50. If their value falls, the bid will become less attractive. This is why companies that make takeover bids with a share exchange offer are always concerned that the market value of their shares should not fall during the takeover negotiations, before the target company's shareholders have decided whether to accept the bid.

4.2 If the market price of the target company's shares rises above the offer price during the course of a takeover bid, the bid price will seem too low, and the takeover is then likely to fail, with shareholders in the target company refusing to sell their shares to the bidder.

EPS before and after a takeover

4.3 If one company acquires another by issuing shares, its EPS will go up or down according to the P/E ratio at which the target company has been bought. If the target company's shares are bought at a **higher P/E ratio** than the predator company's shares, the predator company's shareholders will suffer a fall in EPS. If the target company's shares are valued at a **lower P/E ratio**, the predator company's shareholders will benefit from a rise in EPS.

4.4 EXAMPLE: AMALGAMATIONS AND TAKEOVERS (1)

Giant plc takes over Tiddler Ltd by offering two shares in Giant for one share in Tiddler. Details about each company are as follows.

	Giant plc	*Tiddler Ltd*
Number of shares	2,800,000	100,000
Market value per share	£4	-
Annual earnings	£560,000	£50,000
EPS	20p	50p
P/E ratio	20	

By offering two shares in Giant worth £4 each for one share in Tiddler, the valuation placed on each Tiddler share is £8, and with Tiddler's EPS of 50p, this implies that Tiddler would be acquired on a P/E ratio of 16. This is lower than the P/E ratio of Giant, which is 20.

If the acquisition produces no synergy, and there is no growth in the earnings of either Giant or its new subsidiary Tiddler, then the EPS of Giant would still be higher than before, because Tiddler was bought on a lower P/E ratio. The combined group's results would be as follows.

	Giant group
Number of shares (2,800,000 + 200,000)	3,000,000
Annual earnings (560,000 + 50,000)	610,000
EPS	20.33p

If the P/E ratio is still 20, the market value per share would be £4.07, which is 7p more than the pre-takeover price.

4.5 EXAMPLE: AMALGAMATIONS AND TAKEOVERS (2)

Redwood plc agrees to acquire the shares of Green Ltd in a share exchange arrangement. The agreed P/E ratio for Green's shares is 15.

	Redwood plc	*Green Ltd*
Number of shares	3,000,000	100,000
Market price per share	£2	-
Earnings	£600,000	£120,000
P/E ratio	10	

The EPS of Green Ltd is £1.20, and so the agreed price per share will be £1.20 × 15 = £18. In a share exchange agreement, Redwood would have to issue nine new shares (valued at £2 each) to acquire each share in Green, and so a total of 900,000 new shares must be issued to complete the takeover.

After the takeover, the enlarged company would have 3,900,000 shares in issue and, assuming no earnings growth, total earnings of £720,000. This would give an EPS of:

$$\frac{£720,000}{3,900,000} = 18.5p$$

The pre-takeover EPS of Redwood was 20p, and so the EPS would fall. This is because Green has been bought on a higher P/E ratio (15 compared with Redwood's 10).

Buying companies on a higher P/E ratio, but with profit growth

4.6 Buying companies on a higher P/E ratio will result in a fall in EPS unless there is profit growth to offset this fall. For example, suppose that Starving plc acquires Bigmeal plc, by offering two shares in Starving for three shares in Bigmeal. Details of each company are as follows.

	Starving plc	*Bigmeal plc*
Number of shares	5,000,000	3,000,000
Value per share	£6	£4
Annual earnings		
Current	£2,000,000	£600,000
Next year	£2,200,000	£950,000
EPS	40p	20p
P/E ratio	15	20

4.7 Starving plc is acquiring Bigmeal plc on a higher P/E ratio, and it is only the profit growth in the acquired subsidiary that gives the enlarged Starving group its growth in EPS.

	Starving group	
Number of shares (5,000,000 + 2,000,000)	7,000,000	
Earnings		
If no profit growth (2,000,000 + 600,000) £2,600,000		EPS would have been 37.24p
With profit growth (2,200,000 + 950,000) £3,150,000		EPS will be 45p

If an acquisition strategy involves buying companies on a higher P/E ratio, it is therefore essential for continuing EPS growth that the acquired companies offer prospects of strong profit growth.

Reverse takeovers

4.8 A **reverse takeover** occurs when the smaller company takes over the larger one, so that the 'predator' company has to increase its voting equity by over 100% to complete the takeover.

Further points to consider: net assets per share and the quality of earnings

4.9 It might be concluded from what has been said above that dilution of earnings must be avoided at all costs. However, there are three cases where a dilution of earnings might be accepted on an acquisition if there were other advantages to be gained.

(a) Earnings growth may hide the dilution in EPS as above.

(b) A company might be willing to accept earnings dilution if the quality of the acquired company's earnings is superior to that of the acquiring company.

(c) A trading company with high earnings, but with few assets, may want to increase its assets base by acquiring a company which is strong in assets but weak in earnings so that assets and earnings get more into line with each other. In this case, dilution in earnings is compensated for by an increase in net asset backing.

4.10 EXAMPLE: AMALGAMATIONS AND TAKEOVERS (3)

Intangible plc has an issued capital of 2,000,000 £1 ordinary shares. Net assets (excluding goodwill) are £2,500,000 and annual earnings average £1,500,000. The company is valued by the stock market on a P/E ratio of 8. Tangible Ltd has an issued capital of 1,000,000 ordinary shares. Net assets (excluding goodwill) are £3,500,000 and annual earnings average

BPP PUBLISHING

£400,000. The shareholders of Tangible Ltd accept an all-equity offer from Intangible plc valuing each share in Tangible Ltd at £4. Calculate Intangible plc's earnings and assets per share before and after the acquisition of Tangible Ltd.

4.11 SOLUTION

(a) Before the acquisition of Tangible Ltd, the position is as follows.

$$\text{Earnings per share (EPS)} = \frac{£1,500,000}{2,000,000} = 75p$$

$$\text{Assets per share (APS)} = \frac{£2,500,000}{2,000,000} = £1.25$$

(b) Tangible Ltd's EPS figure is 40p (£400,000 ÷ 1,000,000), and the company is being bought on a multiple of 10 at £4 per share. As the takeover consideration is being satisfied by shares, Intangible plc's earnings will be diluted because Intangible plc is valuing Tangible Ltd on a higher multiple of earnings than itself. Intangible plc will have to issue 666,667 shares valued at £6 each (earnings of 75p per share at a multiple of 8) to satisfy the £4,000,000 consideration. The results for Intangible plc will be as follows.

$$\text{EPS} = \frac{£1,900,000}{2,666,667} = 71.25p \text{ (3.75p lower than the previous 75p)}$$

$$\text{APS} = \frac{£6,000,000}{2,666,667} = £2.25 \text{ (£1 higher than the previous £1.25)}$$

If Intangible plc is still valued on the stock market on a P/E ratio of 8, the share price should fall by approximately 30p (8 × 3.75p, the fall in EPS) but because the asset backing has been increased substantially the company will probably now be valued on a higher P/E ratio than 8.

The shareholders in Tangible Ltd would receive 666,667 shares in Intangible plc in exchange for their current 1,000,000 shares, that is, two shares in Intangible for every three shares currently held.

(a) *Earnings* £
Three shares in Tangible earn (3 × 40p) 1.200
Two shares in Intangible will earn (2 × 71.25p) 1.425
Increase in earnings, per three shares held in Tangible 0.225

(b) *Assets* £
Three shares in Tangible have an asset backing of (3 × £3.5) 10.50
Two shares in Intangible will have an asset backing of (2 × £2.25) 4.50
Loss in asset backing, per three shares held in Tangible 6.00

The shareholders in Tangible Ltd would be trading asset backing for an increase in earnings.

Dividends and dividend cover

4.12 A further issue which may create some difficulties before a merger or takeover can be agreed is the level of **dividends** and **dividend cover** expected by shareholders in each of the companies concerned. Once the companies merge, a single dividend policy will be applied.

5   OTHER MATTERS IN TAKEOVERS   6/94, 6/96, 12/99

Service contracts for key personnel

5.1   When the target company employs certain **key personnel**, on whom the success of the company has been based, the predator company might want to ensure that these key people do not leave as soon as the takeover occurs. To do this, it might be necessary to insist as a condition of the offer that the key people should agree to sign service contracts, tying them to the company for a certain time (perhaps three years). Service contracts would have to be attractive to the employees concerned, perhaps through offering a high salary or other benefits such as share options in the predator company. Where key personnel are shareholders, they might be bound not to sell shares for a period.

The Takeover Panel and the City Code on Takeovers and Mergers

5.2   The **City Code** is a code of behaviour which companies are expected to follow during a takeover or merger, as a measure of self-discipline. The code has no statutory backing, although it is administered and enforced by the **Takeover Panel**. Once adopted, the 13th Company Law Directive of the EU will have statutory power in EU member states, bringing an end to the non-statutory approach to the regulation of bids and takeover deals currently used in the UK.

5.3   The nature and purpose of the City Code is described within the code itself as follows.

> 'The code represents the collective opinion of those professionally involved in the field of takeovers on a range of business standards. It is not concerned with the financial or commercial advantages or disadvantages of a takeover, which are matters for the company and its shareholders, or with those wider questions which are the responsibility of the government, advised by the Monopolies and Mergers Commission.

> The code has not, and does not seek to have, the force of law, but those who wish to take advantage of the facilities of the securities markets in the United Kingdom should conduct themselves in matters relating to takeovers according to the Code. Those who do not so conduct themselves cannot expect to enjoy those facilities and may find that they are withheld.'

5.4   Companies subject to the code include all public companies (listed or unlisted) and also some classes of private company.

The City Code: general principles

5.5   The City Code is divided into general principles and detailed rules which must be observed by persons involved in a merger or takeover transaction. The general principles include the following.

(a)   'All shareholders of the same class of an offeree company must be treated similarly by an offeror.' In other words, a company making a takeover bid cannot offer one set of purchase terms to some shareholders in the target company, and a different set of terms to other shareholders holding shares of the same class in that company.

(b)   'During the course of a takeover, or when such is in contemplation, neither the offeror nor the offeree company ... may furnish information to some shareholders which is not made available to all shareholders.'

(c)   'Shareholders must be given sufficient information and advice to enable them to reach a properly informed decision and must have sufficient time to do so. No relevant information should be withheld from them.'

(d) 'At no time after a *bona fide* offer has been communicated to the board of an offeree company ... may any action be taken by the board of the offeree company in relation to the affairs of the company, without the approval of the shareholders in general meeting, which could effectively result in any *bona fide* offer being frustrated or in the shareholders being denied an opportunity to decide on its merits.' In other words, directors of a target company are not permitted to frustrate a takeover bid, nor to prevent the shareholders from having a chance to decide for themselves.

(e) 'Rights of control must be exercised in good faith and the oppression of a minority is wholly unacceptable.' For example, a holding company cannot take decisions about a takeover bid for one of its subsidiaries in such a way that minority shareholders would be unfairly treated.

(f) 'Where control of a company is acquired ... a general offer to all other shareholders is normally required.' Control is defined as a 'holding, or aggregate holdings, of shares carrying 30% of the voting rights of a company, irrespective of whether that holding or holdings gives *de facto* control.'

The City Code: rules

5.6 In addition to its general principles, the City Code also contains a number of **detailed rules,** which are intended to govern the conduct of the parties in a takeover bid. These rules relate to matters such as:

(a) How the approach to the target company should be made by the predator company

(b) The announcement of a takeover bid

(c) The obligation of the board of a target company to seek independent advice (for example from a merchant bank)

(d) Conduct during the offer

(e) A time barrier to re-bidding if an offer fails

Other legislative requirements

5.7 **Legislative requirements** potentially affecting takeovers and mergers include the following.

(a) Sections 428 to 430 of the Companies Act 1985 allow a company which has acquired over 90% of the shares of another company to purchase compulsorily the remaining shares on the same terms, and gives the minority shareholders similar rights to require the company to buy their shares.

(b) Financial assistance given by a company for the purchase of its own shares is prohibited by section 151 of the Companies Act 1985. This outlaws the tactics of offering such financial assistance so as to inflate share values prior to a share-for-share exchange offer or to arrange for blocks of the target company's shares to be held by 'friendly' parties.

(c) Dealing in shares by various individuals who possess unpublished price-sensitive information ('insider dealing') is prohibited by law (Criminal Justice Act 1993). It is also an offence to *receive* price sensitive information with a view to making again by the use of that knowledge.

6   POST-ACQUISITION INTEGRATION AND AUDIT

Post-acquisition integration

6.1   Failures of takeovers often result from inadequate integration of the companies after the takeover has taken place. There is a tendency for senior management to devote their energies to the next acquisition rather than to the newly-acquired firm. The particular approach adopted will depend upon the culture of the organisation as well as the nature of the company acquired and how it fits into the amalgamated organisation (eg horizontally, vertically, or as part of a diversified conglomerate).

6.2   P F Drucker has suggested Five Golden Rules for the process of **post-acquisition integration.**

Rule 1.   There should be a 'common core of unity' shared by the acquiror and acquiree. The ties should involve overlapping characteristics such as shared technology and markets, and not just financial links.

Rule 2.   The acquiror should ask 'What can we offer them?' as well as 'What's in it for us?'

Rule 3.   The acquiror should treat the products, markets and customers of the acquired company with respect, and not disparagingly.

Rule 4.   The acquiring company should provide top management with relevant skills for the acquired company within a year.

Rule 5.   Cross-company promotions of staff should occur within one year.

6.3   C S Jones has proposed a five-step 'integration sequence'.

Step 1   is to decide on and to communicate initial reporting relationships. This will reduce uncertainty. The issue of whether to impose relationships at the beginning, although these may be subject to change, or to wait for the organisation structure to become more established (see Step 5 below) needs to be addressed.

Step 2   is to achieve rapid control of key factors, which will require access to the right accurate information. Control of information channels needs to be gained without dampening motivation. Note that it may have been poor financial controls which led to the demise of the acquiree company.

Step 3   is the resource audit. Both physical and human assets are examined in order to get a clear picture.

Step 4   is to re-define corporate objectives and to develop strategic plans, to harmonise with those of the acquiror company as appropriate, depending on the degree of autonomy managers are to have to develop their own systems of management control.

Step 5   is to revise the organisational structure.

6.4   Successful post-acquisition integration requires careful management of the 'human factor' to avoid loss of motivation. Employees in the acquired company will want to know how they and their company are to fit into the structure and strategy of the amalgamated enterprise. Morale can, hopefully, be preserved by reducing uncertainty and by providing appropriate performance incentives, staff benefits and career prospects.

BPP PUBLISHING

Post-acquisition audit

12/99

6.5   It is a good idea to conduct a financial post-audit following an acquisition or merger.

6.6   The post-audit can:

   (a)   Identify problems arising following the merger or takeover to which management should direct attention

   (b)   Discourage management from carrying out unwise mergers or takeovers, since they will know that their decisions are to be subjected to close financial scrutiny

   (c)   Examine the accuracy of forecasting, and of the forecasts of individual managers, so that the forecasting process might be improved in the future

   (d)   Examine the merger process itself, so that improvements to this process might be incorporated in future acquisition activity

6.7   **Problems with post-audits**

   (a)   Establishing the financial outcomes that are directly attributable to the acquisition rather than other factors such as the company's changing performance, can be difficult. We need to ask what would have happened if the acquisition had not taken place. This question is more difficult to answer in a company which is growing rapidly either organically or through acquisitions.

   (b)   The timing of the post-audit needs to be decided, as does the question of whether one or a number of post-audits should be undertaken. A relatively long time horizon might be thought necessary in order to trace the financial effects fully, but if the post-audit is carried out too late, it may be that the acquisition can no longer be accurately assessed after say more than one year.

6.8   In conclusion, although financial post-audits are highly desirable, given the extensive restructuring that often arises from an acquisition or merger and the long time period over which its impact will be felt, the data available for the purpose of the post-audit may be of limited accuracy for the purpose.

7   DEMERGERS

6/95

7.1   Mergers and takeovers are not inevitably good strategy for a business. In some circumstances, strategies of internal growth, no growth or even a **demerger** might be preferable.

Case example

ICI plc is one well known example of an enterprise which has undergone demerger, splitting itself into two separate companies some years ago (as ICI and the pharmaceuticals company, Zeneca).

7.2   A demerger is the opposite of a merger. It is the splitting up of a corporate body into two or more separate and independent bodies. For example, the ABC Group plc might demerge by selling its 100% shareholding in a subsidiary, C plc, to an outside buyer, who will then run C plc as an independent company. This would be a case of **disinvestment** by the group, withdrawing from its investment in C plc. Alternatively, shareholders may be offered a package of shares in the demerged parts of the business in exchange for their old shares in the merged company.

7.3   The reasons for demergers could be any of the following.

(a)   An unprofitable subsidiary could be sold. The buyer might perhaps be a group of the subsidiary's managers, with the management buyout team being backed by venture capital finance.

(b)   Subsidiaries which are not 'core businesses' and do not fit in with the group's strategic plans could be sold.

Case example

This was the case when Royal Doulton, the china producer, was demerged from its parent company Pearson, which also owns the Financial Times, in 1993. Pearson said at the time that the demerger was part of its decision to focus on the media.

(c)   A subsidiary with high risk in its operating cash flows could be sold, so as to reduce the business risk of the group as a whole.

(d)   A subsidiary could be sold at a profit. Some companies have specialised in taking over large groups of companies, and then selling off parts of the newly-acquired groups, so that the proceeds of sales more than pay for the original takeovers.

7.4   The potential disadvantages with demergers are as follows.

(a)   Economies of scale may be lost, where the demerged parts of the business had operations in common to which economies of scale applied.

(b)   The smaller companies which result from the demerger will have lower turnover, profits and status than the group before the demerger.

(c)   There may be higher overhead costs as a percentage of turnover, resulting from (b).

(d)   The ability to raise extra finance, especially debt finance, to support new investments and expansion may be reduced.

(e)   Vulnerability to takeover may be increased.

8   MANAGEMENT BUYOUTS   6/95, 6/97

8.1   A **management buyout (MBO)** is the purchase of all or part of a business from its owners by its managers. For example, the directors of a subsidiary company in a group might buy the company from the holding company, with the intention of running it as proprietors of a separate business entity.

Case examples

Management buyouts have remained popular in the UK. Examples include: a £370 million buyout of Dunlop Slazenger from BTR (now Invensys) as the group focuses more closely on its core business; the £800 million sale of HMV Media Group by Thorn EMI; and various sales by British Rail.

8.2   To the managers, the buyout would be a method of setting up in business for themselves. To the group, the buyout would be a method of **disinvestment** - selling off the subsidiary as a going concern. Management buyouts might easily be thought of as attempts by a company to sell loss-making subsidiaries. In fact, management buyouts more commonly involve the sale of **profitable** subsidiaries, which are being sold off simply because they do not fit in well with the group's strategic plans.

The parties to a buyout

8.3 There are usually **three parties** to a management buyout.

(a) There is a **management team** wanting to make a buyout. This team ought to have the skills and ability to convince financial backers that it is worth supporting.

(b) There are the **directors** of a group of companies, who make the disinvestment decision.

(c) There are **financial backers** of the buyout team, who will usually want an equity stake in the bought-out business, because of the venture capital risk they are taking. Often, several financial backers provide the venture capital for a single buyout.

> **KEY TERM**
>
> **Venture capital:** risk capital, normally lent in return for an equity stake.

8.4 The management team making the buyout would probably have the aims of **setting up in business themselves**, being owners rather than mere employees, or **avoiding redundancy**, when the subsidiary is threatened with closure.

8.5 A large organisation's board of directors may agree to a management buyout of a subsidiary for any of a number of different reasons.

(a) The subsidiary may be peripheral to the group's mainstream activities, and may no longer fit in with the group's overall strategy.

(b) The group may wish to sell off a loss-making subsidiary, and a management team may think that it can restore the subsidiary's fortunes.

(c) The parent company may need to raise cash quickly.

(d) The subsidiary may be part of a group that has just been taken over and the new parent company may wish to sell off parts of the group it has just acquired.

(e) The best offer price might come from a small management group wanting to arrange a buyout.

(f) When a group has taken the decision to sell a subsidiary, it will probably get better co-operation from the management and employees of the subsidiary if the sale is a management buyout.

8.6 A private company's shareholders might agree to sell out to a management team because they need cash, or they want to retire, or the business is not profitable enough for them.

8.7 The buyout team will have to find willing **financial backers**, and so it must convince them that it can run the business successfully. To help with the task of convincing the bank or other institution, the management team should prepare a **business plan** and **estimates of sales, costs, profits and cash flows**, in reasonable detail. If the parent company's existing shareholders have already indicated their willingness to sell, the management team should have reasonably free access to the sort of figures they need about revenues, costs, areas for improved efficiency and cost savings, and so on.

The appraisal of proposed buyouts

How likely is a management buyout to succeed?

8.8 Management-owned companies often seem to get better performance out of their company, probably because of:

(a) A favourable buyout price having been achieved
(b) Personal motivation and determination
(c) Quicker decision making and so more flexibility
(d) Keener decisions and action on pricing and debt collection
(e) Savings in overheads, eg costs of a large head office

However, many management buyouts, once they occur, begin with some redundancies to cut running costs.

8.9 The prospects of success for a management buyout ought to be evaluated:

(a) By the managers who are thinking of making the buyout

(b) By the institutional investors who are being asked to put in venture capital to finance the buyout

(c) By the vendor, where the vendor continues to have a trading interest

How should an institutional investor evaluate a buyout?

8.10 An institutional investor should evaluate a buyout before deciding whether or not to finance. Aspects of any buyout that ought to be checked are as follows.

(a) Does the management team have the full range of management skills that are needed (for example a technical expert and a finance director)? Does it have the right blend of experience? Does it have the commitment?

(b) Why is the company for sale? The possible reasons for buyouts have already been listed. If the reason is that the parent company wants to get rid of a loss-making subsidiary, what evidence is there to suggest that the company can be made profitable after a buyout?

(c) What are the projected profits and cash flows of the business? The prospective returns must justify the risks involved.

(d) What is being bought? The buyout team might be buying the shares of the company, or only selected assets of the company. Are the assets that are being acquired sufficient for the task? Will more assets have to be bought? When will the existing assets need replacing? How much extra finance would be needed for these asset purchases? Can the company be operated profitably?

(e) What is the price? Is the price right or is it too high?

(f) What financial contribution can be made by members of the management team themselves?

The financial arrangements in a typical buyout

8.11 Typically, the buyout team will have a minority of the equity in the bought-out company, with the financial backers holding a majority of the shares between them. A buyout might have several financial backers, each providing finance in exchange for some equity.

8.12 The financial institutions may regard their investment as a medium-term one, but they might hope that if the company is successful, it will eventually be floated on a stock market, perhaps the second tier **Alternative Investment Market (AIM)**, thus giving a market value to their equity, and the option to sell their shares if they wish to realise their investment.

8.13 Investors of venture capital usually want the managers to be financially committed. Individual managers could borrow personally from a bank, say £20,000 to £50,000. This should be enough to commit them without hurting them too much.

8.14 The suppliers of equity finance might insist on investing part of their capital in the form of **redeemable convertible preference shares**. These often have voting rights should the preference dividend fall in arrears, giving increased influence over the company's affairs. They are issued in a redeemable form to give some hope of taking out part of the investment if it does not develop satisfactorily, and in convertible form for the opposite reason: to allow an increased stake in the equity of a successful company.

Possible problems with buyouts

8.15 A common problem with management buyouts is that the managers may lack sufficient experience in financial management or financial accounting.

Other problems are:

(a) Tax and legal complications

(b) Difficulties in deciding on a fair price to be paid

(c) Convincing employees of the need to change working practices

(d) Inadequate cash flow to finance the maintenance and replacement of tangible fixed assets

(e) The maintenance of previous employees' pension rights

(f) Accepting the board representation requirement that many sources of funds will insist upon

(g) The loss of key employees if the company moves geographically, or wage rates are decreased too far, or employment conditions are unacceptable in other ways

(h) Maintaining continuity of relationships with suppliers and customers

Buy-ins

8.16 **'Buy-in'** is a term used when a team of outside managers, as opposed to managers who are already running the business, mount a takeover bid and then run the business themselves. A management buy-in might occur when a business venture is running into trouble, and a group of outside managers see an opportunity to take over the business and restore its profitability.

> **KEY TERMS**
>
> **Management buy-in**: the purchase of all or part of a business from its owners by new managers from outside the business.
>
> **Management buy-out**: the purchase of all or part of a business from its owners by its managers.

Sell-offs

8.17 A **sell-off** is a form of divestment involving the sale of part of a company to a third party, usually another company. Generally, cash will be received in exchange. A company may carry out a sell-off for one of the following reasons.

   (a) As part of its strategic planning, it has decided to restructure, concentrating management effort on particular parts of the business. Control problems may be reduced if peripheral activities are sold off.

   (b) It wishes to sell off a part of its business which makes losses, and so to improve the company's future reported consolidated profit performance.

   (c) In order to protect the rest of the business from takeover, it may choose to sell a part of the business which is particularly attractive to a buyer.

   (d) The company may be short of cash.

Liquidations

8.18 The extreme form of a sell-off is where the entire business is sold off in a **liquidation**. In a voluntary dissolution, the shareholders might decide to close the whole business, sell off all the assets and distribute net funds raised.

Spin-offs

8.19 In a **spin-off,** a new company is created whose shares are owned by the shareholders of the original company which is making the distribution of assets. There is no change in the ownership of assets, as the shareholders own the same proportion of shares in the new company as they did in the old company. Assets of the part of the business to be separated off are transferred into the new company, which will usually have different management from the old company. In more complex cases, a spin-off may involve the original company being split into a number of separate companies.

8.20 For a number of possible reasons such as those set out below, a spin-off appears generally to meet with favour from stock market investors.

   (a) The change may make a merger or takeover of some part of the business easier in the future, or may protect parts of the business from predators.

   (b) There may be improved efficiency and more streamlined management within the new structure.

   (c) It may be easier to see the value of the separated parts of the business now that they are no longer hidden within a conglomerate.

   (d) The requirements of regulatory agencies might be met more easily within the new structure, for example if the agency is able to exercise price control over a particular part of the business which was previously hidden within the conglomerate structure.

   (e) After the spin-off, shareholders have the opportunity to adjust the proportions of their holdings between the different companies created.

Going private

8.21 A public company 'goes private' when a small group of individuals, possibly including existing shareholders and/or managers and with or without support from a financial institution, buys all of the company's shares. This form of restructuring is relatively common in the USA and may involve the shares in the company ceasing to be listed on a stock exchange. In some cases, a small group of shareholders who prefer private company status buy the shares in a company from all the other shareholders.

8.22 Advantages in **going private** could include the following.

(a) The costs of meeting listing requirements can be saved.

(b) The company is protected from volatility in share prices which financial problems may create.

(c) The company will be less vulnerable to hostile takeover bids.

(d) Management can concentrate on the long-term needs of the business rather than the short-term expectations of shareholders.

(e) Shareholders are likely to be closer to management in a private company, reducing costs arising from the separation of ownership and control (the 'agency problem').

Case examples

One example of going private was Richard Branson's repurchase of shares in the Virgin Company from the public and financial institutions.

Another example was SAGA the tour operator which changed status from public to private in 1990. While public, 63% of the company was owned by one family. The family raised finance to buy all of the shares, to avoid the possibility of hostile takeover bids and to avoid conflicts between the long-term needs of the business and the short-term expectations which institutional shareholders in particular are often claimed to have.

---

9   SHARE REPURCHASE   12/96

Why buy back the company's shares?

9.1 Until relatively recently, it was illegal for a UK company to repurchase its issued shares. The Companies Act 1981, and now the Companies Act 1985, have given companies rights to **buy back shares from shareholders** who are willing to sell them, subject to certain conditions.

9.2 For a **smaller private company** with few shareholders, the reason for buying back the company's own shares may be that there is no immediate willing purchaser at a time when a shareholder wishes to sell shares. For a public company, share repurchase could provide a way of withdrawing from the share market and 'going private'. **Larger public companies** also sometimes repurchase their own shares. Recently, for instance, a number of the privatised UK electricity companies have made significant share repurchases having gained shareholder approval to do so at the companies' annual meetings.

9.3 Repurchase of own shares is common among US companies and is gaining popularity in the UK. However, the practice remains rare in the rest of Europe. Share buybacks are indeed illegal in a number of European countries including Germany and in Scandinavia, although in some countries, including Sweden, Switzerland, and Ireland, there have been recent moves towards legalisation.

9.4 Among the possible **benefits of a share repurchase scheme** are the following.

(a) Finding a use for surplus cash, which may be a 'dead asset'.

(b) Increase in earnings per share through a reduction in the number of shares in issue. This should lead to a higher share price than would otherwise be the case, and the company should be able to increase dividend payments on the remaining shares in issue.

(c) Increase in gearing. Repurchase of a company's own shares allows debt to be substituted for equity, so raising gearing. This will be of interest to a company wanting to increase its gearing without increasing its total long-term funding.

(d) Readjustment of the company's equity base to more appropriate levels, for a company whose business is in decline.

(e) If certain conditions are met, share repurchase can be treated as a capital rather than an income distribution. ACT is not due in respect of capital distributions.

(f) Share repurchase may also fulfil special purposes, such as preventing a takeover or enabling a quoted company to withdraw from the stock market.

There are also possible **disadvantages**.

(a) It can be hard to arrive at a price which will be fair both to the vendors and to any shareholders who are not selling shares to the company.

(b) A repurchase of shares could be seen as an admission that the company cannot make better use of the funds than the shareholders.

(c) Some shareholders may suffer from being taxed on a capital gain following the purchase of their shares rather than receiving dividend income.

Case examples

In October 1994 it was reported that Midlands Electricity plc had purchased 21.16 million of its own shares. In making such a large repurchase, it had to pay a price of 725 pence, compared with a general market price on the day of 713 pence, up 25 pence on the previous day. There have been many other examples of share repurchase by major companies, such as PowerGen in 1996, and you may notice mention of share buy-backs in the press.

For Midlands Electricity in 1994, the objectives of the buy-back were to boost earnings per share and to help create a 'progressive' dividend policy at a time when the company had cash available for the repurchase. An investment analyst was quoted in the press as approving of the move. Given what he saw as the utilities companies' poor record on diversification, he said that he would prefer seeing the company do this with its money than investing it abroad.

Chapter roundup

- **Mergers** and **takeovers** take place for various reasons. A takeover bid may be viewed as welcome or hostile by the directors of the target company. The acquiring company will need to examine carefully whether its shareholders will regard a takeover as desirable.

- Poor **strategic thinking**, overestimation of **synergistic factors** and poor **internal controls** are examples of why an acquisition may fail.

- Takeover bids are relatively common, and it is worth following one or two in the financial press, so as to see how the considerations set out in this chapter translate into practice.

- **Demergers**, **divestment** and **repurchase of a company's own shares** represent other forms of restructuring.

- **Management buyouts** are a special sort of transaction, involving several parties. A buyout cannot go ahead unless all the parties are satisfied with the arrangements.

Quick quiz

1 What might be the reasons for an amalgamation or takeover? (1.4)

2 Why might the shareholders of the bidding company disapprove of a bid for a target company by their board of directors? (3.6)

3 What factors might affect the choice between a cash offer and a paper offer in a takeover bid? (3.25)

4 What is mezzanine finance? (3.27)

5 If a bidding company issues shares to buy a target company on a *lower* P/E ratio than the bidding company shares are valued at, what will happen to the bidding company's own EPS after the takeover? (4.3)

6 What are the steps which should be followed in ensuring that an acquired company is successfully integrated into the enterprise? (6.3)

7 What are the reasons for demergers? (7.3)

8 How should an institutional investor evaluate a management buyout? (8.10)

9 Why might an investor in a management buyout ask for redeemable convertible preference shares in return for his investment? (8.14)

10 What advantages are there in a public company 'going private'? (8.22)

Question to try	Level	Marks	Time
13	Exam standard	25	45 mins

Chapter 14

THE VALUATION OF COMPANIES

Chapter topic list	Syllabus reference
1 Reasons for share valuations	2(e)
2 Methods of valuing shares	2(e)

Introduction

In the previous chapter, we explored various issues which should be addressed in **business amalgamations.**

We have mentioned different possible methods which could be used to value a company to be acquired. In this chapter, we explain different **valuation methods** in more detail.

1 REASONS FOR SHARE VALUATIONS

1.1 Our main interest in this chapter is with methods of valuing the entire equity in a company, perhaps for the purpose of making a takeover bid, rather than with the value of small blocks of shares which an investor might choose to buy or sell on the stock market. Given quoted share prices on the Stock Exchange, why devise techniques for estimating the value of a share? A share valuation will be necessary:

(a) For **quoted companies,** when there is a takeover bid and the offer price is an estimated 'fair value' in excess of the current market price of the shares

(b) For **unquoted companies,** when:

   (i)   The company wishes to 'go public' and must fix an issue price for its shares
   (ii)   There is a scheme of merger
   (iii) Shares are sold
   (iv)   Shares need to be valued for the purposes of taxation
   (v)   Shares are pledged as collateral for a loan

(c) For **subsidiary companies,** when the group's holding company is negotiating the sale of the subsidiary to a management buyout team or to an external buyer

1.2 Valuing **unquoted companies** presents some special considerations. **It may not be sensible to use P/E ratios** of a quoted company for comparative purposes because the market value of a quoted company is likely to include a premium to reflect the marketability of its shares. A small unquoted company may be highly sensitive to the **loss of key employees** which may follow a merger or buyout. An arrangement to tie key employees in to the enterprise could be costly.

2   METHODS OF VALUING SHARES   6/94, 6/95, 6/96, 6/98

2.1   Common methods of valuing shares

- The **earnings method (P/E ratio method)**
- The **accounting rate of return method**
- The **net assets method**
- The **dividend yield method**
- Use of the **CAPM**
- The **super-profits method**
- **DCF-based valuations**

2.2   It is unlikely that one method would be used in isolation. Several valuations might be made, each using a different technique or different assumptions. The valuations could then be compared, and a final price reached as a compromise between the different values.

The P/E ratio (earnings) method of valuation

2.3   This is a common method of valuing a controlling interest in a company, where the owner can decide on dividend and retention's policy. The **P/E ratio** relates earnings per share to a share's value. The P/E ratio is often called an earnings 'multiple'.

Since P/E ratio $=\dfrac{\text{Market value}}{\text{EPS}}$,

market value per share $=$ EPS $\times$ P/E ratio

Case example

You will find frequent references to the P/E ratio in the financial press. For example, the *Financial Times* on 8 July 1997 reported the first day's trading in shares of the newly demutualised bank Woolwich plc as follows.

'"This is now the most expensive bank in Europe" said one analyst when Woolwich shares ended their first day of trading at 334p. By the close of trading, Woolwich stood at between 18 and 21 times prospective earnings. That compares with 16 times for Lloyds TSB and is considered unsustainable by many brokers unless a bid or merger offer appears.'

2.4   The P/E ratio produce an earnings-based valuation of shares. This is done by deciding a suitable P/E ratio and multiplying this by the EPS for the shares which are being valued. The EPS could be a historical EPS or a prospective future EPS. For a given EPS figure, a higher P/E ratio will result in a higher price. A high P/E ratio may indicate:

(a)   **Expectations** that the EPS will grow rapidly in the years to come, so that a high price is being paid for future profit prospects. Many small but successful and fast-growing companies are valued on the stock market on a high P/E ratio. Some stocks (for example those of some internet companies in the late 1990s) have reached high valuations before making any profits at all, on the strength of expected future earnings.

Case examples

By April 1999, the internet 'portal' company 'Yahoo!', with only very limited assets, commanded a higher stock market value than Boeing the aircraft manufacturer.

Amazon.com, the online bookseller, is valued at $20 billion but had yet to make a profit.

eBay, the internet auctioneer was valued at 2,000 times prospective earnings.

Press comment suggested that private investors, many of them trading through the internet, are mainly responsible for the volatility in internet stocks. These are 'momentum investors' who care little about the economic fundamentals underlying a business. If enough people pile in to buy stocks whose prices seem to rise inexorably, the prices are driven even higher perhaps until the 'bubble' bursts, and investors panic and sell *en masse*, when the price drops again sharply.

By mid-2000, such falls in the share prices of internet stocks were being seen.

(b) **Security of earnings.** A well-established low-risk company would be valued on a higher P/E ratio than a similar company whose earnings are subject to greater uncertainty.

(c) **Status.** If a quoted company made a share-for-share takeover bid for an unquoted company, it would normally expect its own shares to be valued on a higher P/E ratio than the target company's shares. This is because a quoted company ought to be a lower-risk company; but in addition, there is an advantage in having shares which are quoted on a stock market: the shares can be readily sold. The P/E ratio of an unquoted company's shares might be around 50% to 60% of the P/E ratio of a similar public company with a full Stock Exchange listing (and perhaps 70% of that of a company whose shares are traded on the AIM).

2.5 EXAMPLE: EARNINGS METHOD OF VALUATION

Spider plc is considering the takeover of an unquoted company, Fly Ltd. Spider's shares are quoted on the Stock Exchange at a price of £3.20 and with a recent EPS of the company of 20p, the company's P/E ratio is 16. Fly Ltd is a company with 100,000 shares and current earnings of £50,000, 50p per share. How might Spider plc decide on an offer price?

2.6 SOLUTION

The decision about the offer price is likely to be based on deciding first of all what a reasonable P/E ratio would be.

(a) If Fly Ltd is in the same industry as Spider plc, its P/E ratio ought to be lower, because of its lower status as an unquoted company.

(b) If Fly Ltd is in a different industry, a suitable P/E ratio might be based on the P/E ratio that is typical for quoted companies in that industry.

(c) If Fly Ltd is thought to be growing fast, so that its EPS will rise rapidly in the years to come, the P/E ratio that should be used for the share valuation will be higher than if only small EPS growth is expected.

(d) If the acquisition of Fly Ltd would contribute substantially to Spider's own profitability and growth, or to any other strategic objective that Spider has, then Spider should be willing to offer a higher P/E ratio valuation, in order to secure acceptance of the offer by Fly's shareholders.

Of course, the P/E ratio on which Spider bases its offer will probably be lower than the P/E ratio that Fly's shareholders think their shares ought to be valued on. Some haggling over the price might be necessary.

(a) Spider might decide that Fly's shares ought to be valued on a P/E ratio of 60% × 16 = 9.6, that is, at 9.6 × 50p = £4.80 each.

(b) Fly's shareholders might reject this offer, and suggest a valuation based on a P/E ratio of, say, 12.5, that is, 12.5 × 50p = £6.25.

BPP PUBLISHING

(c)   Spider's management might then come back with a revised offer, say valuation on a P/E ratio of 10.5, that is, $10.5 \times 50p = £5.25$.

General guidelines for a P/E ratio-based valuation

2.7   When a company is thinking of acquiring an **unquoted company** in a takeover, the final offer price will be agreed by negotiation, but a list of some of the factors affecting the valuer's choice of P/E ratio is given below.

(a)   General **economic and financial conditions**.

(b)   The type of **industry** and the prospects of that industry.

(c)   The **size** of the undertaking and its **status** within its industry. If an unquoted company's earnings are growing annually and are currently around £300,000 or so, then it could probably get a quote in its own right on the AIM and a higher P/E ratio should therefore be used when valuing its shares.

(d)   **Marketability**. The market in shares which do not have a Stock Exchange quotation is always a restricted one and a higher yield is therefore required. Because of restrictions on transfer given in their Articles, any 'private' market in the shares of private companies is likely to be particularly small. It is not uncommon for a quoted company to have a P/E ratio twice the size of that attributed to a private company in the same industry. For examination purposes, you should normally take a figure around one half to two thirds of the industry average when valuing an unquoted company.

(e)   The **diversity of shareholdings** and the financial status of any principal shareholders.

(f)   The reliability of profit estimates and the past **profit record**.

(g)   **Asset backing** and **liquidity**.

(h)   The **nature of the assets**, for example whether some of the fixed assets are of a highly specialised nature, and so have only a small break-up value.

(i)   **Gearing**. A relatively high gearing ratio will generally mean greater financial risk for ordinary shareholders and call for a higher rate of return on equity.

(j)   The extent to which the business is **dependent** on the technical skills of one or more individuals.

2.8   A predator company may sometimes use their higher P/E ratio to value a target company. This assumes that the predator can improve the target's business - a dangerous assumption. It would be better to use an adjusted industry P/E ratio or some other method.

Forecast growth in earnings

2.9   When one company is thinking about taking over another, it should look at the target company's **forecast earnings,** not just its historical results. Forecasts of the future earnings of a target company might be attempted by managers in the company which is planning to make the takeover bid. Often the management of the predator company will make an initial approach to the directors of the target company, to sound them out about a possible takeover bid. If the target company's directors are amenable to a bid, they might agree to produce forecasts of their company's future earnings and growth. These forecasts (for the next year and possibly even further ahead) might then be used by the predator company in choosing an offer price.

2.10 Forecasts of earnings growth should only be used the earnings growth is expected to be achieved; if a reasonable estimate of growth can be made; and if any forecasts supplied by the target company's board of directors are made in good faith.

The accounting rate of return (ARR) method of share valuation

2.11 This method considers the **accounting rate of return** which will be required from the company whose shares are to be valued. It is therefore distinct from the P/E ratio method, which is concerned with the market rate of return required. The following formula should be used.

$$\text{Value} = \frac{\text{Estimated future profits}}{\text{Required return on capital employed}}$$

2.12 For a takeover bid valuation, it will often be necessary to adjust the profits figure to allow for expected changes after the takeover. Those arising in an examination question might include:

(a) New levels of directors' remuneration

(b) New levels of interest charges (perhaps because the predator company will be able to replace existing loans with new loans at a lower rate of interest, or because the previous owners had lent the company money at non-commercial rates)

(c) A charge for notional rent where it is intended to sell existing properties or where the rate of return used is based on the results of similar companies that do not own their own properties

(d) The effects of product rationalisation and improved management

2.13 EXAMPLE: ARR METHOD

Chambers Ltd is considering acquiring Hall Ltd. At present Hall Ltd is earning, on average, £480,000 after tax. The directors of Chambers Ltd feel that after reorganisation, this figure could be increased to £600,000. All the companies in the Chambers group are expected to yield a post-tax accounting return of 15% on capital employed. What should Hall Ltd be valued at?

2.14 SOLUTION

$$\text{Valuation} = \frac{\pounds 600,000}{15\%} = \pounds 4,000,000$$

This figure is the maximum that Chambers should be prepared to pay. The first offer would probably be much lower.

2.15 An ARR valuation might be used in a takeover when the acquiring company is trying to assess the maximum amount it can afford to pay. This is because it is a measure of management efficiency and the rate used can be selected to reflect (among other things) the return which the acquiring company thinks should be obtainable after any post-acquisition reorganisation has been completed. A valuation on this basis should then be compared with the stock market price (for quoted companies) or a price arrived at using the P/E ratio of similar quoted companies.

The net assets method of share valuation

2.16 Using this method of valuation, the value of a share in a particular class is equal to the **net tangible assets** attributable to that class, divided by the number of shares in the class. Intangible assets (including goodwill) should be excluded, unless they have a market value (for example patents and copyrights, which could be sold).

(a) **Goodwill**, if shown in the accounts, is unlikely to be shown at a true figure for purposes of valuation, and the value of goodwill should be reflected in another method of valuation (for example the earnings basis, the dividend yield basis or the super-profits method).

(b) **Development expenditure**, if shown in the accounts, would also have a value which is related to future profits rather than to the worth of the company's physical assets.

2.17 EXAMPLE: NET ASSETS METHOD

The summary balance sheet of Cactus Ltd is as follows.

Fixed assets	£	£	£
Land and buildings			160,000
Plant and machinery			80,000
Motor vehicles			20,000
			260,000
Goodwill			20,000
Current assets			
Stocks		80,000	
Debtors		60,000	
Short-term investments		15,000	
Cash		5,000	
		160,000	
Current liabilities			
Creditors	60,000		
Taxation	20,000		
Proposed ordinary dividend	20,000		
		(100,000)	
			60,000
			340,000
12% debentures			(60,000)
Deferred taxation			(10,000)
			270,000
Ordinary shares of £1			80,000
Reserves			140,000
			220,000
4.9% preference shares of £1			50,000
			270,000

What is the value of an ordinary share using the net assets basis of valuation?

2.18 SOLUTION

If the figures given for asset values are not questioned, the valuation would be as follows.

	£	£
Total value of net assets		340,000
Less intangible asset (goodwill)		20,000
Total value of tangible assets (net)		320,000
Less: Preference shares	50,000	
Debentures	60,000	
Deferred taxation	10,000	
		120,000
Net asset value of equity		200,000
Number of ordinary shares		80,000
Value per share		£2.50

2.19 The difficulty in an asset valuation method is establishing realistic asset values. The figure attached to an individual asset may vary considerably depending on whether it is valued on a going concern or a break-up basis. The following list should give you some idea of the factors to be considered.

(a) Do the assets need professional valuation? If so, how much will this cost?

(b) Have the liabilities been accurately quantified, for example deferred taxation? Are there any contingent liabilities? Will any balancing tax charges arise on disposal?

(c) How have the current assets been valued? Are all debtors collectable? Is all stock realisable? Can all the assets be physically located and brought into a saleable condition? (May be difficult where assets are situated abroad.)

(d) Can any hidden liabilities be accurately assessed? Would there be redundancy payments and closure costs?

(e) Is there an available market in which the assets can be realised (on a break-up basis)? If so, do the balance sheet values truly reflect these break-up values?

(f) Are there any prior charges on the assets?

When is the net assets basis of valuation used?

2.20 It is always advisable to calculate the net assets per share. The net assets basis of valuation should be used on the following basis.

(a) **As a measure of the 'security' in a share value**. A share might be valued using the earnings basis, and this valuation might be:

(i) **Higher than the net asset value per share.** If the company went into liquidation, the investor could not expect to receive the full value of his shares when the underlying assets were realised.

(ii) **Lower than the net asset value per share.** If the company went into liquidation, the investor might expect to receive the full value of his shares (maybe more).

The asset backing for shares thus provides a measure of the possible loss if the company fails to make the expected earnings or dividend payments. It is often thought to be a good thing to acquire a company with valuable tangible assets, especially freehold property which might be expected to increase in value over time.

(b) **As a measure of comparison in a scheme of merger**. If company A, with a low asset backing, is planning a merger with company B, with a high asset backing, the shareholders of B might consider that their shares' value ought to reflect this. It might therefore be agreed that something should be added to the value of the company B shares to allow for this difference in asset backing.

Exam focus point
You might come across reference to the Berliner method of share valuation. This involves taking the average of the prices calculated using the earnings method and the net assets method.

The dividend yield method of share valuation

2.21 The **dividend yield method** of share valuation is suitable for the valuation of small shareholdings in unquoted companies. It is based on the principle that small shareholders are mainly interested in dividends, since they cannot control decisions affecting the company's profits and earnings. A suitable offer price would therefore be one which compensates them for the future dividends they will be giving up if they sell their shares.

2.22 The simplest dividend capitalisation technique is based on the assumption that the level of dividends in the future will be **constant**. A dividend yield valuation would be:

$$\text{Value} = \frac{\text{Dividend in pence}}{\text{Expected dividend yield \%}}$$

2.23 It may be possible to use expected **future** dividends for a share valuation and to predict dividend growth. For this purpose, it is first necessary to predict future earnings and then to decide how changes in earnings will be reflected in the company's dividend policy.

2.24 The dividend growth model for share valuation, you may recall, is as follows.

$$P_0 = \frac{D_0(1+g)}{(r-g)}$$

where P_0 is the current market value ex dividend
            D_0 is the current dividend
            g is the expected annual growth in dividend, so
                    $D_0(1+g)$ is the expected dividend next year
            r is the return required.

Question

A company expects to pay no dividends in years 1, 2 or 3, but a dividend of 7.8p per share each year from year 4 in perpetuity. Value its shares on a dividend yield basis, assuming a required yield of 12%.

Answer

$$\frac{7.8p}{(1.12)^4} + \frac{7.8p}{(1.12)^5} + \ldots\ldots = \frac{7.8p}{0.12} \times \frac{1}{(1.12)^3} = \frac{65p}{(1.12)^3} = 46.26p, \text{ say } 46p$$

The CAPM and share price valuations

2.25 The **capital asset pricing model (CAPM)** might be used to value shares, particularly when pricing shares for a stock market listing. The CAPM would be used to establish a required equity yield.

2.26 EXAMPLE: CAPM AND SHARE PRICE VALUATIONS

Suppose that Mackerel plc is planning to obtain a Stock Exchange listing by offering 40% of its existing shares to the public. No new shares will be issued. Its most recent summarised results are as follows.

	£
Turnover	120,000,000
Earnings	1,500,000
Number of shares	3,000,000

The company has low gearing.

It regularly pays 50% of earnings as dividends, and with reinvested earnings is expected to achieve 5% dividend growth each year. Summarised details of two listed companies in the same industry as Mackerel plc are as follows.

	Salmon plc	*Trout plc*
Gearing (total debt/total equity)	45%	10%
Equity beta	1.50	1.05

The current Treasury bill yield is 7% a year. The average market return is estimated to be 12%. The new shares will be issued at a discount of 15% to the estimated post-issue market price, in order to increase the prospects of success for the share issue. What will the issue price be?

2.27 SOLUTION

Using the CAPM, we begin by deciding on a suitable β value for Mackerel's equity. We shall assume that since Mackerel's gearing is close to Trout's, a β of 1.05 is appropriate.

The cost of Mackerel equity is $7\% + (12 - 7) \times 1.05\% = 12.25\%$

This can now be used in the dividend growth model. The dividend this year is 50% of £1,500,000 = £750,000.

The total value of Mackerel's equity is $\dfrac{£750,000(1.05)}{(0.1225 - 0.05)} = £10,862,069$

There are 3,000,000 shares, giving a market value per share of £3.62. Since the shares that are offered to the public will be offered at a discount of about 15% to this value, the share price for the market launch should be about 85% of £3.62 = £3.08.

The super-profits method of share valuation

2.28 This method, which is rather out-of-fashion now, starts by applying a 'fair return' to the net tangible assets and comparing the result with the expected profits. Any excess of profits (the **super-profits**) is used to calculate goodwill. The goodwill is normally taken as a fixed number of years super-profits. The goodwill is then added to the value of the target company's tangible assets to arrive at a value for the business.

2.29 EXAMPLE: SUPER-PROFITS METHOD

Light Ltd has net tangible assets of £120,000 and present earnings of £20,000. Doppler Ltd wants to take over Light Ltd and considers that a fair return for this type of industry is 12%, and decides to value Light Ltd taking goodwill at three years super-profits.

	£
Actual profits	20,000
Less fair return on net tangible assets: 12% × £120,000	14,400
Super-profits	5,600
Goodwill: 3 × £5,600	£16,800
Value of Light Ltd: £120,000 + £16,800	£136,800

2.30 The principal drawbacks to this valuation method are as follows.

(a) The rate of return required is chosen subjectively.
(b) The number of years purchase of super-profits is arbitrary.

The discounted future profits method of share valuation

2.31 The **discounted future profits** method of share valuation may be appropriate when one company intends to buy the assets of another company and to make further investments in order to improve profits in the future.

2.32 EXAMPLE: DISCOUNTED FUTURE PROFITS METHOD

Diversification Ltd wishes to make a bid for Tadpole Ltd. Tadpole Ltd makes after-tax profits of £40,000 a year. Diversification Ltd believes that if further investments are made, the after-tax cash flows (ignoring the purchase consideration) could be as follows.

Year	Cash flow (net of tax) £
0	(100,000)
1	(80,000)
2	60,000
3	100,000
4	150,000
5	150,000

The after-tax cost of capital of Diversification Ltd is 15% and the company expects all its investments to pay back, in discounted terms, within five years. What is the maximum price that the company should be willing to pay for the shares of Tadpole Ltd?

2.33 SOLUTION

The maximum price is one which would make the return from the total investment exactly 15% over five years, so that the NPV at 15% would be 0.

Year	Cash flows ignoring purchase consideration £	Discount factor 15%	Present value £
0	(100,000)	1.000	(100,000)
1	(80,000)	0.870	(69,600)
2	60,000	0.756	45,360
3	100,000	0.658	65,800
4	150,000	0.572	85,800
5	150,000	0.497	74,550
Maximum purchase price			101,910

Free cash flow

2.34 One approach to the valuation of a business is to treat its value as the sum of future discounted free cash flows, where **free cash flow** is given by the following.

Free cash flow = Revenues – operating costs + depreciation – investment expenditure

2.35 This approach, however, presents the following problems when used in financial planning and strategy.

(a) Due to movement of working capital items, accounting information on revenues and operating costs may fail to reflect cash flows. For example, if sales increase, they may do so on longer credit terms than previously, and the cash flow effect may therefore be delayed. Also, stock building may have adverse effects on cash flows while having no effects on profits.

(b) The timing of tax payments in a particular year will be based on profits earned in previous time periods. As a result, the free cash flow for the current period less this year's tax liability does not equal cash flow for the current year.

2.36 These problems mean that estimating free cash flow involves not just forecasting sales, costs and profits, but also working capital movements and taxation.

Chapter roundup

- There are a number of different ways of putting a **value** on a **business**, or on **shares** in an **unquoted company**. It makes sense to use several methods of valuation, and to compare the values they produce.

- What matters ultimately is the final **price** that the buyer and the seller agree. The purchase price for a company will usually be discussed mainly in terms of:

    ° **P/E ratios**, when a large block of shares, or a whole business is being valued;
    ° alternatively, **a DCF valuation**;
    ° to a lesser extent, the **net assets per share**.

- The dividend yield method is more relevant to **small shareholdings**.

Quick quiz

1 Why are valuations of companies sometimes necessary? (see para 1.1)

2 What guidelines should help to determine the P/E ratio on which to base an offer price for shares in an unquoted target company? (2.9)

3 How should the net assets of a company be valued, for a net assets method valuation? (2.17 - 2.19)

4 What is 'free cash flow'? (2.34)

Question to try	Level	Marks	Time
14	Introductory	n/a	45 mins

Chapter 15

CAPITAL RECONSTRUCTION SCHEMES

Chapter topic list	Syllabus reference
1 Business failures	2(e)
2 Capital reconstruction schemes	2(e)

Introduction

In Chapter 13, we concentrated mainly on acquisitions but also mentioned some other forms of restructuring such as demergers and disinvestment.

In this chapter, we look at situations in which a **restructuring of capital** is to be carried out.

1   BUSINESS FAILURES

1.1   Not all businesses are profitable. Some incur losses in one or more years, but eventually achieve profitability. Others remain unprofitable, or earn only very small and unsatisfactory profits. Other companies are profitable, but run out of cash. (We looked at **indicators of business failure** in Chapter 12.)

   (a)   A poorly performing company which is unprofitable, but has enough cash to keep going, might eventually decide to go into liquidation, because it is not worth carrying on in business. Alternatively, it might become the target of a successful takeover bid.

   (b)   A company which runs out of cash, even if it is profitable, might be forced into liquidation by unpaid creditors, who want payment and think that applying to the court to wind up the company is the best way of getting some or all of their money.

1.2   However, a company might be on the brink of going into liquidation, but hold out good promise of profits in the future. In such a situation, the company might be able to attract fresh capital and to persuade its creditors to accept some securities in the company as 'payment', and achieve a **capital reconstruction** which allows the company to carry on in business.

1.3   In the event of a liquidation, the assets of the business are sold off and distributed, in the following order or 'priority list'.

   (a)   Secured creditors with a fixed charge on certain assets

   (b)   Liquidation expenses

   (c)   Preferential creditors (eg up to a given time limit, unpaid income tax, VAT and national insurance, some arrears of unpaid wages and salaries)

   (d)   Secured creditors with a floating charge on certain assets

   (e)   Unsecured creditors

(f)   Preference shareholders

(g)   Ordinary shareholders

Fixed and floating charges

1.4   A creditor or lender may hold a **fixed charge** on certain assets of the business as security for a loan. An example would be a mortgage on a factory. When a company goes into liquidation the creditor is 'secured' and is entitled to first claim on the proceeds from the sale of the assets.

(a)   If a bank is owed £60,000 by a company and holds as security a fixed charge on property which is later sold for £75,000, the bank will receive £60,000 out of the proceeds. The remaining £15,000 will be given to the liquidator, to go towards the payment of other debts of the company.

(b)   If a bank is owed £60,000 by a company and its security is a fixed charge on an asset which only realises £35,000 on sale, the bank will receive the £35,000, but will become an **unsecured creditor** for the remaining £25,000 of the total debt.

1.5   A **second charge** on an asset means that the lender has a prior claim on any surplus receipts from the sale of the asset once payment has been made **in full** to another lender who holds a first charge on the asset. For example, suppose that a debenture loan of £60,000 is secured by a fixed charge on freehold property, and a bank overdraft of £20,000 is secured by a second charge on the same property. If the property is sold in a liquidation for £75,000, the debenture holders would be paid back in full (£60,000) and the bank would be paid the balance (£15,000) leaving £5,000 of the overdraft as an unsecured creditor.

1.6   A lender may hold a **floating charge** on certain assets of the business. A floating charge applies to assets such as stocks, which are continually being bought and sold in the course of normal trading operations. When a liquidation occurs, the floating charge 'crystallises' and becomes a fixed charge on the relevant assets which are in the business at that time. For example, if a creditor holds a floating charge on the stocks of a company as security for a debt, and the company goes into liquidation on, say, 31 December 19X4, then the creditor will have as his security for the debt the stocks of the business as at 31 December 19X4. The two forms of charge may be combined in one security document. This is known by bankers as a '**fixed and floater**'.

2   CAPITAL RECONSTRUCTION SCHEMES   12/97

2.1   A **capital reconstruction scheme** is a scheme whereby a company reorganises its capital structure. A reconstruction scheme might be agreed when a company is in danger of being put into liquidation, owing debts that it cannot repay, and so the creditors of the company agree to accept securities in the company, perhaps including equity shares, in settlement of their debts.

2.2   There are certain **general principles** that you should observe in designing a scheme of reconstruction.

(a)   If a company is in difficulties, it will probably need more finance to keep going, eg an injection of capital from existing shareholders or from another source, such as a bank.

(b)   Anyone providing extra finance for an ailing company must be persuaded that the expected return from the extra finance is attractive. A **profit forecast** and a **cash forecast** or a **funds flow forecast** will be needed to provide reassurance about the company's future, to creditors and to any financial institution that is asked to put new capital into the company.

(c) A scheme of reconstruction might involve the creation of new share capital of a different nominal value than existing share capital, or the cancellation of existing share capital.

(d) For a scheme of reconstruction to be acceptable it needs to treat all parties fairly (for example, preference shareholders must not be treated with disproportionate favour in comparison with equity shareholders), and it needs to offer creditors a better deal than if the company went into liquidation. If it did not, the creditors would press for a winding up of the company. A reconstruction might therefore include an arrangement to pay off the company's existing debts in full.

2.3 EXAMPLE: CAPITAL RECONSTRUCTION SCHEMES

Crosby and Dawson Ltd is a private company that has for many years been making mechanical timing mechanisms for washing machines. The management was slow to appreciate the impact that new technology would have and the company is now faced with rapidly falling sales.

In July 20X1, the directors decided that the best way to exploit their company's expertise in the future was to diversify into the high precision field of control linkages for aircraft, rockets, satellites and space probes. By January 20X2, some sales had been made to European companies and sufficient progress had been made to arouse considerable interest from the major aircraft manufacturers and from NASA in the USA. The cost, however, had been heavy. The company had borrowed £2,500,000 from the Vencap Merchant Bank plc and a further £500,000 from other sources. Its bank overdraft was at its limit of £750,000 and the dividend on its cumulative preference shares, which was due in December, had been unpaid for the fourth year in succession. On 1 February 20X2, the company has just lost another two major customers for its washing machine timers. The financial director presents the following information.

If the company remains in operation, the expected cash flows for the next five periods are as follows.

	9 months to 31.12.X2	20X3	Years ending 31 December 20X4	20X5	20X6
	£'000	£'000	£'000	£'000	£'000
Receipts from sales	8,000	12,000	15,000	20,000	30,000
Payments to suppliers	6,000	6,700	7,500	10,800	18,000
pPurchase of equipment	1,000	800	1,600	2,700	2,500
Other expenses	1,800	4,100	4,200	4,600	6,400
Interest charges	800	900	700	400	100
	9,600	12,500	14,000	18,500	27,000
Net	(1,600)	(500)	1,000	1,500	3,000

The above figures are based on the assumption that the present capital structure is maintained by further borrowings as necessary.

BALANCE SHEETS

	31.12.X0	31.12.X1	31.3.X2
			Projected
	£'000	£'000	£'000
Assets employed			
Fixed assets			
Freehold property	2,780	2,770	2,760
Plant and machinery	3,070	1,810	1,920
Motor vehicles	250	205	200
Deferred development expenditure	-	700	790
Current assets			
Stock	890	970	1,015
Debtors	780	795	725
	1,670	1,765	1,740
Current liabilities			
Trade creditors	1,220	1,100	1,960
Bank overdraft (unsecured)	650	750	750
	1,870	1,850	2,710
	(200)	(85)	(970)
	5,900	5,400	4,700
Long-term liabilities			
10% debentures 19X8 (secured on freehold property)	(1,000)	(1,000)	(1,000)
Other loans (floating charges)	-	(3,000)	(3,000)
	4,900	1,400	700
Ordinary shares of £1	3,500	3,500	3,500
8% Cumulative preference shares	1,000	1,000	1,000
Accumulated reserves/(accumulated deficit)	400	(3,100)	(3,800)
	4,900	1,400	700

Other information

1   The freehold property was revalued on 31 December 20X0. It is believed that its net disposal value at 31 March 20X2 will be about £3,000,000.

2   A substantial quantity of old plant was sold during the second six months of 20X1 to help pay for the new machinery needed. It is estimated that the break up value of the plant at 31 March 20X2 will be about £1,400,000.

3   The motor vehicles owned at 31 March 20X2 could be sold for £120,000.

4   Much of the work done on the new control linkages has been patented. It is believed that these patents could be sold for about £800,000, which can be considered as the break-up value of development expenditure incurred to 31 March 20X2.

5   On liquidation, it is expected that the current assets at 31 March 20X2 would realise £1,050,000. Liquidation costs would be approximately £300,000.

Suggest a scheme of reconstruction that is likely to be acceptable to all the parties involved. The ordinary shareholders would be prepared to invest a further £1,200,000 if the scheme were considered by them to be reasonable.

A full solution follows. Complete the first step yourself as a short question.

Question

Ascertain the likely result of Crosby & Dawson Limited (see above) going into liquidation as at 31 March 20X2.

Answer

Break-up values of assets at 31 March 20X2	£'000
Freehold	3,000
Plant and machinery	1,400
Motor vehicles	120
Patents	800
Current assets	1,050
	6,370

Total liabilities at 31 March 20X2	£'000
Debentures	1,000
Other loans	3,000
Bank overdraft	750
Trade creditors	1,960
	6,710

2.4 SOLUTION TO REMAINDER OF THE EXAMPLE

If the company was forced into liquidation, the debentures and other loans would be met in full but that after allowing for the expenses of liquidation (£300,000) the bank and trade creditors would receive a total of £2,070,000 or 76p per pound. The ordinary and preference shareholders would receive nothing.

If the company remains in operation, the cash position will at first deteriorate but will improve from 20X4 onwards. By the end of 20X6 net assets will have increased by £11,800,000 before depreciation (plant £8,600,000 and cash £3,400,000). If the figures can be relied on and the trend of results continues after 20X6 the company will become reasonably profitable.

In the immediate future, after taking into account the additional amounts raised from the existing ordinary shareholders, the company will require finance of £400,000 in 20X2 and £500,000 in 20X3.

Vencap might be persuaded to subscribe cash for ordinary shares. It is unlikely that the company's clearing bank would be prepared to accept any shares, but as they would only receive 76p per pound on a liquidation they may be prepared to transfer part of the overdraft into a (say) five year loan whilst maintaining the current overdraft limit. It is unlikely that a suitable arrangement can be reached with the trade creditors as many would be prepared to accept 76p per pound, rather than agree to a moratorium on the debts or take an equity interest in the company.

A possible scheme might be as follows.

1   The existing ordinary shares to be cancelled and ordinary shareholders to be issued with £1,200,000 new £1 ordinary shares for cash.

2   The existing preference shares to be cancelled and the holders to be issued with £320,000 new £1 ordinary shares at par.

3   The existing debentures to be cancelled and replaced by £800,000 15% secured Debentures with a 15 year term and the holders to be issued with £400,000 of new £1 ordinary shares at par.

4   The loan 'from other sources' to be repaid.

5   The Vencap Bank to receive £2,000,000 15% secured debentures with a 15 year term in part settlement of the existing loan, to be issued £680,000 new ordinary shares in settlement of the balance and to subscribe cash for £800,000 of new ordinary shares.

6   The clearing bank to transfer the existing overdraft to a loan account repayable over five years and to keep the overdraft limit at £750,000. Both the loan and overdraft to be secured by a floating charge.

Comments

1   *Debenture holders*. The debentures currently have more than adequate asset backing, and their current nominal yield is 10%. If the reconstruction is to be acceptable to them, they must have either the same asset backing or some compensation in terms of increased nominal value and higher nominal yield. Under the scheme they will receive securities with a total nominal value of £1,200,000 (an increase of £200,000) and an increase in total yield before any ordinary dividends of £20,000. The new debentures issued to Vencap can be secured on the freehold property (see below).

2   *Loans from other sources*. It has been suggested that the 'loans from other sources' should be repaid as, in general, it is easier to arrange a successful reconstruction that involves fewer parties.

3   *Vencap*. Vencap's existing loan of £2,500,000 will, under the proposed scheme, be changed into £2,000,000 of 15% debentures secured on the property and £680,000 of ordinary shares. This gives total loans of £2,800,000 secured on property with a net disposal value of £3,000,000. This is low asset cover which might increase if property values were to rise. The scheme will increase the nominal value of Vencap's interest by £180,000 with an improvement in security on the first £2,000,000 to compensate for the risk involved in holding ordinary shares. It has also been suggested that Vencap should be asked to subscribe £800,000 for new ordinary shares. The money is required to repay the 'loans from other sources' and to provide additional working capital. The issue of share capital would give the bank a total of 1,480,000 ordinary shares or 43.5% of the equity. From the company's point of view issuing new equity is to be preferred to loan stock as it will improve the gearing position.

4   *The clearing bank*. In a liquidation now, the clearing bank would receive approximately £573,000. In return for the possibility of receiving the full amount owed to them they are being asked under the scheme to advance a further £750,000. By way of compensation, they are receiving the security of a floating charge.

5   *Preference shares*. In a liquidation at the present time, the preference shareholders would receive nothing. The issue of 320,000 £1 ordinary shares should be acceptable as it is equivalent to their current arrears of dividend. If the preference shares were left unaffected by the scheme, the full arrears of dividend would become payable on the company's return to profitability, giving preference shareholders an undue advantage.

6   *Ordinary shareholders*. In a liquidation, the ordinary shareholders would also receive nothing. Under the scheme, they will lose control of the company but, in exchange for their additional investment, will still hold about 35.3% of the equity in a company which will have sufficient funds to finance the expected future capital requirements.

7   *Cash flow forecast, on reconstruction*   £'000

Cash for new shares from equity shareholders   1,200
Cash for new shares from Vencap   800
                                                                               _____
                                                                               2,000
Repayment of loan from other sources   (500)
                                                                               _____
Cash available   1,500
                                                                               _____

The overdraft of £750,000 is converted into a long-term loan, leaving the company with a further £750,000 of overdraft facility to use.

8   *Adequacy of funds.* The balance sheet below shows the company's position after the implementation of the scheme but before any repayments to creditors.

	£'000	£'000
Fixed assets		
Freehold property		2,760
Plant and machinery		1,920
Motor vehicles		200
Deferred development expenditure		790
		5,670
Current assets		
Stocks	1,015	
Debtors	725	
Cash	1,500	
	3,240	
Less current liabilities: Trade creditors	1,960	
		1,280
		6,950
Less long-term liabilities		
15% debentures		(2,800)
Loan from clearing bank		(750)
		3,400
Ordinary shares of £1		3,400

It would seem likely that the company will have to make a bigger investment in working capital (ignoring cash) for the following reasons.

(a)   Presumably a substantial proportion of the sales will be exports which generally have a longer collection period than domestic sales.

(b)   It is unlikely that the trade creditors will accept the current payment position (average credit takes over two months) in the long term.

9   *Will the reconstructed company be financially viable?*

Assuming that net current assets excluding cash and any overdraft will, by the end of 20X2, rise from –£220,000 to £500,000 and increase in proportion to sales receipts thereafter, that the equipment required in 20X2 and 20X3 will be leased on five year terms and that the interest charges (including the finance elements in the lease rentals) will be approximately the same as those given in the question, then the expected cash flows on implementation could be as shown below.

	9 months to 31.12.X2	20X3	20X4	20X5	20X6
	£'000	£'000	£'000	£'000	£'000
Receipts from sales	8,000	12,000	15,000	20,000	30,000
Purchase of equipment	-	-	1,600	2,700	2,500
Payments to suppliers	6,000	6,700	7,500	10,800	18,000
Other expenses	1,800	4,100	4,200	4,600	6,400
Interest charges	800	900	700	400	100
Lease rentals (excluding finance element) (say)	200	360	360	360	360
Bank loan repayment (say)	150	150	150	150	150
Invt. in working capital	720	250	190	310	630
	9,670	12,460	14,700	19,320	28,140
Net movement	(1,670)	(460)	300	680	1,860
Cash balance b/f	1,500	(170)	(630)	(330)	350
Cash balance c/f	(170)	(630)	(330)	350	2,210

These figures suggest that with an agreed overdraft limit of £750,000 the company will have sufficient funds to carry it through the next five years, assuming that the figures are reliable and that no dividends are paid until perhaps 20X4 at the earliest.

This scheme of reconstruction might not be acceptable to all parties, if the future profits of the company seem unattractive. In particular, Vencap and the clearing bank might be reluctant to agree to the scheme. In such an event, an alternative scheme of reconstruction must be designed, perhaps involving another provider of funds (such as another venture capitalist). Otherwise, the company will be forced into liquidation.

Exam focus point

In the question set on a scheme of reconstruction in the 12/97 exam, some candidates tried to estimate the net present value of the reconstruction even though insufficient data was provided to do this. The examiner has said that if a specific calculation technique is expected, then enough data will be provided to allow that technique to be used. Although assumptions may sometimes need to be made (and should be stated), you would not be expected to 'invent' basic financial data.

Chapter roundup

- Any **capital reconstruction scheme** must be carefully designed. Such schemes are only required when companies have already got into difficulties. Some parties will already stand to lose money, and they will only be persuaded to risk more money if they can see really good prospects of eventual success.

Quick quiz

1   Why might a company go into liquidation? (see para 1.1)

2   What is a fixed charge? (1.4)

3   What is a floating charge? (1.6)

4   What is a capital reconstruction scheme? (2.1)

5   What are the general principles to be observed in designing a scheme of reconstruction? (2.2)

Question to try	Level	Marks	Time
15	Exam standard	30	54 mins

Part C
The international environment

Chapter 16

MULTINATIONALS AND INTERNATIONAL TRADE

Chapter topic list	Syllabus reference
1 Multinational enterprises and global trends	5(a), (b)
2 Advantages of international trade	5(c)
3 Protectionism and free trade agreements	5(e), (f)
4 The balance of payments	5(d)

Introduction

In this part of the Study Text, we look at aspects of the **international environment** faced by enterprises. In this first chapter of Part C, we look at some **trends in global competition** and at the theory and practice of **international trade**. We ask what are the **economic arguments** in favour of free trade and what **international agreements** exist to try to ensure that free trade takes place.

Knowledge brought forward from Paper 4

For Paper 14, you need to develop an awareness of the international environment and the economic influences on international decisions. Paper 4 *The Organisational Framework* provided an introduction to these topics, which we revise in this chapter. If you recall these topics well, you may not need to read Sections 2, 3 and 4 of this chapter in detail.

Exam focus point

Bear in mind that the topics of international financial strategy together with risk management account for approximately 45% of the paper.

1   MULTINATIONAL ENTERPRISES AND GLOBAL TRENDS   12/98, 6/99

The nature of multinational enterprises

1.1   A company does not become 'multinational' simply by virtue of exporting or importing products: ownership and control of facilities abroad is involved.

KEY TERM

A **multinational enterprise** is one which owns or controls production facilities or subsidiaries or service facilities outside the country in which it is based.

BPP PUBLISHING

The size and significance of multinationals

1.2 Multinational enterprises range from medium-sized companies having only a few facilities (or 'affiliates') abroad to giant companies having an annual turnover larger than the gross national product (GNP) of some smaller countries of the world. Indeed, the largest - such as the US multinationals Ford, General Motors and Exxon - each have a turnover similar to the GNP a medium-sized national economy.

1.3 The **size and significance of multinationals** is increasing. Many companies in 'middle-income' countries such as Singapore are now becoming multinationals, and the annual growth in output of existing multinationals is in the range 10-15%. The extensive activities of multinational enterprises, particularly the larger ones, raises questions about the problems of controlling them. Individual governments may be largely powerless if multinationals are able to exploit the tax regimes of '**tax haven**' countries through **transfer pricing** policies or if the multinationals' production is switched from one country to another.

> ### KEY TERM
>
> **Tax havens:** countries with lenient tax rules or relatively low tax rates, which are often designed to attract foreign investment.

1.4 Most of the two-way traffic in investment by multinational companies (**foreign direct investment** or **FDI**) is between the developed countries of the world. While the present pattern of FDI can be traced back to the initial wave of investment in Europe by the USA following the Second World War, more recently Europe and Japan have become substantial overseas investors.

Changes in the pattern of FDI

1.5 There have been significant changes affecting the pattern of multinationals' activities over the last twenty years or so.

(a) The **destination countries** have changed. The focus has shifted from Canada and Latin America in the days when the USA was the major source of FDI to other areas, including the countries of South East Asia which receive significant direct investment from Japanese companies in particular. The group of 'newly industrialised countries' (NICs) - Taiwan, South Korea, the Philippines, Brazil and Mexico - have become significant recipients of FDI. For example, Taiwan's five largest electronic exporters are all US-owned companies.

(b) The *reasons* for foreign direct investment have changed. Previously the rationale may have been to supply local markets abroad or to exploit natural resources situated in the foreign country. Now FDI is likely to take place in the context of a worldwide corporate strategy which takes account of relative costs and revenues, tax considerations and **process specialisation.** Process specialisation refers to the specialisation of processes within particular production facilities. For example, companies may locate labour-intensive processes in lower wage countries, leaving the final stage of the production process to be located nearer the intended market. This form of specialisation is characteristic of motor vehicle manufacture.

(c) **Centralised control** of production activities within multinationals has increased, prompted partly by the need for strategic management of production planning and worldwide resource allocation. This process of centralisation has been facilitated by the development of sophisticated worldwide computer and telecommunications links.

Globalisation

1.6 Developments in international capital markets have provided an environment conducive to FDI. **Globalisation** describes the process by which the capital markets of each country have become internationally integrated. The process of integration is facilitated by improved telecommunications and the deregulation of markets in many countries (for example, the UK stock market's so-called Big Bang of 1986).

1.7 Securities issued in one country can now be traded in capital markets around the world. For example, shares in UK companies are traded in the USA. The shares are bought by US banks, which then issue ADRs (American depository receipts) which are a form in which foreign shares can be traded in US markets without a local listing.

1.8 For companies planning international investment activities, easy access to large amounts of funds denominated in foreign currencies can be very useful. Such funds are available in the eurocurrency markets (see Chapter 17), whose continued expansion during the 1980s, although slower than during the 1970s, encouraged FDI. The eurocurrency markets can also help to bypass official constraints on international business activities.

Why do multinationals make direct foreign investments?

Strategic reasons

1.9 Eiteman, Stonehill and Moffett (*Multinational Business Finance, 1992*) set out five main strategic reasons for engaging in FDI, as follows.

(a) **Market seeking**. 'Market seeking' firms engage in FDI either to meet local demand or as a way of exporting to markets other than the home market. Examples of this are the manufacturing operations of US and Japanese car producers in Europe.

(b) **Raw material seeking**. Firms in industries such as oil, mining, plantation and forestry will extract raw materials in the places where they can be found, whether for export or for further processing and sale in the host country.

(c) **Production efficiency seeking**. The labour-intensive manufacture of electronic components in Taiwan, Malaysia and Mexico is an example of locating production where one or more factors of production are cheap relative to their productivity.

(d) **Knowledge seeking**. Knowledge seeking firms choose to set up operations in countries in which they can gain access to technology or management expertise. For example, German, Japanese and Dutch companies have acquired technology by buying US-based electronics companies.

(e) **Political safety seekers**. Firms which are seeking 'political safety' will acquire or set up new operations in those countries which are thought to be unlikely to expropriate or interfere with private enterprise. An example of this strategy has been the heavy investment by Hong Kong firms in manufacturing, service industries and property in the USA, Canada and Australia, in anticipation of the possible consequences of the recent (1997) takeover of Hong Kong by China.

1.10 Of course, the five strategic reasons identified above are not mutually exclusive. For example firms which locate electronics factories in Taiwan, Malaysia and Mexico will also find a market for their products in those countries.

BPP PUBLISHING

Strategic considerations versus financial considerations

1.11 Strategic reasons seem to weigh more heavily than financial considerations in the FDI decision. Empirical studies support this conclusion, including one carried out by Stonehill and Nathanson (1968), which showed the following.

> 'Financial investment criteria were used most often in evaluating relatively small cost-saving projects, replacement projects, and other projects which would fall under the purview of local managers. For relatively large or strategic investments, however, financial investment criteria were used only as a rough screening device to prevent obviously unprofitable projects from wasting the time of the board of directors.'

1.12 The business of determining an appropriate risk-adjusted required rate of return for a foreign project is often complicated by the perceived political and foreign exchange risks. The range of possible expected outcomes may become so wide that it becomes difficult to produce a credible discounted cash flow analysis which produces a single expected net present value. Thus, although discounted cash flow techniques are still used to analyse specific projects, they do not usually become the deciding factor.

Economic theories

1.13 Modern extensions of international economic theory which view the executives of multinationals as operating under conditions of worldwide oligopolistic competition, in ways which are consistent with the rational economic motive of profit maximisation. The traditional economic theory of international trade (examined later in this chapter) assumes that markets are perfectly competitive and that products are homogeneous in quality. These assumptions do not apply generally to multinational enterprises, in which two-way trade within the firm among the parent company and its subsidiaries forms a major element. To explain FDI and the growth of multinational enterprises, we need a theory which recognises the imperfections of markets.

1.14 The modern economic theory of FDI stems from the work of Stephen Hymer (1960), subsequently developed by Charles Kindleberger (1969). The **Hymer-Kindleberger theory** sees imperfections in product and factor markets as opening the way to FDI. Market imperfections may be natural, but more usually they are the result of the policies of **firms**, as for example when oligopolists seek competitive advantage through product differentiation, for instance by creating a multiplicity of brands; and the policies of **governments**, which create market imperfections through tariffs, non-tariff barriers to trade, preferential procurement policies, tax incentives, exchange controls and so on.

1.15 An example of market imperfections created by governments is the formation of trade blocs such as the European Economic Community (now called the European Union or EU) in 1957 and the European Free Trade Area (EFTA) in 1958. The establishment of these trading blocs involved the removal of barriers to trade among member countries together with the imposition of a common external tariff on trade with non-member countries, and these changes led to a major influx of foreign direct investment by multinationals seeking to take advantage of the removal of barriers within the blocs.

1.16 Eiteman *et al* (1992) point out that although government policies, the actions of firms themselves or natural factors may lead to large protected markets being established, foreign firms with operations in such markets must have some **competitive advantages** over local firms to compensate for disadvantages such as their relative lack of knowledge of local customs and unfamiliar laws, as well as greater costs of communication and control. These competitive advantages must be such as to earn for the firm a higher rate of return from direct foreign investment than it would earn from comparable projects with a similar level of risk in the home market. Otherwise, the firm would prefer to enter foreign markets through **other means such as exporting or licensing**.

1.17 The most significant competitive advantages which multinationals enjoy are as follows.

(a) **Size economies of scale**. There are advantages to be gained in production, marketing, finance, research and development, transport and purchasing by virtue of firms being large. Production economies can arise from use of large-scale plant or from the possibility of rationalising production by adopting worldwide specialisation. Multinational car manufacturers produce engines in one country, transmissions in another, bodies in another, and assemble cars in yet another country, often selecting the location on the basis of the comparative advantage of having each type of production in a particular location.

(b) **Managerial and marketing expertise**. Although there is little empirical evidence to show whether managerial expertise enhances firms' success in worldwide oligopolistic markets, intuitively it would seem reasonable to assume that this is the case. Managerial expertise may be fostered in the environment of the larger multinational enterprise, and can be developed from previous knowledge of foreign markets. Empirical studies show that multinationals tend to export to markets before establishing production operations there, thus partly overcoming the possibly superior local knowledge of firms based in the host country.

(c) **Technology**. Empirical studies suggest a link between research and development (R & D) work, which enhances technological, scientific and engineering skills and the larger multinationals engaged in FDI. Vernon's **product cycle theory** is based on the idea that multinational firms originate much new technology as a result of R&D activities on new products initially launched in their home markets. Host nations are often interested in FDI for the reason that technology transfer may result from it.

(d) **Financial economies**. Multinationals enjoy considerable cost advantages in relation to finance. They have the advantage of access to the full range of financial instruments such as eurocurrency and eurobonds, which reduces their borrowing costs. Multinationals' financial strength is also achieved through their ability to reduce risk by diversifying their operations and their sources of borrowing. Although government exchange controls will often forbid it, where possible multinational enterprises can reduce their borrowing costs by borrowing funds where costs are lowest for use in the locations where funds are needed.

(e) **Differentiated products**. Firms create their own firm-specific advantages by producing and marketing differentiated products, which are similar products differentiated mainly by branding. Once the firm has developed differentiated products for the home market, it can maximise return on the heavy marketing costs by marketing them worldwide. Competitors will find it expensive and possibly difficult to imitate such products.

1.18 **Buckley and Casson's theory of internalisation** is an extension of the theories of FDI based on market imperfections. These theorists argue that the existence of imperfect markets and competitive advantage for oligopolistic firms is not alone sufficient to ensure FDI. For FDI to occur, according to this theory, the competitive advantage must be internal to the firms. In other words it must be **specific to the firm, not easily imitated, and transferable to foreign subsidiaries**.

1.19 **Advantages of FDI for the host country** 12/98

- Stimulation of economic activity and creation of employment
- Import of capital, which may be a scarce resource
- Introduction of new technology, leading to increased productivity
- Possibly, training opportunities for the local workforce
- Introduction of more advanced management techniques
- Initial balance of payments benefit: inflow of capital

Disadvantages of FDI for the host country

- Longer-term balance of payments loss, as funds are remitted overseas

- Loss of political and economic sovereignty

- Local tax avoidance through transfer pricing and other measures

- Possible destabilisation of the country's monetary policy and large international currency flows

- Undermining of indigenous cultures by introduction of different cultural values and lifestyles

2 ADVANTAGES OF INTERNATIONAL TRADE

Theory of international trade

2.1 In the modern economy, production is based on a high degree of specialisation. Within a country individuals specialise, factories specialise and whole regions specialise. Specialisation increases productivity and raises the standard of living. International trade extends the principle of the division of labour and specialisation to countries. International trade originated on the basis of nations exchanging their products for others which they could not produce for themselves. Britain for example imports tea and coffee and exports oil to non-oil producing countries (although there is also plenty of trade in different types of oil between oil-producing countries themselves).

2.2 International trade arises for a number of reasons.

(a) Different goods require different proportions of factor inputs in their production
(b) Economic resources are unevenly distributed throughout the world
(c) The international mobility of resources is extremely limited

2.3 Since it is difficult to move resources between nations, the goods which 'embody' the resources must move. Hence nations which have an abundance of land relative to labour will concentrate on land intensive commodities such as agricultural products. These will be exchanged for labour-intensive products such as manufactured goods made by countries with an abundance of labour and capital relative to land. The main reason for trade therefore is that there are differences in the relative efficiency with which different countries can produce different goods and services.

2.4 In the theory of international trade, economists distinguish the concepts of comparative advantage and absolute advantage. To explain this distinction we make the following assumptions in what follows.

(a) There are only two countries, country X and country Y.
(b) Only two goods are produced, lorries and wheat.
(c) There are no transport costs and no barriers to trade.
(d) Resources within each country are easily transferred from one industry to another.

Absolute advantage

2.5   A country is said to have an **absolute advantage** in the production of a good when it is more efficient than another country in the production of that good, ie when it can produce more of a particular good with a given amount of resources than another country. It is a fairly common situation for one country to be more efficient than another in the production of a particular good.

2.6   Assuming that Y produces wheat more efficiently than country X, while country X has an absolute advantage in producing lorries, a simple arithmetical example can illustrate the potential gains from trade. The table below shows the amounts of lorries and wheat that each country can produce, assuming that each country has an equal quantity of resources and devotes half of its resources to lorry production and half to wheat production.

	Lorries	*Wheat (tons)*
Country X	20	100
Country Y	10	150
World total	30	250

2.7   The relative or comparative cost of lorry production is lower in country X than country Y, but the situation is reversed in the case of wheat production. Country X has an absolute advantage in lorry production and country Y has an absolute advantage in wheat production.

2.8   Greater specialisation will, however, increase total output. If each country specialises in the production of the good in which it is most efficient, ie possesses absolute advantage, then total output would be as shown below.

	Lorries	*Wheat (tons)*
Country X	40	0
Country Y	0	300
World total	40	300

2.9   By specialising, total world output is now greater with ten more lorries and 50 tons more wheat now available for consumption. In order to obtain the benefits of specialisation these countries must exchange some part of their individual outputs. It is not possible to specify the exact rate of exchange but the limits of the exchange rate must be somewhere between the domestic opportunity cost ratios of the two countries. One country will not benefit from international trade if the exchange rate is not between these ratios.

Comparative advantage

2.10 When two countries produce the same two goods, as in the example above, and each has an absolute advantage in the production of one good, then it is easy to show that specialisation will lead to an increase in their combined output. Specialisation and trade can still be mutually advantageous, however, even if one country has an absolute advantage in the production of both goods. This will be the case if each country has a comparative advantage in the production of one good. This is summed up in the law of **comparative advantage** (or comparative costs) which states that two countries can gain from trade when each concentrates on the production of that good in which it has greatest comparative cost advantage. Comparative cost relates to the **opportunity costs** of producing the goods and not the **absolute costs**.

2.11 The principle of comparative costs can be shown by an arithmetical example. It is now assumed that country X is more efficient in the production of both lorries and wheat. If each country devotes half its resources to each industry the assumed production totals are shown below.

	Lorries	Wheat (tons)
Country X	20	200
Country Y	10	150
World total	30	350

2.12 In terms of resources used, the costs of production in both industries are lower in country X. If we consider the opportunity costs, however, the picture is rather different. In country X the 'cost' of one lorry is ten tons of wheat, ie in devoting resources to the production of one lorry in country X there is a sacrifice in terms of ten tons of wheat forgone. The opportunity cost of one lorry in country Y is fifteen tons of wheat. Country X therefore has a comparative advantage in the production of lorries.

2.13 In country X the cost of a ton of wheat is 1/10 of a lorry, while in country Y the cost is 1/15 of a lorry. In terms of the output of lorries forgone, wheat is cheaper in country Y than in country X. Country Y has a comparative advantage in wheat. If each country completely specialises in the production of the good where it has a comparative advantage, the figures below show that total output of lorries increases, but the total output of wheat falls.

	Lorries	Wheat (tons)
Country X	40	0
Country Y	0	300
World total	40	300

2.14 The figures above show that the world total of lorry production has risen by ten lorries but that the world production of wheat has fallen by fifty tons. It is possible to show that the increase in the output of lorries, in value terms, more than offsets the fall in the output of wheat. This is not necessary, however, because by only partially specialising in the more efficient country - country X - it is possible to have more of both commodities. If country X devotes 80% of its resources to lorry production and 20% of its resources to wheat production, while country Y specialises completely in wheat, the total output will be as shown below.

	Lorries	Wheat (tons)
Country X	32	80
Country Y	0	300
World total	32	380

2.15 These figures show that total output of both goods is greater than that which was obtained when both countries were producing only for domestic consumption. Since the opportunity cost ratios are different in the two countries, beneficial trade is possible. If the opportunity cost ratios were the same in the two countries, the countries will not benefit from specialisation and international trade.

2.16 Generalising from this example, we can state the law of comparative advantage: **Each country should export goods in which it has a comparative cost advantage.** (By 'cost' we mean opportunity cost of resources.)

The significance of the law of comparative advantage

2.17 The significance of the law of comparative advantage is that it provides a justification for the following beliefs.

(a) Countries should specialise in what they produce, even when they are less efficient (in absolute terms) in producing every type of good. They should specialise in the goods where they have a comparative advantage.

(b) International trade should be allowed to take place without restrictions on imports or exports - ie there should be free trade. Free trade plus specialisation will result in an increase in the world's output, and all countries will share in the benefits (admittedly, however, the more efficient countries benefiting more than the less efficient ones).

Does the law apply in practice?

2.18 The law of comparative advantage does apply in practice, and countries do specialise in the production of certain goods. However, there are certain limitations or restrictions on how it operates.

(a) Free trade does not always exist. Some countries take action to protect domestic industries and discourage imports. This means that a country might produce goods in which it does not have a comparative advantage.

(b) Transport costs (assumed to be nil in the examples above) can be very high in international trade so that it is cheaper to produce goods in the home country rather than to import them.

The advantages of free international trade

2.19 The law of comparative advantage states perhaps the major advantage of encouraging international trade. However, there are other advantages to the countries of the world from encouraging international trade. These are as follows.

(a) Some countries have a surplus of raw materials to their needs, and others have a deficit. A country with a surplus (eg of oil) can take advantage of its resources to export them. A country with a deficit of a raw material must either import it, or accept restrictions on its economic prosperity and standard of living.

(b) International trade increases competition amongst suppliers in the world's markets. Greater competition reduces the likelihood of a market for a good in a country being dominated by a monopolist. The greater competition will force firms to be competitive and so will increase the pressures on them to be efficient, and also perhaps to produce goods of a high quality.

(c) International trade creates larger markets for a firm's output, and so some firms can benefit from **economies of scale** by engaging in export activities. Economies of scale improve the efficiency of the use of resources, reduce the output costs and also increase the likelihood of output being sold to the consumer at lower prices than if international trade did not exist.

(d) There may be political advantages to international trade, because the development of trading links provides a foundation for closer political links. An example of the development of political links based on trade is the European Union.

3   PROTECTIONISM AND FREE TRADE AGREEMENTS   6/95

Exam focus point
Elements of economics, such as trade barriers, may form 10-mark questions, or subsections of longer questions.

BPP PUBLISHING

Free trade and protection

3.1   Free trade exists where there is no restriction on imports from other countries or exports to other countries. The **European Union** (EU) is a free trade area for trade between its member countries. In practice, however, there exist many barriers to free trade because governments wish to protect home industries against foreign competition. Protectionism would in effect be intended to hinder the operation of the law of comparative advantage.

3.2   Protectionist measures may be implemented by a government, but popular demand for protection commonly exceeds what governments are prepared to allow. In the UK, for example, some protectionist measures have been taken against Japanese imports (eg a voluntary restriction on car imports by Japanese manufacturers) although more severe measures are called for from time to time by popular demand or lobbying interests. For example, in recent years, a strong protectionist lobby built up in Congress in the USA, with pressure being applied in particular for measures against Japanese imports.

Protectionist measures

3.3   Protection can be applied in several ways, including the following. Items (b) to (f) below are sometimes called **non-tariff barriers to trade**.

(a)   Tariffs or customs duties
(b)   Import quotas
(c)   Embargoes
(d)   Hidden subsidies for exporters and domestic producers
(e)   Import restrictions
(f)   Deliberately restrictive bureaucratic procedures ('red tape') or product standards
(g)   Government action to devalue the domestic currency

Tariffs or customs duties

3.4   Tariffs or customs duties are taxes on imported goods. The effect of a tariff is to raise the price paid for the imported goods by domestic consumers, while leaving the price paid to foreign producers the same, or even lower. The difference is transferred to the government sector.

For example, if goods imported to the UK are bought for £100 per unit, which is paid to the foreign supplier, and a tariff of £20 is imposed, the full cost to the UK buyer will be £120, with £20 going to the government.

An **ad valorem** tariff is one which is applied as a percentage of the value of goods imported. A **specific** tariff is a fixed tax per unit of goods.

Import quotas

3.5   Import quotas are restrictions on the **quantity** of a product that is allowed to be imported into the country. The quota has a similar effect on consumer welfare to that of import tariffs, but the overall effects are more complicated.

(a)   Both domestic and foreign suppliers enjoy a higher price, while consumers buy less.
(b)   Domestic producers supply more.
(c)   There are fewer imports (in volume).
(d)   The government collects no revenue.

3.6   An **embargo** on imports from one particular country is a total ban, ie effectively a zero quota.

Hidden export subsidies and import restrictions

3.7   An enormous range of government subsidies and assistance for exports and deterrents against imports have been practised, such as:

(a)   **For exports** - export credit guarantees (government-backed insurance against bad debts for overseas sales), financial help (such as government grants to the aircraft or shipbuilding industry) and state assistance via the Foreign Office

(b)   **For imports** - complex import regulations and documentation, or special safety standards demanded from imported goods and so on

3.8   When a government gives grants to its domestic producers, for example regional development grants for new investments in certain areas of the country, or grants to investments in new industries, the effect of these grants is to make unit production costs lower. These give the domestic producer a cost advantage over foreign producers in export markets as well as domestic markets.

Government action to devalue the currency

3.9   If a government allows its currency to fall in value, imports will become more expensive to buy. This will reduce imports by means of the price mechanism, especially if the demand and supply curves for the products are elastic. For example, if the exchange rate between sterling and the US dollar is £1 = $1.60, a good imported from the USA to the UK at a cost of $8,000 would cost the UK buyer £5,000. Now if the government takes action to reduce interest rates, say, which has the effect of weakening the value of sterling, the exchange rate might change to £1 = $1.50. The same good costing $8,000 will now cost a UK buyer £5,333 - ie £333 more than before. At this higher price, the total UK demand for the US good will probably fall.

The extent of the fall in imports will thus depend on the price elasticity of demand in the UK for the US good, in other words on the degree to which demand changes when a change in price occurs.

Arguments in favour of protection

3.10   Arguments for protection are as follows.

(a)   Protectionist measures can be taken against **imports of cheap goods** that compete with higher priced domestically produced goods, and so preserve output and employment in domestic industries. In the UK, advocates of protection have argued that UK industries are declining because of competition from overseas, especially the Far East, and the advantages of more employment at a reasonably high wage for UK labour are greater than the disadvantages that protectionist measures would bring.

(b)   Measures might be necessary to counter '**dumping**' of surplus production by other countries at an uneconomically low price. For example, if the European Union (EU) were to over-produce quantities of steel, wine, beef or butter, it might decide to dump the surpluses on other countries. The 'losses' from overproduction would in effect be subsidised by the EU governments, and so the domestic industries of countries receiving dumped goods would be facing unfair competition from abroad. Although dumping has short-term benefits for the countries receiving the cheap goods, the longer term consequences would be a reduction in domestic output and employment, even when domestic industries in the longer term might be more efficient.

(c) Protectionist measures by one country are often implemented in **retaliation** against measures taken by another country that are thought to be unfair. This is why protection tends to spiral once it has begun. Any country that does not take protectionist measures when other countries are doing so is likely to find that it suffers all of the disadvantages and none of the advantages of protection.

(d) There is an argument that protectionism is necessary, at least in the short term, to protect a country's **'infant industries'** that have not yet developed to the size where they can compete in international markets. **Less developed countries** in particular might need to protect industries against competition from advanced or developing countries.

(e) Protection might also help a country in the short term to deal with the problems of a **declining industry**. Without protection, the industry might quickly collapse and there would be severe problems of sudden mass unemployment amongst workers in the industry - workers who must somehow be channelled into other industries. By imposing some protectionist measures, the decline in the industry might be slowed down, and so the task of switching resources to new industries could be undertaken over a longer period of time.

(f) Protection is often seen as a means for a country to reduce its **balance of trade deficit**, by imposing tariffs or quotas on imports. However, because of retaliation by other countries, the success of such measures by one country would depend on the demand by other countries for its exports being inelastic with regard to price and its demand for imports being fairly elastic.

The 'optimal tariff' argument

3.11 In each of the above cases, tariffs and other protectionist measures are being advocated instead of alternative policies specifically targeted on the objectives sought. For example, alternative policies addressing the problem of labour immobility in industries affected by low-cost foreign competition could include retraining grants or relocation incentives. As an indirect method of attaining objectives in these cases, a tariffs policy has the disadvantage of imposing a **'deadweight burden'** of welfare loss, which we shall explain below.

3.12 Another argument in favour of tariffs targets directly the problem of a divergence between social and private marginal costs arising from trade itself. This **optimal tariff argument** provides a clearer demonstration of the possibility of gains in welfare from a tariff than the earlier arguments cited.

3.13 If a country's imports make up a significant share of the world market for a particular good, an increase in imports is likely to result in the world price of the good rising. In demanding an additional unit of imports, the country raises the price it has to pay for what is already imported. The economic agents in the country collectively 'bid up' the price of imports. In a free market, each individual will buy imports up to the point at which the benefit to the individual equals the world price. Because of the price-raising effect referred to above, the cost to the economy as a whole of the last import exceeds the world price, and therefore exceeds its benefit.

3.14 In such a case, society can gain by restricting imports up to the point at which the benefit of the last import equals its cost to society as a whole. A tariff set to achieve this result is called an 'optimal tariff'.

3.15 Tariffs would decrease the welfare of a country in circumstances in which the optimal tariff is zero and there is no longer a need to discourage imports. This is when a country does not 'bid up' the world price of imports, as with a relatively small country in a large world market for a good. This is the basis of the free trade argument, which is illustrated in Figure 1 below.

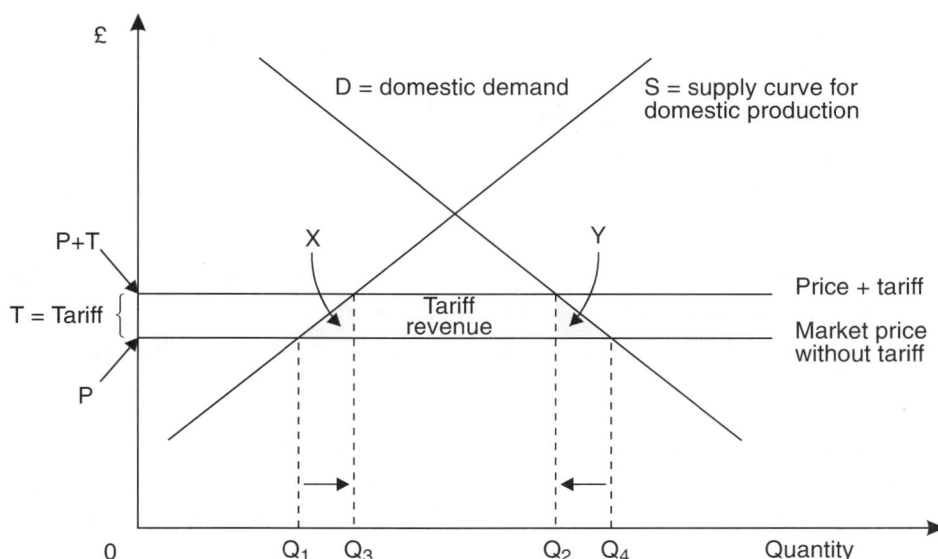

Figure 1 Effects of a tariff on prices and output

3.16 The world market purchase price of the good is initially P. At that price, domestic suppliers are willing to supply Q_1 but consumers are willing to buy Q_4. The difference $(Q_4 - Q_1)$ is then the amount of imports. An import tariff will raise the price to the consumer to (P + T). The domestic suppliers need not, of course, raise their prices, but at the higher price, consumers demand Q_2. If the domestic producers were to raise their prices to (P + T) then they would expand their output to Q_3. Imports would fall from $(Q_4 - Q_1)$ to $(Q_2 - Q_3)$.

3.17 The result of imposing the tariff is to benefit the domestic producers and the government, but to harm the consumer. Domestic producers supply more to the market, while domestic consumers buy fewer units. The government earns some tax revenue $(Q_2 - Q_3) \times T$, but foreign suppliers provide less to the market.

3.18 The areas of triangles X and Y represent waste and net loss to society. Triangle X is the additional amount that is spent by producing the commodity domestically rather than importing it at the world price; area Y is the excess of consumer benefits over social marginal cost which the economy loses by reducing its consumption from Q_4 to Q_2.

Arguments against protection

3.19 Arguments against protection are as follows.

(a) Because protectionist measures taken by one country will almost inevitably provoke retaliation by others, protection will reduce the volume of international trade. This means that the following benefits of international trade will be reduced.

(i) **Specialisation**: the principle of comparative advantage shows that countries will specialise in the production of goods which they can make with greater efficiency than other countries, and specialisation will increase total output and increase the economic wealth of the countries of the world.

BPP PUBLISHING

(ii) **Greater competition**, and so greater efficiency amongst producers.

(iii) The advantages of **economies of scale** amongst producers who need world markets to achieve their economies and so produce at lower costs.

(b) Obviously it is to a nation's advantage if it can apply protectionist measures while other nations do not. But because of **retaliation by other countries**, protectionist measures to reverse a balance of trade deficit are unlikely to succeed. Imports might be reduced, but so too would exports.

(c) It is generally argued that widespread protection will damage the **prospects for economic growth** amongst the countries of the world, and protectionist measures ought to be restricted to 'special cases' which might be discussed and negotiated with other countries.

(d) Although from a nation's own point of view, protection may improve its position, protectionism leads to a **worse outcome for all**. Protection also creates political ill-will amongst countries of the world and so there are **political disadvantages** in a policy of protection.

3.20 As an alternative to protection, a country can try to stimulate its export competitiveness by making efforts to improve the productivity and lower the costs of domestic industries, thus making them more competitive against foreign producers. **Hidden subsidies** and **exchange rate devaluation** are examples of indirect protectionist measures, but other measures, such as **funding industrial training schemes and educational policies**, might in the longer term result in improvements in domestic productivity.

The World Trade Organisation (WTO)

3.21 The **World Trade Organisation (WTO)** was formed in 1995 to continue to implement the General Agreement on Tariffs and Trade (GATT). The GATT was originally signed by 23 countries in 1947 to promote free trade. WTO is effectively the successor to GATT. The aims of GATT were:

(a) To reduce existing barriers to free trade

(b) To eliminate discrimination in international trade

(c) To prevent the growth of protection by getting member countries to consult with others before taking any protectionist measures

3.22 The '**most favoured nation**' principle applies whereby one country (which is a member of GATT) which offers a reduction in tariffs to another country must offer the same reduction to all other member countries of GATT.

KEY TERM

Most favoured nation: a principle in the GATT international trade agreement binding the parties to grant to each other treatment which is as favourable as that offered to any other GATT member in respect of tariffs and other trading conditions.

3.23 GATT membership has reached over 120, including many newly industrialising countries. GATT has succeeded in reducing world tariffs, which averaged around 40% in 1947 compared with below 5% in the 1990s. However there are problems which can arise.

(a)   A country wishing to join GATT must consider the effect of reducing tariffs on its balance of payments and domestic economy.

(b)   Special circumstances (for example economic crises, the protection of an infant industry, the rules of the EU) may be admitted whereby protection or special low tariffs between a group of countries are allowed.

(c)   A country in GATT may prefer not to offer a tariff reduction to another country because it would have to offer the same reduction to all other GATT members.

(d)   In spite of much success in reducing tariffs, the GATT agreements have had less effect in dealing with many non-tariff barriers to trade which countries may set up. Such non-tariff barriers include excessively lengthy customs procedures and licensing agreements which must be met before trading. Some such barriers, for example those in the guise of health and safety requirements, can be very difficult to identify.

3.24   The GATT talks took place over the years in a series of 'rounds' of negotiation, each dealing with different areas of trade.

(a)   The **Kennedy round** of the 1960s was particularly successful and led to tariff cuts of about 30%, bringing the average duty on manufactured goods down to about 10% by 1972.

(b)   The **Tokyo round** of the late 1970s led to further tariff reductions of approximately 30%. Trade between advanced industrialised nations in particular was favoured, with tariff cuts of 38%. The cut was a lower 25% in the case of trade between advanced industrialised and newly industrialised countries.

(c)   The talks in the **Uruguay round** which were concluded in December 1993 represented seven years of work on a very ambitious programme for the liberalisation of world trade.

3.25   The December 1993 conclusion of the 'Uruguay round' has revised, improved and updated many of the GATT rules which were originally drafted in the 1940s. It also brings the following changes, some of which are to be phased in over a period of time.

(a)   **Industrial tariffs**. Before the 1993 deal, tariffs on manufactures averaged 5% in richer countries (down from around 40% in the late 1940s). There is now the prospect of richer countries' tariffs on industrial goods being cut by more than one third. Over 40% of imports of specific types will be duty-free. These changes will bring easier access to world markets and lower prices for consumers.

(b)   **Agriculture**. Subsidies and import barriers which distort trade will be cut over the next six years. For example, domestic farm support, including that in Europe and the USA, will be reduced by 20%. These changes should bring better market opportunities for efficient producers, reduced overproduction and lower food prices for consumers in currently protected countries.

(c)   **Services**. A framework of rules on basic fair trading principles such as non-discrimination has been established, with further talks on telecommunications and financial services planned. Previously, there were no rules governing international trade in most services.

(d)   **Intellectual property**. Agreements were reached on patents, copyright, trademarks, designs and so on. This should facilitate technology transfer and reduce trade in counterfeit goods.

BPP PUBLISHING

(e) **Textiles and clothing**. The quotas imposed by richer countries since 1974 under the Multi-Fibre Arrangement are to be progressively dismantled over ten years and tariffs are to be reduced. Normal GATT rules will apply at the end of the ten year period. These changes will allow less developed countries to sell more textiles and clothing abroad and are likely to reduce prices for consumers worldwide.

(f) **Anti-dumping measures**. Clearer rules will make it more difficult for countries to introduce anti-dumping measures which have often been seen as a disguised form of protectionism.

(g) **Subsidies**. Tighter rules have been introduced on the use of subsidies, with some types of subsidy being prohibited.

(h) **Technical barriers**. Better rules have been introduced to establish international norms for product regulations and standards, which up to now have been fairly extensively used as a disguised form of competition.

(i) **Government procurement**. The coverage of the agreement on government procurement among 12 signatories (including the EU as one) in the Tokyo Round has been enlarged to cover more areas.

3.26 In an article published in the *Students' Newsletter* (October 1994), Len Ross makes the following points about GATT and trade liberalisation.

(a) In spite of the benefits of free trade, virtually all governments intervene to protect their domestic industries from foreign competition, often for **political reasons** as governments perceive electoral as well as **financial advantage** from protection of domestic interests.

(b) GATT's important success in reducing industrial tariffs has been dimmed by its failure to curb other forms of protection, especially **non-tariff barriers to trade (NTBs)** not directly covered by GATT, and by its inability to prevent countries from bypassing GATT rules. GATT has also generally turned a blind eye to the widespread and heavy protection of agriculture; national support for farmers has been viewed as politically sensitive, allowing agricultural protection to rise to very high levels.

(c) The Uruguay Round was the first GATT negotiating round fully to address agricultural protection, NTBs to trade in goods *and* services and issues relating to intellectual property, as well as the main issue in earlier rounds: import tariffs.

(d) In contrast to the previous GATT arrangements, the new **WTO** will be a permanent body with comprehensive responsibility for trade in goods and services and for intellectual property rights. WTO member countries must accept all of the provisions of the Uruguay agreement.

(e) The WTO has a procedure for **settling disputes** and is able to **impose sanctions** on countries breaking the rules, for example by authorising multilateral reprisals against them.

(f) A danger of the new world trade order is that of **regionalism,** with the rich industrial countries organised into inward-looking regional trading blocs centred in North America, Europe and Japan. Such **regional blocs** might continue to pursue increasingly protectionist policies in their own self-interest, leaving the rest of the world, especially the poorest countries, to 'pick up the crumbs from the negotiating table'.

The European Union

3.27 The **EU** is one of several international economic associations. It dates back to 1957 (the Treaty of Rome) and now consists of France, Germany, Italy, Belgium, the Netherlands, Luxembourg, the UK, Denmark, Eire, Greece, Spain, Portugal, Austria, Finland, and Sweden. Over the coming years, it can be expected that more nations will be admitted to membership, including some of the Eastern European countries which were formerly operated as centrally planned economies under Communist regimes.

3.28 The EU incorporates a **common market** combining different aspects, including a **free trade area** and a **customs union.**

    (a) A free trade area exists when there is no restriction on the movement of goods and services between countries. This may be extended into a customs union when there is a free trade area between all member countries of the union, and in addition, there are common external tariffs applying to imports from non-member countries into any part of the union. In other words, the union promotes free trade among its members but acts as a protectionist bloc against the rest of the world.

    (b) A common market encompasses the idea of a customs union but has a number of additional features. In addition to free trade among member countries there is also complete mobility of the factors of production. A British citizen has the freedom to work in any other country of the European Union, for example. A common market will also aim to achieve stronger links between member countries, for example by harmonising government economic policies and by establishing a closer political confederation.

    (c) The **single European currency**, the **euro**, was adopted by eleven countries of the EU from the inception of the currency at the beginning of 1999.

The customs union

3.29 The customs union of the EU **establishes a free trade area between member states**, and erects **common external tariffs** to charge on imports from non-member countries. The EU thus promotes free trade among member states, while acting as a **protectionist bloc** against the rest of the world. It is accordingly consistent that the EU negotiates in GATT talks as a single body.

The Common Agricultural Policy (CAP)

3.30 Because demand for agricultural produce tends to be inelastic, farmers tend to lose revenue with bumper harvests. Most countries provide some financial support for farmers; in the past, Britain offered a guaranteed price to its farmers, but no customs duty on food imports, and made up the difference between the market price and the (higher) guaranteed price as a 'deficiency payment' to British farmers.

3.31 The CAP on the other hand has protected farming by forcing up prices in the home market.

    (a) A target price is set for agricultural prices in the following year.

    (b) A threshold price is used to set customs duties on imported foods (so that imports cannot reach the EU market below this price).

    (c) An intervention price is the price at which various agencies will buy up surplus stocks of agricultural produce, usually after a bumper harvest, to prevent the price falling. The surplus would be stored, disposed of, or 'dumped' abroad - producing the often publicised 'butter mountains', 'wine lakes', or 'beef mountains'.

BPP PUBLISHING

Measures introduced to reform the CAP in 1992 aim to control surplus production. For example, cereal farmers were required to put 15% of their land into 'set aside' (ie take it out of production) and price guarantees for cereals were reduced by around 29% between 1992 and 1995/96.

The single European market

3.32   The EU set the end of 1992 as the target date for the removal of all existing physical, technical and fiscal barriers among member states, thus creating a large multinational **European Single Market**. This objective was embodied in the Single European Act of 1985. In practice, these changes have not occurred 'overnight', and many of them are still in progress.

3.33   **Elimination of trade restrictions** covers the following areas.

(a)   Physical barriers (eg customs inspection) on good and services have been removed for most products. Companies have had to adjust to a new VAT regime as a consequence.

(b)   Technical standards (eg for quality and safety) should be harmonised.

(c)   Governments should not discriminate between EU companies in awarding public works contracts.

(d)   Telecommunications should be subject to greater competition.

(e)   It should be possible to provide financial services in any country.

(f)   There should be free movement of capital within the community.

(g)   Professional qualifications awarded in one member state should be recognised in the others.

(h)   The EU is taking a co-ordinated stand on matters related to consumer protection.

3.34   At the same time, you should not assume that there will be a completely 'level playing field'. There are many areas where harmonisation is a long way from being achieved. Here are some examples.

(a)   **Company taxation.** Tax rates, which can affect the viability of investment plans, vary from country to country within the EU.

(b)   **Indirect taxation (VAT).** Whilst there have been moves to harmonisation, there are still differences between rates imposed by member states.

(c)   **Differences in prosperity.** There are considerable differences in prosperity between the wealthiest EU economies (eg Germany), and the poorest (eg Greece). The UK comes somewhere in the middle. This has meant that grants are sometimes available to depressed regions, which might affect investment decisions; and that different marketing strategies are appropriate for different markets.

(d)   **Differences in workforce skills.** Again, this can have a significant effect on investment decisions. The workforce in Germany is perhaps the most highly trained, but also the most highly paid, and so might be suitable for products of a high added value.

(e)   **Infrastructure.** Some countries are better provided with road and rail than others. Where accessibility to a market is an important issue, infrastructure can mean significant variations in distribution costs.

The European Free Trade Area (EFTA)

3.35   The European Free Trade Area (EFTA) was established in 1959, with seven member countries, one of which was the UK. The UK, Denmark and Portugal have since transferred to the EU, while Finland and Iceland joined the other original member states, Sweden, Norway, Austria and Switzerland. More recently, Finland, Sweden and Austria have also joined the EU. There is free trade between EFTA member countries but there is no harmonisation of tariffs with non-EFTA countries.

The European Economic Area (EEA)

3.36   In 1993, EFTA forged a link with the EU to create a European Economic Area (EEA) with a population of 380 million, so extending the benefits of the EU single market to the EFTA member countries (excluding Switzerland, which stayed out of the EEA). The membership of the EEA comprises the EU countries plus Norway and Iceland.

North American Free Trade Agreement (NAFTA)

3.37   Canada, the USA and Mexico formed the North American Free Trade Agreement (NAFTA) which came into force in 1994. This free trade area covering a population of 360 million and accounting for economic output of US$6,000 billion annually is almost as large as the European Economic Area, and is thus the second largest free trade area after the EEA.

3.38   Under NAFTA, virtually all tariff and other (non-tariff) barriers to trade and investment between the NAFTA members are to be eliminated over a 15-year period. In the case of trade with non-NAFTA members, each NAFTA member will continue to set its own external tariffs, subject to obligations under GATT. The NAFTA agreement covers most business sectors, with special rules applying to especially sensitive sectors, including agriculture, the automotive industry, financial services and textiles and clothing.

4   THE BALANCE OF PAYMENTS

The nature of the balance of payments

4.1   The balance of payments is a statistical 'accounting' record of a country's international trade transactions (the purchase and sale of goods and services) and capital transactions (the acquisition and disposal of assets and liabilities) with other countries during a period of time.

4.2   Under the current method of presentation of the UK balance of payments statistics, the broad classifications of transactions are as follows.

    (a)   **Current account** transactions are sub-divided into:

        (i)   Trade in goods
        (ii)   Trade in services
        (iii)   Investment income
        (iv)   Transfers

        Before 1996, the term **visibles** was used in official statistics for (i) and the term **invisibles** was used for (ii), (iii) and (iv). These terms have now been dropped in order to give more emphasis to the balances for trade in goods and services, although you may still find them mentioned.

(b) The **capital account** shows changes in the UK's external assets and liabilities, sub-divided into:

    (i)   Changes in the UK's external assets. External assets include:

        (1)   Holdings of foreign currency by anyone resident in the UK

        (2)   Holdings of shares or other investments in overseas companies by anyone resident in the UK (including UK firms)

        (3)   Loans to anyone overseas by UK banks

    (ii)   Changes in the UK's external liabilities. External liabilities include:

        (1)   Investments in the UK, for example in UK government stocks or shares of UK firms, by overseas residents (such as overseas firms)

        (2)   Borrowing from abroad by anyone in the UK

The sum of the balance of payments accounts is zero

4.3   The sum of the balance of payments accounts must always be zero (ignoring statistical errors in collecting the figures). This is because every transaction in international trade has a double aspect (in much the same way that accountants regard all business transactions as having matching debit and credit items). In the balance of payments, every *plus* item should have a matching *minus* item.

The UK balance of payments accounts

4.4   To show how the balance of payments figures are presented, the UK balance of payments for 1995 is summarised below.

UK balance of payments, 1995

	£bn
Current account	
Trade in goods	
Exports (credits)	152.3
Imports (debits)	(163.9)
Trade in goods balance	(11.6)
Services balance	6.1
Total goods and services balance	(5.5)
Investment income	9.6
Transfers	(7.0)
Current account balance	(2.9)
Capital account	
Long-term capital account (investments)	
Overseas investment in UK	37.3
UK investment overseas	(65.9)
Long-term capital balance	28.6
Short-term capital balance (Overseas deposits in UK and borrowing from overseas residents (credits), *less* deposits overseas by UK residents and lending to overseas residents (debits))	(28.8)
Reserves (drawing on + adding to –)	0.7
Net transactions in external assets and liabilities (capital balance)	0.5
Balancing item	2.4
	-

(Source: Annual Abstract of Statistics)

Current account

Goods

4.5 **Goods** include foods, beverages and tobacco, raw materials, fuels and manufactured goods.

Services

4.6 **Services** consist of:

(a) Transport services (by sea and air, both passenger and cargo)
(b) Tourism
(c) Financial services (banking, insurance, brokerage etc)
(d) Government (chiefly due to military and diplomatic presence overseas)

Trade in services has grown in importance in recent years, particularly inward tourism and earnings from financial services.

Investment income

4.7 **Investment income** consists of items such as the following.

(a) **Direct investment earnings.** These are the share of profits in overseas branches, overseas subsidiary companies and overseas associated companies. Direct investment earnings might bring income into the country (for example, the profits of UK firms operating overseas) or cause outflows (profits of overseas firms investing in the UK).

(b) **Portfolio investment earnings** (interest and dividends on stocks and shares held in overseas securities by UK residents, or held in UK securities by overseas residents).

(c) **Interest on borrowing and lending** abroad by UK banks.

Transfers

4.8 **General government transfers** include grants to overseas countries, subscriptions and contributions to international organisations and other transfers by the UK government overseas or to the UK government from overseas. Examples of these transfers are payments by the UK into the EU budget, foreign aid and payments into UN budgets. **Private transfers** include gifts of goods, payments by UK residents to dependants overseas and transfers of sums by relief organisations.

Capital account

4.9 The capital account section of the balance of payments is officially called **Transactions in external assets and liabilities** and records investment and other financial flows. The balance of payments records only 'new' transactions in assets and liabilities during the course of the period. It is not a record of the grand total of external assets or liabilities that have built up over time. The capital account comprises the following sections.

(a) **Long-term capital account**, recording long-term capital investments. Investment by foreigners (for example, a new UK factory for a Japanese car manufacturer) comprises a credit item (inflow of money). UK investment abroad is an outflow of money, representing a debit item. When UK overseas investment exceeds foreign investment in the UK, as it often has in recent years, this section of the balance of payments is in substantial deficit.

(b) **Short-term capital flows**. These flows represent short-term flows between the UK and the rest of the world. Foreign deposits in UK banks and loans from abroad to the UK are inflows of money (a credit item). Deposits by UK residents in overseas banks and loans by UK banks to overseas residents are outflows of money (debit items).

(c) **Flows to and from reserves**. The official reserves consist mainly of gold and convertible foreign currencies, held in the government's Exchange Equalisation Account with the Bank of England. (Other countries similarly have official reserves, which are kept and managed on behalf of the government by the central bank.) Governments use these reserves to balance the overseas accounts and also to deal in the foreign exchange markets. Drawing on reserves represents a credit item in the balance of payments accounts, as it is an inflow to the balance of payments but an outflow from the reserve account; an addition to reserves is a debit item. Official reserves may be used to support a deficit in another part of the balance of payments account. If there is, on the other hand, a surplus elsewhere in the balance of payments accounts, the Bank of England may use it to allow the reserves to build up.

4.10 In past years, movements on the official reserves were given greater prominence in the UK balance of payments statistics, but other international capital transactions are so large that they now 'dwarf' any changes in official reserves, and so changes in the official reserves are no longer given the same prominence as before. Instead, they are included as just another item in the assets section of the balance of payments account.

Balancing item

4.11 There is one final figure in the balance of payments account. This is a **balancing item**, which arises because of errors and omissions in collecting statistics for the accounts (eg sampling errors for items such as foreign investment and tourist expenditure and omission in the data gathered about exports or imports). *Try writing an answer to the following exercise before moving on.*

Question

If the balance of payments always balances why do we hear about deficits and surpluses?

Answer

The sum of the three balance of payments accounts must always be zero because every transaction in international trade has a double aspect. Just as accounting transactions are recorded by matching debit and credit entries, so too are international trade and financing transactions recorded by means of matching plus and minus transactions

If a UK exporter sells goods to a foreign buyer:

(a)   The value of the export is a plus in the current account of the balance of payments

(b)   The payment for the export results in a reduction in the deposits held by foreigners in UK banks (A minus in the assets and liabilities section)

When we use the phrase deficit or surplus on the balance of payments what we actually mean is a deficit or surplus on the current account. If there is a surplus (+) on the current account we would expect this to be matched by a similar negative amount on the assets and liabilities section. This will take the form of:

(a)   Additional claims on non-residents (eg overseas loans)
(b)   Decreased liabilities to non-residents (paying off our loans abroad)

This will involve not only banks and other firms but it may also involve the government too, since it is responsible for the 'reserves'.

If there is a deficit (-) on the current account the result will be a similar positive account on the assets and liabilities section. This will consist of inward investment and/or increased overseas indebtedness. This means that banks and other firms will owe more money abroad and the government may also be borrowing from abroad. Increased indebtedness cannot go on forever.

A country's balance of payments position

4.12 A country's balance of payments position is perhaps best analysed by a consideration of its long-term surplus or deficit on its current account.

4.13 If a country has a **surplus** on its current account year after year, it might invest the surplus abroad or add it to official reserves. The balance of payments position would be strong. There is the problem, however, that if one country which is a major trading nation (eg Japan) has a continual surplus on its balance of payments current account, other countries must be in a continual deficit. These other countries can run down their official reserves, perhaps to nothing, and borrow as much as they can to meet the payments overseas, but eventually, they will run out of money entirely and be unable even to pay their debts. Every country must have a reasonably sound balance of payments position if international trade is to prosper. It might therefore be argued that a country has a good balance of payments position, if in the long run, it has neither surplus nor deficit on its current account.

4.14 **Deficits** on the current account must be financed by a run down of official reserves, or borrowing. A country cannot finance deficits in this way indefinitely. Its official reserves

will run out completely one day! Clearly, if a country has a long-term deficit, its balance of payments position will be very weak, and it must eventually take action to improve the position.

Rectifying a balance of payments deficit or surplus   12/97

4.15 Which solution to a balance of payments problem is best may well depend on the cause of the problem on the balance of payments itself. A change in the balance of payments might be caused by, or made to happen by means of:

(a) A change in the assets and liabilities section - for example, changes in assets held abroad, or debts to firms, individuals or governments abroad - or

(b) A change in the current account balance

A change in the assets and liabilities section

4.16 A change in the 'transactions in external assets and liabilities' section might be caused by any of the following items.

(a) **A change in interest rates.** Higher real interest rates in one country relative to another will attract more capital into that country and *vice versa*.

(b) An **expected change in the exchange rate.** For example, if overseas investors holding sterling assets expected sterling to fall in value, they would sell sterling assets in order to prevent a loss.

(c) **Prospects for economic growth and stability.** If overseas firms consider that a country has economic stability and the potential for growth, they might be persuaded to make a direct investment. The government's economic policies will help foreign investors to assess the country's prospects. Direct investment might also be attracted by the offer of government grants, subsidies or other assistance in setting up operations in that country.

(d) **Exchange control regulations.** In the UK exchange control regulations were removed in 1979, and this left UK residents free to invest abroad. As a consequence, there has been a substantial outflow of capital in subsequent years in the form of private investments overseas.

(e) **Changes occurring in the current account.** If we are selling more goods abroad we would expect an increase in the debts owed to UK exporters by non-residents.

A change in the current account balance

4.17 The UK's current account balance is determined by:

(a) The price of exports

(b) The volume of demand for goods in overseas markets, which in turn is dependent on:
   (i) The price of goods (in the domestic currency), and
   (ii) General economic conditions in those markets

(c) The price of imports

(d) The volume of demand for imported goods, which in turn is dependent on:
   (i) The price of goods (in sterling)

(ii)   General economic conditions in the UK (eg manufacturing industry's output, since manufacturers purchase imported raw materials, and also the level of incomes and unemployment)

(e)   The quality and lengths of delivery periods of UK goods and services in comparison with foreign goods competing in the same markets

Of these items, (a) - (d) are perhaps the more significant. They are certainly the factors which the authorities are most able to influence.

Practical ways of rectifying a current account deficit   12/97

4.18   We now consider the following three measures aimed at rectifying a deficit on current account:

- A **depreciation** or **devaluation** of the currency
- **Direct measures** to restrict imports, such as tariffs or import quotas
- Domestic **deflation**

A depreciation (or devaluation) of the currency

> **KEY TERMS**
>
> A decline or **depreciation** in the value of a currency against other currencies is called a **devalaution** when it involves a reduction in a fixed or pegged exchange rate within a managed exchange rate system.

4.19   Assuming that changes in exchange rates are translated into changes in the prices of goods and services, **devaluation** of the currency would make exports relatively cheaper to foreign buyers, and so the demand for exports would probably rise. The extent of the increase in export revenue would depend on:

(a)   The elasticity of demand for the goods in export markets (ie the extent of change in demand following a change in price), and

(b)   The extent to which industry is able to respond to the export opportunities by either producing more goods, or switching from domestic to export markets

4.20   The cost of imports would probably rise because more domestic currency would be needed to obtain the foreign currency to pay for imported goods. Whether or not the total value of imports would fall too would depend on the **elasticity of demand for imports**.

4.21   Because the effect of depreciation or devaluation depends on price elasticities of demand in this way, it might be the case that depreciation of the currency on its own would be insufficient to rectify the balance of payments deficit, unless an extremely large depreciation took place.

4.22   After a time lag, production of exports and import substitutes will rise, so that the volume of exports will rise, thereby increasing the sterling value of exports (regardless of sterling's lower exchange rate), and the volume of imports will fall further. This will improve the current account balance.

4.23   The improvement in the balance of payments will thus have some limit, and the current balance should eventually level off. The effect of the falling exchange rate on the current balance might therefore be described by a **'J' curve** as illustrated in Figure 2.

BPP PUBLISHING

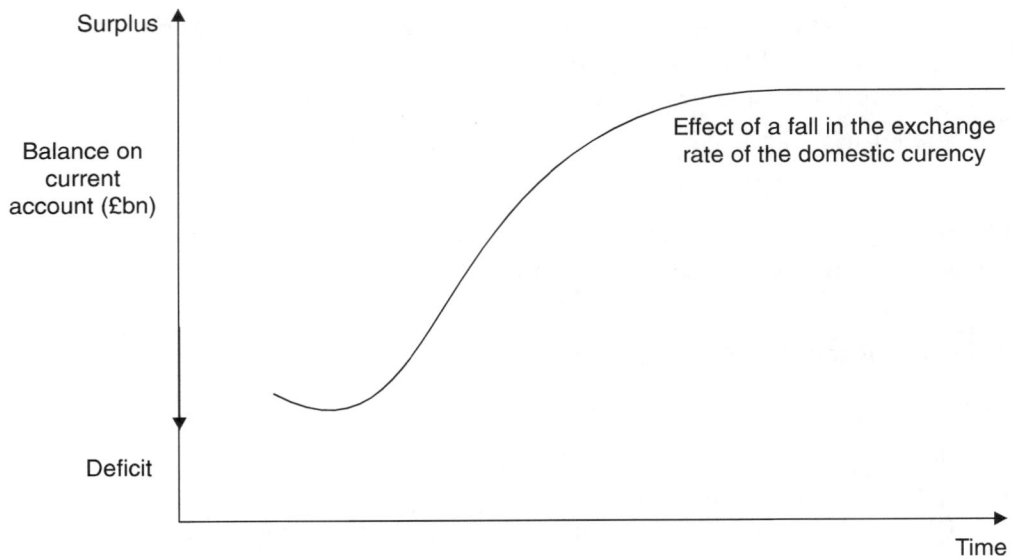

Figure 2   J curve

Direct measures

4.24   Direct measures to restrict the volume of imports or to encourage exports might consist of **tariff** and **non-tariff** barriers to trade, as mentioned earlier in Section 3 of this chapter. **Export subsidies** might also be considered. Another direct measure is to introduce **exchange control regulations** restricting flows of currency in and out of the country. Direct measures such as these may be contrary to World Trade Organisation (WTO) agreements. Such measures may also give rise to counter-measures by other countries. They could therefore be dangerous for a country whose economy relies heavily on external trade.

Domestic deflation

4.25   The most common method for dealing with balance of payments problems and probably the only successful long term measure is to deflate the economy. The term **deflation** might make you think of falling prices - ie the opposite of inflation. It means, however, more than this. When the total volume of expenditure and demand for goods in a county's economy is too high, the government can take steps to reduce it, by reducing its own expenditure, raising interest rates to deter borrowing, and cutting private consumption by raising taxes. This fall in demand should lead to a fall in prices or at least to a reduction in the rate of domestic inflation. Unfortunately, it might also lead, in the short term at least, to a reduction in industrial output and a loss of jobs in the **country's economy**.

4.26   Deflationary measures include cutting government spending, increasing taxation and raising interest rates. The purpose of deflationary measures would be:

(a)   To reduce the demand for goods and services at home, and so to reduce imports
(b)   To encourage industry to switch to export markets, because of the fall in domestic demand
(c)   To tackle domestic inflation

4.27   Sometimes, a government's domestic economic policies are not deflationary, despite a balance of payments deficit, and on the contrary, the government's economic policies might encourage increasing demand, which will both boost demand for imports, and cause more inflation and a falling exchange rate. Economic policies which boost demand in the economy in spite of a balance of payments deficit will worsen, rather than improve, the deficit.

The balance of payments and the domestic economy

4.28 You should try to view any country's balance of payments position in the context of its domestic economy.

(a) When a country's exports exceed its imports, or *vice versa*, there may be a lack of equilibrium between:

    (i) Withdrawals from the circular flow of income in the domestic economy (remember that these withdrawals include imports), and

    (ii) Injections into the circular flow of income (which include exports)

Equilibrium in the balance of payments ('external equilibrium') will also help a country to achieve equilibrium in its circular flow of income ('internal equilibrium').

(b) If a country's international trade is only small in size compared with its domestic economy, problems with any balance of payments deficit will be much less than for a country which relies heavily on international trade.

Interest rates and the balance of payments

4.29 **Comparative interest rates** between one country and another, and changes in interest rates, affect the balance of payments both:

(a) Directly, by stimulating or discouraging foreign investment, and so inflows and outflows of capital, and

(b) Indirectly, through the exchange rate (High interest rates attract foreign investors, thus creating a demand for the currency and keeping the exchange rate at a high level.)

4.30 Is a high interest rate policy a good solution to the problem of a deficit on the balance of payments current account?

(a) If a country relies on inflows of capital to finance a continuing balance of trade deficit, the country's balance of payments will never get into equilibrium. High interest rates will keep the exchange rate high for the country's currency, and this will make it more difficult to export (high export prices to foreign buyers) and encourage imports (cheaper prices). The country might therefore be unable to rectify its balance of trade deficit.

(b) If there is a continuing balance of trade deficit, there will always be a threat that the country's currency will eventually depreciate in value. This will deter investors.

4.31 Investors will only put money into capital investments abroad if they have satisfactory expectations about what the exchange rate for the foreign currency will be. Interest rates alone are not the only factor on which to base an investment decision. After all, what is the value to an investor of high interest rates from investments in a foreign currency when the exchange value of the currency is falling?

Chapter roundup

- We have examined the significance of **multinational enterprises**. We have looked at reasons why a firm would engage in **foreign direct investment (FDI)** and at **economic theories** taking into account the imperfect markets within which multinational companies typically operate.

- We have seen how world output of goods and services will increase if countries specialise in the production of goods/services in which they have a **comparative advantage**. Business enterprises are now also becoming increasingly '**internationalised**' by the development of multinational activities beyond pure import and export trade.

- There are various arguments in favour of both **protection** and **free trade**, although the balance of opinion favours free trade.

- Dismantling protectionism is a matter of **cooperation** to secure a better outcome for world nations as a whole. Although individual nations may gain from self-interested protectionism, this will lead to retaliation and a worse outcome for all than if nations cooperate to lower barriers to trade.

- We have examined the nature of the **balance of payments** of a country and have seen that a country can rectify a balance of payments deficit by:
  - Allowing its currency to depreciate or devalue in foreign exchange value
  - Imposing protectionist measures or exchange control regulations
  - Deflationary economic measures in the domestic economy (Such measures are usually a precondition of any IMF financial assistance to countries in balance of payments difficulties.)

Quick quiz

1   Outline the main changes in the pattern of multinationals' activities over the past twenty years or so. (see paras 1.5, 1.6)
2   What are the five main strategic reasons why a firm might engage in FDI? (1.9)
3   Explain how the establishment of the EEC and EFTA created market imperfections influencing the pattern of foreign direct investment. (1.18)
4   Outline the main competitive advantages which multinational enterprises enjoy. (1.20)
5   What is meant by the law of comparative advantage? (2.16)
6   List the various methods of protection against foreign imports. (3.3)
7   Outline the arguments for protection. (3.10)
8   Outline the arguments against protection. (3.19)
9   List the elements of the UK balance of payments. (4.2)
10   Why might a current account deficit matter? (4.14)
11   By which methods may a government try to reduce or eliminate a current account deficit? (4.18)

Question to try	Level	Marks	Time
16	Introductory	n/a	20 mins

Chapter 17

INTERNATIONAL FINANCE

Chapter topic list	Syllabus reference
1 International borrowing and investment	6(b)
2 International monetary institutions	5(h)
3 The global debt problem	5(i)

Introduction

In this chapter, we are mainly concerned with financial **markets** and **institutions**. The various **'euromarkets'** are of increasing importance to larger companies. You are expected to be aware of the so-called **global debt problem**. There has been less about this in the media than there used to be, but the problem has not gone away.

1   INTERNATIONAL BORROWING AND INVESTMENT   12/95, 6/96

Global financial markets

1.1   Small and medium-sized companies and other enterprises are usually limited in their sources of finance to their domestic markets. Larger companies are able to seek funds in international financial markets. Funds are not only sought on these global markets by multinationals: funds from overseas might be used by larger companies to finance fixed asset acquisitions or working capital in domestic business operations.

International banks

1.2   The period since World War II has seen the development of international financial centres as well as growth in international trade and multinational business activities. The most important such centres are London, New York and Tokyo.

1.3   **International banks,** most of whom are themselves large multinational enterprises, are the most important financial intermediaries in these financial centres.

Question

See if you can list the ways in which international banks might assist multinational enterprises.

Answer

Banks assist in the following ways, with some specialising in particular areas:

(a) The financing of foreign trade
(b) The financing of capital projects
(c) International cash management services
(d) Providing full local banking services in different countries

BPP PUBLISHING

(e) Trading in foreign exchange and currency options
(f) Lending and borrowing in the eurocurrency market
(g) Participating in syndicated loan facilities
(h) Underwriting of eurobonds
(i) Provision of advice and information

Developments in international financial markets

1.4 Among the more important developments affecting international financial markets in recent years are the following.

(a) **Globalisation.** Globalisation describes the process by which the capital markets of each country have become internationally integrated. Securities issued in one country can now be traded in capital markets around the world.

(b) **Securitisation of debt.** Securitisation of debt refers to international borrowing by large companies, not from a bank, but by issuing securities instead. This has been possible because of the deregulation of capital markets, and in the UK because of the opening of overseas markets to borrowers since the abolition of exchange controls in 1979. Securitisation of debt has been popular with borrowers because this form of borrowing is cheaper - no intermediaries' fees - and more flexible than a bank loan. Examples of securitised debt are eurobonds and eurocommercial paper.

(c) **Risk management** (and **risk assessment).** Various techniques have been developed for companies to manage their financial risk. Such techniques are discussed later in this text. The existence of such transactions, which are harder to monitor where they are off balance sheet, make it difficult for banks and other would-be lenders to assess the financial risk of a company that is asking to borrow more money.

(d) **Competition.** There is much fiercer competition between financial institutions for business. Building societies are emerging as potential competitors to the banks. Foreign banks have competed successfully in the UK with the big clearing banks. The 1986 'Big Bang' deregulation measures in the City of London brought greater competition between stockbroking firms, with the abolition of fixed commissions for broking/market-making services.

International money markets

1.5 The international money markets or 'international banking market' are markets for short and medium-term funds, as distinct from the international capital markets. The international money markets include the **eurocurrency market,** one of the 'euromarkets'.

Exam focus point
Do not get confused in the exam by the 'euro' prefix, which is a misnomer: eurocurrency markets provide funds in various currencies, not just European ones.

1.6 A company or other organisation might invest surplus funds on the market by placing the money on deposit with a bank for a period ranging from overnight to five years. Borrowers of funds on the international money markets will generally wish to borrow for shorter periods of time, although loans for three years or more are possible.

International capital markets

1.7 Larger companies may arrange borrowing facilities from their bank, in the form of bank loans or bank overdrafts. Instead, however, they might prefer to borrow from private investors. In other words, instead of obtaining a £10,000,000 bank loan, a company might issue 'bonds', or 'paper' in order to borrow directly from investors, with the bank merely acting as a go-between, finding investors who will take up the bonds or paper that the borrowing company issues and interest being payable to the investors themselves, not to a bank. In recent years, a strong **international capital market** has built up which allows very large companies to borrow in this way, long-term or short-term.

Eurocurrency markets

1.8 A UK company might borrow money from a bank or from the investing public, in sterling. But it might also borrow in a foreign currency, especially if it trades abroad, or if it already has assets or liabilities abroad denominated in a foreign currency. When a UK company borrows in a foreign currency from a UK bank, the loan is known as a **eurocurrency loan**. For example, if a UK company borrows US $50,000 from its bank, the loan will be a 'eurodollar' loan.

1.9 The eurocurrency markets involve the deposit of funds with a bank outside the country of origin of the funds and re-lending these funds for a fairly short term, typically three months, normally at a floating rate of interest. **Eurocredits** are medium to long-term international bank loans which may be arranged by individual banks or by syndicates of banks. Much eurocurrency lending in fact takes place between banks of different countries, and takes the form of negotiable certificates of deposit.

Eurobonds

> **KEY TERM**
>
> A **eurobond** is a bond issued in a capital market (the eurobond market being another of the 'euromarkets'), denominated in a currency which often differs from that of the country of issue and sold internationally.

1.10 **Eurobonds** are long-term loans raised by international companies or other institutions in several countries at the same time. Such bonds can be sold by one holder to another. The term of a eurobond issue is typically ten to 15 years. Although eurobond funds may be raised at a lower cost than direct borrowing from banks, issue costs are generally higher than the costs of using the eurocurrency markets. Eurobonds would only be used by a company to raise fairly large sums of money (normally in excess of £1 million).

1.11 Eurobonds may be the most suitable source of finance for a large organisation with an excellent credit rating, such as a large successful multinational company, which:

(a) Requires a long-term loan to finance a big capital expansion programme (with a loan for at least five years and up to 20 years)

(b) Requires borrowing which is not subject to the national exchange controls of any government (a company in country X could raise funds in the currency of country Y by means of a eurobond issue, and thereby avoid any exchange control restrictions which might exist in country X). In addition, domestic capital issues may be regulated by the government or central bank, with an orderly queue for issues. In contrast, eurobond issues can be made whenever market conditions seem favourable

1.12 The interest rate on a bond issue may be fixed or variable (**floating rate notes**). Many variable rate issues have a minimum interest rate which the bond holders are guaranteed, even if market rates fall even lower. These bonds convert to a fixed rate of interest when market rates do fall to this level. For this reason, they are called 'drop lock' floating rate bonds.

1.13 Other variants from conventional ('straight' or 'vanilla') bonds are **zero coupon (deep discount) bonds**, **convertible bonds** and **multi-currency bonds** (for example, **ecu bonds**), used to reduce risks of, or hedge against, currency movements.

Eurobond issues and currency risk

1.14 A borrower contemplating a eurobond issue must consider the exchange risk of a long-term foreign currency loan.

(a) If the money is to be used to purchase assets which will earn revenue in a currency different to that of the bond issue, the borrower will run the risk of exchange losses. These losses would be due to adverse movements in exchange rates, if the currency of the loan strengthens against the currency of the revenues out of which the bond (and interest) must be repaid. Borrowers cannot obtain long-term forward cover in the forward exchange market, and would have to accept the risks of foreign exchange exposure.

(b) If the money is to be used to purchase assets which will earn revenue in the same currency, the borrower can match these revenues with payments on the bond, and so remove or reduce the exchange risk.

Eurobonds and the investor

1.15 An investor subscribing to a bond issue will be concerned about the following factors.

(a) **Security**. The borrower must be of high quality. A standard condition of a bond issue is a 'negative pledge clause' in which the borrower undertakes not to give any prior charge over its assets, during the life of the bond issue, that would rank ahead of the rights of the investors in the event of a liquidation.

(b) **Marketability**. Investors will wish to have a ready market in which bonds can be bought and sold. If the borrower is of high quality the bonds or notes will be readily negotiable.

(c) **Anonymity**. Investors in eurobonds tend to be attracted by the anonymity of this type of issue, as the bonds are generally issued to bearer.

(d) The **return on the investment**. This is paid tax-free.

Euro-equity issues

1.16 A **euro-equity issue** may be defined as an issue of equity in a market outside the company's own domestic market. The euro-equity market has not developed to such an extent as the comparable eurobond market. The market started in 1965 when bonds were issued with the option to convert them into equity. Later, bonds were issued with warrants attached, meaning that the bond does not have to be surrendered if the warrant is used to obtain shares. Furthermore, the warrant can be traded separately from the bond.

1.17 Conventional share issues have also been made on the euro-equity markets, as for example when there were attempts to place large numbers of shares of US corporations and of Japanese companies in Europe. These attempts were largely unsuccessful: the absence of a sufficiently liquid after-market or secondary market in such shares is the main limitation on such euro-equity issues.

1.18 'Sweeteners' are often added to the shares issued on the market, to make the issue more attractive to investors. For example, a 'rolling put option' might be added to a convertible preference share, giving the purchaser the right to sell the convertible preference share back to the company at any time between, say, five and ten years after the issue.

1.19 A company may find it appropriate to raise funds by selling shares outside its domestic capital market if this is too small for its needs. Another reason why a company may seek a euro-equity issue is to attract shareholders based in the markets in which it trades overseas. The liquidity of the company's shares and the international standing of the firm can be improved. The wider spread of shareholdings which might be achieved could act as a defence against hostile takeovers. An issue overseas may also be convenient if compliance with domestic capital market listing requirements is a complex or lengthy process.

Case example

The flotation of British Telecom involved an international issue alongside the main issue of shares on the UK stock market.

Commercial paper

1.20 A large company can raise short-term finance by issuing commercial paper. Businesses were first allowed to issue sterling commercial paper (SCP) in 1986, following the success of euro-commercial paper (ECP) in the early 1980s.

1.21 **Commercial paper (CP)** is a short-term financial instrument:

(a) Issued in the form of unsecured promissory notes with a fixed maturity of up to one year, typically between seven days and three months (A promissory note is a written promise to pay.)

(b) Issued in bearer form

(c) Issued on a discount basis (so the rate of interest on the CP is implicit in its sale value)

1.22 The term **eurocommercial paper** refers to CP issued in any currency (often US dollars or ecus). Similar instruments issued with a maturity of over one and up to five years, at a rate of interest rather than a discount, are known as **medium term notes (MTNs)** or medium term 'euronotes'. The market is most active among multinationals and other very large companies, frequently involving very large sums on a revolving or standby basis. Commercial paper is an example of **securitisation** - the raising of loans in the form of debt securities. Banks raise finance for their customers by packaging and selling the customers' securities, such as commercial paper, rather than by lending them money.

1.23 The following organisations are entitled to issue CP and medium term notes.

(a) Companies with net assets of at least £25 million

(b) Overseas public sector bodies (as long as the relevant government's debt securities are traded on a Stock Exchange or equivalent exchange)

    (c)   Certain UK local authorities

1.24   Qualifying companies can now issue CP and MTNs in any currency. The minimum amount is £100,000 or currency equivalent, although a minimum of £1,000,000 is more usual. The market is most active among multinationals and very large domestic companies, frequently involving very large sums on a revolving or standby basis. Issues are 'investor-driven' in that CP is only issued to meet demand from specific investors.

1.25   The flexibility of CP arises because the borrower is able to choose the period to maturity (in practice, between 7 and 364 days). For example, a company might decide that it wants to issue some new paper at the end of November, with maturity in the middle of March. However, if the interest rates that would be payable are not attractive enough at the time for this term of borrowing, the borrower can decide instead to issue paper with a maturity in (say) mid-February. Corporate borrowers are therefore able to schedule borrowing for when they expect interest rates to be most favourable to themselves.

1.26   Other advantages of CP include the following.

    (a)   Interest rates are determined by market conditions but companies which issue commercial paper can hope to obtain slightly lower interest rates on their borrowing than if they borrowed direct from a bank.

    (b)   A company that issues CP does not have to be formally 'rated'. However, companies that are rated will be able to issue paper at finer rates.

    (c)   If a company has surplus cash, it can invest it in commercial paper rather than in a bank deposit, and hope to earn a slightly higher interest rate on its short-term investment.

    (d)   The 'paper' is tradeable.

    (*Note*. These are among the advantages of dispensing with financial intermediaries, ie **financial disintermediation,** of which CP is an example.)

Syndicated credits

1.27   A 'credit' in this context is a facility whereby a borrower can borrow funds when required, but might in fact not take up the full amount of the facility. This differs from a loan, which involves an actual transaction for a specified sum for a particular period of time.

1.28   The **syndicated credit market** provides credit facilities at relatively high rates of interest, typically at a substantial margin above LIBOR. The market is frequently used by highly geared companies.

    (a)   Such a company might need such a facility if it is involved in a takeover bid, in which case it will use the standby credit to fund the acquisition if the bid is successful.

    (b)   The market is used in the re-financing of debts incurred in past takeovers in cases where the company has been unable to obtain alternative funds to pay off the debt.

    (c)   The market is also used for local and overseas government borrowings and for project financing (eg Eurotunnel).

1.29   Because much of the takeover activity of the late 1980s was of US corporations, the majority of syndicated credits relating to mergers was denominated in US dollars.

Multiple option facilities

1.30 **Multiple option facilities (MOFs)** comprise a variety of instruments through which companies can raise funds. Such instruments gained popularity in the late 1980s, and include **Note Issuance Facilities (NIFs)** and **Revolving Underwriting Facilities (RUFs)**. In a typical MOF arrangement, the company may get a bank to put together a panel of banks who agree to provide an amount of 'standby' loans over a period of, say, five years, perhaps at an interest rate set to vary by reference to LIBOR. Another 'tender panel' of banks is set up and is invited to bid to provide loans when the company requires cash. The company is able to choose the lowest bid, or alternatively use the standby facility.

1.31 MOFs allow short-term loans (say, for three months) to be arranged in succession, effectively enabling medium-term finance to be obtained, if required, at competitive rates of interest. As implied by their name, MOFs allow the money required to be raised in various different forms, including foreign currency loans and bills of exchange.

Should a company borrow on the euromarkets or in domestic markets?

1.32 The factors which are relevant to choosing between borrowing on the euromarkets or through the domestic banking system are as follows.

   (a) Spreads between borrowing and lending are likely to be closer on the euromarket, because domestic banking systems are generally subject to tighter regulation and more stringent reserve requirements.

   (b) Euromarket loans generally require no security, while borrowing on domestic markets is quite likely to involve fixed or floating charges on assets as security.

   (c) Availability of euromarket funds is enhanced by the fact that euromarkets are attractive to investors as interest is paid gross without the deduction of withholding tax which occurs in many domestic markets.

   (d) With interest normally at floating rates on euromarkets, draw-down dates can be flexible, although there may be early redemption penalties, and commitment fees to pay if the full amount of the loan is not drawn down.

   (e) It is often easier for a large multinational to raise very large sums on the euromarkets than in a domestic financial market.

2   INTERNATIONAL MONETARY INSTITUTIONS   12/96

The International Monetary Fund

> **Exam focus point**
> A general discussion of the role and significance of the IMF was worth 10 marks in the 12/96 paper. Perhaps that suggests that the topic is unlikely to come up again in the same way soon, but it also illustrates the point that significant marks can be available in Paper 14 for some relatively straightforward narrative essay-style questions. Look out for them!

2.1 The **IMF** was established at the **Bretton Woods** conference in 1944. Most countries of the world have membership of the IMF. The three broad aims of the IMF are:

   (a) To promote international monetary co-operation, and to establish a code of conduct for making international payments

(b) To provide financial support to countries with temporary balance of payments deficits

(c) To provide for the orderly growth of international liquidity, through its Special Drawing Rights (SDR) scheme (launched in 1970). SDRs are a form of international currency, whose use is restricted

The IMF and financial support for countries with balance of payment difficulties

2.2   If a country has a balance of payments deficit on current account, it must **either borrow capital** or use up official reserves to offset this deficit. Since a country's official reserves will be insufficient to support a balance of payments deficit on current account for very long, it must borrow to offset the deficit.

2.3   Until the eurocurrency markets emerged in the 1970s, international lending was mainly carried out by means of lending to governments by the IMF and World Bank, and the problem was seen mainly as one of providing governments with funds to top up their official reserves, to help them to overcome a short-term balance of payments problem.

2.4   The IMF can provide financial support to member countries. Most IMF loans are repayable in 3 to 5 years.

(a) Unconditional loans are available for up to 25% of a member's own quota.

(b) A further 25% is available to members which 'demonstrate reasonable efforts' to rectify balance of payments problems.

(c) Credit of up to 75% of the quota is available conditionally, usually as a standby facility.

2.5   Of course, to lend money, the IMF must also have funds. Funds are made available from subscriptions or 'quotas' of member countries. The IMF uses these subscriptions to lend foreign currencies to countries which apply to the IMF for help.

(a) Loans under the IMF's Compensating Financing Facility are intended to cover unforeseen problems such as harvest failures.

(b) Medium-term loans under the Extended Fund Facility of up to 10 years are made to countries with severe structural balance of payments problems.

(c) Special supplementary borrowing facilities are sometimes made available to countries with severe problems.

IMF loan conditions

2.6   The pre-conditions that the IMF places on its loans to debtor countries vary according to the individual situation of each country, but the general position is as follows.

(a) The IMF regards its lending as fairly short-term in nature; this means that countries which borrow from the IMF should get into a position to start repaying the loans fairly quickly. To do this, the countries must take effective action to improve their balance of payments position.

(b) To make this improvement, the IMF generally believes that a country should take action to reduce the demand for goods and services in the economy (eg by increasing taxes and cutting government spending). This will reduce imports and help to put a brake on any price rises. The country's industries should then also be able to divert more resources into export markets.

(c)   With 'deflationary' measures along these lines, standards of living will fall (at least in the short term) and unemployment may rise. The IMF regards these short-term hardships to be necessary if a country is to succeed in sorting out its balance of payments and international debt problems.

Borrowing to supplement liquidity

2.7   Countries which have balance of payments deficits can borrow their way out of trouble, at least temporarily. There are various sources of borrowing:

(a)   The IMF (IMF lending has already been described)

(b)   Other institutions, such as the World Bank, the International Development Association (IDA), and the Bank for International Settlements (BIS)

(c)   Borrowing from private banks (in the eurocurrency markets)

The World Bank (IBRD)

2.8   The **World Bank** (more properly called the **International Bank for Reconstruction and Development** or **IBRD**) began operations in 1946, with the reconstruction of war-damaged economies as one of its objectives. Its chief aim now is to supplement private finance and lend money on a commercial basis for capital projects. Loans are usually direct to governments or government agencies, for a long-term period of over 10 years (typically 20 years). Lending is usually tied to specific projects, although the Bank's lending policy has been more flexible in recent years.

Case example

During 1995, the World Bank provided large loans to Mexico as part of a programme to support that country after the Mexican financial crisis occurring late in 1994. The support programme was assisted by the IMF and by a multi-billion dollar economic assistance package from the USA.

2.9   The World Bank's funds are obtained from capital subscriptions by member countries of the IMF, its profits, and borrowing. The major source of funds is borrowing, and the World Bank makes bond issues on the world's capital markets (eg New York).

The IDA

2.10 World Bank lending is for projects concerned with the development of agriculture, electricity, transport and so on. The cost of World Bank loans was (and still is) high to developing countries, and in 1960, the **International Development Association (IDA)** was set up to provide 'soft' loans - ie loans at a low cost with easy repayment terms - to less developed countries, for similar types of projects financed by the World Bank.

2.11 The IDA is a subsidiary of the World Bank and member countries of the IDA are also members of the World Bank. All member countries make subscriptions to provide funds, but the main source of funds is a once-every-three-years 'replenishment' from the developed countries. The IDA's funding programme is therefore dependent on the attitudes of the governments of the developed countries, especially the USA.

2.12 Because the IDA acts a concessionary arm of the World Bank, lending money on easy terms, it is a potentially valuable source of finance for developing countries. The IDA makes loans for 50 years without interest and charges only a 0.75% service fee.

Capital repayments are:

(a) Nothing for 10 years
(b) 1% per annum in each of the next 10 years
(c) 3% per annum in each of the next 30 years

2.13 Lending had risen to $2.9 billion by 1994, with another $0.9 billion lent through the African Development Bank. Many of the IDA's most needy members in Africa have seen their economies contract over the past 15 years and the World Bank has given a warning that they will continue to shrink for much of the next decade. The appeal of IDA loans to these countries, and the need for such loans to help development, should therefore be readily apparent.

Unfortunately, the debt continues to outpace African economies' capacity to service it. (See below on the global debt problem.)

The BIS

2.14 The **Bank for International Settlements (BIS)** is the banker for the central banks of other countries. It is situated in Basle, where it was founded in 1930. Most of its deposits are from the central banks of various countries and some are shareholders and represented on its board. It is a profit making institution, and lends money at commercial rates. The Bank of England, for example, has a 10% stake in the BIS.

2.15 The main functions of the BIS are to **promote co-operation between central banks** and to **provide facilities for international co-operation**.

3 THE GLOBAL DEBT PROBLEM   12/95

The IMF and lending by the commercial banks

3.1 Since the 1970s, countries with balance of payments difficulties have borrowed large sums of money from international banks and by 1982 it became clear that many countries were unable to repay these debts on schedule. The problem of rescheduling debts therefore arose - ie giving debtor countries more time to pay.

3.2 The international debt crisis forged an 'alliance' between the IMF and the international commercial banks. The role of the IMF was important because banks were now relying on the IMF to impose economic policies on the borrowing country which would enable the country concerned to repay its loans. From 1982, however, in spite of this alliance, the international debt crisis developed and is still a long way from being resolved.

The global debt crisis

3.3 **Sovereign debt** refers to debt owed to non-residents (for example, overseas banks) by governments, government agencies or autonomous public bodies (for example, public corporations) and also any debt which is guaranteed by a government.

3.4 A **global debt crisis** arose as governments in **less developed countries (LDCs)** took on levels of debt to fund their development programmes which are beyond their ability to finance. As a result, the level of debt rose and their ability to repay decreased, as increasing amounts of GDP were absorbed in servicing the debt rather in financing development. A further factor was that, in some countries with substantial oil reserves, banks were keen to lend against the fact of these reserves combined with high world oil prices. Examples of such countries include Nigeria and Venezuela. As the oil price fell, the fall in oil revenues to the LDCs precipitated a debt crisis.

Case examples

'Most of the 41 countries classified as heavily indebted are in sub-Saharan Africa (SSA), including 25 of the 32 countries rated as severely indebted. In 1962, SSA owed $3bn (£1.8bn). Twenty years later it had reached $142bn. Today it's about $235bn - or 76 per cent of GNP. The most heavily indebted countries are: Nigeria ($35bn), followed by Côte D'Ivoire ($19bn) and Sudan ($18bn).

Latin America's debt is much bigger - about $650bn - but the nature of its problem has been very different. Most of its 1980s debt was owed to commercial banks, and a series of relief agreements and stronger economic growth combined to make it more manageable for all but a few countries, including Nicaragua, Bolivia and Guyana.

'Unlike Latin America, Africa owes more than two-thirds of its debt to foreign government and multilateral lenders. Multilateral lenders - including the IMF, the World Bank, and the African Development Bank - account for 32 per cent of the debt; governments are owed 42 per cent, and private lenders, mainly commercial banks, account for the balance - 26 per cent.'

(Financial Times, 15 September 1997)

3.5   Various approaches have been taken in attempts to overcome these problems. Where the situation has arisen due to a sudden (and hopefully temporary) fall in commodity prices, one solution may be for the country to take on additional short-term debt to cover the temporary shortfall.

3.6   Where the problem is of a longer term nature, approaches include the following.

(a)   The debt may be restructured and/or rescheduled in order to allow the government a longer time to repay the loan.

(b)   Restructuring is often linked to a package of economic reforms which are aimed at improving the balance of trade and stimulating growth. Some countries may initiate such reforms themselves as a way out of their problem - in other cases, reforms are linked to the rescheduling package and are approved and monitored by the IMF.

(c)   Some of the debt may be written off by the lending governments and banks thereby reducing the interest burden and enhancing the prospects of eventual payment.

(d)   Some of the debt may be converted to equity, giving foreign companies a stake in local industries and reducing the level of interest payments.

Effects of the global debt crisis on multinational firms

3.7   The debt crisis has a number of adverse consequences for multinational firms which undertake FDI in less developed countries. Many of these adverse consequences result from the policies of 'economic adjustment' which are imposed on debtor countries by the IMF.

(a)   **Effects of deflationary policies**. Deflationary policies imposed on LDCs by the IMF are likely to damage the profitability of multinationals' subsidiaries by reducing their sales in the local market. These deflationary policies are designed to improve the balance of payments position of the debtor countries by reducing their imports and boosting exports. Higher interest rates are likely to be introduced to suppress domestic consumer's demand for imports. However, higher interest rates will tend to dampen domestic investment and could result in increased unemployment and loss of business confidence.

(b) **Effects of devaluation.** Devaluation of the domestic currency is a policy which the debtor country may adopt to try to boost exports. The country will be able to sell its exports more cheaply in foreign currency terms - while imports to the country will become more expensive. This will adversely affect the level of operating costs for multinational firms which make use of imported inputs to their production process.

(c) **Sourcing of imports.** Debtor countries' lack of foreign currency (arising from the need to service their debt) means that less can be imported. Host countries may require that multinationals increase their use of local inputs which may be of higher cost or lower quality than the same goods obtained from elsewhere.

(d) **Lack of capital inflows.** Measures such as the Baker Plan were intended to increase the level of lending available to debtor countries. Nevertheless, as already indicated, the international banks have not been willing to provide these increased capital inflows to the less developed countries. As a result, multinational firms operating in these countries have been forced to rely more heavily on host country funding for their activities in those countries, which they may have preferred not to do.

3.8 As well as there being adverse consequences of the debt crisis on multinationals, some positive effects can also be identified.

(a) **Deregulation.** The debtor countries have been encouraged to become more oriented to free market policies by the interventions of the IMF and the World Bank having the objective of improving the countries' export cost efficiency through the increased competition. Apart from the increased freedom of action for multinationals arising from the IMFs encouragement of fewer government restrictions, the freeing up of markets also allows multinationals to take advantage of lower real labour costs in the less developed countries.

(b) **Increased incentives.** Given the lack of lending to the debt ridden countries, many of their governments have sought to encourage multinationals to engage in FDI. This encouragement may be in the form of production subsidies or tax incentives for foreign investment. The need to encourage FDI as a means of compensating for the lack of inflows of funds has also encouraged the debtor governments to minimise regulatory interference with the activities of the multinationals.

(c) **Expanded markets.** Improved economic performance in the LDCs should increase the size of the local market available to the multinationals. As well as improving their operating performance, an increased ability to match local payments with local revenues should reduce their foreign exchange exposure and simplify their foreign exchange management.

Chapter roundup

- The **international money and capital markets** provide various possibilities in the form of financial instruments which the treasurer of large companies may use for borrowing or for financial investment.

- The **IMF** was set up partly with the role of providing finance for any countries with temporary balance of payments deficits.

- The **World Bank** and the **IDA** have tried to provide long-term finance for developing countries, to help them to continue developing.

- The funds of the IMF, World Bank and IDA have been insufficient to meet the finance needs of developing countries.

- The **sovereign debt problem** of South American countries has attracted much attention, but similar problems have been suffered by other countries - eg in Africa and Asia.

Quick quiz

1 What are eurobonds? (see para 1.10)

2 What is eurocommercial paper? (1.22)

3 What are multiple option facilities? (1.30, 1.31)

4 What are the factors to consider for a company choosing between borrowing in a foreign currency or in the domestic currency? (1.32)

5 What are the broad aims of the International Monetary Fund? (2.1)

6 What is the purpose of the World Bank? (2.8)

7 What are the effects (both positive and negative) of the sovereign debt crisis on multinational firms engaging in foreign direct investment? (3.7, 3.8)

Question to try	Level	Marks	Time
17	Introductory	n/a	20 mins

BPP PUBLISHING

Chapter 18

FOREIGN TRADE FINANCE

Chapter topic list	Syllabus reference
1 Methods of international finance	6(a)
2 Export credit insurance	6(a)
3 Countertrade	6(a)

Introduction

In this chapter, we look at different methods of **financing foreign trade** and at methods of **insuring** against the risk of non-payment by enterprises overseas. Trading with enterprises in other countries is sometimes transacted by **barter** or **countertrade**, which is discussed in the final section of the chapter.

1 METHODS OF INTERNATIONAL FINANCE

Finance for foreign trade

1.1 **Foreign trade** raises special **financing problems**, including the following.

(a) When goods are sold abroad, the customer might ask for credit. The period of credit might be 30 days or 60 days, say, after receipt of the goods; or perhaps 90 days after shipment. Exports take time to arrange, and there might be **complex paperwork**. Transporting the goods can be slow, if they are sent by sea. These delays in foreign trade mean that exporters often build up large investments in stocks and debtors. These working capital investments have to be financed somehow.

(b) The risk of bad debts can be greater with foreign trade than with domestic trade. If a foreign debtor refuses to pay a debt, the exporter must pursue the debt in the debtor's own country, where procedures will be subject to the laws of that country.

There are various measures available to exporters to overcome these problems. (Apart from credit risks, there are other risks, including the risk of currency (exchange rate) fluctuations (see Chapter 20) and political risks (see Chapter 23).)

Reducing the investment in foreign debtors

1.2 A company can reduce its **investment in foreign debtors** by insisting on earlier payment for goods. Another approach is for an exporter to **arrange for a bank to give cash for a foreign debt**, sooner than the exporter would receive payment in the normal course of events. There are several ways in which this might be done.

(a) **Advances against collections**. Where the exporter asks his bank to handle the collection of payment (of a bill of exchange or a cheque) on his behalf, the bank may be prepared to make an advance to the exporter against the collection. The amount of the advance might be 80% to 90% of the value of the collection. The bank will expect repayment of the advance from the proceeds of the bill or the cheque. Advances against collections would be arranged where the bill or cheque is payable in the exporter's own country.

(b) **Documentary credits**. These are described later.

(c) **Negotiation of bills or cheques**. This is similar to an advance against collection, but would be used where the bill or cheque is payable outside the exporter's country (for example in the foreign buyer's country).

The advantages of using bills of exchange in international trade

1.3 The advantages of payment by means of a bill of exchange are as follows.

(a) They provide a convenient method of collecting payments from foreign buyers.

(b) The exporter can seek immediate finance, using term bills of exchange, instead of having to wait until the period of credit expires (ie until the maturity of the bill). At the same time, the foreign buyer is allowed the full period of credit before payment is made.

(c) On payment, the foreign buyer keeps the bill as evidence of payment, so that a bill of exchange also serves as a receipt.

(d) If a bill of exchange is dishonoured, it may be used by the drawer to pursue payment by means of legal action in the drawee's country.

(e) The buyer's bank might add its name to a term bill, to indicate that it **guarantees** payment at maturity. On the continent of Europe, this procedure is known as **'avalising'** bills of exchange.

Reducing the bad debt risk

1.4 Methods of minimising bad debt risks are broadly similar to those for domestic trade. An exporting company should vet the creditworthiness of each customer, and grant credit terms accordingly. Methods of reducing the risks of bad debts in foreign trade include **export factoring, forfaiting, documentary credits**, and **international credit unions. Export credit insurance** is also an important facility which we shall examine in Section 2 of this chapter.

Export factoring

1.5 **Export factoring** is essentially the same as factoring domestic trade debts, a topic covered in Paper 8 and revised below.

> **KEY TERM**
>
> **Factoring:** an arrangement to have debts collected by a factor company, which advances a proportion of the money it is due to collect.

1.6 The main aspects of factoring are:

(a) Administration of the client's invoicing, sales accounting and debt collection services.

(b) Credit protection for the client's debts, whereby the factor takes over the risk of loss from bad debts and so 'insures' the client against such losses. This service is also referred to as 'debt underwriting' or the 'purchase of a client's debts'. The factor usually purchases these debts 'without recourse' to the client, which means that if the client's debtors do not pay what they owe, the factor will not ask for his money back from the client.

(c) Making payments to the client in advance of collecting the debts. This is sometimes referred to as 'factor finance' because the factor is providing cash to the client against outstanding debts.

1.7 The benefits of factoring for a business customer include the following.

(a) The business can pay its suppliers promptly, and so be able to take advantage of any early payment discounts that are available.

(b) Optimum stock levels can be maintained, because the business will have enough cash to pay for the stocks it needs.

(c) Growth can be financed through sales rather than by injecting fresh capital.

(d) The business gets finance linked to its volume of sales. In contrast, overdraft limits tend to be determined by historical balance sheets.

(e) The managers of the business do not have to spend their time on the problems of slow paying debtors.

(f) The business does not incur the costs of running its own sales ledger department.

1.8 Factoring, as compared with forfaiting (which we discuss below), is widely regarded as an appropriate mechanism for trade finance and collection of receivables for small to medium-sized exporters, especially where there is a flow of small-scale contracts. A factoring service typically offers prepayment of up to 80% against approved invoices. Service charges vary between around 0.75% and 3% of total invoice value, plus finance charges at levels comparable to bank overdraft rates for those taking advantage of prepayment arrangements.

Forfaiting

1.9 **Forfaiting** is a method of providing medium-term (say, three to five years) export finance, which originated in Switzerland and Germany where it is still very common. It has normally been used for export sales involving capital goods (machinery etc), where payments will be made over a number of years. Forfaiting is also used as a short-term financing tool.

KEY TERM

Forfaiting: a method of export finance whereby a bank purchases from a company a number of sales invoices or promissory notes, usually obtaining a guarantee of payment of the invoices or notes.

1.10 Forfaiting works as follows.

(a) An exporter of capital goods finds an overseas buyer who wants medium-term credit to finance the purchase. The buyer must be willing:

(i) To pay some of the cost (perhaps 15%) at once

(ii)   To pay the balance in **regular instalments** (perhaps every six months) normally for the next five years

(b)   The buyer will either:

(i)   Issue a series of promissory notes, or

(ii)   Accept a series of drafts

with a final maturity date, say, five years ahead but providing for regular payments over this time: in other words, a series of promissory notes maturing every six months, usually each for the same amount.

(c)   If the buyer has a very good credit standing, the exporter might not ask for the promissory notes (or drafts) to be guaranteed. In most cases, however, the buyer will be required to find a bank which is willing to guarantee (**avalise**) the notes or drafts.

(d)   At the same time, the exporter must find a bank that is willing to be a 'forfaiter'. Some banks specialise in this type of finance.

(e)   Forfaiting is the business of **discounting** (negotiating) medium-term promissory drafts or bills. Discounting is normally at a fixed rate, notified by the bank (**forfaiter**) to the exporter when the financing arrangement is made. If the exporter arranges forfaiting with a bank before the export contract is signed with the buyer, the exporter will be able to incorporate the cost of discounting into the contract price.

(f)   The exporter will deliver the goods and receive the avalised promissory notes or accepted bills. He will then sell them to the forfaiter, who will purchase them **without recourse to the exporter.** The forfaiter must now bear the risk, ie:

(i)   Risks of non-payment

(ii)   Political risks in the buyer's country

(iii) The transfer risk that the buyer's country might be unable to meet its foreign exchange obligations

(iv)   The foreign exchange risk (The forfaiter holds the promissory notes and has paid cash to the exporter, and therefore it is the forfaiter who accepts the exchange risk.)

(v)   The collection of payment from the avalising bank

1.11   Forfaiting can be an expensive choice, and arranging it takes time. However, it can be a useful way of enabling trade to occur in cases where other methods of ensuring payment and smooth cash flow are not certain, and in cases where trade may not be possible by other means. The diagram below should help to clarify the procedures.

BPP PUBLISHING

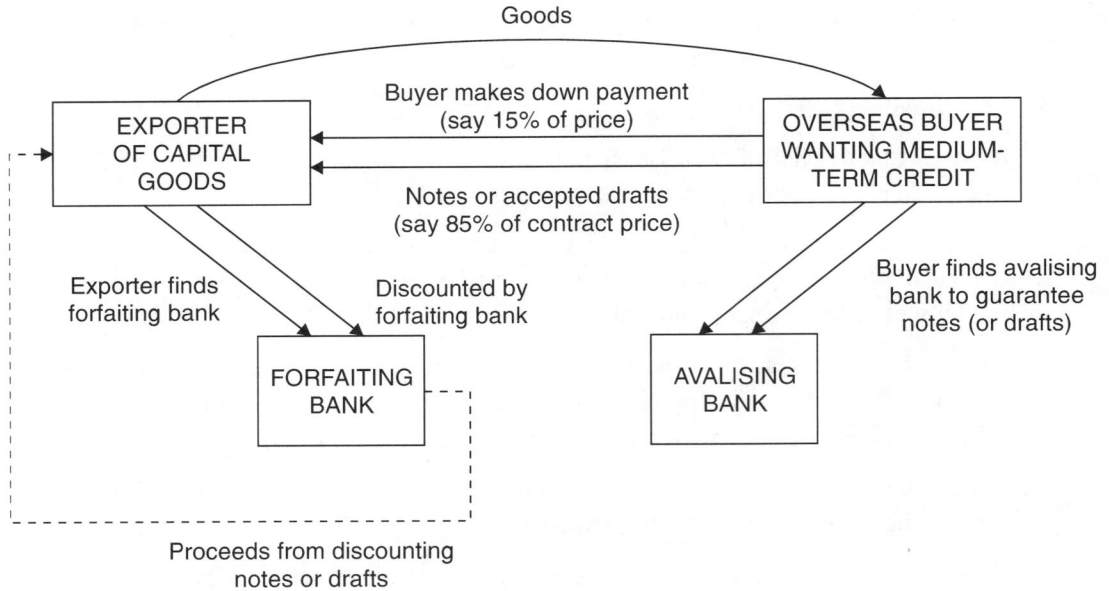

Proceeds from discounting
notes or drafts

Documentary credits

1.12 **Documentary credits ('letters of credit')** provide a method of payment in international trade which gives the exporter a risk-free method of obtaining payment. At the same time, documentary credits are a method of obtaining short-term finance from a bank, for working capital. This is because a bank might agree to discount or negotiate a bill of exchange, and so:

(a) The exporter receives immediate payment of the amount due to him, less the discount, instead of having to wait for payment until the end of the credit period allowed to the buyer

(b) The buyer is able to get a period of credit before having to pay for the imports.

Banks may advance pre-shipment finance to help with manufacture.

1.13 The buyer (a foreign buyer, or a UK importer) and the seller (a UK exporter or a foreign supplier) first of all agree a contract for the sale of the goods, which provides for payment through a documentary credit. The **buyer** then requests a bank in his country to issue a **letter of credit** in favour of the exporter. This bank which issues the letter of credit is known as the **issuing bank**. The buyer is known as the **applicant** for the credit and the exporter is known as the **beneficiary** (because he receives the benefits). The issuing bank, by issuing its letter of credit, guarantees payment to the beneficiary. Banks are involved in the credits, not in the underlying contracts.

1.14 The issuing bank asks a bank in the exporter's country to advise the credit to the exporter. This bank is known as the **advising bank**. The advising bank agrees to handle the credit (on terms arranged with the issuing bank) but does not normally make any commitment itself to guarantee payment to the exporter.

1.15 The advising bank (in the exporter's country) might be required by the issuing bank to add its own 'confirmation' to the credit. The advising bank would then be adding its own guarantee of payment to the guarantee already provided by the issuing bank. If it does confirm the credit, it is then known as the **confirming bank**. Thus, a **confirmed** letter of credit carries the guarantees of two banks, usually one in the exporter's country (the confirming bank) and one in the buyer's country (the issuing bank). The cost of issuing a letter of credit is usually borne by the buyer.

1.16 A documentary credit arrangement must be made between the exporter, the buyer and participating banks **before the export sale takes place**. Documentary credits are slow to arrange, and administratively cumbersome; however, they might be considered essential where the risk of non-payment is high, or when dealing for the first time with an unknown buyer.

International credit unions

1.17 **International credit unions** are organisations or associations of finance houses or banks in different countries (in Europe). The finance houses or banks have reciprocal arrangements for providing instalment credit finance. When a buyer in one country wants to pay for imported goods by instalments the exporter can approach a member of the credit union in his own country which will then arrange for the finance to be provided through a credit union member in the importer's country. The exporter receives immediate payment without recourse to himself. The buyer obtains instalment credit finance. Without the existence of international co-operation between members of a credit union, importers would have more difficulty in obtaining instalment credit finance.

1.18 Suppose, for example, that an exporter in the UK wishes to sell some capital goods to a customer in Germany and the customer wants to pay for the goods by instalment. The exporter can approach a member of an international credit union in the UK, and ask for the necessary instalment finance to be arranged through a German member of the credit union. Details of the proposed sale will be given to the German finance house or bank, which will then decide on the terms of instalment credit it will offer to the German buyer (in accordance with the German laws and practice). The UK finance house will receive full payment for the goods from the German finance house and pay the exporter. The German finance house is then left with a normal hire purchase agreement with the German buyer.

1.19 This type of scheme has advantages for small exporters who cannot afford to allow lengthy credit periods to its overseas customers. Examples of international credit unions are the European Credit Union and Eurocredit.

2 EXPORT CREDIT INSURANCE

The purpose of export credit insurance

> **KEY TERM**
>
> **Export credit insurance** is insurance against the risk of non-payment by foreign customers for export debts.

2.1 Not all exporters take out export credit insurance because premiums are very high and the benefits are sometimes not fully appreciated; but, if they do, they will obtain an insurance policy from a private insurance company that deals in **export credit insurance**. The largest provider of export credit insurance in the UK is **NCM UK,** which insures more than 6,000 British companies in trade with 200 countries. The government's **Export Credit Guarantee Department (ECGD)** also exists, providing long-term guarantees to banks on behalf of exporters.

2.2 Export credit insurance is not essential, if exporters are reasonably confident that all their customers are trustworthy, but it helps cover for some of the special risks involved in exporting. If an export customer defaults on payment, the task of pursuing the case through the courts will be lengthy, and it might be a long time before payment is eventually obtained. Export credit insurance also provides insurance against non-payment for a variety of risks (described later below) in addition to the buyer's failure to pay on time.

The short-term guarantee

2.3 NCM UK provides of credit insurance for short-term export credit business. A credit insurance policy for export trade on short-term credit (up to 180 days) or on cash terms is known as a short-term guarantee.

2.4 Exporters can choose to obtain credit insurance **for all their export business on a regular basis**, for **selected parts of their export business** or for **occasional, high-value export sales**. However, NCM UK prefers to provide comprehensive insurance for an exporter's entire export business. Cover is also available for UK manufacturers and merchants (but not confirming houses) dealing in **foreign** goods, under an **endorsement** to the short-term guarantee. This is referred to as a **multi-sourcing endorsement**.

2.5 The risks covered by the short-term guarantee are non-payment by an overseas customer under any of the following circumstances:

(a) Insolvency of the buyer

(b) The buyer's failure to pay within six months of the due date, in cases where the buyer has accepted the goods sent to him by the exporter

(c) The buyer's failure to accept the goods sent to him (*provided* non-acceptance of the goods has not been caused or excused by the exporter's own actions, and the insurer decides it would serve no useful purpose for the exporter to take up or pursue legal proceedings against the buyer)

(d) A general moratorium on debts to overseas suppliers which might be decreed by the government of the buyer's country

(e) Any other action by the government of the buyer's country which prevents performance of the contract

(f) Political events, economic difficulties, legislative measures or administrative measures arising outside the UK which prevent or delay payments under the contract

(g) A 'shortfall' in revenue to the exporter caused by foreign exchange losses when the exporter has to accept payment in a local currency for a debt which should be paid in sterling

(h) War, and similar disturbances outside the UK, which prevent performance of the contract

(i) The cancellation or non-renewal of the UK export licence or a prohibition by law on the export of goods from the UK (This risk, however, is only covered for insurance policies with a *pre-credit* risk section.)

(j) In the case of 'public buyers' in the overseas country ('government' departments), the short-term guarantee also covers the risk of failure or refusal of the buyer to perform the contract, through no fault of the exporter

2.6 These risks fall into two broad categories: the creditworthiness of the foreign buyer (**buyer risks**); and economic and political risks in the overseas country (**country risks**).

2.7 The following risks are *not* covered by the short-term guarantee:

(a) Non-payment because of the exporter's failure to comply with the provisions of the insurance policy

(b) Non-payment due to causes within the exporter's control

(c) Losses due to a breach of the sale contract by the exporter

(d) Losses covered by a normal commercial insurance policy (eg damage to the exported goods, or theft of the goods)

(e) Losses due to illegal activities by the exporter in either the UK or an overseas country

(f) Insolvency or default over payment by either the collecting bank or the exporter's agent

(g) Exchange risks normally covered by forward exchange contracts

(h) Any loss due to a breach of existing exchange control regulations in the buyer's country

(i) Failure on the part of the buyer to obtain the required *authority* to import the goods or make payment for them

(j) Losses incurred on the contract itself (due to the exporter's own costs in the UK)

2.8 Unless the exporter has additional pre-credit risk cover, this policy does not protect him from cancellation of the contract by the buyer before the goods are dispatched from the UK.

The percentage of cover

2.9 The **percentage of the loss incurred** by the exporter that this policy covers varies according to the cause of the loss.

(a) The short-term guarantee covers 90% of the loss arising from the insolvency of the buyer, or the buyer's failure to pay within six months of the due date, that is losses due to poor creditworthiness of the buyer.

(b) When the buyer fails to take up the goods dispatched to him the exporter must bear a 'first loss' of 20% of the full original invoiced price of the goods, and NCM UK will then bear 90% of the balance.

(c) For the other risks, the short-term guarantee covers 95% of the loss. These are losses due to economic and political risks in the overseas country.

Premiums

2.10 As a general guide, the **premiums** payable by the exporter for a comprehensive short-term guarantee comprise a **fixed basic premium** at the start of the year, plus **additional monthly premiums** that vary with the amount of exports declared by the exporter during the month.

3   COUNTERTRADE

KEY TERM

Countertrade is a general term used to describe a variety of commercial arrangements for reciprocal international trade or barter between companies or other organisations (for example, state controlled organisations) in two or more countries.

3.1 **Countertrade** involving exchange of petroleum and manufacturing goods became popular in the early 1980s as such deals provided a way of avoiding OPEC export quotas for oil-producing countries. It is also common in deals with East European countries which are short of foreign exchange. The huge debts of many Third World and Eastern European countries have also contributed to the growth of countertrade as the only way of arranging international trade in the absence of cash or credit facilities to finance imports. It is now estimated that around 10% to 15% of international trade is conducted by some means of countertrade.

3.2 The following notes are based on the booklet *Countertrade: some guidance for exporters* issued by the Department of Trade and Industry. The quotations in these notes are all taken from this booklet.

3.3 'The common characteristic of countertrade arrangements is that export sales to a particular market are made conditional upon undertakings to accept imports from that market. For example, a British exporter may sell machinery to country X on condition that he accepts agricultural products from X in payment. Simple barter deals like this are unusual and most countertrade deals are much more involved... Even at its simplest, countertrade can be a complex, expensive and uncertain mode of trading. It is fraught with pitfalls. In an ideal market it would not arise. It is, however, growing, fast becoming a fact of international trade and cannot be ignored.'

3.4 Countertrade can be costly for the exporter: it creates lengthy and cumbersome administrative problems just to set up a countertrade arrangement. It is fraught with uncertainty, and deals can easily collapse or go wrong. Small and medium-sized firms might be unable and unwilling to accept the costs and administrative burdens of exporting by means of countertrade arrangements. However, in some situations, countertrade might be the only way of securing export orders.

Case example

The furnishings retailer Ikea engages in numerous countertrade deals with its suppliers in order to overcome the difficult trading conditions which prevail in Eastern Europe.

Why do countries use countertrade?

3.5 Some countries have insisted on imposing countertrade requirements for some of their international trade. The reasons for countertrade are chiefly that as follows.

(a) Some countries lack commercial credit or convertible foreign currency to pay for imports, and so countertrade is needed to finance imports.

(b) Some developing countries (such as Brazil and India) use countertrade to boost their developing manufacturing industries, which can export more goods by means of countertrade arrangements than they would otherwise be able to.

(c) Some centrally planned countries have in the past used countertrade as an instrument of their political and economic policies (to achieve a balance of trade, or long-term commercial and industrial relationships with other countries).

(d) In a buyer's market, to obtain more trade or obtain new technology from another country (offset arrangements, especially for defence equipment).

Which countries have countertrade requirements?

3.6 Countertrade is unusual between industrial countries, with the exception of defence, aviation and big advanced technology deals. However, Australia and New Zealand have mandatory countertrade requirements (offset arrangements) for public sector purchases. Eastern European countries have used countertrade since 1945, and in 1989 this affected about 20% of their trade with the West.

3.7 Some oil exporting countries (Libya, Iran and Iraq) have sometimes required exporters bidding for large public sector contracts to accept payment in oil. The exporter will then have to find an oil distributor willing to buy the oil (at a discount on market prices) and much depends on the current market prices, whether there is a large surplus of oil and the size of the discount asked for by the oil distributor.

3.8 The main growth in countertrade has been among the less developed and developing countries of Latin America (such as Brazil), Africa and Asia. 'Although many LDCs have on occasion sought countertrade arrangements... the number of deals actually transacted has been constrained by the lack of effective organisational arrangements in the LDCs and by their inability to provide sufficient marketable goods for the counterpurchase.'

Question

Countertrade can involve problems for the exporter, in addition to 'normal' export risks. See if you can think what problems might arise, before looking at the next paragraph.

Problems with countertrade

3.9 The problems which may arise in countertrade include the following.

(a) The *costs* of countertrade (see below) might exceed the exporter's expectations. The exporter might increase the export price to cover the extra costs, or he might try to absorb the extra costs himself.

(b) The exporter might be pushed into agreeing to accept large quantities of unmarketable goods without any means of disposing of them.

(c) The importer's country might place an unrealistically high value on the goods they wish to countertrade.

(d) Several parties are likely to be involved in a countertrade arrangement, and this increases the risks of cancellation of the export order, due to one party failing to fulfil its contractual obligations.

What are the costs of countertrade?

3.10 The costs of countertrade include:

(a) Fees of specialist consultants who advise on countertrade negotiations

(b) The discount or 'disagio' necessary to dispose of the goods in countertrade (The size of the discount varies from 2-3% for high grade materials and commodities to 25-30% (and sometimes as much as 40-50%) for low-quality manufactured goods.)

(c) Any fees payable to a third party trading house or broker for assigning counterpurchase obligations

BPP
PUBLISHING

(d) Insurance costs

(e) Bank fees, where a bank provides advice and help on countertrade matters (eg negotiations, disposal of countertraded goods)

Chapter roundup

*   The various methods of providing export and import finance should be understood. **Export factoring** provides all the advantages of factoring generally and is especially useful in assessing credit risk. **International credit unions** and **forfaiting** provide medium term finance for importers of capital goods.

*   It is worth remembering that the exporter can obtain finance from the foreign buyer (by insisting on **cash with order**) and the importer can obtain finance from the foreign supplier (by means of normal trade credit, perhaps evidenced by a term bill of exchange).

*   Various forms of **credit insurance** are available to exporters.

*   **Countertrade** is a complex and possibly expensive means of trading with poor and less developed countries. It can take several forms.

Quick quiz

1   What services do factors provide? (see para 1.6)

2   In what type of situation might forfaiting be used? (1.9)

3   How are documentary credits used? (1.12, 1.13)

4   What is an international credit union? (1.17)

5   What is the purpose of export credit insurance, and when is it needed? (2.1, 2.2)

6   Outline the various forms of countertrade. (3.5)

Question to try	Level	Marks	Time
18	Exam standard	10	18 mins

Chapter 19

EXCHANGE RATES

Chapter topic list	Syllabus reference
1 Exchange rates	4(c), 5(g)
2 Influences on exchange rates	5(g)
3 Exchange rate systems	5(g)
4 European monetary cooperation	5(g)

Introduction

In this chapter, we discuss **exchange rates**, the factors influencing them, and the various attempts which have been made to coordinate and stabilise exchange rates. An understanding of exchange rates is important for financial managers.

Financial managers working in businesses engaged in foreign trade need to understand how exchange rates influence **foreign trade transactions**. Chapters 17 and 18 covered aspects of foreign trade, while in Chapters 20 to 22 we go on to look at the related area of risk management.

All financial managers and accountants should have an appreciation of the importance of exchange rates in **macroeconomic developments** which affect their firms, such as inflation and economic recession.

1   EXCHANGE RATES   12/94, 6/95

Exchange rates

1.1   An **exchange rate** is the rate at which one country's currency can be traded in exchange for another country's currency. Although it is convenient to refer to the 'exchange rate' for currency - eg the exchange rate for sterling - every traded currency in fact has many exchange rates. There is an exchange rate with every other traded currency on the foreign exchange markets, so that there is an exchange rate for sterling with the US dollar, the Canadian dollar, the yen, the deutschmark, the French franc, and so on. Foreign exchange dealers make their profit by buying currency for less than they pay for it, and so there are really two exchange rates, a selling rate and a buying rate.

Exchange rates and EMU

1.2   Exchange rates between currencies of countries in EMU (European Monetary Union) have been fixed in terms of the new European single currency the **euro** since the beginning of 1999, and will continue to be fixed between each other, at the rates shown below. These are irrevocable conversion rates, for as long as EMU exists in its current form.

BPP PUBLISHING

Exchange rates for one euro in EMU currencies

Country	Currency
Belgium	BFr 40.34
France	FFr 6.560
Germany	DM 1.956
Ireland	I£ 0.788
Italy	L 1936
Netherlands	Fl 2.204
Portugal	Es 200.5
Spain	Pta 166.4

1.3 Other EMU countries not included in the above table are Austria, Finland and Luxembourg. The currencies of these countries also have a fixed exchange rate again the euro. The **UK** is not yet a member of EMU, and so the sterling exchange rate against the euro is not fixed and changes from day to day.

1.4 Although euro notes and coins are not yet in circulation, bank accounts can be denominated in euros. Since the euro came into existence on 1 January 1999, it has been common for prices in EMU countries to be quoted in both the euro and the old currency. Some (or all) of a company's transactions may already be denominated in euros even for transactions within the UK, since a contract can be denominated in euros by agreement of the parties.

1.5 Euro notes and coin are due to be introduced to EMU countries on 1 January 2002 followed by a period of up to six months in which there will be double circulation with old notes and coin. At the end of this period, the old currencies will cease to be legal tender.

Spot rates and forward rates

1.6 Broadly speaking, there are two ways in which currencies are bought and sold: **spot** - for immediate 'delivery'; and **forward** - for delivery at a date in the future. Thus, a UK firm might receive US$100,000 from a US customer, and sell it 'spot' to a bank, to receive sterling immediately (in practice normally two business days after the contract is made). If the exchange rate is $1.8000 to £1, the UK firm would receive £55,555.56.

1.7 If a firm knows that it is going to receive some foreign currency in the near future, which it will want to sell in exchange for domestic currency, it can make a forward exchange contract with a bank, at an exchange rate that is specified in the contract. Thus, if a firm knows that it is going to receive US$100,000 in three months' time, it can make a forward exchange contract 'now' to sell the US dollars in three months' time at a specified exchange rate. If the 'spot' rate is $1.8000 to £1, the 'forward' rate may be higher or lower than $1.8000 depending on comparative interest rates in the USA and the UK.

The foreign exchange (FX) markets

1.8 The foreign exchange (or 'forex') markets are worldwide, and are continuing to expand. The main dealers are banks. By far the largest currency dealing centre in the world is London, with a huge **daily** turnover of US$637 billion, 85% of this being in the US dollar, according to a 1998 survey. (Turnover is 37% up on three years earlier). Around 350 banks deal regularly in the London forex market. The next largest centre is New York, with around half of the level of business in London, followed by Tokyo, Singapore, Hong Kong, Zurich and Frankfurt.

1.9 Banks buy currency from customers and sell currency to customers - typically, **exporting and importing firms**. Banks may buy currency from the **government** or sell currency to the government - this is how a government builds up its official reserves. Banks also buy and sell currency **between themselves**. Consider what is actually happening when currencies are bought and sold: essentially, bank deposits denominated in one currency are being exchanged for bank deposits denominated in another currency.

1.10 International trade involves foreign currency, for either the buyer, the seller, or both (for example, a Saudi Arabian firm might sell goods to a UK buyer and invoice for the goods in US dollars). As a consequence, it is quite likely that exporters might want to sell foreign currency earnings to a bank in exchange for domestic currency, and that importers might want to buy foreign currency from a bank in order to pay a foreign supplier.

1.11 Although demand to buy and sell currencies arises from the demand of individuals (for example, tourists going abroad) and firms (for example, importers, exporters, firms investing overseas and governments) the bulk buying and selling of foreign currencies is done mainly by banks in the foreign exchange markets of the world, such as London. Since most foreign exchange rates are not fixed but are allowed to vary, rates are continually changing and each bank will offer new rates for new customer enquiries according to how its dealers judge the market situation. Dealers are kept continually informed of rates at which deals are currently being made, by means of computerised information services.

1.12 Although exchange rates in the market are influenced by the forces as exercised through the actions of the central bank of supply and demand, a **government's policy on the exchange rate** for its currency can have an important effect on how the exchange rate is determined. In the case of the common European currency, the **euro**, the actions of the **European central bank** influence its exchange rate.

Foreign currency quotations

1.13 The price of foreign currency (the exchange rate) is normally quoted in terms of the local currency. The closing (end-of-day) exchange rates between pounds sterling and various foreign currencies are shown in the *Financial Times*. The rates for 9 June 1999 are shown below.

BPP
PUBLISHING

POUND SPOT FORWARD AGAINST THE POUND

Jun 9		Closing mid-point	Change on day	Bid/offer spread	Day's Mid high	low	One month Rate	%PA	Three months Rate	%PA	One year Rate	%PA	Bank of Eng. Index
Europe													
Austria*	(Sch)	21.1104	−0.0537	014 - 194	21.1454	21.0686	21.0628	2.7	20.9687	2.7	20.576	2.5	102.0
Belgium*	(BFr)	61.8877	−0.1572	612 - 141	61.9900	61.7640	61.7482	2.7	61.472	2.7	60.3209	2.5	101.2
Denmark	(DKr)	11.3987	−0.0278	929 - 045	11.4172	11.3776	11.377	2.3	11.3353	2.2	11.1715	2.0	104.3
Finland*	(FM)	9.1217	−0.0232	178 - 256	9.1370	9.1040	9.1011	2.7	9.0604	2.7	8.8908	2.5	80.0
France*	(FFr)	10.0634	−0.0256	591 - 677	10.0801	10.0434	10.0407	2.7	9.9958	2.7	9.8087	2.5	104.3
Germany*	(DM)	3.0006	−0.0076	993 - 018	3.0060	2.9932	2.9937	2.7	2.9804	2.7	2.9246	2.5	101.9
Greece	(Dr)	496.782	−1.1760	417 - 147	498.606	495.985	498.646	−4.5	502.089	−4.3	510.545	−2.8	61.7
Ireland*	(I£)	1.2083	−0.0030	077 - 088	1.2102	1.2058	1.2055	2.7	1.2001	2.7	1.1777	2.5	91.1
Italy*	(L)	2970.54	−7.5400	927 - 181	2975.45	2964.64	2963.84	2.7	2950.59	2.7	2895.34	2.5	74.5
Luxembourg*	(LFr)	61.8877	−0.1572	612 - 141	61.9900	61.7640	61.7482	2.7	61.472	2.7	60.3209	2.5	101.2
Netherlands*	(Fl)	3.3809	−0.0086	794 - 823	3.3864	3.3742	3.3733	2.7	3.3582	2.7	3.2953	2.5	100.4
Norway	(NKr)	12.5976	−0.0151	912 - 039	12.6162	12.5620	12.6152	−1.7	12.639	−1.3	12.6608	−0.5	95.3
Portugal*	(Es)	307.570	−0.7820	439 - 702	308.079	306.960	306.876	2.7	305.504	2.7	299.784	2.5	90.9
Spain*	(Pta)	255.262	−0.6480	153 - 371	255.690	254.760	254.686	2.7	253.547	2.7	248.8	2.5	75.8
Sweden	(SKr)	13.6977	−0.0047	871 - 083	13.7122	13.6539	13.6725	2.2	13.6231	2.2	13.4331	1.9	80.9
Switzerland	(SFr)	2.4411	−0.0066	398 - 424	2.4458	2.4363	2.4323	4.4	2.4149	4.3	2.3458	3.9	106.4
UK	. (£)	-	-	-	-	-	-	-	-	-	-	-	104.6
Euro	(€)	1.5342	−0.0039	335 - 348	1.5367	1.5309	1.5308	2.7	1.5238	2.7	1.4953	2.5	86.13
SDR†	—	1.195900		-	-		-		-		-		-
Americas													
Argentina	(Peso)	1.6000	−0.0034	996 - 003	1.6066	1.5996	-		-		-		-
Brazil	(R$)	2.7980	−0.0044	966 - 993	2.8121	2.7982	-	-	-	-	-	-	-
Canada	(C$)	2.3571	−0.0016	559 - 583	2.3702	2.3559	2.3561	0.5	2.3547	0.4	2.356	0.0	80.1
Mexico	(New Peso)	15.3299	+0.1433	190 - 408	15.3888	15.1691	15.5744	−19.1	16.0218	−18.1	18.2868	−19.3	-
USA	($)	1.6002	−0.0035	999 - 005	1.6069	1.5997	1.5998	0.3	1.5998	0.1	1.6041	−0.2	109.0
Pacific/Middle East/Africa													
Australia	(A$)	2.4227	−0.0102	204 - 250	2.4516	2.4147	2.422	0.3	2.4208	0.3	2.4223	0.0	85.6
Hong Kong	(HK$)	12.4121	−0.0275	090 - 152	12.4622	12.4098	12.4131	−0.1	12.4235	−0.4	12.5972	−1.5	-
India	(Rs)	68.9046	−0.1085	757 - 335	69.6350	68.8757	69.1311	−3.9	69.7182	−4.7	73.1911	−6.2	-
Indonesia	(Rupiah)	12409.56	+197.76	723 - 189	12916.20	12235.50	12574.75	−16.0	12870.21	−14.8	13883.54	−11.9	-
Israel	(Shk)	6.5410	−0.0160	322 - 497	6.5497	6.5276	-		-		-		-
Japan	(Y)	190.392	−2.1580	308 - 476	192.090	189.990	189.552	5.3	187.872	5.3	180.587	5.1	132.6
Malaysia‡	(M$)	6.0808	−0.0139	516 - 541	6.1054	6.0800	-		-		-		-
New Zealand	(NZ$)	2.9967	−0.0257	933 - 000	3.0436	2.9933	2.9952	0.6	2.9925	0.6	2.99	0.2	92.6
Philippines	(Peso)	60.4876	−0.1304	962 - 789	60.5789	60.3962	60.73	−4.8	61.1859	−4.6	63.8505	−5.6	-
Saudi Arabia	(SR)	6.0016	−0.0128	003 - 028	6.0267	6.0002	6.0015	0.0	6.0072	−0.4	6.0564	−0.9	-
Singapore	(S$)	2.7400	−0.0050	387 - 413	2.7501	2.7387	2.7322	3.4	2.7173	3.3	2.6712	2.5	-
South Africa	(R)	9.8029	+0.0246	970 - 087	9.8296	9.7894	9.8783	−9.2	10.0147	−8.6	10.5466	−7.6	-
South Korea	(Won)	1865.83	−23.2700	468 - 698	1890.83	1862.13	-		-		-		-
Taiwan	(T$)	52.0466	−0.1964	968 - 963	52.3155	51.9968	51.8429	4.7	51.8408	1.6	51.9248	0.2	-
Thailand	(Bt)	59.1194	−0.1596	683 - 705	59.5270	59.0683	59.1133	0.1	59.1597	−0.3	59.7126	−1.0	-

† Rates for Jun 8. Bid/offer spreads in the Pound Spot table show only the last three decimal places. Sterling index calculated by the Bank of England. Base average 1990 = 100. Index rebased 1/2/95. * EMU member. The exchange rates printed in this table are also available on the internet at http://www.FT.com.

1.14 The difference between the offer price and the bid price, covering dealers' costs and profit, is called the **spread**. Only the last three decimal places of the bid/offer spread are shown in the *FT* table.

1.15 The closing spot rate between sterling and the US dollar was thus £1 = $1.5999 - 1.6005 on the day in question. The lower price is the **offer price**. A dealer will offer $1.5999 in exchange for £1. The higher price is the **bid price**. A dealer will give £1 for every $1.6005 received. The **mid-point** between these two rates is £1 = $1.6002.

1.16 We can say that the one month forward $/£ price is at a **premium** to the spot rate because it is *lower* than the spot rate. The '%PA' column shows the *annualised* percentage premium (or discount, if negative) reflected in the forward rate.

1.17 The table shows that the one month forward price is at a premium of $1.6002 minus $1.5998 = 0.04 cents on the spot price. This premium (or discount if the forward rate is higher than the spot rate) is sometimes called the **swap rate**. The fact that there is a premium reflects the fact that interest rates in sterling are higher than interest rates in US dollars for deposits over the next month. (This reflects the principle of **interest rate parity**, which we will return to later.) For a one month forward transaction, less dollars will be paid per pound than the spot price. If the forward rate was higher than the spot rate, we would say it was at a **discount** to the spot rate. We should bear in mind that **the forward rate may be higher or lower than the spot rate turns out to be at the relevant future date**. The forward rate is the rate for a transaction *now* on delivery of a currency at a future date.

Question

Using the table above, set out the following rates (offer and bid prices) for (a) the Deutschmark and (b) the Thailand baht against the pound sterling as they were at the end of the day's trading. Are the forward rates of these currencies at a premium or a discount to the spot rates?

Answer

(a) DM2.9993 - DM3.0018; premium.
(b) Baht 59.0638 - 59.1705; premium at 1 month; discount at 3 months and 1 year.

---

2 INFLUENCES ON EXCHANGE RATES   6/95, 12/96, 12/97

Factors influencing the exchange rate for a currency

2.1 The exchange rate between two currencies - ie the buying and selling rates, both 'spot' and forward - is determined primarily by **supply and demand** in the foreign exchange markets. Demand comes from individuals, firms and governments who want to buy a currency and supply comes from those who want to sell it.

2.2 Supply and demand in turn are influenced by:

- The **rate of inflation**, compared with the rate of inflation in other countries
- **Interest rates**, compared with interest rates in other countries
- The **balance of payments**
- **Sentiment** of foreign exchange market participants regarding economic prospects
- **Speculation**
- **Government policy** on intervention to influence the exchange rate

2.3 Other factors influence the exchange rate through their relationship with the items identified above. For example:

(a) Total income and expenditure (demand) in the domestic economy determines the demand for goods, including:

(i)   Imported goods

(ii) Goods produced in the country which would otherwise be exported if demand for them did not exist in the home markets

(b) Output capacity and the level of employment in the domestic economy might influence the balance of payments, because if the domestic economy has full employment already, it will be unable to increase its volume of production for exports.

(c) The growth in the money supply influences interest rates and domestic inflation.

Purchasing power parity theory   6/97, 12/99

2.4 If the rate of inflation is higher in one country than in another country, the value of its currency will tend to weaken against the other country's currency. **Purchasing power parity theory,** which developed in the 1920s, attempted to explain changes in the exchange rate exclusively by the rate of inflation in different countries. The theory predicts that the exchange value of a foreign currency depends on the relative purchasing power of each currency in its own country and that spot exchange rates will vary over time according to relative price changes. This is sometimes referred to as the **law of one price**. The theory can be used to estimate future exchange rates in financial strategy problems.

KEY TERM

Purchasing power parity theory: the theory that, in the long run at least, exchange rates between currencies will tend to reflect the relative purchasing powers of each currency.

2.5 Formally, purchasing power parity is expressed in the following equation.

$$\frac{S_t - S_o}{S_o} = \frac{i_f - i_{uk}}{1 + i_{uk}} \quad \text{or} \quad S_t = S_o \times \frac{1 + i_f}{1 + i_{uk}}$$

where

S_o is the current lower foreign currency spot exchange rate (at time 0)
S_t is the expected spot rate at time t
i_f is the expected inflation in the foreign country to time t (expressed as a decimal)
i_{uk} is the expected inflation in the home country to time t (expressed as a decimal)

EXAM FORMULA

$$\frac{i_f - i_{uk}}{1 + i_{uk}}$$

2.6 EXAMPLE: PURCHASING POWER PARITY

The exchange rate between UK sterling and the French franc is £1 = 8.00 francs. Assuming that there is now purchasing parity, an amount of a commodity costing £110 in the UK will cost 880 French francs. Over the next year, price inflation in France is expected to be 5% while inflation in the UK is expected to be 8%. What is the expected spot exchange rate at the end of the year?

Using the formula above:

$$\frac{S_t - 8.00}{8.00} = \frac{0.05 - 0.08}{1 + 0.08}$$

$$S_t - 8.00 = 8.00 \times \frac{-0.03}{1.08}$$

$$S_t = 8.00 - 0.22 = 7.78$$

or, using the second version of the formula:

$$S_t = 8.00 \times \frac{1.05}{1.08} = 7.78$$

This is the same figure as we get if we compare the inflated prices for the commodity. At the end of the year:

UK price   =   £110 × 1.08 = £118.80

France price $=$ FF880 $\times$ 1.05 $=$ FF924

S_t $=$ 924 $\div$ 118.80 $=$ 7.78

2.7 In the real world, exchange rates move towards purchasing power parity *only over the long term*. However, the theory is sometimes used to predict future exchange rates in investment appraisal problems where forecasts of relative inflation rates are available.

> **Exam focus point**
> The use of purchasing power parity theory to estimate future exchange rates is a favoured topic of the Paper 14 examiner.

Interest rates and the exchange rate

2.8 It would seem logical to assume that if one country raises its interest rates, it will become more profitable to invest in that country, and so an increase in (mainly short-term) investment from overseas will push up the exchange rate because of the extra demand for the currency from overseas investors. This is true, but there is a limit to the amount of investment capital that will flow into a country because of higher interest rates. A major reason this is that investors may expect a **risk premium** for investing in a high interest rate currency if they fear that the currency will depreciate in value.

The Fisher effect

2.9 The term **Fisher effect** is sometimes used in looking at the relationship between interest rates and expected rates of inflation. The rate of interest can be seen as made up of two parts: the real required rate of return plus a premium for inflation. Then:

(1+ nominal rate of interest) = (1 + real rate of interest) $\times$ (1 + expected rate of inflation)

2.10 Countries with relatively high rates of inflation will generally have high nominal rates of interest, partly because high interest rates are a mechanism for reducing inflation and partly because of the Fisher effect: higher nominal interest rates serve to allow investors to obtain a high enough real rate of return where inflation is relatively high.

2.11 According to the **international Fisher effect**, interest rate differentials between countries provide an unbiased predictor of future changes in spot exchange rates. The currency of countries with relatively high interest rates is expected to depreciate against currency's with lower interest rates, because the higher interest rates are considered necessary to compensate for the anticipated currency depreciation. Given free movement of capital internationally, this idea suggests that the real rate of return in different countries will equalise as a result of adjustments to spot exchange rates.

2.12 The Fisher effect can be expressed as:

$$\frac{1+r_f}{1+r_{uk}} = \frac{1+i_f}{1+i_{uk}}$$

where

r_f is the nominal interest rate in the foreign country
r_{uk} is the nominal interest rate in the home country

The balance of payments and the exchange rate

2.13 Although the influence of flows of money within the balance of payments is obvious, it is not predominant. This is apparent from the fact that if exchange rates did respond to demand and supply for current account items, then the balance of payments on the current account of all countries would tend towards equilibrium. This is not so, and in practice other factors influence exchange rates more strongly.

2.14 Demand for currency to invest in overseas capital investments and supply of currency from firms disinvesting in an overseas currency have more influence on the exchange rate, in the short term at least, than the demand and supply of goods and services. However, if a country has a **continual deficit in its balance of payments current account**, international confidence in that country's currency will eventually be eroded, and in the long term, its exchange rate will fall as capital inflows are no longer sufficient to counterbalance the country's trade deficit.

Speculation and the exchange rate

2.15 Speculators in foreign exchange are investors who buy or sell assets in a foreign currency, in the expectation of a rise or fall in the exchange rate, from which they seek to make a profit. **Speculation** could be a **stabilising** influence. For example, if a country has a deficit on its current account in the balance of payments, there will be pressure on its currency to weaken. However, if speculators take the view that the deficit is only temporary, they might purchase assets in the currency when there is a balance of payments deficit and sell them, perhaps at a small profit, when the balance returns to surplus later. However, speculation is more likely to be **destabilising** by creating such a high volume of demand to buy or sell a particular currency that the exchange rate moves to a level where it is overvalued or under-valued in terms of what 'hard economic facts' suggest it should be. Speculation, when it is destabilising, could damage a country's economy because the uncertainty about exchange rates disrupts trade in goods and services.

2.16 In an article published in the *Bank of England Quarterly Bulletin* (August 1995), Professor Alan Kirkman argues that the large fluctuations in exchange rates which are commonplace are based not on the arrival of new information about fundamental economic changes, but rather on a kind of 'herd instinct' as dealers seek to follow each other's moves ever more closely. Speculative dealers will often do better by following the movements of the 'herd', even if these are based on a false reading of the fundamentals.

2.17 Speculation in a currency might be carried out by traders as well as investors of capital. When a currency is expected to devalue or depreciate, debtors who owe money in that currency will pay their debts more slowly, hoping that the currency will become cheaper by the time they have to pay. Debtors owing money in a currency which is expected to appreciate will pay more quickly, before the currency becomes more expensive. Quicker payments temporarily increase the demand for the currency in the foreign exchange market and slower payments temporarily reduce demand for a currency. These leads and lags add to the speculative pressure on currencies by altering supply and demand.

Other factors influencing the exchange rate

2.18 Before we consider government intervention as an influence on exchange rates, there are a number of other factors to note which influence the exchange rate of a currency because they affect the trade in goods and services and capital investments.

(a) The **natural resources of the country**. A country which is rich in natural resources should benefit not only from a net surplus on its current account (exports less payments of interest and dividends) but also from long term capital investment from overseas investors wanting to invest in the future exploitation of the resources. The country's currency should therefore be strong in the foreign exchange market.

(b) The **political stability of the country**. A country with an uncertain political or economic future is likely to suffer from disinvestment and speculation against its currency.

(c) Government intervention taking the form of **exchange controls, import controls or import tariffs**. If there is no retaliation by other countries against such measures, their effect should be to strengthen the exchange rate.

(d) Some currencies (especially the US dollar but also the yen and deutschmark, for example) being held as **reserve currencies** by other countries. (A reserve currency is a currency used as part of the official reserves of another country.) Trading in a reserve currency by the governments of these other countries will influence the exchange rate of the currency.

Forecasting exchange rates

2.19 A variety of foreign exchange forecasting services are offered by banks and independent consultants. Long-term forecasts of exchange rates provided by such services are likely to be based on fundamental economic analysis, for example of the balance of payments, relative rates of inflation and interest rates and purchasing power parities. Short-term forecasts could be based on technical analyses of a type similar to that used in technical analysis of share prices. Some multinational enterprises carry out their own foreign exchange forecasting in-house.

2.20 Can exchange rates be successfully forecast? As with equity markets, the success of the forecasts depends on the forecaster being able to 'beat the market'. The more efficient the foreign exchange market is, the more likely it is that changes in exchange rates are instances of **random walks**, in which case past price changes provide no guide to the future. If markets are less efficient, it is more likely that a forecaster is able to discover some relationship which holds and makes for successful forecasts.

Government intervention

2.21 The government can intervene in the foreign exchange markets to **sell** its own domestic currency in exchange for foreign currencies, when it wants to keep down the exchange rate of its domestic currency. The foreign currencies it buys can be added to the official reserves. Alternatively, it may **buy** its own domestic currency and pay for it with the foreign currencies in its official reserves. It will do this when it wants to keep up the exchange rate when market forces are pushing it down.

2.22 The government can also intervene indirectly, by changing domestic interest rates, and so either attracting or discouraging investors in financial investments which are denominated in the domestic currency. Purchases and sales of foreign investments create a demand and supply of the currency in the FX markets, and so changes in domestic interest rates are likely to cause a change in the exchange rate.

Consequences of an exchange rate policy

2.23 Reasons for a policy of controlling the exchange rate may be:

(a) To rectify a balance of trade deficit, by trying to bring about a fall in the exchange rate

(b) To prevent a balance of trade surplus from getting too large, by trying to bring about a limited rise in the exchange rate (Japan has been under international pressure to do this in recent years, and the Japanese government has attempted to 'manage' an appreciation of the yen to a level consistent with its general economic policy.)

(c) To emulate economic conditions in other countries

Stabilising the exchange rate

2.24 A country's government might have a policy of wanting to stabilise the exchange rate of its currency. A stable currency increases confidence in the currency and promotes international trade. **Exporters** do not want their profit on trading to be wiped out by an adverse movement in exchange rates, which means that their foreign currency earnings are worth less in domestic currency than they anticipated when the export sale was made. Similarly, **importers** do not want to find that the cost of imported goods rises unexpectedly because of an adverse exchange rate movement, which means that they must spend more domestic currency to buy the foreign currency to pay their overseas suppliers.

Exchange rate policy and inflation

2.25 Suppose sterling is devalued. What would happen?

(a) **Exports**, priced mainly in pounds, would become cheaper to foreign buyers. The volume and value of exports would rise.

(b) **Imports**, priced mainly in foreign currencies, would become more expensive to UK buyers. However, since demand for imports is price inelastic, UK buyers continue to buy imports in large quantities, even at higher prices. For a country such as the UK, which depends heavily on imports, these higher import prices could add to the rate of inflation.

(c) **Inflation**. There could be an increase in the rate of inflation, because of:

(i) Higher import prices
(ii) Higher wage settlements by UK firms

If UK firms export goods abroad, a depreciation in sterling would help to boost their export sales and profits. This could encourage them to agree to higher wage settlements for employees, which could also be inflationary.

(d) **Balance of trade**. As a result of a depreciation in sterling, exports would rise, but so too would imports (due to inelastic demand). The balance of trade *might* improve, but not necessarily by much.

(e) **Capital transactions**. As a result of a depreciation in sterling, or a threatened depreciation, investors would switch capital out of sterling and into other currencies. These capital movements would result in sales of sterling on the FX markets, and create pressures for further depreciation.

3   EXCHANGE RATE SYSTEMS   6/96, 6/99

3.1   We shall now go on to consider in more detail the different exchange rate policies which are open to governments. These may be categorised as **fixed exchange rates**, **free floating exchange rates**, **margins around a moveable peg** and **managed floating**.

Fixed exchange rates

3.2   A policy of rigidly fixed exchange rates means that the government of every country in the international monetary system must use its official reserves to create an exact match between supply and demand for its currency in the FX markets, in order to keep the exchange rate unchanged. Using the official reserves will therefore cancel out a surplus or deficit on the current account and non-official capital transactions in their balance of payments. A balance of payments surplus would call for an addition to the official reserves, and a deficit calls for drawings on official reserves.

3.3   The official reserves could in theory consist of any foreign currency (or gold) within the fixed exchange rate agreement. The exchange rates of the various currencies in the system might all be fixed against each other. However, for simplicity and convenience, it is more appropriate to fix the exchange rate for every currency against a standard. The standard might be:

(a)   **Gold**. If every currency is valued in terms of gold, official reserves would consist mainly, or even entirely, of gold.

(b)   A **major currency**, such as the US dollar. If every currency is valued in terms of the dollar, the fixed exchange rate between currencies is easily calculated. The dollars would then be the major reserve currency.

(c)   A **basket of major trading currencies**. For example, the ecu (European Currency Unit) was an 'international currency' which is based on a 'basket' of currencies of EU countries. Before **European Monetary Union (EMU)** the exchange rates of currencies in the **Exchange Rate Mechanism (ERM)** of the **European Monetary System (EMS)** were linked (but not rigidly fixed) to the value of the ecu. In 1999, the **euro** was set up as a common currency in terms of which the currencies of EMU countries are fixed. The euro is a currency in its own right and not a composite 'basket' of currencies.

3.4   A fixed exchange rate system removes exchange rate uncertainty and so encourages international trade. It also imposes economic disciplines on countries in deficit (or surplus). However, this restricts independence of domestic economic policies. A government might be forced to keep interest rates high or to reduce demand in the domestic economy (for example by raising taxes and so cutting the demand for imports) in order to maintain a currency's exchange rate and avoid a devaluation.

3.5   If levels of inflation differ widely in countries subscribing to a fixed exchange rate regime, the regime may not survive for long. The high inflation countries will be forced to devalue in order to keep their exports competitive and to reduce imports.

3.6   There is inevitably some **loss of flexibility in economic policy** making once a country joins a fixed exchange rate regime. The UK is a case in point: Norman Lamont, the (then) Chancellor of the Exchequer, acknowledged in his 1992 Budget speech that within the semi-fixed ERM system 'monetary policy is primarily directed at the maintenance of sterling's parity' within the system.

Floating exchange rates

3.7   Free floating exchange rates are at the opposite end of the spectrum to rigidly fixed rates. Exchange rates are left to the free play of market forces and there is no official financing at all. There is no need for the government to hold any official reserves, because it will not want to use them.

3.8   Floating exchange rate systems (free floating and managed floating) have been criticised in the past because they allow wide fluctuations in exchange rates. Certainly, in the foreign exchange markets today, there are large fluctuations which are unsettling for international trade. However, the (then) Governor of the Bank of England said in a speech (September 1981) that: 'Wide fluctuations in exchange rates are not a reason for criticising floating rate policies, since the underlying economic turbulence would have made a fixed rate system difficult, if not impossible, to work.'

3.9   Floating exchange rates (whether free floating or managed floating) are the only option available to governments when other systems break down and fail. Professor Friedman remarked (1967) that 'floating exchange rates have often been adopted by countries experiencing financial crises when all other devices have failed. That is a major reason why they have such a bad reputation'. In practice, countries would operate 'managed floating' of their currency and a policy of allowing a currency to float freely is rare.

A moveable peg or adjustable peg system

3.10   A moveable or adjustable peg system is a system of fixed exchange rates, but with a provision for:

(a)   The **devaluation** of a currency, for example when the country has a persistent balance of payments deficit

(b)   The **revaluation** of a currency, for example when the country has a persistent balance of payments surplus

Margins around a moveable peg

3.11   A moveable peg system provides some flexibility. Exchange rates, although fixed, are not rigidly fixed, because adjustments are permitted. Even so, it is still fairly inflexible, because governments only have the choice between a revaluation/devaluation or holding the exchange rate steady. A more flexible system would allow some minor variations in exchange rates. For example, the exchange rate between sterling and the US dollar might be fixed at $2 to £1, but governments might only be required to maintain the exchange rate within a margin of, say, 2% on either side of this rate. If this were the case, the UK government would undertake to keep the exchange rate for sterling between $1.96 and $2.04 to £1. However, if the UK were to run into a fundamental balance of payments disequilibrium, a devaluation (or revaluation) of sterling would occur and the UK government would then undertake to maintain exchange rates within the required margins of the new exchange rate.

The historical context

3.12   The European ERM was an adjustable peg system. If has been largely superseded by EMU, although non-EMU members Greece and Denmark remain within it. The advantages and disadvantages of an adjustable peg system will be discussed firstly below within the context of the Bretton Woods agreement.

The Bretton Woods agreement 1944-1971

3.13 The Bretton Woods agreement was formulated in 1944 near the end of the Second World War but it was adopted only gradually as national economies recovered from the devastations of war. The terms of the international monetary system created by the agreement, which was eventually adopted by most advanced Western countries, were as follows.

   (a) There was agreement on fixed exchange rates, but with:

      (i) An **adjustable peg**. Countries were permitted to devalue or revalue their currency when their balance of payments was in 'fundamental disequilibrium'. The exchange rates were fixed ('pegged') against gold, but it became common practice to express exchange rates against the US dollar.

      (ii) A **permitted margin on either side of the pegged rate**. The monetary authorities of each country undertook to use their official reserves to keep their currency's exchange value within plus or minus 1% of the par value.

   (b) The US dollar was pegged to gold at the rate of $35 per ounce. The US authorities were prepared to buy and sell dollars for gold at this rate, with any other central bank in the system. All currencies in the system were therefore convertible into gold via the US dollar (Initially, this was perfectly workable, because the USA's official reserves contained more gold than other countries had dollars in their official reserves.)

3.14 The system succeeded for a while in achieving its main aim. Exchange rate stability did appear to improve business confidence, and in the 1960s, international trade expanded at an unprecedented rate. Most national economies had high rates of growth, output and employment.

3.15 Eventually, however, problems crept into the system and it collapsed in 1971. Why?

   (a) The system depended on exchange rates remaining fixed for long periods of time, but for a devaluation or revaluation to be made as soon as a fundamental disequilibrium in a country's balance of payments became apparent.

      (i) Countries with a balance of payments surplus did not want to revalue their currency and pursue inflationary policies. The entire burden of 'correcting' imbalances in international payments was borne by deficit countries.

      (ii) Deficit countries were reluctant to recognise a fundamental disequilibrium in their balance of payments, because a devaluation of the currency was considered a 'failure'.

   (b) Fixing the nominal value of exchange rates did not protect real values, because the rate of inflation differed from one country to another. The problem of inflation meant that exchange rates would need to be adjusted more frequently, thereby removing a major reason for having a fixed exchange rate/adjustable peg system.

   (c) Speculation could put excessive pressure on a currency, and force a devaluation. The gains of speculators were effectively paid for out of the official reserves.

(d) The amount of capital which was invested overseas expanded in volume during the 1960s, with the early development of the eurocurrency market. Banks and large international firms became aware of the advantages of switching funds between currencies to make a speculative gain or avoid a loss. Speculative capital therefore came to exceed the volume of official reserves, and so governments were unable to prevent successful, co-ordinated speculation.

(e) International liquidity also became a problem because of loss of confidence in the US dollar.

Managed floating

3.16 By 1973, most major currencies had abandoned official par rates and were allowed to float. Floating was adopted because the alternatives had failed, and not for any more positive reason. However, **floating** has always been 'dirty' or '**managed**'.

3.17 A major problem with floating exchange rates in the 1980s was the wide fluctuations in foreign exchange rates for the leading international currencies. **Short-term variability** is inconvenient to traders and travellers abroad, but traders can protect themselves by using the forward exchange markets. A **long-term under-valuation of a currency**:

(a) Affects export competitiveness and makes the country more receptive to imports
(b) Makes investments seem worthwhile that might later turn out to be unprofitable
(c) Discourages long-term investment

3.18 Concern about the volatility of exchange rates led to some efforts of the authorities of the major Western countries to give the markets a lead, and make a more conscious attempt at managed floating of exchange rates.

3.19 Two international agreements were reached.

(a) The **Plaza agreement** of 1985 was an agreement by the authorities of five major countries (the Group of Five: the USA, Japan, West Germany, France and the UK) to co-operate in securing an orderly fall in the value of the US dollar, which they thought had become seriously over-valued. The outcome of the Plaza agreement was a steady fall in the value of the US dollar over the next fifteen months, encouraged by a policy of managed floating from the governments of all five countries concerned.

(b) The 1987 **Louvre accord** between the 'Group of Seven' (G7) countries, (the USA, West Germany, Japan, the UK, France, Canada and Italy) was a further agreement at international co-operation on managing exchange rates with the aim of securing greater stability in exchange rates.

3.20 There were some subsequent instances of concerted intervention by the G7 group, for example in February 1991, indicating that international monetary cooperation was not yet dead. By the mid-1990s however, it came to be accepted that effective international cooperation on exchange rates is hindered by the limited powers of governments to influence prevailing rates in the foreign exchange markets, where flows of funds are very large in relation to governments' foreign exchange reserves. (In 1998 the group turned into the 'Group of Eight' (G8), with the admission of Russia.)

3.21 Within the European Union, monetary and economic convergence has been fostered within the European Monetary System (and more recently by European Monetary Union).

4   EUROPEAN MONETARY COOPERATION   6/96, 6/98

The European Monetary System (EMS)

4.1   The purposes of the EMS are:

(a)   To **stabilise exchange rates** between the currencies of the member countries

(b)   To promote **economic convergence** in Europe, pushing inflation rates down by forcing economic policies on partner governments similar to the policies of the more successful members

(c)   To develop **European Economic and Monetary Union (EMU)**

4.2   The EMS provided for the system of exchange rates for member currencies known as the **exchange rate mechanism (ERM).**

(a)   Each currency had a **central rate** in the ERM.

(b)   The exchange rate of the currency of each member country was permitted to **vary within a margin** on either side of its central rate.

With the creation of the new **euro** currency in 1999, European Monetary Union, the old ERM ceased to exist, although (as already mentioned) some of the non-EMU currencies remain within a new version of the ERM.

European Economic and Monetary Union   6/97

4.3   EMU was a long-standing objective of the EU, reaffirmed in the Single European Act of 1985 and in the Maastricht agreement of 1991.

(a)   **Monetary union** can be defined as a single currency area, which requires a monetary policy for the area as a whole, implemented by the **European Central Bank**.

(b)   **Economic union** can be described as an unrestricted common market for trade, with some economic policy co-ordination between different regions in the union.

4.4   Although the package of measures included in European EMU is not paralleled anywhere else in the world, there have been many international monetary unions. For example, Belgium and Luxembourg were in a monetary union before EMU, and the UK and the Republic of Ireland (Eire) were in currency union until the 1970s.

4.5   Gordon Brown, the UK's Chancellor of the Exchequer, has explained in the House of Commons that the UK Treasury has 'made a detailed assessment of five economic tests' believed to define whether a clear and unambiguous case could be made to support Britain joining a single currency. These are:

(a)   Convergence between the UK and the economies of a single currency
(b)   Whether there is sufficient flexibility to cope with economic change
(c)   The effect on investment
(d)   The impact on the financial services industry
(e)   Whether it is good for employment

4.6   He concluded that applying these economic tests revealed that it was not in the interest of the UK to join in the first wave of EMU starting on 1 January 1999. However, he went on to urge the Government and businesses to prepare intensively, so that the UK will be in a position to join early in the next parliament, should that be desired.

For and against EMU

4.7   The arguments for and against EMU can be summarised as shown below, with particular reference to the UK's position.

For	Against
Economic policy stability.	**Loss of national control over economic policy.**
• EMU members are expected to keep to strict economic criteria. • Politicians in member countries will be less able to pursue short-term economic policies, for example just before an election, to gain political advantage.	• Under EMU, monetary policy is largely in the hands of the new European central bank. • Individual countries' fiscal policies also need to stay in line with European policy criteria. • The European economic policy framework puts greater emphasis on price stability than some individual governments may want. • Restrictive monetary policies could result in disproportionate unemployment and output effects.
Facilitation of trade.	
• Eliminates risk of currency fluctuations affecting trade and investment between EMU member countries • Eliminates need to 'hedge' against such risks • Savings in foreign exchange transaction costs for companies, as well as tourists. • Enhances ease of trade with non EU countries	
	The need to compensate for weaker economies.
	• For the UK, the possible benefits of being economically linked to stronger European economies are reduced and possibly even outweighed by the need to compensate for weaker economies. • Stronger economies could be under pressure to 'bail out' member countries which borrow too much in order to hold the system together.
Lower interest rates.	
• Reduces risk of inflation and depreciating currencies, reducing interest rates • Stabilises interest rates at a level closer to that of Germany, reducing interest costs for businesses and government.	**Confusion in the transition to EMU**. • Introduction of a new currency and coinage may cause confusion to businesses and consumers.
Preservation of the City's position.	**Lower confidence arising from loss of national pride**.
• If the UK stays out of EMU, the City's position as one of the major European financial capitals will be threatened. • In turn, the City's role as a leading global financial market would also be jeopardised. • Inward investment from the rest of the EU would also be likely to diminish.	• Sterling is a symbol of national cohesion. • EMU puts its members on the road to a federal Europe, it is suggested, making the UK parliament into little more than a regional town hall within Europe, with no more power than local government. Such a move might dent national pride and adversely affect economic confidence.

Exam focus point

You may be asked, as in 6/97, about the implications of the single European currency *for a company*. The following case example concerns this issue. (Note that Sweden, like the UK, currently remains outside EMU.)

Case example

What will be the impact of EMU and the euro on individual companies? Here we look at the example of Volvo, which was reported in the *Financial Times* on 14 January 1997.

According to Mr Peter Sandberg, Volvo's head of corporate finance, 'EMU presents us with an enormous challenge with many aspects affecting the whole business. But we can't say yet what the net advantages or disadvantages will be - too many parameters are still open.'

Volvo is based in Sweden and accounts in kronor. It is unlikely that Sweden will join EMU at the outset. Volvo has production operations in Sweden and other EU and non-EU European countries. It has major purchasing contracts in Europe, particularly in Germany. European countries, some of which will be in EMU and some not, account for large parts of Volvo's car and truck sales. Volvo also has major operations in North and South America. The USA is its largest single market for cars.

Volvo has been heavily exposed to the Deutschmark (purchasing exposure) against the US dollar (sales exposure). The planned single European currency, the euro, may have the effect of smoothing this exposure. 'It should be easier to manager our euro/dollar - and our euro/yen - exposure,' says Mr Sandberg.

Other currency complexities which currently arise should also be easier to manage. In France, Volvo's truck division earns more in francs than it spends, while the car division spends more francs than it earns. If the Franc and the Deutschmark no longer exist as separate currencies, such exposure is likely to be reduced. With EMU, says Mr Sandberg, 'there won't be so many currencies to juggle'.

Chapter roundup

- **Factors influencing the exchange rate** include the comparative rates of inflation in different countries, comparative interest rates in different countries, the underlying balance of payments, speculation and government policy on managing or fixing exchange rates.

- Exchange rates are essentially determined by **supply and demand**, but governments can **intervene** to influence the exchange rate. Government policies on exchange rates might be **fixed exchange rates** or **floating exchange rates** as two extreme policies. In practice, 'in-between' schemes have been:

  ° Fixed rates, but with provision for devaluations or revaluations of currencies from time to time ('**adjustable pegs**') and also some fluctuations ('**margins**') around the fixed exchange value permitted - eg Bretton Woods, the EMS

  ° **Managed floating** - eg sterling, the US dollar, the yen

- The weaknesses and strengths of each of these systems and **EMU** should be understood.

Quick quiz

1   Distinguish 'spot' and 'forward' exchange rates. (see para 1.2)

2   What does purchasing power parity theory say? (2.4, 2.5)

3   How might the government intervene in the foreign exchange markets? (2.21 - 2.22)

4   What are the advantages and disadvantages of fixed exchange rates? (3.2 - 3.6)

5   What are the advantages and disadvantages of floating exchange rates? (3.7 - 3.9)

Question to try	Level	Marks	Time
19	Exam standard	25	45 mins

Chapter 20

CURRENCY RISK

Chapter topic list	Syllabus reference
1 Risk and foreign exchange	4(b), 4(c)
2 Managing transaction exposure	4(c)
3 Forward exchange contracts	4(c)
4 Hedging using the money markets	4(c)
5 Choosing between a forward contract and a money market hedge	4(c)
6 Futures and currency risk	4(b)
7 Deciding how to hedge with currency futures	4(b)
8 Choosing between forward contracts and futures contracts	4(b), 4(c)
9 Hedging economic and translation exposure	4(c)

Introduction

In Chapters 20, 21 and 22, all of which are lengthy chapters, we look at various techniques for the management of risk, in particular **foreign exchange (currency) risk** and **interest rate risk** - very important and often difficult topics in Paper 14. In this chapter, we are particularly concerned with risks related to exchange rate fluctuations.

1 RISK AND FOREIGN EXCHANGE   12/98

Risk and risk management

1.1 **Risk management** describes the policies which a firm may adopt and the techniques it may use to manage the risks it faces. **Exposure** means being open to or vulnerable to risk. If entrepreneurship is about risk, why should businesses want to 'manage' risk? Broadly, there are two reasons why risk management makes good business sense.

(a) Firstly, a business may wish to reduce **risks** to which it is exposed to acceptable levels. What is an acceptable level of risk may depend upon various factors, including the scale of operations of the business and the degree to which its proprietors or shareholders are risk-averse.

(b) Secondly, a business may wish to avoid **particular kinds of risks**. For example, a business may be averse to taking risks with exchange rates, for good reasons. The good reasons may include the fact that the risks are simply too great for the business to bear, for example if exchange rate movements could easily bankrupt the business. Or the business, lacking any real expertise in foreign exchange dealings, may wish to minimise its exposure to risks such as foreign exchange risk which derive from conditions external to its business.

BPP PUBLISHING

1.2 For any particular kind of risk faced by a business, it is in general possible to say that someone somewhere will probably be prepared to accept that risk. Some may be happy to bear the risk because they already bear an opposing risk which would cancel out its effect. Others may be prepared to take on the risk if there is the prospect of them making a profit. For example, insurance companies are prepared to accept the pooled risks of fire damage which householders or businesses are unwilling to take individually. Foreign exchange dealers take risks with exchange rates in the anticipation of making profits if exchange rate movements are favourable.

1.3 There are basically two ways in which exposure to risk may be reduced.

(a) **Pooling** of risks. This method underlies insurance, in which risks which may be unacceptable to individual policyholders are aggregated or 'pooled' by being taken on by the insurance company. Pooling of risk also underlies the diversification of a portfolio of investments.

(b) **Hedging** of risks. In the case of hedging, different parties come to an agreement which cancels one of the parties' risks against the other's. The different parties may be subject to similar but opposite risks which they wish to hedge. Alternatively, one party may wish to hedge a risk while the other party may be a speculator.

1.4 Two types of risk with which corporate risk management is often concerned are **currency risk** (or **exchange rate risk**) - the risk of exchange rate movements - and **interest rate risk** - the risk of adverse interest rate movements. The inherent risks of the trade or business can be managed within the company. Other risks, including currency risk and interest rate risk, are due to factors beyond the control of the enterprise and hedging ought therefore to be considered.

Choosing not to hedge

1.5 Risk minimisation is not the only possible strategy. A company may, instead of hedging, choose to remain exposed to risks, hoping to profit from its risk-taking positions. A company's shareholders may prefer a higher risk strategy in the hope of achieving higher returns. As we shall see, the financial markets also provide a range of methods by which risks can be **partially hedged**.

Currency risk   6/98

1.6 A company may become exposed to currency risk in a number of ways, including the following:

(a) As an exporter of goods or services
(b) As an importer of goods or services
(c) Through having an overseas subsidiary
(d) Through being the subsidiary of an overseas company
(e) Through transactions in overseas capital markets

1.7 The variability of exchange rates can be appreciated by examining the following table. Note, for example, that between 1985 and 1995, the pound depreciated by $(3.784 - 2.260)/3.784 = 40\%$ against the deutschmark, while it appreciated by $(1.5783 - 1.2976)/1.2976 = 22\%$ against the US dollar over the same period.

Sterling exchange rates (average of daily rates)

	US dollar	Japanese yen	Swiss franc	European currency unit	Deutsch-mark	French franc	Italian lira
1985	1.2976	307.08	3.155	1.6998	3.784	11.5495	2,463
1986	1.4672	246.80	2.635	1.4948	3.183	10.1569	2,186
1987	1.6392	236.50	2.439	1.4200	2.941	9.8369	2,123
1988	1.7796	227.98	2.603	1.5060	3.124	10.5969	2,315
1989	1.6383	225.66	2.678	1.4886	3.079	10.4476	2,247
1990	1.7864	257.38	2.469	1.4000	2.876	9.6891	2,133
1991	1.7685	237.56	2.529	1.4284	2.925	9.9473	2,187
1992	1.7665	223.72	2.476	1.3620	2.751	9.3248	2,163
1993	1.5015	166.73	2.218	1.2845	2.483	8.5073	2,360
1994	1.5329	156.40	2.090	1.2924	2.481	8.4852	2,467
1995	1.5783	148.37	1.865	1.2211	2.260	7.8730	2,571
1996	1.5617	170.00	1.931	1.2467	2.350	7.9890	2,408
1997	1.6382	198.12	2.376	1.4499	2.840	9.5606	2,789

(Source: Economic Trends)

1.8 The following different types of currency risk may be distinguished.

(a) **Transaction exposure** is the risk of adverse exchange rate movements occurring in the course of normal international trading transactions. This arises when the prices of imports or exports are fixed in foreign currency terms and there is movement in the exchange rate between the date when the price is agreed and the date when the cash is paid or received in settlement. The different methods of reducing this type of exposure form a large part of the syllabus on currency risk and will be the main concern of this chapter and the next.

(b) **Translation exposure** is the risk that the organisation will make exchange losses when the accounting results of its foreign branches or subsidiaries are translated into the home currency. Translation losses can result, for example, from restating the book value of a foreign subsidiary's assets at the exchange rate on the balance sheet date.

(c) **Economic exposure** refers to the effect of exchange rate movements on the international competitiveness of a company. For example, a UK company might use raw materials which are priced in US dollars, but export its products mainly within the EU. A depreciation of sterling against the dollar or an appreciation of sterling against other EU currencies will both erode the competitiveness of the company. Economic exposure can be difficult to avoid, although diversification of the supplier and customer base across different countries may reduce this kind of exposure to risk.

Selling and buying currency

1.9 If an importer has to pay a foreign supplier in a foreign currency, he might ask his bank to sell him the required amount of the currency. For example, suppose that a bank's customer, a trading company, has imported goods for which it must now pay US$10,000.

(a) The company will ask the bank to sell it $10,000. If the company is buying currency, the bank is selling it.

(b) When the bank agrees to sell US$10,000 to the company, it will tell the company what the range of exchange will be for the transaction. If the bank's selling rate (known as the 'offer', or 'ask' price) is, say $1.7935, the bank will charge the company the following amount for the currency.

$$\frac{\$10,000}{\$1.7935 \text{ per } £1} = £5,575.69$$

1.10 Similarly, if an exporter is paid, say, US$10,000 by a customer in the USA, he may wish to exchange the dollars to obtain sterling. He will therefore ask his bank to buy the dollars from him. Since the exporter is selling currency to the bank, the bank is buying the currency. If the bank quotes a buying rate (known as the 'bid' price) of, say $1.8075, the bank will pay the exporter for the currency.

$$\frac{\$10,000}{\$1.8075 \text{ per } £1} = £5,532.50$$

1.11 A bank expects to make a profit from selling and buying currency, and it does so by offering a rate for selling a currency which is different from the rate for buying the currency. If a bank were to buy a quantity of foreign currency from a customer, and then were to re-sell it to another customer, it would charge the second customer more (in sterling) for the currency than it would pay the first customer. The difference would be profit. For example, the figures used for illustration in the previous paragraphs show a bank selling some US dollars for £5,575.69 and buying the same quantity of dollars for £5,532.50, at selling and buying rates that might be in use at the same time. The bank would make a profit of £43.19.

Spot rates

1.12 As we saw earlier, the **spot rate** is the rate of exchange on currency for immediate delivery. All the rates so far mentioned in this chapter have been spot rates.

Direct and indirect currency quotes

1.13 A **direct quote** is the amount of domestic currency which is equal to one foreign currency unit. An **indirect quote** is the amount of foreign currency which is equal to one domestic currency unit. In the UK indirect quotes are invariably used but, in most countries, direct quotes are more common. Currencies may be quoted in either direction. For example the US dollar and German mark might be quoted as DM/$ = 1.723 or $/DM = 0.580. In other words, DM1.723 = $1 and $0.580 = DM1. One rate is simply the reciprocal of the other.

1.14 A further complication to be aware of is that the offer rate in one country becomes the bid rate in the other. For example, Malaysian Ringgit (MR) are quoted in London as:

	Bank sells (offer)		Bank buys (bid)
MR/£	4.0440	-	4.0910

However, in Kuala Lumpur you would see:

	Bank sells (offer)		Bank buys (bid)
MR/£	4.0910	-	4.0440

> **Exam focus point**
>
> The Paper 14 examination is by no means confined to the activities of UK companies. Exchange rates given in the examination could be as quoted in foreign countries. Because of these complications you should always double-check which rate you are using when choosing between the bid or offer rate. One sure method is to recognise that the bank makes money out of the transaction and will therefore offer you the worse of the two possible rates!

Foreknowledge of foreign currency receipts and payments: transaction exposure

1.15 Much international trade involves credit. An importer will take credit often for several months and sometimes longer, and an exporter will grant credit. One consequence of taking and granting credit is that international traders will know in advance about the receipts and payments arising from their trade. They will know:

    (a) What foreign currency they will receive or pay

    (b) When the receipt or payment will occur

    (c) How much of the currency will be received or paid

1.16 **Importers and exporters** alike will be concerned about the profit they can expect to make from trade. An exporter who invoices a foreign buyer in the buyer's currency will expect to be able to exchange his foreign currency proceeds from the buyer for his domestic currency and earn enough domestic currency to cover his costs and make a profit. Similarly, an importer might buy goods from abroad for which he is invoiced in foreign currency. If he plans to sell the imports, he will produce a price list for his customers, or agree prices with his customers, so as to earn enough domestic currency from selling the goods to pay the foreign supplier in foreign currency, and make a profit.

1.17 The great danger to profit margins is in the **movement in exchange rates**. The risk faces (i) exporters who invoice in a foreign currency and (ii) importers who pay in a foreign currency.

Question 1

Bulldog Ltd, a UK company, buys goods from Redland which cost 100,000 Reds (the local currency). The goods are re-sold in the UK for £32,000. At the time of the import purchase the exchange rate for Reds against sterling is R/£ 3.5650 - 3.5800.

Required

(a) What is the expected profit on the re-sale?

(b) What would the actual profit be if the spot rate at the time when the currency is received has moved to:

    (i)   3.0800 - 3.0950

    (ii)   4.0650 - 4.0800?

Ignore bank commission charges.

Answer

(a) Bulldog must buy Reds to pay the supplier, and so the bank is selling Reds. The expected profit is as follows.

	£
Revenue from re-sale of goods	32,000.00
Less cost of 100,000 Reds in sterling (÷ 3.5650)	28,050.49
Expected profit	3,949.51

(b) (i) If the actual spot rate for Bulldog to buy and the bank to sell the Reds is 3.0800, the result is as follows.

	£
Revenue from re-sale	32,000.00
Less cost (100,000 ÷ 3.0800)	32,467.53
Loss	(467.53)

(ii) If the actual spot rate for Bulldog to buy and the bank to sell the Reds is 4.0650, the result is as follows.

	£
Revenue from re-sale	32,000.00
Less cost (100,000 ÷ 4.0650)	24,600.25
Profit	7,399.75

2   MANAGING TRANSACTION EXPOSURE   6/94, 6/95

2.1   The forward exchange contract is perhaps the most important method of obtaining cover against transaction exposure, where a firm decides that it does not wish to speculate on foreign exchange. This is discussed later in the chapter. However, there are other methods of reducing risks which we shall look at first.

Currency of invoice

2.2   One way of avoiding exchange risk is for an **exporter** to **invoice his foreign customer in his domestic currency**, or for an **importer** to **arrange with his foreign supplier to be invoiced in his domestic currency**. However, although either the exporter or the importer can avoid any exchange risk in this way, only one of them can deal in his domestic currency. The other must accept the exchange risk, since there will be a period of time elapsing between agreeing a contract and paying for the goods (unless payment is made with the order).

2.3   If a UK exporter is able to quote and invoice an overseas buyer in sterling, then the foreign exchange risk is in effect transferred to the overseas buyer. Similarly, a UK-based importer may be able to persuade the overseas supplier to invoice in sterling rather than in a foreign currency. An **alternative method** of achieving the same result is to negotiate contracts expressed in the foreign currency but specifying a fixed rate of exchange as a condition of the contract.

2.4   There are certain advantages in invoicing in a foreign currency which might persuade an exporter to take on the exchange risk. One of the most important is the possible marketing advantage by proposing to invoice in the buyer's own currency, when there is competition for the sales contract.

(a) The foreign buyer, invoiced in his own currency, will not have the problem of deciding whether to protect himself against exchange risks. The risks are borne by the exporter.

(b) If the exporter is in danger of losing the contract to overseas competition, and if the buyer's own currency is weak and likely to depreciate against sterling, the exporter might offer to invoice the buyer in his own (weak) currency. The exporter is in effect offering the buyer a price discount due to the probability of a movement in exchange rates favourable to the buyer and therefore unfavourable to the exporter.

(c) In some export markets, foreign currency (often the US dollar) is the normal trading currency, and so UK exporters might have to quote prices in that currency for customers to consider buying from them.

(d) The exporter may be able to offset payments to his own suppliers in a particular foreign currency against receipts in that currency. For example, if a UK company regularly imports goods which it pays for in US$, and it then exports those goods and invoices its own customer in US$, it will be able to offset payments against receipts in US$ and thereby eliminate exchange risks in both directions. (See *Matching receipts and payments* below.)

(e) By arranging to sell goods to customers in a foreign currency, a UK exporter might be able to obtain a loan in that currency at a lower rate of interest than in the UK, and at the same time obtain cover against exchange risks by arranging to repay the loan out of the proceeds from the sales in that currency. The exporter's asset (the money due from the overseas buyer) will then match his liability (his foreign currency borrowing), whatever happens to the exchange rate.

2.5 There are certain other aspects to invoicing in foreign currency that an exporter might wish to consider.

(a) **Pricing and price lists**. If the exporter issues price lists in foreign currency, he should be aware of the need to make frequent revisions to the price lists as the exchange value of his domestic currency fluctuates. For example, if a UK exporter issues a price list in US dollars, and sterling strengthens against the US dollar, the exporter will earn less sterling when he sells his US dollar receipts, and so his profit margins will be cut. He might therefore need to raise his prices to maintain profit margins. On the other hand, if the US dollar strengthened against sterling, the UK exporter could cut his prices whilst still maintaining his sterling profit margins. Whether an exporter has price lists or not, invoicing in a foreign currency should focus his attention on pricing policy and the reaction of the overseas market to price changes.

(b) **Customer relations**. A switch from invoicing in sterling to invoicing in a foreign currency might not be easy to achieve, at least not without giving adequate warning to the customer. The ability of an exporter to make a change might be thwarted by the resistance of a customer who is in a position of some bargaining strength (who can stop buying the exporter's goods).

(c) **Accounting systems**. Accounting procedures for invoicing in foreign currency, or borrowing in a foreign currency, are a little more complex than for invoicing and borrowing in sterling.

(d) **Pricing policy**. Pricing in a foreign currency should focus the exporter's attention on market prices in the buyer's country, and so create greater market awareness.

(e) **Credit control**. When a foreign customer is late with a payment, the exporter would suffer extra costs. It is therefore essential that credit control systems should be effective, to ensure that customers do pay on time.

(f) The customer might wish to consider taking out **credit insurance cover** for foreign currency debts.

Matching receipts and payments

2.6 A company can reduce or eliminate its foreign exchange transaction exposure by matching receipts and payments. Wherever possible, a company that expects to make payments and have receipts in the same foreign currency should plan to offset its payments against its receipts in the currency. Since the company will be setting off foreign currency receipts against foreign currency payments, it does not matter whether the currency strengthens or weakens against the company's 'domestic' currency because there will be no purchase or sale of the currency.

2.7 The process of matching is made simpler by having **foreign currency accounts** with a bank. UK residents are allowed to have bank accounts in any foreign currency. Receipts of foreign currency can be credited to the account pending subsequent payments in the currency. (Alternatively, a company might invest its foreign currency income in the country of the currency - for example it might have a bank deposit account abroad - and make payments with these overseas assets/deposits.)

2.8   Since a company is unlikely to have exactly the same amount of receipts in a currency as it makes payments, it will still be exposed to the extent of the surplus of income, and so the company may wish to avoid exposure on this surplus by arranging forward exchange cover. **Offsetting** (matching payments against receipts) will be cheaper than arranging a forward contract to buy currency and another forward contract to sell the currency, provided that receipts occur before payments, and the time difference between receipts and payments in the currency is not too long. Any differences between the amounts receivable and the amounts payable in a given currency should be covered by a forward exchange contract to buy/sell the amount of the difference.

Leads and lags

2.9   Companies might try to use **lead payments** (payments in advance) or **lagged payments** (delaying payments beyond their due date) in order to take advantage of foreign exchange rate movements. With a lead payment, paying in advance of the due date, there is a finance cost to consider. This is the interest cost on the money used to make the payment.

2.10   EXAMPLE: LEADS AND LAGS

A company owes $30,000 to a US supplier, payable in 90 days. It might suspect that the US dollar will strengthen against sterling over the next three months, because the US dollar is quoted forward at a premium against sterling on the foreign exchange market. The spot exchange rate is $1.50 = £1.

2.11   The company could pay the $30,000 now, instead of in 90 days time. This would cost £20,000 now, which is a payment that could have been delayed by 90 days. The cost of this lead payment would be interest on £20,000 for 90 days, at the company's borrowing rate or its opportunity cost of capital.

2.12   Of course, if the company has a dollar bank account, it could buy the dollars today and simply put them on deposit for 90 days before paying the US supplier. This would earn interest to at least partially off-set its interest cost on the £20,000. This technique is known as a **money market hedge**, or **synthetic forward contract**, and is dealt with in detail later.

Matching assets and liabilities

2.13   A company which expects to receive a substantial amount of income in a foreign currency will be concerned that this currency may weaken. It can hedge against this possibility by borrowing in the foreign currency and using the foreign receipts to repay the loan. For example, US dollar debtors can be hedged by taking out a US dollar overdraft. In the same way, US dollar trade creditors can be matched against a US dollar bank account which is used to pay the creditors.

2.14   A company which has a long-term foreign investment, for example an overseas subsidiary, will similarly try to match its foreign assets (property, plant etc) by a long-term loan in the foreign currency. For example, a Japanese company may raise a long-term sterling loan to finance the cost of setting up a production facility in the UK. The loan will be repaid out of the operating profits of the UK subsidiary. If the pound weakens for a long period, the reduction in the yen value of the subsidiary's earnings is offset by the exchange gain on the repayment of the loan. The matching of assets and liabilities thus provides an effective hedge not just against transaction exposure but also against economic and translation exposure.

Netting   6/94

2.15 Unlike matching, netting is not technically a method of managing exchange risk. However, it is conveniently dealt with at this stage. The objective is simply to save transactions costs by netting off inter-company balances before arranging payment. Many **multinational groups** of companies engage in **intra-group trading**. Where related companies located in different countries trade with one another, there is likely to be inter-company indebtedness denominated in different currencies.

> ### KEY TERM
>
> **Netting** is a process in which credit balances are netted off against debit balances so that only the reduced net amounts remain due to be paid by actual currency flows.

2.16 In the case of **bilateral netting,** only two companies are involved. The lower balance is netted off against the higher balance and the difference is the amount remaining to be paid.

2.17 EXAMPLE: BILATERAL NETTING

A and B are respectively UK and US based subsidiaries of a German based holding company. At 31 March 19X5, A owed B DM300,000 and B owed A DM220,000. Bilateral netting can reduce the value of the intercompany debts: the two intercompany balances are set against each other, leaving a net debt owed by A and B of DM 80,000 (DM300,000 – 220,000).

Multilateral netting

2.18 As you will have guessed, **multilateral netting** is a more complex procedure in which the debts of more than two group companies are netted off against each other. There are different ways of arranging multilateral netting. The arrangement might be co-ordinated by the company's own central treasury or alternatively by the company's bankers.

2.19 The **common currency** in which netting is to be effected needs to be decided upon, as does the method of establishing the exchange rates to use for netting purposes. So that it is possible to agree the outstanding amounts in time but with minimum risk of exchange rate fluctuations in the meantime, this may involve using the exchange rates applying a few days before the date at which payment is to be made.

2.20 Netting has the following advantages.

   (a) Foreign exchange purchase costs, including commission and the spread between selling and buying rates, and money transmission costs are reduced.

   (b) There is less loss in interest from having money in transit.

2.21 **Local laws and regulations** need to be considered before netting is used, as netting is restricted by some countries. In some countries, bilateral netting is permitted but multinational netting is prohibited; in other cases, all payments can be combined into a single payment which is made on a 'gross settlements' basis.

2.22 EXAMPLE: MULTILATERAL NETTING

A group of companies controlled from the USA has subsidiaries in the UK, South Africa and France. Below, these subsidiaries are referred to as UK, SA and FR respectively. At 30 June 19X5, inter-company indebtedness is as follows.

Debtor	Creditor	Amount
UK	SA	1,200,000 South African rand (R)
UK	FR	480,000 French francs (FF)
FR	SA	800,000 South African rand
SA	UK	£74,000 sterling
SA	FR	375,000 French francs

It is the company's policy to net off inter-company balances to the greatest extent possible. The central treasury department is to use the following exchange rates for this purpose.

US$1 equals R 6.126 / £0.6800 / F 5.880.

You are required to calculate the net payments to be made between the subsidiaries after netting off of inter-company balances.

2.23 SOLUTION

The first step is to convert the balances into US dollars as a common currency.

Debtor	Creditor	Amount in US dollars
UK	SA	1,200,000 ÷ 6.126 = $195,886
UK	FR	480,000 ÷ 5.880 = $81,633
FR	SA	800,000 ÷ 6.126 = $130,591
SA	UK	£74,000 ÷ 0.6800 = $108,824
SA	FR	375,000 ÷ 5.880 = $63,776

		Paying subsidiaries		
Receiving subsidiaries	UK	SA	FR	Total
	$	$	$	$
UK	-	108,824	-	108,824
SA	195,886	-	130,591	326,477
FR	81,633	63,776	-	145,409
Total payments	(277,519)	(172,600)	(130,591)	580,710
Total receipts	108,824	326,477	145,409	
Net receipt/(payment)	(168,695)	153,877	14,818	

The UK subsidiary should pay $153,877 to the South African subsidiary and $14,818 to the French subsidiary.

3 FORWARD EXCHANGE CONTRACTS   6/94

3.1 Foreign exchange transaction exposure may be overcome by a **forward exchange contract**, whereby the importer or exporter arranges for a bank to sell or buy a quantity of foreign currency at a future date, at a rate of exchange determined when the forward contract is made. This allows a trader, who knows that he will have to buy or sell foreign currency at a date in the future, to make the purchase or sale at a predetermined rate of exchange. The trader will know in advance either how much local currency he will receive (if he is selling foreign currency to the bank) or how much local currency he must pay (if he is buying foreign currency from the bank).

KEY TERM

A **forward exchange contract** is:

(a) An immediately firm and binding contract, eg between a bank and its customer

(b) For the purchase or sale of a specified quantity of a stated foreign currency

(c) At a rate of exchange fixed at the time the contract is made

(d) For performance (delivery of the currency and payment for it) at a future time which is agreed when making the contract (This future time will be either a specified date, or any time between two specified dates.)

The forward rate compared with the spot rate

3.2 The rate quoted by a bank for selling a currency forward will be slightly different from the spot rate. For example the spot rate for US\$/£ might be 1.6362 - 1.6370 but the 'one month forward' rate is quoted as 1.6352 - 1.6361 and 'three months forward' as 1.6331 - 1.6342. Suppose a British company, which needs to pay \$1,000,000 to a US supplier in one month's time, is given these quotes by a bank. It can fix the exchange rate with absolute certainty by entering into a forward contract to buy \$1,000,000 at the rate of \$/£1.6352, giving a cost of £611,546. This cost is slightly more expensive than the spot rate 1.6362 which gives £611,172. On the forward markets, the dollar is stronger against the pound than on the spot market.

3.3 On the day that these forward rates were quoted, the bank could earn interest on one month pound deposits at the rate of 6.25% per annum but the equivalent US dollar interest rate was 5.53125% per annum. This gives monthly interest of 6.25%/12 = 0.52083% in pounds and 0.46094% in dollars. When the company agrees to buy \$1,000,000 in one month's time, the bank will hedge its own position by immediately transferring money from pounds to dollars for one month.

3.4 For every £1 transferred, the bank will lose interest in one month of 0.52083%, giving a total loss of £1.0052083. The £1 will be converted at the spot rate to \$1.6362 and will earn interest in one month of \$1.6362 × 0.46094% = \$0.0075419, resulting in a total of \$1.6437419. Thus, after one month, the effective exchange rate between dollars and pounds is \$1.6437419/£1.0052083 = \$/£1.6352, which is the forward rate quoted by the bank to its customer.

£ $

1.6362

1.00 ◄ – – – – ► 1.6362

0.52083%   0.46094%

£1.0052083 ◄ – – – – ► $1.6437419

1.6352

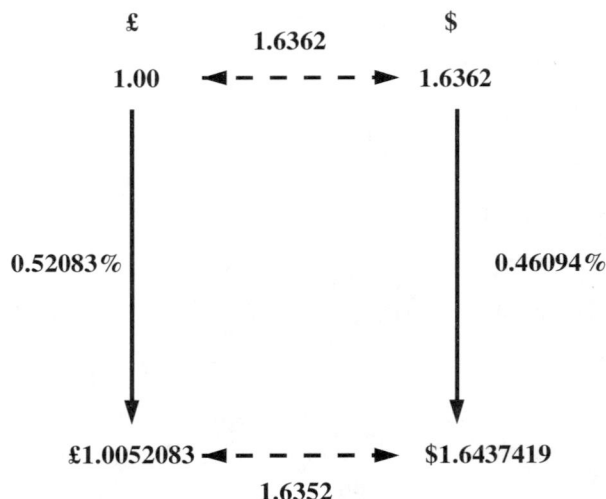

3.5   The forward currency exchange rate is therefore seen to be dependent on the spot rate and the short-term fixed interest rates in each currency. All of these figures are available with certainty when the contract is signed. The forward rate can be calculated today without making any estimates of future exchange rates. **Future exchange rates** depend largely on future events and will often turn out to be very different from the forward rate. However, the forward rate is probably an **unbiased predictor of the expected value of the future exchange rate**, based on the information available today. That is, if the dollar is at a premium on the forward market, it is likely to strengthen on the spot market in future.

Interest rate parity

3.6   The difference between spot and forward rates reflects differences in interest rates. If this were not so, then investors holding the currency with the lower interest rates would switch to the other currency for (say) three months, ensuring that they would not lose on returning to the original currency by fixing the exchange rate in advance at the forward rate. If enough investors acted in this way (known as **arbitrage**), forces of supply and demand would lead to a change in the forward rate to prevent such risk-free profit making.

3.7   The principle of **interest rate parity** (not to be confused with purchasing power parity, which we explained earlier) links the foreign exchange markets and the international money markets. The principle can be stated as follows.

$$\frac{1+r_\$}{1+r_\£} = \frac{f_{\$/\£}}{s_{\$/\£}}$$

3.8   This equation, based here on dollar/pound exchange and interest rates but of course generalisable to other cases, shows that the difference between the spot and forward rates depends on the difference between the interest rates:

     where $r_\$$ is the dollar ($) interest rate on a deposit for a certain time period
                    $r_\£$ is the sterling interest rate on a deposit for the same time period
                    $f_{\$/\£}$ is the forward exchange rate $/£ for the same time period
                    $s_{\$/\£}$ is the spot exchange rate $/£

3.9   Applying this formula to the example above:

$$\frac{1+0.0046094}{1+0.0052083} = \frac{f_{\$/\£}}{1.6362}, \text{ from which } f_{\$/\£} = 1.6352.$$

3.10 EXAMPLE: INTEREST RATE PARITY

Exchange rates between two currencies, the Northland florin (NF) and the Southland dollar (S$) are listed in the financial press as follows.

Spot rates	4.7250	NF/$S
	0.21164	$S/NF
90 day rates	4.7506	NF/$S
	0.21050	$S/NF

The money market interest rate for 90 day deposits in Northland florins is 7.5% annualised. What is implied about interest rates in Southland?

Assume a 365 day year. (*Note*. In practice, foreign currency interest rates are often calculated on an alternative **360-day basis**, one month being treated as 30 days.)

3.11 SOLUTION

Today, $S1.000 buys NF4.7250.

NF4.7250 could be placed on deposit for 90 days to earn interest of NF$(4.7250 \times 0.075 \times 90/365)$ = NF0.0874, thus growing to NF$(4.7250 + 0.0874)$ = NF4.8124.

This is then worth $S1.0130 at the 90 day exchange rate. This tells us that the annualised expected interest rate on 90-day deposits in Southland is $0.013 \times 365/90$ = 5.3%.

3.12 Alternatively, we can reach the same answer as follows.

Northland interest rate on 90 day deposit = r_n = $7.5\% \times 90/365$ = 1.85%

Southland interest rate on 90 day deposit = r_s

90-day forward exchange rate = $f_{s/n}$ = 0.21050

Spot exchange rate = $s_{s/n}$ = 0.21164

$$\frac{1+ r_s}{1 + 0.0185} = \frac{0.21050}{0.21164}$$

$$1 + r_s = 1.0185 \times 0.21050 \div 0.21164$$

$$= 1.013$$

$$r_s = 0.013, \text{ or } 1.3\%$$

Annualised, this is $0.013 \times 365/90$ = 5.3%

Fixed and option contracts

3.13 A forward exchange contract may be either **fixed** or **option**.

(a) **'Fixed'** means that performance of the contract will take place on a specified date in the future. For example, a two months forward **fixed** contract taken out on 1 September will require performance on 1 November.

(b) **'Option'** means that performance of the contract may take place, at the option of the customer, either:

   (i) At any date from the contract being made up to and including a specified final date for performance, or

   (ii) At any date between two specified dates

It is important to note that option forward exchange contracts are different from **currency options**, which are explained in Chapter 21.

Premiums and discounts: quoting a forward rate

3.14 Let us recap on **premiums and discounts** in quoting forward rates. As you will already appreciate, a forward exchange rate might be higher or lower than the spot rate. If it is higher, the quoted currency will be cheaper forward than spot. For example, if in the case of Italian lire against sterling (i) the spot rate is 2,156 - 2,166 and (ii) the three months forward rate is 2,207 - 2,222:

   (a) A bank would sell 2,000,000 lire:

   (i)   At the spot rate, now, for £927.64 $(\frac{2,000,000}{2,156})$

   (ii) In three months time, under a forward contract, for £906.21 $(\frac{2,000,000}{2,207})$

   (b) A bank would buy 2,000,000 lire:

   (i)   At the spot rate, now, for £923.36 $(\frac{2,000,000}{2,166})$

   (ii) In three months time, under a forward contract, for £900.09 $(\frac{2,000,000}{2,222})$

3.15 In both cases, the quoted currency (lire) would be worth less against sterling in a forward contract than at the current spot rate. This is because it is quoted forward cheaper, or 'at a discount', against sterling.

3.16 If the forward exchange rate is lower than the spot rate, the quoted currency will be more expensive forward than spot. For example:

   (a) If the spot rate for DM against sterling is 2.790 - 2.800
   (b) The one month forward rate is 2.770 - 2.785

   then DM are more expensive (quoted 'at a premium') forward than spot.

3.17 Forward rates are sometimes quoted as adjustments to the spot rates. If the forward rate for a currency is **cheaper** than the spot rate, it is quoted as a **discount** to the spot rate. The forward rate will be higher than the spot rate by the amount of the discount. If the forward rate for a currency is **more expensive** than the spot rate, it is quoted as a **premium** to the spot rate. The forward rate will be lower than the spot rate by the amount of the premium.

The rule for adding or subtracting discounts and premiums

3.18 A **discount** is therefore **added** to the spot rate, and a **premium** is therefore **subtracted** from the spot rate. (The mnemonic **ADDIS** may help you to remember that we ADD DIScounts and so subtract premiums.) The longer the duration of a forward contract, the larger will be the quoted premium or discount. Thus premiums or discounts will be larger three months forward than one month forward.

3.19 EXAMPLE: FORWARD EXCHANGE CONTRACTS (1)

A UK importer knows on 1 April that he must pay a foreign seller 26,500 Swiss francs in one month's time, on 1 May. He can arrange a forward exchange contract with his bank on 1

April, whereby the bank undertakes to sell the importer 26,500 Swiss francs on 1 May, at a fixed rate of say 2.64.

The UK importer can be certain that whatever the spot rate is between Swiss francs and sterling on 1 May, he will have to pay on that date, at this forward rate:

$$\frac{26,500}{2.64} = £10,037.88$$

If the spot rate is **lower than 2.64**, the importer would have successfully protected himself against a weakening of sterling, and would have avoided paying more sterling to obtain the Swiss francs. If the spot rate is **higher than 2.64**, sterling's value against the Swiss franc would mean that the importer would pay more under the forward exchange contract than he would have had to pay if he had obtained the francs at the spot rate on 1 May. He cannot avoid this extra cost, because a forward contract is binding.

Option forward exchange contracts   6/94

3.20   Option forward contracts are forward exchange contracts where the customer has the option to call for performance of the contract:

   (a)   At any date from the contract being made up to a specified date in the future or
   (b)   At any date between two dates both in the future

Performance must take place at some time: it cannot be avoided altogether.

3.21   Option forward contracts are normally used to cover whole months straddling the likely payment date, where the customer is not sure of the exact date on which he will want to buy or sell currency. (The purpose of an option forward contract is to avoid having to renew a forward exchange contract and extend it by a few days, because extending a forward contract can be expensive.) Option forward contracts can also be used bit by bit. For example, if a customer makes an option forward contract to sell DM100,000 at any time between 3 July and 3 August, he might sell DM20,000 on 5 July, DM50,000 on 15 July and DM30,000 on 1 August.

3.22   When a customer makes an option forward exchange contract with his bank, the bank will quote the rate which is most favourable to itself out of the forward rates for all dates within the option period. This is because the customer has the option to call for performance of the contract on any date within the period, and the bank will try to ensure that the customer does not obtain a favourable rate at the bank's expense.

3.23   EXAMPLE: OPTION FORWARD CONTRACT

A company is expecting to receive 32 billion Italian lire at some time between three and six months from now. The spot and forward rates for Lire/£ are:

Spot	2703 - 2708
Three months forward	2717 - 2724
Six months forward	2725 - 2732

The company covers the receipt with an option forward contract, to be fulfilled at any time between three and six months from now. What rate will apply to the contract?

3.24 SOLUTION

The relevant rates for selling Lire to the bank are 2724 and 2732. Of these, the worse rate is 2732, which will give fewer pounds than the rate of 2724. The contract will be agreed at an exchange rate of Lire/£ 2732.

What happens if a customer cannot satisfy a forward contract?

3.25 A customer might be unable to satisfy a forward contract for any one of a number of reasons.

(a) An **importer** might find that:

    (i)   His supplier fails to deliver the goods as specified, so the importer will not accept the goods delivered and will not agree to pay for them

    (ii)   The supplier sends fewer goods than expected, perhaps because of supply shortages, and so the importer has less to pay for

    (iii)   The supplier is late with the delivery, and so the importer does not have to pay for the goods until later than expected

(b) An **exporter** might find the same types of situation, but in reverse, so that he does not receive any payment at all, or he receives more or less than originally expected, or he receives the expected amount, but only after some delay.

Close-out of forward contracts

3.26 If a customer cannot satisfy a forward exchange contract, the bank will make the customer fulfil the contract.

(a) If the customer has arranged for the bank to buy currency but then cannot deliver the currency for the bank to buy, the bank will:

    (i)   Sell currency to the customer at the spot rate (when the contract falls due for performance)

    (ii)   Buy the currency back, under the terms of the forward exchange contract

(b) If the customer has contracted for the bank to sell him currency, the bank will:

    (i)   Sell the customer the specified amount of currency at the forward exchange rate
    (ii)   Buy back the unwanted currency at the spot rate

3.27 Thus, the bank arranges for the customer to perform his part of the forward exchange contract by either selling or buying the 'missing' currency at the spot rate. These arrangements are known as **closing out** a forward exchange contract.

3.28 EXAMPLE: FORWARD EXCHANGE CONTRACTS (2)

Shutter Ltd arranges on 1 January with a US supplier for the delivery of a consignment of goods costing US$96,000. Shutter Ltd will have to pay for the goods in six months time, on 1 July. The company therefore arranges a forward exchange contract for its bank to sell it US$96,000 six months hence.

In the event, the size of the consignment is reduced, and on 1 July, Shutter Ltd only needs US$50,000 to pay its supplier. The bank will therefore arrange to close out the forward exchange contract for the US$46,000 which Shutter Ltd does not need. This is called a partial close-out. Compute the cost to Shutter Ltd of the whole transaction, ignoring commission.

Exchange rates between the US dollar and sterling are as follows.

1 January:
Spot	$1.5145 - 1.5155
6 months forward	0.95 - 0.85c pm

1 July:
Spot	$1.5100 - 1.5110

3.29 SOLUTION

(a) The bank will sell Shutter Ltd US$96,000, to fulfil the original forward contract. The six months forward rate on 1 January was as follows.

Spot rate	1.5145
Less premium	0.0095
Forward rate	1.5050

(b) The bank will buy back the unwanted US$46,000 at the spot rate on 1 July, thus closing out the contract.

	£
Sale of US$96,000 at $1.5050	63,787.38
Purchase of US$46,000 at $1.5110	30,443.41
Cost to Shutter Ltd	33,343.97

Extensions of forward contracts

3.30 When a forward exchange contract reaches the end of its period, a customer might find that he has not yet received the expected currency from an overseas buyer, or does not yet have to pay an overseas seller. The customer still wants to buy or sell the agreed amount of currency in the forward exchange contract, but he wants to defer the delivery date for the currency under the contract. The customer can then ask the bank to close out the old contract at the appropriate spot rate, and ask for a new contract for the extra period, with the rate being calculated in the usual way.

3.31 An alternative would be for the bank to extend the contract, by changing the bank's selling or buying rate in the contract. The bank would then arrange a new forward exchange contract with the customer at a rate that is slightly more favourable to the customer than for an ordinary forward exchange contract. This type of arrangement is, however, frowned upon by the Bank of England as it might encourage companies to conceal losses, and banks will only permit it in the rarest of cases.

4 HEDGING USING THE MONEY MARKETS 6/98

4.1 Because of the close relationship between forward exchange rates and the interest rates in the two currencies, it is possible to 'manufacture' a forward rate by using the spot exchange rate and money market lending or borrowing. This technique is known as a **money market hedge** or **synthetic forward**. Indeed such hedges were historically used by traders long before forward contracts were available and are still useful today, either as a direct alternative to forward contracts or for currencies where forward contracts are not available.

Money market hedges

4.2 Suppose a British company needs to **pay** a French creditor in French francs in three months time. It does not have enough cash to pay now, but will have sufficient in three months time. Instead of negotiating a forward contract, the company could:

Step 1. Borrow the appropriate amount in pounds now

Step 2. Convert the pounds to francs immediately

Step 3. Put the francs on deposit in a French franc bank account

Step 4. When the time comes to pay the creditor:

    (a) Pays the creditor out of the franc bank account

    (b) Repays the pound loan account

4.3   The effect is exactly the same as using a forward contract, and will usually cost almost exactly the same amount. If the results from a money market hedge were very different from a forward hedge, speculators could make money without taking a risk (see *Covered interest arbitrage* which follows). Therefore market forces ensure that the two hedges produce very similar results.

4.4   EXAMPLE: MONEY MARKET HEDGE

A UK company owes a French creditor FF3,500,000 in three months time. The spot exchange rate is FF/£ 7.5509 - 7.5548. The company can borrow in Sterling for 3 months at 8.60% per annum and can deposit FF for 3 months at 10% per annum. What is the cost in pounds with a money market hedge and what effective forward rate would this represent?

4.5   SOLUTION

The interest rates for 3 months are 2.15% to borrow in pounds and 2.5% to deposit in FF. The company needs to deposit enough French francs now so that the total including interest will be FF3,500,000 in three months' time. This means depositing:

FF3,500,000/(1 + 0.025) = FF3,414,634.

These French francs will cost £452,215 (spot rate 7.5509). The company must borrow this amount and, with three months interest of 2.15%, will have to repay:

£452,215 × (1 + 0.0215) = £461,938.

Thus, in three months, the French creditor will be paid out of the French bank account and the company will effectively be paying £461,938 to satisfy this debt. The effective forward rate which the company has 'manufactured' is 3,500,000/461,938 = 7.5768. This effective forward rate shows the French franc at a discount to the pound because the franc interest rate is higher than the sterling rate.

£	Convert at 7.5509	FF
Borrow		**Deposit**
£452,215 — — — — ►		**FF3,414,634**
Interest paid: 2.15%		**Interest earned: 2.5%**
£461,938 ◄ — — — — ►		**FF3,500,000**

4.6 A similar technique can be used to cover a foreign currency **receipt** from a debtor. To manufacture a forward exchange rate, follow the steps below.

Step 1. Borrow an appropriate amount in the foreign currency today

Step 2. Convert it immediately to home currency

Step 3. Place it on deposit in the home currency

Step 4. When the debtor's cash is received:

  (a) Repay the foreign currency loan
  (b) Take the cash from the home currency deposit account

> **Exam focus point**
> Variations on these money market hedges are possible. In an examination question, follow the instructions given. If none are given, then follow the procedure above.

Covered interest arbitrage

4.7 Because the spot rate and the short-term fixed interest rates are all known with certainty today, if the forward rate is out of alignment with the money market rates it will be possible for speculators to make a risk-free gain by buying in one market and selling in the other. The activities of such 'arbitrageurs' helps to ensure that forward rates and interest rates have a very close relationship. The technique of covered interest arbitrage is one method that can be used.

4.8 EXAMPLE: COVERED INTEREST ARBITRAGE

A London-based investor has surplus cash of US$ 1,000,000 to invest in a three-month money market account. The three-month deposit rates are 7.2% per annum in sterling and 4% per annum in US dollars. The current spot exchange rate is $/£ 1.5000 - 1.5020. The three-month forward offer price for US dollars quoted to the investor is 1.4930. Show how he can make a risk-free gain.

4.9 SOLUTION

Three-month interest rates are 1.8% in sterling and 1% in dollars. The investor originally intended to deposit $1,000,000, making interest of 1% in three months = $10,000.

After studying the market rates:

Step 1 He sells the dollars at spot, getting £ 1,000,000 / 1.5020 = £665,779.

Step 2 He deposits the £665,779 in a sterling account for three months.

Step 3 He accepts a forward contract for the bank to sell him $1,011,900 at 1.4930.

After three months the sterling account will yield £665,779 × 1.018 = £677,763. This is used to buy the $1,011,900 at the agreed rate of 1.4930. The investor has made effective dollar interest of $11,900, which is a gain of $1,900 above target. The actions of arbitrageurs like this will cause the forward rate to strengthen from 1.4930. If it moves to 1.4902, no further gains can be made (1,010,000 / 677,763).

Use of interest rate parity to forecast future exchange rates 12/96

4.10 As seen above, the **interest rate parity** formula links the forward exchange rate with interest rates in a fairly exact relationship, because risk-free gains are possible if the rates are out of alignment. We have previously noted that the forward rate tends to be an unbiased predictor of the future exchange rate. So does this mean that future exchange rates can be predicted using interest rate parity, in the same way as **purchasing power** parity can be used? The simple answer is 'yes', but of course the prediction is subject to very large inaccuracies, because events which arise in the future can cause large currency swings in the opposite direction to that predicted by interest rate parity. In general, interest rate parity is regarded as less accurate than purchasing power parity for predicting future exchange rates.

> **Exam focus point**
> The Paper 14 examiner favours the purchasing power parity method over the interest rate parity method in predicting future exchange rates, and so PPP is more likely to be tested in the exam.

4.11 The general formula for interest rate parity can be extended to:

$$\frac{1 + r_n}{1 + r_d} = \frac{\text{Forward rate}_{(n/d)}}{\text{Spot rate}_{(n/d)}} = \frac{\text{Expected future exchange rate}_{(n/d)}}{\text{Spot rate}_{(n/d)}}$$

where:

r = rate of interest
n = currency which is the numerator (top line) in the exchange rate
h = currency which is the denominator (bottom line) in the exchange rate

4.12 EXAMPLE: INTEREST RATE PARITY

An Italian company is expecting to receive Kuwaiti dinars in one year's time. The spot rate is lire/dinar 5,467. The company could borrow in dinars at 9% or in lire at 14%. There is no forward rate for one year's time. Predict what the exchange rate is likely to be in one year.

4.13 SOLUTION

Using interest rate parity, lire is the numerator and dinar is the denominator. So the expected future exchange rate lire/dinar is given by:

$$5,467 \times \frac{1.14}{1.09} = 5,718$$

This prediction is subject to great inaccuracy, but note that the company could 'lock into' this exchange rate, working a money market hedge by borrowing today in dinars at 9%, converting the cash to lire at spot and repaying some of its 14% lire overdraft. When the dinar cash is received from the customer, the dinar loan is repaid.

Alternative version of the interest rate parity formula

4.14 As with purchasing power parity, an alternative version of the formula can be used. If you remember from the previous chapter, the formula for purchasing power parity given on the

Paper 14 formula sheet is $\dfrac{i_f - i_{uk}}{1 + i_{uk}}$ which, applied to interest rate parity, would give

$\dfrac{r_f - r_{uk}}{1 + r_{uk}}$ or, in the more general terms we have used above, $\dfrac{r_n - r_d}{1 + r_d}$.

4.15 Applying this formula to the above example:

$\dfrac{r_n - r_d}{1 + r_d} = \dfrac{0.14 - 0.09}{1.09} = 0.04587$ or 4.587%. This implies that the Italian lire will depreciate

by 4.587% against the dinar, predicting an exchange rate of $5{,}467 \times 1.04587 = 5{,}718$.

> **Exam focus point**
> In the examination, you may use whichever version of the formula you feel happier with.

Use of interest rate parity to compute the effective cost of foreign currency loans

4.16 As we have seen, loans in some currencies are cheaper than in others. However, when the likely strengthening of the exchange rate is taken into consideration, the cost of apparently cheap foreign loans becomes a lot more expensive. This is illustrated in the following example.

4.17 EXAMPLE: EFFECTIVE COST OF FOREIGN CURRENCY LOANS

Chateau SA, a French company, needs a one year loan of about FF50million. It can borrow in French francs at 10.80% pa but is considering taking out a US$ loan which would cost only 6.56% pa. The current spot exchange rate is FFr/US$ 5.1503. The company decides to borrow US$10million at 6.56% per annum. Converting at the spot rate, this will provide FF51.503 million. Interest will be paid at the end of one year along with the repayment of the loan principal.

Assuming the exchange rate moves in line with interest rate parity, you are required to show the French franc values of the interest paid and the repayment of the loan principal. Compute the effective interest rate paid on the loan.

4.18 SOLUTION

By interest rate parity, the French franc will have weakened in one year to:

$5.1503 \times \dfrac{1.1080}{1.0656} = 5.3552$

Time		$'000	Exchange rate	FFr'000
Now	Borrows	10,000	5.1503	51,503
In 1 year	6.56% interest	(656)		
	Repayment	(10,000)	5.3552	(57,065)
		(10,656)		

The effective interest rate paid is $\dfrac{57{,}065}{51{,}503} - 1 = 10.80\%$, the same as it would have paid in US$.

4.19 The general principle is that, when exchange rate movements are taken into account, interest rates in different currencies are very similar. However, in practice and in exam questions, there may sometimes be genuine opportunities to pick up loans at cheaper rates in other currencies.

5 CHOOSING BETWEEN A FORWARD CONTRACT AND A MONEY MARKET HEDGE

5.1 When a company expects to receive or pay a sum of foreign currency in the next few months, it can choose between using the forward exchange market and the money market to hedge against the foreign exchange risk. Other methods may also be possible, such as making lead payments. The cheapest method available is the one that ought to be chosen.

5.2 EXAMPLE: CHOOSING THE CHEAPEST METHOD

Trumpton plc has bought goods from a US supplier, and must pay $4,000,000 for them in three months time. The company's finance director wishes to hedge against the foreign exchange risk, and the three methods which the company usually considers are:

(a) Using **forward exchange contracts**
(b) Using **money market borrowing or lending**
(c) Making **lead payments**

The following annual interest rates and exchange rates are currently available.

	US dollar		Sterling	
	Deposit rate	Borrowing rate	Deposit rate	Borrowing rate
	%	%	%	%
1 month	7	10.25	10.75	14.00
3 months	7	10.75	11.00	14.25

	$/£ exchange rate ($ = £1)
Spot	1.8625 - 1.8635
1 month forward	0.60c - 0.58c pm
3 months forward	1.80c - 1.75c pm

Which is the cheapest method for Trumpton plc? Ignore commission costs (the bank charges for arranging a forward contract or a loan).

5.3 SOLUTION

The three choices must be compared on a similar basis, which means working out the cost of each to Trumpton either now or in three months time. In the following paragraphs, the cost to Trumpton now will be determined.

Choice 1: the forward exchange market

5.4 Trumpton must buy dollars in order to pay the US supplier. The exchange rate in a forward exchange contract to buy $4,000,000 in three months time (bank sells) is:

	$
Spot rate	1.8625
Less 3 months premium	0.0180
Forward rate	1.8445

The cost of the $4,000,000 to Trumpton in three months time will be:

$$\frac{\$4,000,000}{1.8445} = £2,168,609.38$$

5.5 This is the cost in three months. To work out the cost now, we could say that by deferring payment for three months, the company is:

(a) Saving having to borrow money now at 14.25% a year to make the payment now, or
(b) Avoiding the loss of interest on cash on deposit, earning 11% a year

The choice between (a) and (b) depends on whether Trumpton plc needs to borrow to make any current payment (a) or is cash rich (b). Here, assumption (a) is selected, but (b) might in fact apply.

5.6 At an annual interest rate of 14.25% the rate for three months is approximately 14.25/4 = 3.5625%. The 'present cost' of £2,168,609.38 in three months time is:

$$\frac{£2,168,609.38}{1.035625} = £2,094,010.26$$

Choice 2: the money markets

5.7 Using the money markets involves **borrowing in the foreign currency**, if the company will eventually receive the currency, or **lending in the foreign currency**, if the company will eventually pay the currency. Here, Trumpton will pay $4,000,000 and so it would lend US dollars.

5.8 It would lend enough US dollars for three months, so that the principal repaid in three months time plus interest will amount to the payment due of $4,000,000.

(a) Since the US dollar deposit rate is 7%, the rate for three months is approximately 7/4 = 1.75%.

(b) To earn $4,000,000 in three months time at 1.75% interest, Trumpton would have to lend now:

$$\frac{\$4,000,000}{1.0175} = \$3,931,203.93$$

5.9 These dollars would have to be purchased now at the spot rate of (bank sells) $1.8625. The cost would be:

$$\frac{\$3,931,203.93}{1.8625} = £2,110,713.52$$

By lending US dollars for three months, Trumpton is matching eventual receipts and payments in US dollars, and so has hedged against foreign exchange risk.

Choice 3: lead payments

5.10 Lead payments should be considered when the currency of payment is expected to strengthen over time, and is quoted forward at a premium on the foreign exchange market. Here, the cost of a lead payment (paying $4,000,000 now) would be $4,000,000 ÷ 1.8625 = £2,147,651.01.

5.11 **Summary**

	£
Forward exchange contract	2,094,010.26 (cheapest)
Currency lending	2,110,713.52
Lead payment	2,147,651.01

6 FUTURES AND CURRENCY RISK 6/96, 6/99

The development of futures contracts

6.1 **Futures** are a form of forward contract which have their origins in the markets for commodities such as wheat, coffee, sugar, meat, oil, base metals and precious metals. The prices of all of these commodities fluctuate seasonally and are also subject to large changes because of unpredictable events such as storms, drought, wars and political unrest. To avoid the uncertainty arising from large swings in prices, buyers and sellers of these commodities would agree quantities and prices in advance. This encouraged investment in production and benefited buyers and sellers alike by enabling them to plan in advance.

6.2 Originally the buyer and seller would agree a forward price for settlement by actual delivery of an agreed amount of the commodity on an agreed date. As a protection against defaulting on the deal, both parties would put down a deposit. However, the commodity futures markets developed rapidly when the contracts were **standardised** in terms of **delivery date** and **quantity**. This enabled the futures contracts to be traded purely on the basis of price, like shares on a stock exchange. Speculators, with no particular interest in the underlying commodity, entered the futures markets and greatly increased their liquidity and efficiency. Today commodity futures contracts are traded on futures exchanges all over the world, the largest and most important of which are in Chicago: the **Chicago Board of Trade (CBOT)** and **Chicago Mercantile Exchange (CME)**.

6.3 The abolition of US exchange control regulations in 1971 led to volatility in exchange rates and bond prices. This encouraged the futures exchanges to introduce **financial futures contracts** in interest rates, exchange rates and stock exchange indices. For example, CME set up a specialist division called the International Monetary Market (IMM) which has become the world's largest financial futures market. CME also has a special link with Singapore International Monetary Exchange (SIMEX). The London International Financial Futures and Options Exchange (LIFFE) was set up in 1982. A European rival to LIFFE, created from the German, Swiss and Austrian futures markets, is **Eurex**, based in Frankfurt.

Difference between forward contracts and futures contracts

6.4 The key difference between a forward contract and a futures contract is as follows.

(a) A forward contract is negotiated **'over the counter'** between a buyer and a seller. For example, a currency forward contract is negotiated between a bank and its customer and a commodity forward contract is negotiated between a producer and a buyer. This means that the contract can be **tailored** to the customer's exact requirements. Three things must be negotiated: quantity to be delivered, delivery date and price.

(b) A futures contract is bought and sold on a futures exchange, which operates like a stock exchange. In order to make a futures contract tradeable it must be **standardised** as to quantity and delivery date. The only factor which is traded is the price. The prices of futures contracts change continuously and are quoted by the futures exchange and in the financial press like share prices or currency prices.

6.5 For example:

(a) Cotton futures are traded on NYCE (New York Cotton Exchange) with a standard contract size of 50,000 lbs and only five standard delivery dates each year in March, May, July, October and December

(b) Deutschmark currency futures are traded on the IMM (International Monetary Market, Chicago) with a standard contract size of DM 125,000 and only four standard delivery dates per year, in March, June, September and December

6.6 The standardisation of contract sizes means that amounts required must be rounded to the nearest whole number of contracts. For example, a requirement to buy DM 950,000 must be dealt with on the futures market by buying 8 contracts (DM950,000/DM125,000 = 7.6, which is 8 contracts to the nearest whole number). This introduces some inaccuracies when transactions are being hedged.

6.7 However, it is the standardisation of delivery dates which results in the biggest difference between the way that futures contracts and forward contracts are used. Whereas most forward contracts are settled by delivery of the actual currency or commodity, it is very unlikely that the person who buys deutschmark futures or cotton futures will need the commodity at exactly the same time as the standardised date when the futures contract is settled. For this reason the vast majority of futures contracts are not settled by delivery but by 'closing out'.

Closing out futures contracts

6.8 **Closing out a futures contract** means entering into a second futures contract which reverses the effect of the first one. If, on 1 July, a company buys 8 deutschmark contracts, it closes out by selling 8 deutschmark contracts at a later date, say 31 July. The effect is that the company now has no liability to buy or sell any deutschmark, but it will have made a gain or loss resulting from the difference in price between 1 July and 31 July.

6.9 EXAMPLE: CLOSING OUT

On IMM (International Monetary Exchange) on 1 July the price of deutschmark futures with a 30 September settlement date is $/DM 0.5800 (i.e. US$ 0.5800 = DM 1). By 31 July the price of these futures contracts has moved to $/DM 0.6000. Your company buys 8 deutschmark futures contracts on 1 July and sells 8 deutschmark futures contracts on 31 July. What gain or loss has been made?

6.10 SOLUTION

Each deutschmark futures contract has a standard size of DM125,000 (see above). Deutschmark futures contracts with a standard settlement date of 30 September are called 'D-Mark September contracts'. **On 1 July**, when you buy 8 D-Mark September contracts at $/DM 0.5800, you have contracted to buy DM 125,000 × 8 = DM1,000,000 on 30 September, paying a price in US$ of 0.5800 × 1,000,000 = $580,000. Like a forward contract, this is a binding obligation. **On 31 July**, when you sell 8 D-Mark contracts, you incur a second obligation. This is to sell DM1,000,000 on 30 September, receiving the price of US$ 0.6000 × 1,000,000 = $600,000. Combining the two transactions, the deutschmarks cancel out, leaving you with a profit in dollars of $20,000.

6.11 Closing out of futures contracts is a technique used both by hedgers and speculators. In the above example, a speculator with no particular interest in deutschmarks could have made a profit by buying futures contracts on 1 July and selling them on 31 July. Likewise a company which actually needed to buy one million deutschmarks on 31 July could have hedged by using the same technique. Let us extend the example a little.

6.12 EXAMPLE: HEDGING BY CLOSING OUT FUTURES CONTRACTS

On July 1 the spot exchange rate for US dollars against the D-Mark is $/DM 0.5830. D-Mark September futures are trading at a price of $/DM 0.5800.

Note that the spot rate and the futures price will be close together, but not exactly the same. As with currency forward contracts, the difference represents the interest rate differential between dollars and deutschmarks for the period 1 July to 30 September. Future events will normally cause the spot rate and the futures price to move *in the same direction*. If the deutschmark spot price strengthens, the futures price will also strengthen.

Your company needs to buy one million deutschmarks with US dollars on July 31. You are happy with the July 1 exchange rate but are afraid that the deutschmark might strengthen over the next month. You decide to 'lock into' today's exchange rate by buying 8 deutschmark September contracts at $/DM 0.5800. If the deutschmark strengthens on the spot market, you will be able to sell the futures contracts at a profit which will pay for the more expensive deutschmarks.

You are required to illustrate the effect of using the futures hedge under the following two scenarios.

(a) The deutschmark spot exchange rate strengthens to $/DM 0.6030 and the September futures price moves to $/DM 0.6000.

(b) The deutschmark spot exchange rate weakens to $/DM 0.5630 and the September futures price moves to $/DM 0.5600.

6.13 SOLUTION

The company's **target payment** at the July 1 spot exchange rate is $0.5830 × 1,000,000 = $583,000. As in the previous example, buying the 8 deutschmark contracts gives you an obligation to buy DM 1,000,000 for $580,000 on 30 September. However, the company needs to buy the deutschmarks on 31 July, not 30 September, so it will achieve this by closing out its futures contracts and buying the deutschmarks on the spot market on 31 July. The results which follow are different under the two scenarios.

		Scenario 1		Scenario 2	
Futures hedge (8 contracts)	*$/DM*	*$*		*$/DM*	*$*
July 1: Buy DM 1,000,000 at	0.5800	(580,000)		0.5800	(580,000)
July 31: Sell DM 1,000,000 at	0.6000	600,000		0.5600	560,000
Gain/(loss) from futures market		20,000			(20,000)
Cash transaction					
July 31: DM 1,000,000 are					
actually bought at	0.6030	(603,000)		0.5630	(563,000)
Net cost of the deutschmarks		(583,000)			(583,000)

In **Scenario 1**, the deutschmark strengthens and the additional cost of buying the currency on July 31 is exactly offset by a gain from the futures market. In **Scenario 2**, the deutschmark weakens and the cheaper cost of buying the currency is offset by a loss from the futures market.

The net result is that the company has 'fixed' or 'locked into' its target exchange rate of $/DM 0.5830. The hedge achieves the same type of result as using a forward foreign exchange contract. Unfortunately futures hedges are not always as perfect as the one illustrated in the above example but, before looking at the complications, we will define a few terms.

Futures: definitions, terminology and background facts

> **KEY TERMS**
>
> A **futures contract** can be defined as 'a standardised contract covering the sale or purchase at a set future date of a set quantity of a commodity, financial investment or cash'. A **financial future** is a futures contract which is based on a financial instrument, rather than a physical commodity. There are financial futures for interest rates, currencies and stock market indices. A **currency future** is a futures contract to buy or sell a currency.

6.14   **Currency futures** - our main concern in this chapter - are not nearly as common as forward contracts, and their market is much smaller. On the currency futures markets, currencies such as the pound, deutschmark, yen, Swiss franc and French franc are all priced in US dollars. There is no contract for the US dollar itself.

6.15   On financial futures exchanges, most trading is in **interest rates** and **stock exchange indices**. **LIFFE** started trading in currency futures in 1982 but quickly abandoned them because of competition from the huge London-based forward foreign exchange market. LIFFE now trades futures and options concerned with short-term and long-term interest rates, the FTSE 100 and 250 indices and some commodities (eg wheat, coffee).

6.16   A London-based firm wishing to deal in currency futures could not therefore use LIFFE but would need to use a foreign exchange. The largest market for currency futures is the International Monetary Market (IMM), a division of the Chicago Mercantile Exchange. Another alternative is Singapore International Monetary Exchange (SIMEX).

6.17   The **contract size** is the fixed minimum quantity of commodity which can be bought or sold using a futures contract. Dealing in this amount is referred to as buying or selling one contract. In general, dealing on futures markets must be in a whole number of contracts.

6.18   The **contract price** is the price at which the futures contract can be bought or sold. For all currency futures the contract price is in US dollars (e.g. $/DM 0.5800 as used in the last example). Most commodities are also priced in dollars, though other currencies (eg pounds) are also used. The contract price is the figure which is traded on the futures exchange. It changes continuously and is the basis for computing gains or losses.

6.19   The **settlement date** (or delivery date, or expiry date) is the date when trading on a particular futures contract stops and all accounts are settled. On IMM, the settlement dates for all currency futures are at the end of March, June, September and December. The period for which a currency contract is traded before the settlement date is normally a maximum of nine months. This means that for each currency there will be three contracts being traded

BPP PUBLISHING

at any time, each to a different settlement date. For example from April to June, the currency futures being traded will be the June contract, the September contract and the December contract.

6.20 A buyer of a futures contract is said to take a **long position**. A seller is said to take a **short position**.

6.21 One tick (or the **tick size**) is the smallest measured movement in the contract price. For currency futures this is a movement in the fourth decimal place. A movement in the price of the D-Mark contract from $/DM 0.5800 to 0.5801 is a one-tick movement. The **value of a tick** is the gain or loss which is made if there is one tick price movement. This value depends on the contract size. Examples of tick values and contract sizes are shown in the following table.

Currency future	Contract size	Tick size	Value of one tick
Deutschmark	DM 125,000	$0.0001 per DM	$12.50
Swiss franc	SFr 125,000	$0.0001 per SFr	$12.50
Japanese yen	Y 12.5 million	$0.0001 per Y100	$12.50
Sterling	£62,500	$0.0001 per £	$6.25

The value of one tick = contract size × tick size.

6.22 Market traders will compute gains or losses on their futures positions by reference to the number of ticks by which the contract price has moved. For instance, the futures market gain in the previous example could have been computed as follows.

Bought at	0.5800
Sold at	0.6000
Gain	0.0200 = 200 ticks.

200 ticks × $12.50 × 8 contracts = $20,000.

6.23 When futures contracts are bought or sold, a deposit known as the **initial margin** must be advanced. The size of this margin depends on the actual contract but might typically amount to about 5% of the value of contracts dealt in. This deposit is refunded when the contract is closed out. The objective of the initial margin is to cover any possible losses made from the first day's trading. Thereafter, any variations in the contract price are covered by a **variation** margin. Profits are advanced to the trader's account but losses must be covered by advancing further collateral. This process is known as **marking to market**.

6.24 The fact that futures trading can be carried out **on the margin** in this fashion makes it very attractive to speculators. For example, if you buy $580,000 worth of futures contracts, you might only have to advance $29,000 initial margin. Thereafter, if the value of the contract increases steadily over the next month to $600,000, you need advance no more. When you close out you make a gain of $20,000 and your $29,000 is refunded. Your percentage return in one month is $20,000/$29,000 = 69% compared with the 3.45% you would have made if you had to advance the full $580,000. Under volatile trading conditions, percentage gains can be far higher than this. It goes without saying, however, that similar percentage *losses* can be made, sometimes amounting to several times the initial outlay.

6.25 A future's price may be different from the spot price, and this difference is the **basis**.

Basis = spot price – futures price

(Some books show it the other way round, so that the basis is the amount by which the futures price exceeds the spot price.) The basis will move towards zero at the delivery date.

If it did not, arbitrage profits would be possible. If, for example, the basis was negative at the delivery date, profits could be earned by selling futures contracts (at the higher price) and simultaneously buying in the cash market (at the lower price) goods - gold, pork bellies, dollars or whatever - for delivery to the futures buyers.

6.26 The futures markets have grown rapidly as more and more speculators have become involved and this has increased short-term volatility. However, hedgers who need to buy or sell the underlying currency or commodity do not use the margin to trade more than they otherwise would and can use the futures markets quite safely provided they understand how the system operates. The only risk to hedgers is that the futures market does not always provide a perfect hedge. This can result from two causes.

(a) The first reason is that amounts must be **rounded to a whole number of contracts**, causing inaccuracies.

(b) The second reason is **basis risk** - the risk that the futures contract price may move by a different amount from the price of the underlying currency or commodity. The actions of speculators may increase basis risk. A measure of **hedge efficiency** compares the profit made on the futures market with the loss made on the cash or commodity market, or *vice versa*.

6.27 EXAMPLE: HEDGE EFFICIENCY

Palace Inc, a company based in the USA, imports glassware products from Krystal AG, a company in Germany, and pays for them in deutschmarks. The company is due to pay DM650,000 in 30 days time and wishes to hedge the risk that the mark will strengthen against the dollar using currency futures. The spot rate today is \$/DM 0.5803 and the deutschmark futures contract is trading at \$/DM 0.5725.

Required

(a) Show how the futures hedge is set up.

(b) Show the net cost of the payment after using the futures hedge under the following two scenarios:

   Scenario 1. After 30 days the spot price moves to 0.6112 and the futures price moves to 0.6030.

   Scenario 2. After 30 days the spot price moves to 0.5680 and the futures price moves to 0.5610.

   In each case, compute the hedge efficiency.

6.28 SOLUTION

(a) The company needs to buy deutschmarks and hedges against a strengthening in the mark by buying deutschmark futures now. They will be sold in 30 days time. The number of contracts to be bought is DM650,000/DM125,000 = 5.2. Rounding to the nearest whole number gives 5 contracts. Note that there is nothing necessarily to be gained by rounding *up* because the futures market may give a gain or a loss.

   Summary: Buy 5 D-Mark contracts at \$/DM 0.5725.

(b) The company wishes to hedge today's spot rate. Its **target payment** is \$0.5803 × 650,000 = \$377,195.

The results of the hedge under each scenario are given below.

	Scenario 1		Scenario 2	
Futures hedge (5 contracts)	$/DM	$	$/DM	$
Today: Buy 5 at	0.5725		0.5725	
In 30 days: Sell 5 at	0.6030		0.5610	
Gain/(loss) per contract in ticks	305		(115)	
Total gain/(loss) on 5 contracts:				
5 × $12.50 × no. of ticks		19,063		(7,187)
Cash transaction				
In 30 days: DM650,000 are				
actually bought at	0.6112	(397,280)	0.5680	(369,200)
Net cost of the deutschmarks		(3 78,217)		(376,387)

6.29 The futures hedge gives slightly more or less than the target payment of $377,195 because of hedge inefficiency. To compute the hedge efficiency in each case, compute gain/loss as a percentage. In scenario 1 the gain comes from the futures market. In scenario 2 the gain comes from the cash market.

Hedge efficiency

	$	$
Target payment	377,195	377,195
Actual cash payment	397,280	369,200
Gain/(loss) on spot market	(20,085)	7,995
Futures gain / (loss)	19,063	(7,187)
Hedge efficiency	94.9%	111.2%

The hedge efficiency can be further analysed as follows.

6.30 In scenario 1, the futures market gave a gain of 305 ticks on 5 contracts. The spot market price lost 309 ticks on the equivalent of 5.2 contracts. Hedge efficiency $= \dfrac{305 \times 5}{309 \times 5.2} =$ 94.9%.

In scenario 2, the spot market gained 123 ticks on 5.2 contracts. The futures price lost 115 ticks on 5 contracts. Hedge efficiency $= \dfrac{123 \times 5.2}{115 \times 5} = 111.2\%$.

7 DECIDING HOW TO HEDGE WITH CURRENCY FUTURES

7.1 In the preceding section we showed how futures contracts are traded and how they can be used for speculation or for hedging by the technique of 'closing out'. In this section we discuss the factors a treasurer must consider when deciding how to set up a currency futures hedge.

7.2 When deciding to use futures to hedge currency risk, the questions to be asked are:

- Should the futures contracts be bought or sold?
- How many contracts?
- Which settlement date?

To buy or to sell?

7.3 One of the limitations of currency futures is that currencies can only be bought or sold for US dollars. The basic rules are given below.

- If you need to **buy** a currency on a future date with US dollars, take the following action.

  Step 1. Buy the appropriate currency futures contracts now

  Step 2. Close out by selling the same number of futures contracts on the date that you buy the actual currency

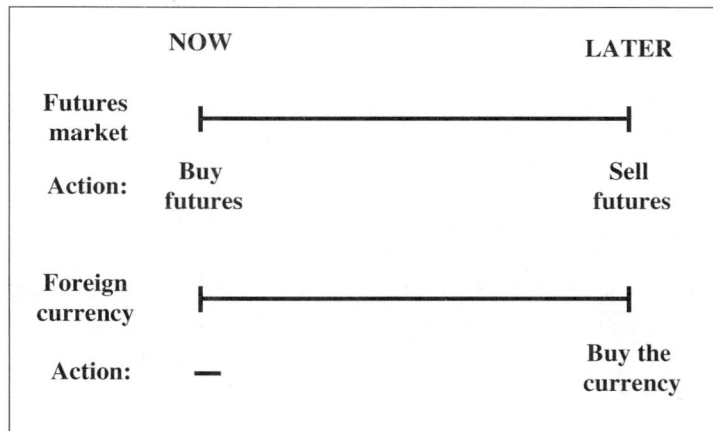

This was the procedure we used in the examples involving deutschmarks in the previous section.

- If you need to **sell** a currency on a future date for US$, take the following steps.

  Step 1. Sell the appropriate currency futures contracts now

  Step 2. Close out by buying the same number of futures contracts on the date that you sell the actual currency

7.4 EXAMPLE: CURRENCY FUTURES (1)

Natterjack Inc, an American company, will receive a dividend of three million Swiss francs in 70 days' time. What action should it take on the futures market to hedge currency risk?

7.5 SOLUTION

In 70 days, the Swiss francs will need to be sold for dollars. The company should **sell** Swiss franc futures now and buy them in 70 days when it sells the actual Swiss francs. The contract size is SFr125,000, so 24 contracts should be sold.

Non-US companies

7.6 If companies are not based in the United States but wish to hedge the receipt or payment of US dollars, they must re-state their requirements in a format which shows whether their **own currency** needs to be bought or sold.

7.7 EXAMPLE: CURRENCY FUTURES (2)

Starburst plc, a British company, expects a large receipt of US dollars in six months' time. How can it hedge this receipt on the futures market?

7.8 SOLUTION

The company cannot sell US dollar futures. They do not exist. Instead it must restate its requirements as a need to buy pounds with dollars in six months' time. It must therefore **buy sterling futures** now and sell them in six months.

7.9 EXAMPLE: CURRENCY FUTURES (3)

Geheim AG, a German company, needs to pay US dollars to an American supplier in 90 days. How can it hedge the transaction using currency futures?

7.10 SOLUTION

In 90 days the company will need to sell deutschmarks for US dollars. It should sell deutschmark futures now and buy them in 90 days.

Transactions not involving US dollars

7.11 If a company wishes to buy or sell a currency with another currency, neither of which are US dollars, it needs to deal in more than one type of contract. This complication makes the use of the currency futures markets much more complex than the use of forward markets and contributes to their relative lack of popularity.

7.12 EXAMPLE: CURRENCY FUTURES (4)

Great Eastern plc, a British company, has purchased steel from Japan and needs to pay for this in 90 days' time. How can it hedge the cost of the purchase by using currency futures?

7.13 SOLUTION

The company needs to buy Japanese yen. On the futures market, it can hedge this by buying Japanese yen futures. On the futures market yen are bought with US dollars. The company therefore needs to **sell sterling futures** (to get dollars) and **buy yen futures** (with dollars). In 90 days it will close out by buying sterling futures and selling yen futures.

How many contracts?

7.14 We have already made the point that futures can only be bought or sold as a whole number of contracts. When hedging, there is no necessary advantage in rounding **up** because futures trading can produce a loss as regularly as a profit. The problem which has not yet been covered is **how many contracts to use when the receipt or payment is in US dollars**. The method normally used is to convert to the other currency using the exchange rate implicit in the futures contract (i.e. today's contract price).

7.15 EXAMPLE: CURRENCY FUTURES (5)

Starburst plc, a British company, expects to receive 5 million US dollars in six months' time. How can it hedge this receipt on the futures market? The current spot rate is $/£ 1.5320 and the sterling futures contract is trading at $/£ 1.5275.

7.16 SOLUTION

Using the futures contract price, $5 million = £5,000,000/1.5275 = £3,273,322.
The sterling contract size = £62,500.
Number of contracts to be used = £3,273,322/£62,500 = 52.37, rounded to 52.
The company should buy 52 sterling contracts now and sell 52 contracts in six months.

7.17 EXAMPLE: CURRENCY FUTURES (6)

Great Eastern plc, a British company, has purchased steel worth Y100 million from Japan and needs to pay for this in 90 days' time. How can it hedge the cost of the purchase by using currency futures? On IMM the Japanese yen future is trading at $0.8106 per 100 yen and the Sterling future is trading at $1.6250 per pound.

7.18 SOLUTION

The company must buy yen futures and sell sterling futures. The size of the Japanese yen futures contract is Y12.5 million. The number of yen futures to buy is 100/12.5 = 8.

8 contracts represent $\dfrac{8 \times 12,500,000 \times \$0.8106}{100} = \$810,600$.

$810,600, converted at the sterling futures price, gives £ 810,600/1.6250 = £498,831. The sterling contract size is £62,500. The company should sell £498,831/£62,500 = 7.98 contracts, rounded to 8 contracts.

Summary. Today, buy 8 yen contracts and sell 8 sterling contracts. In 90 days, close out by selling 8 yen contracts and buying 8 sterling contracts.

Which settlement date?

7.19 Currency futures are traded for a period of about nine months before the settlement date is reached. This means that at any time there will be a choice of three settlement dates to choose from. To hedge currency receipts and payments a futures contract must have a settlement date *after* the date that the actual currency is needed. Usually the best hedge is achieved by selecting the contract which matures *next after* the actual cash is needed.

7.20 EXAMPLE: CURRENCY FUTURES (7)

For example, in July, suppose the following figures are quoted.

Sterling futures: contract size £62,500: price in $ per £

	12 July price
Sep	1.5552
Dec	1.5556
Mar	1.5564

Your company, based in Britain, will receive US$2,000,000 on 13 December. How should you hedge the receipt using futures?

7.21 SOLUTION

The receipt of dollars is hedged by buying sterling futures now (12 July) and selling sterling futures on 13 December. The September contract will be no use because it expires on 30 September. Either of the other two contracts can be used. It is usual to choose the contract which expires next after 13 December. This is the December contract which expires on 31 December.

Assuming the December contract is chosen, the receipt of $2,000,000 converts, using the futures contract price, to £ 2,000,000/1.5556 = £1,285,678. The contract size is £62,500. The number of contracts to be bought is £1,285,678/£62,500 = 20.57, rounded to 21 contracts.

Summary. On 12 July, buy twenty-one December sterling contracts at $/£ 1.5556. On 13 December, sell twenty-one December sterling contracts.

8 CHOOSING BETWEEN FORWARD CONTRACTS AND FUTURES CONTRACTS

8.1 A futures market hedge attempts to achieve the same result as a forward contract, that is to fix the exchange rate in advance for a future foreign currency payment or receipt. As we have seen, hedge inefficiencies mean that a futures contract can only fix the exchange rate subject to a margin of error. It is useful at this stage to consider the advantages and disadvantages of futures hedges over forward contracts and then to work some examples which compare the two.

8.2 Forward contracts are agreed 'over the counter' between a bank and its customer. Futures contracts are standardised and traded on futures exchanges. This results in the following advantages and disadvantages.

Advantages of futures over forward contracts

(a) Transaction costs should be lower.

(b) The exact date of receipt or payment of the currency does not have to be known, because the futures contract does not have to be closed out until the actual cash receipt or payment is made. In other words, the futures hedge gives the equivalent of an 'option forward' contract, limited only by the expiry date of the contract.

Disadvantages of futures compared with forward contracts

(a) The contracts cannot be tailored to the user's exact requirements.

(b) Hedge inefficiencies are caused by having to deal in a whole number of contracts and by basis risk.

(c) Only a limited number of currencies are the subject of futures contracts (although the number of currencies is growing, especially with the rapid development of Asian economies).

(d) The procedure for converting between two currencies neither of which is the US dollar is twice as complex for futures as for a forward contract.

In general, the disadvantages of futures mean that the market is much smaller than the currency forward market.

Question 2

Allbrit plc, a company based in the UK, imports and exports to the USA. On 1 May it signs three agreements, all of which are to be settled on 31 October:

(a) A sale to a US customer of goods for $205,500
(b) A sale to another US customer for £550,000
(c) A purchase from a US supplier for $875,000

On 1 June the $/£ spot rate is 1.5500 - 1.5520 and the October forward rate is at a premium of 4.00 - 3.95 cents per pound. Sterling futures contracts are trading at the following prices:

Sterling futures (IMM) Contract size £62,500

Contract settlement date	Contract price $ per £
Jun	1.5370
Sep	1.5180
Dec	1.4970

Required

(a) Compute the net amount receivable or payable in pounds if the transactions are covered on the forward market.

(b) Show how a futures hedge could be set up.

(c) Compute the result of the futures hedge if, by 31 October, the spot market price for dollars has moved to 1.5800 - 1.5820 and the December sterling futures price has moved to 1.5650.

(d) Discuss the efficiency of the futures hedge.

Answer

Before covering any transactions with forward or futures contracts, match receipts against payments. The sterling receipt does not need to be hedged. The dollar receipt can be matched against the payment giving a net payment of $669,500 on 31 October.

The appropriate spot rate for buying dollars on 1 May (bank sells) is 1.5500. The forward rate for October is *spot – premium* = 1.5500 – 0.0400 = 1.5100.

Using a forward contract, the sterling cost of the dollar payment will be 669,500/1.5100 = £443,377. The net cash received on October 31 will therefore be £550,000 – 443,377 = £106,623.

To set up a futures hedge, December contracts must be used. The June and September contracts will have expired by October. To hedge a payment of $699,000 means that the company will have to *sell* pounds to get dollars. It therefore needs to *sell* sterling futures in May and buy them in October.

The number of contracts to be sold is found by using the December futures price:

$669,500/1.4970 = £447,228, which is 447,228/62,500 contracts = 7.16 contracts, rounded to 7 contracts. The futures hedge is set up by selling seven December sterling contracts at $/£ 1.4970.

The tick value of the sterling contract is $0.0001 per pound × 62,500 = $6.25 per contract. Between May and October the dollar weakens against the pound, which means the payment in October will be cheaper than the original target, but unfortunately it also means that the futures hedge gives the company a loss.

Futures hedge

May 1: sell at	1.4970
Oct 31: buy at	1.5650
Loss in ticks	680

The total loss made on the futures hedge is 7 contracts × 680 ticks × $6.25 = $29,750. This dollar loss must be purchased at the same time as the net dollar payment of $669,500. Total dollars required is therefore $669,500 + $29,750 = $699,250. This is purchased at the spot rate on 31 October.

Cost in £ = 699,250/1.5800 = £442,563, which is slightly cheaper than the cost on the forward market. The net receipt in £ on 31 October is therefore £550,000 – £442,563 = £107,437.

The futures contract has produced a slightly better hedge than the forward rate.

In this example, the futures contract exhibits substantial basis risk because, although in May the dollar is at a substantial premium on the forward and futures markets, by October it has weakened and the December contract is much nearer its settlement date. The futures price therefore swings by more than the spot rate and gives a bigger loss than we would like. The original target payment for the US dollars at the 1 May spot rate would have been 669,500/1.5500 = £431,935. The actual payment for $669,500 at the October spot rate would have been 669,500/1.5800 = £423,734. The gain on the spot market is only £431,935 – £423,734 = £8,201.

Meanwhile the futures hedge has given a loss of $29,750, which must be paid for with pounds at $/£ 1.5800 = £18,829. The hedge efficiency is $\dfrac{\text{gain}}{\text{loss}}$ = £8,201/£18,829 = 43.6%.

Alternatively the hedge efficiency can be analysed as follows.

The spot price has increased by 300 ticks from 1.5500 to 1.5800. The futures price has increased by 680 ticks from 1.4970 to 1.5650. The hedge efficiency is $\dfrac{300 \times 7.16 \text{ contracts}}{680 \times 7 \text{ contracts}}$ = 45.1%. This is a slightly different figure from that above because of the difference in spot exchange rate between May and June.

However, in this situation it is probably fairer to measure the hedge efficiency of the future against the forward payment of £443,377 rather than the 'target' of £431,935, because the future is attempting to achieve the same result as the forward hedge.

	£
Target at forward rate	443,377
Actual at October spot rate	423,734
Gain	19,643

Hedge efficiency = 19,643/18,829 = 104.3%.

9 HEDGING ECONOMIC AND TRANSLATION EXPOSURE

Economic exposure

9.1 Earlier in this chapter we described **economic exposure** as the risk that exchange rate movements might reduce the international competitiveness of a company. More formally we might define it as the risk that the present value of a company's future cash flows might be reduced by adverse exchange rate movements. **Transaction exposure**, which has been the main subject of this chapter, can be seen as a short-term version of economic exposure. Economic exposure reveals itself in many different ways, as shown in the following examples.

9.2 Suppose a UK company invests in setting up a subsidiary in Eastern Europe. The currency of the Eastern European country depreciates continuously over a five year period. The cash flows remitted back to the UK are worth less in sterling terms each year, causing a reduction in the value of the investment project.

9.3 Another UK company buys raw materials which are priced in US dollars. It converts these materials into finished products which it exports mainly to Spain. Over a period of several years, the pound depreciates against the dollar but strengthens against the Spanish peseta. The sterling value of the company's income declines while the sterling cost of its materials increases, resulting in a drop in the value of the company's cash flows.

9.4 The value of a company depends on the present value of its expected future cash flows. If there are fears that a company is exposed to the sort of exchange rate movements described above, this may reduce the company's value. Protecting against economic exposure is therefore necessary to protect the company's share price.

9.5 A company need not even engage in any foreign activities to be subject to economic exposure. For example if a company trades only in the UK but the pound strengthens appreciably against other world currencies, it may find that it loses UK sales to a foreign competitor who can now afford to charge cheaper sterling prices.

9.6 None of these examples are as simple as they seem, however, because of the compensating actions of economic forces. For example, if the exchange rate of an Eastern European country depreciates significantly, it is probably because of its high inflation rate. We discussed **purchasing power parity**, which describes this effect, in the last chapter. So if the Eastern European subsidiary of a UK company increases its prices in line with inflation, its cash flows in the local currency will increase each year. These will be converted at the depreciating exchange rate to produce a fairly constant sterling value of cash flows. Alternatively, if the subsidiary does not increase its prices, it may increase its sales volume by selling at more competitive prices.

9.7 From this it can be seen that in the long run economic exposure is not always as bad as it seems at first sight. However, exchange rate movements can be very large, as seen in the table at the beginning of this chapter, and it may take much longer for compensating economic forces to take effect. When the pound became devalued after Britain left the European exchange rate mechanism (ERM) in 1992, many British companies benefited from increased exports but suffered when the pound strengthened in 1996. Sometimes the short or medium term makes the difference between success or bankruptcy. It is therefore very important to consider how economic exposure can be hedged.

Hedging economic exposure

9.8 Various actions can reduce economic exposure, including the following.

(a) **Matching assets and liabilities**. A foreign subsidiary can be financed, so far as possible, with a loan in the currency of the country in which the subsidiary operates. A depreciating currency results in reduced income but also reduced loan service costs. A multinational will try to match assets and liabilities in each currency so far as possible.

(b) **Diversifying the supplier and customer base**. For example, if the currency of one of the supplier countries strengthens, purchasing can be switched to a cheaper source.

(c) **Diversifying operations world-wide**. On the principle that countries which confine themselves to one country suffer from economic exposure, international diversification is a method of reducing economic exposure.

Translation exposure

9.9 **Translation exposure** is the risk that the organisation will make exchange losses when the accounting results of its foreign branches or subsidiaries are translated into the home currency. Translation losses can result, for example, from restating the book value of a foreign subsidiary's assets at the exchange rate on the balance sheet date. Such losses will not have an impact on the firm's cash flow unless the assets are sold.

9.10 There are opposing arguments as to whether translation exposure is important. The arguments centre on whether the reporting of a translation gain or loss will affect the company's share price. There is a powerful argument that, to the extent that cash flows are not affected, translation exposure can be ignored. On the other hand, those who believe that accounting results are an important determinant of share price argue that translation losses should be reduced to a minimum.

9.11 The argument can be perhaps resolved by saying that it is important to consider potential losses arising from changes to the **economic value** of assets whereas changes to their **book values** are unimportant if there is no change to the economic value. In other words, **translation exposure** is unimportant to the extent that it does not represent **economic exposure**. Following this argument, translation exposure does not need to be specifically managed if economic exposure is being properly managed. For example, the matching of assets and liabilities in each currency will hedge translation exposure as well as economic exposure.

Chapter roundup

- **Currency risk** occurs in three forms: **transaction exposure** (short-term), **economic exposure** (effect on present value of longer term cash flows) and **translation exposure** (book gains or losses). Most of this chapter has been concerned with how to reduce transaction exposure.

- The main methods discussed have been **forward contracts, money market hedges** and **futures**. Other more basic methods such as **matching** are also important in practice.

- At the end of the chapter we concluded that it is also important to hedge **economic exposure** but that **translation exposure** probably does not need to be specifically hedged.

- Two other important methods of hedging currency risk which have not yet been covered are **foreign currency options** and **currency swaps**. These will be covered in Chapters 21 and 22.

Quick quiz

1 Distinguish and briefly explain the three types of currency risk. (see para 1.8)
2 What are the main advantages of netting? (2.15)
3 Define a forward exchange contract. (3.1)
4 What is the meant by the principle of interest rate parity? (3.7)
5 What happens if a company cannot satisfy a forward exchange contract? (3.29)
6 What is a 'synthetic forward' or 'money market hedge'? (4.1)
7 What are futures? (6.1)
8 Compare the relative merits of futures and forward contracts. (8.2)
9 How can economic exposure be hedged? (9.8)

Questions to try	Level	Marks	Time
20	Introductory	n/a	35 mins

Chapter 21

OPTIONS AND OPTION VALUATION

Chapter topic list	Syllabus reference
1 The nature of options	4(b)
2 Share options	4(b)
3 Currency options	4(b)
4 Traded currency options - some complications	4(b)
5 A graphical approach to options	4(b)
6 Collars and other option combinations	4(b)
7 Theory of the valuation of options	4(b)
8 Applications of options theory	4(b)

Introduction

Options can take various forms and are important as a form of hedging instrument. Your syllabus requires a working knowledge of options, especially currency options and interest rate options. **Currency options**, the main subject of this chapter, provide a flexible method of hedging currency transactions exposure in the same sorts of situation where forward contracts, money market hedges or futures were used in the last chapter. **Interest rate options** are dealt with in detail in the next chapter. The syllabus also requires a general understanding of how options can be **valued**. This is dealt with at the end of this chapter. The chapter opens with a general introduction to options, including **share options**.

1   THE NATURE OF OPTIONS

Share option schemes

1.1   You are probably aware that share options may be issued by a company, giving their holders the right to subscribe for new ordinary shares at a predetermined price, at a certain date in the future. When options are eventually exercised, the company will issue new shares for cash. Companies which are 'floated' on the Stock Exchange main market or the second tier Alternative Investment Market might use the flotation as an opportunity to set up a share option scheme for employees.

1.2   **Share options** can also be issued by a company as a way of rewarding employees. The feature of share options is that they give the right to apply for shares at a date in the future, at a specified price that will probably be favourable to the applicant. For example, a public company whose shares are currently traded at £2 on the stock market might award share options to some of its employees, giving them the right to apply for a quantity of shares at a date in the future at a price of, say, £2. Provided that the market price of the shares rises above £2 by the time the options can be exercised, the employees would then be able:

(a)   To obtain some shares, and so get an equity interest in their company, or

BPP
PUBLISHING

(b) To obtain some shares and then sell them at a profit - the share options would then give, in effect, a cash bonus

1.3 Share option schemes are an example of options, which can take various forms, as we shall see below.

Exam focus point

Although they serve as a useful model for understanding how options in general work, **share options** are more important for fund managers than for treasurers, and so the focus in the exam will remain on **interest rate** and **currency options**.

The nature of an option

KEY TERM

An **option** is an agreement giving the **right but not the obligation** to buy or to sell a specific quantity of something (eg shares in a company, a foreign currency or a commodity) at a known or determinable price within a stated period.

1.4 The key to options of all types is that they give the holder a right but not an obligation. For example, the holder of share options at a £2 exercise price has a right to buy the shares at £2 but need not exercise this right if it is not to his or her advantage. If the market price of the shares has fallen to £1.80 then the option will not be exercised. **Options offer a choice** between:

(a) **Exercising** your right to buy or sell at a pre-determined price (known as the **exercise price**, or **strike price**), and

(b) Not exercising this right: allowing the option to lapse, sometimes known as **abandoning** the option - an option which is not used is either discarded or, possibly, sold to somebody else who might find it valuable, if the rules allow this

It is this element of choice which is the big distinction between options and futures or forward contracts. This distinction will be explored in detail later in the chapter.

1.5 An employee share option scheme involves the **issue of new shares** by the company if the options are exercised, and earnings per share will be diluted. Exactly the same thing happens if warrants are issued (see Chapter 4). A rights issue is another example of this type of option. The shareholders are given the right but not the obligation to buy new shares at the discounted issue price. If they choose not to exercise their rights they can sell their rights (ie sell the option) to another investor.

1.6 However, not all options are of this type. Most options are options to buy or sell assets which already exist. They are known as **pure options.** A pure share option is an option to buy or sell shares which are already in issue. If one person exercises the option to buy shares then another person must sell, but the company does not issue new shares. Similarly a currency option is an option to buy or sell currency which already exists. No new currency is issued by the government. The remainder of this chapter is concerned with pure options and their use both for speculation and to hedge risk.

> ## KEY TERM
>
> **Derivative**: a financial security whose value is derived partly from the value and characteristics of an underlying security. Option contracts, financial futures and swaps are types of derivative.

Option writers and option purchasers

1.7 A pure option is created by an **option writer**. As an example, suppose that the writer drafts an option contract and gives it to another party (whom we will call the **holder**) which allows the holder to buy one hundred shares in Cresco plc (a fictional company) at 400 pence each on 30 June. The company's share price is at the moment 390 pence. Consider the holder's position if the share price on 30 June (a) rises to 450 pence (b) falls to 330 pence.

1.8 In situation (a) the option holder exercises the right to buy 100 shares at 400p each and immediately sells them on the market for 450 pence each, making a total gain of £50. Where does the holder buy the shares at 400p? No new shares are issued, so the option holder must buy them from the option writer. If the option writer does not own Cresco shares, he must buy them on the market for 450p and sell them to the option holder for 400p, making a loss of £50. So in situation (a), the holder makes a profit out of the writer.

1.9 In situation (b) the holder does not exercise the option, but allows it to lapse, destroying the option agreement and forgetting about it. Both the holder and the writer have made no gain and no loss.

1.10 The option holder will clearly be very happy with this option agreement. If Cresco shares rise she makes a gain, but if they fall she makes no loss. The writer, however, is in a no-win situation. If the shares rise, he loses, and if they fall he makes no gain.

1.11 So why would anybody want to write options? The answer is because the writer does not give the options away but **sells** them. If we assume that the two situations (a) and (b) above are equally likely, the expected value of the writer's loss from the option is $0.5 \times £50 + 0.5 \times 0 = £25$. Ignoring the time value of money, the writer should sell the option on Cresco shares for at least £25.

1.12 In order to acquire an option, then, you have to **purchase** it. Note that this is different from a forward contract or a future. You have to purchase an option because it gives you a powerful choice, which you can use to limit your risk. The option writer accepts the risk which the purchaser avoids. The writer therefore needs to be paid in compensation.

1.13 Let us take another example, involving foreign currencies. Suppose a British company needs to buy one million Singapore dollars to pay for imports of computer disk drives in one month's time. Suppose also that the Singapore dollar (S$) is expected to weaken over the next month but that a hedge should be taken out against a possible strengthening in the exchange rate. An option writer sells the company an option to buy S$ with pounds at the exercise price of S$/£ 2.20.

1.14 If the S$ strengthens to say S$/£ 2.10, the option is exercised to buy S$1 million at S$/£ 2.20 (cost = £454,545) because this is cheaper than using the spot market exchange rate of S$/£ 2.10 (cost = £476,190). But what the company is really hoping for is that the S$ will weaken,

BPP PUBLISHING

say to S$/£ 2.30, in which case the option will be abandoned and the S$ will be bought at the spot rate of S$/£ 2.30, giving a cost of only £434,783.

In this example the company has purchased an option as a hedge, **but it hopes that it will not have to use it**. In this respect an option hedge is like an insurance policy. The company purchases the option from the writer in the same way as an individual may purchase medical insurance. It is there if you need it, but you hope you will not need it.

1.15 To pursue the analogy a bit further, the price at which an option writer sells an option to a purchaser is known as the **option premium** - the same term as the price of an insurance policy. The insurer takes the risk off the insured party's shoulders in exchange for a premium. The option writer takes the risk off the option purchaser's shoulders in exchange for an option premium.

1.16 Where can the prospective purchaser of an option find an option writer? Either by approaching a financial institution directly or by using a traded options exchange. The following paragraphs use share options to illustrate the different types of options and the terminology involved.

2 SHARE OPTIONS

Negotiated share options

2.1 A company or an investor can arrange a tailor-made option for their specific needs with a financial institution, and this is called a **negotiated option** or an **over-the-counter** option. Negotiated share options may be for any number of shares or other stocks (except gilts). In practice, negotiated options are often for either 16 days or 3 months, the latter being more common.

> **KEY TERMS**
>
> An investor may acquire a **call option**, which means he is entitled to buy the shares at the exercise price within the specified period, or a **put option** which means he has the right to sell the shares at the exercise price within the specified period, or he may take a two-way option or a **double option** (also called a **straddle**) which gives the right to buy or sell (and costs about twice as much). A **naked option** is one that is held on its own, and not as a hedge against loss.

2.2 The price written into the option (called the **exercise price** or **strike price**) will be slightly lower than the current bid price (the price at which a market maker will buy the share) for a put option and slightly higher than the current offer price for a call option. For example, if the current quotation were 393-397 for shares in ABC the striking price for a call option might be 400 and for a put option, 390.

Traded options in shares

2.3 One of the disadvantages of negotiated options is that because they are all different, there is no ready market for them. This problem is overcome by **traded options**, which are traded on LIFFE and similar exchanges.

2.4 Share option contracts are normally for 1,000 shares. Where there has been a change which affects the number of the underlying shares in issue, such as a share split or a bonus issue, the option contract may be for a different amount. Traded options are available only in about 60 financially strong companies, and in the FT-SE 100 index. (Index options are explained further below.)

> **KEY TERMS**
>
> An **American-style option** is an option that can be exercised on any day until the expiry date. A **European-style option** is one which can only be exercised on the expiry date. This terminology is however potentially misleading, since most options traded in the UK and Europe are in fact American options.

2.5 There are two parties to each traded option contract: the person who receives the option money in exchange for granting an option (the seller) and the person who buys the option. Someone who sells an option he does not already own is known as a 'writer'. Anybody who can satisfy the Stock Exchange of his creditworthiness can write traded options but, as with negotiated options, it is usually done by institutions. Unlike negotiated options, a traded option position can be closed at any time by either party. The writer simply buys an option of the same series and the original buyer simply sells one. Positions may also be closed by matching call and put options with the same exercise price and the same expiry date. In practice, only a few traded options are ever actually exercised, and so no actual shares are involved in the transaction.

Prices of traded options

2.6 Prices of traded share options are quoted in tables, such as the following for options on shares in Reuters.

LIFFE: Reuters - underlying security price 679   (7 May)

		Calls			Puts	
Exercise price	*Jul*	*Oct*	*Jan*	*Jul*	*Oct*	*Jan*
650	52	67	84	14½	24	31½
700	25	41	58	37½	44½	55

2.7 The table shows that, on the day in question, Reuters shares are trading at 679 pence. Both call (buy) and put (sell) options are available, with expiry dates at the end of July, October and January. There are two possible exercise prices, one at below the current share price (650p) and one above it (700p). The figures in the table show the price (premium) per share of each option contract.

2.8 An option is said to be **in the money** when, if it were exercised today, a profit would be made. A call option is in the money if the exercise price is below the underlying security price. All the 650 call options are in the money. A put option is in the money if the exercise price is above the underlying security price. All the 700 put options are in the money.

2.9 An option is said to be **out of the money** when, if it were exercised today, a loss would be made (consequently it would not be exercised today). A call option is out of the money if the exercise price is above the underlying security price. All the 700 call options are out of the money. A put option is out of the money if the exercise price is below the underlying security price. All the 650 put options are out of the money.

2.10 An option is said to be **at the money** when the exercise price equals the underlying security price. If the Reuters share price were to rise to 700p, all the 700 options would be at the money.

2.11 For all traded options there will be at least one exercise price above the current share price and another below it. If the Reuters share price were to rise above 700p (for at least three days) a new series of options with exercise price 750p would be created.

Intrinsic value and time value

2.12 The **intrinsic value** of an option is computed by assuming that its expiry date is today. 'In the money' options would be exercised and have a value equal to the difference between the exercise price and the current share price. 'Out of the money' options would not be exercised and would therefore have zero intrinsic value. The intrinsic value of calls and puts can be summarised in the following formulae.

(a) The **intrinsic value of a call option** is the higher of (i) share price *minus* exercise price; and (ii) zero.

(b) The **intrinsic value of a put option** is the higher of (i) exercise price *minus* share price; and (ii) zero.

2.13 Intrinsic values of the Reuters options as at 7 May in a particular year are shown in the table below.

Intrinsic values - Reuters share options

	Calls			Puts		
Exercise price	*Jul*	*Oct*	*Jan*	*Jul*	*Oct*	*Jan*
650	29	29	29	0	0	0
700	0	0	0	21	21	21

2.14 By comparing with the original table, we can see that in all cases the actual option prices are higher than the intrinsic value. This is because options also have a **time value**. In the period between today (in this example, 7 May) and the expiry date of the options there is a chance that the share price might rise, giving greater gains for call options, or it might fall, benefiting put options. The time value can be computed for each option as the difference between the option's actual value and its intrinsic value.

Time values - Reuters share options

	Calls			Puts		
Exercise price	*Jul*	*Oct*	*Jan*	*Jul*	*Oct*	*Jan*
650	23	38	55	14½	24	31½
700	25	41	58	16½	23½	34

2.15 Note that the **time value** of *all* options increases with the **time period to expiry**. The time value actually depends on a number of factors, which include:

(a) The time period to expiry of the option
(b) The volatility of the underlying security price
(c) The general level of interest rates (the time value of money)

How these different factors combine to give an option its value is discussed later in this chapter.

Exercise and assignment

2.16   An investor may choose to exercise a share option which he holds rather than to sell it back into the market, for a number of reasons.

  (a) If he had been expecting a bid for the company to emerge or if he was expecting funds to become available which he wanted to invest in a popular company, he might exercise the appropriate call option in order to claim the shares once either of these events had occurred.

  (b) If he had been holding shares in order to receive the dividend or to vote in a shareholders' meeting, or if bad news had been announced affecting the company's prospects, he might exercise a put option to rid himself of the shares.

2.17   When an option is exercised, all writers stand an equal chance of being selected on any one of the options they have written. This process is known as **assignment**. Once notice of assignment has been received (by means of computer), the writer cannot trade the option but must buy or sell shares in order to complete his side of the bargain.

  (a) Someone who has written call options against shares which he already owns has written a **covered call**. He simply sells his shares through the market at the exercise price.

  (b) Writers of **naked calls** hold no shares. They must buy shares in the market at whatever price they can in order to satisfy their side of the bargain.

  (c) Writers of **naked puts** must buy shares at the exercise price whether they want them or not. If they do not wish to hold the shares, they can close their position by selling them into the market at whatever price they can obtain.

Attractions of traded options

2.18   Traded options can be very speculative investments. However, they may also be used in many other ways. The majority of traded options are dealt in by institutional investors who:

  (a) Write call options or buy put options to protect the portfolios which they manage

  (b) Buy call options as part of their overall portfolio management. Call options allow them to control their cashflows very effectively while leaving them free to take advantage of stockmarket changes

  (c) Take 'covered' option positions which allow them the chance to make profits for a known amount of risk

2.19   The private investor who favours traded options is likely to be wealthy. He may:

  (a) Buy puts or calls as a pure gamble

  (b) Sell call options against shares which he owns in the hope of increasing his gain on those shares

  (c) Buy put options to protect the value of shares which he owns

Index options

Exam focus point
Index options are unlikely to be examined in detail, but you should be aware of their existence.

BPP
PUBLISHING

2.20 As already mentioned, traded options are available on the FT-SE 100 share index. This class of **index options** was introduced following the popularity of similar investment instruments in the USA.

2.21 Each **contract** is for a notional value of the index value multiplied by £10. Thus, if the index stands at 4,500, the notional value of a contract is £45,000. Exercise prices are set at intervals of 50 index points (eg 4,400, 4,450, 4,500, 4,550 etc). Prices (or **premiums**) are quoted in pence as the price of 1/1,000th of the contract. Thus, if an option is bought at 35p, the price per contract will be £350 (1,000 × 35p). The procedure for creation and valuation of the options is the same as for other traded options. However, there are different expiry dates. There are also four series, set one month apart.

2.22 Index options can be useful to an investor in a number of ways, either for speculative purposes or as a 'hedge' against risk of adverse movements in market prices generally. For example, an investor may be convinced that the market is set to rise but he is not completely confident of any individual stock nor does he have sufficient funds to acquire a well-diversified equity portfolio. He may then buy index call options which he hopes will rise in value with the market. Suppose he bought one 4,600 call contract at 36p. He would have paid £360 before expenses (see above). If the index rises to 4,690, he may be able to sell his contract at (say) 96p or £960 in total, giving a profit before expenses of £600. When the index stands at 4,690, a 4,600 call option will have an intrinsic value of £10 × (4,690 – 4,600) = £900, or, in terms of the quoted price, £900 ÷ 1,000 = 90p. In other words, of the 96p price 90p is intrinsic value and 6p is time value. This reflects the fact that the index has time to rise further before the expiry of the option. If the investor exercised his option instead of selling it, he would realise only the intrinsic value.

2.23 Consider the position of another investor who acquires 10,000 shares in Superprofit plc (a company in which traded options are not available) when the share price is standing at 450 pence and the index is 4500. The investor is convinced that Superprofit will outperform the market but is worried that share prices in general will fall. The value of his shares is currently £45,000. He decides to buy one FT-SE 100 put option contract, exercise price 4500 at a premium price of 40p, total cost 1,000 × 40p = £400. Some time later his fears have been justified. The index has fallen to 3600 (a 20% fall) and the price of Superprofit shares to 405p (a 10% fall). The value of the put options (which still have some time to run before expiry) has risen to 920p, at which price he sells them. His overall position is as follows:

	£
Gain on options: 1000 × (920p – 40p)	8,800
Loss on shares: 10,000 × (450p – 405p)	4,500
Overall gain	4,300

2.24 The gain from the FT-SE option is nearly twice the loss from the fall in the value of the shares, reflecting the relative movement of the index compared with the share price. When the FT-SE option was purchased it had an intrinsic value of zero and a time value of 40p. When it was sold, its intrinsic value was (4500 – 3600) × £10/1,000 = 900p, implying a time value of 20p reflecting the fact that there is still some time before the expiry of the option.

3 CURRENCY OPTIONS 6/94, 6/95, 12/96, 6/98

3.1 Forward exchange contracts and currency futures contracts are contracts to buy or sell a given quantity of foreign exchange, which must be carried out because they are binding contracts. Some exporters might be uncertain about the amount of currency they will earn in several months time, and so would be unable to enter forward exchange contracts or futures contracts without the risk of contracting to sell more or less currency to their bank than they will actually earn when the time comes. An alternative method of obtaining foreign exchange cover which overcomes much of the problem is the **foreign currency option**.

> ## KEY TERM
>
> A **currency option** is an agreement involving a right, but not an obligation, to buy or to sell a certain amount of currency at a stated rate of exchange (the **exercise price**) at some time in the future.

3.2 As with other types of option, **buying** a currency option involves paying a premium, which is the most the buyer of the option can lose. **Selling** (or 'writing') options, unless covered by other transactions, is risky because the seller ('writer') bears the whole of the cost of the variation and can face potentially unlimited losses. Such risks received much publicity with the Barings Bank failure in 1995.

3.3 Some terminology relating to traded options was explained in the previous section of the chapter in the context of options to buy and sell shares. Much of the same terminology applies to currency options.

(a) **Call options** give the buyer of the option the right to buy the underlying currency at a fixed rate of exchange (and the seller of the option would be required to sell the underlying currency at that rate). **Put options** give the buyer of the option the right to sell the underlying currency at a fixed rate of exchange (and the seller of the option would be required to buy the underlying currency at that rate).

(b) The **exercise price** may be the same as the current spot rate, or it may be more favourable or less favourable to the option holder than the current spot rate. Options are **at the money, in the money** or **out of the mone**y accordingly.

(c) **Over the counter (OTC)** or **negotiated currency options** are tailor-made options available from a bank, suited to the company's specific needs. **Traded options** or **exchange-traded** options are standardised options, available from an options exchange in certain currencies only.

3.4 A company wishing to purchase an option to buy or sell sterling might use currency options traded on the important Philadelphia Stock Exchange. The schedule of prices for £/$ options is set out in tables such as the one shown below.

Philadelphia SE £/$ options £31,250 (cents per pound)

Strike price	Aug	Calls Sep	Oct	Aug	Puts Sep	Oct
1.575	2.58	3.13	-	-	0.67	-
1.580	2.14	2.77	3.24	-	0.81	1.32
1.590	1.23	2.17	2.64	0.05	1.06	1.71
1.600	0.50	1.61	2.16	0.32	1.50	2.18
1.610	0.15	1.16	1.71	0.93	2.05	2.69
1.620	-	0.81	1.33	1.79	2.65	3.30

3.5 Note the following points.

(a) The contract size is £31,250.

(b) If a firm wished to have the option to buy pounds (selling dollars) in September, it can buy a call option on sterling. To have the option to buy pounds at an exchange rate of $1.580/£, it would need to pay a premium of 2.77 cents per pound (check for yourself in the table). For a higher exchange rate, the premium is lower, since the higher exchange rate is less favourable to the buyer of the option: more dollars are needed to buy the same number of pounds.

(c) A put option here is the option to sell sterling in exchange for dollars. Note that a put option with a strike price of 1.600 $/£ exercisable in September is, at 1.50 cents per pound, cheaper than a September put option exercisable at 1.610 $/£, which is available at a premium of 2.05 cents per pound. The premium on put options is higher for the higher exchange rate since the purchaser will receive more dollars for each pound sold than with the lower exchange rate.

(d) Note that a call option with a strike price of 1.600 $/£ exercisable in September will cost more than an option with the same strike price which is exercisable in August. This difference reflects the fact that for the September option there is a longer period until the exercise date and consequently the likelihood of it being beneficial to exercise the option is increased (ie it is more likely to be 'in the money' at the exercise date). The difference also reflects the market's view of the direction in which the exchange rate is likely to move between the two dates.

The purpose of currency options

3.6 The main purpose of currency options is to reduce exposure to adverse currency movements, while allowing the holder to profit from favourable currency movements. They are particularly useful for companies in the following situations:

(a) Where there is uncertainty about foreign currency receipts or payments, either in timing or amount. Should the foreign exchange transaction not materialise, the option can be sold on the market (if it has any value) or exercised if this would make a profit.

(b) To support the tender for an overseas contract, priced in a foreign currency (see example below).

(c) To allow the publication of price lists for its goods in a foreign currency.

(d) To protect the import or export of price-sensitive goods. If there is a favourable movement in exchange rates, options allow the importer/exporter to profit from the favourable change (unlike forward exchange contracts, when the importer/exporter is tied to a fixed rate of exchange by the binding contract). This means that the gains can be passed on in the prices to the importer's or exporter's customers.

3.7 In both situations (b) and (c), the company would not know whether it had won any export sales or would have any foreign currency income at the time that it announces its selling prices. It cannot make a forward exchange contract to sell foreign currency without becoming exposed in the currency.

3.8 EXAMPLE: CURRENCY OPTIONS (1)

Tartan plc has been invited to tender for a contract in Blueland with the bid priced in Blues (the local currency). Tartan thinks that the contract would cost £1,850,000. Because of the fierce competition for the bid, Tartan is prepared to price the contract at £2,000,000, and since the exchange rate is currently B2.80 = £1, it puts in a bid of B5,600,000. The contract will not be awarded until after six months.

3.9 What can happen to Tartan with the contract? There are two 'worst possible' outcomes.

(a) Tartan plc decides to hedge against the currency risk, and on the assumption that it will be awarded the contract in six months time, it enters into a forward exchange contract to sell B5,600,000 in six months time at a rate of B2.8 = £1.

As it turns out, the company fails to win the contract and so it must buy B5,600,000 spot to meet its obligation under the forward contract. The exchange rate has changed, say, to B2.5 = £1.

	£
At the outset:	
Tartan sells B5,600,000 forward at B2.8 to £1	2,000,000
Six months later:	
Tartan buys B5,600,000 spot to cover the hedge, at B2.5 to £1	(2,240,000)
Loss	(240,000)

(b) Alternatively, Tartan plc might decide not to make a forward exchange contract at all, but to wait and see what happens. As it turns out, Tartan is awarded the contract six months later, but by this time, the value of the Blue has fallen, say, to B3.2 = £1.

	£
Tartan wins the contract for B5,600,000, which has a sterling value of	
(B3.2 = £1)	1,750,000
Cost of the contract	(1,850,000)
Loss	(100,000)

A currency option would, for a fixed cost, eliminate these risks for Tartan plc. When it makes its tender for the contract, Tartan might purchase an over-the-counter currency option to sell B5,600,000 in six months time at B2.8 to £1, at a cost of £40,000.

The worst possible outcome for Tartan plc is now a loss of £40,000. If the company **fails to win the contract**, Tartan will abandon the option (unless the exchange rate has moved in Tartan's favour and the Blue has weakened against sterling so that the company can make a profit by buying B5,600,000 at the spot rate and selling it at B2.8 = £1). If the company **wins the contract** and the exchange rate of the Blue has weakened against sterling, Tartan will exercise the option and sell the Blues at 2.80.

	£	£
Proceeds from selling B5,600,000		2,000,000
Cost of contract	1,850,000	
Cost of currency option	40,000	
		1,890,000
Net profit		110,000

(c) If the Blue has strengthened against sterling, Tartan will abandon the option. For example, if Tartan wins the contract and the exchange rate has moved to B2.5 = £1, Tartan will sell the B5,600,000 at this rate to earn £2,240,000, and will incur costs, including the abandoned currency option, of £1,890,000.

	£	£
Proceeds from selling B5,600,000		2,240,000
Cost of contract	1,850,000	
Cost of currency option	40,000	
		1,890,000
Net profit		350,000

Tutorial note. In practice the currency option could be used to cover the period between the date when Tartan makes the tender offer and the date when the Blueland purchaser awards the contract, if this date is known in advance. Any further period until the sales proceeds are received could be covered by a forward contract or a money market hedge.

Comparison of currency options with forward contracts and futures contracts

3.10 In the last chapter, we saw that a hedge using a currency future will produce approximately the same result as a currency forward contract, subject to hedge inefficiencies. When comparing currency options with forward or futures contracts we usually find the following.

(a) If the currency movement is adverse, the option will be exercised, but the hedge will not normally be quite as good as that of the forward or futures contract; this is because of the **premium cost of the option**.

(b) If the currency movement is favourable, the option will not be exercised, and the result will normally be better than that of the forward or futures contract; this is because the option allows the holder to **profit from the improved exchange rate**.

These points are illustrated by the next series of examples.

3.11 EXAMPLE: CURRENCY OPTIONS (2)

Crabtree plc is expecting to receive 20 million Austrian schillings (Sch) in one month's time. The current spot rate is Sch/£ 19.3383 - 19.3582. Compare the results of the following actions.

(a) The receipt is hedged using a forward contract at the rate 19.3048.

(b) The receipt is hedged by buying an over-the-counter (OTC) option from the bank, exercise price Sch/£ 19.30, premium cost 12 pence per 100 schillings.

(c) The receipt is not hedged.

In each case compute the results if, in one month, the exchange rate moves to:

(a) 21.00;
(b) 17.60.

3.12 SOLUTION

The target receipt at today's spot rate is 20,000,000/19.3582 = £1,033,154.

(a) The receipt using forward contract is fixed with certainty at 20,000,000/19.3048 = £1,036,012. This applies to both exchange rate scenarios.

(b) The cost of the option is 20,000,000/100 × 12/100 = £24,000. This must be paid at the start of the contract.

The results under the two scenarios are as follows.

Scenario	(a)	(b)
Exchange rate	21.00	17.60
Exercise price	19.30	19.30
Exercise option?	YES	NO
Exchange rate used	19.30	17.60
	£	£
Pounds received	1,036,269	1,136,364
Less option premium	24,000	24,000
Net receipt	1,012,269	1,112,364

(c) The results of not hedging under the two scenarios are as follows.

Scenario	(a)	(b)
Exchange rate	21.00	17.60
Pounds received	£952,381	£1,136,364

Summary. The option gives a result between that of the forward contract and no hedge. If the Austrian schilling weakens to 21.00, the best result would have been obtained using the forward market (£1,036,012). If it strengthens to 17.60, the best course of action would have been to take no hedge (£1,136,364). In both cases the option gives the second best result, being £24,000 below the best because of its premium cost.

3.13 EXAMPLE: CURRENCY OPTIONS (3)

In *Example: currency options (2)*, by how much would the exchange rate have moved if the forward and option contracts gave the same result? Comment on your answer.

3.14 SOLUTION

The forward contract gives a receipt of £1,036,012 whatever the movement in exchange rate. If the option is to give a net receipt of £1,036,012, it must give a gross amount (before deducting the premium) of £1,036,012 + £24,000 = £1,060,012. This implies that the exchange rate has moved to 20,000,000/1,060,012 = 18.87 schillings to the pound.

The option will not be exercised at this exchange rate. It is allowed to lapse, giving an exchange gain which just covers the premium cost. The option becomes advantageous over a forward contract if the exchange rate strengthens beyond 18.87 schillings to the pound.

3.15 EXAMPLE: CURRENCY OPTIONS (4)

Prices (premiums) on 1 June for Sterling traded currency options on the Philadelphia Stock Exchange are shown in the following table:

Sterling £31,250 contracts (cents per £)

Exercise price	Calls		Puts	
$/£	September	December	September	December
1.50	5.55	7.95	0.42	1.95
1.55	2.75	3.85	4.15	6.30
1.60	0.25	1.00	9.40	11.20

Prices are quoted in cents per £. On the same date, the September sterling futures contract (contract size £62,500) is trading at $/£ 1.5390 and the current spot exchange rate is $1.5404 - $1.5425. Stark Inc, a US company, is due to receive sterling £3.75 million from a debtor in four months' time at the end of September. The treasurer decides to hedge this receipt using either September £ traded options or September £ futures.

Required

Compute the results of using futures and options hedges (illustrating the results with all three possible option exercise prices) if by the end of September the spot exchange rate moves to (i) 1.48; (ii) 1.57; (iii) 1.62. Assume that the futures price moves by the same amount as the spot rate and that by the end of September the options contracts are on the last day before expiry.

3.16 SOLUTION

The target receipt is 3,750,000 × 1.5404★ = $5,776,500.

★The American company gets the lower number of dollars for selling sterling.

A receipt of £3.75 million will represent 3,750,000/62,500 = 60 futures contracts or 3,750,000/31,250 = 120 option contracts. The value of a one-tick movement will be $6.25 on the futures contract (and $3.125 on the options contract, although this figure will not be needed in the calculation).

3.17 The results of using futures hedges are shown first. If we make the assumption that the futures price moves by the same amount as the spot rate, there will be no basis risk and the future will give a perfect hedge.

On 1 June, 60 sterling futures contracts are sold for $1.5390 (a price which is $0.0014 below the spot rate). The results of his hedge are as follows.

Scenario	(i)	(ii)	(iii)
Spot rate, 30 Sept	1.4800	1.5700	1.6200
Sell 60 at	1.5390	1.5390	1.5390
Buy 60 at (spot - 0.0014)	1.4786	1.5686	1.6186
Gain/(loss) in ticks	604	(296)	(796)
	$	$	$
Value of gain/(loss)	226,500	(111,000)	(298,500)
£3.75 million sold at spot for	5,550,000	5,887,500	6,075,000
Total net receipt	5,776,500	5,776,500	5,776,500

3.18 Using options, the treasurer will purchase 120 September *put* options. The premium cost will vary with the exercise price as follows.

Exercise price	Cost $
1.50	120 × 0.42/100 × 31,250 = $15,750
1.55	120 × 4.15/100 × 31,250 = $155,625
1.60	120 × 9.40/100 × 31,250 = $352,500

Scenario 1 - spot rate moves to 1.48

In all cases, exercise the option and sell £3.75 million at the exercise price.

Exercise price $/£	Cash received $	Premium cost $	Net $	
1.50	5,625,000	(15,750)	5,609,250	
1.55	5,812,500	(155,625)	5,656,875	← *Best result*
1.60	6,000,000	(352,500)	5,647,500	

In practice, the options will probably be sold (closed out) rather than exercised. On the last day before expiry, the option premium will be equal to its intrinsic value (no time value), so the gain made from closing out the option will be exactly equivalent to exercising the option. For ease of demonstration in exam questions, it is usually easier to assume the option is exercised rather than sold, unless there is a significant time before expiry of the option.

Scenario 2

Spot rate moves to 1.57.

Exercise price	Exercise option?	Exchange rate used	Cash received $	Premium cost $	Net $	
1.50	No	1.57	5,887,500	(15,750)	5,871,750	←*Best*
1.55	No	1.57	5,887,500	(155,625)	5,731,875	
1.60	Yes	1.60	6,000,000	(352,500)	5,647,500	

Scenario 3

Spot rate moves to 1.62.

In all cases, abandon the option.

Cash received = $6,075,000

Exercise price	Cash received $	Premium cost $	Net $	
1.50	6,075,000	(15,750)	6,059,250	←*Best*
1.55	6,075,000	(155,625)	5,919,375	
1.60	6,075,000	(352,500)	5,722,500	

Summary. The futures hedge achieves the target exactly. The options give a range of possible results around the target. As in the previous example when the option is exercised, it does not give as good a result as the future. However, when the option is allowed to lapse because of a favourable movement in the exchange rate, it allows the company to make a gain over target.

3.19 It is possible to do a simple computation to predict the best exercise price under each scenario. If the pound strengthens, as in scenarios (ii) and (iii), the options are not needed, so, with the benefit of hindsight, the best option is the one with the cheapest premium (just as the best car insurance is the cheapest, provided you don't need to use it!) In this case it is the 1.50 exercise price.

3.20 However, if the pound weakens the options will be exercised. The best exercise price will be the one which gives the highest net $ per £ when the premium is deducted. For this purpose, the premium must be expressed as $ per £ (ie divide the quoted premium by 100).

Best option if exercised

Exercise price $/£	Premium $/£	Net $/£	
1.50	(0.0042)	1.4958	
1.55	(0.0415)	1.5085	← *Best*
1.60	(0.0940)	1.5060	

Thus, in scenario (i), the best option is the 1.55 exercise price.

3.21 *Note*. A similar computation can be carried out to determine the best *call* option if exercised. This will be the exercise price which gives the minimum total $ cost per £ when the exercise price and the premium are added together. For example, suppose the company needed to *buy* £3.75 million at the end of September. The best option, if exercised, would be found by adding the exercise prices and premiums of the September call options.

Exercise price $/£	Premium $/£	Total $/£	
1.50	0.0555	1.5555	← *Best* (cheapest cost per £)
1.55	0.0275	1.5775	
1.60	0.0025	1.6025	

On the other hand, if the dollar strengthens and the options are not exercised, the best option would have been the one with the cheapest premium (i.e. the 1.60 exercise price).

4 TRADED CURRENCY OPTIONS - SOME COMPLICATIONS

4.1 The last example showed how traded options can be used as a hedge to reduce currency losses while allowing the possibility of exchange gains if there are favourable exchange rate movements. As with futures, a number of complications are encountered when using traded options. The most important of these complications are:

- Choosing the correct type of option (call or put)
- Choosing the exercise price and the number of contracts to be used
- Surplus cash when the number of contracts is rounded
- Closing out when traded options still have time to run
- Use of collars to reduce the option premium cost

Choosing the correct type of option

4.2 In the previous example the American company needed to sell pounds sterling. It therefore purchased options to sell pounds, which are sterling put options. Note that the vast majority of options examples which we consider are concerned with **hedgers** who **purchase** options in order to reduce risk. We are seldom concerned with option writers. The only times that we normally consider selling options are either when we wish to close out options which have already been purchased or when we wish to create a 'collar'. Both of these situations are dealt with later.

4.3 So, given that we are normally going to *purchase* options, should we purchase puts or calls? With OTC options there is usually no problem in making this decision. If, for example, we may need to buy US dollars at some stage in the future, we can hedge by purchasing a US dollar call option. With traded options, however, we run into the same problem as with futures. Only a limited number of currencies are available and there is no US dollar option as such. We have to rephrase the company's requirements, as we did with futures.

4.4 For example, a UK company wishing to sell US dollars in the future can hedge by purchasing £ sterling call options (ie options to buy sterling with dollars). Similarly, a German company which needs to buy US dollars can hedge by purchasing D-Mark put options.

Choosing the exercise price and the number of contracts to be used

4.5 When the American company wished to sell £3.75 million, the computation of the number of contracts was easy (£3,750,000/£31,250 = 120 option contracts). A problem arises when a non-US company wishes to buy or sell US dollars using traded options. The amount of US dollars must first be converted into the home currency. For this purpose the best exchange rate to use is the exercise price, which means that the number of contracts may vary according to which exercise price is chosen. The following example demonstrates this problem.

4.6 EXAMPLE: CURRENCY OPTIONS (5)

A British company needs to hedge the receipt of US$ 10 million from an American customer at the end of June. The spot rate is (US$/£) 1.4461 - 1.4492 and the 30 June forward rate is 1.4050 - 1.4101. The following currency options are available.

Sterling £31,250 contracts (cents per £)

Exercise price	Calls	Puts
$/£	June	June
1.400	5.74	7.89
1.425	3.40	9.06
1.450	1.94	11.52
1.475	0.89	14.69

4.7 The company needs to purchase sterling call options. If the exercise price chosen is 1.40, the value of $10 million is £7,142,857, which is 228.57 contracts. If the exercise price of 1.475 is used, the $10 million becomes £6,779,661, which is 216.95 contracts. Under such circumstances it becomes too lengthy (in exam-style questions) to test out the results of all possible exercise prices in detail. It is usually better to choose one exercise price to demonstrate how the option works.

4.8 There are various ways of choosing an exercise price and an appropriate number of contracts and in the end the choice is subjective. However the following method is suggested for exam questions. The company wants to pay as little as possible for its pounds. Assuming the options are to be exercised, it can find this cheapest figure by adding together the exercise prices and the premiums, as in the example in the previous section.

Exercise price	Premium	Total	
$/£	$/£	$/£	
1.4000	0.0574	1.4574	← *Best* (cheapest cost per £)
1.4250	0.0340	1.4590	
1.4500	0.0194	1.4694	
1.4750	0.0089	1.4839	

4.9 The cheapest total cost per pound is $1.4574 resulting from an exercise price of 1.4000. At this exercise price, the receipt of $10 million converts to £7,142,857 which, with a contract size of £31,250, represents 228.57 contracts, rounded to 229.

4.10 As stated above, many alternatives are available for choosing an exercise price. Some might choose the 1.475 exercise price, simply because it has the cheapest premium. This would be the best option if the dollar strengthens and the option is abandoned. Others might choose the exercise price nearest the spot rate, and still others might choose the exercise price nearest the June forward rate. In the end there is no right answer, because the future is unknown. If you knew the future, you would not need an option. You would either need a forward contract or no hedge at all.

Surplus cash when the number of contracts is rounded

4.11 Assume that the company chooses to hedge the receipt of $10 million by purchasing 229 June £ call option contracts, exercise price 1.400 $/£. Demonstrate the result if the spot rate on June 30 is (i) 1.55; (ii) 1.35.

4.12 The premium cost is 229 × $0.0574 × 31,250 = $410,769. This must be purchased at today's spot $/£ rate, which is 1.4461, giving a cost of £284,053.

Scenario (i)

The option will be exercised and £31,250 × 229 = £7,156,250 will be purchased with 7,156,250 × 1.40 = $10,018,750. The customer provides $10,000,000, but $18,750 has to be purchased at the June 30 spot rate of 1.55 $/£, giving an additional cost of £12,097. (Note that this additional amount *could* have been covered on the forward market, but that this would have created an exchange loss under Scenario (ii) when the option is abandoned. We therefore assume that forward cover is not taken).

The total sterling amount received from the sale of $10 million is:

	£
Option premium paid	(284,053)
£ purchased by exercising option	7,156,250
Purchase of surplus $ on 30 June	(12,097)
Net £ received	6,860,100

Note. An approximate result can be obtained by converting $10,000,000 at 1.4574 (the sum of the exercise price and the option premium) giving £6,861,534. However, this method ignores the fact that the premium is paid in advance and that surplus $ must be purchased at the end.

Scenario (ii)

The option is abandoned. $10,000,000 is converted at the spot rate 1.35, giving £7,407,407. After subtracting the option premium of £284,053, the net receipt is £7,123,354.

By way of comparison, a forward contract would have yielded 10,000,000/1.4101 = £7,091,696.

Closing out when traded options still have time to run

4.13 The above example assumes that the traded option is at its expiry date when the decision needs to be made between exercising or abandoning. In practice, most traded options are closed out, like futures contracts, because the date when the cash is required does not match the option expiry date.

4.14 Suppose that the company in the above example was due to receive $10 million on 10 June. Then June option contracts would still be used, but on 10 June the decision that needs to be made is whether to close out the option, to exercise it or to allow it to lapse. Closing out will be more beneficial than exercising or allowing to lapse if the option still has a positive time value.

4.15 Assume that the company purchased 229 June sterling call option contracts, exercise price 1.400, and that on 10 June two possible scenarios are as follows.

(a) Spot rate is 1.55 and the 1.400 call option premium has risen to 15.35 cents per pound
(b) Spot rate is 1.35 and the 1.400 call option premium has fallen to 0.43 cents per pound

In *Scenario (a)* the intrinsic value of the option is $(1.55 - 1.40) = 15 cents. If the option is exercised, a gain of 15 cents per £ will be made, as opposed to a gain of 15.35 cents per £ if the call option is sold. Consequently the contracts will be sold for a premium of $0.1535 × 31,250 × 229 = $1,098,484.

	$	£
Option premium paid at start		(284,053)
Option premium received at end	1,098,484	
Cash from customer	10,000,000	
Total dollars received	11,098,484	
Converted to sterling at 1.55:		7,160,312
Net sterling received		6,876,259

In *Scenario (b)* the intrinsic value of the option is zero, so it will be sold in order to realise the small time value: $0.0043 × 31,250 × 229 = $30,772.

	$	£
Option premium paid at start		(284,053)
Option premium received at end	30,772	
Cash from customer	10,000,000	
Total dollars received	10,030,772	
Converted to sterling at 1.35:		7,430,202
Net sterling received		7,146,149

Using collars

4.16 Various combinations of options are possible, the most important of which, for our purposes, is a **collar**. The premium cost of purchasing an option can be expensive. A collar reduces this premium cost by sacrificing some of the potential gains which the option would allow. It is constructed by buying a call option and simultaneously selling a put option, or *vice versa*. Collars are illustrated after the following section.

The drawbacks of currency options

4.17 The major drawbacks of currency options are as follows.

(a) The cost is about 5% of the total amount of foreign exchange covered, although the exact amount depends on the expected volatility of the exchange rate.

(b) Options must be paid for as soon as they are bought.

(c) Tailor-made options lack negotiability.

(d) Traded options are not available in every currency.

5 A GRAPHICAL APPROACH TO OPTIONS

5.1 A **graphical approach** to options may help you to understand options more fully and may provide a means of illustrating options in answers to exam questions. The **examples** illustrated below generally refer to share prices. In the case of other types of option (eg index options or currency options), then it will be the value or price of the particular underlying investment (eg the stock index or the currency) which is relevant. Firstly, Figure 1 shows the position of a **call option holder**.

5.2 The holder of the call option will not exercise the option unless the share price is at least equal to the **exercise price** (or **strike price**) at the exercise date. If the share price is above that level, he can cut his losses (up to the break-even price) or make profits (if the share price is above the break-even price). Holding a call option is referred to as having a **long call position** in the option.

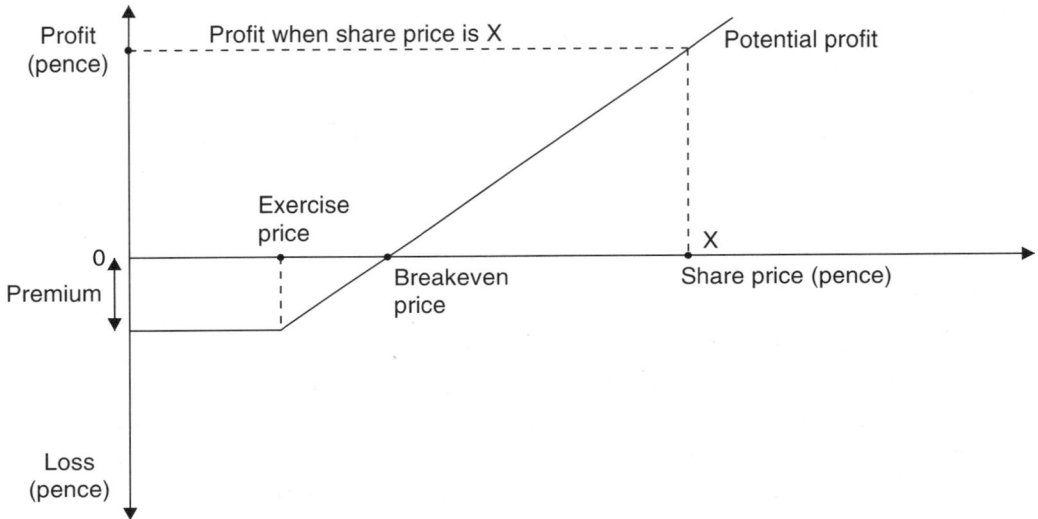

Figure 1 Call option holder ('long call position')

5.3 Any profit made by the holder of the option is reflected by the loss of the other party to the transaction - the writer of the option. Accordingly, Figure 2, illustrating the potential outcomes for the **writer of the option**, looks like a 'mirror image' of Figure 1. Selling or writing a call option is called taking a **short call position**. It can be seen from Figure 2 that the writer of the call option is exposed to potentially unlimited losses.

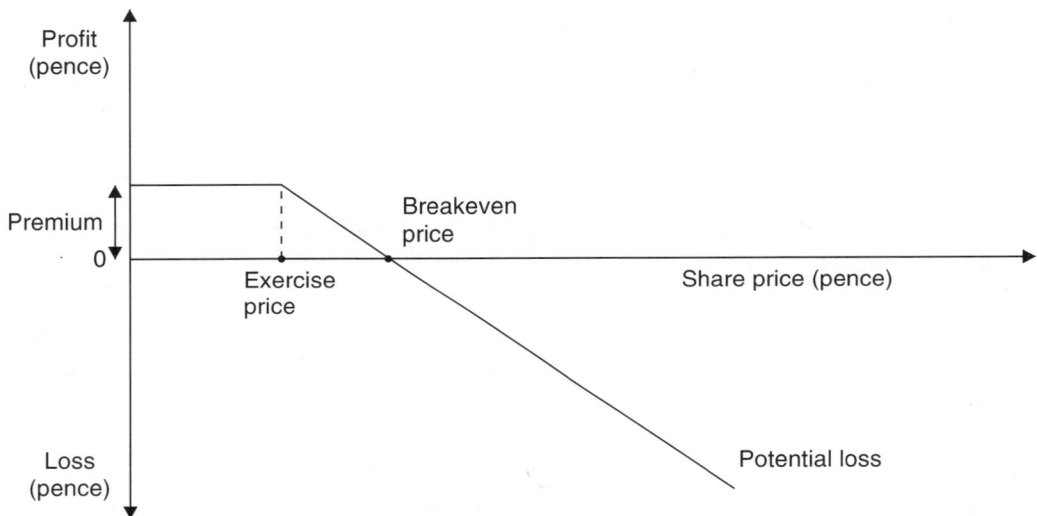

Figure 2 Call option writer ('short call position')

5.4 The position of the **buyer of a put option** is illustrated in Figure 3. The maximum potential profit is equal to the exercise price, which is the position if the share price falls to zero. Then, the put option holder has the option to sell worthless shares at the exercise price. You should be able to appreciate that the put option can be used to protect a holder of shares against a fall in their value. As Figure 3 shows, the loss on the option is limited to the size of the premium. You will probably by now be able to guess what a graph illustrating the position of a **put option writer** will look like (Figure 4).

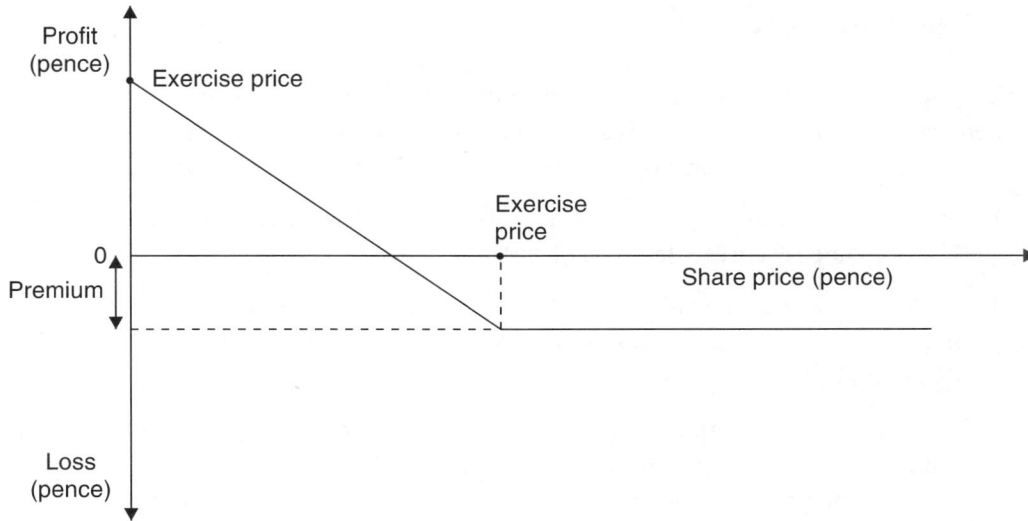

Figure 3 Put option holder ('long put position')

Question 1

See if you can sketch such a graph and then look at Figure 4.

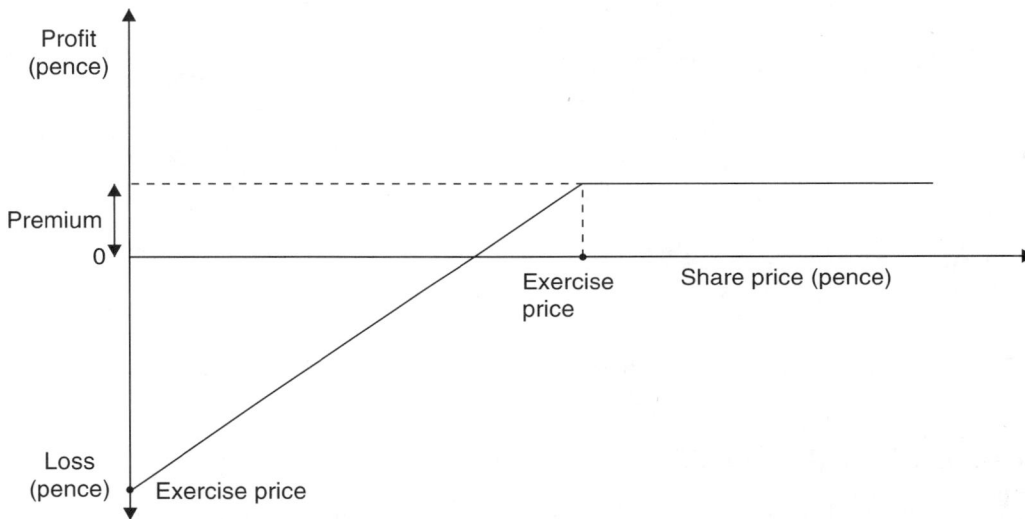

Figure 4 Put option writer ('short put position')

Question 2

Reasoning from what you have already learned about options, check that you can explain Figure 4. Note that the maximum loss for the writer or seller of the put option is the exercise price.

5.5 Figures 1 to 4 illustrate the basic positions which can be taken in options. It is also possible to combine different option positions in various ways, depending on the combination of risks and returns which are sought from different outcomes.

BPP PUBLISHING

Graphical illustration of currency options

5.6 The graphical approach can also be used to illustrate **currency options**. Suppose that a UK-based company expects to receive an amount of export income in dollars ($) in three months' time. Figure 5 illustrates the profit/loss profile of different strategies.

(a) Selling dollars and buying sterling in the forward market eliminates all uncertainty. The outcome is represented by a horizontal line.

(b) Relying on the spot market results in a net gain or loss compared with the forward market if the spot exchange rate in three months' time turns out to be below or above $X per pound respectively.

(c) If a call option is used, it will not be exercised if the exchange rate is less than $X per pound. A currency call option reduces the potential gain compared with the spot market strategy (b) by the amount of the premium on the option, but has the advantage that potential losses are contained as they will not exceed the value of the premium.

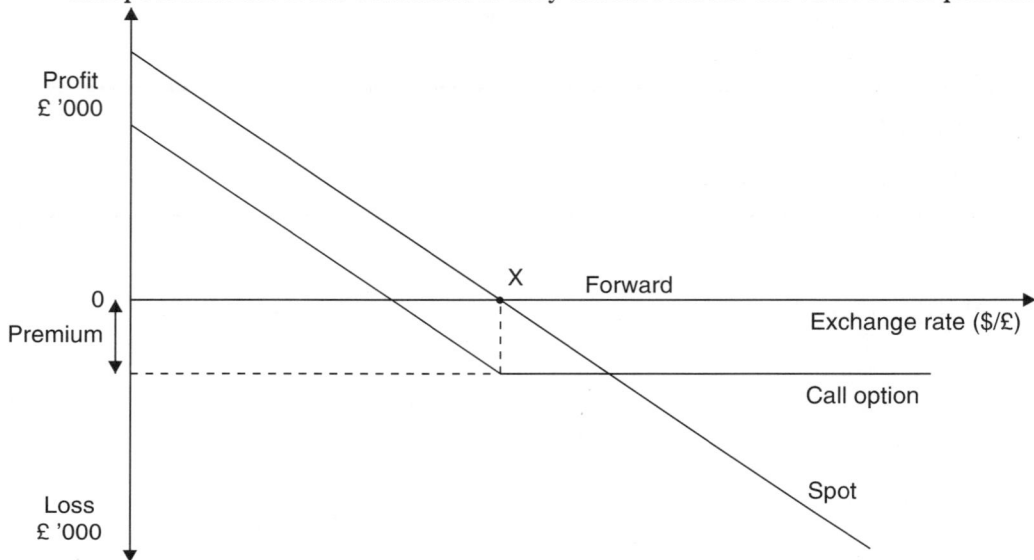

Figure 5 Currency call option, forward and spot markets: profit/loss profile

6 COLLARS AND OTHER OPTION COMBINATIONS

6.1 Speculators and hedgers have devised many combinations of purchasing and writing options. One of the most important combinations for hedgers is the **collar**. This is illustrated in the following paragraphs, after which other possible combinations will be described in outline.

How to construct a collar

6.2 One of the main problems with purchasing an option is that the premium cost reduces the value of the hedge and tends to wipe out any potential gains that might be made. A collar is an attempt to reduce the premium cost. It is achieved by simultaneously purchasing and writing options. The premium received from writing an option (ie selling it to another party) is used to offset the cost of purchasing another option.

6.3 **A collar can work in one of two ways.** We can **either** purchase a call option and simultaneously sell a put option **or** purchase a put option and simultaneously sell a call option. As we shall see, the advantage of the reduced premium cost is balanced by the fact that we allow a limit to be imposed on our potential gains. The techniques can be illustrated using over-the-counter currency options.

(a) **A collar if we fear that a currency will strengthen**. If we need to buy a currency at some future date and we fear that it may strengthen, we can purchase a call option from a bank (to protect us in case the currency strengthens) and, at the same time, sell a put option to the bank (in order to get some money to offset against the cost of our call option). **Both options should be for the same amount of currency**. The premium which we receive for writing the put option will be offset against the premium cost of the call option, lowering our initial outlay substantially without reducing the protection against a strengthening currency. However, as a result of this strategy, we will place a limit on the gains we can make if the currency weakens.

For example, suppose we will need to purchase deutschmarks with US dollars in one month's time and the current spot rate is $0.61 per DM. We can protect ourselves by purchasing a deutschmark call option (exercise price, say, $0.62 per DM) and then get some money back by selling a deutschmark put option (exercise price, say, $0.60 per DM). In a collar of this type, the exercise price of the call option needs to be a higher figure than that of the put option. Why is this?

Our objective is to place a ceiling on the **maximum** cost for the currency (in this case $0.62 to be paid for every DM purchased). This maximum cost is determined by the **call** option we have purchased. However, if the exchange rate weakens below $0.60 per DM, the bank will exercise its put option. Since we wrote the put option, the bank has the right to sell us DM for $0.60. In other words we will be forced to buy DM for $0.60. The **put** option determines the **minimum** cost we must pay for the currency. Consequently, the exercise price for the call option will need to be a larger figure than the exercise price for the put option.

In summary, the collar can be achieved by purchasing a deutschmark call option at an exercise price of $0.62 per DM and selling a deutschmark put option at an exercise price of $0.60 per DM.

Question 3

Show what happens if the exchange rate moves to (i) 0.63 $/DM; (ii) 0.59 $/DM; (iii) What happens if it remains at 0.61 $/DM?

Answer

(i) If the DM strengthens to $0.63 we will exercise our call option to buy at $0.62. The bank will not exercise its put option. The DM are therefore bought at $0.62.

(ii) If the DM weakens to $0.59 we will not want to exercise our call option, but the bank will exercise the right to sell DM to us at the agreed price of $0.60. We will therefore be forced to purchase DM at $0.60. The overall effect of the collar is that we have a maximum cost of $0.62 per DM and a minimum cost of $0.60. The premium cost must be added to these figures, but this will be small because the proceeds from selling the put option are offset against the cost of the call option.

(iii) If the spot rate stays between the two exercise prices of $0.60 and $0.62 then neither of the options will be exercised and the D-Marks are simply bought at the spot rate. So if the spot rate stays at $0.61, the DM will be bought at $0.61.

The 'profile' of the collar can be seen in the following graph. *(The premium cost has been omitted.)*

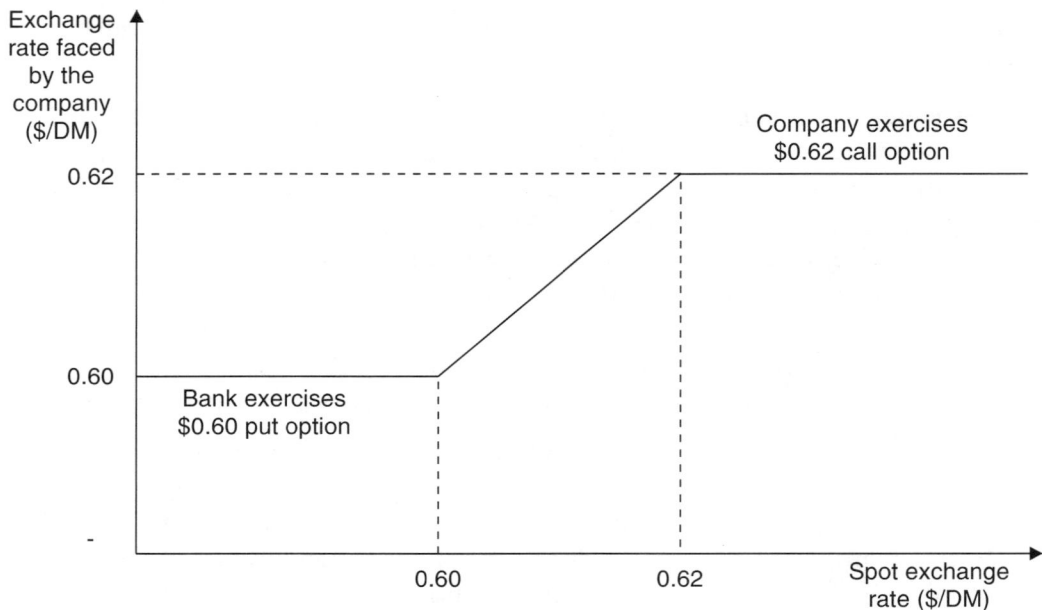

Profile of the collar

(b) **A collar if we fear that a currency will weaken**. If we need to sell a currency at some future date and we fear that it may weaken, we can purchase a put option and simultaneously sell (write) a call option for the same amount of currency. The premium which we receive for selling the call option will offset our premium cost of the put option. The exercise price for the put option will need to be a lower figure than the exercise price for the call option.

For example, if we need to sell DM for US$, we might *purchase a deutschmark put option at an exercise price of $0.60 per DM and sell (write) a deutschmark call option at an exercise price of $0.62 per DM*. The profile of this collar will be the same as that in the diagram above, except that our company exercises the put option and the bank exercises the call option. The result is that we can sell deutschmarks for at least $0.60 but no more than $0.62.

The net premium cost of a collar

6.4 The net premium cost of the collar will depend on the exercise prices used and whether these exercise prices are 'in the money' or 'out of the money'. For example, a collar constructed by buying an in-the-money call and selling an out-of-the-money put will be relatively expensive, whereas a collar made up by buying an out-of-the-money call and selling an in-the-money put will actually have a negative cost: that is, it will earn premium income for the investor. In between, it is possible to construct **zero cost collars** where the premium paid is exactly compensated by the premium earned.

6.5 EXAMPLE: COLLAR USING OVER-THE-COUNTER OPTIONS

Blackberry Inc, a US company, needs to pay £300,000 to a British supplier in six month's time. The current spot rate is 1.50 $/£. The company purchases an OTC sterling call option on £300,000 at an exercise price of 1.51 $/£. The premium cost is 2.5 cents per pound. At the same time the company writes a put option on £300,000 for the bank at an exercise price of 1.47 $/£, earning a premium of 1.2 cents per pound.

Show the results of the hedge assuming that the spot rate moves to (i) 1.55; (ii) 1.53; (iii) 1.48; (iv) 1.45; (v) 1.43.

6.6 SOLUTION

At today's spot rate of 1.50 \$/£, the 'target cost' of £300,000 is \$450,000. The cost of the call option is 300,000 × \$0.025 = \$7,500. The premium received from the put option sold is 300,000 × \$0.012 = \$3,600. The net cost of the collar is \$7,500 – \$3,600 = \$3,900.

Scenario	(i)	(ii)	(iii)	(iv)	(v)
Spot rate \$/£	1.55	1.53	1.48	1.45	1.43
Does the company exercise its \$1.51 call?	Yes	Yes	No	No	No
Does the bank exercise its \$1.47 put?	No	No	No	Yes	Yes
Exchange rate obtained by the company \$/£:	1.51	1.51	1.48	1.47	1.47
	\$	\$	\$	\$	\$
Cost of £300,000	453,000	453,000	444,000	441,000	441,000
Add: premium cost	3,900	3,900	3,900	3,900	3,900
Total cost	456,900	456,900	447,900	444,900	444,900
	Maximum			*Minimum*	

The company has used the collar to fix a maximum cost of \$456,900 but must accept a minimum cost of \$444,900.

Constructing collars from traded currency options

6.7 Using traded options, a number of different collars can be created. The put and call should have the same expiry date and the same number of contracts but a range of exercise prices is possible. Consider the following prices for Philadelphia Stock Exchange sterling options.

Philadelphia SE £ sterling options (contract size £31,250, premium in cents per £)

Strike price	.... Calls			.... Puts		
	May	Jun	Jul	May	Jun	Jul
1.620	1.78	2.34	2.75	0.28	0.93	1.46
1.630	1.09	1.75	2.23	0.59	1.33	1.90
1.640	0.59	1.26	1.75	1.10	1.85	2.42

6.8 Suppose a British company needs to pay \$500,000 at the end of June. It will need to sell sterling to get dollars, so it can protect its position by *buying* June sterling *put* options. It can make a collar by simultaneously *selling* June sterling *call* options. The *put* options which it purchases are intended to give a guaranteed *minimum* to the number of dollars it will get for each pound. The *call* options will force a *maximum* to the number of dollars per pound. The exercise price for the put options must therefore be a lower figure than that for the call options.

Three collars are available (June options):

Collar 1 Buy puts at 1.620 and sell calls at 1.630; net premium *received:* –0.93 + 1.75 = 0.82 cents per pound = \$0.0082 per pound.

Collar 2 Buy puts at 1.620 and sell calls at 1.640; net premium *received:* –0.93 + 1.26 = 0.33 cents per pound = \$0.0033 per pound.

Collar 3 Buy puts at 1.630 and sell calls at 1.640; net premium *paid:* –1.33 + 1.26 = 0.07 cents per pound = \$0.0007 per pound.

6.9 Collar 3 is virtually a zero cost collar. The other two produce premium income. $500,000 converts to £308,642 at 1.62 $/£, which is 9.88 contracts, rounded to 10. At 1.63 or 1.64 $/£ the number of contracts is also 10. The hedge is therefore set up by buying 10 June sterling put options and selling 10 June sterling call options.

6.10 A detailed demonstration of the range of possible outcomes from the collars would be a lengthy task, because the number of contracts has been rounded and surplus cash will result. However an approximation to the possible results can easily be made if:

(a) Surplus cash is ignored, and

(b) It is assumed that the options are either exercised or abandoned, since they are at their expiry date at the end of June

6.11 Consider two exchange rate scenarios.

Scenario 1. The dollar strengthens: at the end of June, the spot rate is 1.60 $/£.

6.12 In this case, we exercise our put option but the call is not exercised. We obtain our guaranteed minimum dollars per pound, as follows.

Collar	(i)	(ii)	(iii)
Buy put	1.62	1.62	1.63
Sell call	1.63	1.64	1.64
	$	$	$
£1 sold for	1.6200	1.6200	1.6300
Premium received/(paid)	0.0082	0.0033	(0.0007)
Guaranteed minimum $ per £:	1.6282	1.6233	1.6293

Scenario 2. The dollar weakens: at the end of June, the spot rate is 1.65 $/£.

6.13 We allow our put to lapse but the call is exercised, forcing our maximum dollars per pound.

Collar	(i)	(ii)	(iii)
Buy put	1.62	1.62	1.63
Sell call	1.63	1.64	1.64
	$	$	$
£1 sold for	1.6300	1.6400	1.6400
Premium received/(paid)	0.0082	0.0033	(0.0007)
Maximum $ per £:	1.6382	1.6433	1.6393

6.14 In summary, Collar (i) gives an exchange rate between $1.6282 and $1.6382 per pound. Collar (ii) gives between $1.6233 and $1.6433 and Collar (iii) gives between $1.6293 and $1.6393. Collar (iii) gives the best protection if the dollar strengthens. Collar (ii) allows the greatest gain if the dollar weakens.

6.15 From the above example, it can be seen that collars tend to give a range of possible results between that of a straight option and that of a future.

Collars on the same strike price

6.16 If collars are made from puts and calls on the same strike price, and if the markets are in equilibrium, the result should be identical to that of a future. This can be seen by investigating the figures in the table of sterling options given above and comparing the result with the futures price on the same day, which was 1.6341 $/£. There are three possible collars, as seen in the table below.

Collar	(iv)	(v)	(vi)
Buy put	1.62	1.63	1.64
Sell call	1.62	1.63	1.64
	Cents per £	Cents per £	Cents per £
Premium cost of put	(0.93)	(1.33)	(1.85)
Premium received from call	2.34	1.75	1.26
Net premium received/(paid)	1.41	0.42	(0.59)
	$	$	$
£1 sold for	1.6200	1.6300	1.6400
Net premium in $	0.0141	0.0042	(0.0059)
Total $ per £	1.6341	1.6342	1.6341

All three collars give $ per £ equal to the futures price of 1.6341 (subject to small differences). In other words, buying a put and selling a call on the same strike price is the same as selling a future. In the same way, buying a call and selling a put on the same strike price is the same as buying a future.

6.17 There are several other possible combinations which give the same results. For example:

- Buying a future and buying a put is the same as buying a call
- Selling a future and buying a call is the same as buying a put

If these relationships were not true, speculators could make gains without incurring extra risk.

Other combinations of options

6.18 There are many other combinations of options which can be devised, all of which have different characteristics. Some of them are described in outline below, in relation to currencies.

> **Exam focus point**
> You do not need to learn the terms set out below for the exam: they are described here to give you an idea of the variety of combinations available.

(a) A **straddle** is made by buying a put and a call at the same time. This has an expensive premium cost and provides protection against exchange rate movements in either direction. It is unlikely to be of much use to a treasurer. If the company has both receipts and payments in the same currency, the hedge is already provided by matching.

(b) A **vertical bull spread** can be made by purchasing a call with a lower exercise price and selling a call with a higher exercise price. If the currency increases in value, a profit is made from the difference between the exercise prices. If the currency decreases in value, both the options lapse.

(c) A **horizontal bull spread** involves purchasing a long-dated call (eg July) and selling a shorter dated call (eg May).

(d) **Other terms** used in the options markets include bear spreads, diagonal spreads, variable ratio spreads and butterfly spreads.

7 THEORY OF THE VALUATION OF OPTIONS

The time value of an option

7.1 Earlier we stated that the value of an option is made up of its 'intrinsic value' and its 'time value' and that the time value of an option is affected by the **time period to expiry**, the **volatility of the underlying security**, and the **general level of interest rates**. In this section we will use a share call option to illustrate how the three factors listed affect the option's value. We will then describe in outline the **Black-Scholes model** for valuing options.

Time to expiry

7.2 The value of all options will increase with the length of the expiry period, because in this period the underlying security has time to rise and create a gain for the option holder. If the underlying security falls in value, the option holder makes no loss other than the initial premium cost.

Volatility of the underlying security

7.3 Options on volatile securities will be more valuable than options on securities whose prices do not change much. This is because volatile securities will either show large increases or large decreases in value. The holder of a call option will gain a lot from a large increase in the value of the security but will lose nothing if it falls in value. The following example illustrates this point.

7.4 EXAMPLE: EFFECT OF SHARE PRICE VOLATILITY ON THE VALUE OF A CALL OPTION

Shares in A plc have a value of 200 pence. Within the next six months, it is estimated that there is a 50% chance that the share price will rise to 220 pence and a 50% chance that it will fall to 180 pence.

Shares in B plc are also priced at 200 pence, but the market price per share is much more volatile. Within the next six months, it is estimated that there is a 50% chance that the share price will rise to 280 pence and a 50% chance that it will fall to 120 pence.

Call options with an exercise price of 200 pence and a six month expiry date are available on the shares of both A plc and B plc.

By using expected values, illustrate why the options on share B are worth more than those on share A.

7.5 SOLUTION

Consider the potential profits when the expiry date is reached in six months.

	Pence	Pence
A plc - share price in six months	220	180
Call option exercise price	200	200
Exercise option?	YES	NO
Gain	20	0
Probability	0.5	0.5
Expected value of gain	10 pence	

	Pence	Pence
B plc - share price in six months	280	120
Call option exercise price	200	200
Exercise option?	YES	NO
Gain	80	0
Probability	0.5	0.5
Expected value of gain	40 pence	

7.6 The call option on shares in B plc gives a much higher expected gain than the option on shares in A plc. This is because a large upswing in share price gives a gain whereas a large down-swing gives no loss. It will therefore be more expensive to purchase the options on B's shares than on A's shares.

The general level of interest rates

7.7 The intrinsic value of an in-the-money call option is equal to the share price minus the exercise price. If the option has time to run before expiry, the exercise price will not have to be paid until the option is exercised. The option's value will therefore depend on the current share price minus the **present value of the exercise price.** If interest rates increase, this present value will decrease and **the value of the call option will increase.**

Put-call parity

7.8 The relationship between the values of put and call options (with the same exercise price) can be expressed by a formula known as **put-call parity**. To understand this formula, first consider a short example.

7.9 Mr X has one share in J plc and a put option to sell the share for 350 pence. The put option is at its expiry date. The value of his holding will be equal to the share price unless this is below 350 pence, in which case he will exercise the put option to get 350 pence cash.

Mr Y has cash of 350 pence and a call option to buy a share in J plc for 350 pence. The call option is at its expiry date. The value of his holding is 350 pence unless the share price is higher than 350 pence in which case he will exercise the option to buy the share.

The value of Mr X's holding (share + put) is equal to that of Mr Y's holding (call + exercise price). Both are worth a minimum of 350 pence but are equal to the share price if this is higher. Thus:

Value of put + value of share = value of call + exercise price

When the options still have time to expiry, we must replace exercise price with the 'present value of exercise price'. This leads to the formula for put-call parity which is:

Value of put + value of share = value of call + present value of exercise price

The Black-Scholes model

7.10 The **Black-Scholes** model for the valuation of European-style options was developed in 1973. The basic model makes the assumption that shares pay no dividends, although the model can be varied to take dividends into account. It is also assumed that there are no transaction costs, while in practice of course there always will be.

7.11 Another problem is that the model requires an estimate to be made of the variation in return on the shares. A simple way of making such an estimate is to measure the variation in the share price in the recent past and to make the assumption that this variability will apply during the life of the option.

7.12 Variants of the model are applied by practitioners in the field, who often make use of programmed electronic calculators or computers to determine option prices. Alternatively, option tables based on the model can be used.

Exam focus point

Although *application* of the Black-Scholes option valuation model is beyond the scope of the Paper 14 *Financial Strategy* syllabus, it will be useful to be aware of the variables on which it is based. Your understanding of these may be enhanced by looking at the model in the form of mathematical notation, as we do below. Understanding of the term $N(d_1)$ is also necessary to understand the *delta hedge* (covered below).

7.13 The Black-Scholes model states that the current value (P_0) of a European call option is given by the following formula.

$$P_0 = P_S N(d_1) - \frac{E}{e^{rt}} N(d_2)$$

where:

$$d_1 = \frac{\log_n(P_S / E) + (r + \frac{1}{2}\sigma^2)t}{\sigma\sqrt{t}}$$

d_2 = $d_1 - \sigma\sqrt{t}$

P_s = the current price of the share

E = the exercise price of the option

r = the compound risk-free rate of return (as a decimal)

σ = the standard deviation of the rate of return on the share

e = the exponential constant 2.7183

t = the time in years to expiration of the option

$\log_n(P_s/E)$ = the natural logarithm of P_s/E

$N(d)$ = the probability that a deviation of less than d will occur in a normal distribution with a mean of zero and a standard deviation of 1

7.14 The formula may well seem daunting, but fortunately you do not need to learn it! As already mentioned, what is important is to be aware of the variables which it includes. You should however note from the formula that the value of a share option depends upon:

(a) The **current share price** (P_s): if the share price rises, the value of a call option will increase. (For currency options, the relevant 'price' is the exchange rate.)

(b) The **exercise price of the option** (E): the higher the exercise price, the lower is the value of a call option.

(c) The **standard deviation of the return on the underlying share** (σ): the higher the standard deviation of the return, the higher is the value of a call option;

(d) The **time to expiration of the option** (t): the longer the period to expiration, the higher is the value of a call option;

(e) The **risk-free rate of interest** (r): the higher the risk-free rate of interest, the higher is the value of a call option. (In the case of currency options, the risk-free interest rate differential between the currencies involved is a relevant factor).

The delta value

7.15 If we accept the Black-Scholes model, the value of $N(d_1)$ can be used to indicate the amount of the underlying shares (or other instrument) which the writer of an option should hold in order to hedge (eliminate the risk of) the option position. The appropriate 'hedge ratio' $N(d_1)$ is referred to as the **delta value**: hence the term **delta hedge**. The delta value is valid if the price changes are small.

Delta = change in call option price ÷ change in the price of the underlying share

7.16 For example, if a change in share price of 3 pence results in a change in the option price of 1 pence, then:

Delta = 1p ÷ 3p = $^1/_3$

7.17 The writer of the option needs to hold one-third of the number of shares on which there are options in order to achieve a delta hedge. If the writer loses 1 pence per share on the option, this will be offset by 1 pence gain on the share held. The delta value is liable to change during the period of the option, and so the option writer may need to change his holding of the underlying share from time to time in order to maintain a delta hedge position.

Exam focus point

A short or part-question could be set on a delta hedge - a topic which the Examiner has specifically referred to.

7.18 EXAMPLE: DELTA HEDGE

How can the writer of a 3 month call option on 10,000 shares in R plc with an exercise price of 384 pence achieve a delta hedge? The delta value is given by $N(d_1)$, whose value is 0.745.

7.19 SOLUTION

A delta hedge would be achieved by holding the following number of shares:

$10,000 \times 0.745 = 7,450$ shares

Other points about delta values

7.20 Note also the following points about delta values.

(a) If an option is 'at the money' (ie if the share price equals the exercise price) then the delta value is approximately 0.5.

(b) As an option moves 'out of the money' (ie the share price moves below the exercise price), the delta value falls towards zero. Delta will be zero when the share price is zero: the shares are then worthless.

(c) As an option moves further 'into the money', the delta hedge ratio increase towards a value of 1.

(d) A small change in the share price can result in a large change in the delta value.

7.21 The factors influencing delta when the option is either in the money or out of the money can be appreciated by looking at the variables in the $N(d_1)$ formula given earlier. These factors are:

- The exercise price of the option relative to the share price (ie its intrinsic value)
- The time to expiration
- The risk-free rate of return
- The volatility of returns on the share

The gamma value

7.22 The **gamma value** measures the amount by which the delta value changes as the share price changes:

Gamma = Change in delta value ÷ Change in the price of the underlying share

7.23 The higher the gamma value, the more difficult it is for the option writer to maintain a delta hedge. As a result, a higher gamma value will mean that the option will carry a higher premium.

7.24 Gamma values will be highest for a share which is close to expiry and is 'at the money'. For example, suppose that an option has an exercise price of 340 pence and is due to expire in a few minutes' time.

   (a) If the share price is 338 pence, there is a very low chance of the option being exercised. The delta hedge ratio will be approximately zero: in other words, no hedge is necessary.

   (b) If the share price rises suddenly to 342 pence, it becomes highly probable that the option will be exercised and the delta hedge ratio will approximate to 1, suggesting the need to hedge through holding the underlying shares.

8 APPLICATIONS OF OPTIONS THEORY

8.1 Options theory is relevant to financial decisions beyond the areas of financial instruments such as traded options, currency options and interest rate options. The following examples should give some idea of the range of possible applications.

   (a) **Convertible loan stock** provides a combination of a conventional loan with a call option. If the option is exercised, the loan is exchanged for a specified number of shares in the company.

   (b) **Share warrants** provide the holder with an option to purchase shares from the company at a specified exercise price during a specified time period.

   (c) **Government loan guarantees** effectively provide a put option to holders of risky loans, giving the holders an opportunity to exercise an option of obtaining reimbursement from the government if a borrower defaults.

   (d) **Insurance** more generally is a form of put option which is exercised when an insurance claim is made.

   (e) **Share purchase** at the prevailing market price can be seen as equivalent to the purchase of a call option combined with the sale of a put option, while putting the remaining amount on deposit at a risk-free rate of return over the option period.

   (f) Option valuation theory which is used in valuing share options can be extended to various options which financial managers may meet in making **capital investment decisions,** such as:

   (i) The **option to make further 'follow-on' investments** if an initial project is successful, which is equivalent to a call option

(ii) The **option to abandon** a project, which is equivalent to a put option

(iii) The **option to delay** the start of a project (and gain knowledge in the meantime), which is equivalent to a call option

8.2 Most practical option problems require the use of a computer model; using such a model effectively demands informed judgement. The **binomial model for option valuation**, for example, provides a basis for such a task and is basically a method of solving decision trees. The model involves starting at a future date and working back through the tree to the present time, determining the best future action at each decision point. Eventually, the various possible cash flows generated by future events are related back to establish a present value. In practice, such decision trees tend to be complex: hence the need for computer power to solve them.

8.3 The application of option pricing theory such as the binomial model allows discounting to be carried out within decision trees. Standard discounted cash flow methods do not work within decision trees: there can be no single constant discount rate for options because the risk of the option changes as time progresses and the price of underlying assets change. Therefore, the market value of the future cash flows described by the decision tree needs to be calculated by option pricing methods.

8.4 These examples suggest the wider scope there is for financial managers and strategists to use options theory in a variety of situations which an enterprise may face. However, where there is no market for the option concerned, such as there is with traded options, the exercise is likely to be a more subjective one involving a greater level of estimation to be made of the different factors affecting the value of the option.

Chapter roundup

- **Options** give the right but not the obligation to buy or sell an asset. The examples considered in this chapter have mainly concerned share options and currency options.

- **Currency options** protect against adverse exchange rate movements while allowing the investor to take advantage of favourable exchange rate movements. They are particularly useful in situations where the cash flow is not certain to occur (eg when tendering for overseas contracts).

- Various combinations of options are possible. **Collars** are an important example.

- The **value of an option** depends on:
  ° The current price of the asset
  ° The exercise price
  ° The volatility (standard deviation) of the asset value
  ° The time period to expiry
  ° The risk-free rate of interest

- Many decision making situations can be analysed as examples of **options**.

- Options on interest rates are considered in the next chapter, together with interest rate futures and other related financial instruments.

Quick quiz

1 Distinguish between a 'call option' and a 'put option'. (see para 2.1)

2 What is the 'intrinsic value' of a share option? (2.12)

3 In what circumstances are currency options useful? (3.6)

4 What different effects are there between currency options and forward or futures contracts? (3.10)

5 What are the possible drawbacks of currency options? (4.17)

6 Sketch a graph showing the position of a call option writer ('short call position'). (5.2)

7 According to the Black-Scholes model, on what does the value of an option depend? (7.14)

8 What is the 'delta value'? (7.15)

Question to try	Level	Marks	Time
21	Exam standard	30	54 mins

Chapter 22

INTEREST RATE RISK

Chapter topic list	Syllabus reference
1 Interest rate risk	4(b)
2 Interest rate futures	4(b)
3 Over-the-counter interest rate options	4(b)
4 Traded interest rate options	4(b)
5 Interest rate swaps	4(b)
6 Currency swaps	4(b)

Introduction

Here we extend our discussion of risk and its management to consider **interest rate risk** and some more of the **financial instruments** which are now available for managing financial risks. Bear in mind, however, that the risk of interest rate changes is less significant in most cases than the risk of currency fluctuations which, in some circumstances, can wipe out profits entirely if it is not hedged.

1   INTEREST RATE RISK   12/94

Managing a debt portfolio

1.1   There are three important considerations for corporate treasurers in managing a debt portfolio, that is, in deciding how a company should obtain its short-term funds so as to be able to repay debts as they mature and to minimise any inherent risks, notably foreign exchange risk, in the debts the company owes and is owed.

(a)   **Maturity mix.** The treasurer must avoid having too much debt becoming repayable within a short period.

(b)   **Currency mix.** Foreign currency debts create a risk of losses through adverse movements in foreign exchange rates before the debt falls due for payment. Foreign currency management involves hedging against foreign currency risks, for example by means of forward exchange contracts, or having debts in several currencies, some of which will strengthen and some of which will weaken over time.

(c)   The **mix of fixed interest and floating rate debts**

(i)   Too much fixed interest rate debt creates an unnecessary cost when market interest rates fall. A company might find itself committed to high interest costs that it could have avoided.

(ii)   Too much borrowing at a variable rate of interest (such as bank overdrafts and medium-term bank lending) leads to high costs when interest rates go up.

Interest rate exposure and hedging

1.2   The variability of interest rates over time can be appreciated from the table below.

Selected UK interest rates (end-of-year rates)

	Treasury bill yield	Selected retail bank base rates	Inter-bank 3 month offer rate	Sterling certificates of deposit 3 months offer rate	Euro-dollar 3 month rate	Long dated (20 years) UK gilts yields
1990	13.50	14.00	14.00	13.88	7.50	11.08
1991	10.45	10.50	11.00	10.88	4.22	9.92
1992	6.44	7.00	7.19	6.91	3.37	9.12
1993	4.95	5.50	5.31	5.25	3.31	7.87
1994	6.00	6.25	6.56	6.44	6.44	8.05
1995	6.31	6.50	6.50	6.47	5.54	8.26
1996	6.26	6.00	6.44	6.41	5.50	8.10
1997	7.13	7.25	7.63	7.59	5.69	7.09

(Source: Economic Trends)

1.3   There are a number of situations in which a company might be exposed to **risk** from interest rate movements.

(a)   **Fixed rate versus floating rate debt.** A company can get caught paying higher interest rates by having fixed rather than floating rate debt, or floating rather than fixed rate debt, as market interest rates change.

(b)   **Currency of debt.** This is also a foreign currency exposure. A company can face higher costs if it borrows in a currency for which exchange rates move adversely against the company's domestic currency. The treasurer should seek to match the currency of the loan with the currency of the underlying operations/assets that generate revenue to pay interest/repay the loans.

(c)   **Term of loan.** A company can be exposed by having to repay a loan earlier than it can afford to, resulting in a need to re-borrow, perhaps at a higher rate of interest.

(d)   **Term loan or overdraft facility?** A company might prefer to pay for borrowings only when it needs the money as with an overdraft facility: the bank will charge a commitment fee for such a facility. Alternatively, a term loan might be preferred, but this will cost interest even if it is not needed in full for the whole term.

To hedge or not to hedge?

1.4   Where the magnitude of the risk is immaterial in comparison with the company's overall cash flows, one option is to *do nothing* and to accept the effects of any movement in interest rates which occur. **Hedging** means taking action to reduce or 'cover' an exposure to risk: hedging is the process of financial risk management. Hedging has a cost, either a fee to a financial institution or a reduction in profit, but companies might well consider the costs to be justified by the reduction in financial risks that the hedging achieves. The degree to which the exposure is covered is the **hedge efficiency**: a perfect hedge has 100% efficiency.

Interest rate risk management methods

1.5   Methods of reducing **interest rate risk** include forward rate interest agreements (FRAs), interest rate futures, interest rate options (or interest rate guarantees), interest rate swaps and options on interest rate swaps ('swaptions'). In the remainder of this chapter, we look at FRAs, before considering interest rate futures, options and swaps.

Forward interest rate agreements (FRAs)

1.6   **FRAs** are agreements, typically between a company and a bank, about the interest rate on future borrowing or bank deposits. For example, a company can enter into a FRA with a bank that fixes the rate of interest for borrowing at a certain time in the future. If the actual interest rate proves to be higher than the rate agreed, the bank pays the company the difference. If the actual interest rate is lower than the rate agreed, the company pays the bank the difference.

> **KEY TERM**
>
> **Forward interest rate agreement (FRA):** an agreement to borrow or to lend a sum of money in the future at an interest rate which is fixed at the time the agreement is made.

1.7   One limitation on FRAs is that they are usually only available on loans of at least £500,000. They are also likely to be difficult to obtain for periods of over one year.

1.8   An advantage of FRAs is that, for the period of the FRA at least, they protect the borrower from adverse market interest rate movements to levels above the rate negotiated for the FRA. With a normal variable rate loan (for example linked to a bank's base rate or to LIBOR) the borrower is exposed to the risk of such adverse market movements. On the other hand, the borrower will similarly not benefit from the effects of favourable market interest rate movements.

1.9   The interest rates which banks will be willing to set for FRAs will reflect their current expectations of interest rate movements. If it is expected that interest rates are going to rise during the term for which the FRA is being negotiated, the bank is likely to seek a higher fixed rate of interest than the variable rate of interest which is current at the time of negotiating the FRA.

Question 1

Explain what is meant by hedging in the context of interest rate risk.

Outline answer

Hedging is a means of reducing risk. Hedging involves coming to an agreement with another party who is prepared to take on the risk that you would otherwise bear. The other party may be willing to take on that risk because he would otherwise bear an opposing risk which may be 'matched' with your risk; alternatively, the other party may be a speculator who is willing to bear the risk in return for the prospect of making a profit. In the case of interest rates, a company with a variable rate loan clearly faces the risk that the rate of interest will increase in the future as the result of changing market conditions which cannot now be predicted.

Many financial instruments have been introduced in recent years to help corporate treasurers to hedge the risks of interest rate movements. These instruments include forward rate agreements, financial futures, interest rate swaps, options, and options on interest rate swaps ('swaptions').

Gap analysis of interest rate risk

1.10   The degree to which a firm is exposed to interest rate risk can be identified by using the method of **gap analysis**.

1.11 Some of the interest rate risks to which a firm is exposed may cancel each other out, where there are both assets and liabilities with which there is exposure to interest rate changes. If interest rates rise, more interest will be payable on loans and other liabilities, but this will be compensated for by higher interest received on assets such as money market deposits.

1.12 The effect of interest rate changes depends upon whether interest rates for the assets and liabilities are floating or fixed. Floating interest rates, of course, move up and down according to general market conditions. With fixed interest rates, the interest on the asset or liability will only be repriced at the date of maturity in the light of prevailing market conditions. If a fixed interest rate liability matures at the same time as a fixed rate asset, then the interest rate risks arising from the repricing of the two instruments will cancel each other out.

1.13 Gap analysis is based on the principle of grouping together assets and liabilities which are sensitive to interest rate changes according to their maturity dates. Two different types of 'gap' may occur.

   (a) A **negative gap**. A negative gap occurs when a firm has a larger amount of interest-sensitive liabilities maturing at a certain time or in a certain period than it has interest-sensitive assets maturing at the same time. The difference between the two amounts indicates the net exposure.

   (b) A **positive gap**. There is a positive gap if the amount of interest-sensitive assets maturing in a particular time exceeds the amount of interest-sensitive liabilities maturing at the same time.

1.14 With a negative gap, the company faces exposure if interest rates rise by the time of maturity. With a positive gap, the company will lose out if interest rates fall by maturity. The company's interest rate hedge should be based on the size of the gap.

Duration analysis

1.15 In the case of bonds, the return is comprised of both interest and a capital gain or loss accruing during the bond's life. Therefore, it is not possible simply to match bonds on the basis of a period to maturity. What can be done is to base the analysis on the 'notional' time to maturity or the **duration** of the bond.

Exam focus point
The calculations necessary for duration analysis are beyond the scope of the Paper 14 syllabus, and so here we deal only with the general principles.

1.16 The duration of the bond is calculated as the weighted average period to maturity of the cashflows of a bond, the weights being the present value of the cashflows arising from the bond. Note that for a **zero coupon bond**, the duration is the same as the period to actual maturity, and for **coupon bearing bonds**, the duration is less than the period to maturity.

1.17 The duration of a portfolio of bonds can be calculated to indicate the sensitivity of the market price of a bond to a change in the level of interest rates. The duration of the bond portfolio is the weighted average of the durations of the bonds within the portfolio, the weights being the market prices of the bonds. The duration can be used to find the hedge ratio for the portfolio, representing the size of the hedge needed to hedge the interest rate risk of the portfolio. Calculating a hedge ratio based on the duration is beyond the scope of your syllabus.

2   INTEREST RATE FUTURES   12/94, 6/96, 6/97, 12/98, 12/99

2.1   Most LIFFE futures contracts involve interest rates (**interest rate futures**), and these offer a means of hedging against the risk of interest rate movements. Such contracts are effectively a gamble on whether interest rates will rise or fall. Like other futures contracts, interest rate futures offer a way in which speculators can 'bet' on market movements just as they offer others who are more risk-averse a way of hedging risks.

2.2   Recall that a **futures contract** is an agreement to buy or sell a standard quantity of a particular financial instrument at a specified future date at an agreed price - the price being determined by trading on the floor of a futures exchange. For example, a company can contract to buy (or sell) £100,000 of a notional 30-year Treasury bond bearing an 8% coupon, in say, 6 months time, at an agreed price.

(a)   The futures price is likely to vary with changes in interest rates, and this acts as a hedge against adverse interest rate movements.

(b)   The outlay to buy futures is much less than for buying the financial instrument itself, and so a company can hedge large exposures of cash with a relatively small initial employment of cash.

2.3   **LIFFE** provides a market for futures contracts in long-dated, medium-dated and short-dated gilt-edged stocks, American, German and Japanese government bonds, short-term sterling and eurocurrency interest rates. **The Chicago Mercantile Exchange (CME)** and the **Chicago Board of Trade (CBOT)** are other important exchanges for the trading of interest rate futures. Interest rate futures are similar in effect to FRAs, except that the terms, the amounts and the periods are standardised.

Short-term interest rate futures

2.4   Most of the interest rate futures we shall encounter are for short term interest rates in sterling, eurodollars and other eurocurrencies. These **short-term interest rate futures** contracts normally represent interest receivable or payable on notional lending or borrowing *for a three month period* beginning on a standard future date. The contract size depends on the currency in which the lending or borrowing takes place.

2.5   For example, the 3-month sterling interest rate futures March contract represents the interest on notional lending or borrowing of £500,000 for three months, starting at the end of March. £500,000 is the contract size. As with all futures, a whole number of contracts must be dealt with. Note that the notional period of lending or borrowing starts when the contract expires, at the end of March. On LIFFE, futures contracts are available with maturity dates at the end of March, June, September and December. The 3-month eurodollar interest rate futures contract is for notional lending or borrowing in US dollars. The contract size is $1 million.

2.6   Note that with interest rate futures what we *buy* is the entitlement to interest *receipts* and what we *sell* is the promise to make interest *payments*. So when an investor buys one 3-month sterling contract he has the right to receive interest for three months in pounds. When he sells a 3-month sterling contract he incurs an obligation to make interest payments for three months.

BPP
PUBLISHING

2.7 The price at which a short term interest rate future can be bought or sold is determined by the three-month interest rate r% which the investor contracts for. It is calculated as (100 – r). For example, an investor who buys one 3-month sterling interest rate futures March contract at the price of 92.00 is notionally contracting to lend £500,000, receiving interest for three months at 8% (because 100 – 8 = 92). Note that the interest rate must be stated as a percentage, not a decimal. If, over the next week, the futures price *increases* to 92.20, this implies that interest rates at the end of March are now expected to be *lower* at 7.8% (because 100 – 7.8 = 92.20).

2.8 The investor can close out his position by selling one 3-month sterling interest rate futures March contract at 92.20. This means that he is notionally contracting to borrow £500,000 for 3 months at 7.8%. A gain has therefore been made by notionally borrowing £500,000 at 7.8% and lending it at 8%. The value of the gain is 0.2% × 3/12 × £500,000 = £250. The gain on closing out can be calculated directly from the prices at which the future was bought and sold:

Sell at	92.20
Buy at	92.00
Gain	0.20

0.2% × 3/12 × £500,000 = £250.

2.9 As with other futures, the gain is normally calculated by means of ticks. Remember that a tick is the smallest measured movement in the price of a futures contract, which in this case is 0.01, which represents 0.01% interest for 3 months on £500,000. So the value of one tick on the 3-month sterling contract is 0.01% × 3/12 × £500,000 = £12.50. The value of the investor's gain in the example above can be computed as 20 ticks × £12.50 × 1 contract = £250.

2.10 The tick value of other short-term interest rate futures contracts are shown in the table above. For example the contract size of the 3-month eurodollar is $1000,000. The tick value is 0.01% × 3/12 × $1,000,000 = $25. Note from the table that the tick values of interest rate futures are always in the same currency as the contract itself. Contrast this with currency futures, where the tick values were always in US dollars.

Margins

2.11 Initial margins and variation margins work in exactly the same way as with currency futures. In order to buy or sell one 3-month sterling futures contract, the investor does not have to advance the full £500,000, but only an initial margin of £300. Similarly the 3-month eurodollar contract has an initial margin of $500. Variation margin represents the change in price of the contract from day to day.

Long-term interest rate futures

2.12 Long-term interest rate futures are priced differently from the short-term interest rate futures described above. They represent the present value of interest to be received or paid over a long period; in other words they represent the value of a notional long-dated fixed interest government bond. Pricing for long-term bond futures is as a percentage of par value, similarly to the pricing of bonds themselves.

(a) In the case of US Treasury bond futures and Notional UK gilt futures, prices are quoted in 32nds of each full percentage point of price. The number of 32nds is shown as a number following a hyphen. For example, 91-23 denotes a price of $91^{23/32}$ per 100 nominal value and 91-16 denotes a price of $91^{1/2}$ per 100 nominal value.

(b) For other types of bond future, decimal pricing is used, so that if Italian government bond futures are quoted at 92.75, this indicates a price of $92^{3/4}$ per 100 nominal value.

2.13 Notional UK gilts have a nominal interest rate of 9%. If the price is quoted as 113-16, this shows that the notional bond has a value of 113.5. The long-term yield implied is therefore approximately $9\% \times 100/113.5 = 7.93\%$ (although the accurate figure needs to take into account the period to maturity of the underlying gilt).

2.14 EXAMPLE: FUTURES PRICE MOVEMENTS

September long gilts sterling futures fell in price on a particular day from 99-9 to 98-27. Privet plc has sold September futures, having a short position of 10 contracts. You are required to calculate the change in value of the contract on the day concerned.

2.15 SOLUTION

The fall in price represents 14 ticks ($99^{9/32} - 98^{27/32} = {}^{14/32}$ and the tick size is $^{1/32}$ of 1%). The value of one tick for long gilts sterling futures is £15.625. Each contract has fallen in value by $£15.625 \times 14 = £218.75$. For Privet plc, which has sold 10 contracts, the day's price movement represents a profit of $£218.75 \times 10 = £2,187.50$.

Question 2

The following futures price movements were observed during a week in October.

Contract	Price at start of week	Price at end of week
December short sterling	90.40	91.02
December US Treasury bonds	92-16	92-06
December Japanese government bond	93.80	94.25

Hawthorn plc has the following positions in these contracts:

(a) A short position (seller) of ten December short sterling contracts
(b) A long position (buyer) of six December US Treasury bonds contracts
(c) A long position of eight December Japanese government bonds contracts

Interest rate futures

	Notional amount of deposit	Tick size	Tick value
3-month (short sterling)	£500,000	0.01	£12.50
US Treasury bonds	$100,000	1/32 of 1	$31.25
Japanese government bond	Y100,000	0.01	Y10,000

Required

Calculate the profit or loss to the company on the futures contracts.

Answer

Short sterling

Increase in price (91.02 – 90.40 = 0.62)	62 ticks
Value per tick	£12.50
Increase in value of one contract (62 × £12.50)	£775

The company is a seller of ten contracts and would lose £7,750 (£775 × 10)

US Treasury bond futures

Fall in price ($92^{16}/_{32} - 92^{6}/_{32} = 10/32$)	10 ticks
Value per tick	$31.25
Fall in value of one contract (10 × $31.25)	$312.50

The company is a buyer of six contracts and would lose $1,875 ($312.50 × 6)

Japanese government bonds

Increase in price (94.25 − 93.80 = 0.45)	45 ticks
Value per tick	Y10,000
Increase in value of one contract (45 × Y10,000)	Y450,000

The company is a buyer of eight contracts and would gain Y3,600,000 (Y450,000 × 8)

Hedging using interest rate futures

2.16 The hedges illustrated here are initially concerned with short-term lending or borrowing for periods of up to about one year.

To hedge borrowing

2.17 If a corporate treasurer knows that his company needs to borrow at some future date but is concerned about the risk of interest rates rising before the start date of the borrowing, he can set up a hedge using interest rate futures which will produce the same sort of result as a forward rate agreement with a bank. In the language of interest rate futures, borrowing equals selling, so the treasurer must *sell* interest rate futures now and *buy* them on the date that actual borrowing starts. If interest rates rise over the period, the futures price will fall. The futures will therefore be sold at a higher price than they are bought for and the resulting gain will compensate for the increase in interest rates. As with all other futures, however, the company cannot take advantage of falling interest rates because the futures hedge will produce a compensating loss.

2.18 EXAMPLE: HEDGE OF A BORROWING TRANSACTION

In three months time, at the beginning of May, Yew plc will need to borrow £10 million for a three month period. The company can currently borrow at 9% per annum, but the treasurer is concerned that interest rates will rise before May. The 3-month sterling interest rate futures June contract is currently trading at 93.34.

Required

(a) Show how a futures hedge can be set up.

(b) Illustrate the result of the hedge if by May:

  (i) Interest rates have risen by 1% and the futures price has fallen by 1.00
  (ii) Interest rates have fallen by 0.5% and the futures price has risen by 0.48

2.19 SOLUTION

(a) £10,000,000 borrowing for three months is £10,000,000/£500,000 contracts = 20 contracts. The futures hedge is set up by selling 20 3-month sterling June contracts at the price of 93.34.

(b) The target interest payable at today's interest rate of 9% per annum is £10 million × 9% × 3/12 = £225,000.

The actual results under the two interest rate scenarios in May are as follows.

Scenario	(i)	(ii)
Company borrows at	10.00%	8.50%
Actual interest paid	£250,000	£212,500
Result of futures hedge:		
Sold 20 contracts at	93.34	93.34
Bought 20 contracts at	92.34	93.82
Gain /(loss) in ticks	100	(48)
Total gain /(loss) on 20 contracts at £12.50 per tick	£25,000	£(12,000)
Net payment	£225,000	£224,500

In Scenario (i), the actual interest less the futures gain gives a total exactly on target. The hedge efficiency is 100%. In Scenario (ii), the actual interest is a gain of £12,500 on target and the future gives a loss of £12,000. The hedge efficiency is 12,500/12,000 = 104.2%. Since £10 million is a whole number of contracts, the hedge efficiency is caused entirely by basis risk. The interest saving was 0.5% and the futures loss was 0.48% giving hedge efficiency of 0.5/0.48 = 104.2%.

To hedge lending

2.20 In the language of interest rate futures, lending equals buying. The treasurer hedges against the possibility of falling interest rates by buying futures now and selling futures on the date that the actual lending starts. The calculation proceeds in a similar way to the example above.

2.21 EXAMPLE: HEDGING BY A LENDER

Beech plc will have a surplus of 2 million US dollars for three months starting in August. The cash will be placed on fixed interest deposit, for which the current rate of interest is 5% pa. How can the deposit income be hedged using futures contracts? The September 3-month eurodollar futures contract is currently trading at 94.00.

2.22 SOLUTION

The target interest to be earned is $2 million × 5% × 3/12 = $25,000. The 3-month eurodollar contract size is $1 million and the tick value is $25. To hedge lending, buy two 3-month eurodollar September futures contracts now and sell two contracts in August.

Suppose that by August, interest rates have fallen by 1%. The $2 million is deposited at 4% for three months, yielding $20,000, a shortfall on target of $5,000. If the futures market has also moved by 1%, the contract price will have risen to 95.00, giving a gain of 100 ticks. The gain from selling 2 contracts at the higher price is 2 × 100 ticks × $25 = $5,000. This compensates for the shortfall in actual interest.

Maturity mismatch

2.23 **Maturity mismatch** occurs if the actual period of lending or borrowing does not match the notional period of the futures contract (three months). The number of futures contracts used has to be adjusted accordingly. Since fixed interest is involved, the number of contracts is adjusted in proportion to the time period of the actual loan or deposit compared with three months. For example, if the period of borrowing is six months the number of contracts is doubled. This leads to the following formula.

$$\text{Number of futures contracts} = \frac{\text{Amount of actual loan or deposit} \times \text{time period}}{\text{Futures contract size} \times 3 \text{ months}}$$

2.24 EXAMPLE: MATURITY MISMATCH (1)

On 5 June, a corporate treasurer decides to hedge a short-term deficit of 17 million Swiss francs which is predicted to arise for 2 months from 4 October to 3 December. Three month Euro Swiss franc futures, December contract, are trading at 98.15. The contract size is SFr 1 million. Show the action taken.

2.25 SOLUTION

$$\text{Number of futures contracts} = \frac{\text{SFr 17 million} \times 2 \text{ months}}{\text{SFr 1 million} \times 3 \text{ months}}$$

= 11.33 contracts, rounded to 11.

2.26 EXAMPLE : MATURITY MISMATCH (2)

In three months' time (June), Hawthorn plc will need to borrow £10 million for a six month period. Current interest rates for such a loan are 8% per annum. The company treasurer expects interest rates to rise by 2% over the next three months.

LIFFE *Three months sterling futures £500,000 points of 100*% are available, with June futures priced at 92.50. Tax, margin requirements and the time value of money can be ignored. What is the effect of using the futures market if the interest rate rises by 2% and the futures price moves by, say, 1.8%?

2.27 SOLUTION

'Points of 100%' indicates that the tick size on a three month contract is £500,000 × 0.01% × 3/12 = £12.50. The company's anticipated additional interest costs, which need to be matched by the expected gain on the futures, are:

£10 million × 2% × 6/12 = £100,000

A 2% movement in the futures price would represent 200 ticks. The gain on a single contract would be 200 × £12.50 = £2,500. The company needs 40 futures contracts to make the gain of £100,000 required, assuming that the futures price moves in line with interest rates. The futures market gain will be 40 × 180 ticks × £12.50 = £90,000, not quite enough to offset fully the £100,000 additional interest costs. The **hedge efficiency** is 90,000/100,000 = 90%.

Use of short-term interest rate futures to hedge interest rates on a long-term floating rate loan

2.28 The above examples have concentrated on short-term lending and borrowing, but 3-month interest rate futures can also be used to hedge interest on longer term floating rate loans.

Typically these loans are subject to a 'rollover' every three months. In other words, every three months the loan interest rate is reviewed and set for the next three months.

2.29 EXAMPLE: LONG-TERM FLOATING RATE LOAN

Ash plc has a 5-year £5 million floating rate loan at an interest rate of LIBOR + 2%. (LIBOR = London Inter-Bank Offered Rate). Interest is reviewed every three months on 1 February, May, August and November. It is now 25 November and the treasurer is worried that sterling interest rates are about to rise. 3-month sterling interest rate futures (contract size £500,000) are available with March and June maturity dates. Show how the next two rollover periods can be hedged (no computations required).

2.30 SOLUTION

The floating rate loan is regarded as a series of 3-month short-term loans and the treasurer hedges the interest in 3-month blocks. The next two rollover periods are 1 February to 30 April and 1 May to 31 July. The interest rate for the three month periods will be set on 1 February and 1 May. For the 1 February rollover date, March or June futures can be used but for the May rollover date June futures must be used. The value of the £5 million loan represents 10 contracts.

The most likely action taken by the treasurer is:

Now: Sell 10 March futures contracts and 10 June futures contracts.
1 Feb: Buy 10 March futures contracts.
1 May: Buy 10 June futures contracts.

Use of interest rate futures

2.31 The **standardised nature** of interest rate futures is a limitation on their use by the corporate treasurer as a means of hedging, because they cannot always be matched with specific interest rate exposures. Futures contracts are frequently used by banks and other financial institutions as a means of hedging their portfolios: such institutions are often not concerned with achieving an exact match with their underlying exposure.

2.32 The seller of a futures contract does not have to own the underlying instrument, but may need to deliver it on the contract's delivery date if the buyer requires it. Most, but not all, interest rate contracts are **settled for cash** rather than by delivery of the underlying instrument.

2.33 Interest rate futures offer a means of **speculation** for some investors, because there is no requirement that buyers and sellers should actually be lenders and borrowers (respectively) of the nominal amounts of the contracts. A relatively small investment can lead to substantial gains, or alternatively to substantial losses. The speculator is in effect 'betting' on future interest rate movements.

Basis risk

2.34 The concept of hedge efficiency was introduced earlier. Remember that there are two reasons why it is often not possible to achieve a perfect (100%) hedge with currency futures or interest rate futures, as follows.

BPP
PUBLISHING

(a) The fact that futures are available only in certain standard sizes means that the contracts may not fit exactly the company's needs.

(b) There is **basis risk** arising from the fact that the price of the futures contract may not move as expected in relation to the value of the instrument which is being hedged. There are two main reasons for this basis risk.

    (i) Cashflow requirements may differ, altering the relative values of the underlying financial instrument and the derivative futures contract. This is because usually no payment is required when a forward contract is entered into, while an initial margin must be deposited for a futures contract.

    (ii) The financial instrument which the firm is seeking to hedge may be different from the financial instrument which underlies the futures contract. For example, a firm may wish to hedge interest rates which are linked to bank base interest rates using a futures contract which is based on the London Inter-Bank Offered Rate (LIBOR). This type of hedge is called cross hedging, and there will be basis risk because LIBOR will not always move exactly in line with bank base interest rates.

2.35 The basis risk can be calculated as the difference between the futures price and the current price ('**cash market' price**) of the underlying security.

2.36 EXAMPLE: BASIS AND BASIS RISK

To give an example, if three-month LIBOR (the London Inter-Bank Offered Rate) is 7% and the September price of the three-month sterling future is 92.70 now (at the end of March, say) then the basis is:

Libor (100-7)	93.00
Futures	92.70
	0.30 %
	or 30 basis points

2.37 If a firm takes a position in the futures contract with a view to closing out the contract before its maturity, there is still likely to be basis, and the firm can only estimate what effect this will have on the hedge. '**Basis risk**' refers to the problem that the basis may result in an imperfect hedge. The basis will be **zero** at the **maturity date of the contract**.

2.38 In the above example, suppose that the future is being used to hedge a borrowing commitment which begins in 5 months' time, one month before the maturity date. We may estimate the expected basis by assuming that it reduces steadily to zero. $30 \times 1/6 = 5$ basis points.

2.39 The expected movement in basis will be disadvantageous to the company. If interest rates rise by 1% (to the equivalent of 92.00), then with five basis points, the futures price is expected to move to $(92.00 - 0.05) = 91.95$. The loss of 1% in the cash market is offset by a $(92.70 - 91.95) = 0.75\%$ gain in the futures market, resulting in an imperfect hedge. However, there is no guarantee that the basis will turn out to be the figure estimated: movement in the yield curve could change the basis.

Hedge ratio

2.40 The **hedge ratio** is the ratio of the amount of the futures contracts bought or sold to the amount of the underlying financial instrument being hedged. For example, if a company is exposed to interest rate risk on a loan of £210,000 and it takes a position in futures contracts for £200,000, the hedge ratio is:

$$\frac{200,000}{210,000} = 95.2\%$$

Optimal hedge ratio

2.41 The **optimal hedge ratio** is given by the formula:

$$p\frac{\sigma_i}{\sigma_f}$$

where $p =$ the coefficient of correlation between the change in price of the underlying instrument and the change in price of the futures contract, each measured over the period of the hedge

$\sigma_i =$ the standard deviation of the change in the price of the underlying instrument

$\sigma_f =$ the standard deviation of the change in the price of the futures contract

2.42 As you can probably appreciate, establishing values for the variables p, σ_i and σ_f is more of a problem than calculating the optimal hedge ratio using the formula.

2.43 EXAMPLE: OPTIMAL HEDGE RATIO

Melbury plc wishes to hedge the interest rate risk on a 1 year floating rate loan of £2,000,000. The futures price is more volatile than the price of the debt, such that $\sigma_i = 0.08$ and $\sigma_f = 0.10$. $p = 0.6$. What is the optimal hedge ratio?

2.44 SOLUTION

Optimal hedge ratio = $p\dfrac{\sigma_i}{\sigma_f} = 0.6 \times \dfrac{0.08}{0.10} = 0.48$

It follows that Melbury plc should take a position in interest rate futures for:

$2,000,000 \times 0.48 = £960,000$

3 OVER-THE-COUNTER INTEREST RATE OPTIONS 12/94, 6/96, 12/99

3.1 An **interest rate option** grants the buyer of it the right, but not the obligation, to deal at an agreed interest rate (strike rate) at a future maturity date. On the date of expiry of the option, the buyer must decide whether or not to exercise the right. Clearly, a buyer of an option to borrow will not wish to exercise it if the market interest rate is now below that specified in the option agreement. Conversely, an option to lend will not be worth exercising if market rates have risen above the rate specified in the option by the time the option has expired. The term **interest rate guarantee (IRG)** refers to an interest rate option which hedges the interest rate for a single period of up to one year.

3.2 Tailor-made (**over-the-counter**) interest rate options can be purchased from major banks, with specific values, periods of maturity, denominated currencies and rates of agreed interest. The cost of the option is the 'premium'. Interest rate options offer more flexibility than and are more expensive than FRAs.

Caps, floors and collars

3.3 Various **cap** and **collar** agreements are possible. An **interest rate cap** is an option which sets an interest rate ceiling. A **floor** is an option which sets a lower limit to interest rates. Using a 'collar' arrangement, the borrower can buy an interest rate cap and at the same time sell an interest rate floor which fixes a minimum cost for the company. The cost is lower than for a cap alone. However, the borrowing company forgoes the benefit of movements in interest rates below the floor limit in exchange for this cost reduction. A **zero cost collar** can be negotiated sometimes, if the premium paid for buying the cap equals the premium received for selling the floor.

3.4 EXAMPLE: CAP AND COLLAR (1)

Suppose the prevailing interest rate for a company's borrowing is 10%. The company treasurer considers that a rise in rates above 12% will cause serious financial difficulties for the company. How can the treasurer make use of a 'cap and collar' arrangement?

3.5 SOLUTION

The company can buy an interest rate cap from the bank. The bank will reimburse the company for the effects of a rise in rates above 12%. As part of the arrangements with the bank, the company can agree that it will pay at least 9%, say, as a 'floor' rate. The bank will pay the company for agreeing this. In other words, the company has sold the floor to the bank, which partly offsets the costs of the cap. The bank benefits if rates fall below the floor level.

3.6 EXAMPLE: CAP AND COLLAR (2)

Arabella plc has £20 million of borrowings at floating rate, LIBOR + 0.75%, with a three month rollover. The treasurer is considering hedging the interest rate for the period starting on the next rollover date and has been offered an FRA at 10% interest, and a cap at 10% interest for a premium of 1% per annum. The bank is prepared to buy a floor from Arabella plc at 8% interest for a premium of 0.75% per annum.

Show the effective interest rate paid for the quarter if Arabella:

(a) Does not hedge
(b) Agrees the FRA
(c) Buys the cap
(d) Buys the collar

under each of the following conditions:

LIBOR moves to (1) 6.25% (2) 8.25% (3) 10.25%.

3.7 SOLUTION

Scenario	*1*	*2*	*3*
LIBOR	6.25%	8.25%	10.25%
(a) *No hedge* (LIBOR + 0.75%)	7.00%	9.00%	11.00%
(b) *FRA*			
Interest paid at	7.00%	9.00%	11.00%
(Refunded)/paid to bank	3.00%	1.00%	(1.00)%
Effective net interest payment	10.00%	10.00%	10.00%

Scenario	1	2	3
(c) *Option (cap)*			
Exercise?	NO	NO	YES
Interest rate paid	7.00%	9.00%	10.00%
Add: Premium cost	1.00%	1.00%	1.00%
	8.00%	10.00%	11.00%
(d) *Collar*			
Exercise cap?	NO	NO	YES
Floor exercised by bank?	YES	NO	NO
Interest paid	8.00%	9.00%	10.00%
Add: Net premium paid	0.25%	0.25%	0.25%
	8.25%	9.25%	10.25%

3.8 The FRA fixes the interest rate at 10%. The option (cap) fixes a maximum effective interest rate of 11% but allows the company to benefit from falling interest rates. The collar fixes a maximum effective interest rate of 10.25% and a minimum rate of 8.25%.

Types of collar

3.9 A collar for **borrowing** (as above) is constructed by buying a cap and selling a floor at a lower interest rate. A collar for **lending** is constructed by selling a cap and buying a floor at a lower interest rate.

Hedging strategy alternatives

3.10 Different hedging instruments often offer alternative ways of managing risk in a specific situation. In this section, we work through an example in which different ways in which a company can hedge interest rate risk are evaluated, covering both interest rate futures and interest rate options (interest rate guarantees).

3.11 EXAMPLE: HEDGING STRATEGY (1)

It is 31 December. Octavo plc needs to borrow £6 million in three months' time for a period of six months. For the type of loan finance which Octavo would use, the rate of interest is currently 13% per year and the Corporate Treasurer is unwilling to pay a higher rate. The treasurer is concerned about possible future fluctuations in interest rates, and is considering the following possibilities:

(a) Forward rate agreements (FRAs)
(b) Interest rate futures
(c) Interest rate guarantees or short-term interest rate caps

The Corporate Treasurer of Octavo decides to hedge the interest rate risk by using interest rate futures. Her expectation is that interest rates will increase by 2% over the next three months. The current price of March sterling three months time deposit futures is 87.25. The standard contract size is £500,000, while the minimum price movement is one tick, the value of which is 0.01% per year of the contract size.

You are required to set out calculations of the effect of using the futures market to hedge against movements in the interest rate and estimate the hedge efficiency:

(a) If interest rates increase by 2% and the futures market price moves by 2%
(b) If interest rates increase by 2% and the futures market price moves by 1.75%

BPP PUBLISHING

(c)   If interest rates fall by 1.5% and the futures market price moves by 1.25%

The time value of money, taxation and margin requirements can be ignored.

3.12   SOLUTION

(a)   One tick has a value of: $0.0001 \times 500,000 \times {}^{3}/_{12} = £12.50$.

$2\% \equiv 200$ ticks

If interest rates rise by 2%, the extra interest over 6 months is:

$£6,000,000 \times 2\% \times {}^{6}/_{12} = £60,000$

Therefore a £60,000 gain from the futures contracts is required.

2% (200 ticks) movement on one contract would produce a gain of:

$200 \times £12.50 = £2,500$

Therefore, to hedge £60,000, 24 contracts are required for the hedge.

£500,000 March sterling time deposit contracts to be sold at 87.25 (effectively 12.75% interest) on 31 December. 24 to be bought in March or when interest rates change at 85.25 (effectively 14.75% interest), closing out the position.

Gain: 24×200 ticks at £12.50 = £60,000

There is 100% hedge efficiency (the perfect hedge).

(b)   In this case, the futures gain will be 24×175 ticks at £12.50 = £52,500.

The hedge efficiency is £52,500 ÷ £60,000 = 87.5%

(c)   In this case, there is a gain on the cash market arising from the fall in interest rates, and a loss on the futures market.

Cash market gain: $£6,000,000 \times 1.5\% \times {}^{6}/_{12} = £45,000$

A futures market loss arises from selling at 87.25 and closing out the position at 88.50.

Futures market loss: 24×125 ticks at £12.50 = £37,500

                          ie $£6m \times 1.25\% \times {}^{6}/_{12} = £37,500$

The hedge efficiency is: $\dfrac{£45,000}{£37,500} = 120\%$

3.13   EXAMPLE: HEDGING STRATEGY (2)

We now extend the example to look at an alternative hedging method.

Required

Calculate, for situations (a) to (c) in Paragraph 3.12 above, whether the total cost of the loan after hedging would have been lower with the futures hedge chosen by the treasurer or with an interest rate guarantee which she could have purchased at 13% for a premium of 0.25% of the size of the loan to be guaranteed. Again, the time value of money, taxation and margin requirements are to be ignored.

3.14   SOLUTION

Futures hedge costs

(a)   Interest $£6m \times 15\% \times {}^{6}/_{12} = £450,000$
      Less gain £60,000 = £390,000

(b)   Interest (as in (i)) £450,000
      Less gain £52,500 = £397,500

(c)   Interest £6m × 11.5% × $^6/_{12}$ =£345,000
      Add loss £37,500 = £382,500

The premium for the guarantee is £6m × 0.25% = £15,000.

The guarantee would be used in cases (a) and (b) when interest rates increase.

Then, total cost limiting interest rates to 13% is:

£6m × 13% × $^6/_{12}$ = £390,000
Plus premium of £15,000, equals £405,000.

This costs more than the futures contracts hedge in cases (a) and (b).

In case (c), the guarantee is not used.

Interest costs at 11.5% are:

£6m × 11.5% × $^6/_{12}$ = £345,000
Plus £15,000 premium, equals £360,000.

This costs less than the futures hedge, reflecting the fact that declining to take up the interest rate option in the case of the guarantee has allowed the company to take advantage of the lower interest rates in the cash market.

4   TRADED INTEREST RATE OPTIONS   12/98, 12/99

4.1   Exchange-traded interest rate options are available as **options on interest rate futures,** which give the holder the right to buy (call option) or sell (put option) one futures contract on or before the expiry of the option at a specified price. The best way to understand the pricing of interest rate options is to look at a schedule of prices. The schedule below (from the *Financial Times*) is for 8 August in a particular year.

Long gilt futures options (LIFFE) £50,000 64th of 100%

Strike	Calls				Puts			
price	Sep	Oct	Nov	Dec	Sep	Oct	Nov	Dec
106	0-61	1-09	1-34	1-54	0-31	1-13	1-38	1-58
107	0-29	0-46	1-05	1-25	0-63	1-50	2-09	2-29
108	0-11	0-26	0-47	1-01	1-45	2-30	2-51	3-05

4.2   The tick size (minimum price movement) is $^1/_{64}$% and the tick value is thus $^1/_{64}$% × 50,000 = £7.8125.

4.3   The price of an October call contract at a strike price of 106 is $1^9/_{64}$% × 50,000 = £570.31. This means that an investor could pay £570.31 and buy one long gilt futures option which would allow him to purchase a notional 9% UK gilt in October at a price of £106 per £100 stock.

4.4   Here is another schedule of prices for options on interest rate futures (again, for 8 August).

Short sterling options (LIFFE) £500,000 points of 100%

Strike	Calls			Puts		
price	Sep	Dec	Mar	Sep	Dec	Mar
9300	0.19	0.31	0.38	0.05	0.21	0.40
9325	0.05	0.17	0.26	0.16	0.32	0.53
9350	0.01	0.09	0.17	0.37	0.49	0.69

BPP PUBLISHING

4.5 The short sterling option is an option to buy (call) or sell (put) the 3-month sterling interest rate futures contract. Note that the contract size (£500,000) is the same as that of the future, which is true of all traded interest rate options (for example three month eurodollar options have a contract size of $1 million which is the same as that of the eurodollar futures contract).

4.6 The schedule shows that options are available to buy or sell the 3-month sterling futures contract at strike prices varying between 9300 and 9350. For traded options these strike prices are traditionally shown in ticks (0.01%). A call option with a strike price of 9300 is simply an option to buy the 3-month sterling futures contract at the price of 93.00.

4.7 Special attention must be paid to the premium on **short interest rate option contracts**. As an example, consider the premium on 9300 September call options. This is shown as 0.19 and is described at the top of the table as 'points of 100%'. There are two ways of calculating the premium cost:

(a) The premium is 0.19% per annum of £500,000 **for three months:**

$0.19\% \times £500,000 \times 3/12 = £237.50$; or

(b) The premium is 19 ticks at £12.50 per tick = £237.50.

4.8 The premium cost of this option is thus £237.50 per contract. It can be exercised at a profit if the September 3-month sterling futures contract price is higher than 93.00. For example, suppose the futures contract price moves to 93.70 because interest rates are falling. The option can be exercised thus:

Exercise the option to buy one futures contract at:	93.00
Close out by simultaneously selling one futures contract at market price:	93.70
Gain in ticks	70

	£
Value of gain (70 × £12.50)	875.00
Less: option premium cost	237.50
Net profit	637.50

Note: In practice, of course, the option would probably not be exercised if it still had a significant time value. Closing out by selling a 9300 call option would produce a better result.

Question 3

Using the above table, what is the premium cost in pounds of 10 March short sterling put option contracts, strike price 9325? What gain would be made if the options were exercised when the futures price was 92.95?

Answer

The premium is listed as 0.53, which means 0.53% × £500,000 × 3/12 = £662.5 per contract (alternatively 53 ticks × £12.50 = £662.5). The cost of 10 option contracts is £6,625.

If the option is exercised when the futures price is 92.95:

Exercise the option to sell 10 futures contract at:	93.25
Close out by simultaneously buying 10 futures contract at market price:	92.95
Gain in ticks	30

	£
Value of gain: 10 contracts × 30 ticks × £12.50:	3,750
Less: option premium cost	6,625
Net loss	(2,875)

In this case the option did not make sufficient gain to cover its premium cost.

4.9 A quick method of calculating the net gains or losses from exercising traded interest rate options is to work entirely in terms of ticks. In the last example, we could have done the calculation like this:

	Ticks
Sell 10 at strike price	9325
Buy 10 at market price	9295
Gain	30
Less: premium	53
Net loss	(23)

Value of net loss = 10 contracts × 23 ticks × £12.50 = £2,875.

Using traded interest rate options for hedging

4.10 To use traded interest rate options for hedging, follow exactly the same principles as for traded currency options, noting the following specific points.

(a) If a company needs to hedge borrowing at some future date, it should purchase put options. Instead of selling futures now and buying futures later, it purchases an option to sell futures now and only exercises the option if interest rates have risen causing a fall in the price of the futures contract.

(b) Similarly, if a company needs to lend money, it should purchase call options.

The use of traded options is best demonstrated in comparison with the use of futures contracts, as in the following example.

4.11 EXAMPLE: COMPARING FUTURES AND TRADED OPTIONS

It is now 1 November. The treasury department of Intopt plc has predicted a temporary surplus of US$ 7.2 million which will arise towards the end of March next year. The surplus is predicted to last four months. It is intended to put this money on deposit for that period. The company can currently deposit US dollars at 6% per annum. In case of further reductions in interest rates, it is decided to hedge, using futures or traded options.

The following data is available.

1 November

Three month eurodollar futures $1,000,000 points of 100%

	Contract price
Dec	93.30
Mar	92.40
Jun	91.74
Sep	91.28

Short eurodollar options (LIFFE) $1,000,000 points of 100%

Strike price	....	*Calls*	....	....	*Puts*	....
	Dec	*Mar*	*Jun*	*Dec*	*Mar*	*Jun*
9325	0.27	0.09	0.12	0.22	0.94	1.63
9350	0.13	0.04	0.08	0.33	1.14	1.84
9375	0.05	0.02	0.05	0.50	1.37	2.06

Required

Illustrate the use of futures and options hedges under the following scenarios.

(1)   Interest rates fall by 1.5%. The futures market moves by 80% of this amount.
(2)   Interest rates rise by 2%. The futures market moves by 90% of this amount.

4.12 SOLUTION

Target interest to be earned = 6% × $7.2 million × $\frac{4}{12}$ = $144,000.

In Scenario (1), interest rates fall: the receipt will be 4.5% × $7.2 million × $\frac{4}{12}$ = $108,000.

In Scenario (2), interest at 8% will be $192,000.

Hedge using the futures market

Number of contracts = $\dfrac{\$7.2\text{million} \ \times \ 4 \text{ months}}{\$1\text{million} \ \times \ 3 \text{ months}}$ = 9.6 contracts; round to 10.

On 1 November, buy 10 March 3-month Eurodollar futures contracts at 92.40.

At end of March:

Scenario	(1)	(2)
Interest rate moves to	4.5%	8.0%
Price of futures contract moves to	93.60	90.60

Sell the futures at this price.

Result of futures hedge:		
Sell 10 at	93.60	90.60
Buy 10 at	92.40	92.40
Gain/(loss) per contract in ticks	120.00	(180.00)

Value of one tick = $25.

	$	$		
Value of futures gain/(loss)	30,000	(45,000)		
Actual interest received:	108,000	192,000		
Total net receipt	138,000	147,000	Target:	$144,000

The futures hedge 'fixes' the target receipt of $144,000, subject to small inefficiencies.

Hedge using traded options

Buy 10 March call option contracts. The best call option, if exercised, can be determined by finding the minimum of: strike price *plus* premium.

Strike price	Premium (ticks)	Total
9325	9	9334
9350	4	9354
9375	2	9377

Choose the *9325 March call option,* with a premium cost of 9 ticks. In Scenario (1) the option will be exercised to give a gain, but in Scenario (2) the option is allowed to lapse.

Scenario	(1)	(2)
Interest rate moves to	4.50%	8.00%
Futures price in March	93.60	90.60
Exercise option to buy at 93.25?	Yes	No
	Ticks	*Ticks*
Sell at	9360	-
Buy at	9325	-
Gain	35	-
Premium (ticks)	(9)	(9)
Net gain/(cost):	26	(9)
	$	$
Value of net gain/(cost):	6,500	(2,250)
Actual interest received	108,000	192,000
Total net receipt:	114,500	189,750

4.13 The option does not provide such a good hedge as the future when it is exercised (Scenario (1)). But when interest rates rise (Scenario (2)) it allows the company to benefit.

Collars using traded interest rate options   6/96

4.14 When we used OTC interest rate options to make collars, we saw that a **collar for borrowing** is made by buying a cap and selling a floor at a lower interest rate., and a **collar for lending** is made by selling a cap and buying a floor at a lower interest rate. Converting this into the language of traded options, buying a **cap**, which fixes our maximum borrowing rate, means buying a traded **put** option. When we buy a **floor**, we are buying a **call** option.

4.15 Remembering that lower interest rates mean higher futures prices and higher option strike prices, we can deduce that when we use traded options the floor must be at a *higher* strike price than the cap. Thus a **collar for borrowing** is made by buying a put and selling a call at a higher strike price, and a **collar for lending** is made by selling a put and buying a call at a higher strike price.

4.16 EXAMPLE: COLLARS USING TRADED INTEREST RATE OPTIONS

Continuing with the example of Intopt plc, above, you are asked to demonstrate how collars can be used to hedge the company's interest receipt.

(a) Demonstrate the result of using a collar with options on strike prices of 9375 and 9325.
(b) Identify the best collar under each of the two scenarios given.

4.17 SOLUTION

(a) A collar for lending is constructed by buying a call option on a high strike price and selling a put option at a low strike price. We therefore consider buying the March 9375 call options and selling the March 9325 put options. The net premium in ticks is 2 – 94 = 92 ticks *received* per contract. Buy 10 March 9375 call options and sell 10 March 9325 put options.

Scenario	(1)	(2)
Interest rate moves to	4.5%	8.0%
Futures price in March (ticks)	9360	9060
Exercise option to buy at 9375?	No	No
Is the 9325 put option exercised?	No	Yes
	Ticks	Ticks
We must buy from the other party at	-	9325
We sell at market price	-	9060
Loss made	-	(265)
Net premium received (ticks)	92	92
Net gain/(loss) in ticks	92	(173)
	$	$
Total value of gain/(loss) on 10 contracts	23,000	(43,250)
Actual interest received:	108,000	192,000
Total net receipt	131,000	148,750

The collar gives a result somewhere between that of the future and that of the option as shown in the summary results below.

Scenario	(1)	(2)
Total receipt:	$	$
Target interest	144,000	144,000
Future	138,000	147,000
Collar: 9375 call/9325 put	131,000	148,750
9325 call option	114,500	189,750

(b) *Choosing the best collar*

As with currency hedges, the 'best' interest rate collar is different under different scenarios. Three possible collars can be identified, labelled (i), (ii) and (iii) in the workings below. We can identify the best one under each scenario by the following method.

Collar	(i)	(ii)	(iii)
Buy call at	9375	9375	9350
Sell put at	9350	9325	9325
Premium:	Ticks	Ticks	Ticks
Cost of call	(2)	(2)	(4)
Received from put	114	94	94
Net premium received:	112	92	90
Scenario (1): Future moves to 9360			
Exercise call option?	No	No	Yes
Is put exercised?	No	No	No
	Ticks	Ticks	Ticks
Gain from call option	-	-	10
Loss from put option	-	-	-
Net premium received	112	92	90
Total gain in ticks	112	92	100
Total value of gain on 10 contracts	$28,000	$23,000	$25,000
	Best		

Collar	(i)	(ii)	(iii)
Scenario (2): Future moves to 9060			
Exercise call option?	No	No	No
Is put exercised?	Yes	Yes	Yes
	Ticks	*Ticks*	*Ticks*
Gain from call option	-	-	-
Loss from put option	(290)	(265)	(265)
Net premium received	112	92	90
Net loss in ticks	(178)	(173)	(175)
Total value of loss on			
10 contracts	$(44,500)	$(43,250)	$(43,750)
		Best	

Summary. Collar (ii), which we examined in the first part of this question, is the best performer in scenario (2), producing the lowest loss when interest rates rise. However, it is the worst performer in Scenario (1) when interest rates fall and protection is needed. The best protection in Scenario (1) is given by Collar (i).

5 INTEREST RATE SWAPS 6/96, 12/97

5.1 **Interest rate swaps** involve two parties agreeing to exchange interest payments with each other over an agreed period. Because the Paper 14 syllabus is concerned mainly with corporate finance, we will usually assume that at least one of the parties is a limited company. In practice, however, the major players in the swaps market are banks and many other types of institution can become involved, for example national and local governments and international institutions.

> **KEY TERM**
>
> **Interest rate swap:** an agreement whereby the parties to the agreement exchange interest rate commitments.

5.2 In the simplest form of interest rate swap, party A agrees to pay the interest on party B's loan, while party B reciprocates by paying the interest on A's loan. If the swap is to make sense, **the two parties must swap interest which has different characteristics**. Assuming for the moment that the interest swapped is in the same currency, the usual motivation for the swap is to switch from paying floating rate interest to fixed interest or *vice versa*. A typical swap arrangement may arise as follows.

5.3 Company A has borrowed £10 million at a fixed interest rate of 9% per annum. Company B has also borrowed £10 million but pays interest at LIBOR + 1%. LIBOR is currently 8% per annum. The directors of company A feel that interest rates are going to fall and would prefer to be paying floating rate interest. The feeling at company B is that interest rate risk could be removed if they were paying fixed interest and that this would facilitate cash planning. The two companies agree to swap interest payments. A pays LIBOR + 1% to B and B pays 9% to A. No loan principals are swapped and both parties retain the obligation to repay their original loans. A summary of the arrangements can be shown as follows.

	Company A		Company B
Interest paid on original loan	(9%)		(LIBOR + 1%)
A pays to B	(LIBOR + 1%)	→	LIBOR + 1%
B pays to A	9%	←	(9%)
Net payment after swap	(LIBOR + 1%)		(9%)

5.4 Both parties have achieved their objective of switching the nature of their interest payments and, if LIBOR stays at 8%, neither party gains or loses. However, if LIBOR falls, A gains at the expense of B and the reverse happens if LIBOR rises.

5.5 Note that the parties to a swap retain their obligations to the original lenders. If company B defaults, company A still has liability to pay the interest on its 9% loan. This means that the parties must accept **counterparty risk**, which is the risk that the swap partner defaults.

5.6 Obvious questions to ask are: 'Why do the companies bother swapping interest payments with each other? Why don't they just terminate their original loan and take out a new one?' The answer is that transaction costs may be too high. Terminating an original loan early may involve a significant termination fee and taking out a new loan will involve issue costs. Arranging a swap can be significantly cheaper, even if a banker is used as an intermediary. Because the banker is simply acting as an agent on the swap arrangement and has to bear no default risk, the arrangement fee can be kept low.

5.7 Most interest rate swap deals are more complex than the simple arrangement illustrated above. It is unlikely that both parties will have loans outstanding of exactly the same amount or that they will want to arrange an exact swap of each others' interest payments. In practice, a notional amount of loan principle is agreed and interest payments made to each other are negotiated. This can result in one party making a gain out of the other or, in some cases, both parties making a gain out of the loan markets. The following example illustrates a situation where both parties gain.

5.8 EXAMPLE: INTEREST RATE SWAPS

Goodcredit plc has been given a high credit rating. It can borrow at a fixed rate of 11%, or at a variable interest rate equal to LIBOR, which also happens to be 11% at the moment. It would like to borrow at a variable rate. Secondtier plc is a company with a lower credit rating, which can borrow at a fixed rate of 12½% or at a variable rate of LIBOR plus ½%. It would like to borrow at a fixed rate.

(a) Without a swap, Goodcredit would borrow at LIBOR which is currently 11%, and Secondtier would borrow at 12½% fixed.

(b) With a swap:

    (i) Goodcredit would borrow at a fixed rate (11%)

    (ii) Secondtier would borrow at a variable rate (LIBOR plus ½%), currently 11½%

    (iii) They would then agree a rate for swapping interest, perhaps with:

        (1) Goodcredit paying Secondtier variable rate interest, at LIBOR

        (2) Secondtier paying Goodcredit fixed rate interest, say at 11½%

5.9 The net result is as follows.

Goodcredit plc		*Secondtier plc*	
Pays		Pays	
to bank	(11%)	to bank	(LIBOR plus ½%)
in swap	(LIBOR)	in swap	(11½%)
Receives		Receives	
in swap	11½%	in swap	LIBOR
Net interest cost	(LIBOR less ½%)	Net interest cost	(12%)

The results of the swap are that Goodcredit ends up paying variable rate interest, but at a lower cost than it could get from a bank, and Secondtier ends up paying fixed rate interest, also at a lower cost than it could get from investors or a bank.

5.10 If both parties ended up paying interest at a lower rate than was obtainable from the bank, where did this gain come from? To answer this question, set out a table of the rates at which both companies could borrow from the bank.

	Goodcredit	*Secondtier*	*Difference*
Can borrow at fixed rate	11%	12½%	1½%
Can borrow at floating rate	LIBOR	LIBOR + ½%	½%
Difference between differences			1%

5.11 Goodcredit has a better credit rating than Secondtier in both types of loan market, but its advantage is comparatively higher in the fixed interest market. The 1% differential between Goodcredit's advantage in the two types of loan may represent a market imperfection or there may be a good reason for it. Whatever the reason, it represents a potential gain which can be made out of a swap arrangement.

5.12 Assume that the gain is split equally between Goodcredit and Secondtier, ½% each. Then Goodcredit will be targeting a floating rate loan of LIBOR less ½% (½% less than that at which it can borrow from the bank). Similarly, Secondtier will be targeting a fixed interest loan of 12½% – ½% = 12%. These are precisely the rates which are obtained by the swap arrangement illustrated above. Note that for the swap to give a gain to both parties:

(a) Each company must borrow in the loan market in which it has **comparative advantage**. Goodcredit has the greatest advantage when it borrows fixed interest. Secondtier has the least disadvantage when it borrows floating rate.

(b) The parties must actually **want** interest of the opposite type to that in which they have comparative advantage. Goodcredit wants floating and Secondtier wants fixed.

5.13 Once the target interest rate for each company has been established, there is an infinite number of swap arrangements which will produce the same net result. The example illustrated above is only one of them.

Question 4

Enter swap interest payments into this *pro-forma* to move from the original interest paid to the desired result.

	Goodcredit	*Secondtier*
Pays		
to bank	(11%)	(LIBOR + ½%)
in swap		
Receives		
in swap		
Net interest cost	(LIBOR – ½%)	(12%)

BPP PUBLISHING

Answer

Enter any figure into any slot of the pro-forma and the other figures must automatically balance out. Here is one of many possible solutions.

	Goodcredit	Secondtier
Pays		
to bank	(11%)	(LIBOR + ½%)
In swap	(LIBOR + ½%)	(12%)
Receives		
in swap	12%	LIBOR + ½%
Net interest cost	(LIBOR – ½%)	(12%)

5.14 Section summary

In summary, the advantages of interest rate swaps in a single currency are as follows.

(a) They enable a switch from floating rate to fixed rate interest, or *vice versa*, for use as a hedge against interest rate risk.

(b) The arrangement costs are often significantly less than terminating an existing loan and taking out a new one.

(c) They can be used to make interest rate savings, either out of the counterparty or out of the loan markets, by using the principle of comparative advantage.

(d) They are available for longer periods than the short-term methods of hedging risk (FRAs, futures, options) that we have considered in this chapter.

(e) They are flexible and can be easily reversed.

Like all financial instruments, swaps can be used for speculation as well as hedging. In cases receiving much publicity, some local authority treasurers in the UK have engaged in such speculation with disastrous results.

6 CURRENCY SWAPS

6.1 In a **currency swap**, the parties agree to swap equivalent amounts of currency for a period. This effectively involves the exchange of debt from one currency to another. As with interest rate swaps, liability on the principal is not transferred and the parties are liable to counterparty risk: if the other party defaults on the agreement to pay interest, the original borrower remains liable to the lender. This can present complicated legal problems, and some borrowers are unwilling to get involved in swap transactions for this reason.

6.2 Swaps are flexible since they can be arranged in any size and are reversible. Transaction costs are low, only amounting to legal fees, since there is no commission or premium to be paid.

(a) Currency swaps can provide a hedge against exchange rate movements for longer periods than the forward market. If A Ltd gives £1 million to B Inc in return for $1.5 million, and the amounts are repaid after five years, then the effective exchange rate both at the beginning and at the end of the period is $1.50 = £1, whatever happens to the spot exchange rate in that time. Currency swaps can be similarly useful when using currencies for which no forward market is available.

(b) With a currency swap, a company could benefit from gaining access to debt finance in another country and currency where it is little known, and consequently has a poorer credit rating, than in its home country. It can therefore take advantage of lower interest rates than it could obtain if it arranged the loan itself.

(c) A further purpose of currency swaps is to restructure the currency base of the company's liabilities. This may be important where the company is trading overseas and receiving revenues in foreign currencies, but its borrowings are denominated in the currency of its home country. Currency swaps therefore provide a means of reducing exchange rate exposure.

(d) A third benefit of currency swaps is that at the same time as exchanging currency, the company may also be able to convert fixed rate debt to floating rate or vice versa. Thus it may obtain some of the benefits of an interest rate swap in addition to achieving the other purposes of a currency swap.

(e) A currency swap could be used to absorb excess liquidity in one currency which is not needed immediately, to create funds in another where there is a need.

6.3 A simple example would be one in which a UK company agrees with a US company to swap capital amounts at an agreed rate of exchange. Suppose a UK company is selling satellite equipment to NASA in the USA but will not be paid (in US dollars) for two years. The UK company could agree with another company to swap capital at an agreed rate of exchange in two years' time. The UK company will give the counterparty US dollars and receive sterling in return.

6.4 Consider a UK company X with a subsidiary in France which owns vineyards. Assume a spot rate of £1 = 10 French francs. Suppose the parent company wishes to raise a loan of 10 million French francs for the purpose of buying another French wine company. At the same time, the French subsidiary Y wishes to raise £1 million to pay for new up-to-date capital equipment imported from the UK. The UK parent company X could borrow the £1 million sterling and the French subsidiary Y could borrow the 10 million francs, each effectively borrowing on the other's behalf. This last example is known as a back-to-back loan.

6.5 A variation on currency swaps is **international interest arbitrage financing** or **arbiloans**. This can be of value for an enterprise which operates in a country where interest rates are high and credit is hard to obtain. A subsidiary in a low-interest country borrows the amount required, converting it into the domestic currency of the parent company at the spot rate. The UK parent signs an agreement to repay the amount in the foreign currency at the end of the term, and purchases a forward contract for repayment at the same date.

6.6 A term which you may come across in relation to swaps is **warehousing** which refers to the activity of an intermediary who enters into contracts for one side of a swap even though it does not yet have a client firm to enter into the other side of the swap. In practice, many currency swaps are conducted between banks and their customers. An agreement may only be necessary if the swap were for longer than, say, one year.

6.7 EXAMPLE: HEDGING STRATEGY USING A SWAP

Adventurer Ltd, a UK company, is considering a contract to supply a telephone system to Blueland Telecom. All operating cash flows would be in the local currency, the Blue, as follows.

Time from start	Cash flow
	Blues
0	(700,000)
6 months	(400,000)
12 months	1,800,000

Because of high inflation in Blueland, the directors of Adventurer Ltd are very concerned about the foreign exchange risk. However, the only available form of cover is a currency swap at a fixed rate of 9 Blues to the pound, for 1,100,000 Blues, to take effect in full at the start of the project and to last for a full year. The interest rate chargeable on the Blues would be 18% a year. This compares to a UK opportunity cost of capital for Adventurer Ltd of 22%.

The alternative to the swap is to convert between sterling and Blues at the spot rate, currently 10 Blues to the pound. The Blue floats freely on world currency markets. Inflation in Blueland and the UK over the year for which the project will last is forecast to be as follows.

UK	Blueland	Probability
%	%	
2	10	0.2
3	30	0.3
4	70	0.5

You are required to show whether or not Adventurer Ltd should use the available swap. Do not discount receipts and payments to a single time.

6.8 SOLUTION

The first step is to calculate the exchange rate in each of the different inflation scenarios. The rates can be found if we assume purchasing power parity between the two countries.

Then, with inflation rate expressed as decimals:

$$\text{Exchange rate after a year} = \text{current spot rate} \times \frac{1 + \text{Blueland inflation rate}}{1 + \text{UK inflation rate}}$$

$$\text{Exchange rate after six months} = \text{current spot rate} \times \sqrt{\frac{1 + \text{Blueland inflation rate}}{1 + \text{UK inflation rate}}}$$

Month	Inflation Blueland	UK	Exchange rate B/£
0			10.00
6	0.10	0.02	10.38
12	0.10	0.02	10.78
0			10.00
6	0.30	0.03	11.23
12	0.30	0.03	12.62
0			10.00
6	0.70	0.04	12.79
12	0.70	0.04	16.35

The expected values will not be calculated since these have little real meaning. Instead, the swap will be evaluated using the currency markets for each of the three scenarios.

The effects of the exchange rate on the investments and returns can now be calculated. It is assumed that Adventurer Ltd will have to borrow funds in the UK to finance the deal, and therefore interest will be calculated at the opportunity cost of funds, 22%. The interest rate for six months will be $\sqrt{1.22} - 1 = 0.1045 = 10.45\%$.

(a) *Using the currency markets*

    (i)   Inflation rates 2% and 10%:

	Blues	£	*Interest* £
Investment - month 0	(700,000)	(70,000)	(15,400)
Investment - month 6	(400,000)	(38,536)	(4,027)
		(108,536)	(19,427)
Interest		(19,427)	
Total cost		(127,963)	
Price received	1,800,000	166,976	
Net profit/(loss)		39,013	

    (ii)   Inflation rates 3% and 30%:

		£	*Interest* £
Investment - month 0	(700,000)	(70,000)	(15,400)
Investment - month 6	(400,000)	(35,619)	(3,722)
		(105,619)	(19,122)
Interest		(19,122)	
Total cost		(124,741)	
Price received	1,800,000	142,631	
Net profit/(loss)		17,890	

    (iii)   Inflation rates 4% and 70%:

	Blues	£	*Interest* £
Investment - month 0	(700,000)	(70,000)	(15,400)
Investment - month 6	(400,000)	(31,274)	(3,268)
		(101,274)	(18,668)
Interest		(18,668)	
Total cost		(119,942)	
Price received	1,800,000	110,092	
Net profit/(loss)		(9,850)	

(b) *Using the currency swap*

Adventurer Ltd will have to borrow sterling funds in the UK to finance the swap. The cost of funds in the UK is 22%. However, swaps involve the transfer of interest rate liabilities as well as of principal, and therefore the interest cost will be calculated at the swap rate of 18%.

It is assumed that no interest will be earned on the 400,000 Blues which will be lying idle until month 6. The sterling investment required before interest is £1,100,000/9 = £122,222.

The price received will depend on the inflation rates. 1,100,000 Blues will be at the swap rate of 9 Blues to the pound, yielding £122,222, equal to the initial sterling outlay; the balance (700,000 Blues) will be at the prevailing year end rate. The sterling value of interest payments (198,000 Blues) will also depend on the exchange rate. It is assumed that no interest will be paid until the end of the year.

Inflation rates	Spot rate receipts £'000	Interest £'000	Profit £'000	Profit/(loss) without swap £'000
2% and 10%	64,935	18,367	46,568	39,013
3% and 30%	55,468	15,689	39,779	17,890
4% and 70%	42,813	12,110	30,703	(9,850)

Whatever the inflation rates, Adventurer Ltd will make a bigger profit with the swap than without it. It should therefore use the swap.

Fixed to floating rate currency swaps

6.9   A **fixed to floating rate currency swap** is a combination of a straight currency swap and an interest rate swap. For example, a UK company borrows £100,000 at LIBOR + 1% and an American company borrows $150,000 at 6% fixed interest. The two companies agree to swap loan principals at the exchange rate $1.50 = £1. Each company then pays the interest on each other's loan. At the end of the loan period, the principals are swapped back giving the same effective exchange rate of $1.50 = £1. (See the diagram below.)

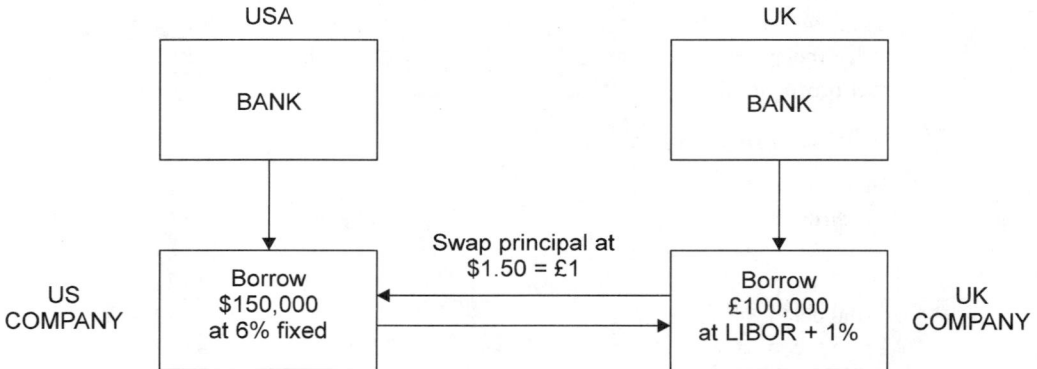

Fixed to floating rate currency swap

6.10   EXAMPLE: FIXED TO FLOATING RATE CURRENCY SWAP

Swapster plc wishes to borrow DM 300 million for five years at a floating rate to finance an investment project in Germany. The cheapest rate at which it can raise such a loan on the euromarkets is DM LIBOR + 0.75%. This would be cheaper than borrowing or from the German domestic market.

The company's bankers have suggested that one of their German client companies would be interested in a swap arrangement. This German company needs a fixed interest sterling loan. The cheapest rate at which it can arrange the sterling loan is 10.5% per annum. It could, however, borrow in DM at the floating rate of DM LIBOR + 1.5%.

Swapster plc can issue a fixed interest sterling 5 year bond at 9% per annum interest. The banker would charge a swap arrangement fee of 0.15% per year to both parties. The current exchange rate is DM2.3077 = £1. You are required to devise a swap by which both parties can benefit.

6.11   SOLUTION

Consider the interest rates at which the companies can issue their own debt and determine whether their is any comparative advantage.

	Swapster	*German company*	*Difference*
Can borrow fixed rate in £	9%	10.5%	1.5%
Can borrow floating rate in DM	LIBOR + 0.75%	LIBOR + 1.5%	0.75%
Difference between differences			0.75%

If the potential gain of 0.75% is split equally, this gives a gain of 0.375% each. Even after deducting the banker's commission of 0.15%, both parties can make a gain of 0.225% per annum over the best rate at which they could issue their own debt in the foreign currency.

Swapster is targeting DM LIBOR + 0.75% – 0.375% gain = DM LIBOR + 0.375% before banker's commission. The German company is targeting £ borrowing at 10.5% – 0.375% = 10.125% before commission. To determine the terms of the swap, set up the proforma shown earlier and suggest one of an infinite number of possible arrangements.

	Swapster	*German company*
Pays		
own loan interest	(9%)	(LIBOR + 1.5%)
in swap	(LIBOR + 0.375%)	(9%)
Receives		
in swap	9%	LIBOR + 0.375%
Net interest cost before commission	(LIBOR + 0.375%)	(10.125%)
Add: Banker's commission	(0.15%)	(0.15%)
Net annual payment	(LIBOR + 0.525%)	(10.275%)

Both companies make a net gain of 0.225% over the best rate at which they could borrow in the foreign currency. The swap proceeds as follows.

Step 1. At the spot rate, DM 300 million = 300/2.3077 = £130 million

Step 2. Swapster raises a fixed interest 5 year loan for £130 million at 9% interest.

Step 3. The German company raises a floating rate DM 300 million loan at DM LIBOR + 1.5%.

Step 4. The companies swap loan principals.

Step 5. Each year, each company pays its own loan interest and the interest to the counter-party, and receives interest from the counter-party.

Step 6. At the end of 5 years, the loan principals are swapped back (resulting in a hedged exchange rate of 2.3077 DM/£) and the companies repay their original loans.

Swaptions
12/95

6.12 Among the various 'hybrid' hedging instruments available which combine the features of different financial instruments is the **swaption.** A swaption is an instrument which is traded on a market in the writing/purchasing of **options to buy an interest rate swap**. For example, A Ltd might buy a swaption from a bank, giving A Ltd the right, but not the obligation, to enter into an interest rate swap arrangement with the bank at or before a specified time in the future.

Exam focus point
You may hear of various 'exotic' hybrid derivatives other than the swaption, with equally exotic names. You will probably be pleased to know that the examiner does not intend to set questions on these, but the swaption remains examinable.

6.13 A swaption offers a borrower protection against rises in interest rates and at the same time allows it to take advantage of falls in rates. A **European-style swaption** is exercisable only on the maturity date while an **American-style swaption** is exercisable on any business day during the exercise period.

BPP PUBLISHING

6.14 EXAMPLE: SWAPTIONS

It is now 1 January 19X6. Towyn plc pays a variable rate of interest on a $1,000,000 eurodollar loan which is due to mature on 30 June 19X9. The interest rate currently payable on this loan is 6.75% per annum. The company treasurer is now concerned about the possibility of interest rates rises over the near future. The company's bank has indicated that an American-style dollar swaption is available with the following features.

Interest rate 7.5%
Exercise period 1 July 19X6 to 31 December 19X6
Maturity date 30 June 19X9
Premium $20,000

You are required to assess under what circumstances Towyn plc will gain from exercising the swaption. Ignore the time value of money.

6.15 SOLUTION

The swaption would be likely to be exercised if interest rates rose above 7.5% during the next nine months. To evaluate the benefit of the swaption, ignoring the time value of money, it is first necessary to evaluate its cost over the remaining three year period of the loan.

	$
Interest: $1,000,000 \times 7.5\% \times 3$	225,000
Premium	20,000
Total cost	245,000

This represents an effective annual rate of interest of 8.17% ($245,000/($1,000,000 $\times$ 3)). The average rate of interest payable by the company without the swap would therefore have to exceed 8.17% for the swaption to be beneficial. If interest rates fall, the swaption will not be exercised and the company will be able to advantage of the lower interest payments.

The company should also take into account the fact that if it enters into the agreement the premium will be payable whether or not the swaption was exercised. The premium is effectively the price paid for the possibility of taking advantage of lower interest rates.

Chapter roundup

- **Interest rates**, like exchange rates, can be very volatile.
- Factors involving interest rate risk include the following.
  - **Fixed rates versus floating rate debt**
  - The **term of the loan**
- A variety of financial instruments are available for reducing exposure to interest rate risk, including **FRAs, futures, swaps** and **options**.
- An **interest rate guarantee** is a form of interest rate option.

Quick quiz

1 Define 'hedge efficiency'. (see para 1.5)

2 What is a forward interest rate agreement? (1.7)

3 Briefly explain the principles of gap analysis of interest rate risk. (1.14)

4 Who might use interest rate futures? (2.17, 2.20, 2.28)

5 What is basis risk? (2.34)

6 Outline what is meant by a 'collar'. (3.3)

7 What is a 'zero cost collar'? (3.3)

8 What is an interest rate swap? (5.1)

9 How might currency swaps be used? (6.2)

10 What is a 'swaption'? (6.12)

Question to try	Level	Marks	Time
22	Exam standard	10	18 mins

Chapter 23

FORMS OF INTERNATIONAL OPERATION. TRANSFER PRICING

Chapter topic list	Syllabus reference
1 Forms of foreign investment	6(d)
2 Financing overseas subsidiaries	6(d)
3 Obtaining returns from subsidiaries	6(c)
4 Evaluating performance of overseas operations	6(c)

Introduction

In this chapter, we examine the **different types of entity** which are available for **international operations** by a company. We also discuss various problems which countries face in relation to **foreign direct investment (FDI)**.

1 FORMS OF FOREIGN INVESTMENT   12/94, 12/99

1.1 **Foreign direct investment (FDI)** and the activities of multinational enterprises were previously discussed in Chapter 16 of this Text. Here we explore FDI from the perspective of the company undertaking it.

1.2 A firm might develop **horizontally** in different countries, replicating its existing operations on a global basis. **Vertical integration** might have an international dimension through FDI to acquire raw material or component sources overseas (**backwards integration**) or to establish final production and distribution in other countries (**forward integration**). **Diversification** might alternatively provide the impetus to developing international interests.

1.3 Different forms of expansion overseas are available to meet various strategic objectives.

   (a) Firms may expand by means of **new 'start-up' investments**, for example in manufacturing plants. This does allow flexibility, although it may be slow to achieve, expensive to maintain and slow to yield satisfactory results.

   (b) A firm might **take over or merge** with established firms abroad. This provides a means of purchasing market information, market share and distribution channels. If speed of entry into the overseas market is a high priority, then acquisition may be preferred to start-up. However, enterprises available for takeover tend to be those which have high debt gearing, poor market performance and poor management. The better acquisitions will only be available at a premium.

   (c) **A joint venture with a local overseas partner** might be entered into. A joint venture may be defined as 'the commitment, for more than a very short duration, of funds, facilities and services by two or more legally separate interests to an enterprise for their mutual benefit.' Different forms of joint venture are distinguished below.

Joint ventures

1.4   The two distinct types of joint venture are **industrial co-operation (contractual)** and **joint-equity**. A **contractual joint venture** is for a fixed period and the duties and responsibility of the parties are contractually defined. A **joint-equity venture** involves investment, is of no fixed duration and continually evolves. Depending on government regulations, joint ventures may be the **only** means of access to a particular market.

Case examples

There is a growing trend towards a contractual form of joint venture as a consequence of the high research and development costs and the 'critical mass' necessary to take advantage of economies of scale in industries such as automobile engineering.

Japanese car manufacturers have for some time been forming joint ventures and alliances as well as establishing links with suppliers and customers. Contractual joint ventures have become a common means of establishing a presence in the newly emerging mixed economies of Eastern Europe.

As well as in the car industry, this form of joint venture is common in the aerospace industry. A joint-equity venture may be the only way of establishing a presence in countries where full foreign ownership is discouraged, such as Nigeria, Japan and some Middle Eastern countries.

1.5   **Advantages of joint ventures**

   (a)   Relatively low cost access to new markets

   (b)   Easier access to local capital markets, possibly with accompanying tax incentives or grants

   (c)   Use of joint venture partner's existing management expertise, local knowledge, distribution network, technology, brands, patents and marketing or other skills

   (d)   Sharing of risks

   (e)   Sharing of costs, providing economies of scale

Disadvantages of joint ventures

   (a)   Managerial freedom may be restricted by the need to take account of the views of all the joint venture partners.

   (b)   There may be problems in agreeing on partners' percentage ownership, transfer prices, reinvestment decisions, nationality of key personnel, remuneration and sourcing of raw materials and components.

   (c)   Finding a reliable joint venture partner may take a long time.

   (d)   Joint ventures are difficult to value, particularly where one or more partners have made intangible contributions.

Economic interest groups

1.6   Economic interest groups are organisations set up to help parties to joint ventures cooperate with one another and to overcome the problems which can arise from differences in local legislation and culture. **European economic interest groups (EEIGs)** form one example of economic interest groups which are of particular benefit to small and medium-sized enterprises. EEIGs are governed by European law rather than national laws and have full legal capacities. They cannot hold stakes in members' businesses, and thus the members remain independent.

Alternatives to FDI

1.7 **Exporting** and **licensing** stand as alternatives to FDI. **Exporting** may be direct selling by the firm's own export division into the overseas markets, or it may be indirect through agents, distributors, trading companies and various other such channels. **Licensing** involves conferring rights to make use of the licensor company's production process on producers located in the overseas market.

> ### KEY TERM
>
> **Licensing** is an alternative to foreign direct investment by which overseas producers are given rights to use the licensor's production process in return for royalty payments.

1.8 **Exporting** may be unattractive because of tariffs, quotas or other import restrictions in overseas markets, and local production may be the only feasible option in the case of bulky products such as cement and flat glass.

1.9 **Advantages of licensing**

   (a) It can allow fairly rapid penetration of overseas markets.

   (b) It does not require substantial financial resources.

   (c) Political risks are reduced since the licensee is likely to be a local company.

   (d) Licensing may be a possibility where direct investment is restricted or prevented by a country.

   (e) For a multinational company, licensing agreements provide a way for funds to be remitted to the parent company in the form of licence fees.

1.10 **Disadvantages of licensing**

   (a) The arrangement may give to the licensee know-how and technology which it can use in competing with the licensor after the license agreement has expired.

   (b) It may be more difficult to maintain quality standards, and lower quality might affect the standing of a brand name in international markets.

   (c) It might be possible for the licensee to compete with the licensor by exporting the produce to markets outside the licensee's area.

   (d) Although relatively insubstantial financial resources are required, on the other hand relatively small cash inflows will be generated.

1.11 **Management contracts** whereby a firm agrees to sell management skills are sometimes used in combination with licensing. Such contracts can serve as a means of obtaining funds from subsidiaries, and may be a useful way of maintaining cash flows where other remittance restrictions apply. Many multinationals use a **combination** of various methods of servicing international markets, depending on the particular circumstances.

Overseas subsidiaries

1.12 The basic structure of many multinationals consists of a parent company (a holding company) with subsidiaries in several countries. The subsidiaries may be wholly owned or just partly owned, and some may be owned through other subsidiaries. For example a UK parent company could own the holding company of a US group. Large multinationals have many subsidiaries in a large number of different countries and many of them are household names, for example Ford and Unilever.

The purpose of setting up subsidiaries abroad

1.13 Reasons for foreign direct investment were set out in some detail in Chapter 16. To summarise points made there, the following are some reasons why a parent company might want to set up subsidiary companies in other countries.

   (a) The **location of markets**. If, say, there is a big market in Australia for the products of a UK company, it might be cheaper for the UK company to establish a manufacturing subsidiary in Australia, in order to save the costs of shipping finished goods from the UK to Australia.

   (b) The **need for a sales organisation**. Some subsidiaries are not manufacturing subsidiaries, but provide a sales and marketing organisation in their country for the parent company's goods. For example, a US parent company might set up a subsidiary in the UK, in order to sell goods in the UK which are shipped over from the USA.

   (c) The **opportunity to produce goods more cheaply**. If labour costs are much lower in one country than in another, it might be profitable for a multinational to set up a manufacturing subsidiary in the low-cost country, provided that the labour force in that country has the skills that are needed to produce good quality output. For example, a UK company might design a new type of computer and set up a subsidiary in the Far East, where labour costs are lower, to manufacture the computers. They would then be shipped to the UK for sale in the UK market.

   (d) The **need to avoid import controls**. When a country has regulations which restrict the import of certain goods, or impose high tariffs on imports, a multinational might decide to set up a manufacturing subsidiary in that country.

   (e) The **need to obtain access to raw materials**, particularly in less developed countries (LDCs).

   (f) The **availability of grants and tax concessions**.

1.14 Whatever the reason for setting up subsidiaries abroad, the aim is to increase the profits of the multinational's parent company. However there are different approaches to increasing profits that the multinational might take. At one extreme, the parent company might choose **to get as much money as it can** from the subsidiary, and **as quickly as it can**. This would involve the transfer of all or most of the subsidiary's profits to the parent company. At the other extreme, the parent company might encourage a foreign subsidiary to **develop its business gradually**, to achieve long-term growth in sales and profits. To encourage growth, the subsidiary would be allowed to retain a large proportion of its profits, instead of remitting the profits to the parent company.

The risks of multinationals

1.15 Multinational companies, like any other companies, must accept the normal risks of business. However, compared with companies that trade entirely within one country, and

BPP PUBLISHING

even with companies that export from their base in one country, multinationals face additional risks, as follows.

(a) **Foreign exchange risks**. Any country that exports or imports faces the risk of higher costs or lower revenues because of adverse movements in foreign exchange rates. Multinationals that trade between one country and another therefore face this risk. A company that owns assets in different countries (subsidiaries abroad) faces the risk of accounting losses due to adverse movements in exchange rates causing a fall in the value of those assets, as expressed in domestic currency.

(b) **Political risks** and **country risks**. A multinational can face risks of economic or political measures being taken by governments, affecting the operations of its subsidiaries abroad. Political risks are discussed further below.

(c) **Geographical separation**. The geographical separation of the parent company from its subsidiaries adds to the problems of management control of the group of companies as a whole.

Question 1

A management journal expressed the opinion that 'British investors have been bidding high for the acquisition of US companies. They are speculating on a scenario that an improved dollar will make the assets of those companies and the profit streams derived from them look cheap in the future.'

Explain the above statement and discuss its validity, assuming that the exchange rate at the time of a particular acquisition was $1.50 = £1.

Answer

Consider a UK investor who is considering the purchase of a US company when the exchange rate is $1.50 = £1. The US company might cost $3,000,000 and generate annual income of $300,000. The cost would therefore be £2,000,000, and at present rates the annual income would be £200,000, a return of 10%.

If the dollar strengthened, so that the exchange rate became $1 = £1, the annual income would become £300,000, but the initial investment, having already been made at the old exchange rate, would be unaffected. The rate of return would thus rise to 15%.

While the calculations are sound, the statement in the question does not set out an easy way to achieve very high returns. Firstly, exchange rates are unpredictable; if the dollar weakened, the return on the sterling investment would fall rather than rise. Secondly, the sterling investment must be financed. It may well be that interest rates on sterling borrowings are higher than corresponding rates on US dollar borrowings, to reflect the scope for profitable investment overseas. This point will apply however the investment is to be financed, as high rates on borrowings imply high rates forgone on surplus cash not invested in the UK, and also high required rates of return on equity.

Political risks for multinationals   12/98

1.16   When a multinational company invests in another country, by setting up a subsidiary, it may face a **political risk** of action by that country's government which restricts the multinational's freedom. The government of a country will almost certainly want to encourage the development and growth of commerce and industry, but it might also be suspicious of the motives of multinationals which set up subsidiaries in their country, perhaps fearing exploitation.

KEY TERM

Political risk: the risk that political action will affect the position and value of a company.

1.17 On the other hand, the government might try to prevent the exploitation of the country by multinationals, and the various measures it might take include the following.

(a) Import **quotas** could be used to limit the quantities of goods that a subsidiary can buy from its parent company and import for resale in its domestic markets.

(b) Import **tariffs** could make imports (such as from parent companies) more expensive and domestically produced goods therefore more competitive.

(c) Legal standards of safety or quality (**non-tariff barriers**) could be imposed on imported goods to prevent multinationals from selling goods through a subsidiary which have been banned as dangerous in other countries.

(d) **Exchange control regulations** could be applied (see below).

(e) A government could **restrict** the ability of foreign companies to buy domestic companies, especially those that operate in politically sensitive industries such as defence contracting, communications, energy supply and so on.

(f) A government could **nationalise** foreign-owned companies and their assets (with or without compensation to the parent company).

(g) A government could insist on a **minimum shareholding** in companies by residents. This would force a multinational to offer some of the equity in a subsidiary to investors in the country where the subsidiary operates.

Exchange controls

1.18 **Exchange controls** restrict the flow of foreign exchange into and out of a country, usually to defend the local currency or to protect reserves of foreign currencies. Exchange controls are generally more restrictive in developing and less developed countries although some still exist in developed countries. Typically, a government might enforce regulations:

(a) **Rationing the supply of foreign exchange**. Anyone wishing to make payments abroad in a foreign currency will be restricted by the limited supply, which stops them from buying as much as they want from abroad.

(b) **Restricting the types of transaction** for which payments abroad are allowed, for example by suspending or banning the payment of dividends to foreign shareholders, such as parent companies in multinationals, who will then have the problem of **blocked funds**.

2 FINANCING OVERSEAS SUBSIDIARIES   12/95

2.1 The parent company will be largely financed in much the same way as any other large company, with share capital and reserves, loan capital and some short-term finance. But there are some differences in methods of financing the **parent company** itself, and the **foreign subsidiaries**. The parent company itself is more likely than companies which have no foreign interests to raise finance in a foreign currency, or in its home currency from foreign sources.

BPP
PUBLISHING

2.2 The **need to finance a foreign subsidiary** raises the following questions.

    (a) How much equity capital should the parent company put into the subsidiary?

    (b) Should the subsidiary be allowed to retain a large proportion of its profits, to build up its equity reserves, or not?

    (c) Should the parent company hold 100% of the equity of the subsidiary, or should it try to create a minority shareholding, perhaps by floating the subsidiary on the country's domestic stock exchange?

    (d) Should the subsidiary be encouraged to borrow as much long-term debt as it can, for example by raising large bank loans? If so, should the loans be in the domestic currency of the subsidiary's country, or should it try to raise a foreign currency loan?

    (e) Should the subsidiary be encouraged to minimise its working capital investment by relying heavily on trade credit?

2.3 The **method of financing** a subsidiary will give some indication of the nature of the investment that the parent company is prepared to make. A sizeable equity investment (or long-term loans from the parent company to the subsidiary) would indicate a long-term investment by the parent company. In contrast, when a subsidiary is financed largely by debt capital and short-term liabilities (even if the trade creditor is the parent company, for goods supplied by the parent to the subsidiary), this would indicate a short-term investment policy.

2.4 When a UK company wishes to finance operations overseas, there may be a currency (foreign exchange) risk arising from the method of financing used. For example, if a UK company decides on an investment in the USA, to be financed with a sterling loan, the investment will provide returns in US dollars, while the investors (the lenders) will want returns paid in sterling. If the US dollar falls in value against sterling, the sterling value of the project's returns will also fall.

2.5 To reduce or to eliminate the currency risk of an overseas investment, a company might finance it with funds in the same currency as the investment. The advantages of borrowing in the same currency as an investment are as follows.

    (a) Assets and liabilities in the same currency can be matched, thus avoiding exchange losses on conversion in the group's annual accounts.

    (b) Revenues in the foreign currency can be used to repay borrowings in the same currency, thus eliminating losses due to fluctuating exchange rates.

2.6 **Factors influencing the choice of finance** for an overseas subsidiary include the following.

    (a) The **local finance costs**, and any subsidies which may be available

    (b) **Taxation systems** of the countries in which the subsidiary is operating

    (c) Any **restrictions on dividend remittances**

    (d) The possibility of **flexibility in repayments** which may arise from the parent/subsidiary relationship

2.7 Tax-saving opportunities may be maximised by structuring the group and its subsidiaries in such a way as to take the best advantage of the different local tax systems.

2.8   Because subsidiaries may be operating with a guarantee from the parent company, different gearing structures may be possible. Thus, a subsidiary may be able to operate with a higher level of debt that would be acceptable for the group as a whole.

3   OBTAINING RETURNS FROM SUBSIDIARIES   12/95

3.1   When a foreign subsidiary makes a profit, the profit will be included in the total profits of the multinational group. The management of the parent company must decide, however **how the total profit of the group should be divided** between the parent company and each of its subsidiaries, which is likely to depend on the transfer prices adopted, and how the parent company should **obtain the cash returns** that it wants from each of its subsidiaries.

3.2   An example will show how shares of profits can be manipulated by accounting methods.

(a)   Suppose that a US parent company ships some goods to a UK subsidiary. The goods cost US$40,000 to make, and they are sold in the UK by the subsidiary for £50,000, which is the equivalent, say, of US$75,000. The US multinational group will make a total profit of US$35,000. So how much profit from the US$35,000 has been earned by the US parent company, and how much has been earned by the UK subsidiary?

The answer depends on the transfer price at which the US parent sells the goods to its UK subsidiary. The transfer price will be set by management decision, so that the share of total profit between parent company and subsidiary can be manipulated to suit the preferences of management.

(i)   If the transfer price is US$45,000, the US parent company would make a profit of $5,000, leaving a profit of $30,000 for the UK subsidiary.

(ii)   If the transfer price is US$70,000, the US parent company would make a profit of $30,000, leaving only a $5,000 profit for the UK subsidiary.

(b)   The same choice of how to share total profits can be made in fixing a transfer price for goods made by a subsidiary and sold to the parent company or to another subsidiary.

3.3   The question of how profits are shared between parent company and subsidiary leads us on to the question of how a parent company obtains its returns in cash from its subsidiaries. If a subsidiary earns a profit, but then retains and reinvests the profits, the parent company will not get any cash at all. Various ways of obtaining a cash return are as follows.

(a)   The subsidiary could make a profit and **pay a dividend** out of profits.

(b)   The parent company could **sell goods or services** to the subsidiary and obtain payment. The amount of this payment will depend on the volume of sales and also on the transfer price for the sales.

(c)   A parent company which grants a subsidiary the right to make goods protected by patents can charge a **royalty** on any goods that the subsidiary sells. The size of any royalty can be adjusted to suit the wishes of the parent company's management.

(d)   If the parent company makes a **loan** to a subsidiary, it can set the interest rate high or low, thereby affecting the profits of both companies. A high rate of interest on a loan, for example, would improve the parent company's profits to the detriment of the subsidiary's profits.

(e)   **Management charges** may be levied by the parent company for costs incurred in the management of international operations.

3.4 When the subsidiary is in a country where there are **exchange control regulations**, the parent company may have difficulty in getting cash from the subsidiary.

The workings of transfer prices

> **KEY TERM**
>
> A **transfer price** may be defined as the price at which goods or services are transferred from one process or department to another or from one member of a group to another.

3.5 The extent to which costs and profit are covered by the transfer price is a matter of company policy. A transfer price may be based upon any of the following.

- **Marginal cost:** at marginal cost or with a gross profit margin added
- **Full cost:** at full cost, or at a full cost plus price
- **Market price**
- **Market price less a discount**
- **Negotiated price**, which could be based on any of the other bases

3.6 A transfer price based on cost might be at **marginal cost** or **full cost**, with no profit or contribution margin but in a profit centre system it is more likely to be a price based on marginal cost or full cost plus a margin for contribution or profit. This is to allow profit centres to make a profit on work they do for other profit centres, and so earn a reward for their effort and use of resources on the work.

3.7 Transfers based on **market price** might be any of the following.

(a) The actual market price at which the transferred goods or services could be sold on an external market

(b) The actual external market price, minus an amount that reflects the savings in costs (for example selling costs and bad debts) when goods are transferred internally

(c) The market price of similar goods which are sold on an external market, although the transferred goods are not exactly the same and do not themselves have an external market

The level of a transfer price

3.8 The size of the transfer price will affect the costs of one profit centre and the revenues of another. Since profit centre managers are held accountable for their costs, revenues, and profits, they are likely to dispute the size of transfer prices with each other, or disagree about whether one profit centre should do work for another or not. Transfer prices affect behaviour and decisions by profit centre managers.

3.9 In a system of **profit centre accounting**, the transfer price of goods and services between divisions is a focal issue. If managers of individual profit centres are tempted to take decisions that are harmful to other divisions and are not congruent with the goals of the organisation as a whole, the problem is likely to emerge in disputes about the transfer price. One profit centre manager might be reluctant to transfer goods and services to another division, arguing that he is not paid enough for the work. Alternatively, one profit centre manager might refuse to accept transfers of goods from another division, arguing that it would be too costly to do so.

3.10 Disagreements about output levels tend to focus on the transfer price. There is presumably a profit-maximising level of output and sales for the organisation as a whole. However, unless each profit centre also maximises its own profit at the corresponding level of output, there will be inter-divisional disagreements about output levels and the profit-maximising output will not be achieved.

3.11 Ideally, a transfer price should be set at a level that overcomes these problems.

(a) The transfer price should provide a selling price that enables the transferring division to earn a return for its efforts, and the receiving division to incur a cost for benefits received.

(b) The transfer price should be set at a level that enables profit centre performance to be measured commercially. This means that the transfer price should be a fair commercial price.

(c) The transfer price should encourage profit centre managers to agree on the amounts of goods and services to be transferred, which will also be at a level that is consistent with the aims of the organisation as a whole (for example maximising company profits).

3.12 Here is an exercise to revise basic transfer price calculations.

Question 2

A company has two profit centres, X and Y. Each will work at full capacity. X's total annual costs are £3,570,000 and Y's total annual costs excluding purchases from X are £1,500,000. 40% of X's output is transferred to Y, and the remaining 60% is sold externally for £4,800,000. All of Y's output is sold externally for £7,000,000.

Compute the profits of X, Y and the company as a whole:

(a) Using a transfer price equal to market value
(b) Using a transfer price equal to full cost

Answer

(a) *Transfer price equal to market value*

	X	X	Y	Y	Total
	£'000	£'000	£'000	£'000	£'000
External sales		4,800		7,000	11,800
Transfer sales		3,200		0	
		8,000		7,000	
Transfer costs	0		3,200		
Own costs	3,570		1,500		5,070
		3,570		4,700	
Profit		4,430		2,300	6,730

(b) *Transfer price equal to full cost*

	X	X	Y	Y	Total
	£'000	£'000	£'000	£'000	£'000
External sales		4,800		7,000	11,800
Transfer sales*		1,428		0	
		6,228		7,000	
Transfer costs	0		1,428		
Own costs	3,570		1,500		5,070
		3,570		2,928	
		2,658		4,072	6,730

* (3,570 × 0.4)

The advantages of market value transfer prices

3.13 In a decentralised company, divisional managers should have the opportunity to make output, selling and buying decisions which appear to be in the best interests of the division. (If every division optimises its performance, the company as a whole must inevitably achieve optimal results.) Thus a transferor division should be given the freedom to sell output on the open market, rather than to transfer them within the company. The reason for this option is that the selling division might find more profitable opportunities to sell other products: if output is switched to this new option, the transferee division is able to replace the internal supply by buying on the open market.

3.14 Giving profit centre managers the freedom to negotiate prices with other profit centres as though they were independent companies will tend to result in market-based transfer prices. In most cases where the transfer price is at market price, internal transfers should be expected, because the buying division is likely to benefit from a better quality of service, greater flexibility, and dependability of supply. Both divisions may benefit from lower costs of administration, selling and transport. A market price as the transfer price would therefore result in decisions which would be in the best interests of the company or group as a whole.

The disadvantages of market value transfer prices

3.15 **Market value** as a transfer price does have certain disadvantages.

(a) The market price may be a temporary one, induced by adverse economic conditions, or dumping, or the market price might depend on the volume of output supplied to the external market by the profit centre.

(b) A transfer price at market value might, under some circumstances, act as a disincentive to use up any spare capacity in the divisions. A price based on incremental cost, in contrast, might provide an incentive to use up the spare resources in order to provide a marginal contribution to profit.

(c) Many products do not have an equivalent market price, so that the price of a similar product might be chosen. In such circumstances, the option to sell or buy on the open market does not exist.

(d) There might be an imperfect external market for the transferred item, so that if the transferring division tried to sell more externally, it would have to reduce its selling price.

(e) Internal transfers are often cheaper than external sales, with savings in selling costs, bad debt risks and possibly transport costs. It would therefore seem reasonable for the buying division to expect a discount on the external market price, and to negotiate for such a discount.

Tax implications of transfer pricing

3.16 If a UK resident company makes investments abroad it will be liable to corporation tax on the profits made, the taxable amount being before the deduction of any foreign taxes. The profits may be any of the following.

(a) Profits of an overseas branch or agency
(b) Income from foreign securities, for example debentures in overseas companies
(c) Dividends from overseas subsidiaries
(d) Capital gains on disposals of foreign assets

3.17 In many instances, a company will be subject to overseas taxes as well as to UK corporation tax on the same profits. **Double taxation relief** is, however, usually available in respect of the foreign tax suffered.

3.18 EXAMPLE: TRANSFER PRICES

A multinational company based in Beeland has subsidiary companies in Ceeland and in the UK. The UK subsidiary manufactures machinery parts which are sold to the Ceeland subsidiary for a unit price of B$420 (420 Beeland dollars), where the parts are assembled. The UK subsidiary shows a profit of B$80 per unit; 200,000 units are sold annually.

The Ceeland subsidiary incurs further costs of B$400 per unit and sells the finished goods on for an equivalent of B$1,050.

All of the profits from the foreign subsidiaries are remitted to the parent company as dividends. Double taxation treaties between Beeland, Ceeland and the UK allow companies to set foreign tax liabilities against their domestic tax liability.

The following rates of taxation apply.

	UK	*Beeland*	*Ceeland*
Tax on company profits	25%	35%	40%
Withholding tax on dividends	-	12%	10%

Required

Show the tax effect of increasing the transfer price between the UK and Ceeland subsidiaries by 25%.

3.19 SOLUTION

The current position is as follows.

	UK company B$'000	*Ceeland company* B$'000	*Total* B$'000
Revenues and taxes in the local country			
Sales	84,000	210,000	294,000
Production expenses	(68,000)	(164,000)	(232,000)
Taxable profit	16,000	46,000	62,000
Tax (1)	(4,000)	(18,400)	(22,400)
Dividends to Beeland	12,000	27,600	39,600
Withholding tax (2)	0	2,760	2,760
Revenues and taxes in Beeland			
Dividend	12,000	27,600	39,600
Add back foreign tax paid	4,000	18,400	22,400
Taxable income	16,000	46,000	62,000
Beeland tax due	5,600	16,100	21,700
Foreign tax credit	(4,000)	(16,100)	(20,100)
Tax paid in Beeland (3)	1,600	-	1,600
Total tax (1) + (2) + (3)	5,600	21,160	26,760

An increase of 25% in the transfer price would have the following effect.

	UK company B$'000	Ceeland company B$'000	Total B$'000
Revenues and taxes in the local country			
Sales	105,000	210,000	315,000
Production expenses	(68,000)	(185,000)	(253,000)
Taxable profit	37,000	25,000	62,000
Tax (1)	(9,250)	(10,000)	(19,250)
Dividends to Beeland	27,750	15,000	42,750
Withholding tax (2)	0	1,500	1,500
Revenues and taxes in Beeland			
Dividend	27,750	15,000	42,750
Add back foreign tax paid	9,250	10,000	19,250
Taxable income	37,000	25,000	62,000
Beeland tax due	12,950	8,750	21,700
Foreign tax credit	(9,250)	(8,750)	(18,000)
Tax paid in Beeland (3)	3,700	-	3,700
Total tax (1) + (2) + (3)	12,950	11,500	24,450

The total tax payable by the company is therefore reduced by B$2,310,000 to B$24,450,000.

Controlled foreign companies

3.20 A UK resident company may choose to trade abroad through an investment in a local company. Providing there are no exchange control problems and cash flow requirements do not call for the repatriation of all profits to the UK, there will generally be a tax benefit in accumulating income in a foreign company whose effective tax rate is lower than that of the UK company. To prevent undue tax avoidance through the use of 'tax havens' in this way, there are special rules for '**controlled foreign companies**' (CFCs).

3.21 Where UK resident persons have overall control of a company which is resident in a country with a lower level of tax, the profits of the CFC might, under some circumstances, be apportioned to any corporate UK shareholders and taxed accordingly.

The migration of companies

3.22 Because the overseas profits of a UK resident company are chargeable to corporation tax whereas the overseas profits of a non-UK resident company are not, UK companies might wish to transfer their residence in order to avoid paying UK corporation tax. Only companies incorporated abroad can emigrate, as companies incorporated in the UK are automatically UK resident.

3.23 A company may freely transfer its residence out of the UK provided that:

(a) It gives notice to the Inland Revenue, and
(b) It pays an exit charge (based on unrealised capital gains on its assets)

Sales at artificial transfer prices

3.24 Where sales are made to a non-resident fellow group company at an undervalue, or purchases are made from such a company at an overvalue, the Revenue will substitute a market price in computing the profits chargeable to corporation tax. However, no corresponding relief is given for sales at overvalue or purchases at undervalue by the UK company.

Trading abroad

3.25   The controlled foreign companies legislation may reduce the attractiveness of setting up a subsidiary in a tax haven, as opposed to a branch of the UK company. However, a *bona fide* group structure may still be designed, avoiding the CFC rules, with the result that UK tax can be minimised by controlling the timing and amounts of dividends paid by the foreign subsidiary.

3.26   If an overseas operation is expected to make losses at first and then become profitable, it may be sensible to start with a branch and then transfer the trade to a subsidiary. Provided all the assets (or all except cash) are transferred, and the consideration is in the form of shares, gains on the transfers of assets can be deducted from the value of the shares instead of being immediately taxable in the UK. Where the overseas country is a member state of the European Union, an alternative is to allow the gains to be taxable but to claim relief for tax which would have been payable overseas but for the EU Mergers Directive (which gives certain reliefs from tax).

4   EVALUATING PERFORMANCE OF OVERSEAS OPERATIONS   12/96

4.1   In an international context, the **evaluation of performance** takes different forms. For a multinational group as a whole, performance may be of special interest to investors and other outsiders. The diversified nature of the operations of a multinational group mean that caution must be exercised in interpreting the results of the performance analysis of the group and in comparing results with those of other multinational groups. Within a group, the performance of investment centres located in different countries can be assessed.

4.2   We looked earlier at various measures of performance for business enterprises. Measuring and evaluating the performance of overseas subsidiaries presents special problems, particularly because of the need to translate foreign exchange using a particular method. In practice, the method used is often that applying in the financial accounting rules specified in SSAP 20.

Exam focus point
These rules are covered in BPP's Study Texts for ACCA Paper 13 and (excluding consolidated accounts) ACCA Paper 10.

4.3   International differences of various kinds can distort simple international comparisons of performance using financial data, for example as follows. A subsidiary in a low-interest country might finance another subsidiary in a high-interest country. The first subsidiary will have 'excess' interest charges while the second will show an undercharging of interest. A consistent method (for example, involving 'notional' intercompany charges) will be needed to reflect the situation. Also, there may be very different economic environments facing subsidiaries in different countries, national limitations on remittances of funds and variations in work customs.

4.4   Research has shown that **budget analysis** - the comparison of sales and operating expenses with an earlier budget making use of price and volume variances - is the most important criterion for measuring performance of subsidiaries of multinational companies. This emphasis on budgets reflects the underlying principle that **operating management is held responsible** for the variables influencing performance which they can control, and that they are not held responsible for performance variations outside their control.

4.5 The system of control in a multinational enterprise must always allow intercountry comparisons to be made. This means that the overall operating budget must always be expressed in the currency of the parent company. Fluctuations in exchange rates will lead to variances between budget and actual figures. The resulting price variance is different in its implications from other price variances resulting from sales price or cost changes. Where responsibility for the exchange rate variance lies will depend upon the system of financial control in the particular organisation concerned.

4.6 Some argue that local managers should be held responsible for exchange rate variances, since the firm's ultimate goal is profitability in terms of the currency of the parent company and since local managers must be aware of the consequences of exchange rate variances.

(a) A control system which reflects this in the performance measurement process is one which uses projected exchange rates (rather than opening or closing rates) in setting the budget and closing rates (rather than opening or projected rates) in monitoring performance.

(b) Many multinationals using this method of evaluation do, however, show the exchange rate variance as a separate item in variance reports, allowing some latitude in the degree to which the local manager will actually be held responsible.

Chapter roundup

- In this chapter, we have examined problems specific to **multinationals**.
- **Foreign direct investment (FDI)** will generally be undertaken if exporting is more costly than overseas production. However, difficulties in repatriating profits and other political factors complicate the issue.
- **Transfer pricing** is of importance to multinational companies. There are legal provisions affecting transfer pricing which are aimed at preventing avoidance of tax.
- Different methods of transfer pricing also have different **motivational effects** on the cost centres involved.
- Evaluating the **performance of overseas enterprises** presents special problems.

Quick quiz

1 What two different forms of joint venture can be distinguished? (see para 1.4)
2 Why might a company set up subsidiaries abroad? (1.11)
3 What are the main risks faced by multinationals? (1.13)
4 What measures might a government take to control local subsidiaries of a multinational? (1.15)
5 What exchange controls might a government apply? (1.16)
6 How might a parent company extract cash from a subsidiary? (3.3)
7 Identify the advantages and disadvantages of market value transfer prices. (3.13 - 3.15)

Question to try	Level	Marks	Time
23	Exam standard	10	18 mins

Chapter 24

INTERNATIONAL INVESTMENT DECISIONS

Chapter topic list	Syllabus reference
1 International portfolio diversification	6(d)
2 International CAPM	6(d)
3 Capital budgeting for foreign projects	6(d)
4 Taxation in the multinational environment	6(d)

Introduction

In this chapter, we look at aspects of **international investment decisions** in the light of investment techniques and asset pricing theories covered earlier in the Study Text. We also examine here special complications of **investment appraisal** in an international context.

In Chapter 7, we saw how portfolio theory seeks to establish guidelines for building up a portfolio of investments. Given the increased liberalisation of domestic capital markets and the increasing internationalisation of the financial system, the investor seeking a diversified portfolio does not need to restrict choice of securities to domestic securities. We therefore ask what special considerations relate to **international portfolio diversification.**

1   INTERNATIONAL PORTFOLIO DIVERSIFICATION   12/97

1.1   Approximately 7% of total world equities has been estimated to comprise cross-border holdings. Even so, it is arguable that there remains a domestic bias among many types of investor, which can be attributed to a number of barriers to international investment, including the following.

(a) **Legal restrictions** exist in some markets, limiting ownership of securities by foreign investors.

(b) **Foreign exchange regulations** may prohibit international investment or make it more expensive.

(c) **Double taxation** of income from foreign investment may deter investors.

(d) There are likely to be higher **information and transaction costs** associated with investing in foreign securities.

(e) Some types of investor may have a parochial **home bias** for domestic investment.

1.2   There are a number of arguments in favour of **international portfolio diversification**.

BPP PUBLISHING

Diversification of risk

1.3 A portfolio which is diversified internationally should in theory be less risky than a purely domestic portfolio. This is of advantage to any risk-averse investor. As with a purely domestic portfolio, the extent to which risk is reduced by **international diversification** will depend upon the degree of correlation between individual securities in the portfolio. The lower the degree of correlation between returns on the securities, the more risk can be avoided by diversification.

1.4 On the international dimension, a number of factors help to ensure that there is often low correlation between returns on securities in different countries and therefore enhance the potential for risk reduction, including the following.

   (a) Different countries are often at **different stages of the trade cycle** at any one time.

   (b) **Monetary, fiscal and exchange rate policies** differ internationally.

   (c) Different countries have **different endowments of natural resources** and different industrial bases.

   (d) Potentially **risky political events** are likely to be localised within particular national or regional boundaries.

   On the other hand, for countries within the same region having closely linked economies, such as the USA and Canada, correlations are relatively high.

1.5 A study published in *Financial Analysts Journal* (1974) found that a fully diversified international portfolio had less than half the risk (measured as the variance of portfolio return ÷ variance of return on a typical security) of a fully diversified US domestic portfolio.

1.6 Securities markets in different countries differ considerably in the **combination of risk and return** which they offer. For example, a study of fifteen major stock markets over the period 1973 to 1982 found that the Hong Kong, Singapore and UK stock markets were characterised by high risk but high returns while the US market displayed low risk and relatively low returns.

Exchange rates

1.7 **Exchange rate fluctuations** will generally have implications for international portfolio diversification where the investment is in a country whose currency floats against that of the investor's own country's currency. Indeed, the volatility in exchange rates between major currencies in recent years is sometimes cited as a barrier to international investment. Foreign exchange markets can often be almost as volatile as stock markets. Overall, fluctuations in exchange rates make international investment more risky, but this does not negate the fact that international portfolio diversification is worthwhile for investors wishing to reduce the risk of a portfolio.

Multinationals as diversified portfolios

1.8 Some of the costs and other barriers associated with international investment might be reduced if the investor is able to achieve international portfolio diversification by investing in the **shares of a multinational company**. The evidence on this issue suggests that, unlike a portfolio of stocks drawn from different international markets, the share price behaviour of multinational companies closely reflects that of non-multinational domestic firms. It follows that the reduction of risk (ie the reduction in the variance of portfolio return) that international portfolio diversification can achieve is not likely to be gained through the strategy of investing in a home based multinational.

The international cost of capital

1.9 Earlier in this Study Text, we examined the **weighted average cost of capital (WACC)** of a firm. The WACC, you should by now appreciate, is a weighted average of the required returns for the various providers of finance to the firm. The **cost of capital** is important for both the **financing decision** of the firm and for the investment decision.

The financing decision

1.10 The company will wish to keep the cost of funds after tax as low as possible within a reasonable level of risk, since the lower is the cost of capital the higher is the value of the firm. Multinational firms, having access to worldwide capital markets, are likely to be well placed to adjust the mix of the firm's finance so as to reduce the cost of capital.

1.11 There are various factors to consider in deciding the **mix of finance**.

   (a) What are the relative costs of different types of fund? It must be borne in mind that an increase in one type of finance may have an effect on the cost (or return required) on other forms of finance.

   (b) What is the appropriate mix of short-term and long-term finance?

   (c) In the light of the arguments of Modigliani and Miller, what is the appropriate mix of debt and equity? The effect on risk for ordinary shareholders of increasing additional debt needs to be considered.

   (d) Tax rules need to be considered. Because tax relief is available on debt interest, the mix of debt and equity can affect the tax liability of the firm.

The investment decision

1.12 It will be appropriate to adopt the firm's **WACC** as a discount rate if the following two conditions are satisfied.

   (a) The systematic risk associated with the investment should be similar to that of the firm's other investments. In this context, we assume that the company's shareholders hold the shares within a well diversified portfolio.

   (b) The method of financing of the project should not affect the level of gearing of the company.

1.13 An overseas project may alter the firm's total risk. Political risk and currency risk, both of which are unsystematic, are likely to increase. Total risk may be allowed for by:

   (a) Adjusting the discount rate for total risk, or

   (b) Accounting for risk in projected cash flows, using a discount rate adjusted for systematic business risk and financial risk as in the case of a domestic project

1.14 In practice, it is common for firms to add a premium to the discount rate to account for risk. In comparing different approaches to adjusting for risk, the different characteristics of the special risks involved in international investment should be noted.

   (a) **Political risk** is generally the risk of an adverse outcome in the form of possible expropriation of assets resulting from currently unforeseen changes in the political

461

climate that may prevail in the future. Since the risks cannot currently be foreseen, the effect is likely to be on future cash flows. If political risk were to be adjusted for through the discount rate, all cash flows would be affected.

(b) **Currency risk** can have either favourable or adverse effects on the project cashflows. Whether the effect is favourable or adverse depends on the direction of change in exchange rates and on whether the cash flows concerned are inflows or outflows. Instead of adjusting the discount rate, it is more appropriate to adjust for this 'two-way' risk by reflecting alternative outcomes in the cash flow forecasts themselves.

Effects of international portfolio diversification

1.15 As already discussed, internationalisation of a portfolio provides a means of reducing the risk of the portfolio. For a firm contemplating a foreign investment, the degree of correlation between the stock markets of the two countries involved provides an indication of the level of systematic risk associated with the investment: the lower is the correlation coefficient, the lower is the likely level of systematic risk.

1.16 The possibility of lowering systematic risk through international investment suggests that a lower discount rate is appropriate for overseas investments. However, whether this is reasonable depends upon whether it is true that shareholders will accept a lower return on their equity in an internationally diversified firm for the reason that there is a reduction in the domestic (home-country) systematic risk. This is likely to be the case if the multinational firm is enabling shareholders to achieve international diversification that they would not otherwise be able to achieve, perhaps because of regulatory restrictions.

1.17 If the multinational firm is investing in countries in which shareholders can readily invest themselves directly, or via a managed investment fund such as a unit trust or investment trust, then there is no reason to suppose that shareholders will gain from the diversification within the multinational firm. In this case, there would seem to be no reason for the firm to use a lower discount rate for the overseas investment.

2 INTERNATIONAL CAPM

2.1 As we have seen, the possibility of international portfolio diversification increases the opportunities available to investors. Extension of the **capital asset pricing model (CAPM)**, which we examined in Chapter 8, to the international case means that we must take into account exchange rate risk and market imperfections.

2.2 You will recall from Chapter 8 the CAPM formula giving the equilibrium expected return on a risky individual security.

$$E(r_j) = r_f + [E(r_m) - r_f]\beta_j$$

where $E(r_j)$ is the expected return from an individual security
r_f is the risk-free rate of return
$E(r_m)$ is the expected return from the market as a whole
β_j is the beta factor of the individual security

2.3 Recall also that one formula for calculating the beta value of a company's shares is:

$$\beta = \frac{(\text{cov x, y})}{\text{var (x)}}$$

where (cov x,y) is the covariance of returns on an individual company's shares (y) with returns for the market as a whole (x) and var (x) is the variance of returns for the market as a whole.

2.4 CAPM implies that investors receive returns above the risk-free rate only by bearing systematic (non-diversifiable) risk. Investors should diversify as much as possible and avoid unsystematic risk.

2.5 If we assume that the international capital market is simply like an enlarged domestic market, then we have an international CAPM formula as follows.

$$E(r_j) = r_f + [E(r_w) - r_f]\beta_w$$

where $E(r_w)$ is the expected return from the world market portfolio and β_w is a measure of the world systematic risk, given by the following formula:

$$\beta_w = \frac{(cov\ w, y)}{var\ (w)}$$

where (cov w,y) is the covariance of returns on the individual security (y) with returns on the world market (w) and var (w) is the variance of returns on the world market.

2.6 This analysis implies that the risk premium is proportional to the world systematic risk, β_w, and that investors can benefit from maximum diversification by investing in the world market portfolio consisting of all securities in the world economy.

2.7 In practice, such complete diversification will of course not be practicable. However, significant international diversification can be achieved by the following methods:

(a) Direct investment in companies in different countries
(b) Investments in multinational enterprises
(c) Holdings in unit trusts or investment trusts which are diversified internationally

2.8 EXAMPLE: INTERNATIONAL CAPM

A company's shares have a covariance of returns of 17.8% relative to returns for the world market portfolio. The risk-free rate of return is 8% and the expected return on the world market portfolio is 11%. The standard deviation of returns for the world market is 30%.

You are required to calculate the international cost of equity capital for the company. Exchange rate risks and market imperfections can be ignored.

2.9 SOLUTION

The variance is the square of the standard deviation and so the world beta value for the company is:

$$\frac{0.178}{0.3^2} = \frac{0.178}{0.09} = 1.98$$

The cost of equity capital is $8\% + (11 - 8) \times 1.98\% = 13.94\%$.

3 CAPITAL BUDGETING FOR FOREIGN PROJECTS   12/94, 6/97

3.1 **Multinational capital budgeting** can be based on similar concepts to those used in the purely domestic case which we have examined earlier in this Study Text using **net present value (NPV) analysis**, in which project cash flows are discounted using the firm's weighted average cost of capital, or the **internal rate of return** method which finds the rate of return equating project cash inflows with project costs.

3.2 Depending upon the information available, two alternative NPV methods are available. Both methods produce the NPV in domestic currency terms. For a UK company investing overseas, we can:

(a) Convert the project cash flows into sterling and then discount at a sterling discount rate to calculate the NPV in sterling terms, or

(b) Discount the foreign currency cash flows from the project at a discount rate for that currency and then convert the resulting NPV into a sterling NPV at the spot exchange rate

3.3 There are, however, some **special considerations** in the international case.

(a) For the purpose of assessing how expected performance compares with potential performance, it is necessary to compare the project's net present value with those of similar host country projects. This involves measuring the cash flows in terms of the currency of the host country.

(b) A foreign project also needs to be evaluated on its net present value in respect of the funds which can be remitted to the parent. The purpose of this second stage is to evaluate whether the cash flow remitted justifies the cash invested from the home country.

(c) Cash flows from the subsidiary may come about through a variety of means, including licensing fees and payments for imports from the parent company.

(d) The possibility of **differing national rates of inflation** needs to be taken into account.

The APV method

3.4 The **adjusted present value (APV) method**, which we analysed in Chapter 6, may be used for a project which is financed differently from the parent company. However, although the APV is a feasible method of analysis for foreign projects, it is not used nearly as much in practice as the traditional weighted average cost of capital method.

> ### Exam focus point
> The Examiner for Paper 14 has indicated that calculations questions will not be set requiring application of the APV method in an international context.

Foreign exchange risk and overseas operations

3.5 When a UK company wishes to finance operations overseas, there may be a foreign exchange risk arising from the method of financing used. To reduce or eliminate the foreign exchange risk of an overseas investment, a company might finance it with funds raised in the same currency as the investment. As you should appreciate from our earlier discussion of **currency risk**, there are advantages of borrowing in the same currency as an investment. Assets and liabilities in the same currency can be matched, thus avoiding exchange losses on conversion in the group's annual accounts. Revenues in the foreign currency can be used to repay borrowings in the same currency, thus eliminating losses due to fluctuating exchange rates.

Additional factors

3.6 Additional factors to be taken into account when appraising overseas investments are as follows.

    (a) **Political interference** by overseas governments, including exchange controls, extra charges on the profits of overseas companies and employment legislation could be a danger.

    (b) **Differences in tax systems** (and accounting practices) may be significant.

    (c) The investor should allow for the **extra risk** associated with overseas investments, largely as a result of (a) and (b), as well as any foreign exchange risk through not matching foreign currency assets and liabilities, or not matching revenues and finance payments in the foreign currency.

    (d) Some countries offer **special finance incentives** for investment in that country.

    (e) It **might be better to export** than to set up a foreign subsidiary.

Loans in foreign currencies

3.7 A UK company could borrow in a foreign currency to finance an investment in sterling. For example, a company could finance a project in the UK by borrowing in US dollars. The loan could be raised as a **eurocurrency loan** from a bank or, in the case of very large companies, as a **eurobond issue**. The **reason** for financing a project in a foreign currency would be the availability of a lower interest rate than the current market rate for sterling loans.

3.8 However, it is easy to be deceived by lower interest rates on eurocurrency loans, and foreign currency loans at a low interest rate could prove more expensive than a loan in domestic currency at a higher interest rate. Companies need to beware of this 'interest rate trap.' The project will pay back returns in sterling, but the loan, and interest on the loan, must be paid in the foreign currency. If the currency of the loan strengthens against sterling, the **sterling cost** of the loan interest and the loan repayment will increase.

3.9 For example, suppose that a UK company borrows $6,000,000 at an interest rate of 7%, when the exchange rate is $2 = £1. The loan would finance a UK investment costing £3,000,000. Annual interest on the loan would be $420,000, which would cost £210,000 if the exchange rate does not change. But if sterling falls in value against the dollar to, say, $1.50 = £1, the loan interest will cost £280,000 a year, and the capital sum needed to repay the loan at the end of its term will be £4,000,000.

4 TAXATION IN THE MULTINATIONAL ENVIRONMENT

Tax planning

4.1 Tax planning for multinational companies is an extremely complex area. (We looked at the tax implications of transfer pricing in Chapter 23.) Each country has its own range of taxes, and multinational enterprises must usually seek local advice in each country, which may be available through international accounting firms.

Foreign tax credits

4.2 In order to prevent the same income being taxed twice **(double taxation),** most countries give a tax credit for taxes on income paid to the host country. For example, a Japanese subsidiary of a US firm earns the equivalent of $500,000 in yen. The subsidiary pays 40% income tax ($200,000) in Japan. The US parent can claim a credit against US taxes of $200,000 when the earnings are remitted to the parent company.

4.3 **Foreign tax credits** are also available for withholding taxes on sums paid to other countries as dividends, interest, royalties and in other forms.

Tax havens

4.4 **Tax havens** are used by some multinationals as a means of deferring tax on funds prior to their repatriation or reinvestment. A tax haven is likely to have the following characteristics.

(a) Tax on foreign investment or sales income earned by resident companies, and withholding tax on dividends paid to the parent, should be low.

(b) There should be a stable government and a stable currency.

(c) There should be adequate financial services support facilities.

Question

Flagwaver plc is considering whether to establish a subsidiary in the USA, at a cost of $2,400,000. This would be represented by fixed assets of $2,000,000 and working capital of $400,000. The subsidiary would produce a product which would achieve annual sales of $1,600,000 and incur cash expenditures of $1,000,000 a year.

The company has a planning horizon of four years, at the end of which it expects the realisable value of the subsidiary's fixed assets to be $800,000.

It is the company's policy to remit the maximum funds possible to the parent company at the end of each year.

Tax is payable at the rate of 35% in the USA and is payable one year in arrears. A double taxation treaty exists between the UK and the USA and so no UK taxation is expected to arise.

Tax allowable depreciation is at a rate of 25% on a straight line basis on all fixed assets.

Because of the fluctuations in the exchange rate between the US dollar and sterling, the company would protect itself against the risk by raising a eurodollar loan to finance the investment. The company's cost of capital for the project is 16%.

Calculate the NPV of the project.

Answer

The annual writing down allowance (WDA) is 25% of US$2,000,000 = $500,000, from which the annual tax saving would be (at 35%) $175,000.

Year	Invest-ment $m	Contri-bution $m	Tax on contri-bution $m	Tax saving on WDA & tax on realisable value $m	Net cash flow $m	Discount factor 16%	Present value $m
0	(2.4)				(2.400)	1.000	(2.400)
1		0.6		0.175	0.775	0.862	0.668
2		0.6	(0.21)	0.175	0.565	0.743	0.420
3		0.6	(0.21)	0.175	0.565	0.641	0.362
4	1.2*	0.6	(0.21)	0.175	1.765	0.552	0.974
5			(0.21)	(0.28)**	(0.490)	0.476	(0.233)
							(0.209)

*   Fixed assets realisable value $800,000 plus working capital $400,000

** It is assumed that tax would be payable on the realisable value of the fixed assets, since the tax written down value of the assets would be zero. 35% of $800,000 is $280,000.

The NPV is negative and so the project would not be viable at a discount rate of 16%.

Chapter roundup

- **International portfolio diversification** brings advantages resulting from differences in the economies of different countries.

- The **CAPM** can be extended to cover international portfolio risk, but in practice foreign exchange fluctuations and market imperfections also need to be considered.

- The **appraisal of foreign projects** involves a number of complexities which do not arise in the case of domestic projects, including international tax complications and differential rates of inflation.

Quick quiz

1 What barriers are there to international investment? (see para 1.1)

2 What factors ensure that there is low correlation between returns on securities in different national securities markets around the world? (1.5)

3 What does the international CAPM indicate about international portfolio diversification? (2.6)

4 What special considerations are there in applying NPV analysis to the appraisal of foreign projects? (3.3)

5 Why might a multinational company make use of a tax haven, and what characteristics is a tax haven likely to have? (4.5)

Question to try	Level	Marks	Time
24	Exam standard	40	72 mins

Chapter 25

THE TREASURY FUNCTION

Chapter topic list	Syllabus reference
1 Treasury departments	4(a), 6(c)
2 Payments between companies	4(a), 6(c)
3 Cash management services	4(a), 6(c)
4 Short-term investments	4(a), 6(c)

Introduction

We now discuss the work of the **treasury function**, which in larger companies will form a separate department. Whether a treasury department is treated as a **cost centre** or a **profit centre** can have significant implications for how it approaches its role and may reflect the strategy of the organisation as a whole.

1 TREASURY DEPARTMENTS

6/96

1.1 Large companies, including multinationals, often rely heavily for both long-term and short-term funds on the financial and currency markets. These markets are volatile, with interest rates and foreign exchange rates changing continually and by significant amounts. Many large companies have set up separate treasury departments to manage cash and foreign currency.

1.2 **Treasurership** can be defined as the function concerned with the provision and use of finance. It covers provision of capital, short-term borrowing, foreign currency management, banking, collections and money market investment.

1.3 A **treasury department**, even in a large company, is likely to be quite small, with perhaps a staff of three to six qualified accountants, bankers or corporate treasurers working under a Treasurer, who is responsible to the Finance Director. In some cases, where the company or organisation handles very large amounts of cash or foreign currency dealings, and often has large cash surpluses, the treasury department might be a little bigger.

The role of the treasurer

1.4 The Association of Corporate Treasurers has listed the experience it will require from its student members before they are eligible for full membership of the Association. This list of required experience gives a good indication of the roles of treasury departments.

   (a) **Corporate financial objectives**

      (i)   Financial aims and strategies
      (ii)   Financial and treasury policies
      (iii)   Financial and treasury systems

(b) **Liquidity management**: making sure the company has the liquid funds it needs, and invests any surplus funds, even for very short terms.

    (i)   Working capital and money transmission management
    (ii)   Banking relationships and arrangements
    (iii)   Money management

Cash management and liquidity management are probably the most obvious responsibilities of a treasurer. In some organisations, the task is largely one of controlling stocks, debtors, creditors and bank overdrafts.

In cash-rich companies, the treasurer will invest surplus funds to earn a good yield until they are required again for another purpose.

A good relationship with one or more banks is desirable, so that the treasurer can negotiate overdraft facilities, money market loans or longer term loans at reasonable interest rates.

(c) **Funding management**

    (i)   Funding policies and procedures
    (ii)   Sources of funds
    (iii)   Types of funds

Funding management is concerned with all forms of **borrowing**, and alternative sources of funds, such as leasing and factoring.

The treasurer needs to know:

    (i)   Where funds are obtainable
    (ii)   For how long
    (iii)   At what interest rate
    (iv)   Whether security would be required
    (v)   Whether interest rates would be fixed or variable

If a company borrows, say, £10,000,000, even a difference of ¼% in the interest cost of the loan obtained would be worth £25,000 in interest charges each year.

(d) **Currency management**

    (i)   Exposure policies and procedures
    (ii)   Exchange dealing, including futures and options
    (iii)   International monetary economics and exchange regulations

Currency dealings can save or cost a company considerable amounts of money, and the success or shortcomings of the corporate treasurer can have a significant impact on the profit and loss account of a company which is heavily involved in foreign trade.

(e) **Corporate finance**

    (i)   Equity capital management
    (ii)   Business acquisitions and sales
    (iii)   Project finance and joint ventures

Corporate finance is concerned with matters such as raising share capital, its form (ordinary or preference, or different classes of ordinary shares), obtaining a stock exchange listing, dividend policy, financial information for management, mergers, acquisitions and business sales.

(f) **Related subjects**

    (i)   Corporate taxation (domestic and foreign tax)
    (ii)   Risk management and insurance

(iii)   Pension fund investment management

Centralised or decentralised cash management?   6/97

1.5   A large company may have a number of subsidiaries and divisions. In the case of a multinational, these will be located in different countries. It will be necessary to decide whether the treasury function should be centralised.

1.6   With centralised cash management, the central Treasury department effectively acts as the bank to the group and has the job of ensuring that individual operating units have all the funds they need at the right time.

1.7   The following are advantages of having a specialist **centralised treasury department**.

(a)   Centralised liquidity management avoids having a mix of cash surpluses and overdrafts in different localised bank accounts, and facilitates bulk cash flows, so that lower bank charges can be negotiated.

(b)   Larger volumes of cash are available to invest, giving better short-term investment opportunities (for example money markets, high-interest accounts and CDs).

(c)   Any borrowing can be arranged in bulk, at lower interest rates than for smaller borrowings, and perhaps on the eurocurrency or eurobond markets. **Interest rate hedging** will be facilitated.

(d)   **Foreign currency risk management** is likely to be improved in a group of companies. A central treasury department can match foreign currency income earned by one subsidiary with expenditure in the same currency by another subsidiary. In this way, the risk of losses on adverse exchange rate movements can be avoided without the expense of forward exchange contracts or other hedging methods.

(e)   A specialist treasury department will employ experts with knowledge of dealing in forward contracts, futures, options, eurocurrency markets, swaps and so on. Localised departments could not have such expertise.

(f)   The centralised pool of funds required for precautionary purposes will be smaller than the sum of separate precautionary balances which would need to be held under decentralised treasury arrangements.

(g)   Through having a separate profit centre, attention will be focused on the strategy of the group and the contribution to group profit performance that can be achieved by good cash, funding, investment and foreign currency management.

(h)   Transfer prices can be set centrally, thus minimising the global tax burden of the group.

1.8   Possible advantages of decentralised cash management are as follows.

(a)   Sources of finance can be **diversified** and can **match local assets.**

(b)   **Greater autonomy** can be given to subsidiaries and divisions because of the closer relationships they will have with the decentralised cash management function.

(c)   A decentralised Treasury function may be able to be **more responsive** to the needs of individual operating units.

(d)   Since cash balances will not be aggregated at group level, there will be more **limited opportunities to invest** such balances on a short-term basis.

The treasury department as cost centre or profit centre

1.9 A treasury department might be managed either as a **cost centre** or as a **profit centre**. For a group of companies, this decision may need to be made for treasury departments in separate subsidiaries as well as for the central corporate treasury department.

1.10 In a cost centre, managers have an incentive only to keep the costs of the department within budgeted spending targets. The cost centre approach implies that the treasury is there to perform a service of a certain standard to other departments in the enterprise. The treasury is treated much like any other service department.

1.11 However, some companies (including BP, for example) have been able to make significant profits from their treasury activities. Treating the treasury department as a profit centre recognises the fact that treasury activities such as **speculation** may earn revenues for the company, and may as a result make treasury staff more motivated. The profit centre approach is probably going to be appropriate only if the company has a high level of foreign exchange transactions.

> **KEY TERM**
>
> **Speculation:** the acceptance of risk in undertaking uncovered transactions.

1.12 If a profit centre approach is being considered, the following issues should be addressed.

(a) **Competence of staff**. It may be unreasonable to expect local managers to have sufficient expertise in the area of treasury management to carry out speculative treasury operations competently. Mistakes in this specialised field may be costly. It may only be appropriate to operate a larger centralised treasury as a profit centre, and additional specialist staff demanding high salaries may need to be recruited.

(b) **Controls**. Adequate controls must be in place to prevent costly errors and overexposure to risks such as foreign exchange risks. It is possible to enter into a very large foreign exchange deal over the telephone.

(c) **Information**. A treasury team which trades in futures and options or in currencies is competing with other traders employed by major financial institutions who may have better knowledge of the market because of the large number of customers they deal with. In order to compete effectively, the team needs to have detailed and up-to-date market information.

(d) **Attitudes to risk**. The more aggressive approach to risk-taking which is characteristic of treasury professionals may be difficult to reconcile with the more measured approach to risk which may prevail within the board of directors. The recognition of treasury operations as profit making activities may not fit well with the main business operations of the company.

(e) **Internal charges**. If the department is to be a true profit centre, then market prices should be charged for its services to other departments. It may be difficult to put realistic prices on some services, such as arrangement of finance or general financial advice.

(f) **Performance evaluation**. Even with a profit centre approach, it may be difficult to measure the success of a treasury team for the reason that successful treasury activities sometimes involve **avoiding** the incurring of costs, for example when a currency devalues. For example, a treasury team which hedges a future foreign currency receipt

BPP PUBLISHING

over a period when the domestic currency undergoes devaluation (as sterling did in 1992 when it left the European exchange rate mechanism) may avoid a substantial loss for the company.

The treasury function in the multinational firm 6/94

1.13 Cash management in a multinational firm may be improved by both **centralisation** and **multilateral netting.**

1.14 If **cash management within a multinational firm is centralised**, each subsidiary holds only the minimum cash balance required for transaction purposes. All excess funds will be remitted to the central Treasury department. Funds held in the central pool of funds can be returned quickly to the local subsidiary by telegraphic transfer or by means of worldwide bank credit facilities. The firm's bank can instruct its branch office in the country in which the subsidiary is located to advance funds to the subsidiary. Multinationals' central pools of funds are generally maintained in major financial centres such as London, New York, Tokyo and Zurich.

Multilateral netting

1.15 Where there is a large number of separate foreign currency transactions between different subsidiaries, the obligations of different subsidiaries may be **netted off against each other on a multilateral basis**, in the ways explained in an earlier chapter. This may bring the advantage of reduced transaction costs because there will be a reduced level of transfers between different currencies. However, in some countries, including France and Italy for example, there are regulations limiting or prohibiting netting. We looked at multilateral netting in Chapter 20.

2 PAYMENTS BETWEEN COMPANIES 6/98

2.1 Various methods of payment used in trade, including international trade, each have their own distinguishing features, and will now be described in turn.

Payment by cheque

2.2 **Payment by cheque** is a *slow* method of settlement, because the payee must wait for the cheque to be returned to the drawer's bank for clearance before his own account is credited. The exporter will arrange for his bank to collect the payment. (In international trade, cheques must always be sent for collection.)

2.3 A cheque can be made out in any currency, not just the currency of the drawer's bank account. The cost of a cheque for the **buyer** is low, although the exporter incurs collection charges. These are advantages of payment by cheque. However, the long time it takes to collect payment by cheque is a serious inconvenience. Cheques are often payable in the buyer's country, and so the exporter must arrange for the money to be collected through his bank from abroad.

2.4 Payment by cheque of a debt in international trade might also be unsatisfactory for the following reasons.

    (a) The exporter (payee) will have to ask his bank to arrange to collect the payment for him, and the bank will make a **collection charge**.

(b)   The cheque might contravene the exchange control regulations of the buyer's country, so that settlement would be delayed until the necessary authorisation to make payment has been obtained.

(c)   Many companies are unaware that they are receiving an advance if their account is credited immediately in domestic currency when they present a cheque drawn on an overseas bank to their bank. The bank will charge interest on their advance.

(d)   The cheque might not be paid when presented. If the cheque is unpaid, the bank will reclaim the advance, converting the domestic currency into the currency of the cheque at the prevailing exchange rate, possibly resulting in an exchange loss.

Float

2.5   The term '**float**' is sometimes used to describe the amount of money tied up between the time when a payment is initiated (for example when a debtor sends a cheque in payment, probably by post) and the time when the funds become available for use in the recipient's bank account.

2.6   There are three reasons why there might be a lengthy float.

(a)   **Transmission delay.** When payment is sent through the post, it will take a day or longer for the payment to reach the payee.

(b)   **Delay in banking the payments received (lodgment delay).** The payee, on receipt of a cheque or cash, might delay presenting the cheque or the cash to his bank. The length of this delay will depend on administrative procedures in the payee's organisation.

(c)   The **time needed for a bank to clear a cheque (clearance delay).** A payment is not available for use in the payee's bank account until the cheque has been cleared. This will usually take two or three days for cheques payable in the UK. For cheques payable abroad, the delay is much longer.

2.7   There are several measures that could be taken to reduce the float.

(a)   The payee should ensure that the lodgment delay is kept to a minimum. Cheques received should be presented to the bank on the day of receipt.

(b)   The payee might, in some cases, arrange to collect cheques from the payer's premises. This would only be practicable, however, if the payer is local. The payment would have to be large to make the extra effort worthwhile.

(c)   The payer might be asked to pay through his own branch of a bank. The payer can give his bank detailed payment instructions, and use the credit clearing system of the bank giro. The **bank giro** is a means of making credit transfers for customers of other banks and other branches. The payee might include a bank giro credit slip on the bottom of his invoice, to help with this method of payment.

(d)   **BACS (Bankers' Automated Clearing Services)** is a banking system which provides for the computerised transfer of funds between banks. In addition, BACS is available to corporate customers of banks for making payments. The customer must supply a magnetic tape or disk to BACS, which contains details of payments, and payment will be made in two days. BACS is now commonly used by companies for salary payments.

(e)   For regular payments, **standing orders** or **direct debits** might be used.

(f) **CHAPS** (Clearing House Automated Payments System) is a computerised system for banks to make same-day clearances (that is, immediate payment) between each other. It has been estimated that over £50 billion passes through CHAPS each day. CHAPS replaced the 'walks' system where a bank sent a messenger with a cheque or draft, on foot, to another bank for on the spot payment. Each member bank of CHAPS can allow its own corporate customers to make immediate transfers of funds through CHAPS. However, there is a large minimum size for payments using CHAPS.

(g) For international payments, **lock boxes** may be used (discussed below).

2.8 A lengthy float suggests **inefficient cash management**. But there are other types of delay in receiving payment from debtors, which might also suggest inefficient cash management.

(a) There is the delay created by the length of credit given to customers. There is often a 'normal' credit period for an industry, and companies might be unable to grant less time for payment than this.

(b) There are avoidable delays caused by poor administration (in addition to lodgment delay), such as failure to notify the invoicing department that goods have been despatched, so that invoices are not sent promptly, or cheques from debtors being made out incorrectly, to the wrong company perhaps, because invoices do not contain clear instructions.

2.9 EXAMPLE: CASH MANAGEMENT (1)

Ryan Coates owns a chain of seven clothes shops in the London area. Takings at each shop are remitted once a week on Thursday evening to the head office, and are then banked at the start of business on Friday morning. As business is expanding, Ryan Coates has hired an accountant to help him. The accountant gave him the following advice.

'Turnover at the seven shops totalled £1,950,000 last year, at a constant daily rate, but you were paying bank overdraft charges at a rate of 11%. You could have reduced your overdraft costs by banking the shop takings each day, except on Saturdays. Saturday takings could have been banked on Mondays.'

Comment on the significance of this statement, stating your assumptions. The shops are closed on Sundays.

2.10 SOLUTION

(a) A bank overdraft rate of 11% a year is approximately $11/365 = 0.03\%$ a day.

(b) Annual takings of £1,950,000 would be an average of $£1,950,000/312 = £6,250$ a day for the seven shops in total, on the assumption that they opened for a 52 week year of six days a week (312 days).

(c) Using the approximate overdraft cost of 0.03% a day, the cost of holding £6,250 for one day instead of banking it is $0.03\% \times £6,250 = £1.875$.

(d) Banking all takings up to Thursday evening of each week on Friday morning involves an unnecessary delay in paying cash into the bank. The cost of this delay would be either:

   (i) The opportunity cost of investment capital for the business, or
   (ii) The cost of avoidable bank overdraft charges

   It is assumed here that the overdraft cost is higher and is therefore more appropriate.

Takings on	Could be banked on	Number of days delay incurred by Friday banking
Monday	Tuesday	3
Tuesday	Wednesday	2
Wednesday	Thursday	1
Thursday	Friday	0
Friday	Monday	4
Saturday	Monday	4
		14

In one week, the total number of days delay incurred by Friday banking is 14. At a cost of £1.875 a day, the weekly cost of Friday banking was £1.875 × 14 = £26.25, and the annual cost of Friday banking was £26.25 × 52 = £1,365.

(e) *Conclusion.* The company could have saved about £1,365 a year in bank overdraft charges last year. If the overdraft rate remains at 11% and turnover continues to increase, the saving from daily banking would be even higher next year.

Speeding up settlement by cheque: lock boxes

2.11 In spite of there being quicker ways of getting paid, such as electronic transfer, a large proportion of trade in Europe is still settled by cheque. Cheque payment is often preferred by buyers as it helps to delay payment. After it is received by the creditor, the cheque must be presented to a local bank branch which will then forward it to the national head office of the bank of the creditor company, which must in turn present it to the debtor's bank overseas. This process can take up to 28 days to be completed.

2.12 If electronic transfer is not possible and payment by cheque must be accepted, it is possible to reduce the time taken for the payment process to only five days instead of 28 using a '**lock box**' arrangement. Suppose you export to a customer which is a German company. You set up a 'lock box' bank account with a reputable German bank. You then ask the German customer to present the cheque to the German bank, providing full account details for the 'lock box'. Clearance of the cheque is then as fast as for a domestic cheque, with the funds being remitted electronically to your bank account.

2.13 Lock box arrangements are possible in Europe and North America. Within North America, lock boxes help to overcome delays in the postal service resulting from the large distances involved.

Payment by bill of exchange

2.14 **Bills of exchange** are a commonly used method of settlement in international trade. They are a form of IOU. When A sells goods to B, the settlement of the debt might be arranged by means of a bill of exchange (called **a trade bill** as B is a trader). A will draw a bill on B (asking B to pay a certain sum of money on a certain date in the future, such as 90 days after the date of the bill). B then accepts the bill, by signing it, and returns it to A. By accepting the bill, B is acknowledging its debt to A and is giving a promise to pay. After the credit period (the term of the bill) has expired, B will pay A the money owed.

Payment by banker's draft

2.15 A **banker's draft** is a cheque drawn by a bank on one of its own bank accounts. For example, a banker's draft might be issued by a UK bank instructing payment out of its own bank account with a 'correspondent' bank in an overseas country.

2.16   Banker's drafts are fairly commonly used, but they are a **slow** method of payment and would not be used when quick payment is required. An **advantage** of a banker's draft is that the exporter receives direct notification that the payment is now available to him. If the draft is for an advance payment, and the exporter is waiting to receive it before shipping the goods abroad, this direct notification to the exporter might help to speed up the shipment.

Mail transfer (mail payment orders)

2.17   A **mail transfer** (MT) is:

(a)   A payment order in writing

(b)   Sent by one bank to another bank (overseas)

(c)   Which can be **authenticated** as having been authorised by a proper official in the sending bank

(d)   And which instructs the other bank to pay a certain sum of money

(e)   To a **specified beneficiary** (or on application by a specified beneficiary)

The payment order is sent from the instructing bank to the overseas bank by airmail.

2.18   As is the case with banker's drafts, the overseas bank will have an account in the name of the instructing bank, and it is this account which will be debited with the amount paid to the beneficiary. Unlike a banker's draft, a mail transfer is sent by the bank itself to another bank, not by the bank's customer to the overseas supplier.

2.19   Because mail transfer (MT) involves airmail communication between one bank and another, it is a quicker method of payment than a banker's draft at no extra cost. However, there is always a possibility that instructions sent by airmail will be delayed or lost in the post, and there are quicker methods of arranging payment.

Telegraphic transfer : cable or telex payment orders

2.20   **Telegraphic transfers** (TT) or 'cable payment orders' are the same as mail transfers, except that instructions are sent by cable or telex instead of by airmail. TT is therefore slightly more costly to the paying bank's customer than mail transfer, but it speeds up payment.

2.21   Large payments should be made by TT or by SWIFT (see below) because the marginal extra cost of TT over MT might be outweighed by the extra interest earnings or savings in interest costs which would be achievable if TT were used. A further advantage of TT over MT is that there is no danger of instructions being delayed or lost in the post.

SWIFT

2.22   **SWIFT** (the Society for Worldwide Interbank Financial Telecommunications) provides an electronic funds transfer (EFT) and payment system for its shareholder banks worldwide. Most major North American and Western European banks are members. Since its establishment, non-banks have been admitted as eligible users, and users include securities houses, recognised exchanges, central clearing institutions, moneybrokers and fund managers. SWIFT is a secure telecommunications network which facilitates rapid international transfers between the member banks.

International money orders

2.23 An **international money order** is a means of transferring comparatively small sums of money from one country to another through the agency of the Post Office or possibly an international bank (eg Barclays). Since only small amounts are involved, international money orders are best suited to small orders where the exporter asks for payment in advance since the small amount of money involved would perhaps not financially justify allowing credit to the buyer or the minimum bank charges associated with collections or letters of credit.

Section summary

2.24 Methods of settlement include cheques and banker's drafts. These are relatively slow. Cheque settlement can be speeded up by the use of lock boxes. Mail transfers or international money transfers are quicker and telegraphic transfers or express international money transfers are even quicker. MT is a quicker method of payment than a banker's draft, because a draft is given to the importer to send to the beneficiary, and so there is usually some administrative delay in getting the draft sent to the beneficiary.

2.25 An international money transfer would be sent by ordinary SWIFT message. SWIFT has a computer/switching network which is used to transfer instructions and messages from one bank to another bank in a different country, without the need to use ordinary mail, telex or 'public' cable transmission. An IMT can therefore be sent, provided that a suitable bank in the supplier's country is a member of the SWIFT organisation.

2.26 Telegraphic transfer is a very fast method of settlement, because the payment order is sent to a bank in the supplier's country by means of telex or cable message. An express international money transfer (EIMT) is similar to a TT, with the exception that the payment order will be sent by the SWIFT network as a 'priority SWIFT message'.

3 CASH MANAGEMENT SERVICES

3.1 One of the banks' services is a cash management service for corporate customers. A company with many different bank accounts can obtain information about the cash balance in each account through a computer terminal in the company's treasury department linked to the bank's computer. The company can then arrange to move cash from one account to another and so manage its cash position more efficiently and make optimal use of its funds deposited with banks or in various money market investments. A cash management service can be provided to a company with several bank accounts in the UK, or, through an international network of banks, to a multinational company with accounts in different currencies in various countries.

3.2 The cash management services provided by the banks comprise three basic services.

(a) **Account reporting**

   (i) Information is given about the balances on sterling or currency accounts whether held in the UK or overseas, including details of the cleared balances for the previous day and any uncleared items.

   (ii) Forecast balance reports, which take into account uncleared items and automated entries (BACS credits and debits, standing orders and direct debits) can be obtained.

   (iii) Reports giving details of individual transactions can be obtained.

   (b) **Funds transfer**

      The customer can initiate sterling and currency payments through his terminal. Banks will also give customers with substantial cash floats the opportunity to get in touch with money market dealers directly and deposit funds in the money markets.

   (c) **Decision support services**

      An information service giving information on foreign exchange rates and money market (sterling deposit) interest rates could be used.

Cash pooling

3.3   **Cash pooling** is a procedure whereby debit and credit balances held with the same bank by companies within a group are set off against each other so that interest costs can be reduced. A cash pooling arrangement is administered by the bank at which the accounts are held and involves transferring all account balances to a 'dummy' account. The interest chargeable or payable is that based on the net balance in the dummy account. No actual movement of funds occurs. The group will need to have a policy on how to allocate interest savings resulting from pooling.

3.4 EXAMPLE: CASH POOLING

Two group companies K and L have accounts with the same bank. During September 19X4, K has an overdraft of £120,000 and L has a credit balance of £200,000. The bank charges interest on the group's overdraft balances at a rate of 0.8% per month and pays interest of 0.5% per month on credit balances. Calculate how much interest would be gained by adopting cash pooling for September 19X4.

3.5 SOLUTION

	£
Without cash pooling	
Interest charged (120,000 × 0.008)	(960)
Interest receivable (200,000 × 0.005)	1,000
Net interest receivable	40
With cash pooling	
The net balance is (200,000 − 120,000)	£80,000
Interest receivable (80,000 × 0.005)	£400
The net gain is (400 − 40)	£360

Applying probabilities in cash management problems

> **Exam focus point**
>
> Questions could require you to apply probabilities to cash management problems. The following example illustrates this approach.

3.6 EXAMPLE: CASH MANAGEMENT (2)

Sinkos Wim Ltd has an overdraft facility of £100,000, and currently has an overdraft balance at the bank of £34,000. The company maintains a cash float of £10,000 for transactions and precautionary purposes. It is unclear whether a long awaited economic recovery will take place, and the company has prepared cash budgets as set out below for the next three months using two different assumptions about economic events. The cash flow in months 2 and 3 depend on the cash flows in the previous month.

Estimated net cash flows

	Month 1		Month 2		Month 3	
Probability	*Cash flow* £'000		*Probability*	*Cash flow* £'000	*Probability*	*Cash flow* £'000
			0.8	25	0.5	30
0.7	(40)				0.5	20
			0.2	10	0.5	10
					0.5	0
			0.8	0	0.5	(10)
0.3	(60)				0.5	(20)
			0.2	(10)	0.5	(40)
					0.5	(50)

If the company intends to maintain a cash float of £10,000 at the end of each month, what is the probability that this will be possible at the end of each of months 1, 2 and 3 given the current overdraft limit?

3.7 SOLUTION

The opening balance at the beginning of month 1 is £10,000.

	Month 1				Month 2				Month 3		
Prob.	*Cash flow* £'000	*Clos. bal.* £'000	*Over-draft* £'000	*Prob.*	*Cash flow* £'000	*Clos. bal.* £'000	*Over-draft* £'000	*Prob.*	*Cash flow* £'000	*Clos. bal.* £'000	*Over-draft* £'000
								0.28	30	10	19
				0.56	25	10	49	0.28	20	10	29
0.7	(40)	10	74								
								0.07	10	10	54
				0.14	10	10	64	0.07	0	10	64
								0.12	(10)	6	100
				0.24	0	10	94	0.12	(20)	(4)	100
0.3	(60)	10	94								
								0.03	(40)	(34)	100
				0.06	(10)	6	100	0.03	(50)	(44)	100

The probabilities that the cash float of £10,000 can be maintained at the end of each month are as follows.

Month 1:   0.7 + 0.3 = 1.0
Month 2:   0.56 + 0.14 + 0.24 = 0.94
Month 3:   0.28 + 0.28 + 0.07 + 0.07 = 0.7

Question

Using the figures in the above example, state the probabilities that the company completely runs out of cash at the end of each month.

Answer

Under none of the projected outcomes for months 1 and 2 does the company run out of cash.

For month 3, the probability of the company running out of cash is: 0.12 + 0.03 + 0.03 = 0.18.

4 SHORT-TERM INVESTMENTS

4.1 Companies and other organisations sometimes have a surplus of cash and become 'cash rich'. A cash surplus is likely to be temporary, but while it exists the company should seek to obtain a good return by investing or depositing the cash, without the risk of a capital loss (or at least, without the risk of an excessive capital loss).

4.2 **Three possible reasons for a cash surplus**

   (a) Profitability from trading operations

   (b) Low capital expenditure, perhaps because of an absence of profitable new investment opportunities

   (c) Receipts from selling parts of the business

   The board of directors might keep the surplus in liquid form:

   (a) To benefit from high interest rates that might be available from bank deposits, when returns on re-investment in the company appear to be lower

   (b) To have cash available should a strategic opportunity arise, perhaps for the takeover of another company for which a cash consideration might be needed

   (c) To buy back shares from shareholders in the near future

   (d) To pay an increased dividend to shareholders

Short-term investments

4.3 Temporary cash surpluses are likely to be:

   (a) Deposited with a bank or similar financial institution

   (b) Invested in short-term debt instruments (Debt instruments are debt securities which can be traded.)

   (c) Invested in longer term debt instruments, which can be sold on the stock market when the company eventually needs the cash

   (d) Invested in shares of listed companies, which can be sold on the stock market when the company eventually needs the cash

4.4 The problem with (c) and (d) is the risk of capital losses due to a fall in the market value of the securities. With short-term debt instruments (item (b)) any capital losses should not be large, because of the short term to maturity. With bank deposits (item (a)) the risk of capital losses is minimal.

Short-term deposits

4.5 Cash can of course be put into a bank deposit to earn interest. The rate of interest obtainable depends on the size of the deposit, and varies from bank to bank.

4.6 There are other types of deposit.

BPP PUBLISHING

(a) **Money market lending.** There is a very large money market in the UK for inter-bank lending, with banks lending to each other and borrowing from each other for short terms ranging from as little as overnight up to terms of a year or more. The international money markets, as mentioned elsewhere in this Text, provide a way of earning interest on deposits for periods from overnight up to five years. The interest rates in the market are related to the London Interbank Offered Rate (**LIBOR**) and the London Interbank Bid Rate (**LIBID**).

    (i)   A large company will be able to lend surplus cash directly to a borrowing bank in the market.

    (ii)   A smaller company with a fairly large cash surplus will usually be able to arrange to lend money on the interbank market, but through its bank, and possibly on condition that the money can only be withdrawn at three months notice.

(b) **Local authority deposits.** Local authorities often need short-term cash, and investors can deposit funds with them for periods ranging from overnight up to one year or more.

(c) **Finance house deposits.** These are time deposits with finance houses (usually subsidiaries of banks).

4.7   Deposits with banks, local authorities and finance houses are non-negotiable, which means that the investor who deposits funds cannot sell the deposit to another investor, should an unexpected need for cash arise. The deposit will only be released back to the investor when its term ends.

Short-term debt instruments

4.8   There are a number of short-term debt instruments which an investor can re-sell before the debt matures and is repaid, including **certificates of deposit (CDs)**; **Treasury bills**; **eligible bank bills; bills of exchange** (discussed earlier in connection with foreign trade); **local authority bonds; commercial paper** (CP) – also discussed in an earlier Chapter.

4.9   A **CD** is a security that is issued by a bank, acknowledging that a certain amount of money has been deposited with it for a certain period of time (usually, a short term). The CD is issued to the depositor, and attracts a stated amount of interest. The depositor will be another bank or a large commercial organisation. CDs are negotiable and traded on the CD market (a money market), so if a CD holder wishes to obtain immediate cash, he can sell the CD on the market at any time. This secondhand market in CDs makes them attractive, flexible investments for organisations with excess cash.

4.10   A company with surplus cash can deposit a certain amount of cash with a bank for a fixed period, and receive a certificate of deposit from the bank, or buy an existing CD, which may have a much shorter period to maturity, on the CD market. CDs are mainly denominated in sterling, but there is a growing market in US dollar CDs, and in deposits linked to the value of the European currency unit (ecu).

4.11   **Treasury bills** are issued weekly by the government to finance short-term cash deficiencies in the government's expenditure programme. They are IOUs issued by the government, giving a promise to pay a certain amount to their holder on maturity. Treasury bills have a term of 91 days to maturity, after which the holder is paid the full value of the bill. Most Treasury bills are denominated in sterling, but some are in ecus.

4.12 Treasury bills do not pay interest, but the purchase price of a Treasury bill is less than its face value, the amount that the government will eventually pay on maturity. There is thus an implied rate of interest in the price at which the bills are traded. The secondhand value of Treasury bills in the discount market (the money market in which they are traded) varies with current interest rates but will never exceed their face value. A company can arrange through its bank to invest in Treasury bills. Since they are negotiable, they can be re-sold, if required, on the discount market before their maturity date.

4.13 Bank bills are IOUs issued by a bank. **Eligible bank bills** are bills issued by 'eligible' banks: top-rated banks whose bills the Bank of England will agree to buy on the money market. They are denominated in sterling and are short-term. Like Treasury bills, they are negotiable and traded on the discount market. Most purchasers of bank bills are other banks, including the Bank of England.

4.14 **Local authority bonds** are short-term securities issued by local authorities to raise cash. They carry interest, and are repayable on maturity. They are traded secondhand in the money market, and so, like CDs, are a flexible investment for organisations with excess cash. They are not always available, however.

Chapter roundup

- In this chapter we have looked at aspects of the **treasury function** and various methods of cash transmission and international payment.

- A **small company** may have little choice but to accept the range of services offered by their bank managers or the facilities offered by overseas suppliers. **Larger companies** and **multinational enterprises** are in a position to adopt a more active role in managing deposits, borrowings and foreign debtors.

- **Centralisation** of the treasury function of a group has various advantages.

Quick quiz

1   What is the role of the treasurer? (see para 1.4)

2   What advantages are there in centralised treasury management? (1.7)

3   What are the advantages and disadvantages of settling foreign debts by cheque? (2.3, 2.4)

4   What cash management services are offered by banks? (3.1, 3.2)

5   What is 'cash pooling'? (3.3)

6   What short-term debt instruments are available for the investment of surplus cash? (4.8)

Question to try	Level	Marks	Time
25	Introductory	n/a	35 mins

Appendix: Mathematical tables and formulae

MATHEMATICAL TABLES

PRESENT VALUE TABLE

Present value of 1, ie $(1+r)^{-n}$

where r = discount rate

        n = number of periods until payment

Periods	Discount rates (r)									
(n)	1%	2%	3%	4%	5%	6%	7%	8%	9%	10%
1	0.990	0.980	0.971	0.962	0.952	0.943	0.935	0.926	0.917	0.909
2	0.980	0.961	0.943	0.925	0.907	0.890	0.873	0.857	0.842	0.826
3	0.971	0.942	0.915	0.889	0.864	0.840	0.816	0.794	0.772	0.751
4	0.961	0.924	0.888	0.855	0.823	0.792	0.763	0.735	0.708	0.683
5	0.951	0.906	0.863	0.822	0.784	0.747	0.713	0.681	0.650	0.621
6	0.942	0.888	0.837	0.790	0.746	0.705	0.666	0.630	0.596	0.564
7	0.933	0.871	0.813	0.760	0.711	0.665	0.623	0.583	0.547	0.513
8	0.923	0.853	0.789	0.731	0.677	0.627	0.582	0.540	0.502	0.467
9	0.914	0.837	0.766	0.703	0.645	0.592	0.544	0.500	0.460	0.424
10	0.905	0.820	0.744	0.676	0.614	0.558	0.508	0.463	0.422	0.386
11	0.896	0.804	0.722	0.650	0.585	0.527	0.475	0.429	0.388	0.350
12	0.887	0.788	0.701	0.625	0.557	0.497	0.444	0.397	0.356	0.319
13	0.879	0.773	0.681	0.601	0.530	0.469	0.415	0.368	0.326	0.290
14	0.870	0.758	0.661	0.577	0.505	0.442	0.388	0.340	0.299	0.263
15	0.861	0.743	0.642	0.555	0.481	0.417	0.362	0.315	0.275	0.239

	11%	12%	13%	14%	15%	16%	17%	18%	19%	20%
1	0.901	0.893	0.885	0.877	0.870	0.862	0.855	0.847	0.840	0.833
2	0.812	0.797	0.783	0.769	0.756	0.743	0.731	0.718	0.706	0.694
3	0.731	0.712	0.693	0.675	0.658	0.641	0.624	0.609	0.593	0.579
4	0.659	0.636	0.613	0.592	0.572	0.552	0.534	0.516	0.499	0.482
5	0.593	0.567	0.543	0.519	0.497	0.476	0.456	0.437	0.419	0.402
6	0.535	0.507	0.480	0.456	0.432	0.410	0.390	0.370	0.352	0.335
7	0.482	0.452	0.425	0.400	0.376	0.354	0.333	0.314	0.296	0.279
8	0.434	0.404	0.376	0.351	0.327	0.305	0.285	0.266	0.249	0.233
9	0.391	0.361	0.333	0.308	0.284	0.263	0.243	0.225	0.209	0.194
10	0.352	0.322	0.295	0.270	0.247	0.227	0.208	0.191	0.176	0.162
11	0.317	0.287	0.261	0.237	0.215	0.195	0.178	0.162	0.148	0.135
12	0.286	0.257	0.231	0.208	0.187	0.168	0.152	0.137	0.124	0.112
13	0.258	0.229	0.204	0.182	0.163	0.145	0.130	0.116	0.104	0.093
14	0.232	0.205	0.181	0.160	0.141	0.125	0.111	0.099	0.088	0.078
15	0.209	0.183	0.160	0.140	0.123	0.108	0.095	0.084	0.074	0.065

ANNUITY TABLE

Present value of an annuity of 1, ie $\dfrac{1-(1+r)^{-n}}{r}$

where r = discount rate

n = number of periods

Periods					Discount rates (r)					
(n)	1%	2%	3%	4%	5%	6%	7%	8%	9%	10%
1	0.990	0.980	0.971	0.962	0.952	0.943	0.935	0.926	0.917	0.909
2	1.970	1.942	1.913	1.886	1.859	1.833	1.808	1.783	1.759	1.736
3	2.941	2.884	2.829	2.775	2.723	2.673	2.624	2.577	2.531	2.487
4	3.902	3.808	3.717	3.630	3.546	3.465	3.387	3.312	3.240	3.170
5	4.853	4.713	4.580	4.452	4.329	4.212	4.100	3.993	3.890	3.791
6	5.795	5.601	5.417	5.242	5.076	4.917	4.767	4.623	4.486	4.355
7	6.728	6.472	6.230	6.002	5.786	5.582	5.389	5.206	5.033	4.868
8	7.652	7.325	7.020	6.733	6.463	6.210	5.971	5.747	5.535	5.335
9	8.566	8.162	7.786	7.435	7.108	6.802	6.515	6.247	5.995	5.759
10	9.471	8.983	8.530	8.111	7.722	7.360	7.024	6.710	6.418	6.145
11	10.37	9.787	9.253	8.760	8.306	7.887	7.499	7.139	6.805	6.495
12	11.26	10.58	9.954	9.385	8.863	8.384	7.943	7.536	7.161	6.814
13	12.13	11.35	10.63	9.986	9.394	8.853	8.358	7.904	7.487	7.103
14	13.00	12.11	11.30	10.56	9.899	9.295	8.745	8.244	7.786	7.367
15	13.87	12.85	11.94	11.12	10.38	9.712	9.108	8.559	8.061	7.606

	11%	12%	13%	14%	15%	16%	17%	18%	19%	20%
1	0.901	0.893	0.885	0.877	0.870	0.862	0.855	0.847	0.840	0.833
2	1.713	1.690	1.668	1.647	1.626	1.605	1.585	1.566	1.547	1.528
3	2.444	2.402	2.361	2.322	2.283	2.246	2.210	2.174	2.140	2.106
4	3.102	3.037	2.974	2.914	2.855	2.798	2.743	2.690	2.639	2.589
5	3.696	3.605	3.517	3.433	3.352	3.274	3.199	3.127	3.058	2.991
6	4.231	4.111	3.998	3.889	3.784	3.685	3.589	3.498	3.410	3.326
7	4.712	4.564	4.423	4.288	4.160	4.039	3.922	3.812	3.706	3.605
8	5.146	4.968	4.799	4.639	4.487	4.344	4.207	4.078	3.954	3.837
9	5.537	5.328	5.132	4.946	4.772	4.607	4.451	4.303	4.163	4.031
10	5.889	5.650	5.426	5.216	5.019	4.833	4.659	4.494	4.339	4.192
11	6.207	5.938	5.687	5.453	5.234	5.029	4.836	4.656	4.486	4.327
12	6.492	6.194	5.918	5.660	5.421	5.197	4.988	4.793	4.611	4.439
13	6.750	6.424	6.122	5.842	5.583	5.342	5.118	4.910	4.715	4.533
14	6.982	6.628	6.302	6.002	5.724	5.468	5.229	5.008	4.802	4.611
15	7.191	6.811	6.462	6.142	5.847	5.575	5.324	5.092	4.876	4.675

BPP PUBLISHING

FORMULAE

Formulae provided to Paper 14 candidates are set out below.

Ke   (i) $E(r_j) = r_f + [E(r_m) - r_f]\beta_j$

(ii) $\dfrac{D_1}{P_0} + g$

WACC $Ke_g \dfrac{E}{E+D} + Kd(1-t)\dfrac{D}{E+D}$

or $Ke_u \left[1 - \dfrac{Dt}{E+D}\right]$

2 asset portfolio $\sigma_p = \sqrt{\sigma_a^2 x^2 + \sigma_b^2(1-x)^2 + 2x(1-x)p_{ab}\sigma_a\sigma_b}$

Purchasing power parity $\dfrac{i_f - i_{uk}}{1 + i_{uk}}$

Corporate beta $\beta_a = \beta_e \dfrac{E}{E+D(1-t)} + \beta_d \dfrac{D(1-t)}{E+D(1-t)}$

Exam question
and answer bank

1 REMUNERATION (10 marks)

Assume you are Finance Director of a large multinational company, listed on a number of international stock markets. The company is reviewing its corporate plan. At present, the company focuses on maximising shareholder wealth as its major goal. The Managing Director thinks this single goal is inappropriate and asks his co-directors for their views on giving greater emphasis to the following:

(i)   Cash flow generation

(ii)   Profitability as measured by profits after tax and return on investment

(iii)   Risk-adjusted returns to shareholders

(iv)   Performance improvement in a number of areas such as concern for the environment, employees' remuneration and quality of working conditions and customer satisfaction

The company is already considering improving the methods of remuneration for its senior employees. As a member of the executive board, you are asked to give your opinions on the following suggestions:

(a)   A high basic salary with usual 'perks' such as company car, pension scheme etc but no performance-related bonuses

(b)   A lower basic salary with usual 'perks' plus a bonus related to their division's profit before tax

(c)   A lower basic salary with usual 'perks' plus a share option scheme which allows senior employees to buy a given number of shares in the company at a fixed price at the end of each financial year

Required

Discuss the arguments for and against *each* of the *three* options from the point of view of both the company and its employees. Detailed comments on the taxation implications are *not* required.

2 CORPORATE GOVERNANCE (10 marks)

(a)   Describe the main recommendations of the final report of the Committee on the Financial Aspects of Corporate Governance (the Cadbury Report) published in December 1992.

(4 marks)

(b)   Discuss the arguments for and against the introduction of statutory controls on corporate governance.   (6 marks)

3 HAYWORTH

Hayworth is an electronics company which is considered a project to build a combined television and computer (codenamed the teleputer within the company). This is a new venture involving state of the art technology and the company is eager to be first on to the market with this product.

Extensive market research has already been carried out at a cost of £250,000. Research costs are expected to be £1 million per annum for the next two years. Production of the first model of the teleputer is not expected to commence for a year. Because of expected technological changes it is anticipated that this first model will only be manufactured for a couple of years at an annual production cost of £7.5 million (this figure includes depreciation of £1.5 million per annum). Findings from the market research suggests that the initial high retail price of the first teleputer and its newness will result in only modest sales income of £4.5 million in the first year it is produced, and £7 million in the second year. After this time it is expected that this first model will be replaced by a newer version.

Because of the high risk of this project the company has decided to use a high discount rate of 20% for the investment appraisal.

Required

(a)   Calculate the net present value of this project based on the above figures (you can assume that all relevant cash flows occur at the year end).

(b)   What other factors might Hayworth take into account before making a decision as to whether to carry out this particular project?

4   COMMENTS   *18 mins*

The following two comments were drawn from separate articles in a highly respected financial newspaper.

'Market efficiency does not mean that share prices can be forecast with accuracy.'

'The research department of a large firm of stockbrokers has developed a multiple regression model, based on data collected between 1964 and 1994, which is claimed to give statistically significant results for predicting share prices.'

Required

Discuss these comments and explain why they are not contradictory.

5   CRYSTAL PLC   *35 mins*

The following figures have been extracted from the most recent accounts of Crystal plc.

BALANCE SHEET AS ON 30 JUNE 20X9

	£'000	£'000
Fixed assets		10,115
Investments		821
Current assets	3,658	
Less current liabilities	1,735	
		1,923
		12,859
Ordinary share capital		
Authorised: 4,000,000 shares of £1		
Issued: 3,000,000 shares of £1		3,000
Reserves		6,542
Shareholders' funds		9,542
7% Debentures		1,300
Deferred taxation		583
Corporation tax		1,434
		12,859

Summary of profits and dividends

Year ended 30 June:	19X5	19X6	19X7	19X8	19X9
	£'000	£'000	£'000	£'000	£'000
Profit after interest and before tax	1,737	2,090	1,940	1,866	2,179
Less tax	573	690	640	616	719
Profit after interest and tax	1,164	1,400	1,300	1,250	1,460
Less dividends	620	680	740	740	810
Added to reserves	544	720	560	510	650

The current (1 July 20X9) market value of Crystal plc's ordinary shares is £3.27 per share cum div. An annual dividend of £810,000 is due for payment shortly. The debentures are redeemable at par in ten years time. Their current market value is £77.10 per cent. Annual interest has just been paid on the debentures. There have been no issues or redemptions of ordinary shares or debentures during the past five years.

The current rate of corporation tax is 30%, and the current basic rate of income tax is 25%. Assume that there have been no changes in the system or rates of taxation during the last five years.

Required

(a)   Estimate the cost of capital which Crystal plc should use as a discount rate when appraising new investment opportunities.

(b)   Discuss any difficulties and uncertainties in your estimates.

6   EMMA PLC   *35 mins*

Emma plc is currently financed by 3,000,000 £1 ordinary shares, which have a market value ex div of £3.20 each. The company has always been an all equity company, but is now considering raising some debt finance for a new project.

The after tax operating cash flows of the project would be as follows.

Cost	£3,600,000
Benefit	£500,000 a year in perpetuity

The project would be financed by the issue at par of £3,600,000 of 10% debt capital. The very large increase in gearing that this would involve is thought to be feasible. Indeed, it has been suggested that the resulting gearing (measured in market value rather than book value terms) and weighted average cost of capital would be at the optimum level.

Emma plc's current after tax cost of equity is 16% and the new project would have the same operating risk characteristics as the company's existing projects. The company pays out all its after-tax earnings as dividends.

The corporate tax rate is 30% and there is no delay in receiving the benefit of tax relief.

Ignore issue costs.

Required

(a)   The company's objective is to maximise the wealth of its shareholders. Apply Modigliani and Miller's propositions to calculate whether the project would be worthwhile:

   (i)   If it were all-equity financed

   (ii)   If it were financed by the proposed issue of debt capital

   (iii)   If Emma plc had already been a geared company with its weighted average cost of capital at the optimum level, and if the project had been financed in such a way as to leave this weighted average cost of capital unchanged

(b)   Assuming that the project is financed by the issue of debt capital:

   (i)   Calculate the weighted average cost of capital after undertaking the project

   (ii)   Calculate the incremental cost of capital when compared with the company's previous all equity state. The incremental cost of capital is found by relating the incremental after-tax benefits of the project to the increase in the market value of the company as a consequence of the project

   (iii)   Use the results in (b)(i) and (b)(ii) to support your conclusions in (a)(ii) and (a)(iii) above

7   PORTFOLIO (10 marks)   *18 mins*

You are considering making an investment in one or both of two securities, X and Y, and you are given the following information.

Security	Possible rates of return %	Probability of occurrence
X	30	0.3
	25	0.4
	20	0.3
Y	50	0.2
	30	0.6
	10	0.2

Required

(a)   Calculate the expected return for each security separately and for a portfolio comprising 60% X and 40% Y, assuming no correlation between the possible rates of return from the shares comprising the portfolio.   (4 marks)

(b)   Calculate the risk of each security separately and of the portfolio as defined above. Measure risk by the standard deviation of returns from the expected rate of return.   (6 marks)

8   CANADIAN PLC (35 marks)   *63 mins*

Canadian plc is a regional electricity generating company with several coal, oil and gas powered generating stations. The opportunity to bid for the coal mine supplying one of its local stations has arisen, and you have been asked to assess the project. If Canadian does not bid for the pit, then it is likely to close, in which case coal for the station would have to be obtained from overseas.

Canadian's bid is likely to be successful if priced at £6 million. Regional development fund finance is available at a subsidised interest rate of 4% for the full cost of the purchase, as against Canadian's marginal cost of debt if financed commercially. If Canadian invests a further £6 million in updated machinery, the pit is likely to generate £10 million of coal per annum for the next five years at current UK coal prices. Operating costs will total £3 million per annum, plus depreciation. Thereafter it will have to close, at a net cost after asset sales of £17 million, which includes redundancy, cleanup and associated costs, at present prices.

You have ascertained the following information about the coal industry.

	Coal industry (average)
Gearing (debt/equity):	
Book values	1 to 0.5
Market values	1:1
Equity beta	0.7
Debt beta	0.2

Capital allowances would be available at 25% on a reducing balance basis for all new machinery. The purchase price can be depreciated for tax at 25% per annum straight line. All other costs are tax allowable in full.

Other than the regional development fund loan (repayable after 5 years), the project would be financed by retained earnings. The project is likely to add another £3 million of borrowing capacity to Canadian, in addition to the £6 million regional development fund loan. Corporation tax is expected to remain to 30% during the life of the project. The company as a whole expects to be in a tax payable position for all years except the third year of the project.

Assume that all prices rise with the RPI, currently by 3% pa, except coal prices, which in view of reduced demand are set to remain static. You may assume that original investment cashflows arise at the start of the first year, and that all other cashflows arise at the end of the year in which the costs are incurred, except for tax, which lags one year. Treasury bills currently yield 8%, and the return required of the market portfolio is currently 16%.

You have discovered the following information concerning Canadian.

	Canadian plc
Gearing (debt/equity):	
Book values	1 to 1
Market value	1:2
Equity beta	1.0
Debt beta	0.25
P/E ratio	14
Dividend yield	6%
Share price	220 pence
Number of ordinary shares	8 million

Required

Write a memorandum for the finance director advising on whether the mine should be acquired. you should divide your memorandum into the following sections:

(a)	Overall summary and conclusion	(5 marks)
(b)	Detailed numerical workings	(20 marks)
(c)	Assumptions behind the report	(7 marks)
(d)	Areas for further research	(3 marks)

9 PRISM PLC   *25 mins*

Prism plc obtained a stock exchange listing in November 20X3. Previously 80% of its shares were owned by two families, but since the listing this proportion has fallen to 40%.

Prism's earnings and dividends for its financial years (year end 31 March) prior to the listing are as follows.

Year	Profit (note 1)	Ordinary shares	Dividend per share
20W9	1,200,000	8,000,000	6.0p
20X0	1,500,000	8,000,000	7.5p
20X1	2,412,500	10,000,000	9.65p
20X2	2,800,000	10,000,000	11.2p
20X3	3,288,000	10,000,000	13.15p
20X4	4,225,000 (note 2)	15,000,000	

Notes

1 Profit after tax in pounds.
2 Estimated profit in 20X4

The number of issued ordinary shares (25p nominal) was increased by 50% at the time of the listing to 15 million. The current market value of the company is £35 million. The Board of Directors is considering future dividend policy. An interim dividend of 5.8 per share was paid immediately prior to the listing and the Finance Director has suggested a final dividend should be 4.0p per share. The company's stated objective is to maximise shareholder wealth.

Required

(a) Explain the company's dividend policy prior to the listing and discuss whether this remains suitable for a listed company.

(b) Is the proposed final dividend of 4.0p likely to be suitable if the majority of shares are owned by wealthy individuals?

10 CENAC PLC   *30 mins*

Cenac plc is considering introducing a new product to be called Comboux. Details of the project are as follows.

Production of Comboux will require the purchase and installation of new plant and machinery at a cost of £375,000, payable immediately. This plant will have a useful life of six years. It will have no scrap value at the end of that period.

Sales of Comboux are expected to be £600,000 per annum over the next six years. Production costs for Comboux are expected to be £480,000 per annum.

Cenac plc considers that a discount rate of 16% is appropriate for projects of this type.

Required

(a) Calculate the net present value of the project.

(b) For each of the estimates listed below, calculate the change in the individual estimate which would lead to the project breaking even in present value terms.

  (i)   Sales per annum
  (ii)   Production costs per annum
  (iii) Cost of plant and machinery
  (iv)   Useful life of plant and machinery
  (v)   Discount rate

11 THREE DECISIONS   *18 mins*

For the purpose of achieving the long-term financial objectives of a company, the financial manager will be faced with decisions on investment policy, on financing policy and on dividend policy.

Required

(a) Explain the nature of these three types of decision and the extent to which they are inter-related.

(b)   List the types of current and forecast information which might be relevant to each decision.

12   FINANCIAL OBJECTIVE

45 mins

The primary objective in financial management is usually assumed to be the maximisation (or improvement) of the wealth of ordinary shareholders. One way this can be achieved is to obtain a consistent rate of growth in the earnings per share.

The ability of a company to achieve such consistent growth depends to some extent on:

(a)   The external environment of the company
(b)   The company's operating cost structure
(c)   The company's capital gearing and the cost of debt capital

Required

(a)   Show how these factors are relevant to a consistent growth in earnings per share, using the information provided below about two companies, X Ltd and Y Ltd.

(b)   Discuss the financial management of both companies, insofar as the information provided allows.

	X Ltd				Y Ltd			
Year	20X1	20X2	20X3	20X4	20X1	20X2	20X3	20X4
	£'000	£'000	£'000	£'000	£'000	£'000	£'000	£'000
Profit & loss account								
Turnover	100	124	175	254	400	448	582	728
Variable costs	60	77	112	165	120	140	192	286
Fixed costs	26	31	42	58	180	196	230	256
Total costs	86	108	154	223	300	336	422	542
Earnings before interest and Tax	14	16	21	31	100	112	160	186
Less interest	4	4	7	8	10	16	19	19
Earnings before tax	10	12	14	23	90	96	141	167
Less tax	4	5	6	11	40	44	70	83
Distributable profits	6	7	8	12	50	52	71	84
Less dividends	3	3	4	4	18	18	30	40
Retained earnings	3	4	4	8	32	34	41	44
Balance sheet								
Fixed assets	29	42	56	64	300	318	400	425
Net current assets	31	34	49	72	80	153	207	232
	60	76	105	136	380	471	607	657
Ordinary shares of £1	20	20	20	25	200	200	250	250
Asset revaluation reserve	0	12	16	20	0	0	0	0
Reserves	15	19	23	31	100	134	175	225
Equity funds	35	51	59	76	300	334	425	475
Loans	25	25	46	60	80	137	182	182
	60	76	105	136	380	471	607	657
EPS (pence)	30.0	35.0	40.0	48.0	25.0	26.0	28.4	33.6

13   KILLISICK AND HOLBECK (25 marks)

45 mins

Killisick plc wishes to acquire Holbeck plc. The directors of Killisick are trying to justify the acquisition to the shareholders of both companies on the grounds that it will increase the wealth of all shareholders. The supporting financial evidence produced by Killisick's directors is summarised below.

	Killisick	*Holbeck*
	£'000	*£'000*
Operating profit	12,400	5,800
Less interest payable	4,431	2,200
Profit before tax	7,969	3,600
Less taxation	2,789	1,260
Earnings available to ordinary shareholders	5,180	2,340

	Killisick	*Holbeck*
Earnings per share (pre-acquisition)	14.80 pence	29.25 pence
Market price per share (pre-acquisition)	222 pence	322 pence
Estimated market price (post-acquisition)	240 pence	
Estimated equivalent value of one old Holbeck share (post-acquisition)		360 pence

Payment is to be made with Killisick ordinary shares, at an exchange ratio of 3 Killisick shares for every 2 Holbeck shares.

Required

(a) Show how the directors of Killisick produced their estimates of post-acquisition value and, if you do not agree with these estimates, produce revised estimates of post-acquisition values. All calculations must be shown. State clearly any assumptions that you make. (10 marks)

(b) If the acquisition is contested by Holbeck plc, using Killisick's estimate of its post-acquisition market price calculate the maximum price that Killisick could offer without reducing the wealth of its existing shareholders. (3 marks)

(c) The board of directors of Holbeck plc later informally indicate that they are prepared to recommend to their shareholders a 2 for 1 share offer.

Further information regarding the effect of the acquisition on Killisick is given below.

(i) The acquisition will result in an increase in the total pre-acquisition after tax operating cash flows of £2,750,000 a year indefinitely.

(ii) Rationalisation will allow machinery with a realisable value of £7,200,000 to be disposed of at the end of the next year.

(iii) Redundancy payments will total £3,500,000 immediately and £8,400,000 at the end of the next year.

(iv) Killisick's cost of capital is estimated to be 14% a year.

All values are after any appropriate taxation. Assume that the pre-acquisition market values of Killisick and Holbeck shares have not changed.

Recommend, using your own estimates of post-acquisition values, whether Killisick should be prepared to make a 2 for 1 offer for the shares of Holbeck. (6 marks)

(d) Disregarding the information in (c) above and assuming no increase in the total post-acquisition earnings, assess whether this acquisition is likely to have any effect on the value of debt of Killisick plc. (6 marks)

14 BLACK RAVEN LTD
45 mins

Black Raven Ltd is a prosperous private company, whose owners are also the directors. The directors have decided to sell their business, and have begun a search for organisations interested in its purchase. They have asked for your assessment of the price per ordinary share a purchaser might be expected to offer. Relevant information is as follows.

MOST RECENT BALANCE SHEET

	£'000	£'000	£'000
Fixed assets (net book value)			
Land and buildings			800
Plant and equipment			450
Motor vehicles			55
Patents			2
			1,307
Current assets			
Stock		250	
Debtors		125	
Cash		8	
		383	
Current liabilities			
Creditors	180		
Taxation	50		
		230	
			153
			1,460
Long-term liability			
Loan secured on property			400
			1,060

	£'000
Share capital (300,000 ordinary shares of £1)	300
Reserves	760
	1,060

The profits after tax and interest but before dividends over the last five years have been as follows.

Year	£
1	90,000
2	80,000
3	105,000
4	90,000
5 (most recent)	100,000

The company's five year plan forecasts an after-tax profit of £100,000 for the next 12 months, with an increase of 4% a year over each of the next four years. The annual dividend has been £45,000 (gross) for the last six years.

As part of their preparations to sell the company, the directors of Black Raven Ltd have had the fixed assets revalued by an independent expert, with the following results.

	£
Land and buildings	1,075,000
Plant and equipment	480,000
Motor vehicles	45,000

The gross dividend yields and P/E ratios of three quoted companies in the same industry as Black Raven Ltd over the last three years have been as follows.

	Albatross plc		Bullfinch plc		Crow plc	
	Div. yield	P/E ratio	Div. yield	P/E ratio	Div. yield	P/E ratio
	%		%		%	
Recent year	12	8.5	11.0	9.0	13.0	10.0
Previous year	12	8.0	10.6	8.5	12.6	9.5
Three years ago	12	8.5	9.3	8.0	12.4	9.0
Average	12	8.33	10.3	8.5	12.7	9.5

Large companies in the industry apply an after-tax cost of capital of about 18% to acquisition proposals when the investment is not backed by tangible assets, as opposed to a rate of only 14% on the net tangible assets.

Your assessment of the net cash flows which would accrue to a purchasing company, allowing for taxation and the capital expenditure required after the acquisition to achieve the company's target five year plan, is as follows.

	£
Year 1	120,000
Year 2	120,000
Year 3	140,000
Year 4	70,000
Year 5	120,000

Required

Use the information provided to suggest seven valuations which prospective purchasers might make.

15   BRIVE PLC (30 marks)   *54 mins*

The latest balance sheet for Brive plc is summarised below.

	£'000	£'000	£'000
Fixed assets at net book value			5,700
Current assets			
Stock and work in progress		3,500	
Debtors		1,800	
		5,300	
Less current liabilities			
Unsecured creditors	4,000		
Bank overdraft (unsecured)	1,600		
		5,600	
Working capital			(300)
Total assets less current liabilities			5,400
Liabilities falling due after more than one year			
10% secured debentures			3,000
Net assets			2,400

	£'000
Capital and reserves	
Called up share capital	4,000
Profit and loss account	(1,600)
	2,400

Brive plc's called up capital consists of 4,000,000 £1 ordinary shares issued and fully paid. The fixed assets comprise freehold property with a book value of £3,000,000 and plant and machinery with a book value of £2,700,000. The debentures are secured on the freehold property.

In recent years the company has suffered a series of trading losses which have brought it to the brink of liquidation. The directors estimate that in a forced sale the assets will realise the following amounts.

Freehold premises	£2,000,000
Plant and machinery	£1,000,000
Stock	£1,700,000
Debtors	£1,700,000

The costs of liquidation are estimated at £770,000. However, trading conditions are now improving and the directors estimate that if new investment in plant and machinery costing £2,500,000 were undertaken the company should be able to generate annual profits before interest of £1,750,000. In order to take advantage of this they have put forward the following proposed reconstruction scheme.

(a)   Freehold premises should be written down by £1,000,000, plant and machinery by £1,100,000, stocks and work in progress by £800,000 and debtors by £100,000.

(b)   The ordinary shares should be written down by £3,000,000 and the debit balance on the profit and loss account written off.

(c)   The secured debenture holders would exchange their debentures for £1,500,000 ordinary shares and £1,300,000 14% unsecured loan stock repayable in five years' time.

(d)   The bank overdraft should be written off and the bank should receive £1,200,000 of 14% unsecured loan stock repayable in five years time in compensation.

(e)   The unsecured creditors should be written down by 25%.

(f)   A rights issue of 1 for 1 at par is to be made on the share capital after the above adjustments have been made.

(g)   £2,500,000 will be invested in new plant and machinery.

Required

(a)   Prepare the balance sheet of the company after the completion of the reconstruction.   (8 marks)

(b)   Prepare a report, including appropriate calculations, discussing the advantages and disadvantages of the proposed reconstruction from the point of view of:

    (i)   The ordinary shareholders

      (ii)   The secured debenture holders
      (iii)   The bank
      (iv)   The unsecured creditors

Ignore taxation.   (22 marks)

16   COMMON MARKET   *20 mins*

(a)   State the differences between free trade areas, customs unions and common markets.

(b)   What economic benefits might countries gain from forming a common market?

17   IMF AND EUROMARKETS   *20 mins*

(a)   What is the purpose of the International Monetary Fund and how does it operate?

(b)   Describe the main features of the eurocurrency, eurobond and euroequity markets.

18   AARDVARK LTD (10 marks)   *18 mins*

Aardvark Ltd has been having some difficulty with the collection of debts from export customers. At present the company makes no special arrangements for export sales.

As a result the company is considering either employing the services of a non-recourse export factoring company, or insuring its exports against non-payment through an insurer. The two alternatives also provide possible ways of financing sales.

An export factor will, if required, provide immediate finance of 80% of export credit sales at an interest rate of 2% above bank base rate (the base rate is 8%). The service fee for debt collection is 3% of credit sales. If the factor is used, administrative savings of £35,000 a year should be possible.

A comprehensive insurance policy costs 35 pence per £100 insured and covers 90% of the risk of non-payment for exports. The insurer will probably allow Aardvark Ltd to assign its rights to a bank, in return for which the bank will provide an advance of 70% of the sales value of insured debts, at a cost of 1.5% above base rate.

Aardvark's annual exports total £1,000,000. Export sales are on open account terms of 60 days credit, but on average payments have been 30 days late. Approximately 0.5%, by value, of credit sales result in bad debts which have to be written off. The company is able to borrow on overdraft from its bank, unsecured, at 2.5% above base rate. Assume a 360 day year.

Required

Determine which combination of export administration and financing Aardvark Ltd should use.

19   OVERSEAS INVESTMENT (25 marks)   *45 mins*

(a)   The financial press recently listed the following information about two currencies, the Westland dollar ($W) and the Eastland mark (Em).

      Spot rates: 2.0725 Em/$W
                                         0.4825 $W/Em

      90 day rates: 2.0687 Em/$W
                                         0.4834 $W/Em

      The Westland prime interest rate on the same day was 9.5%. *Note.* Use a 365-day year.

      (i)   Explain what is implied about the Eastland interest rate.

      (ii)   Calculate and comment on the Eastland interest rate if the forward exchange rate was 0.4795 $W/Em.

      (iii)   Calculate and comment on the 90-day forward rate on Em/$W if the Eastland interest rate was 8%.   (7 marks)

(b)   It is currently 20X4. In the late 20W0s R plc, a manufacturing company based in the United Kingdom, developed a substantial market for its products in Eastern Europe. The board decided to establish a subsidiary in Hungary. The assets needed for the new subsidiary were mainly buildings. Plant and equipment were provided from the UK. Most of the raw material for production was, and still is, sourced in the UK. Local labour is used, except for senior managers who are seconded from the UK parent for 2 to 3 years.

Assuming the UK company wished to minimise its exposure to exchange risk:

(i)   discuss the options which were available to the parent company management for financing the new subsidiary. Assume that the parent company did not need to raise new long-term capital to finance this new venture;

(ii)   explain how the UK parent could have minimised its exchange losses arising from either operating transactions or a decline in the value of Hungarian Forints (HUF).

(10 marks)

(c)   R plc went ahead with the overseas investment in June 20X2 when the exchange rate was 150 HUF = £1. In October 20X2 the UK government was forced to devalue the pound sterling and leave the European Exchange Rate Mechanism. The exchange rate of HUF to the pound at the end of 20X2 was 125 = £1.

Discuss how the devaluation of the pound against the HUF might have affected the cash flows generated by the subsidiary and how the parent company could have managed the situation.

(8 marks)

20   EXPO PLC   *35 mins*

Expo plc is an importer/exporter of textiles and textile machinery. It is based in the UK but trades extensively with countries throughout Europe. It has a small subsidiary based in Germany. The company is about to invoice a customer in Germany 750,000 Deutschmarks, payable in three months' time. Expo plc's treasurer is considering two methods of hedging the exchange risk. These are:

Method 1: Borrow DM 750,000 for three months, convert the loan into sterling and repay the loan out of eventual receipts.

Method 2: Enter into a 3-month forward exchange contract with the company's bank to sell DM 750,000.

The spot rate of exchange is DM 2.3834 to £1. The 3-month forward rate of exchange is DM 2.3688 to £1. Annual interest rates for 3 months' borrowing are: Germany 3%, UK 6%.

Required

(a)   Advise the treasurer on:

(i)   Which of the two methods is the most financially advantageous for Expo plc, and

(ii)   The factors to consider before deciding whether to hedge the risk using the foreign currency markets

Include relevant calculations in your advice.

(b)   Assume that Expo plc is trading in and with developing countries rather than Europe and has a subsidiary in a country with no developed capital or currency markets. Expo plc is now about to invoice a customer in that country in the local currency. Advise Expo plc's treasurer about ways in which the risk can be managed in these circumstances. No calculations are required for this part of the question.

21   CURROPT PLC (30 marks)   *54 mins*

It is now 1 March and the treasury department of Curropt plc, a quoted UK company, faces a problem. At the end of June the treasury department may need to advance to Curropt's US subsidiary the amount of $15,000,000. This depends on whether the subsidiary is successful in winning a franchise. The department's view is that the US dollar will strengthen over the next few months, and it believes that a currency hedge would be sensible. The following data is relevant.

Exchange rates US$/£
1 March spot 1.4461 - 1.4492; 4 months forward 1.4310 - 1.4351.

Futures market contract prices

Sterling £62,500 contracts:
March contract 1.4440; June contract 1.4302.

BPP PUBLISHING

Currency options: Sterling £31,250 contracts (cents per £)

	Calls	Puts
Exercise price	June	June
$1.400/£	3.40	0.38
$1.425/£	1.20	0.68
$1.450/£	0.40	2.38

(a) Is the treasury department justified in its belief that the US dollar is likely to strengthen against the pound? (3 marks)

(b) Explain the relative merits of forward currency contracts, currency futures contracts and currency options as instruments for hedging in the given situation. (7 marks)

(c) Assuming the franchise is won, illustrate the results of using forward, future and option currency hedges if the US$/£ spot exchange rate at the end of June is:

(i) 1.35
(ii) 1.45
(iii) 1.55 (20 marks)

22 CARRICK PLC (10 marks) 18 mins

It is currently 1 January 19X7. Carrick plc receives interest of 6% per annum on short-term deposits on the London money markets amounting to £6 million. The company wishes to explore the use of a collar to protect, for a period of seven months, the interest yield it currently earns. The following prices are available, with the premium cost being quoted in annual percentage terms.

LIFFE interest rate options on three month money market futures (Contract size: £500,000).

	Calls		Puts	
Strike price	Jun	Sept	Jun	Sept
9250	0.71	1.40	0.02	0.06
9300	0.36	1.08	0.10	0.14
9350	0.12	0.74	0.20	0.35
9400	0.01	0.40	0.57	0.80
9450	-	0.06	0.97	1.12

Required

Evaluate the use of a collar by Carrick plc for the purpose proposed above. Include calculations of the cost involved and indicate appropriate exercise price(s) for the collar. Ignore taxation, commission and margin requirements.

23 FOREIGN MARKETS (10 marks) 18 mins

Explain briefly the advantages and disadvantages of exporting, licensing and foreign direct investment as alternative forms of involvement in foreign markets.

24 GLOBAL TELECOMMUNICATIONS INC (40 marks) 72 mins

(a) Zenobia is a developing country situated on the coast of Africa. Its government, now democratically elected, has produced a programme of economic reforms aimed at promoting investment in the country and reducing its dependence on foreign aid. A major feature of this programme is the privatisation of companies and corporations which are currently 100% owned by the government, for example hotels, breweries and coffee production. For the time being, the government is not considering privatising services such as post, railways or the provision of basic telecommunications (this is mainly the fixed line, voice telephony service). It does, however, wish to attract private capital to provide new services such as cellular (mobile) telephones and data communication.

Global Telecommunications Inc (GTI) is a company registered in the USA but with global business interests. Its shares are not listed on a stock exchange, but industry sources estimate that it could command a market capitalisation of around US$200 million. It has established itself as a specialist in the provision of mobile telephone (cellular) services. It is currently negotiating with the government of Zenobia (GoZ) for a licence to provide such services in the country and has already spent US$0.5 million in surveys and miscellaneous expenses. If GTI were successful in the negotiations, it would be the company's first experience of working in a developing country.

Based on a recent World Bank report, GTI estimates that there is a market for between 10,000 and 15,000 customers in a rectangular geographical area bounded by the capital city and three other main towns. The proposed cellular service will operate in this relatively prosperous 'urban rectangle' but the poorer, rural areas outside the rectangle will not be covered.

The market for 10,000 lines is, apart from potential disaster, virtually guaranteed. GTI estimates that the initial investment for this number of lines will be US$25 million. The company has asked the GoZ for a five-year exclusivity period (a period when no other company will be allowed to enter the market to compete). Net operating cashflows, based on a network of 10,000 lines, are forecast to be:

Year	1	2	3	4	5
Net operating cashflows (US$ million)	3.5	4.8	5.6	6.8	7.2

Cashflows are after interest and tax payments and are shown in US$ equivalents at today's exchange rate.

In year 6, competitors are likely to enter the market and cashflows are expected to fall to around US$6million per annum. For the purposes of evaluation, GTI assumes this annual net cashflow will maintain indefinitely from year 6 onwards on a network of 10,000 lines. The GoZ is aware that there are other telecommunications companies which are considering investment in the country although to date none has formally declared an interest. It is therefore not prepared to offer a licence based on GTI's terms and has made two counter-proposals for GTI to consider.

Option 1

GTI must provide at least 20% of the 10,000 lines to rural areas and charge rural customers lower rental and call charges than urban customers. In return, the GoZ will allow a ten-year period of exclusivity to GTI. GTI estimates this option will involve US$30million in initial capital costs, and annual net operating cashflows are likely to fall US$0.5 million below those forecast above. However, the ten-year period of exclusivity means that further investment in the network might be advantageous. In considering this option, GTI estimates that an additional investment to provide between 2,000 and 5,000 additional lines at the end of year 3 may be worthwhile. The following information is relevant to GTI's decision.

The capital cost of each additional line is estimated at US$2,000. The average net operating cashflow for each additional line is estimated as US$600 from year 4 onwards. The probabilities for additional demand are:

Number of additional lines	Probability
2,000	0.60
3,000	0.30
5,000	0.10

Note. You should assume that the additional lines will be connected simultaneously at the end of year 3.

Option 2

GTI will be allowed a five-year period of exclusivity, a tax holiday for that five-year period and other cost concessions by the GoZ. In return for these concessions, the GoZ requires a 20% shareholding in GTI's Zenobia subsidiary. Dividends will not be payable on this 20% and GTI may remit all profits during this five-year period free of tax. However, GTI will not be permitted to expand the network during the five-year period and at the end of five years GTI will be required to sell 100% of its Zenobia interests on the Zenobia stock market, which is planned to be operational by that time. GTI estimates that this option will reduce the initial investment needed to US$20million, and increase annual net operating cashflows by 10% over the company's original forecasts. The terminal value of GTI's Zenobia subsidiary is estimated as the capitalised value of year 5's net operating cashflows.

There is some dispute between GTI's directors about the discount rate to be used for the evaluations of this project. The company's cost of capital is 15% per annum constant and this is the rate which is being suggested. However, the Managing Director thinks this is a particularly risky project, not least because all calculations and negotiations with the GoZ are in US$, but also because much of the cash inflow will be in local currency. The Technical Director says that, as the project increases international diversification, it actually reduces the company's risk, so a lower rate should be used. The Financial Director says that, as the three options being evaluated have different life spans, different discount rates should be used to evaluate the three options. He also notes that the cashflows for each year are highly correlated with those of the previous and subsequent years.

Required

(i) Advise the board of GTI of the methods available for evaluating international investment decisions, and on how an appropriate discount rate should be determined for the evaluation of a project such as this. Your discussion should be based on, but not necessarily limited to, the comments of the three directors given in the last paragraph above.   (10 marks)

(ii) Provide the board of GTI with a report which evaluates the net present value of the company's own proposal and the two options suggested by the GoZ. You should also provide in your report reasoned recommendations for which, if either, of the Government of Zenobia's offers should be accepted. You should assume that all cashflows occur at the end of each year, with the exception of the initial investment. Assume also that the board of GTI has agreed on a discount rate of 20% to evaluate all three options for the project.

You should ignore taxation in your calculations.   (20 marks)

(b) GTI is at present all equity financed. The company has sufficient cashflows from other projects to enable it to finance the Zenobia deal internally. However, the IFC (the World Bank's sister company which provides finance for investment in developing countries) is prepared to offer 10% fixed interest rates on loans of up to US$20 million for investments of this nature. Capital is repaid at the end of the loan period which must be a minimum of five years. Interest is paid annually. No early repayment of the loan is permitted without severe financial penalties. If GTI were to raise a similar amount of debt in the capital markets it would currently be obliged to pay 12.5% interest. GTI will be eligible for tax relief at 40% on loan interest payments.

Required

Discuss the advantages and disadvantages of financing the project with an IFC loan.   (10 marks)

25 FINANCIAL CONTROL   *35 mins*

(a) Discuss the possible advantages and disadvantages of centralising the financial functions of a group of companies.

(b) Suppose that you are the managing director of a group of companies. Suggest, giving reasons for your suggestions, what financial ratios (or combinations of financial ratios) you might find useful in order to monitor, evaluate and control the activities of the group.

(c) What problems might exist with the use of financial ratios as a financial control system within a group of companies?

1   REMUNERATION

The choice of an appropriate remuneration policy by a company will depend, among other things, on:

(a)   *Cost*: the extent to which the package provides value for money.

(b)   *Motivation*: the extent to which the package motivates employees both to stay with the company and to work to their full potential.

©   *Fiscal effects*: government tax incentives may promote different types of pay. At present there are tax benefits in offering share options and profit-related pay schemes (although PRP schemes are due to be phased out starting from 1998). At times of wage control and high taxation this can act as an incentive to make the 'perks' a more significant part of the package.

(d)   *Goal congruence*: the extent to which the package encourages employees to work in such a way as to achieve the objectives of the firm - perhaps to maximise rather than to satisfice.

In this context, Option (i) is likely to be relatively expensive with no payback to the firm in times of low profitability. It is unlikely to encourage staff to maximise their efforts, although the extent to which it acts as a motivator will depend on the individual psychological make-up of the employees concerned. Many staff prefer this type of package however, since they know where they are financially. In the same way the company is also able to budget accurately for its staff costs.

Provided that the scheme qualifies, the firm will be able to gain fiscal benefits from operating a profit-related pay scheme (Option (ii)). It also benefits from the fact that costs will be lower, though not proportionately so, during a time of low profits. The effect on motivation will vary with the individual concerned, and will also depend on whether it is an individual or a group performance calculation. There is a further risk that figures and performance may be manipulated by managers in such a way as to maximise their bonus to the detriment of the overall longer term company benefit.

A share option scheme (Option (iii)) carries fiscal benefits in the same way as the performance related pay above. It also minimises the cost to the firm since this is effectively borne by the existing shareholders through the dilution of their holdings. Depending on how pricing is determined, it may assist in achieving goal congruence. However, since the share price depends on many factors which are external to the firm, it is possible for the scheme to operate in a way which is unrelated to the individual's performance. Thus such a scheme is unlikely to motivate directly through links with performance. Staff will continue to obtain the vast majority of their income from salary and perks and are thus likely to be more concerned with maximising these elements of their income than with working to raise the share price.

2   CORPORATE GOVERNANCE

(a)   The main recommendation of the Cadbury report was that the boards of all listed companies should comply with the 'Code of Best Practice' defined in the report. A 'statement of compliance' with the Code should become a listing requirement and the directors of all UK companies should use the Code for guidance. In accounts, directors should state whether the report and accounts comply with the Code and give reasons for any non-compliance.

Some of the principal items in the Code are as follows.

(i)   The board of directors should meet regularly and monitor the performance of the executive management.

(i)   There should be a separation of powers at the top of the firm. This should be achieved either by a separation of the posts of chairman and chief executive, or by ensuring that there is a strong independent group present on the board.

(iii)   There should be a formal schedule of matters that must be referred to the board such as material acquisitions and disposals, capital investments and borrowings.

(iv)   The board should include a number of fully independent non-executive directors.

(v)   Directors' contracts should normally be for a maximum of three years, and all emoluments should be fully disclosed. Directors' pay should be decided by a separate remuneration committee which, following the Greenbury Committee recommendations, should have its report included in the company's annual report and accounts.

(vi)   An audit committee should be appointed with the authority, resources and access to investigate anything within its terms of reference. It should have at least one meeting per year with the auditors when no executive directors are present.

(vii)   The directors should report on the effectiveness of the internal control systems.

(viii)   The board should present a clear and balanced assessment of the company's position, together with a going concern statement supported by any necessary assumptions or qualifications.

(b)   It is not totally correct to talk about the introduction of statutory control on corporate governance since there has been some degree of control for a considerable time through such instruments as the Companies Acts. An example is the regulations governing the appointment and responsibilities of directors. However, many of the controls commonly accepted by firms are not statutory in nature but are generally agreed codes of practice. An example of this is the City Code on Takeovers and Mergers which has no legal backing but is administered and enforced by the Takeover Panel.

Recent incidents in the City, for example the collapse of Maxwell Corporation, have increased the pressure for stricter statutory controls. Particular areas of concern include:

(i)   Accounting policies which are misleading as to the true financial health of the company, for example in the area of the capitalisation of intangibles

(ii)   The weakness of the shareholders' control over the directors' investment decisions

(iii)   The lack of clearly defined rules for the governance and investment of pension funds

From the viewpoint of firms which try to follow the spirit of the law and abide by such regulations as do exist, further legislation will only add to the burden of overheads. There could be a large increase in the amount of litigation, some of it for unintentional breaches of detailed rules. This is happening now in the waste management industry which is subject to much more stringent statutory regulation than most other industries. However, unless all firms do comply not only with the letter but also with the spirit of the legislation it is very likely that more legislation will be introduced in the near future.

3   HAYWORTH

> **Tutorial note**. Although the calculations in this question are quite simple, it is one of those questions that requires careful reading, and a good understanding of the issues surrounding the subject.
>
> In part (a) you should be careful in your treatment of the timing of the various costs and revenues. In part (b) it is helpful to separate the direct financial issues from the more indirect strategic implications.

(a)   The cost of the market research that has already been undertaken will be ignored since this is a sunk cost.

Depreciation will be excluded since this is a non-cash item.

It is assumed that production and sales will both commence in year 2.

	Year 0 £'000	Year 1 £'000	Year 2 £'000	Year 3 £'000	Total £'000
Sales income			4,500	7,000	
Research costs		(1,000)	(1,000)		
Production costs		____	(6,000)	(6,000)	
Net cash flow		(1,000)	(2,500)	1,000	
20% discount factors	1.000	0.833	0.694	0.579	
PV cash flow	0	(833)	(1,735)	579	(1,989)

The NPV of the project is –£1,989,000. On this basis the project should not be undertaken.

(b)   There are a number of additional factors that Hayworth should take into account, some of which relate to the nature of the financial analysis, and some of which address broader business issues. Financial factors include the following.

(i)   It would be helpful to have some information on the nature of the cash flow estimates, in particular, the degree of conservatism within the estimates, and the potential variability. It would then be possible to assign levels of probability to different outcomes and to arrive at an *expected value* for the project.

(ii)   Costs and revenues have been grouped into three very broad headings. It would be useful to consider the detailed costs, their sensitivity to changes in key variables (such as the level of sales), and the likely impact of such changes on the outcome of the project.

(iii) With interest rates currently standing at around 7%, the 20% discount rate that has been used does appear very high. It might be useful to look in more detail at the risks attaching to the project and to arrive at a discount rate that takes specific account of the risks inherent in the project.

(iv) It seems artificial to assume that no further revenues will arise beyond the second year of production. In practice, it is likely that some level of sales will continue to be achieved, and in addition, there may be revenue that arises from sale of any machinery that has been used in the production process. The question of continuing revenue should therefore be addressed further.

Broader business issues include the following.

(i) It may be that the costs of launching the first product in this market are indeed high, but that this is a cost worth paying in order that Hayworth becomes, if not the brand leader, at least a well known supplier within the new market.

(ii) Although the teleputer may be replaced by a newer version within two years of being launched, it is likely that many of the research costs may have to be incurred in any event in order for Hayworth to enter the market with a second generation product. If this is the case, then the potential future revenues from the later model should also be taken into account when making the evaluation.

(iii) The teleputer, although costly to Hayworth, may be necessary in order to ensure that the company can offer a full range of electronics products and so maintain good market share in all its other products.

4 COMMENTS

An efficient market can be defined in terms of information processing as one in which the prices of traded securities reflect all the relevant information which is available to participants, where no individual or group of individuals dominates the market, and where transaction costs are insignificant. Thus it will be supposed that share prices respond quickly to all new information about future prospects. Since it is postulated that prices already reflect all the available information, it follows that at any one point in time future price movements cannot be forecast, since future information is not known and therefore the corresponding price movement is not known. The efficient market hypothesis thus provides a means of explaining the current level of share prices and not of forecasting their future levels. The implication for investors is that it is not possible for an investor consistently to outperform the market.

Mathematical models which attempt to predict movements in share prices are generally, as in this particular case, based on the analysis of a large volume of data over a long period of time. However, they are only likely to be able to predict the future with accuracy if the economic, financial, corporate and political framework that governed the period in question remains stable into the future. In practice, such conditions are in a constant state of change and therefore the predictive value of such models degrades quickly over time thus rendering such models of limited value. However, in the short term they may in themselves become an influence on the market since if sufficient people have faith in them they may influence buying behaviour and hence become something of a self-fulfilling prophecy. In the longer term though, prices will adjust back to their 'underlying' or 'real' values and the utility of the models will decline.

Neither statement claims to be able to predict the price of a given security with significant accuracy for a given point in time, and therefore to this extent they are not contradictory. Similarly, both statements are in fact concerned more with the historical movements in share prices than with their prediction into the future.

5 CRYSTAL PLC

(a) The post-tax weighted average cost of capital should first be calculated.

(i)
	£
Ordinary shares	
Market value of shares cum div.	3.27
Less dividend per share (810 ÷ 3,000)	0.27
Market value of shares ex div.	3.00

The formula for calculating the cost of equity when there is dividend growth is:

$$r = \frac{D_0(1 + g)}{P_0} + g$$

where r = cost of equity
                     D_0 = current dividend
                     g = rate of growth
                     P_0 = current ex div market value.

In this case we shall estimate the future rate of growth (g) from the average growth in dividends over the past four years.

$810 = 620 (1 + g)^4$

$(1 + g)^4$	=	$\dfrac{810}{620}$
	=	1.3065
$(1 + g)$	=	1.069
g	=	0.069 = 6.9%
$r =$	$\dfrac{0.27 \times 1.069}{3}$	+ 0.069 = 16.5%

(ii)   *7% Debentures*

In order to find the post-tax cost of the debentures, which are redeemable in ten years time, it is necessary to find the discount rate (IRR) which will give the future post-tax cash flows a present value of £77.10.

The relevant cash flows are:

(1)   Annual interest payments, net of tax, which are £1,300 × 7% × 70% = £63.70 (for ten years)

(2)   A capital repayment of £1,300 (in ten years time)

It is assumed that tax relief on the debenture interest arises at the same time as the interest payment. In practice the cash flow effect is unlikely to be felt for about a year, but this will have no significant effect on the calculations.

	Present value £'000
Try 8%:	
Current market value of debentures (1,300 at £77.10 per cent)	(1,002.3)
Annual interest payments net of tax £63.70 × 6.710 (8% for ten years)	427.4
Capital repayment £1,300 × 0.463 (8% in ten years time)	601.9
NPV	27.0

	£'000
Try 9%:	
Current market value of debentures	(1,002.3)
Annual interest payments net of tax 63.70 × 6.418	408.8
Capital repayment 1,300 × 0.422	548.6
NPV	(44.9)

$$\text{IRR} = 8\% + \left[\frac{27.0}{27.0 - -44.9} \times (9 - 8) \right]\%$$

$$= 8.38\%$$

(iii)   *The weighted average cost of capital*

	Market value £'000	*Cost* %	*Product*
Equity	9,000	16.50	1,485
7% Debentures	1,002	8.38	84
	10,002		1,569

$$\frac{1,569}{10,002} \times 100 = 15.7\%$$

The above calculations suggest that a discount rate in the region of 16% might be appropriate for the appraisal of new investment opportunities.

(b) Difficulties and uncertainties in the above estimates arise in a number of areas.

(i) *The cost of equity.* The above calculation assumes that all shareholders have the same marginal cost of capital and the same dividend expectations, which is unrealistic. In addition, it is assumed that dividend growth has been and will be at a constant rate of 6.9%. In fact, actual growth in the years 20X5/6 and 20X8/9 was in excess of 9%, while in the year 20X7/8 there was no dividend growth. 6.9% is merely the average rate of growth for the past four years. The rate of future growth will depend more on the return from future projects undertaken than on the past dividend record.

(ii) *The use of the weighted average cost of capital.* Use of the weighted average cost of capital as a discount rate is only justified where the company in question has achieved what it believes to be the optimal capital structure (the mix of debt and equity) and where it intends to maintain this structure in the long term.

(iii) *The projects themselves.* The weighted average cost of capital makes no allowance for the business risk of individual projects. In practice some companies, having calculated the WACC, then add a premium for risk. In this case, for example, if one used a risk premium of 5% the final discount rate would be 21%. Ideally the risk premium should vary from project to project, since not all projects are equally risky. In general, the riskier the project the higher the discount rate which should be used.

6 EMMA PLC

(a) (i)

Year	Cash flow £m	Discount factor 16%	Present value £m
0	(3.6)	1.0	(3.600)
In perpetuity	0.5	$1 \div 0.16$	3.125
		NPV =	(0.475)

The NPV is negative and the project should not be undertaken.

(ii) The tax shield on the debt is represented by Dt, where:

D = £3,600,000
t = 0.30
Dt = £3,600 × 0.30 = £1,080,000

	£m
NPV if all-equity financed	(0.475)
Tax shield on debt	1.080
NPV with debt financing	0.605

Since the NPV is positive, the project is worthwhile if it is financed by debt.

(iii) The gearing of the company after the project is undertaken in (a)(ii) would be:

$$\frac{D}{D + V_{eg}} = \frac{3.6}{(3.6 + (9.6 + 0.605))} = \frac{3.6}{13.805} = 0.260775$$

Using the formula:

$$V_g = V_u + Dt$$

but applying it only to the incremental project, we get:

$$V_g = 3.125m^* + (0.30 \times 0.260775 V_g)$$
$$0.9218 V_g = 3.125m$$
$$V_g = 3.390m$$

(*V_u is the value of benefits calculated in (a)(i)).

	£m
Project benefits	3.390
Project cost	3.600
Loss in value due to project	0.210

Again, as in (a)(i), the project would not be worthwhile.

(b) (i) $WACC_g = Ke_u \left[1 - \dfrac{Dt}{E + D} \right]$

$WACC_g = 0.16 \times \left(1 - \dfrac{3.6 \times 0.30}{(9.6 + 0.605) + 3.6} \right) = 0.1471$, or 14.7%

(ii) The incremental cost of capital is:

Incremental after-tax annual cash benefits in perpetuity
Incremental value of the company

$= \dfrac{£500,000}{£13,805,000 - £9,600,000} \times 100\% = \dfrac{£500,000}{£4,205,000} \times 100\% = 11.9\%$

(iii) The figures in (b)(i) and (b)(ii) can be used to support the solutions in (a)(ii) and (a)(iii) as follows.

(1)

WACC	£m
PV of cost	(3.600)
PV of benefits £500,000 ÷ 0.147	3.401
NPV	(0.199)

This supports the solution in (a)(iii).

(2)

Incremental WACC	£m
PV of cost	(3.600)
PV of benefits £500,000 ÷ 0.119	4.202
Increase in equity value from incremental investment	0.602

This supports the solution in (a)(ii).

7 PORTFOLIO

(a)

		Return	Probability	EV
		%		%
(i)	Security X	30	0.3	9
		25	0.4	10
		20	0.3	6
	Expected return, security X			25
(ii)	Security Y	50	0.2	10
		30	0.6	18
		10	0.2	2
	Expected return, security Y			30

(iii) Portfolio of 60% X and 40% Y
The expected return is (60% of 25%) + (40% of 30%) = 15% + 12% = 27%

(b) (i) Security X. The average return, $\bar{x}$, is 25%.

Return			Probability	
x	$(x - \bar{x})$		p	$p(x - \bar{x})^2$
30	5		0.3	7.5
25	0		0.4	0
20	(5)		0.3	7.5
				15.0

Risk = standard deviation = $\sqrt{15}$ = 3.87%

(ii) Security Y: The average return, $\bar{x}$, is 30%.

Return		Probability	
x	$(x - \bar{x})$	p	$p(x - \bar{x})^2$
50	20	0.2	80
30	0	0.6	0
10	(20)	0.2	80
			160

Risk = standard deviation = $\sqrt{160}$ = 12.65%

(iii) $\sigma_p = \sqrt{\sigma_x^2 w^2 + \sigma_y^2(1-w)^2 + 2w(1-w)p_{xy}\sigma_x\sigma_y}$

The correlation coefficient p_{xy} is 0.

$\sigma = \sqrt{(15)(0.6)^2 + (160)(0.4)^2} = \sqrt{5.4 + 25.6} = \sqrt{31} = 5.6\%$

8 CANADIAN PLC

MEMORANDUM

To: The Finance Director
From: Accountant
Date: 12 December 20X5
Subject: Proposed investment in local coal mine

(a) *Overall summary and conclusion*

I have performed an analysis of the available figures using the adjusted present value technique (APV). This method is appropriate because the project:

(i)   Represents an activity fundamentally different from that of the company
(ii) Has a fundamentally different risk profile, as evidenced by the differing betas, from Canadian
(iii) Is to be financed using a gearing ratio different from the company
(iv) Is a significant investment for the company (ie is not a marginal investment)

An alternative to this method might be the adjusted discount rate method, in which an estimate is made of the appropriate discount rate to use and the project cash flows discounted at this rate. However, insufficient data is available to perform this sort of analysis.

APV demonstrates that while the project appears to be marginally attractive under the stated assumptions (a positive NPV of £86,000), the total project allowing for the financing effects has a positive net present value of £2,010,000. These positive financing effects result from the interest savings on the Regional Development Board loan, plus the tax effects of the additional debt capacity of the firm.

However, I should stress that these figures assume a great deal about the future, both as regards the values of the factors that have been taken into account, and the factors that have been ignored. I would refer you to the later sections of this memo, but broadly:

(i)   There would be substantial implications for power station X if this pit were to close. These costs should also be considered in coming to our conclusion.

(ii) Even if the power station is judged viable in the absence of the pit, buying coal from overseas will expose us to currency fluctuations which would need to be managed

(iii) No sensitivity analysis has been carried out. It would appear likely that the project is highly sensitive to the price of coal, and to the level of redundancy and environmental cleanup costs. This implies a high degree of political risk, which will be outstanding for five years

(b) *Workings*

The adjusted present value represents the NPV of the project based on an all equity financed situation, adjusted for any finance costs/benefits.

The appropriate discount rate is found from the formula:

$$\beta \text{ asset} = \beta_e \frac{E}{E + D(1-t)} + \beta_d \frac{D(1-t)}{E + D(1-t)}$$

This should be based on the betas for the coal mining industry, which obviously has a different risk profile from that of the power generation industry.

$$\beta \text{ asset} = 0.7 \times \frac{1}{1 + 1(1 - 0.3)} + 0.2 \times \frac{(1 - 0.3)}{1 + 1(1 - 0.3)} = 0.494$$

Therefore the appropriate discount rate is:

k_e = 8% + (16% − 8%) × 0.494
= 12%

The cashflows generated by the project are therefore discounted at 12% to find the base NPV.

Cashflow forecast, £000s

Year	0	1	2	3	4	5	6
Inflows							
Value of coal production		10,000	10,000	10,000	10,000	10,000	
Outflows							
Operating costs		(3,090)	(3,183)	(3,278)	(3,377)	(3,478)	
Initial investment	(12,000)						
Final payment (17,000 × 1.03⁵)						(19,708)	
Tax			(1,173)		(1,313)	(1,347)	4,525
Tax from year 3					(1,258)		
Net cashflow	(12,000)	6,910	5,644	6,722	4,052	(14,533)	4,525
NPV factor	1.000	0.893	0.797	0.712	0.636	0.567	0.507
NPV	(12,000)	6,171	4,498	4,786	2,577	(8,240)	2,294
Total NPV	86						

Workings:

Year	1	2	3	4	5
Tax calculations:					
Operating cashflows					
inflows	10,000	10,000	10,000	10,000	10,000
outflows	(3,090)	(3,183)	(3,278)	(3,377)	(3,478)
Capital allowances					
on equipment	(1,500)	(1,125)	(844)	(633)	(1,898)
on mine	(1,500)	(1,500)	(1,500)	(1,500)	
Termination costs					(19,708)
Net taxable flow	3,910	4,192	4,378	4,491	(15,084)
Tax on taxable flow	1,173	1,258	1,313	1,347	(4,525)

Some authors have argued that tax is a certain cashflow, and therefore should not be discounted back at the ungeared discount rate, at least not between the year it is 'earned' and the year it is paid. However, it is common to do so, and indeed, as this case shows in year 3, tax is not always paid in the year in which the project cashflows would predict that it is due.

Financing effects are as follows.

Borrowing effect

The company can borrow a total of £6 million (the regional development loan) plus the £3 million increase in the borrowing capacity as a result of this project. This means that debt benefits flow on a total of £9 million of additional debt. This is worth:

Debt benefit = Total debt × Canadian's borrowing rate × tax rate

Canadian's borrowing rate can be found using CAPM as:

k_d = 8% + (16% − 8%) × 0.25 = 10%

Therefore the increase in debt capacity is worth:

£9 million × 10% × 30% = £270,000 pa

This tax benefit will be received between the years 2 and 6, and should be discounted at the cost of debt (10%).

$$£270,000 \times 3.791 \times \frac{1}{1.10} = £931,000$$

Regional development loan

The value of the subsidy can be related directly to the cost of debt that Canadian plc would otherwise have paid (10%).

Therefore the saving in interest charges is:

£6 million × (10% − 4%) = £360,000 pa

Again, this is discounted at the cost of debt. However, there are two things to notice:

(i)   the benefit of the interest rate reduction is received in years 1-5

(ii) there is an associated reduction in the tax benefit, detrimental in years 2-6, of the interest cost × tax charge.

Present value of interest saved in years 1-5:

£360,000 × 3.791 = £1,365,000

Present value of tax benefit foregone in years 2-6:

$$£6m \times 6\% \times 30\% \times 3.791 \times \frac{1}{1.10} = £372,000$$

The expected APV of the project, including financing effects, will therefore be:

	£'000
NPV of project	86
NPV of tax shelter on interest	931
NPV of interest saved	1,365
NPV of tax benefit forgone on interest saved	(372)
	2,010

© _Assumptions behind this report_

As regards the data used in the report, it assumes the following.

(i)   The various output and costing figures are reasonably accurate.

(ii)   The Regional Development Board loan is obtained.

(iii) The cleanup and redundancy costs are correctly estimated - this assumes a stable political environment over the next five years.

(iv)   The tax regime is at least as favourable as regards capital allowances as at present over the next five years.

(v)   Retained earnings are available to finance the equity component of the project. If additional equity finance were required then issue costs could make this project unviable.

(vi)   The RPI can be accurately used as a measure of the cost inflation factors that will affect the pit.

(vii) The price of coal will stay at the current level for the foreseeable future.

(viii) That the debt capacity added to the firm is accurate. It is not known how this figure is arrived at, but the project might well affect the total perceived risk of the firm for both equity and debt, and therefore change borrowing capacities for the rest of the firm.

As regards the APV model, it assumes the following.

(i)   The value of the tax shield is the full corporate tax rate. This is questionable when shareholders obtain the benefit of a dividend imputation system and annual capital gains tax allowances.

(ii)   The project will contribute a full £9 million to the borrowing capacity of the group for the whole of its useful life. In reality it is likely that the asset base, and hence the borrowing capacity, will diminish over time.

(iii) The CAPM can be used to arrive at an ungeared cost of capital, which can then be used to discount the cash flows over five years. The CAPM is an annual model, so the assumption must be questioned.

(d)   *Areas for further research*

(i)   This memo is incomplete without a detailed sensitivity analysis being carried out. Such an analysis would seek to determine which of the above assumptions was likely to change, and by how much.

(ii) It is also not possible to assess whether this project is advisable in isolation from other capital opportunities and needs of the firm. It is unclear whether capital is in short supply.

(iii) The scenario presumes that there is no alternative bidder for the mine. However, it is possible that supplies to Station X might be secured by offering a fixed price contract to an alternative bidder for the supply of coal. In this case we ourselves can avoid the risks inherent in this industry, about which we know so little, and concentrate on our strengths.

9   PRISM PLC

(a)   The table below shows that prior to the listing Prism's dividend policy was to maintain a constant payout ratio of 40% of profits.

Year	Shares	Div per share pence	Total Div £'000	Profit £'000	Payout ratio
20W9	8,000	6.00	480	1,200	40.0%
20X0	8,000	7.50	600	1,500	40.0%
20X1	10,000	9.65	965	2,413	40.0%
20X2	10,000	11.20	1,120	2,800	40.0%
20X3	10,000	13.15	1,315	3,288	40.0%
20X4	15,000	9.80	1,470	4,225	34.8%

Modigliani and Miller argued that in the absence of tax distortions shareholders are indifferent between dividends and capital gains, the value of a company being entirely dependent on the 'earning power' of its assets. If this theory is true and dividend policy is irrelevant to investor decisions, then Prism should be able to continue its existing policy, cash permitting, with no impact on its financial position.

However, in reality many other factors come into play. Due to differing rates of taxation and the high transaction costs involved in realising capital gains for income, investors may have a preference for either high dividends or for capital growth. If Prism enters a period of capital rationing or has liquidity problems, these will create internal pressures to reduce the level of dividends. Further distortions arise due to imperfections in the availability of information within the market. Shareholders are not always aware of future investment plans and profitability forecasts, or if they are aware they may chose to put a different interpretation on the figures provided.

In practice, companies are normally expected at least to maintain the same level of dividends from one year to the next, if not to increase them. Failure to maintain the level of dividend from year to year can undermine investor confidence in the company. It is therefore unlikely to be appropriate for Prism to continue to work at maintaining a constant payout ratio. The directors need to assess their forecasts of profits and cash and to set dividends at a level that it will be realistic to maintain or increase into the foreseeable future.

(b)   A final dividend of 4.0p per share would mean that Prism is paying a total dividend of 9.8p per share.

Current market value	£35,000,000
Number of shares in issue	15,000
Current market price per share	£2.33
19X4 projected dividend yield (9.8/2.33)	4.20%

It is assumed that there is no other class of shares participating in the market value.

The calculations show that (excluding tax effects) this equates to a dividend yield of 4.2%. If this is the only return to shareholders, then it appears low. However no information is provided about the alternative investment opportunities available to Prism and its projections of future growth in earnings and dividends. It is by some combination of dividends and capital appreciation that Prism will be able to maximise the wealth of the shareholders, the optimum combination depending among other things on the investment position of the company and the tax situation of the investors.

If the majority of the shares are held by wealthy individuals then they will be liable to higher rate taxation on their dividend payments. They are also unlikely to be relying on dividends to provide a source of regular income. On the other hand they may be looking to maximise the use of their tax allowances including the capital gains tax allowance. It is therefore likely that they will have a preference for capital gains over dividend income. Although Prism will need to pay some level of dividends this may not need to be as high as that projected - a dividend yield of 3% may be adequate.

10   CENAC PLC

(a)   The project involves the following costs and revenues:

  Year 0   £375,000 capital expenditure
  Yrs 1-6   £120,000 annual revenues

The net present value can be calculated by discounting the cash flows at 16% as follows:

$$NPV = (£120,000 \times 3.685) - £375,000 = £67,200$$

(b)   (i)   The first step is to calculate the net annual revenue (a) that would be required for the project to break even in net present value terms. This can be found as follows.

$$£375,000 - (a \times 3.685) = 0$$
$$a = £101,764$$

Since it is known that the annual production costs amount to £480,000, the required annual level of sales is £480,000 + £101,764 = £581,764. This represents a reduction in sales of £18,236.

(ii)   On the basis of the calculations above, it is known that the net annual revenue required to break even is £101,764. If sales are £600,000, then production costs would have to be £600,000 − £101,764 = £498,236. This represents an increase of £18,236.

(iii)   The break even cost of machinery (m) can be found as follows.

$$m - (£120,000 \times 3.685) = 0$$
$$m = £442,200$$

This represents an increase in costs of £67,200.

(iv)   The first step is to calculate the annuity value (v) that would need to be applied to the annual earnings for the project to break even.

$$£375,000 - (£120,000 \times v) = 0$$
$$v = 3.125$$

The life of the plant and machinery can then be calculated from the 16% annuity table using interpolation. 3.125 lies between the figures for 4 and 5 years:

$$\frac{3.125 - 2.798}{3.274 - 2.798} = 0.687$$

The useful life of the plant and machinery would therefore be 4.687 years - a reduction of 0.313 years (approximately 16 weeks).

(v)   As calculated above, the annuity value would have to fall to 3.125 for the project to break even. The discount rate that this represents can be found from interpolation of the annuity tables at the six year point. 3.125 lies between the discount rates of 22% and 24%:

$$\frac{3.125 - 3.02}{3.170 - 3.02} = 0.7$$

The discount rate can therefore be estimated as:

$$24\% - (0.7 \times 2) = 22.6\%$$

11   THREE DECISIONS

(a)   *Investment decisions*

These decisions involve the selection of new projects, or of companies or other securities to invest in. Such decisions will be taken in the light of required rates of return and estimated risks. Financial managers should also consider the effect on cash flows, and the ease with which investments can be withdrawn from should it be necessary.

Financing decisions

Once investments have been identified as possibly suitable for the company, methods of financing them must be selected. Possibilities include new share issues, loans, the retention of profits and sales of assets. The costs of different sources of finance will be relevant here.

Dividend decisions

When a company makes profits, they may be distributed to shareholders or retained in the business. The directors must decide how much to distribute, taking into account the needs of the business and the preferences of shareholders for current income or future capital gains.

These three types of decision all interact. The acceptability of an investment depends on the cost of the chosen method of finance. One possible source of finance is the retention of profits, and hence the restriction of dividends. A company's dividend policy may well affect its share price, and hence the scope for financing investments by share issues. Loans for investments may be made conditional on a certain dividend policy. Finally, the selection of profitable investments should give scope for increased dividends in the future.

(b)   *Relevant information*

(i)   *Investment decisions: new projects*

Estimated amounts and timings of cash flows
The level of uncertainty of those estimates
An appropriate discount rate, and the net present value at that rate
The internal rate of return
The impact on accounting profit
Details of alternative projects

(ii)   *Investment decisions: investment in other companies and securities*

Amounts available to invest
Current and forecast returns
Market rates of return
Prospects for capital growth
Levels of risk involved

(iii)   *Financing decisions*

Possible sources of finance
The current share price
The current state of the stock market
Current and forecast interest rates
The company's level of gearing
Cash flow projections

(iv)   *Dividend decisions*

Profits available for distribution
Market expectations
The need to maintain a high share price
Cash flow projections
Opportunities for internal use of retained profits

12   FINANCIAL OBJECTIVE

(a)   In the last three years, each company has achieved a reasonably consistent increase in growth in EPS, with Y Ltd's growth rate doubling in each of these years. The ability of the companies to do this depends partly on:

(i)   *The external environment*. This includes market demand and inflation. The large increase in turnover of both companies, because of price or sales volume increases, has contributed to the increase in EBIT, and therefore to the increase in distributable earnings.

The rate of taxation as a percentage of EBIT appears to have risen slightly between 20X1 and 20X4; this had the effect of reducing the rate of growth in EPS.

(ii) *The companies' operating cost structures.* Although variable costs as a percentage of sales rose in both companies between 20X1 and 20X4, there was a reduction in the ratio of fixed costs to sales, so that the operating profit to sales ratio remained fairly constant over this period. This meant that EBIT increased at about the same rate as the rate of increase in sales. However, since X Ltd operates with a lower contribution/sales ratio than Y Ltd, an increase in turnover will have a much greater effect on the EBIT (and therefore the EPS) of Y Ltd than of X Ltd. In 20X4, each extra pound of sales earned X Ltd 35p contribution before tax, compared with 61p for Y Ltd.

(iii) *Gearing.* X Ltd is more highly geared than Y Ltd. This might explain X Ltd's stronger earnings growth. The gearing ratio of X Ltd remained fairly constant in the period, although it would have been much higher but for the asset revaluation reserve. Y Ltd increased its gearing ratio substantially in 20X2. Interest rates appear to have fallen during the period, so both companies financed their expansion to a considerable extent by acquiring relatively cheap loans.

(b) The financial management of X Ltd shows some cause for concern in spite of the increase in turnover, profits and EPS.

(i) The gearing of the company is rather high. In 20X4 it is 44%, and if the asset revaluation reserve is removed, the gearing ratio is 60/116 = 52%. Although we do not know the working capital structure, the debt ratio is probably in excess of 50%, and it is surprising that the company was able to raise an extra £14,000 in loans in 20X4 (£60,000 - £46,000). The higher rates of interest paid by X Ltd (compared to Y Ltd) probably reflect the higher risk of investing in X Ltd.

(ii) The revaluation of assets (by £12,000 out of £42,000 in 20X2) seems surprisingly high.

(iii) The need for additional sources of funds to finance the growth in sales has meant that earnings have had to be retained. It is perhaps significant that in 20X4 dividends were only a third of distributable profits, whereas in earlier years the fraction was about half.

(iv) It would appear, from results in 20X4 when a high proportion of earnings were retained and a new issue of shares was made, that the company is reaching the limit of its ability to borrow without first reducing its gearing and debt ratios. It should be expected, however, that in view of the increasing profitability, the company should be able to restore itself to a position of financial strength with prudent financial management.

Even so, ROI is quite high, and the company might therefore be attractive to investors.

Y Ltd has lower gearing than X Ltd, and there has been no revaluation of assets. Any such revaluation would reduce the gearing ratio considerably. The interest cover in Y Ltd is very high, and this too suggests good security for lenders.

The company's rate of growth in EPS is high, and if the company wishes to continue to expand rapidly, it appears to be in a sound financial position to do so.

(i) Retained earnings are high.

(ii) At the same time, dividends have risen more quickly than earnings, and shareholders are receiving the benefit of the growth in profits. This is likely to increase the value of Y Ltd's shares.

(iii) The company was able to raise an extra £50,000 in new shares in 20X3, and loan capital has more than doubled. There would appear to be scope for further borrowing if required.

(iv) ROI is about 28% in 20X4, rather higher than for X Ltd.

Y Ltd offers security to lenders, safe gearing, and a fast growth in profits and dividends. In these respects, its financial management appears to be very sound. Some thought should be given, however, to a revaluation of the company's fixed assets, if this seems appropriate.

Workings

		X Ltd					Y Ltd		
	20X1	20X2	20X3	20X4	20X1	20X2	20X3	20X4	
Growth in EBIT (%)		14.3%	31.2%	47.6%		12.0%	42.9%	16.2%	
Growth in EPS (%)		16.7%	14.3%	20.0%		4.0%	9.2%	18.3%	
Growth in EPS (pence)		5	5	8		1	2.4	5.2	
Cost structure	%	%	%	%	%	%	%	%
Variable cost/sales ratio	60	62	64	65	30	31	33	39
Fixed cost/sales ratio	26	25	24	23	45	44	40	35
EBIT/sales ratio	14	13	12	12	25	25	27	26
	100	100	100	100	100	100	100	100
Gearing ratio (Loans/capital employed)	42%	33%	44%	44%	21%	29%	30%	28%
Interest cover (EBIT/interest)	3.5×	4.0×	3.0×	3.9×	10.0×	7.0×	8.4×	9.8×
Average cost of interest (Interest/loan capital)	16%	16%	15%	13%	12.5%	12%	10%	10%

		X Ltd					Y Ltd		
	20X1	20X2	20X3	20X4	20X1	20X2	20X3	20X4	
		£'000	£'000	£'000		£'000	£'000	£'000	
Financing of increases in assets									
Extra shares		0	0	5		0	50	0	
Revaluation		12	4	4		0	0	0	
Retained profits		4	4	8		34	41	50	
Equity		16	8	17		34	91	50	
Loans		0	21	14		57	45	0	
Increase in assets		16	29	31		91	136	50	

ROI								
(i) EBIT/capital employed	23%	21%	20%	23%	26%	24%	26%	28%
(ii) Earnings before tax /equity capital	29%	24%	24%	30%	30%	29%	33%	35%

13 KILLISICK AND HOLBECK

(a)

	Killisick plc	Holbeck plc
Earnings	£5,180,000	£2,340,000
EPS	14.8p	29.25p
Number of shares	35,000,000	8,000,000

An offer of three shares in Killisick for two shares in Holbeck would result in the equity of Killisick increasing to 47,000,000 shares.

In order to establish how the estimated post-acquisition market price of Killisick was reached, we must look at P/E ratios.

	Killisick plc	Holbeck plc
Pre-acquisition price	222	322
EPS	14.8	29.25
P/E ratio, pre-acquisition	15	11

The post-acquisition earnings, assuming no synergy or growth, would be (5,180 + 2,340) £7,520,000 or (÷ 40 million shares) 16p a share.

The estimated post-acquisition share price of Killisick plc is 240p. On the assumption that the post-acquisition EPS is 16p, the P/E ratio would be 15.

It would therefore seem that the estimated post-acquisition market price of Killisick plc shares has been derived by applying the pre-acquisition P/E ratio of Killisick to an estimated post-acquisition EPS (assuming no profits growth through synergy).

The estimated post-acquisition equivalent market value of an old Holbeck share is 1.5 times 240 pence, because three Killisick shares will be exchanged for two Holbeck shares, giving a relative value of 3:2 or 1.5.

These estimates cannot be realistic, because it is incorrect to assume that on a takeover where neither company is minuscule relative to the other, the post-acquisition P/E ratio will be the same as the pre-acquisition P/E ratio of the more highly rated company in the takeover.

Killisick is hoping to take over a public company with a lower P/E ratio than its own, and its directors must expect Killisick's post-acquisition P/E ratio to fall accordingly.

A better estimate of the post acquisition P/E ratio would be the *weighted average* of their pre-acquisition P/Es as follows.

	Earnings £'000		Market value £'000
Killisick	5,180	(35m × 222p)	77,700
Holbeck	2,340	(8m × 322p)	25,760
Combined	7,520		103,460

Weighted average P/E ratio $\frac{103,460}{7,520} = 13.758$

Applying this to a post-acquisition EPS of 16p, an estimated post-acquisition market price of Killisick plc shares would be (13.758 × 16p) 220p each. This would make the post-acquisition equivalent MV of an old Holbeck share (220 × 1.5) = 330p.

There would be a very slight gain for Holbeck plc shareholders at the expense of Killisick plc shareholders, but not much. This is because the share exchange ratio of three for two reflects almost exactly the pre-acquisition market prices per share of 322:222 = 1.45 or nearly 1.50, which is 3:2.

(b)

	£'000
Value of 35 million Killisick shares:	
Estimated post-acquisition value (× 240p)	84,000
Pre-acquisition value (× 222p)	77,700
Gain to Killisick shareholders from acquisition (× 18p)	6,300

Killisick plc could raise its offer by £6,300,000 without reducing the wealth of its shareholders, but only assuming that the 240p estimate of the post-acquisition share price is correct. This extra value might be offered in cash (£0.7875 per share in Holbeck) or in more shares in Killisick.

(c) The pre-acquisition market value of Killisick plc is unchanged at 222p, and so a two-for-one share exchange offer would value each share in Holbeck at 444p as well, compared with its current 322p.

	£'000
Offer value for 8,000,000 shares in Holbeck (× 444p)	35,520
Current value of 8,000,000 shares in Holbeck (× 322p)	25,760
Excess	9,760

The revised offer would only maintain the wealth of current shareholders if the combined share values of the post-acquisition company were to increase by at least £9,760,000.

It is assumed that the value of the post-acquisition company will be increased by the NPV of the asset disposals, savings in running costs and extra redundancy costs, discounted at Killisick's cost of capital of 14% per year.

Year	Item	Amount £'000	Discount factor 14%	Present value £'000
0	Redundancy costs	(3,500)	1.000	(3,500.0)
1	Redundancy costs	(8,400)	0.877	(7,366.8)
1	Fixed asset disposals	7,200	0.877	6,314.4
1 - ∞	Savings in running costs	2,750	(1 ÷ 0.14) = 7.14	19,642.9
			Net present value	15,090.5

We might therefore conclude that because of redundancies and rationalisation, the combined value of the post-acquisition companies will increase by about £15,000,000 which is more than the £9,760,000 needed to fund the extra price being offered for their shares to Holbeck shareholders. Of the increase in share values, Holbeck shareholders would benefit by the first £9,760,000, leaving the remaining £5,240,000 to be shared between all shareholders in the post-acquisition company.

A two for one offer should therefore be made.

(d) Assuming no increase in total post-acquisition earnings, the group will have a fairly low interest cover ratio. The interest cover in the 'old' Killisick is (12,400 ÷ 4,431) 2.8 times and in the 'old' Holbeck is (5,800 ÷ 2,200) = 2.6 times. In the combined company it will be (12,400 + 5,800) ÷ (4,431 + 2,200) = 2.75 times.

Although we do not have balance sheet details, this low interest cover indicates high gearing, and the cost of the existing debt capital might therefore be high.

The takeover will create an enlarged company, and because of this, it is fairly reasonable to assume that the risk of default will be less than with either of the 'old' companies taken individually. This reduction in default risk, if perceived to be significant, might reduce the return that investors in debt capital seek from the company. A reduction in the required return on marketable fixed interest capital would raise its market value. In this respect, the acquisition would have some effect on the market value of Killisick's debt.

Of course, Killisick's debt might be non-marketable bank loans and overdrafts, in which case the acquisition would not have any effect on the market value of the debt, since such debt has no market value.

14 BLACK RAVEN LTD

(a) *An assets basis valuation*
If we assume that a purchaser would accept the revaluation of assets by the independent valuer, an assets valuation of equity would be as follows.

	£	£
Fixed assets (ignore patents, assumed to have no market value)		
Land and buildings		1,075,000
Plant and equipment		480,000
Motor vehicles		45,000
		1,600,000
Current assets		383,000
		1,983,000
Less: current liabilities	230,000	
loan	400,000	
		630,000
Asset value of equity (300,000 shares)		1,353,000

Value per share = £4.51

Unless the purchasing company intends to sell the assets acquired, it is more likely that a valuation would be based on earnings.

(b) *Earnings basis valuations*
If the purchaser believes that earnings over the last five years are an appropriate measure for valuation, we could take average earnings in these years, which were:

$$\frac{£465,000}{5} = £93,000$$

5

An appropriate P/E ratio for an earnings basis valuation might be the average of the three publicly quoted companies for the recent year. (A trend towards an increase in the P/E ratio over three years is assumed, and even though average earnings have been taken, the most recent year's P/E ratios are considered to be the only figures which are appropriate.)

	P/E ratio	
Albatross plc	8.5	
Bullfinch plc	9.0	
Crow plc	10.0	
Average	9.167	(i)
Reduce by about 40% to allow for unquoted status	5.5	(ii)

Share valuations on a past earnings basis are as follows.

	P/E ratio	*Earnings* £'000	*Valuation* £'000	*Number of shares*	*Value per share*
(i)	9.167	93	852.5	300,000	£2.84
(ii)	5.5	93	511.5	300,000	£1.71

Because of the unquoted status of Black Raven Ltd, purchasers would probably apply a lower P/E ratio, and an offer of about £1.71 per share would be more likely than one of £2.84.

Future earnings might be used. Forecast earnings based on the company's five year plan will be used.

		£	
Expected earnings:	Year 1	100,000	
	Year 2	104,000	
	Year 3	108,160	
	Year 4	112,486	
	Year 5	116,986	
	Average	108,326.4	(say £108,000)

A share valuation on an expected earnings basis would be as follows.

P/E ratio	*Average future earnings*	*Valuation*	*Value per share*
5.5	£108,000	£594,000	£1.98

It is not clear whether the purchasing company would accept Black Raven's own estimates of earnings.

(c) *A dividend yield basis of valuation with no growth*

There seems to have been a general pattern of increase in dividend yields to shareholders in quoted companies, and it is reasonable to suppose that investors in Black Raven would require at least the same yield.

An average yield for the recent year for the three quoted companies will be used. This is 12%. The only reliable dividend figure for Black Raven Ltd is £45,000 a year gross, in spite of the expected increase in future earnings. A yield basis valuation would therefore be:

$$\frac{£45,000}{12\%} = £375,000 \text{ or } £1.25 \text{ per share.}$$

A purchasing company would, however, be more concerned with earnings than with dividends if it intended to buy the entire company, and an offer price of £1.25 should be considered too low. On the other hand, since Black Raven Ltd is an unquoted company, a higher yield than 12% might be expected.

(d) *A dividend yield basis of valuation, with growth*

Since earnings are expected to increase by 4% a year, it could be argued that a similar growth rate in dividends would be expected. We shall assume that the required yield is 17%, rather more than the 12% for quoted companies because Black Raven Ltd is unquoted. However, in the absence of information about the expected growth of dividends in the quoted companies, the choice of 12%, 17% or whatever, is not much better than a guess.

$$P_0 = \frac{D_0(1+g)}{(r-g)} = \frac{45,000(1.04)}{(0.17 - 0.04)} = £360,000 \text{ or } £1.20 \text{ per share}$$

(e) *The discounted value of future cash flows*

The present value of cash inflows from an investment by a purchaser of Black Raven Ltd's shares would be discounted at either 18% or 14%, depending on the view taken of Black Raven Ltd's assets. Although the loan of £400,000 is secured on some of the company's property, there are enough assets against which there is no charge to assume that a purchaser would consider the investment to be backed by tangible assets.

The present value of the benefits from the investment would be as follows.

Year	Cash flow	Discount factor	PV of cash flow
	£'000	14%	£'000
1	120	0.877	105.24
2	120	0.769	92.28
3	140	0.675	94.50
4	70	0.592	41.44
5	120	0.519	62.28
			395.74

A valuation per share of £1.32 might therefore be made. This basis of valuation is one which a purchasing company ought to consider. It might be argued that cash flows beyond year 5 should be considered and a higher valuation could be appropriate, but a figure of less than £2 per share would be offered on a DCF valuation basis.

(f) *The accounting rate of return method*

If a company wishing to take over Black Raven Ltd expects to make an accounting rate of return of, say, 20%, and assuming that a return of £100,000 is assumed for this purpose the valuation of Black Raven Ltd might be:

$$\frac{£100,000}{20\%} = £500,000, \text{ or } £1.67 \text{ per share.}$$

(g) *The super-profits method*

If we assume that the normal rate of profit is 5% on net assets, the normal profits might be as follows (although 'net assets' could be defined in other ways).

	£
Asset value of equity (see (a))	1,353,000
Add asset value of loan stock	400,000
Net assets	1,753,000
Actual (current) profit	100,000
Less normal profit after taxation (5%)	87,650
Super-profits	12,350
Goodwill (say two years purchase of super-profits)	£24,700

The total purchase consideration for equity would be £1,353,000 + £24,700 = £1,377,700 or £4.59 per share.

(h) *Summary*

Any of the preceding valuations might be made, but since share valuation is largely a subjective matter, many other prices might be offered. In view of the high asset values of the company an asset stripping purchaser might come forward.

15 BRIVE PLC

REPORT

To: Board of Directors
From: M Accountant
Date: 17 September 20X1
Subject: Proposed capital reconstruction

Introduction

The purpose of this report is to evaluate the implications of the proposed capital reconstruction of Brive plc for the various affected parties, including the shareholders, debenture holders, unsecured creditors and the bank. Calculations showing the effect of the reconstruction on the balance sheet are included as an appendix to this report.

Ordinary shareholders

In the event of Brive going into liquidation, the ordinary shareholders would be most unlikely to receive anything for their shares, since the net proceeds of the liquidation would be as follows.

	£
Property	2,000,000
Plant	1,000,000
Stock	1,700,000
Debtors	1,700,000
Liquidation costs	(770,000)
	5,630,000

The total amount due to the creditors, bank and debenture holders is £8,600,000, leaving nothing available for the shareholders.

If the reconstruction is undertaken, the existing shareholders will have to provide an additional £1m of capital in subscribing to the rights issue. However, if the projections are correct the effect of this should be to bring Brive back into profit, with earnings after interest amounting to £1.4m (£1.75m – £0.35m) per annum. This amounts to earnings per share of 28p which should permit Brive to start paying a dividend and providing some return to the shareholders again. The fact that the company is returning to profit should also make it possible to sell the shares if required which is presumably difficult at the present time. However there would be a substantial shift in the balance of control with the existing shareholders being left with only 40% of the equity, the balance being in the hands of the present debenture holders.

Secured debenture holders

Under the existing arrangements, the amount owing to the debenture holders is £3m. Although the debentures are secured on the property which has a book value of £3m, in the event of a forced sale this would only be likely to realise £2m giving a shortfall of £1m. The debenture holders would rank alongside the bank and the other creditors for repayment of this balance. As has been calculated above, the amount that would be realised on liquidation and available to the unsecured creditors would be £3.63m (net of property proceeds). The total amount owed is:

	£m
Debenture holders	1.0
Bank (overdraft)	1.6
Creditors	4.0
	6.6

The debenture holders would therefore only receive 55 pence in the pound on the balance owing, giving a total payout of 85 pence in the pound ((£2m + £0.55m)/£3.0m).

Under the proposed scheme, the debenture holders would receive £2.8m of new capital in return for the old debentures ie 93.33 pence in the pound in the form of capital rather than cash. Of this, £1.3m would be in the form of 14% unsecured loan stock, and the remainder in the form of equity. They would also have to subscribe an additional £1.5m to take up the rights issue. Their total investment in the reconstruction would therefore be:

	£m
Cash foregone from liquidation	2.55
Additional cash investment	1.50
	4.05

Returns would be:

	£
Interest (£1.3m × 14%)	182,000
Return on equity (£3m × 0.28)	840,000
	1,022,000

This represents a return of 25.23% which is likely to be above that which could be earned elsewhere thus making the scheme attractive to the debenture holders. However, in addition they would have to forgo their security on the property and rank partly with the unsecured creditors and partly with the equity. They should therefore be confident of the ability of the management to deliver the projected returns before consenting to the scheme.

The bank

Since the overdraft is unsecured, the bank would rank for repayment alongside the unsecured creditors. As calculated above, the amount to be repaid would be 55 pence in the pound, and the bank would thus recover £880,000 in the event of a liquidation. In the reconstruction, the bank would have to write off £400,000, but would receive interest of 14% per annum leading to repayment of the balance in five years time.

The investment that the bank would be making would therefore be the cash forgone from the liquidation of £880,000. The annual returns would be £168,000 (14% × £1.2m) which represents a return on the incremental investment of 19.1%. Provided that the bank is confident of the financial projections of the management, it stands to receive £1.2m in five years' time. The effective return of 19.1% in the meantime is in excess of current overdraft rates, and the level of security is improved since there would no longer be secured debenture holders ranking ahead of the bank for repayment. The scheme is therefore likely to be attractive to the bank.

Unsecured creditors

If Brive goes into liquidation the unsecured creditors will receive 55 pence in the pound ie £2.2m. Under the proposed scheme they would stand to receive 75 pence (25% written down) in the pound with apparently no significant delay in payment. If Brive continues to operate they will be able to continue to trade with the company and generate further profits from the business. The proposed scheme therefore seems attractive from their point of view.

Conclusions

The proposed scheme appears to hold benefits for all the parties involved. It is also in the interests of Brive's customers and workforce for the company to continue to trade. However these benefits will only be realised if the directors are correct in their forecast of trading conditions and if the new investment can achieve the projected returns. All parties should satisfy themselves as to these points before considering proceeding further with the reconstruction.

	Before	*a*	*b*	*c*	*d*	*e–g*	*After*
	£'000						£'000
Fixed assets	5,700	(2,100)				2,500	6,100
Current assets							
Stock	3,500	(800)					2,700
Debtors	1,800	(100)					1,700
	5,300						4,400
Creditors	(4,000)					1,000	(3,000)
Overdraft	(1,600)				1,600		0
Working capital	(300)						1,400
Total assets	5,400						7,500
10% Debentures	(3,000)			3,000			0
14% Stock				(1,300)	(1,200)		(2,500)
Net assets	2,400						5,000
Capital and reserves							
Share capital	4,000		(3,000)	1,500		2,500	5,000
P&L account	(1,600)		1,600				0
	2,400						5,000

16 COMMON MARKET

(a) A free trade area exists when there is no restriction on the movement of goods and services between countries. This may be extended into a customs union when there is a free trade area between all member countries of the union, and in addition there are common external tariffs applying to imports from non-member countries into any part of the union. In other words, the union promotes free trade among its members but acts as a protectionist bloc against the rest of the world.

A common market encompasses the idea of a customs union but has a number of additional features. In addition to free trade among member countries there is also complete mobility of the factors of production. A British citizen has the freedom to work in any other country of the European community, for example. A common market will also aim to achieve stronger links between member countries, for example by harmonising government economic policies and by establishing a closer political confederation.

(b) The most obvious benefits which countries might gain from forming a common market are associated with free trade between them. The benefits of free trade are illustrated by the law of comparative advantage which states that countries should specialise in producing those goods where they have a comparative advantage. Specialisation, together with free trade, will result in an increase in total output and all countries will be able, to a great or lesser extent, to share in the benefits.

In particular, different countries have different factor endowments and, as the international mobility of these factors tends to be severely limited, trade increases the range of goods and services available in a particular country. By becoming part of a common market, imports from other member countries are available more cheaply and easily. Imports of certain raw materials or types of capital equipment not otherwise available in a particular country will improve its productive potential, enabling a faster rate of economic growth to be achieved. Similarly, improvements in the range and quality of consumer goods available will tend to enhance a country's standard of living.

In addition, there is a larger market for domestic output and firms may be able to benefit from economies of scale by engaging in export activities. Economies of scale improve efficiency in the use of resources and enable output to be produced at lower cost. This also raises the possibility of benefits to consumers if these cost savings are passed on in the form of lower prices. In addition, the extension of the market in which firms operate increases the amount of competition they face and hence should improve efficiency.

Establishment of a common market is often accompanied by some form of exchange rate agreement between members and this in turn is likely to encourage further trade as it reduces uncertainty for both exporters and importers. Stability of exchange rates is also beneficial to a government in formulating its domestic economic policies.

Membership of a common market may be particularly beneficial to smaller or weaker economies as, in addition to increasing the availability of essential factors of production and the range of goods and services available to domestic consumers, it also enables them to benefit from any economic growth experienced by their fellow members. Spin-offs may be in the form of larger markets for their exports, lower import prices, improved employment opportunities and so on.

In addition to fostering economic ties between countries, common markets provide the basis for stronger political links. Again, this may be particularly important for smaller countries enabling them to benefit from an enhanced position in the world economy. It may also encourage further international economic co-operation, in turn providing an additional stimulus to growth.

17   IMF AND EUROMARKETS

(a) The International Monetary Fund was established in 1944 following the Bretton Woods conference, and it started operations in 1947. The Bretton Woods conference aimed to encourage a more stable pattern of world trade after World War II than that which had existed previously. In the 1930s, there had been floating exchange rates after the abandonment of the gold standard. Bretton Woods introduced a period of fixed exchange rates. The IMF was intended to assist the process of co-operation in monetary matters involving foreign exchange and to help to stabilise exchange rates. The International Bank for Reconstruction and Development (the 'World Bank') was set up alongside the IMF and had the role of promoting capital investment in member countries, following the damage suffered in World War II.

The IMF has three broad aims.

(i)   It aims to promote international monetary co-operation through establishing a code of conduct for making international payments and providing for greater exchange rate stability.

(ii)   The Fund provides financial support to countries which have temporary balance of payments deficits.

(iii)   It aims to provide for an orderly growth in international liquidity, through its scheme of Special Drawing Rights (SDRs), which were launched in 1970.

The Fund operates by making funds for lending available out of the subscriptions or 'quotas' of member countries. 75% of members' quotas are contributed in the member countries' own currency and 25% is in other currencies, mainly US dollars and SDRs. Quota levels are set according to the size of member countries' economies. IMF loans are generally repayable in three to five years.

The SDR was created with the purpose of providing a new form of international liquidity, and ensuring that there is enough international liquidity for the world's needs. The supply of SDRs is subject to periodic review, and is increased by international consent. However, a proposal for a substantial increase in the volume of SDRs in 1989 was resisted, mainly by the USA, on the grounds that an excessive growth of the international money supply would add to inflation rates throughout the world.

SDRs count as part of the member country's official reserves and are in proportion with quotas. Quotas, which have expanded in line with the expansion in international trade, determine the voting rights of members.

A board of directors manages the fund; the directors are nominated by major economies. The USA is a major contributor to the IMF, accounting for about 20% of quotas.

The IMF applies conditions to loans which can be harsh on the borrowing country. The Fund regards its lending as fairly short-term. In order to repay borrowings quickly, a country is expected to take effective action to improve their balance of payments position. The IMF generally takes the position that a country should take deflationary measures which reduce the demand for goods and services in the economy. This may require increases in taxation and cuts in government spending. The deflationary measures necessary may lead to falls in the standard of living in the country and increases in unemployment. The objective from the point of view of the IMF will be to reduce levels of imports. Reductions in price inflation should enable the industries of the country to direct resources into export markets.

(b) The euromarkets are international money and capital markets in which organisations from one country raise funds from lenders in other countries, usually in a currency that is not the domestic currency of the borrowing organisation.

Eurocurrency is a term used to describe funds in a currency deposited with a bank which is outside the currency's country of origin. For example, eurodollars are US dollars deposited with a bank outside the USA. The eurocurrency markets are markets for the lending and borrowing of eurocurrency. Banks with which eurocurrency is deposited will re-lend the currency to borrowers, and so companies which wish to borrow in a foreign currency can borrow eurocurrency from a bank. Eurocurrency borrowing is mainly short term, but can be medium term (up to five years or so).

Interest rates on eurocurrency lending are about the same (but not necessarily exactly the same) as domestic interest rates available in the currency's country of origin.

Eurocurrency loans can be very large, and in the case of large loans, a syndicate of banks might provide the funds to the borrower.

Eurobonds are bonds issued by a borrowing company or other organisation, in two or more financial centres at the same time and often in foreign currency. The term of a eurobond issue is typically 10 to 15 years, and eurobonds are marketable, with fairly well-established 'secondhand' markets for trading in them, the bonds being quoted on one or more stock markets. Only well-established, large, and creditworthy borrowers can issue eurobonds.

The *euro-equity market* relates to the issue of equity shares by multinational companies on two or more international stock markets at the same time. The company's shares are then traded in the two or more markets simultaneously. This has an effect on share prices. If a share is traded on the New York and London exchanges, say, a fall in its price on the New York exchange will result in a matching fall in its price in London.

18 AARDVARK LTD

Aardvark Ltd has the following options.

(a) It can continue its existing policy.

(b) It can use the export factor, either in combination with its existing overdraft, or using the 80% finance offered by the factor.

© It can use the insurer with the assignment of policy rights (since cheaper finance is available at no extra cost.

It is assumed that all export debts will be financed by an overdraft or by special lending arrangements.

(a) *Use of the export factor for debt collection only*

	£
Service fee (3% × £1,000,000)	(30,000)
Bad debts saved (by insurance) (0.5% × £1,000,000)	5,000
Administration costs saved	35,000
Net saving	10,000

(b) *Use of the export factor for debt collection and finance*

That there will be a saving in finance charges of 0.5% a year on 80% of the average debtors required.

	£
Service fee for debt collection	(30,000)
Interest costs saved (0.5% × 80% × £1,000,000 × 90/360)	1,000
Bad debts saved	5,000
Administrative costs saved	35,000
Net saving	11,000

© *Use of the insurer*

If the insurer was used, there is a saving of 1% on 70% of the finance required, since 70% of finance will be obtained at just 1.5% above base rate, instead of 2.5% above base rate.

	£
Insurance costs (0.35% × £1,000,000)	(3,500)
Savings in bank interest (1% × 70% × £1,000,000 ×90/360)	1,750
Savings in bad debts (90% × 0.5% × £1,000,000)	4,500
Net saving	2,750

Conclusion

Aardvark Ltd should use the services of the export factor, and obtain finance for 80% of export credit sales from the factor.

19 OVERSEAS INVESTMENT

(a) (i) Since the forward rate for the Em against the $W is lower than the spot rate, the implication is that the Eastland interest rate is lower than that in Westland. This is based on the interest rate parity theory which states that in equilibrium the difference in interest rates between two countries is equal to the difference between the forward and the spot rates. The Eastland interest rate can be estimated as follows.

Day 1	1.0000 Em buys	0.4825 $W
Day 90	interest at 9.5%	0.0113 $W
	Total value	0.4938 $W

This is now worth 1.0215 Em (at 0.4834). The annualised Eastland interest rate is therefore 8.7% (0.0215 × 365/90).

(ii) If the forward rate was 0.4795 $W/Em, then the total value in the above calculations would become 1.0298 Em (0.4938/0.4795). The annualised Eastland interest rate is therefore 12.09%.

(iii) If the interest rate in Eastland is 8%, then the total value of the money in $W is 0.4938, and in Em is 1.0197. This implies a forward rate of 0.4843 $W/Em.

(b) (i) The new subsidiary will be incurring costs for raw materials and management denominated in sterling. It will be receiving income from sales denominated in HUF and other eastern European currencies. If the HUF weakens against the pound, this will make its raw material and management costs relatively more expensive. At the same time, if the HUF weakens against other eastern European countries, this will make its exports to these areas relatively cheaper. The weakening HUF will also mean that remittances to the UK will be subject to exchange losses.

One of the most effective ways to hedge is to ensure that receipts and payments in different currencies are, so far as is possible, in balanced amounts. By transferring production to Hungary, the company is improving the extent to which matching is achieved since a significant proportion of the labour costs as well as other expenses are now denominated in local currency. However, there is still likely to be some imbalance.

In terms of financing the venture, relatively few assets need to be acquired locally. The decision on whether to lease or buy the buildings will depend on the relative costs of the different options, the availability of funds, and the relative costs of borrowing in the UK and in Hungary. However, it is likely that some form of lease will be appropriate since this will allow the company to retain flexibility as well as providing another opportunity for the matching of receipts and payments denominated in HUF.

(ii) The company has a number of options available to it in detailed terms when it comes to hedging its foreign exchange risk. In the event of the HUF weakening, these will all involve some method of borrowing HUF and depositing sterling. Specific techniques include the use of forward exchange contracts if the size of the transactions are known in advance with reasonable certainty, or the use of options or futures contracts.

© The cash flows which arise locally (sales revenues, labour and overhead costs excluding management) would have been unaffected by the devaluation. Those costs which arose in the UK (management and raw materials) would have become cheaper. The value of remittances to the UK would also have increased on the devaluation.

The effect of these movements means that the group would have been in the best position had it not entered into any hedging transactions but simply taken advantage of favourable exchange rate movements. If it wished to continue to have some protection against a weakening of the HUF, then the best solution would have been to take out option contracts. These allow advantage to be taken of favourable exchange rate movements at the same time as hedging against unfavourable movements. However the cost of this approach would need to be taken into account since options are one of the most expensive forms of hedge on the market.

20 EXPO PLC

(a) To: The Treasurer

From: Assistant

Date: 12 November 20X7

(i) Comparison of two methods of hedging exchange risk

Method 1

Expo borrows DM750,000.

Three months interest is DM750,000 × 3% × 3/12 = DM5,625.

The customer pays DM750,000, which repays the loan principal but not the interest. The interest must be paid by converting pounds. Since the interest is known in advance, this can be covered on the forward market at a cost of 5625/2.3688 = £2,375.

Meanwhile, the DM750,000 is converted to sterling at the original spot rate 2.3834 to give £314,677. Assume that this is used to repay the company's short-term borrowings. Interest saved will be £314,677 × 6% × 3/12 = £4,720.

So, at the end of three months, the net sterling cash from the transaction is:

£314,677 + £4,720 − £2,375 = £317,022.

Method 2

The exchange rate is agreed in advance. Cash received in three months is converted to produce 750,000/2.3688 = £316,616.

Conclusion

On the basis of the above calculations, Method 1 gives a slightly better receipt. Banker's commission has been omitted from the figures.

(ii) *Factors to consider before deciding whether to hedge foreign exchange risk using the foreign currency markets*

The company should have a clear strategy concerning how much foreign exchange risk it is prepared to bear. A highly risk-averse or 'defensive' strategy of hedging all transactions is expensive in terms of commission costs but recognises that floating exchange rates are very unpredictable and can cause losses high enough to bankrupt the company.

An alternative 'predictive' strategy recognises that if all transactions are hedged, then the chance of currency gains is lost. The company could therefore attempt to forecast foreign exchange movements and only hedge those transactions where currency losses are predicted. The fact is that some currencies are relatively predictable (for example, if inflation is high the currency will devalue and there is little to be gained by hedging payments in that currency).

This is, of course, a much more risky strategy but in the long run, if predictions are made sensibly, the strategy should lead to a higher expected value than that of hedging everything and will incur lower commission costs as well. The risk remains, though, that a single large uncovered transaction could cause severe problems if the currency moves in the opposite direction to that predicted.

A sensible strategy for our company could be to set a cash size for a foreign currency exposure above which all amounts must be hedged, but below this limit a predictive approach is taken or even, possibly, all amounts are left unhedged.

Before using any technique to hedge foreign currency transactions, receipts and payments in the same currency at the same date should be offset. This technique is known as 'matching'. For example, if the company is expecting to receive DM750,000 on 31 March and to pay DM600,000 on the same day, only the net amount of DM150,000 needs to be considered.

Matching can be extended to receipts and payments which do not take place on exactly the same day by simply hedging the period and amount of the difference between the receipt and payment. A company like ours which has many receipts and payments in European currencies should consider matching assets with liabilities in the same currency. For example if we have total German debtors of DM2million, we should borrow DM2million on overdraft to match the debtor.

(b) If the foreign subsidiary is selling predominantly in its own country, the principle of matching assets and liabilities says that the subsidiary should be financed as far as possible in the currency of that country. Ideally the subsidiary will be highly geared with loans and overdrafts in the developing country's currency. If local finance has not been used and the sales invoice which is about to be sent is large, then an overdraft in the same currency should be taken out and the receipt converted to sterling immediately.

If it is impossible to borrow in the local currency, Expo plc should attempt to find a hard currency which is highly positively correlated with the local currency. For example, some countries have a policy of pegging their currency to the US dollar. The receipt can then be hedged by selling the US dollar forward.

This technique is, however, open to the risk that the local currency suddenly devalues against the dollar, as happened in 1997 with a number of Asian currencies. The likelihood of this happening is high if there is high inflation in the country and it has low reserves.

If Expo plc is fairly certain that the local currency is going to devalue and that it cannot borrow in that currency, the remaining alternatives are:

(i) To increase the sales price by the amount of the expected devaluation and bear the risk

(ii) To invoice in a hard currency, for example US dollars, which can then be sold forward

(iii) To arrange a 'counter-trade' agreement (ie barter) in which the sale of Expo's textiles is paid for by the purchase of local raw materials or other products

21   CURROPT PLC

(a) The department's view that the US dollar will strengthen is in agreement with the indications of the forward market and the futures market. Forward and futures rates show a stronger dollar than the spot rate. The forward rate is often taken as an unbiased predictor of what the spot rate will be in future. However, future events could cause large currency movements in either direction.

(b) The company needs to buy dollars in June.

A forward currency contract will fix the exchange rate for the date required near the end of June. If the exact date is not known, a range of dates can be specified, using an option forward contract. This will remove currency risk *provided that the franchise is won.* If the franchise is not won and the group has no use for US dollars, it will still have to buy the dollars at the forward rate. It will than have to sell them back for pounds at the spot rate which might result in an exchange loss.

A currency hedge using futures contracts will attempt to create a compensating gain on the futures market which will offset the increase in the sterling cost if the dollar strengthens. The hedge works by selling sterling futures contracts now and closing out by buying sterling futures in June at a lower dollar price if the dollar has strengthened. Like a forward contract, the exchange rate in June is effectively fixed because, if the dollar weakens, the futures hedge will produce a loss which counter-balances the cheaper sterling cost. However, because of inefficiencies in future market hedges, the exchange rate is not fixed to the same level of accuracy as a forward hedge.

A futures market hedge has the same weakness as a forward currency contract in the franchise situation. If the franchise is not won, an exchange loss may result.

A currency option is an ideal hedge in the franchise situation. It gives the company the right but not the obligation to sell pounds for dollars in June. It is only exercised if it is to the company's advantage, that is if the dollar has strengthened. If the dollar strengthens and the franchise is won, the exchange rate has been protected. If the dollar strengthens and the franchise is not won, a windfall gain will result by selling pounds at the exercise price and buying them more cheaply at spot with a stronger dollar.

© *Results of using currency hedges if the franchise is won*

Forward market

Using the forward market, the rate for buying dollars at the end of June is 1.4310 US$/£. The cost in sterling is 15 million/1.4310 = £10,482,180.

Futures market

Using the futures market the hedge is set up by selling sterling futures on 1 March. The June contract must be used because the March one will have expired by the end of June. At the June contract price of 1.4302, the number of contracts to be sold is $\dfrac{15,000,000}{1.4302 \times 62,500}$ = 167.8. (Round to the nearest whole number.)

Action on 1 March

Set up the hedge position by selling 168 sterling June futures contracts at $/£ 1.4302.

Action at end of June

Buy 168 sterling June futures contracts and buy the US$15 million with pounds at spot. Results will differ under the three scenarios, but not by much.

The value of a one-tick movement in the futures contract is $0.0001 \times 62,500 = 6.25.

Assume, at the end of June, that the futures market has moved by the same amount as the spot exchange rate. (This is a convenient assumption to make when you are not told the futures contract price in June.)

The difference between the spot and future rate on 1 March is 1.4461 − 1.4302 = 0.0159. To compute the futures contract price in June, subtract this amount from the spot rate in each of the following scenarios.

Scenario	(i)	(ii)	(iii)
June spot rate	1.3500	1.4500	1.5500
Less:	0.0159	0.0159	0.0159
Futures price - purchase in June	1.3341	1.4341	1.5341
Futures price - sale on 1 March	1.4302	1.4302	1.4302
Gain/(loss) in ticks per contract	961	(39)	(1039)
Total gain/(loss):	$	$	$
Ticks × $6.25 × 168 contracts	1,009,050	(40,950)	(1,090,950)
US$ required for franchise	15,000,000	15,000,000	15,000,000
Net US$ required	13,990,950	15,040,950	16,090,950
Net cost of currency at spot	£10,363,667	£10,373,069	£10,381,258

Traded currency options

Put options are required. It is not feasible to demonstrate the result of using all exercise prices under all three scenarios. The best exercise price should be selected, assuming that the option is going to be exercised, by subtracting the option premium in dollars from the exercise price.

Exercise price	Premium	Net	
1.4000	0.0038	1.3962	
1.4250	0.0068	1.4182	
1.4500	0.0238	1.4262	← Best

The best exercise price, if the option is exercised, is the 1.4500 option. Therefore we will demonstrate the results under all three scenarios of this option.

Exercise price	1.4500

Number of contracts:

$$\frac{15,000,000}{1.45 \times 31,250} \qquad 331.03$$

Rounded to:	331
Total sterling sold if option exercised: £31,250 × 331	£10,343,750
US$ total if option exercised: 10,343,750 × 1.45	$14,998,438
Put option premium (cent per £):	2.38
Total option premium (US$): 31,250 × $0.0238 × 331	$246,181
Premium paid in sterling at 1 January spot rate: 246,181/1.4461	£170,238

Scenario	(i)	(ii)	(iii)
Spot rate in June	1.35	1.45	1.55
Exercise option?	YES	NO	NO
	$	$	$
$ bought	14,998,438	15,000,000	15,000,000
Less paid out to subsidiary:	15,000,000	15,000,000	15,000,000
Shortfall dollars	1,562	0	0
	£	£	£
Purchase shortfall $ at spot 1.35	(1,157)		
£ paid at exercise price	(10,343,750)		
£ paid at spot		(10,344,828)	(9,677,419)
Option premium	(170,238)	(170,238)	(170,238)
Net cost of payment	(10,515,145)	(10,515,066)	(9,847,657)

22   CARRICK PLC

Collars make use of interest rate options to limit exposure to the risk of movement in rates. The company would arrange both a ceiling (an upper limit) and a floor (a lower limit) on its interest yield. The use of the ceiling means that the cost is lower than for a floor alone.

Since Carrick requires protection for the next seven months, it can use September options in order to cover the full period. It is assumed that the floor will be fixed at the current yield of 6%. This implies that it will buy call options at 9400. At the same time, Carrick will limit its ability to benefit from rises in rates by selling a put option at a higher rate, for example 7% (or 9300).

If Carrick does take out the options as described above, the effect will be as follows.

(a)   If interest rates fall below 6%, Carrick will exercise the call option and effectively fix its interest rate at 6%. The loss on the interest rate will be borne by the seller of the call option.

(b)   If interest rates remain between the 6% floor and the 7% ceiling, Carrick will do nothing but will benefit from the effect of any increase in rates above 6% within this band.

(c)   If interest rates rise above 7% the buyer of the put option will exercise their option, provided that the futures price falls below 9300. Carrick will effectively achieve an interest rate of 7%, but the benefit of any premium on rates above 7% will accrue to the buyer of the put option.

The level of premiums payable will depend on the different sizes of collar. The number of three-month contracts required for seven months' cover will be:

$$\frac{£6m}{£0.5m} \times \frac{7}{3} = 28 \text{ contracts } (£14m)$$

The premiums payable at different sizes of collar (in annual percentage terms) will be:

Call	Premium	Put	Premium	Net premium	£ cost*
9400	0.40	9350	0.35	0.05	1,750
9400	0.40	9300	0.14	0.26	9,100
9400	0.40	9250	0.06	0.34	11,900

(* eg £14m × 0.05% × ¼ = £1,750)

The potential gross interest rate gain, and the net gain taking premiums into account if rates do rise to the various exercise prices, are as follows. The interest rate gain is calculated on £6m for seven months.

	Interest rate % rise	Interest gain £	Premium £ cost (above)	Net gain £
9350	0.50	17,500	1,750	15,750
9300	1.00	35,000	9,100	25,900
9250	1.50	52,500	11,900	40,600

This suggests that Carrick could make the greatest potential gain by selling put options at 9250. However, this gain will only be realised if actual rates rise to 7.5%. If they stay at around 6% then Carrick will still incur costs without realising benefits. The actual put price chosen will depend on the view of the directors on the likely movements in rates over the period in question, but if it seems likely that rates will increase by up to 1%, then a put price of 9300 would be the most appropriate.

In practice, costs will be higher due to the transaction costs that will be incurred.

23 FOREIGN MARKETS

Exporting may be direct selling by the firm's own export department into the overseas markets, or it may be indirect through channels such as agents, distributors or trading companies. Provided the product can travel, the main advantage of exporting is that it is the lowest risk option. However, it may be difficult to establish a good customer support system if there is no operational base in the overseas countries. Other disadvantages may include high transport costs as well as tariffs, quotas and unfavourable tax regimes in the foreign countries. Consumers may also have a preference for locally made equipment.

Licensing involves conferring rights to make use of the licensor company's production process on producers located in the overseas market in return for royalty payments. Advantage of licensing over exporting and direct foreign investment include the following.

(a) It can permit rapid penetration of the new markets.

(b) Set-up costs are low compared with foreign direct investment.

(c) Political risks are lessened since the licensee will probably be a local firm, and it is a good option when the overseas country has high import barriers.

(d) License fees allow funds to be remitted to the home country.

Disadvantages include the following.

(a) The licensee company may end up as a direct competitor once the agreement has expired.

(b) Quality standards are difficult to enforce and may be compromised.

(c) Since some profit must accrue to the licensee the financial returns on the agreement may be relatively low.

Foreign direct investment (FDI) may take a variety of forms, including the setting up of a wholly owned subsidiary in the overseas country, taking over an existing firm in that country, or some form of joint venture operation. Whatever the mechanism, however, the size of the investment required is likely to be relatively large and the risks of failure correspondingly greater.

Reasons for FDI are diverse and include the following.

(a) It may offer access to new markets where transportation time and costs make exporting difficult.

(b) The relative costs of production may be cheaper due to access to cheaper local raw materials, lower labour costs and so on.

(c) FDI may overcome the problem of import quotas and tariffs.

(d) Grants and tax concessions may exist to attract foreign inward investment.

24 GLOBAL TELECOMMUNICATIONS INC

(a) (i)

REPORT

To: Board of Directors
From: Management Accountant   Date: 23 May 20X5
Subject: Evaluation of international investment decisions

Introduction

This paper is concerned with the selection of the appropriate method to be used in evaluating international investment decisions with particular regard to the Zenobia opportunity. Choice of an appropriate discount rate for NPV appraisal will be considered, together with the effect of risk on the evaluation method.

Choice of appraisal method

The decision on whether to invest in a particular project in a foreign country is based on exactly the same theory as home investment decisions. The principal aim is to maximise the wealth of the ordinary shareholders as measured by the net present value (NPV) of the projected cash flows. From the point of view of achieving this stated aim therefore, the appraisal should be based on an evaluation of the NPV of the project cashflows discounted at the cost of capital. This approach is superior to others available such as the payback period or the accounting rate of return.

Choice of discount rate

The current cost of capital to GTI is 15%. In situations where the project is small in relation to the size of the company and where the risk profile is similar to that of the existing operations, then the cost of capital provides an appropriate discount rate to use in investment appraisal since it requires each project to increase the net present worth of the organisation and hence to increase shareholder value. However, the Zenobia project does not fit into this category for two reasons.

(1) The investment required is large in relation to the estimated potential market capitalisation of GTI of £200m. It is as yet uncertain how the finance is to be raised, but if the cost of new capital is significantly more expensive than the present rate then this should be taken into account in the evaluation of the project.

(2) It is likely to carry more risk than existing operations due to the following.

    Exchange rate exposure. As the Managing Director points out, receipts and payments are not matched, most of the investment required being in dollars while the revenues are in local currency. Traditional hedging methods are not available since there is no forward market in the local currency, and therefore if the dollar strengthens as is likely, GTI will face a loss on exchange. Since such a depreciation is probable this negates any potential benefits of risk reduction through international diversification.

    Political risk. Although there is a new democratically elected government which has an expressed desire to attract foreign direct investment, there is a history of political instability in this part of the world. Any change in government represents a risk to GTI of a radical change in this policy which could result in the nationalisation of assets and restrictions on currency remittances out of the country. This would result in a discontinuity in the cash flows which as the Finance Director points out would otherwise show a strong correlation from one year to the next.

    Diversification. This will be GTI's first experience of direct investment in a developing country. It is therefore likely that mistakes will be made while the management passes through the learning curve. This means that returns could be lower than projected.

There are various methods available to allow for the higher than normal level of risk associated with this project. Probably the simplest and most effective approach is to add a premium to the existing cost of capital. Since this is cumulative, it should provide sufficient allowance for the fact that the three options have different lifespans.

Conclusions

It is recommended that GTI should undertake an NPV comparison of the different options. A premium should be added to the cost of capital to allow for the significantly higher level of risk attaching to this project as compared with our other investments.

Signed: Management Accountant

(ii)
REPORT

To: Board of Directors
From: Management Accountant   Date: 23 May 20X5
Subject: Evaluation of proposed investment in Zenobia

Introduction

This report is concerned with the financial evaluation of the three options under consideration with regard to the proposed investment in Zenobia. Detailed numerical analysis is provided in the Appendix to this report.

Financial evaluation

The three options have been evaluated at a discount rate of 20% over a five year timescale. The calculations suggest that the GoZ Option 2 provides the best NPV and should therefore be the preferred option. However, it is apparent that the **terminal value** is of key importance in determining the outcome of the calculations. The estimates for all the options are subject to a high degree of uncertainty, and GTI must be very confident of obtaining the projected price for the subsidiary before making a final choice of this option. The terminal values are particularly subject to **political risk** as discussed in a previous paper, and the Board would be well advised to look further into this area before making any decisions as to the investment route.

Signed: Management Accountant

Appendix

Year	0	1	2	3	4	5
20% discount factor	1.000	0.833	0.694	0.579	0.482	0.402
	$m	$m	$m	$m	$m	$m
GTI proposal						
Initial investment	(25.0)					
Operating cashflow		3.5	4.8	5.6	6.8	7.2
Residual (6.0/20%)[1]						30.0
Net cashflow	(25.0)	3.5	4.8	5.6	6.8	37.2
DCF	(25.0)	2.9	3.3	3.2	3.3	15.0
Cumulative DCF	(25.0)	(22.1)	(18.8)	(15.5)	(12.2)	2.7
GoZ Option 1						
Initial investment	(30.0)					
Operating cashflow		3.0	4.3	5.1	6.3	6.7
Further investment[2]				(5.2)		
Extra operating cashflow					1.6	1.6
Residual (6.7 + 1.6)/20%						41.5
Net cashflow	(30.0)	3.0	4.3	(0.1)	7.9	49.8
DCF	(30.0)	2.5	3.0	(0.1)	3.8	20.0
Cumulative DCF	(30.0)	(27.5)	(24.5)	(24.6)	(20.8)	(0.8)
GoZ Option 2						
Initial investment	(20.0)					
Operating cashflow		3.9	5.3	6.2	7.5	7.9
Residual (7.9 × 80%/20%)						31.6
Net cashflow	(20.0)	3.9	5.3	6.2	7.5	39.5
DCF	(20.0)	3.2	3.7	3.6	3.6	15.9
Cumulative DCF	(20.0)	(16.8)	(13.1)	(9.5)	(5.9)	10.0

Notes

¹ Residual values have been capitalised at the cost of capital (20%) and added to the income in the fifth year.

² The further investment required in year 3 under Option 1 is calculated as the expected number of additional lines (2,600) multiplied by the cost of connection ($2,000 per line).

(b) Since the size of the investment required is large in relation to the size of the company, the choice of financing method is likely to have a significant impact on GTI's capital structure. At present the company is 100% equity financed. This guarantees full control to the shareholders and minimises the amount of financial risk, but it also means that the cost of capital, currently estimated at 15% is high when one considers that the market rate of interest is 12.5% and this is tax deductible at 40%. If GTI chose to introduce debt into the capital structure it should be able to achieve a noticeable reduction in its weighted average cost of capital (WACC) due to the effect of the tax shield on the interest payments.

Given the above, GTI should consider taking on some form of debt provided that it has worthwhile alternative opportunities in which to invest the surplus internally generated funds. The benefit of the IFC loan in this situation is that it offers a fixed rate of interest which is below the current market level. If it is expected that market rates will remain stable or rise over the next five years then this loan becomes increasingly attractive. Alternatively, if rates were to fall then this weakens the case for the IFC loan.

A further benefit of obtaining IFC investment is that if political problems do arise during the course of the project, GTI would have an ally with superior political influence which could assist in obtaining a reasonable outcome.

25 FINANCIAL CONTROL

(a) The following are advantages of centralising a group's financial functions.

(i) A centralised department for financial functions could probably afford to employ specialists (such as foreign currency dealers and tax specialists) which individual subsidiaries could not.

(ii) Financial activities can be organised more efficiently in a variety of ways.

(1) There could be better co-ordination of foreign currency inflows and outflows. A centralised treasury function might be able to set up foreign currency bank accounts, and match inflows in one currency earned by one subsidiary with payments in the same currency by another subsidiary. This would eliminate foreign exchange risk in the currency, at little cost, in a way that individual subsidiaries could not do on their own. Centralised foreign exchange management would also avoid the risk that an individual subsidiary might allow itself to become over-exposed to foreign currency risk.

(2) Better co-ordination of fund-raising would be possible. If several subsidiaries need extra finance, a centralised finance department should be able to provide it at a lower cost than individual subsidiaries could achieve on their own, for example by lending cash surpluses of one subsidiary to another in the group, or by raising a single large loan or making an equity issue, instead of leaving individual subsidiaries to obtain their own bank loans.

(3) Centralised tax management would probably be beneficial for the group.

(4) Cash surpluses of some subsidiaries can be pooled with cash deficits of others, so as to minimise bank overdraft requirements.

(iii) The capital expenditure budget can be formulated, evaluated and approved on a group basis.

(iv) Centralised financial control would allow the head office to monitor the performance of individual subsidiaries in the area of financial management. For example, there would be close central monitoring of credit management by subsidiaries.

(v) There might be some savings in administrative costs, with fewer staff needed in total in a centralised department than in a large number of decentralised departments.

There are some disadvantages to having a group's financial functions centralised.

(i)   A centralised department might be slow moving and inefficient, if it is required to carry out many diverse functions.

(ii)   In a multinational group, financial staff at head office might be unaware of local conditions in the country that a subsidiary is operating in. Decision-making from head office could be inefficient. Subsidiaries in other countries would also need some measure of control over their cash, since it would be pointless to transfer funds from one country to another just for the sake of having centralised bank accounts.

(iii)   If key financial decisions are taken at head office, there is likely to be some loss of motivation among senior managers in the subsidiaries.

(iv)   Decisions are likely to be delayed when they are taken at head office. Where speedy decisions are needed, profit-making opportunities might be missed.

(b)   The activities of subsidiaries within the group can be monitored, evaluated and controlled by means of a variety of financial ratios. Ratios can be grouped into those indicating profitability and asset use, those indicating debt and gearing levels, and those indicating liquidity.

Profitability and asset use
The most significant ratio will be return on investment, which compares the profits being earned by the company with the total assets it is using. A target ROI will probably be set for each subsidiary in the group, as well as for the group as a whole.

Profit/sales ratios should be used to measure the profit margin on sales that the company is earning. Both the gross margin (sales minus cost of sales as a percentage of sales turnover) and the net margin (pre-tax profit as a percentage of sales) should be monitored.

Trends in the gross margin percentage or the net margin percentage can be analysed more closely by monitoring a variety of cost/sales ratios, such as materials costs/sales and labour costs/sales.

Return on investment depends on asset use as well as profit margins, and so asset turnover ratios should be monitored. Both working capital and fixed asset use should be controlled, and suitable ratios include:

(i)   Sales: assets employed
(ii)   Sales: fixed assets employed
(iii)   Working capital per £1 sales
(iv)   Stock turnover
(v)   Debtors' collection period

Debt and gearing
Individual subsidiaries should not become over-burdened with debt, and a number of ratios can be used to monitor trends and changes in the debt position of a company. The most useful ratios are:

(i)   The gearing ratio: the ratio of prior charge capital to equity capital
(ii)   The debt ratio: the ratio of total liabilities to total assets
(iii)   The interest cover: the ratio of profit before interest to interest costs
(iv)   The cash flow ratio: the ratio of net cash inflow to total debts

Liquidity
A company should be able to meet its short-term commitments to pay creditors, and trends in liquidity could provide important indications of the ability of a company to continue to do this. The two ratios commonly used to monitor liquidity are the current ratio (current assets: current liabilities) and the quick ratio or acid test ratio (current assets minus stocks: current liabilities). An increasing sales: working capital ratio might also indicate declining liquidity rather than better working capital management.

At a group level, other financial ratios which must be monitored are shareholder ratios. For a quoted company, dividend yield, P/E ratio and EPS are the most important.

©   The problems with using financial ratios for control within a group are as follows.

(i)   The ratios of one subsidiary will be compared with the ratios of another, and some will be judged to have performed better than others. However, inter-company comparisons might be unfair, especially if their fixed assets differ in age or nature. For example, a subsidiary with ageing assets might achieve a much higher ROI in the short term than a subsidiary that has invested in new fixed assets, and a subsidiary with relatively few fixed assets, such as one operating in a service industry, will often achieve a higher ROI than a subsidiary which must invest heavily in fixed assets.

(ii)   Where subsidiaries trade with each other, the level of profitability achieved by each of them will depend to some extent on the transfer prices that have been fixed for this trading. Where transfer prices are below market prices, the buying subsidiary will benefit at the expense of the selling subsidiary.

(iii) Where there are subsidiaries in different countries, a comparison of their ratios might be misleading. For example, in a country where debt capital is much more widely used, gearing levels should be higher.

(iv)   The way in which head office charges are allocated to subsidiaries might affect their profitability significantly.

(v)   The managers of subsidiaries will probably try to manipulate their results to make them appear better to the head office controllers.

(vi)   Unless financial ratios are measured and reported regularly, they might be available too late to be of much practical value for control purposes.

(vii) Financial ratios are unsuitable for monitoring certain decisions by managers in subsidiaries because they are retrospective and take a short-term view of performance. In particular, capital expenditure decisions should be assessed on the basis of their long term expected future costs and benefits. Since profits from capital projects usually take time to build up, the short-term effect of new investment is usually a fall in profits and ROI. If financial ratios are used to measure performance, the managers of subsidiaries might be criticised for deteriorating performance when in fact they have undertaken investment which in the longer term might be highly profitable, and for which they ought to be rewarded.

536

Lecturers' question bank

1 INTEREST YIELD CURVE (10 marks)   *18 mins*

(a) Explain what is meant by the interest yield curve, illustrating your explanation numerically and with a freehand graph. (5 marks)

(b) Suggest what information might be derived from the interest yield curve in the area of financial forecasting. (5 marks)

2 LEISURE INTERNATIONAL PLC   *45 mins*

The following is an extract from the balance sheet of Leisure International plc at 30 June 19X2.

	£'000
Ordinary shares of 50p each	5,200
Reserves	4,850
9% preference shares of £1 each	4,500
14% debentures	5,000
Total long-term funds	19,550

The ordinary shares are quoted at 80p. Assume that the market estimate of the next ordinary dividend is 4p, growing thereafter at 12% per annum indefinitely. The preference shares, which are irredeemable, are quoted at 72p and the debentures are quoted at par. Corporation tax is 30%. Assume income tax at 23% where relevant.

Required

(a) Use the relevant data above to estimate the company's weighted average cost of capital (WACC), ie the return required by the providers of the three types of capital, using the respective market values as weighting factors.

(b) Explain how the capital asset pricing model would be used as an alternative method of estimating the cost of equity, indicating what information would be required and how it would be obtained.

(c) Assume that the debentures have recently been issued specifically to fund the company's expansion programme under which a number of projects are being considered. It has been suggested at a project appraisal meeting that because these projects are to be financed by the debentures, the cutoff rate for project acceptance should be the after-tax interest rate on the debentures rather than the WACC. Comment on this suggestion.

(d) Assume that instead of raising £5 million of 14% debentures, the company had raised the equivalent amount in preference shares giving the same yield as the existing preference capital.

    (i) Demonstrate that the returns offered to investors in the two securities are consistent with investor risk aversion.

    (ii) Calculate how Leisure International plc's equity earnings would have been affected if the preference shares had been issued instead of the loan capital.

3 BETTALUCK PLC   *35 mins*

Bettaluck plc has been enjoying a substantial net cash inflow, and until the surplus funds are needed to meet tax and dividend payments, and to finance further capital expenditure in several months time, they have been invested in a small portfolio of short-term equity investments. Details of the portfolio, which consists of shares in four UK listed companies, are as follows.

Company	Number of shares held	Beta equity coefficient	Market price per share	Latest dividend yield %	Expected return on equity in the next year %
Dashing plc	60,000	1.16	£4.29	6.1	19.5
Elegant plc	80,000	1.28	£2.92	3.4	24.0
Fantastic plc	100,000	0.90	£2.17	5.7	17.5
Gaudy plc	125,000	1.50	£3.14	3.3	23.0

The current market return is 19% a year and the Treasury bill yield is 11% a year.

Required

(a) ` On the basis of the data given, calculate the risk of Bettaluck plc's short-term investment portfolio relative to that of the market.

(b) Recommend, with reasons, whether Bettaluck plc should change the composition of its portfolio.

4   P/E RATIOS (10 marks)   *18 mins*

List and discuss briefly five reasons why companies in the same type of business might have different P/E ratios.

Comment on the view that the P/E ratio is 'an attempt to value a company in terms of its earnings'.

5   LEIVERS   *35 mins*

(a) Discuss how managers' objectives might differ from those of shareholders, especially if managers are not closely monitored by shareholders, and are not subject to constraints and/or incentives imposed by shareholders. For these differing objectives mention the policies that managers might adopt that are likely to be considered sub-optimal from the shareholders' point of view.

(b) In recent years there has been a large increase in the number of management buyouts, often when a company is in financial distress. What are the possible financial advantages of a company's shares being sold to a group of managers rather than the company's being liquidated?

(c) Five managers of Leivers Ltd are discussing the possibility of a management buy-out of the part of the company that they work for. The buy-out would require a total of £700,000, of which £525,000 would comprise the purchase cost, and £175,000 the funds for a small expansion in activity and for working capital. The managers believe that they could jointly provide £70,000.

Required
(i) Discuss possible sources of finance that the managers might use to raise the required funds.

(ii) What are likely to be the major factors that a potential supplier of finance will consider before deciding whether to offer finance? What type of security or other conditions might providers of finance specify?

6   GOVERNMENT   *20 mins*

(a) Outline the major government activities that influence financial management and briefly illustrate how government activities affect companies in achieving their financial objectives.

(b) Your company is subject to an unexpected takeover bid by a rival company. Your board of directors proposes to reject the bid, but believes that increased bids might follow.

Discuss the policies that your company might adopt to defend itself against the takeover bid(s), and comment upon the significance of the City Code on takeovers and mergers in this process.

7   LEADING AND LAGGING (10 marks)   *18 mins*

(a) Explain the terms 'leading' and 'lagging' in relation to foreign currency settlements and state the circumstances under which this technique might be used.

(5 marks)
(b) Explain the procedures for matching foreign currency receipts and payments, having regard to the possibility that these might be on different time scales, and state their possible advantages.

(5 marks)

This question is concerned with internal techniques and does not require reference to methods involving external bodies, such as forward contracts, options or swaps.

8   VEREY PLC (30 marks)   *54 mins*

Verey plc is a quoted manufacturing company trading solely in the UK. It has the following capital structure.

	Book value	Market value
	£'000	£'000
£1 ordinary shares	2,500	4,000
10% secured debentures	1,000	980
14% unsecured loan stock	800	795
	4,300	5,775

The secured debentures were issued ten years ago and will not be redeemed for another 20 years, but the unsecured loan stock must be redeemed at par in six months time. All market values are ex div or ex int, a final dividend and half a year's interest being payable next week. Interest is covered four times.

The company has no cash available in excess of what it needs for working capital. It is contemplating an investment in a factory in Redland which would cost R$800,000 (R$ is the local currency), and which would yield a steady annual operating income of R$90,000. The present exchange rate is R$2 = £1, but this rate could fluctuate. There are no exchange controls.

Required

(a)   Comment on the company's existing capital structure, and on how it might finance the redemption of the loan stock and the investment in Redland. Make any assumptions you need to, but state them clearly. Ignore taxation.   (15 marks)

(b)   Outline the factors that a company should consider when developing a long-term financial plan to cover three years or more.   (6 marks)

(c)   Briefly describe the major types of financial model that might be used to assist in the preparation of such plans, and discuss the problems that companies face in long-term planning.   (9 marks)

9   WOPPIT   *40 mins*

(a)   The managing director of Woppit plc is worried about the volatility of the company's traded option price. He considers that such volatility might be seen as financial weakness and make the company more likely to be the target of a takeover bid.

Required

Explain what factors influence the price of a traded option and whether volatility of a company's share option price is necessarily a sign of financial weakness.

(b)   As a defence against a possible takeover bid the managing director proposes that Woppit make a bid for Grapper plc, in order to increase Woppit's size and, hence, make a bid for Woppit more difficult. The companies are in the same industry.

Woppit's equity beta is 1.2 and Grapper's is 1.05. The risk-free rate and market return are estimated to be 10% and 16% per year respectively. The growth rate of after tax earnings of Woppit in recent years has been 15% per year and of Grapper 12% per year. Both companies maintain an approximately constant dividend payout ratio.

Woppit's directors require information about how much premium above the current market price to offer for Grapper's shares. Two suggestions are:

(i)   the price should be based upon the balance sheet net worth of the company, adjusted for the current value of land and buildings, plus estimated after tax profits for the next five years;

(ii)   the price should be based upon a valuation using the dividend valuation model, using existing growth rate estimates.

Summarised financial data for the two companies are shown below.

BPP PUBLISHING

MOST RECENT BALANCE SHEETS

	Woppit		Grapper	
	£m	£m	£m	£m
Land and buildings (net)[1]		560		150
Plant and machinery (net)		720		280
Stock	340		240	
Debtors	300		210	
Bank	20		40	
		660		490
Less Trade creditors	200		110	
Overdraft	30		10	
Tax payable	120		40	
Dividends payable	50		40	
		400		200
Total assets less current liabilities		1,540		720
Financed by:				
Ordinary shares[2]		200		100
Share premium		420		220
Other reserves		400		300
		1,020		620
Loans due after one year		520		100
		1,540		720

Notes

[1]   Woppit's land and buildings have been recently revalued. Grapper's have not been revalued for four years, during which time the average value of industrial land and buildings has increased by 25% per year.

[2]   Woppit 10 pence par value, Grapper 25 pence par value.

MOST RECENT PROFIT AND LOSS ACCOUNTS

	Woppit £m	Grapper £m
Turnover	3,500	1,540
Operating profit	700	255
Net interest	120	22
Taxable profit	580	233
Taxation	203	82
Profit attributable to shareholders	377	151
Dividends	113	76
Retained profit	264	75

The current share price of Woppit is 310 pence and of Grapper 470 pence.

Required

(i)   Calculate the premium per share above Grapper's current share price that would result from the two suggested valuation methods. Discuss which, if either, of these values should be the bid price.

State clearly any assumptions that you make.

(ii)   Assess the managing director's strategy of seeking growth by acquisition in order to make a bid for Woppit more difficult.

(iii) Illustrate how Woppit might achieve benefits through improvements in operational efficiency if it acquires Grapper.

10   FORECASTING FAILURE (10 marks)   *18 mins*

(a)   Discuss the theories, or arguments, which suggest that financial analysis can be used to forecast the probability of a given firm's failure.

(b)   Explain why such an analysis, even if properly applied, may not always predict failure.

List of Key Terms
and Index

These are terms which we have identified throughout the text as being KEY TERMS. You should make sure that you can define what these terms mean; go back to the pages highlighted here if you need to check.

BPP PUBLISHING

BPP PUBLISHING

See overleaf for information on other
BPP products and how to order

ACCA Order

To BPP Publishing Ltd, Aldine Place, London W12 8AA

Tel: 020 8740 2211. Fax: 020 8740 1184

Mr/Mrs/Ms (Full name) _____

Daytime delivery address _____

Postcode _____

Daytime Tel _____ Date of exam (month/year) _____

	6/00 Texts	1/00 Kits	1/00 Psscrds	2/00 Tapes	2/00 Videos	Master CDs
FOUNDATION						
1 The Accounting Framework	£18.95 ☐	£9.95 ☐	£5.95 ☐	£12.95 ☐	£25.00 ☐	£34.95 ☐
2 The Legal Framework	£18.95 ☐	£9.95 ☐	£5.95 ☐	£12.95 ☐	£25.00 ☐	£34.95 ☐
3 Management Information	£18.95 ☐	£9.95 ☐	£5.95 ☐	£12.95 ☐	£25.00 ☐	£34.95 ☐
4 The Organisational Framework	£18.95 ☐	£9.95 ☐	£5.95 ☐	£12.95 ☐	£25.00 ☐	£34.95 ☐
CERTIFICATE						
5 Information Analysis	£18.95 ☐	£9.95 ☐	£5.95 ☐	£12.95 ☐	£25.00 ☐	
6 The Audit Framework	£18.95 ☐	£9.95 ☐	£5.95 ☐	£12.95 ☐	£25.00 ☐	
7 The Tax Framework (Finance Act 00) (8/00 Text, 1/01 P/C, 1/01 Kit)	£18.95 ☐	£9.95 ☐	£5.95 ☐	£12.95 ☐	£25.00 ☐	
8 Managerial Finance	£18.95 ☐	£9.95 ☐	£5.95 ☐	£12.95 ☐	£25.00 ☐	£39.95 ☐
PROFESSIONAL						
9 Information for Control and Decision Making	£19.95 ☐	£10.95 ☐	£5.95 ☐	£12.95 ☐	£25.00 ☐	£39.95 ☐
10 Accounting and Audit Practice (Accounting)	£15.95 ☐	£10.95 ☐	£5.95 ☐	£12.95 ☐	£25.00 ☐	£39.95 ☐
10 Accounting and Audit Practice (Auditing)	£13.95 ☐	£10.95 ☐	}	£12.95 ☐	£25.00 ☐	
11 Tax Planning (Finance Act 00) (8/00 Text, 1/01 P/C, 1/01 Kit)	£20.95 ☐	£10.95 ☐	£5.95 ☐	£12.95 ☐	£25.00 ☐	
12 Management and Strategy	£20.95 ☐	£10.95 ☐	£5.95 ☐	£12.95 ☐	£25.00 ☐	
13 Financial Reporting Environment	£20.95 ☐	£10.95 ☐	£5.95 ☐	£12.95 ☐	£25.00 ☐	
14 Financial Strategy	£20.95 ☐	£10.95 ☐	£5.95 ☐	£12.95 ☐	£25.00 ☐	
INTERNATIONAL STREAM						
1 The Accounting Framework	£18.95 ☐	£9.95 ☐				
6 The Audit Framework	£18.95 ☐	£9.95 ☐				
10 Accounting and Audit Practice (Accounting)	£15.95 ☐	£10.95 ☐				
10 Accounting and Audit Practice (Audit)	£13.95 ☐	£10.95 ☐				
13 Financial Reporting Environment	£20.95 ☐	£10.95 ☐				

£ [ ]

POSTAGE & PACKING

Study Texts

	First	Each extra
UK	£3.00	£2.00
Europe*	£5.00	£4.00
Rest of world	£20.00	£10.00

£ [ ]

Kits/Passcards/Success Tapes

	First	Each extra
UK	£2.00	£1.00
Europe*	£2.50	£1.00
Rest of world	£15.00	£8.00

£ [ ]

Master CDs/Breakthrough Videos

	First	Each extra
UK	£2.00	£2.00
Europe*	£2.00	£2.00
Rest of world	£20.00	£10.00

£ [ ]

Grand Total (Cheques to *BPP Publishing*) I enclose a cheque for (incl. Postage) £ [ ]

Or charge to Access/Visa/Switch

Card Number [ ][ ][ ][ ]

Expiry date _____ Start Date _____

Issue Number (Switch Only) _____

Signature _____

We aim to deliver to all UK addresses inside 5 working days; a signature will be required. Orders to all EU addresses should be delivered within 6 working days. All other orders to overseas addresses should be delivered within 8 working days. * Europe includes the Republic of Ireland and the Channel Islands.

REVIEW FORM & FREE PRIZE DRAW

All original review forms from the entire BPP range, completed with genuine comments, will be entered into one of two draws on 31 January 2001 and 31 July 2001. The names on the first four forms picked out on each occasion will be sent a cheque for £50.

Name: _____   **Address**: _____

_____

_____

How have you used this Text?
(Tick one box only)

☐ Home study (book only)

☐ On a course: college _____

☐ With 'correspondence' package

☐ Other _____

Why did you decide to purchase this Text?
(Tick one box only)

☐ Have used BPP Texts in the past

☐ Recommendation by friend/colleague

☐ Recommendation by a lecturer at college

☐ Saw advertising

☐ Other _____

During the past six months do you recall seeing/receiving any of the following?
(Tick as many boxes as are relevant)

☐ Our advertisement in *Students' Newsletter*

☐ Our advertisement in *Pass*

☐ Our brochure with a letter through the post

Which (if any) aspects of our advertising do you find useful?
(Tick as many boxes as are relevant)

☐ Prices and publication dates of new editions

☐ Information on Text content

☐ Facility to order books off-the-page

☐ None of the above

Your ratings, comments and suggestions would be appreciated on the following areas

	Very useful	Useful	Not useful
Introductory section (Key study steps, personal study plan etc)	☐	☐	☐
Chapter introductions	☐	☐	☐
Key terms	☐	☐	☐
Explanations	☐	☐	☐
Case examples and examples	☐	☐	☐
Questions and answers	☐	☐	☐
Chapter roundups	☐	☐	☐
Quick quizzes	☐	☐	☐
Exam focus points	☐	☐	☐
Exam question bank	☐	☐	☐
Exam answer bank	☐	☐	☐
List of key terms and index	☐	☐	☐
Icons	☐	☐	☐

	Excellent	Good	Adequate	Poor
Overall opinion of this Text	☐	☐	☐	☐

Do you intend to continue using BPP Study Texts/Kits?   ☐ Yes   ☐ No

Please note any further comments and suggestions/errors on the reverse of this page.

Please return to: Katy Hibbert, BPP Publishing Ltd, FREEPOST, London, W12 8BR

REVIEW FORM & FREE PRIZE DRAW (continued)

Please note any further comments and suggestions/errors below